The Complete 4-String Cigar Box Guitar Chord Book

4-String Cigar Box Guitar Chords in GDGB Tuning

By Brent Robitaille

www.brentrobitaille.com

KALYMI PUBLISHING

Copyright © 2020 by Brent Robitaille
All Rights Reserved

Unauthorized copying, arranging, adapting is an infringemnet of copyright.

OTHER BOOKS BY BRENT ROBITAILLE

The Complete Cigar Box Guitar Chord Book 3-String
Cigar Box Guitar - Jazz & Blues Unlimited Book One & Two
Cigar Box Guitar Blues Overload
101 Riffs for Cigar Box Guitar
Celtic Collection for Cigar Box Guitar
The Ultimate Collection – How to Play Cigar Box Guitar Vol. 1 & 2
Cigar Box Guitar - The Technique Book
The Pop Rock Looper Pedal Book
The Blues Guitar Looper Pedal Book
Standard Guitar Tuning - Celtic Collection
Open D Guitar Tuning - Celtic Collection
Open G Guitar Tuning - Celtic Collection
Improve Your Guitar Chord Playing
Slide Guitar Collection
Celtic Collection Fiddle - Tab & Notes
Holiday Collection for Fiddle - Tab & Notes
Traditional Collection Fiddle - Tab & Notes
Fiddle Tab - Celtic Collection
Celtic Collection for Mandolin
Celtic Collection for Ukulele
Holiday Collection for Cigar Box Guitar

Recordings - Ebooks - Sheet Music
Available at:

www.brentrobitaille.com

Cover Design and Photography by Anton Pickard

KALYMI PUBLISHING

PUBLISHED BY KALYMI PUBLISHING
©2020 Kalymi Publishing

Although the author and publisher have made every effort to ensure that the information in this book is in public domain at press time, the author and publisher do not assume and hereby disclaim any liability to any party. Any copying of this material whole or in part with the express written permission of Kalymi Publishing is a violation of copyright law.

Introduction

The *Complete Cigar Box Guitar Chord Book* is the most extensive library of chords ever assembled for the 4-string cigar box guitar. Incredibly, there are thousands of possible chords with only four strings in GDGB tuning. This extensive chord library will give you the tools to cover all genres of music and perform all styles of music.

I have included as many chords possible in each of the 12 keys in music. There are multiple voicings for each chord group providing many chord choices. You will find chords categorized by note names starting from A - Ab/G#. Each note name has the most used chord suffixes, i.e., Major, Major 6, Major 7, etc. For beginners, there is a convenient summary of easier chords and common chord shapes.

Learning your favourite chords is the first step, followed by learning to switch between chords to play songs and chord progressions. Improve your chords by playing through the chord progressions taken directly from popular songs. There is a good selection of blues chord progressions that cover the standard blues changes in all keys.

Have a look at the popular strumming and fingerpicking patterns to further your chord playing abilities. There is also a review on basic chord theory explaining how chords are formed, the chord numbering system, chord formulas, and understanding chord progressions.

Visit my website for more information and audio tracks:

www.brentrobitaille.com/cbg-chord-book

www.brentrobitaille.com

https://kalymimusic.com

Contents: The Complete 4-String Cigar Box Guitar Chord Book

Introduction..3
How to Read Chords and Tablature 5

Beginner Chords and Moveable Shapes

Basic Chords on the Cigar Box Guitar with Photos 7
Moveable Chords on the Cigar Box Guitar 16
Diatonic Chords..20

Complete Chord Library

A Chords 22
B♭ (A♯) Chords 30
B Chords 38
C Chords 46
C♯ - D♭ Chords...54
D Chords 62
E♭ (D♯) Chords 70
E Chords...78
F Chords...86
F♯ - G♭ Chords 94
G Chords 102
A♭ (G♯) Chords 110

Theory and Chord Progressions

Chord Progressions and Theory..118
Chord Numbering Systems 120
Understanding Chord Formulas..122
Cigar Box Fingerboard and Interval and Note Chart..124

Strumming and Fingerpicking Patterns

Strumming and Picking Techniques...126
Strumming Patterns..128
Tips for Accompanying on Cigar Box Guitar..133
Fingerpicking Patterns 134

Chord Progressions

Chord Progressions - Blues..136
Chord Progressions - Pop...146
Chord Progressions - Rock 162

HOW TO READ CHORD DIAGRAMS

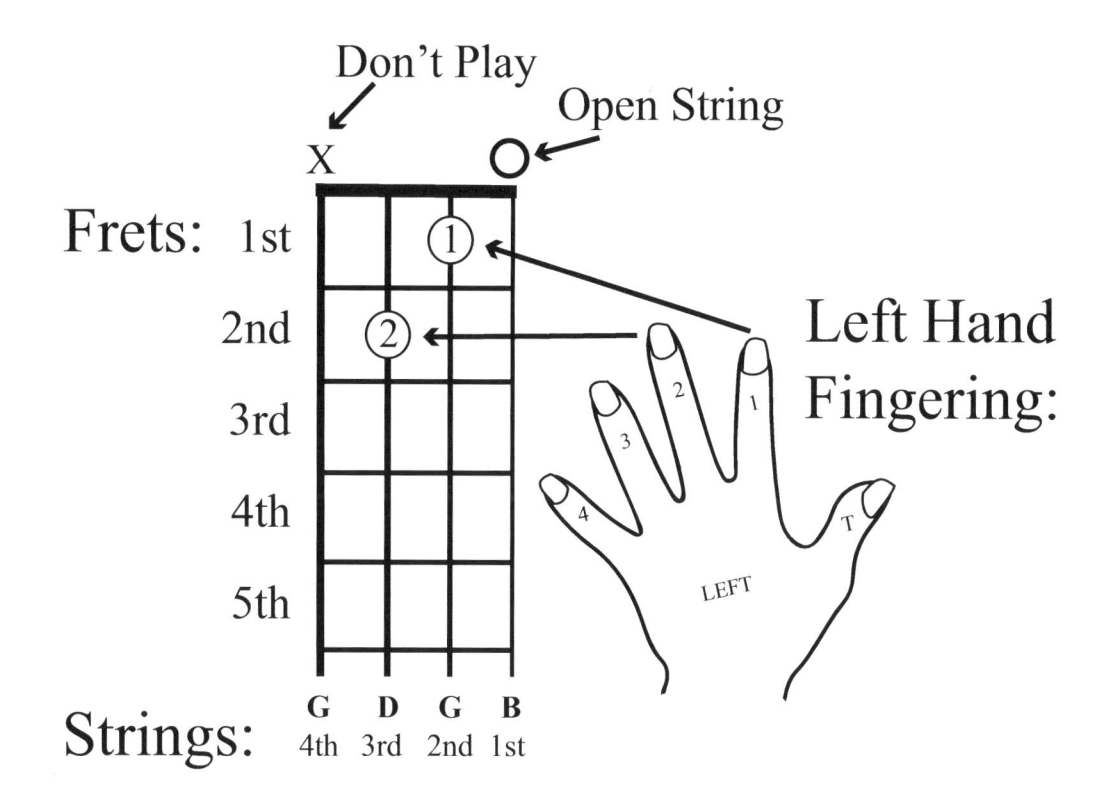

Don't Play
Open String
Frets: 1st, 2nd, 3rd, 4th, 5th
Left Hand Fingering:
Strings: G (4th), D (3rd), G (2nd), B (1st)

Barre Chords

Barre chords require covering several strings with one finger. In this example, place your 1st finger on strings 1 to 4 then add the 2nd and 3rd finger to form the D major chord.

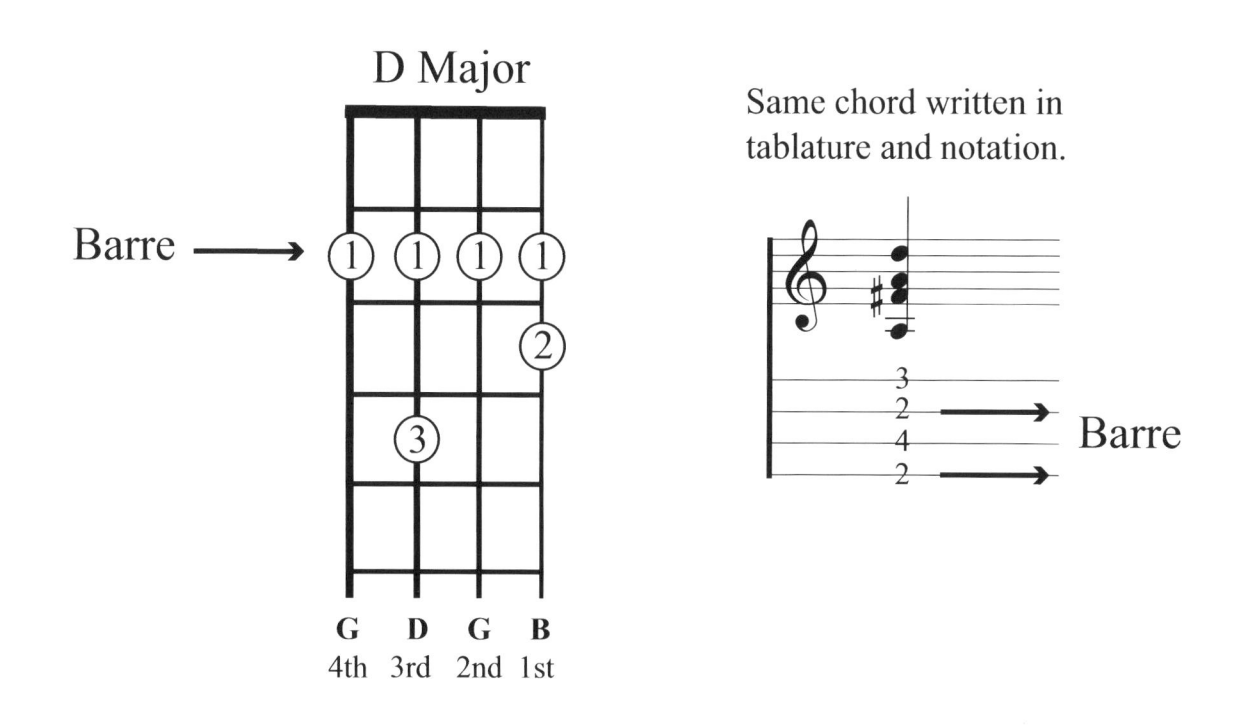

D Major

Barre →

G (4th), D (3rd), G (2nd), B (1st)

Same chord written in tablature and notation.

→ Barre

HOW TO READ TABLATURE (TAB)

To read tablature, you need to know four things:

1) What string is the note on? - Strings are thin (1st) to thick (4th).
2) What fret is the note on? - Fret numbers are left to right.
3) Which finger do I use? - Keep all fingers in position (1-2-3-4) where possible when playing single notes, and most comfortable fingerings for chords.
4) How long to let the note ring? - Based on the song's rhythm but generally keep fingers on fretboard as long as possible to let notes ring throughout.

Fingerboard Number Chart

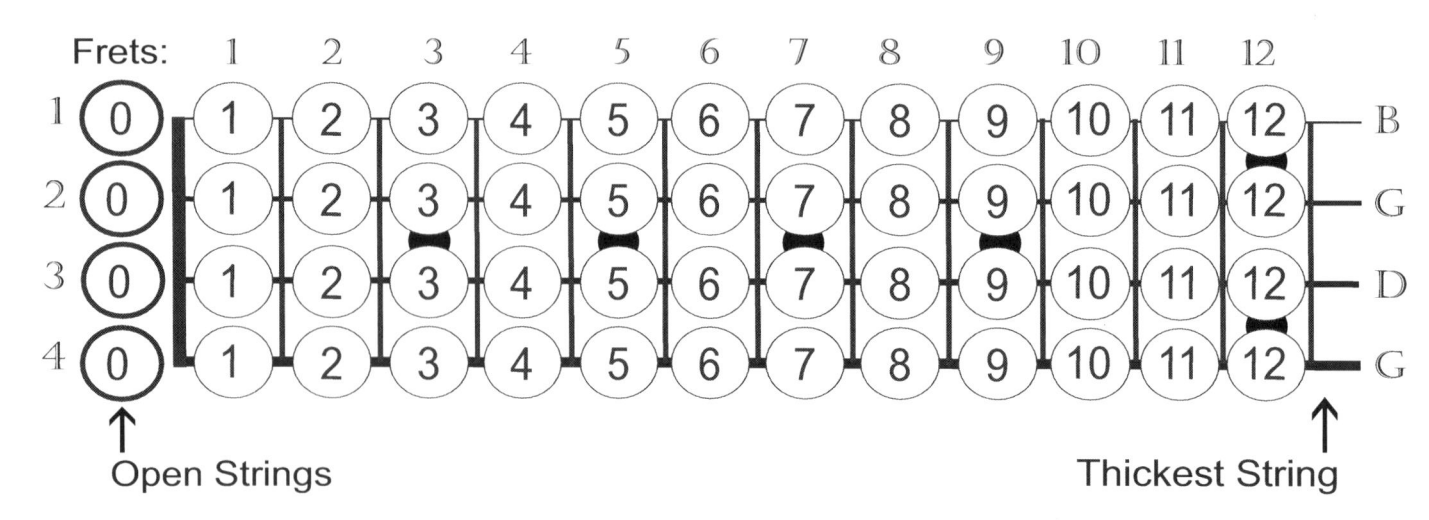

Strings (top to bottom): B, G, D, G — tuned open (0). Frets numbered 1 through 12 left to right. Leftmost circles (0) = Open Strings. Rightmost = Thickest String.

Examples:

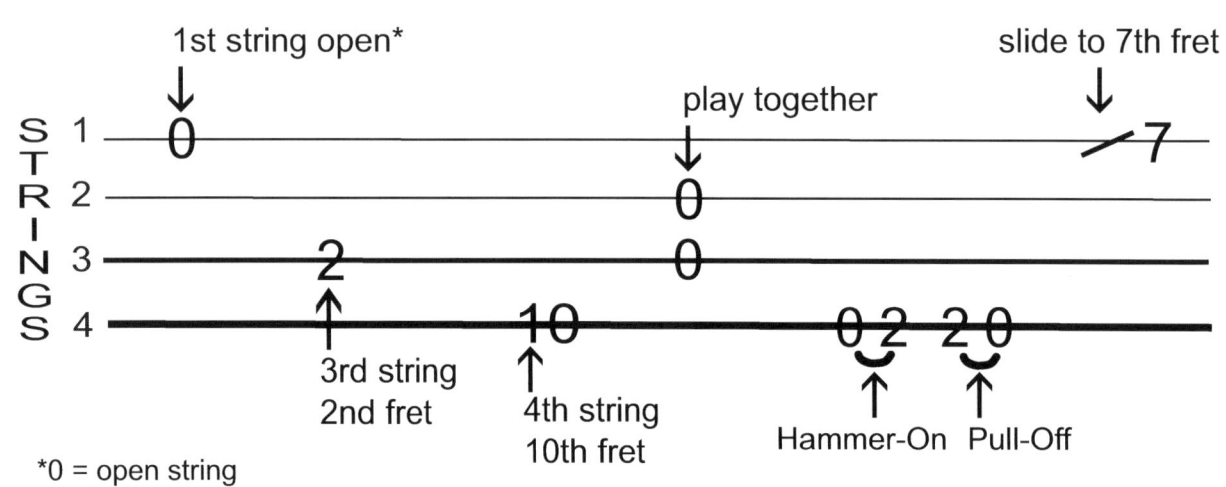

- 1st string open* → 0 on string 1
- 3rd string, 2nd fret → 2 on string 3
- 4th string, 10th fret → 10 on string 4
- play together → 0 on strings 1, 2, 3
- Hammer-On: 0 to 2 on string 4
- Pull-Off: 2 to 0 on string 4
- slide to 7th fret → /7 on string 1

*0 = open string

BASIC CHORDS - MAJOR

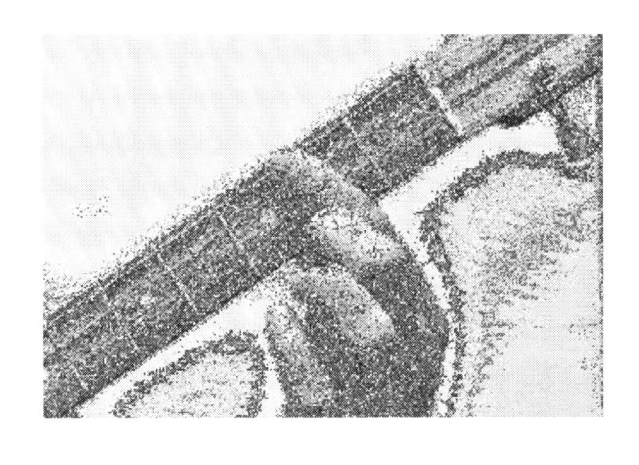

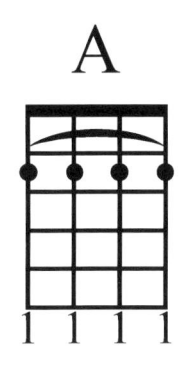

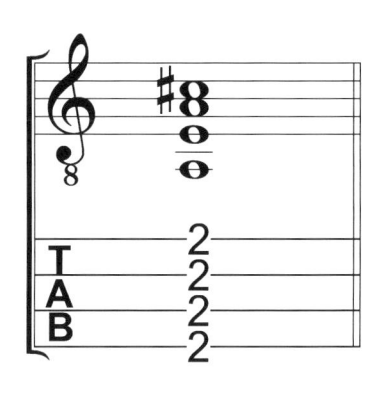

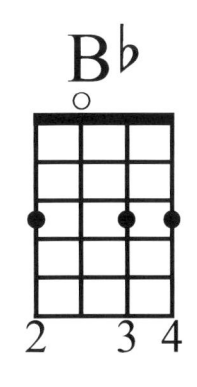

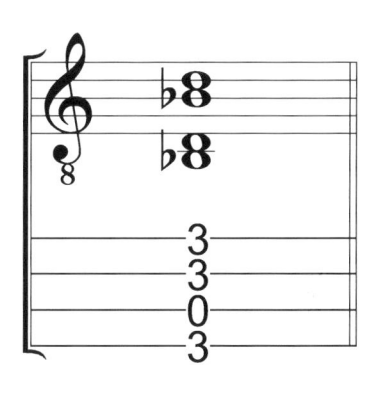

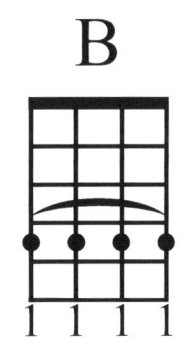

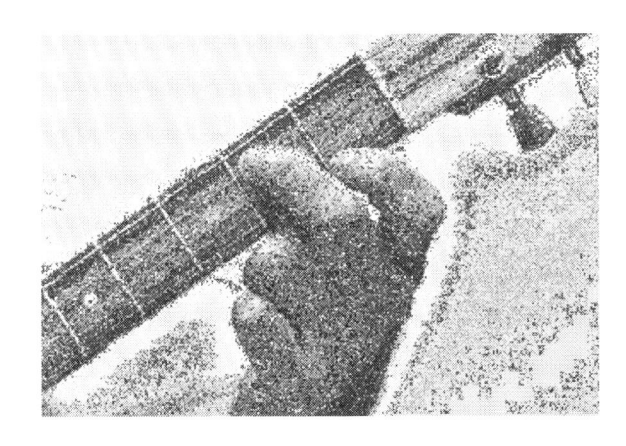

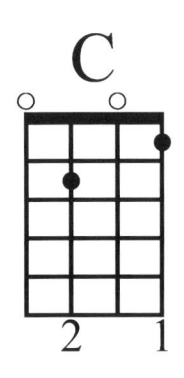

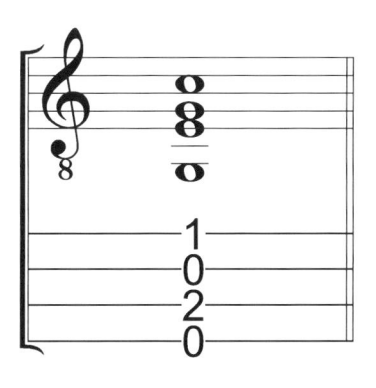

MAJOR CHORDS

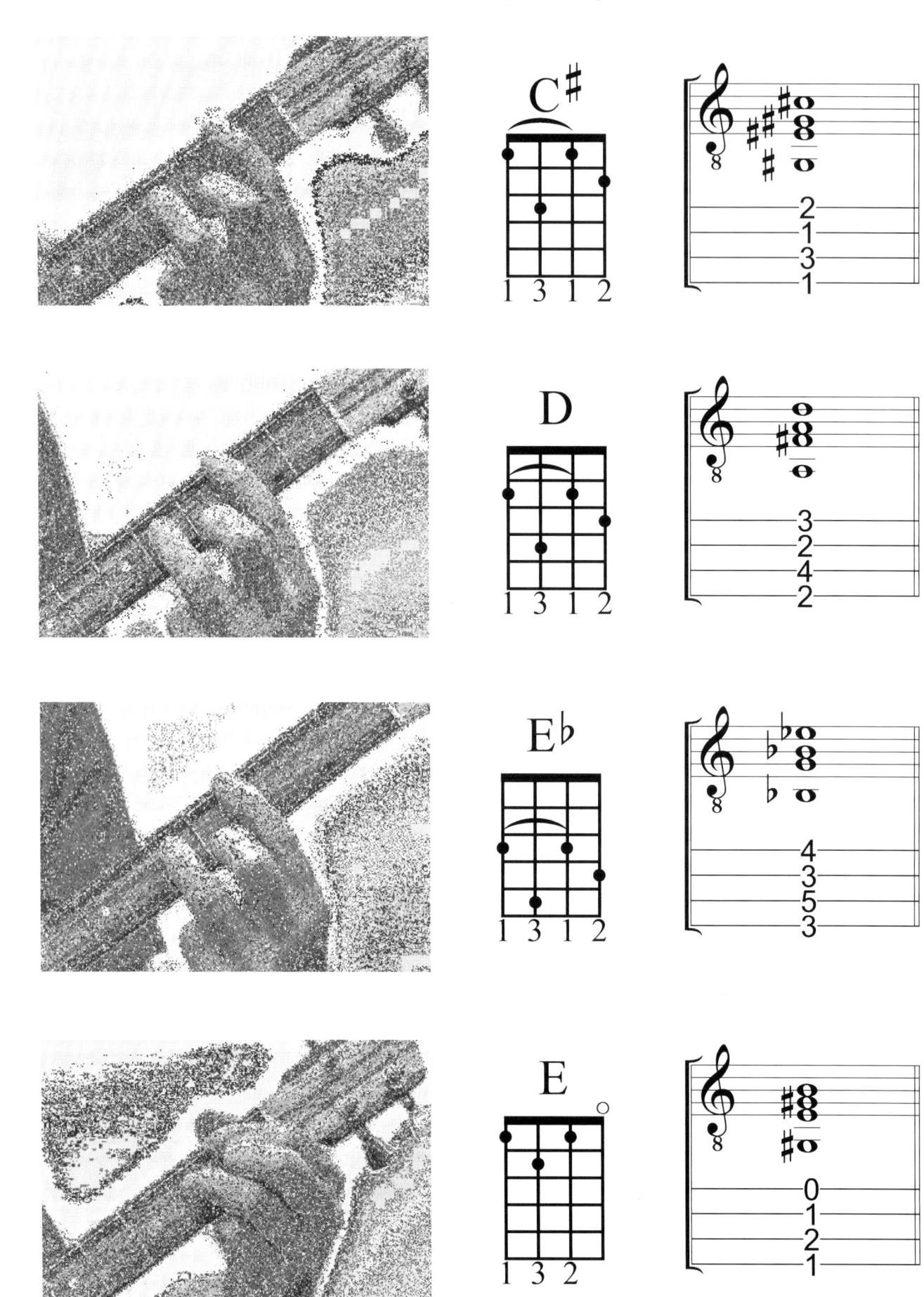

C#

D

E♭

E

MAJOR CHORDS

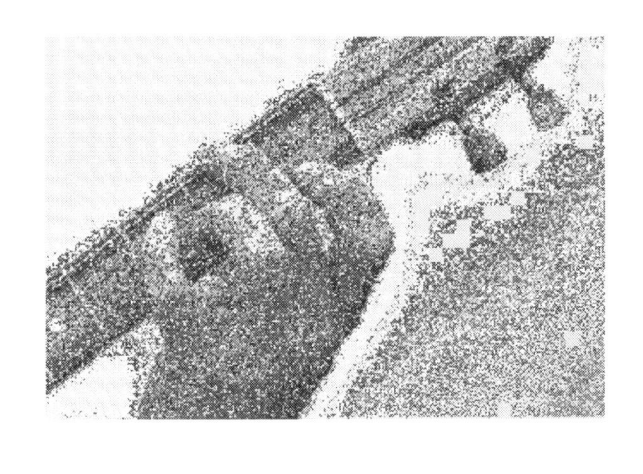

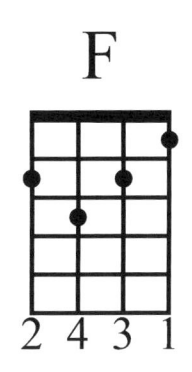

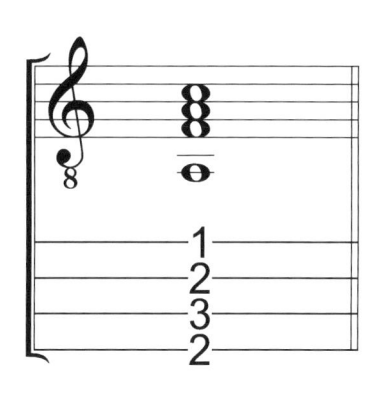

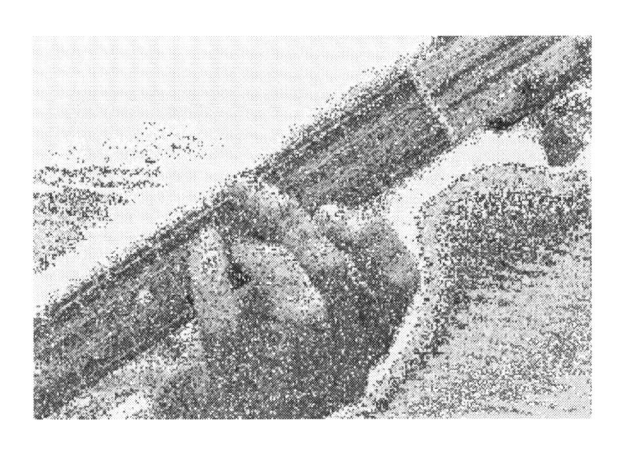

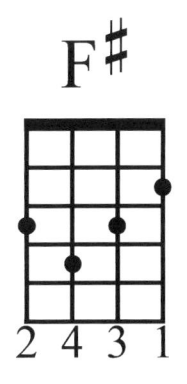

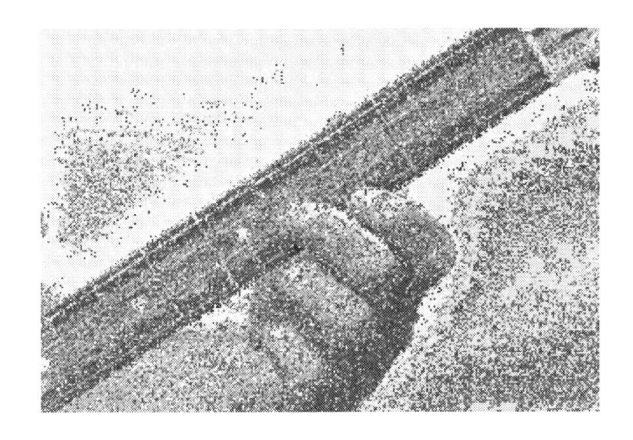

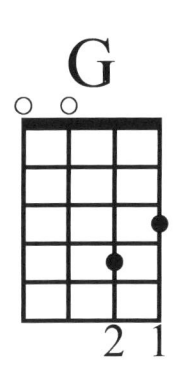

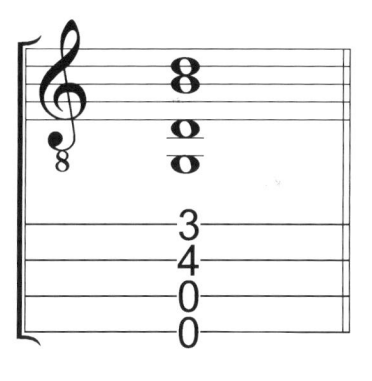

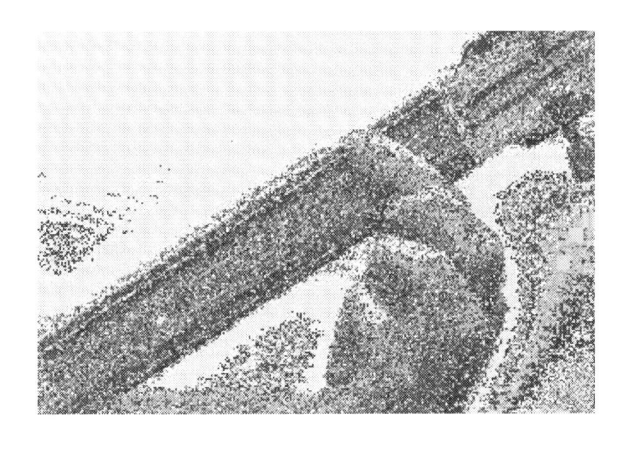

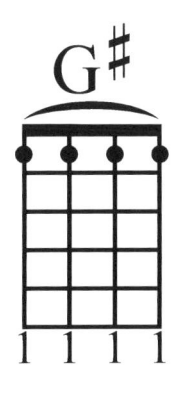

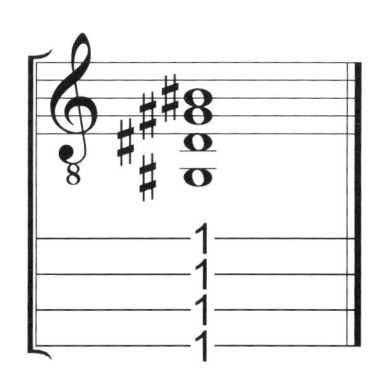

MINOR

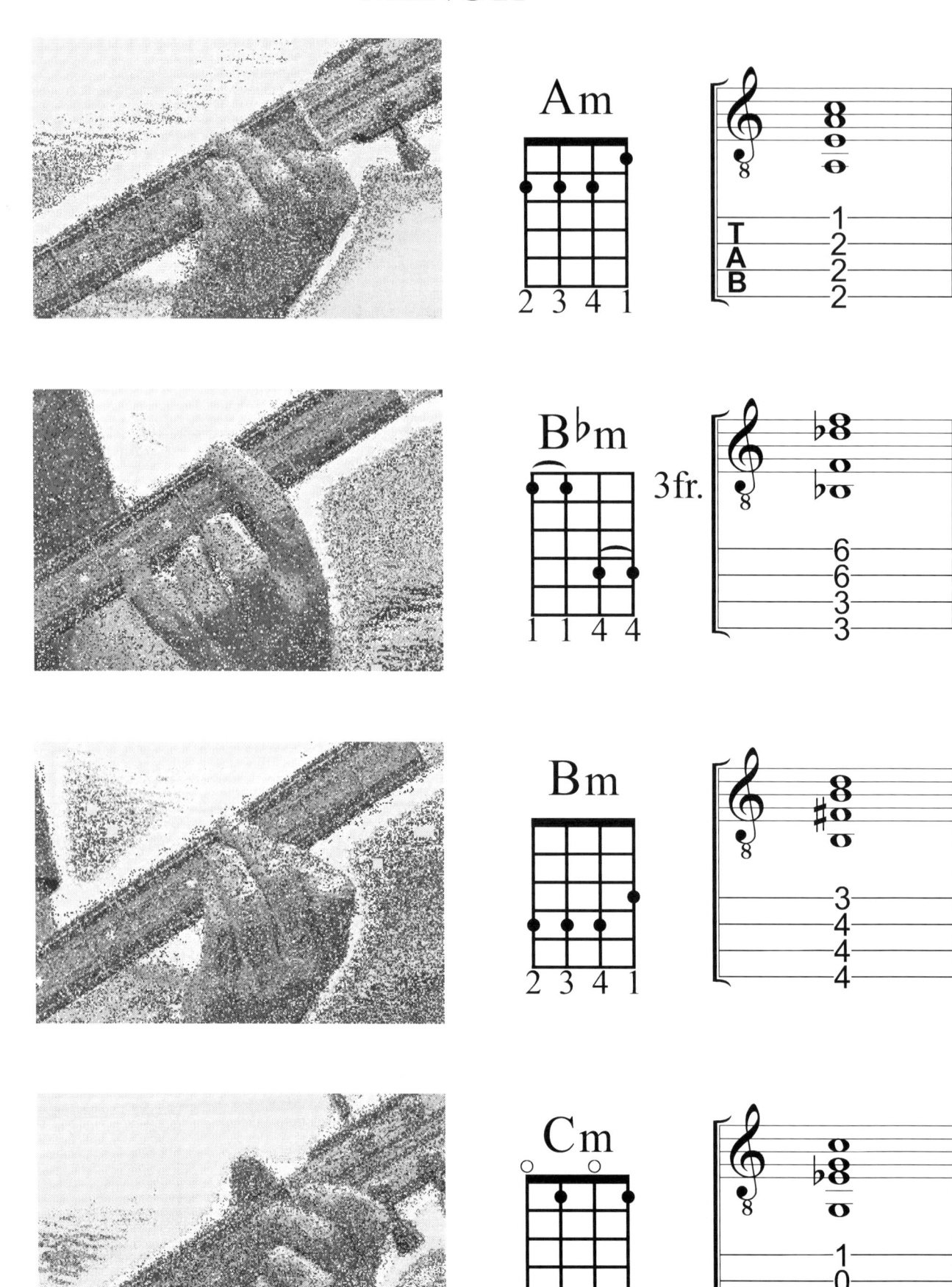

Am

B♭m 3fr.

Bm

Cm

MINOR

C#m

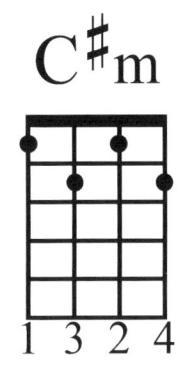

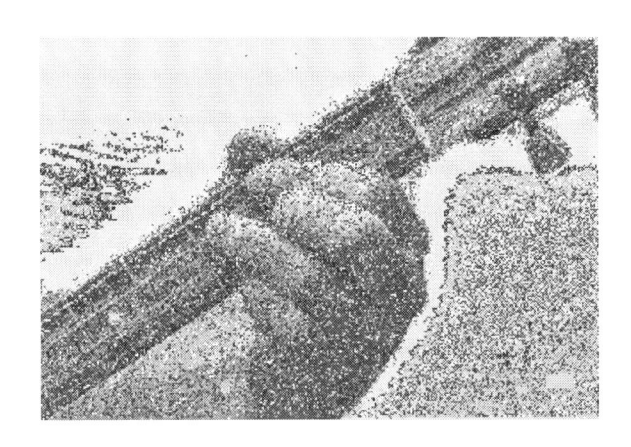

Dm

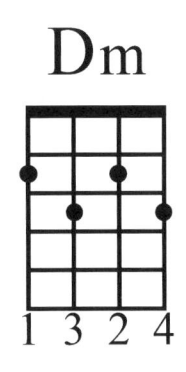

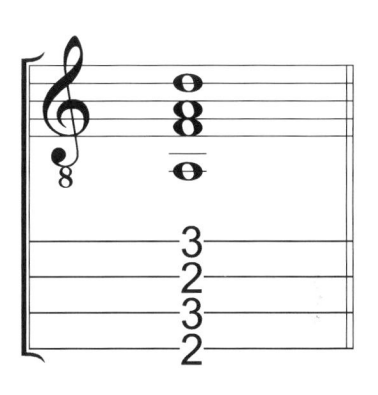

E♭m

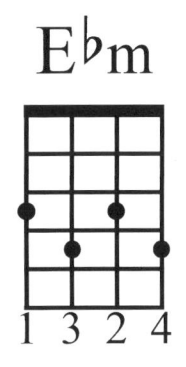

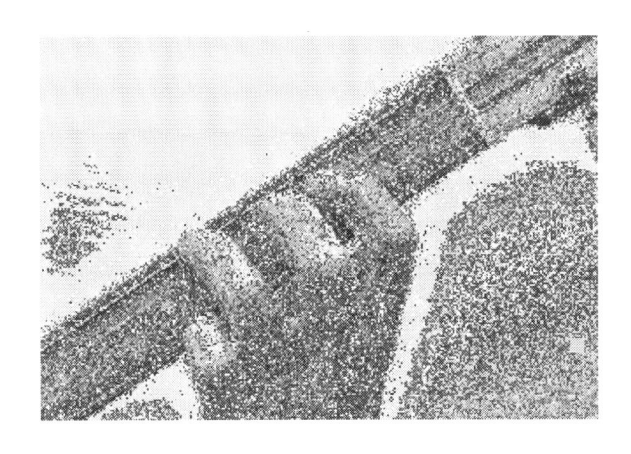

Em

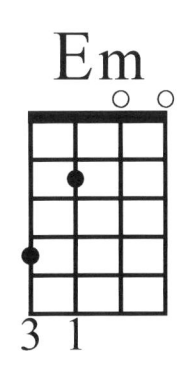

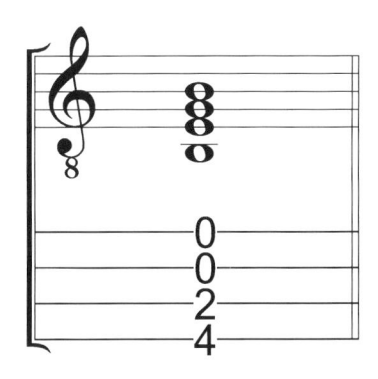

MINOR

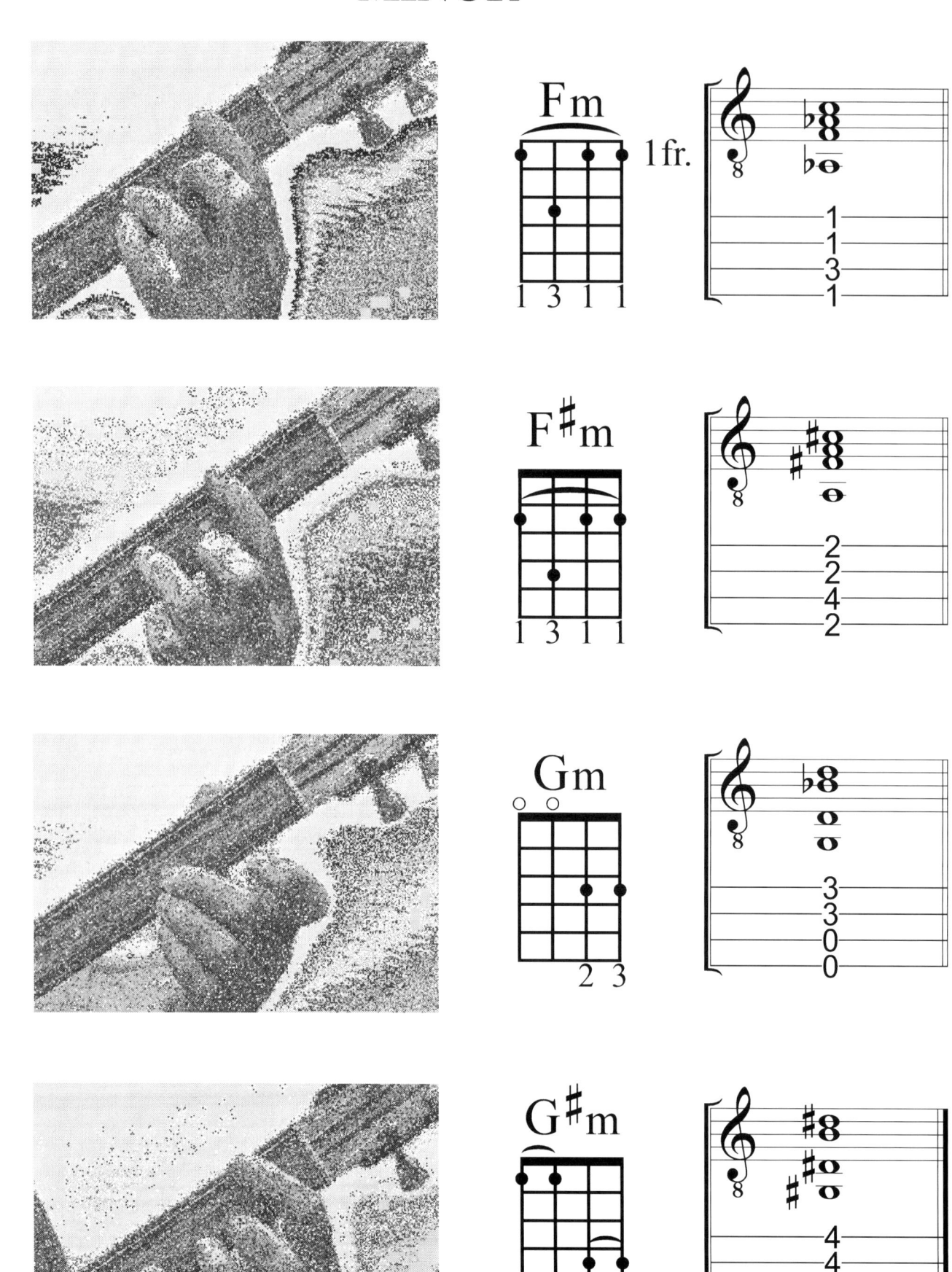

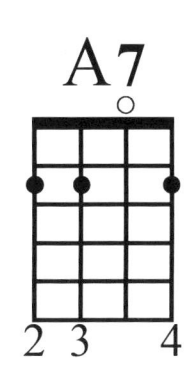

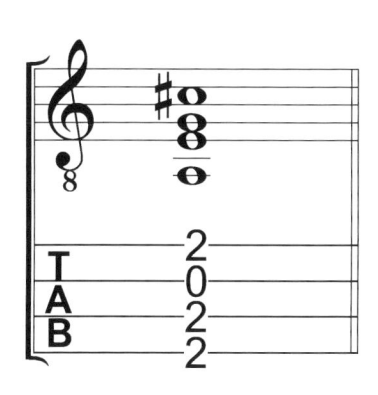

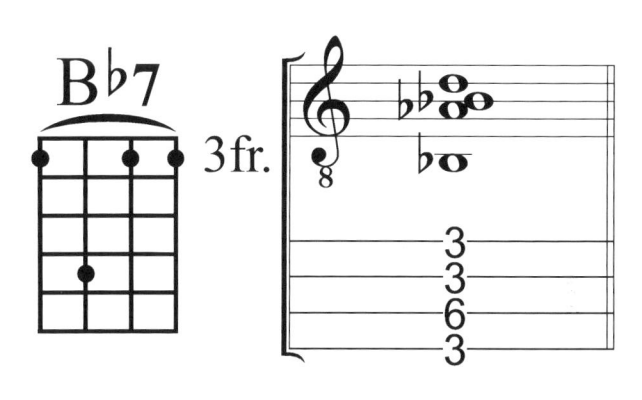

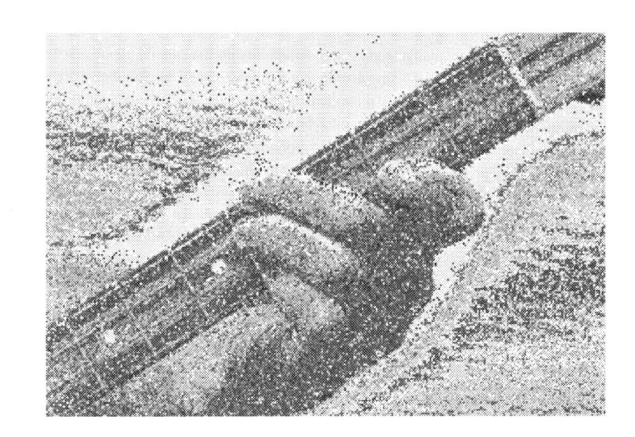

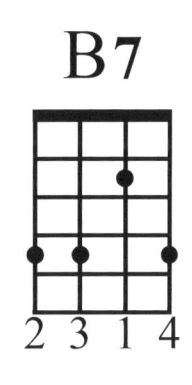

DOMINANT 7th

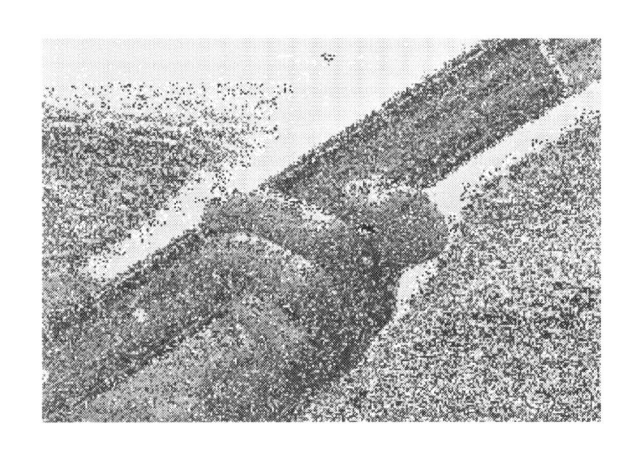

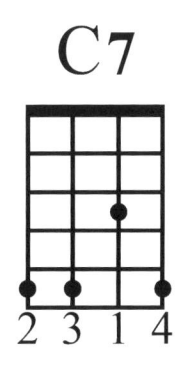

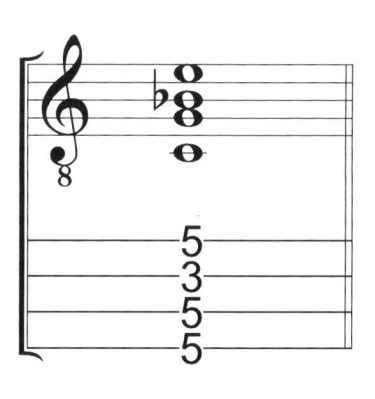

DOMINANT 7th

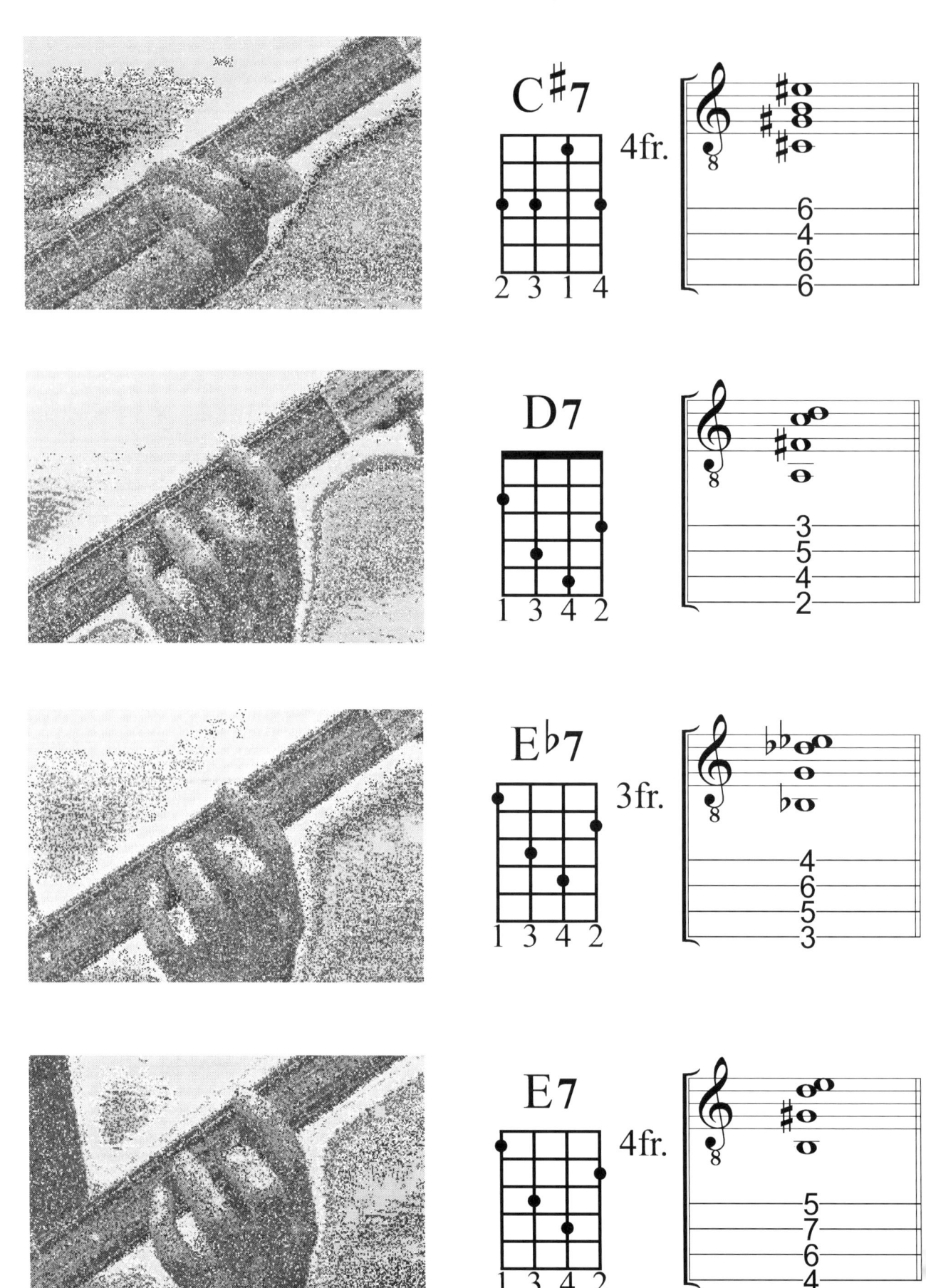

C#7 — 4fr.

D7

Eb7 — 3fr.

E7 — 4fr.

DOMINANT 7th

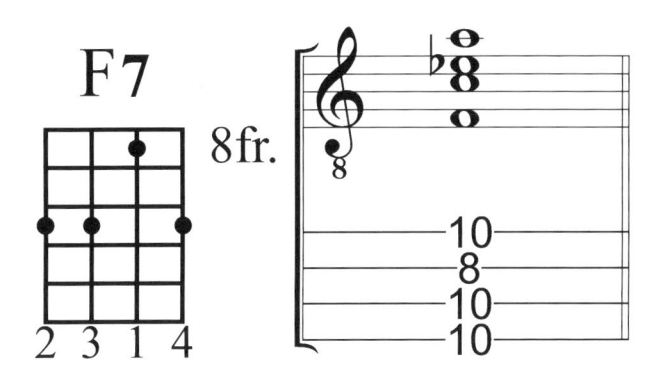

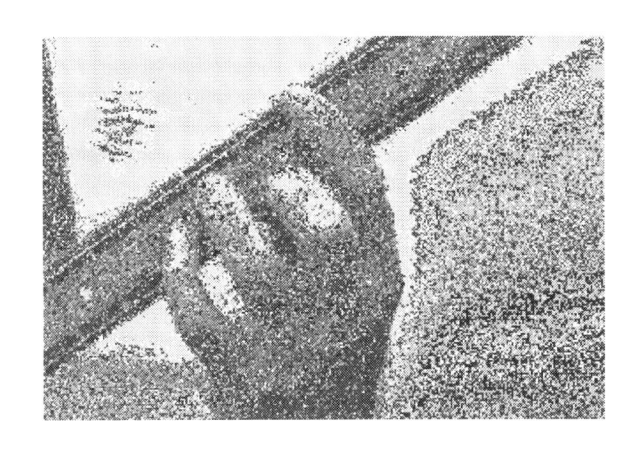

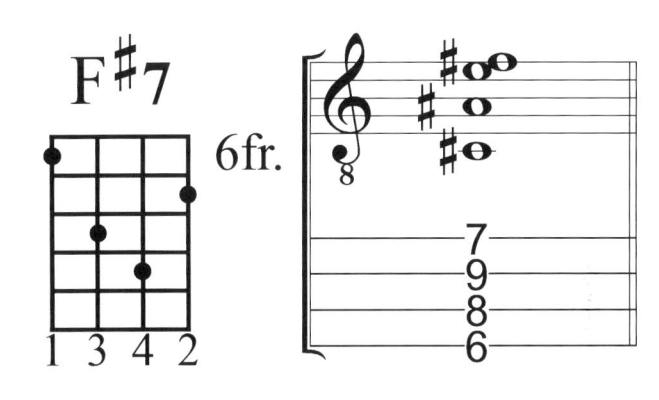

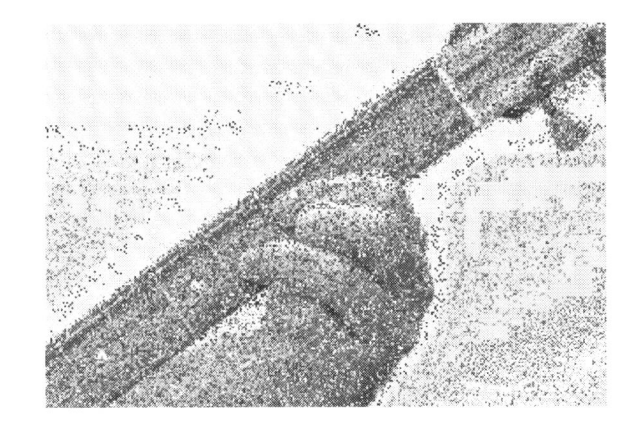

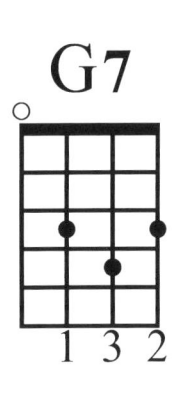

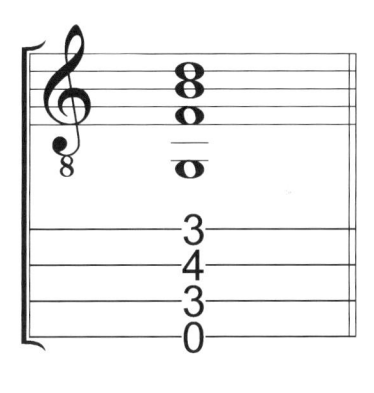

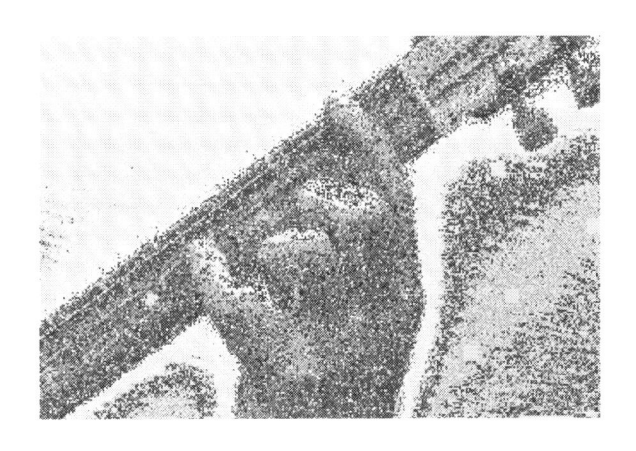

Moveable Chord Shapes

A great way to master chords on the cigar box guitar is to memorize the most common chord shapes, or "moveable chords." Moveable chords allow you to keep your fingers on the same shape and change the chord name by moving to a different fret.

For example, play an A major chord with a barre on the second fret as shown in the diagram below, then move the same chord down to the seventh fret to play a D chord. You will quickly notice moving the shape is easy, but now you have to study where the root for each chord is and the letter names on the fingerboard.

The root of the chord is the note that gives the chord its name – so, the root of a C chord is C. The root can be found on any of the four strings, but I recommend learning the notes on the fourth, then moving to the third string. Fortunately, we have two strings tuned to a G, so when you learn the notes on the fourth string, you are also learning the notes on the second string.

With time and practice, you can learn the note names on the cigar box guitar and expand your chord knowledge exponentially.

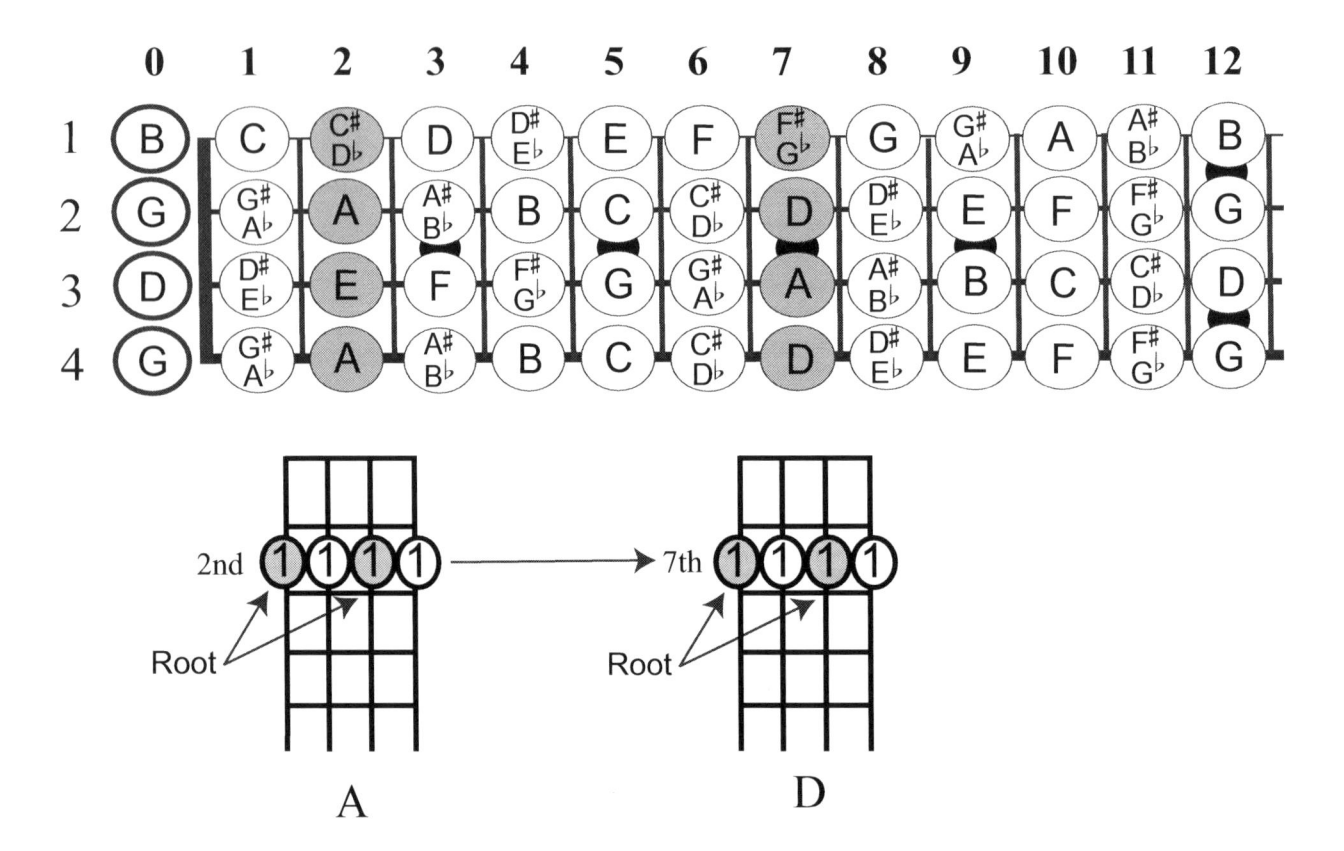

Major

Minor

*Augmented

*Diminished

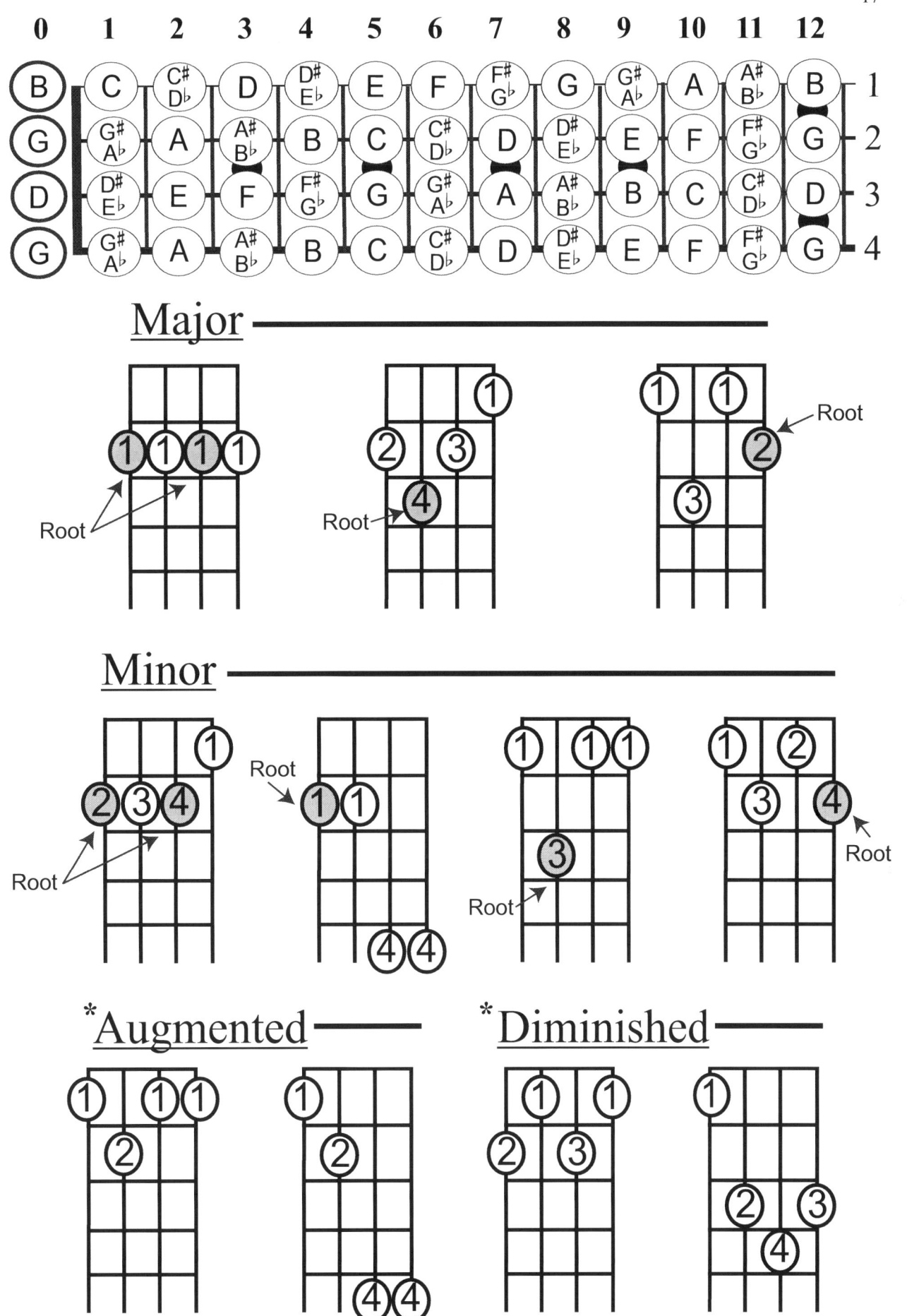

* The root can be any note with augmented and diminished chords.

Minor 7th

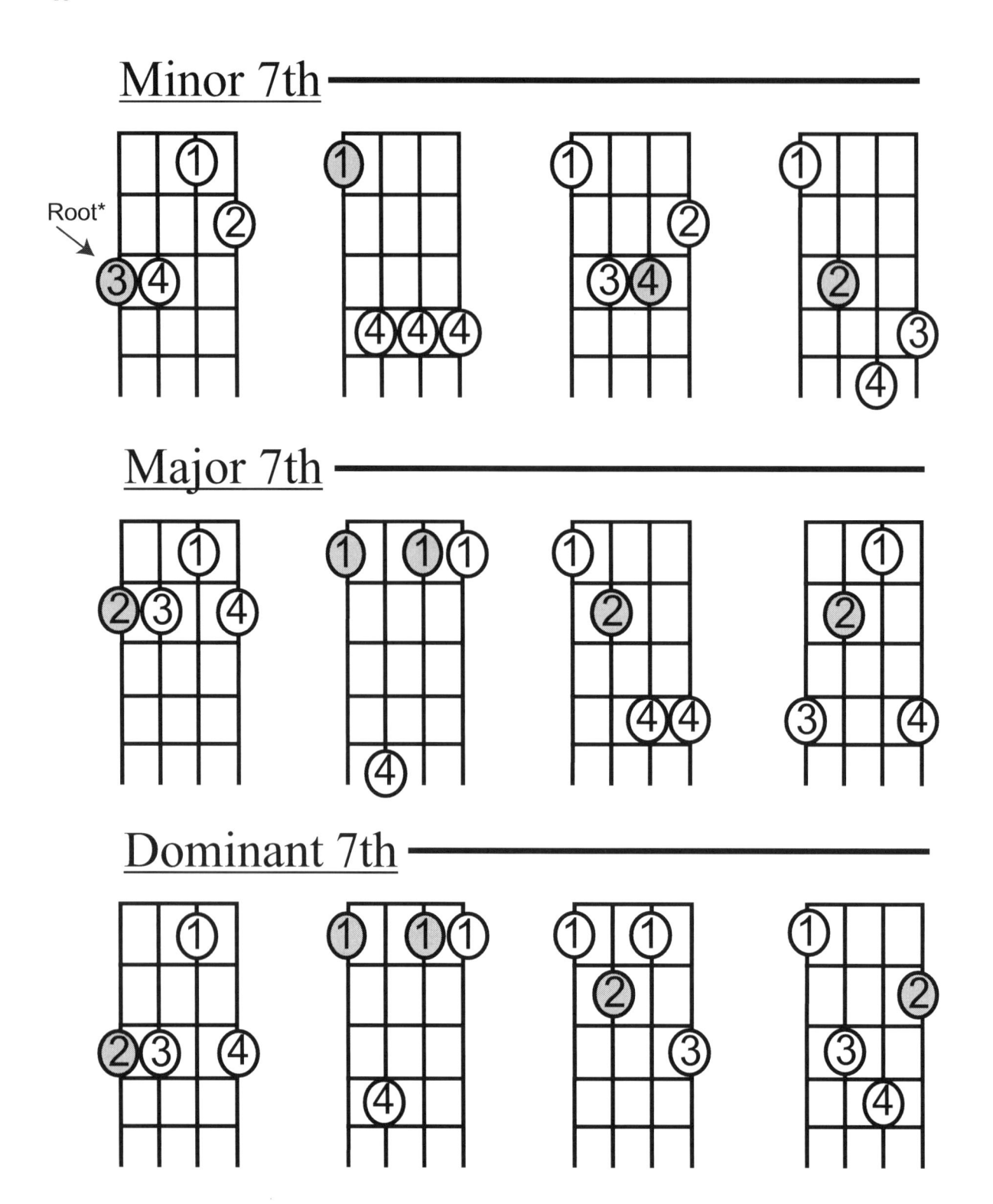

Major 7th

Dominant 7th

Practice moving the following chords around the neck to a song or chord progression you know. Here's a sample progression in the key of G and C:

G | B7 | E7 | Am7 | C | Cm | G7 F#7 F7 | E7 | Am7 | D7 | G ||
C | E7 | A7 | Dm7 | F | Fm | C7 B7 Bb7| A7 | Dm7 | G7 | C ||

*Filled in note is root

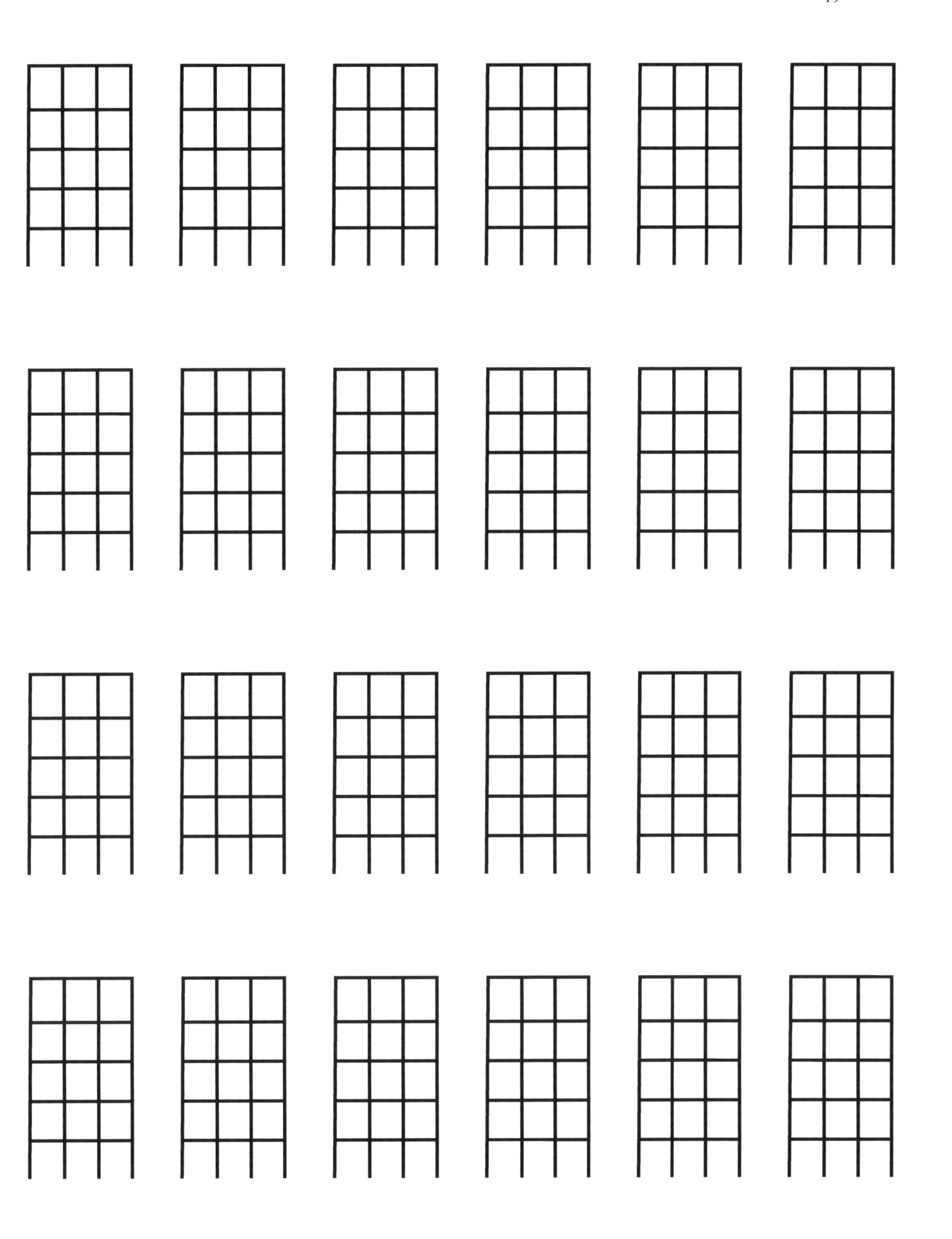

Diatonic Chords in C - G - D

Diatonic chords are when you build a chord on each note of a scale.
In the examples below, triads and 7th chords are shown in the major keys of G, C, and D.

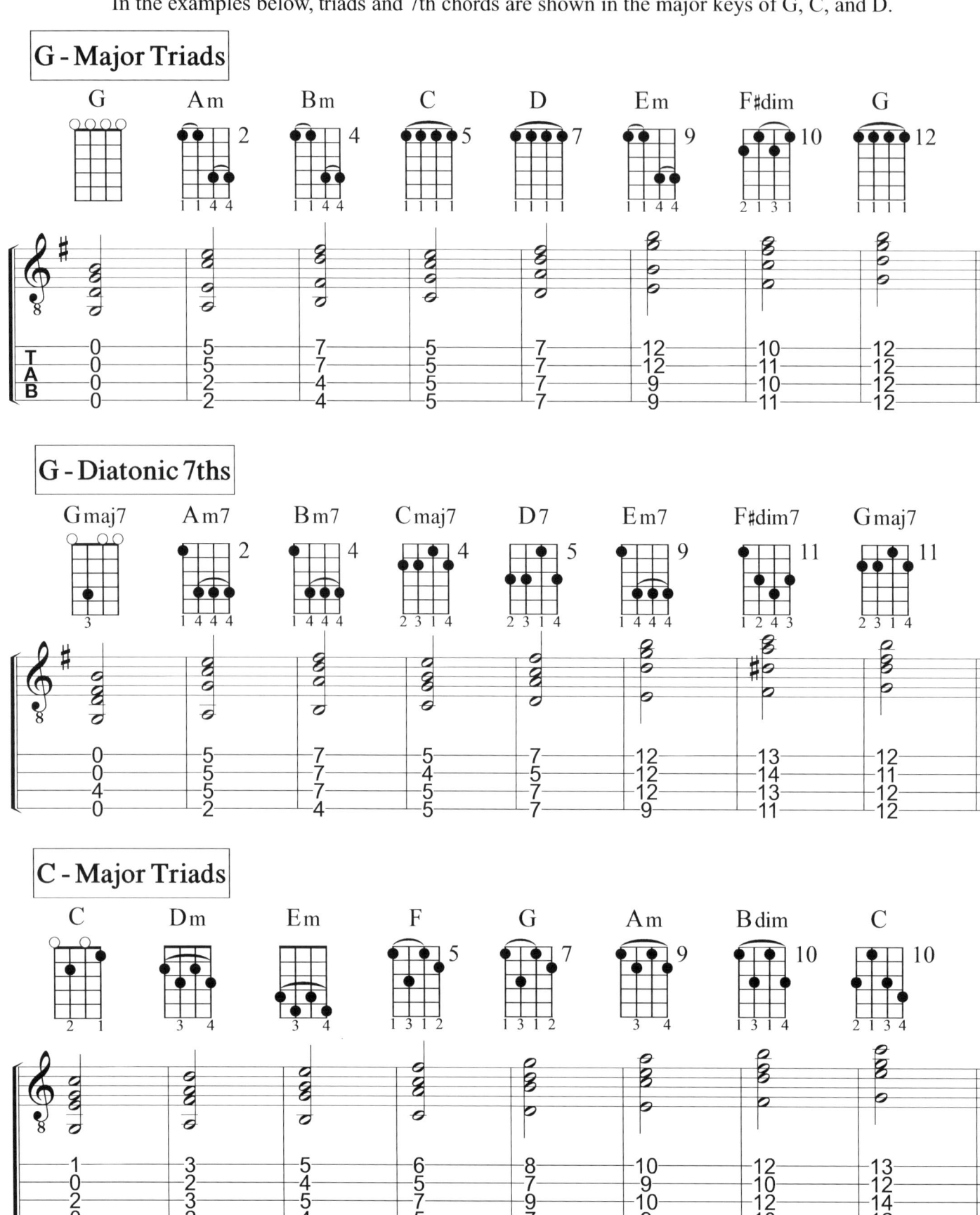

G - Major Triads

G - Diatonic 7ths

C - Major Triads

C - Diatonic 7ths

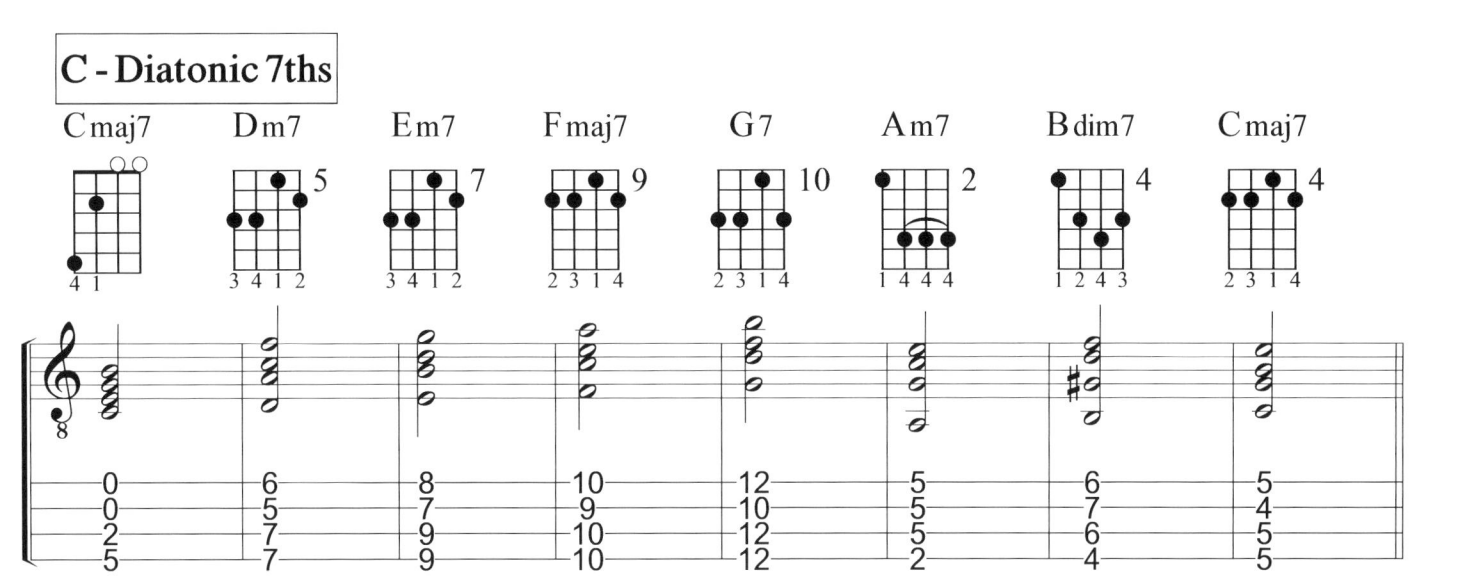

D - Major Triads

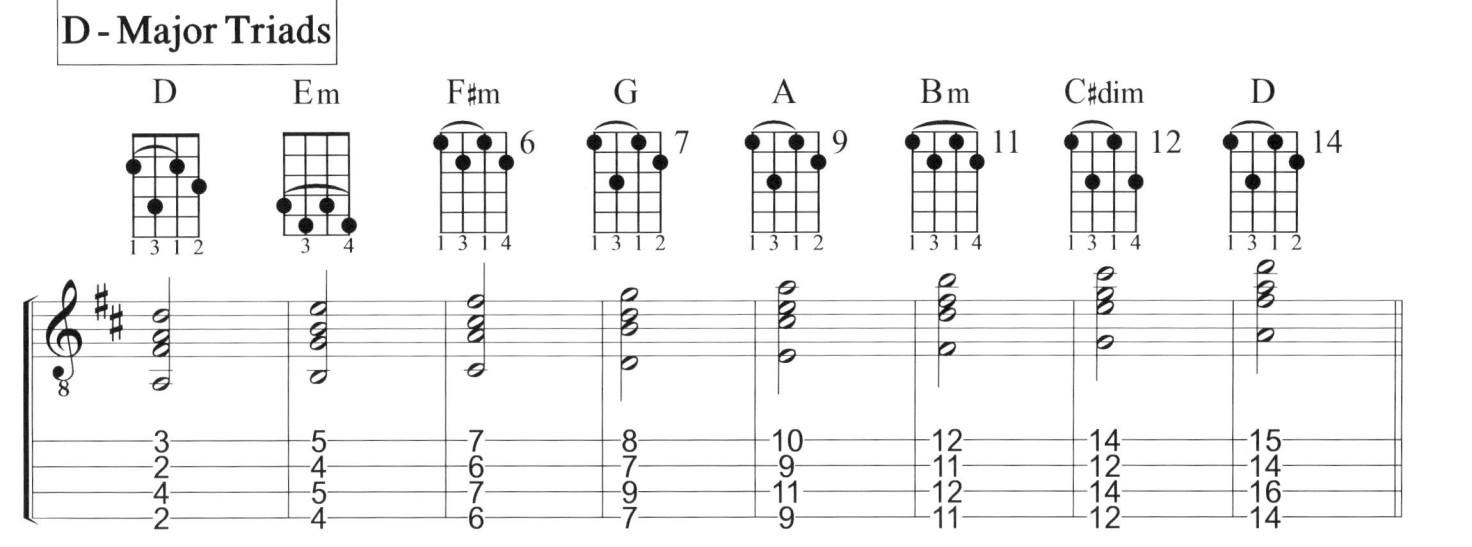

D - Diatonic 7ths

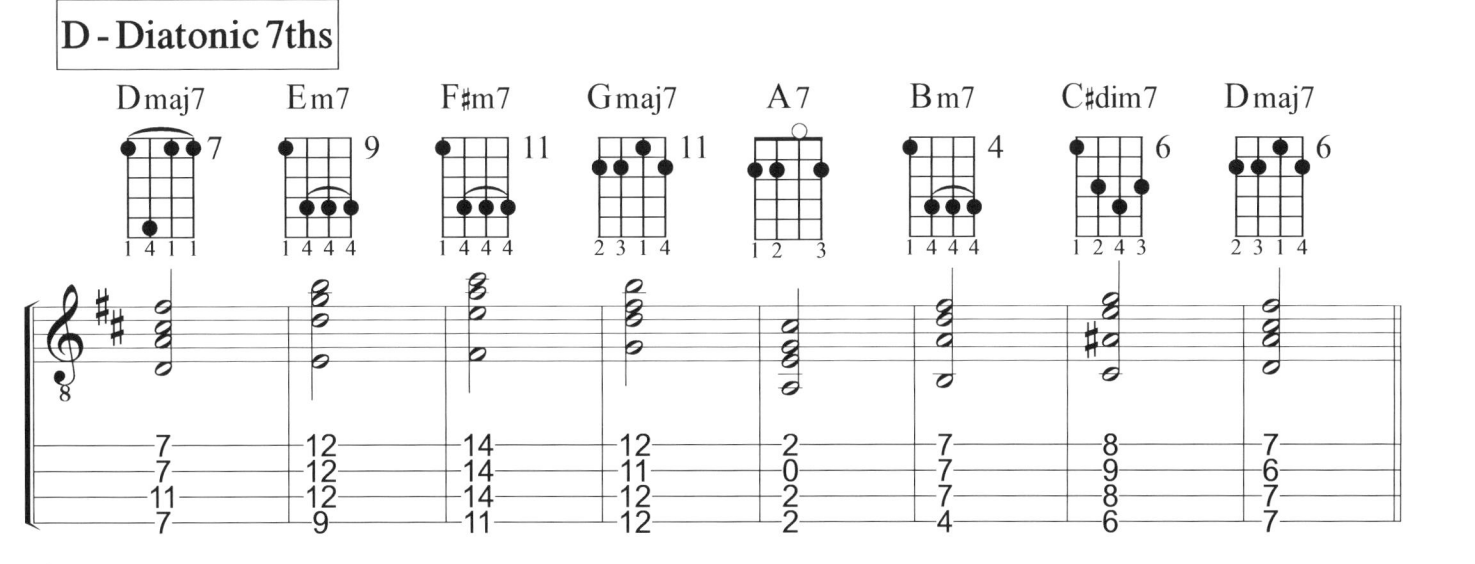

CHORD LIBRARY

A Major - A6 - Amaj7

A Major

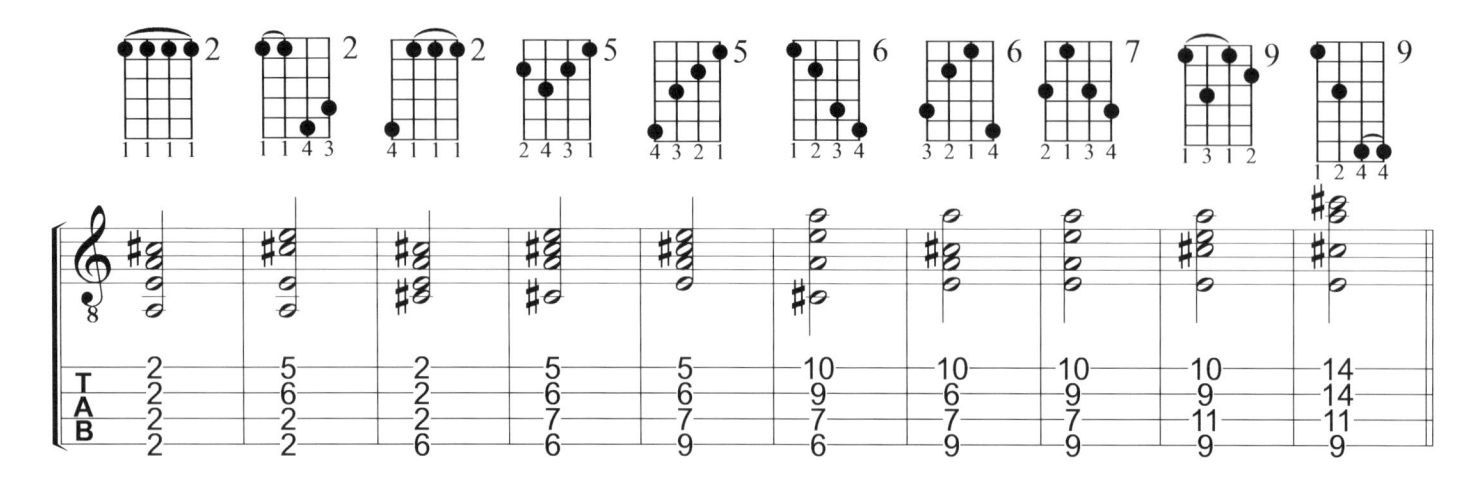

A6

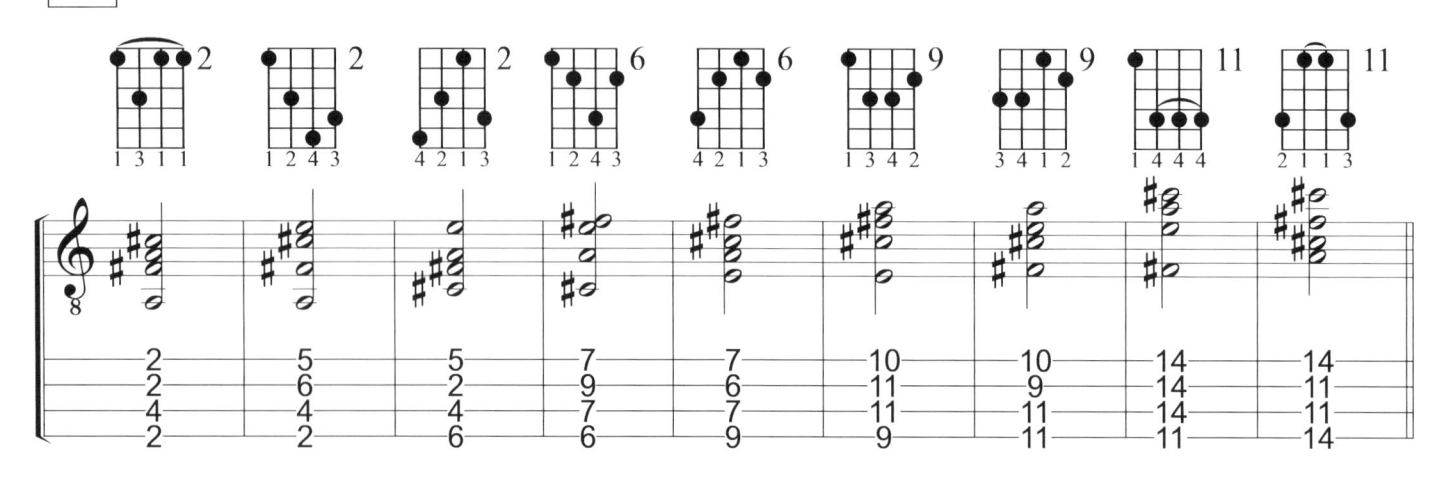

Amaj7

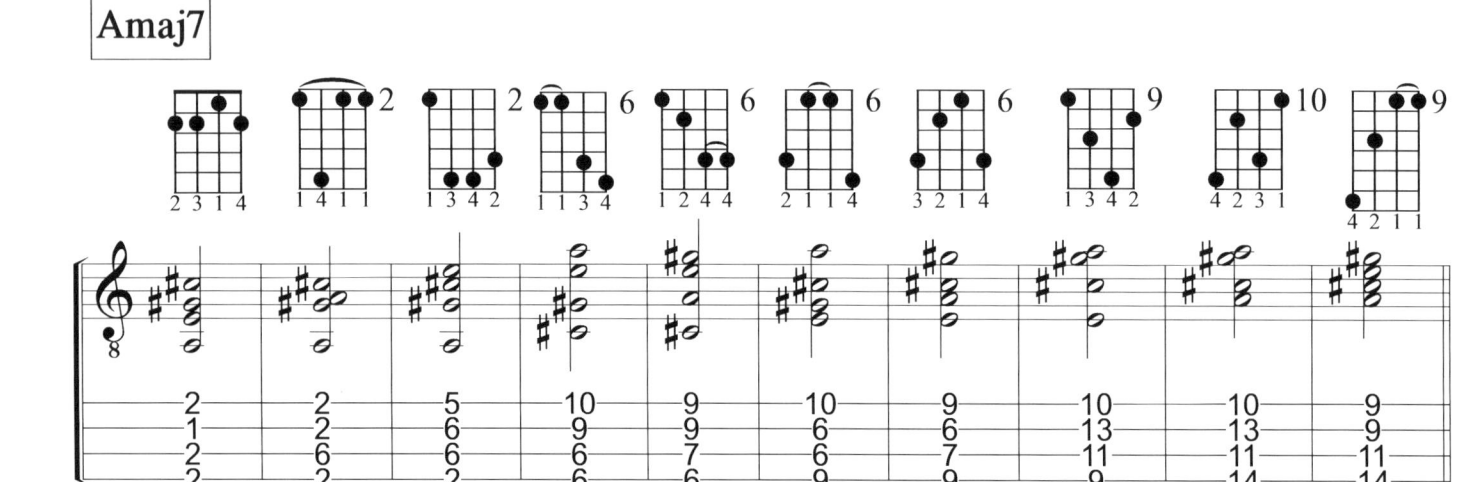

Amaj9 - A6/9 - A augmented +

Amaj9

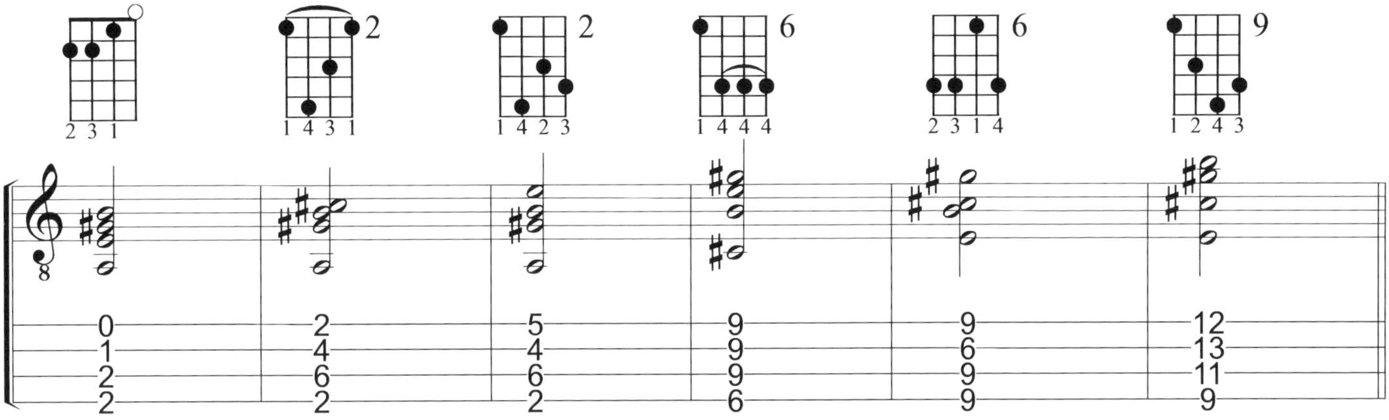

A6/9

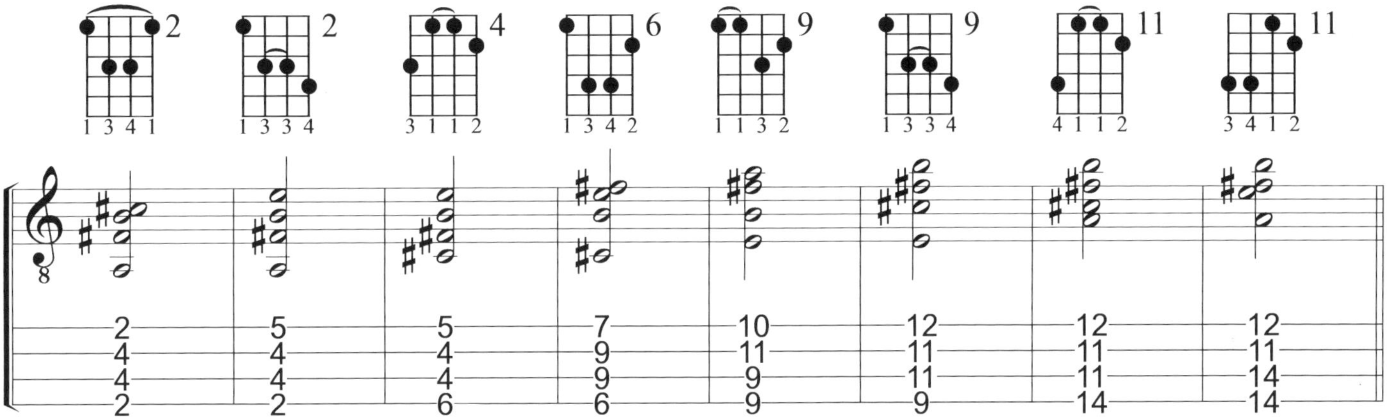

A Augmented (A+)

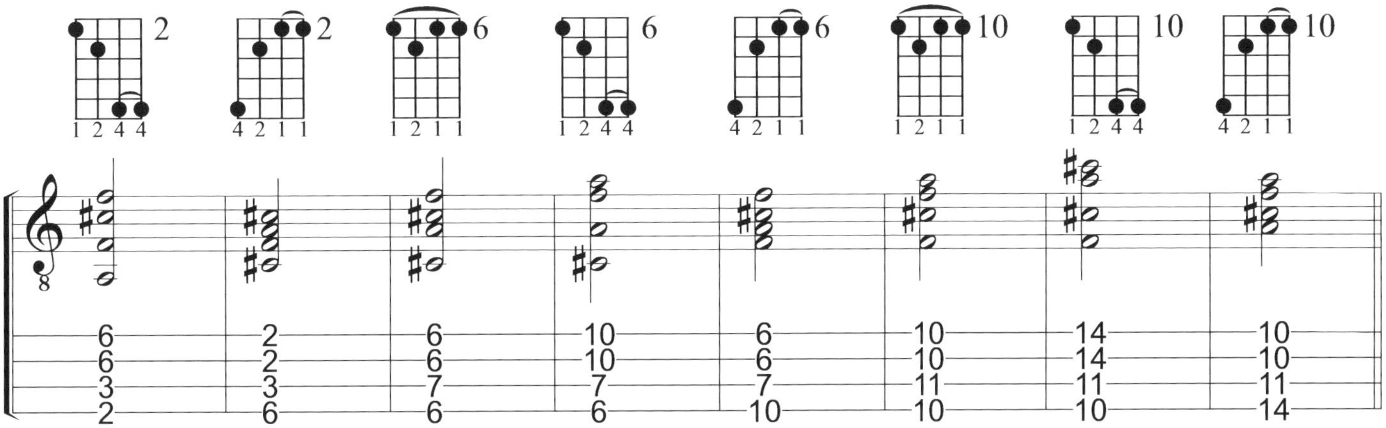

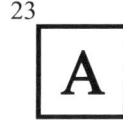

Am - Am6 - Am7

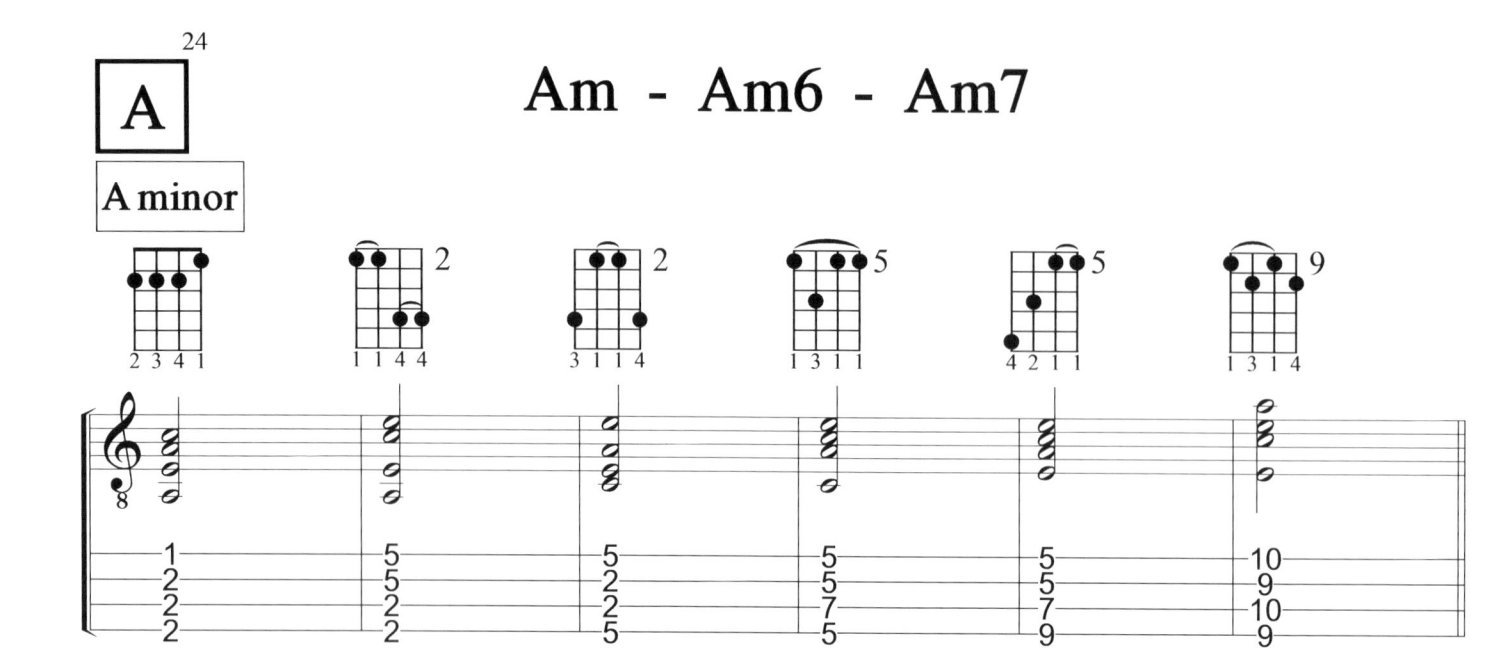

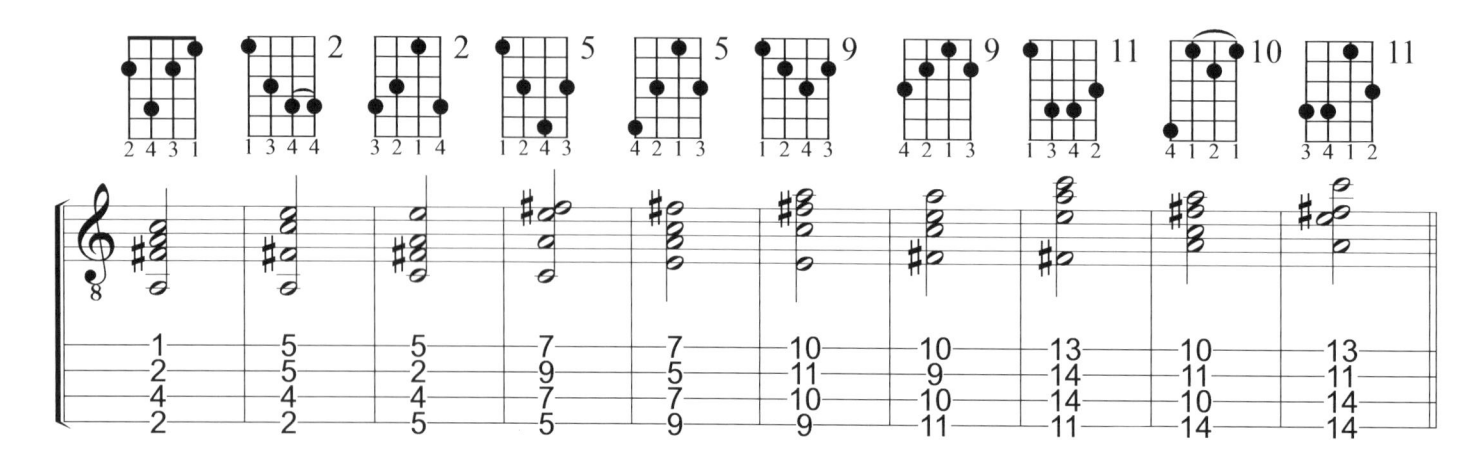

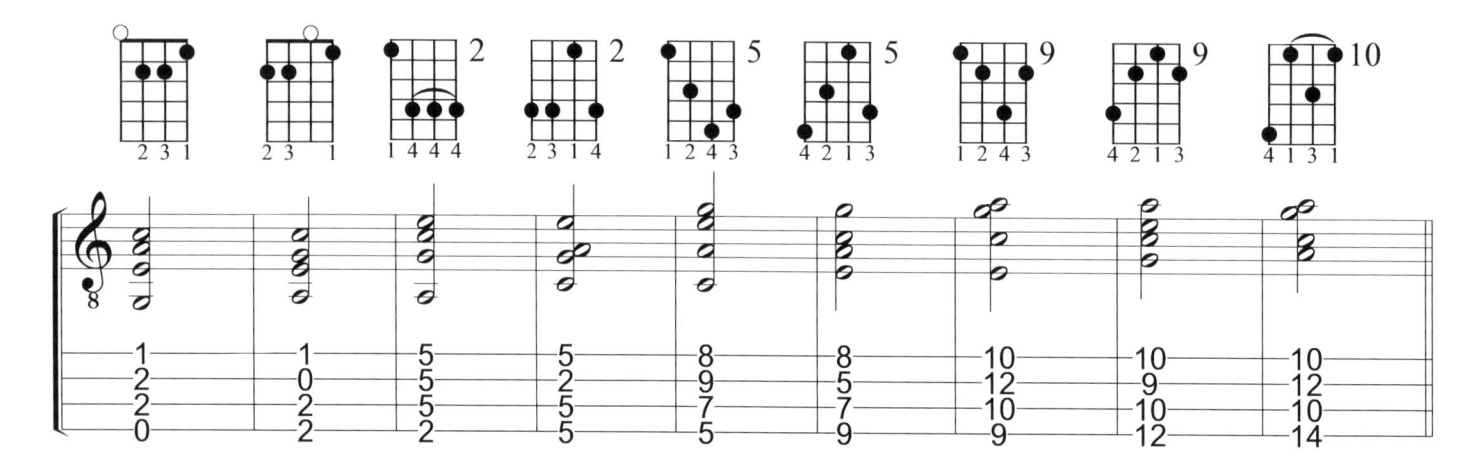

A minor

Am7♭5 - Am9 - Am11 - Am(maj7)

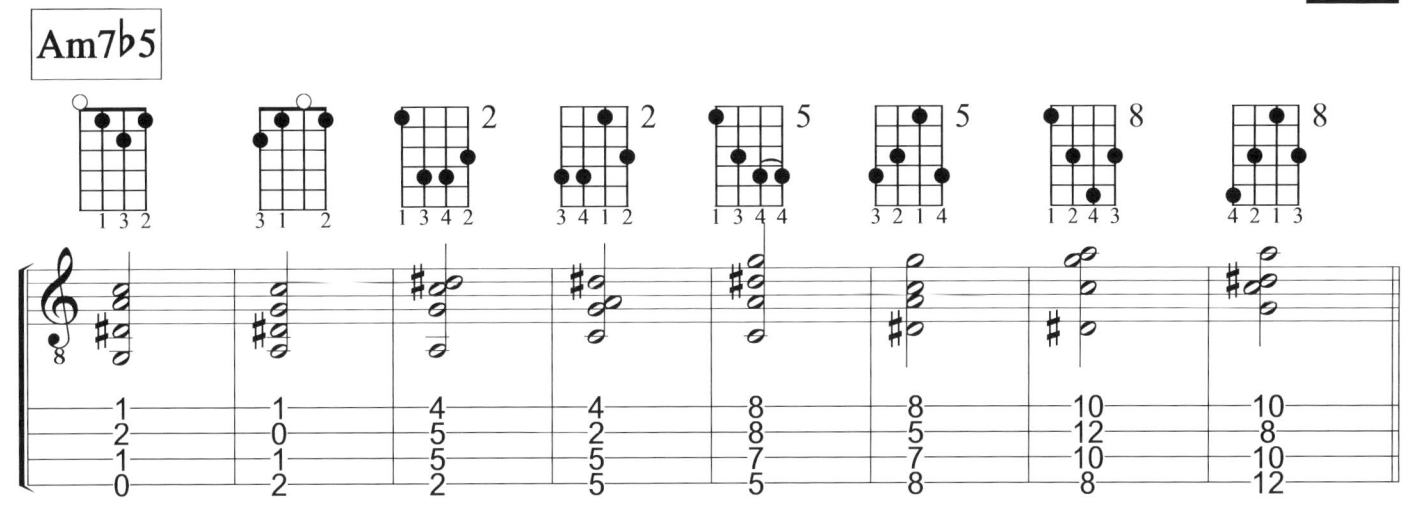

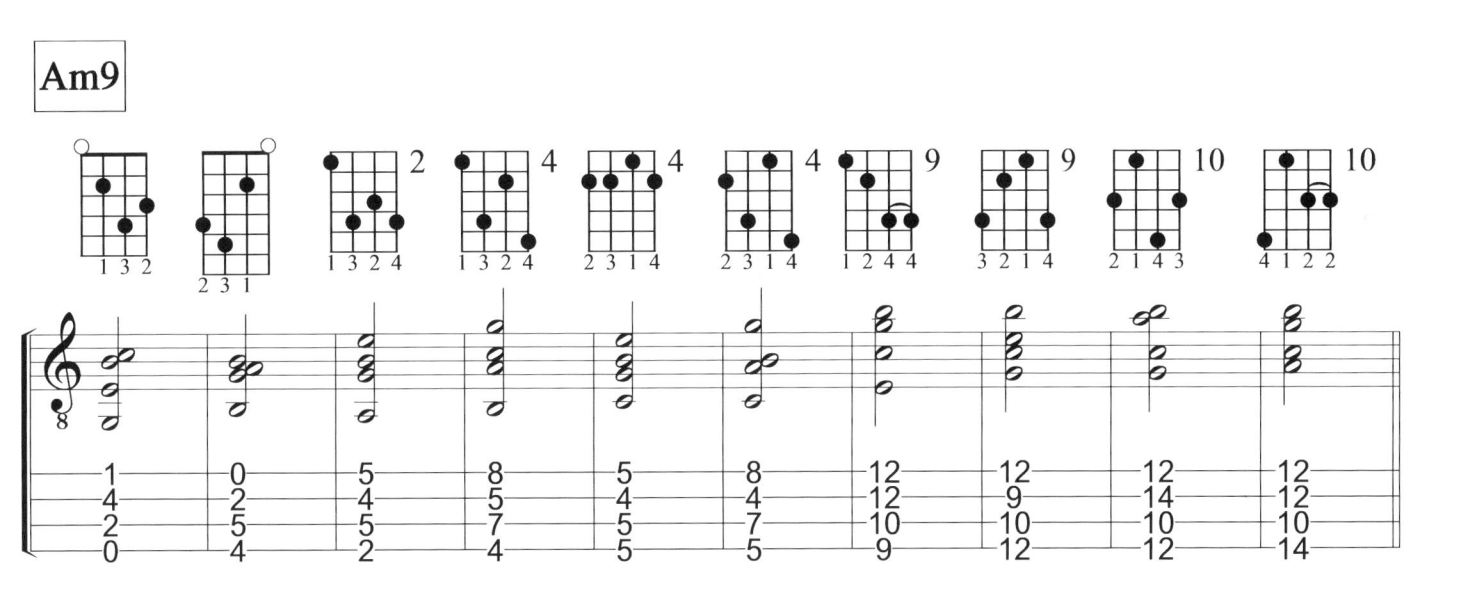

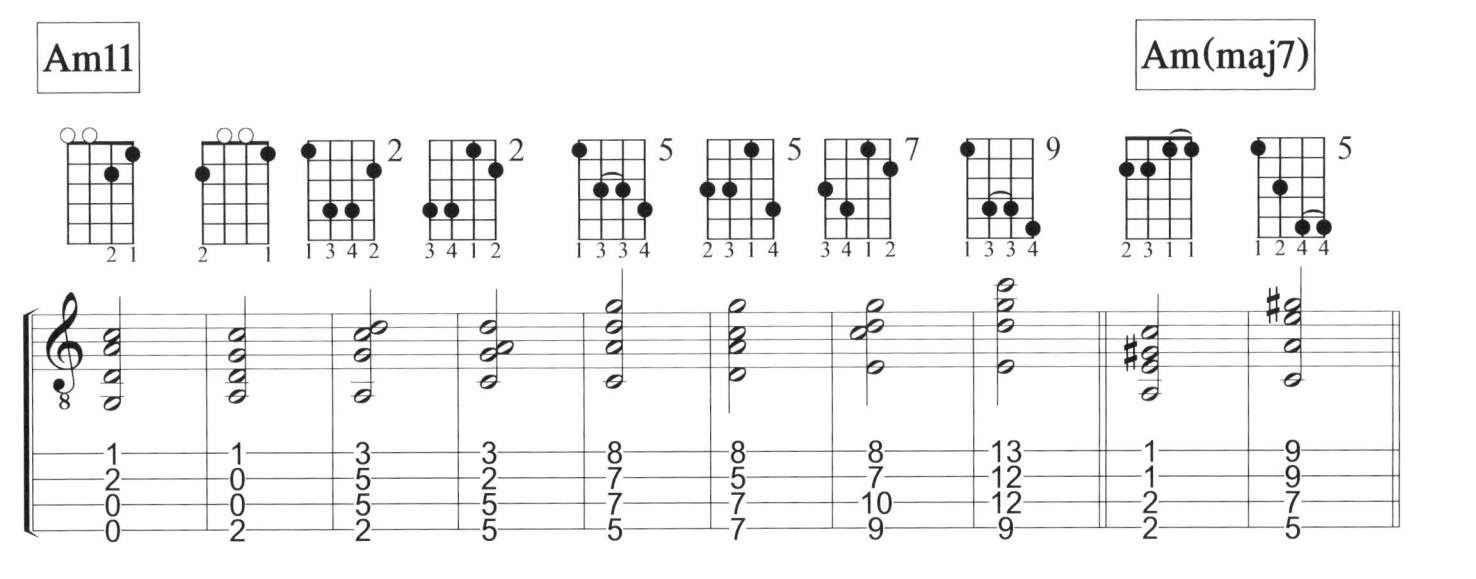

A7 - A9 - A13

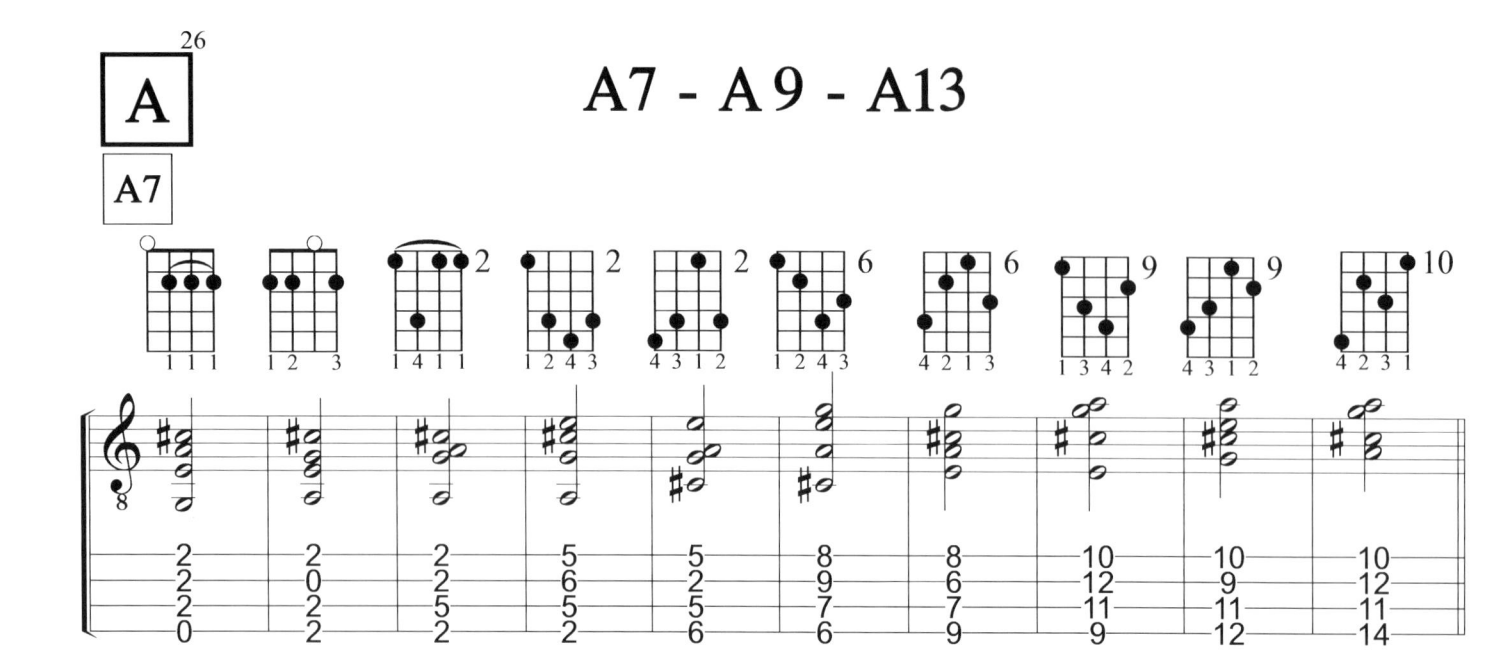

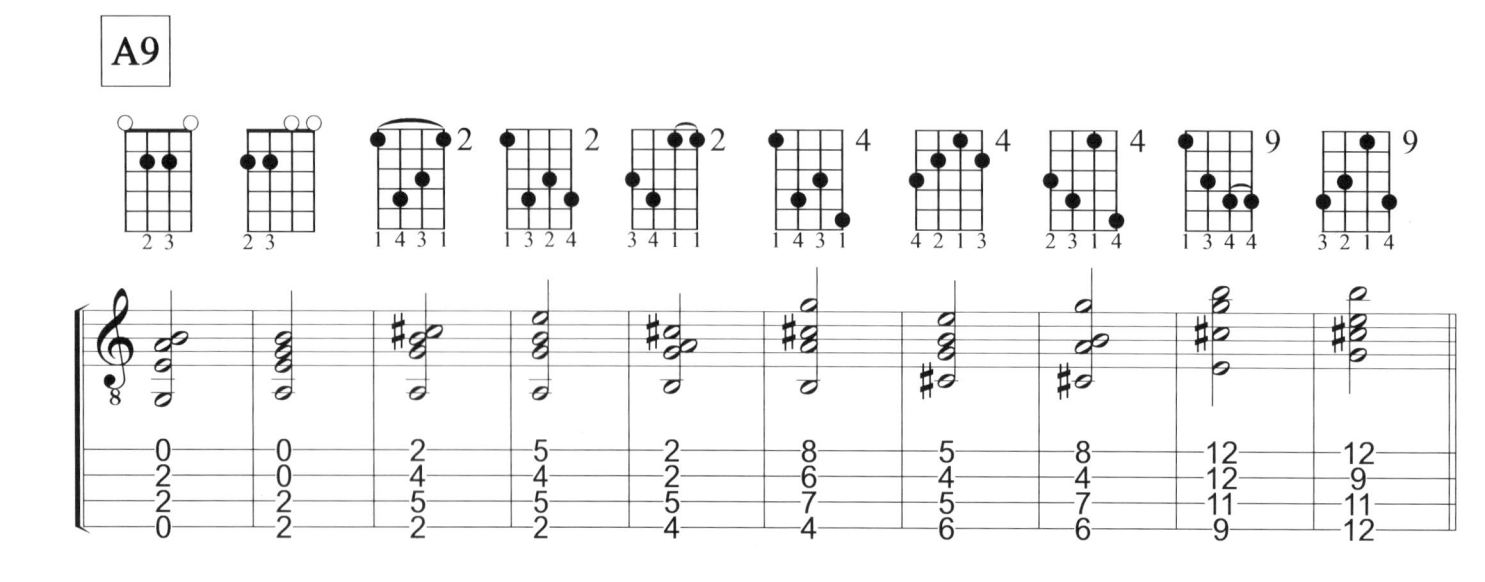

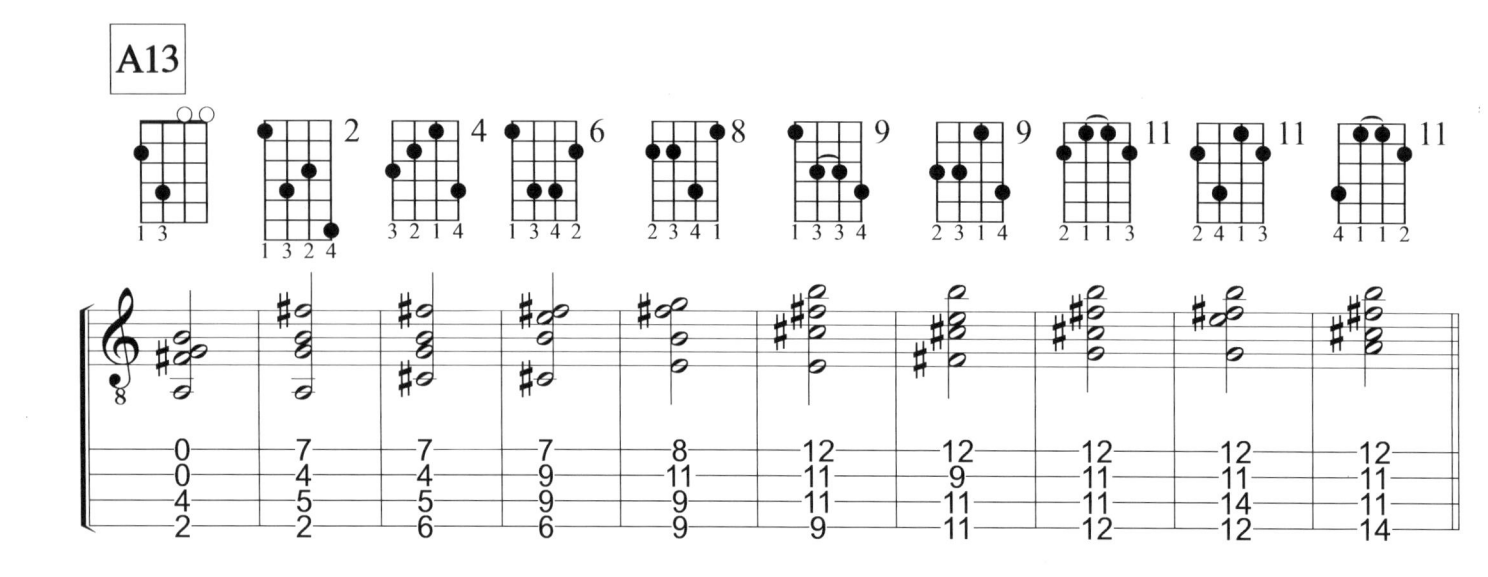

A7♭5 - A7♯5 - A7♯9

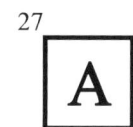

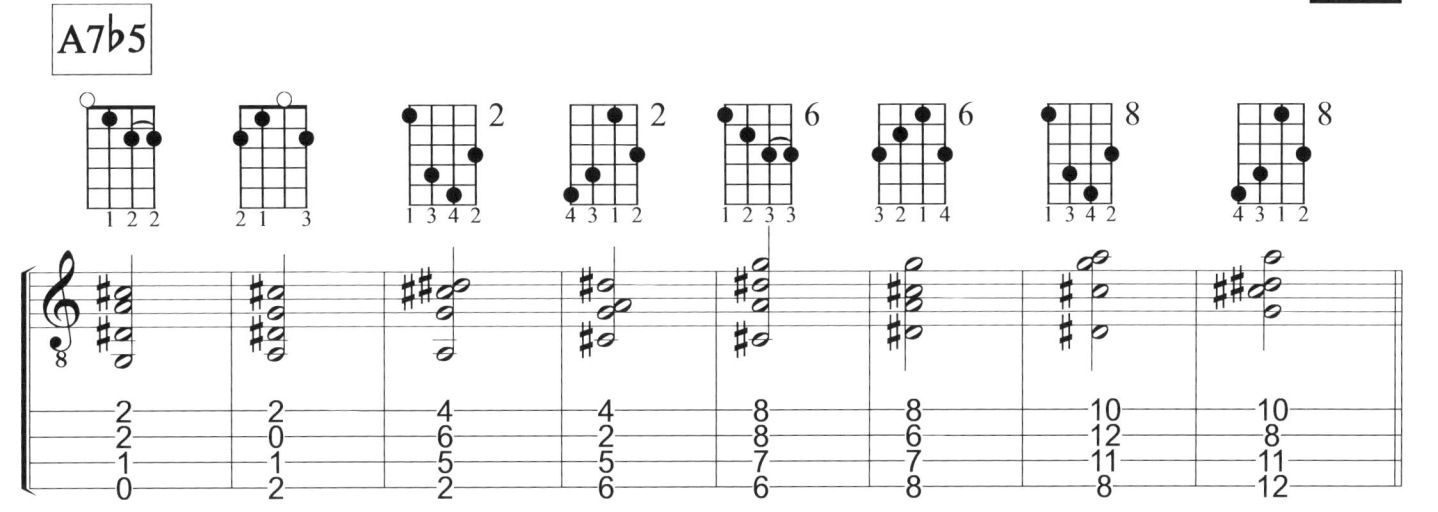

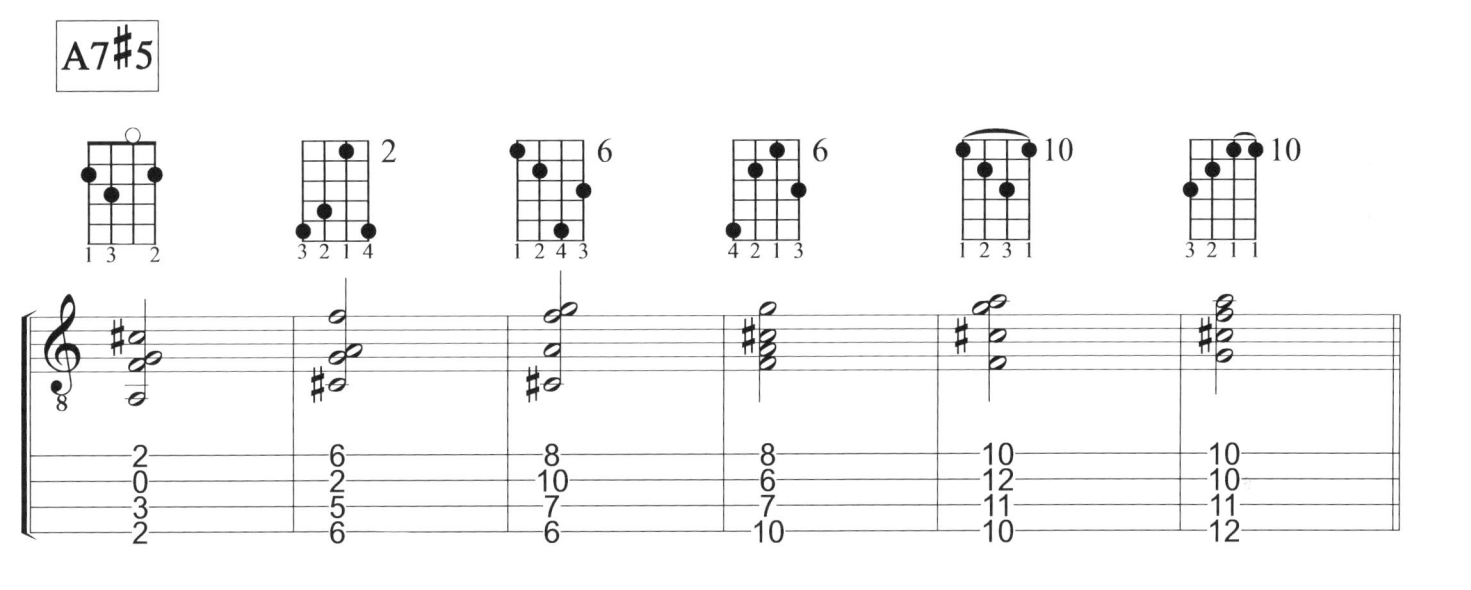

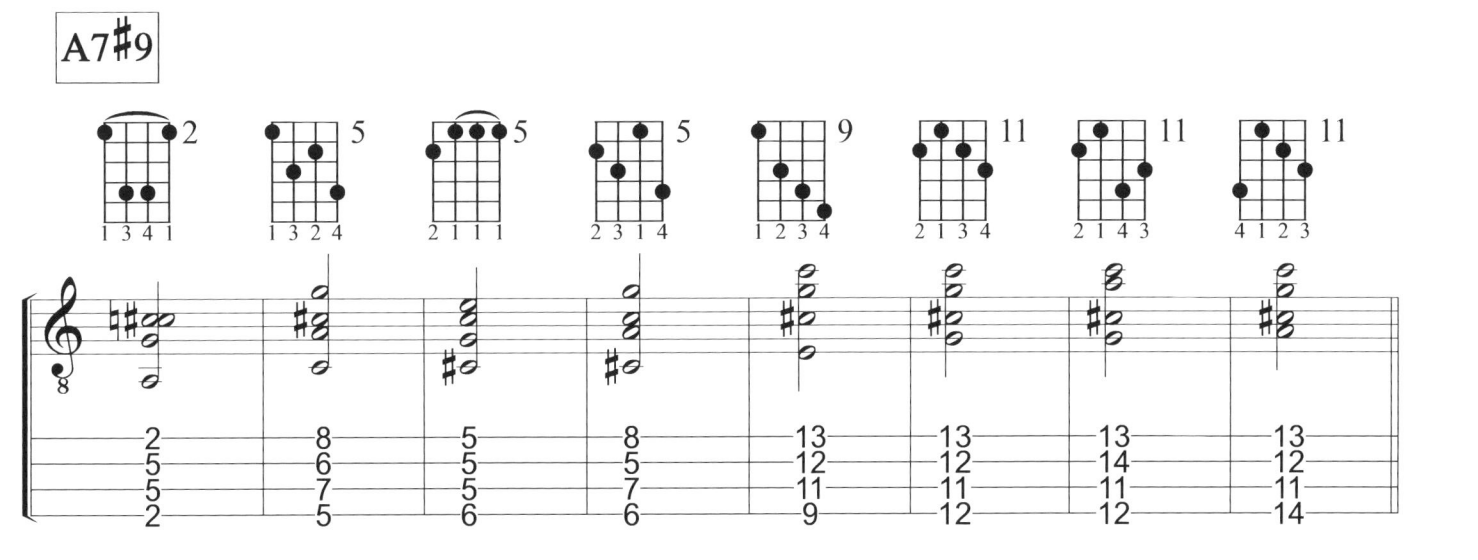

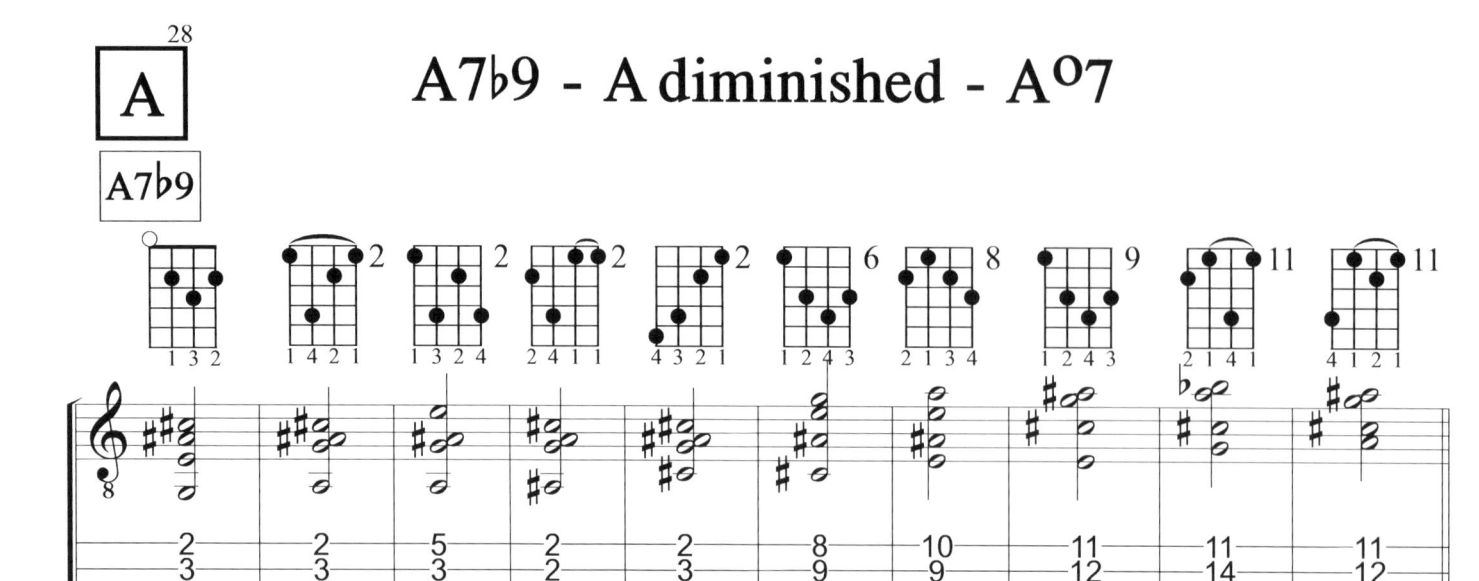

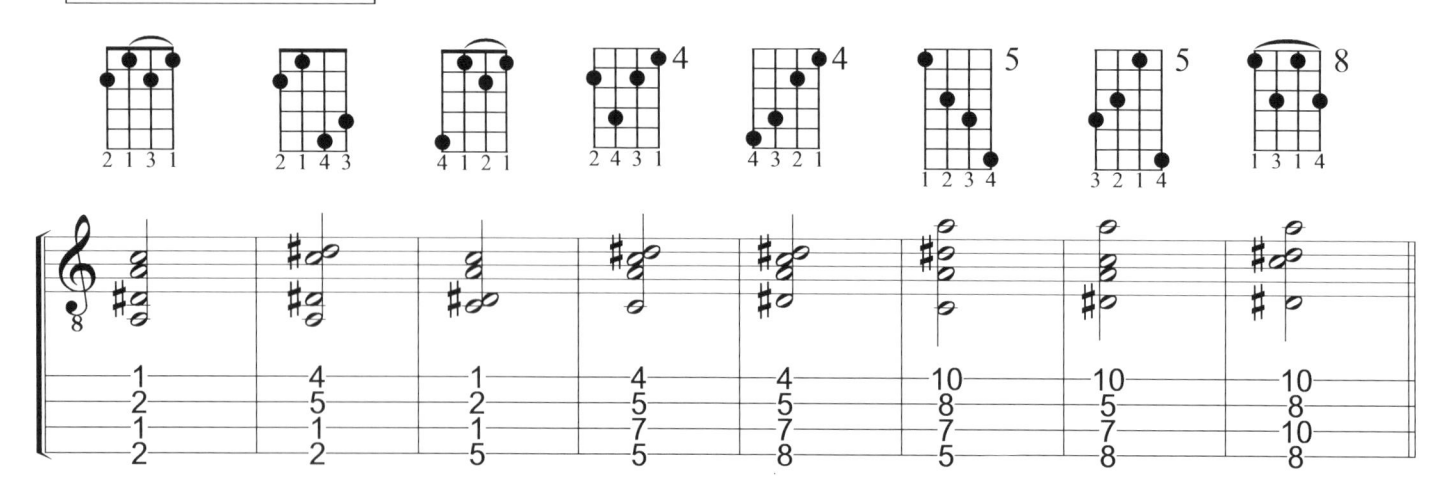

A7♭9 - A diminished - A°7

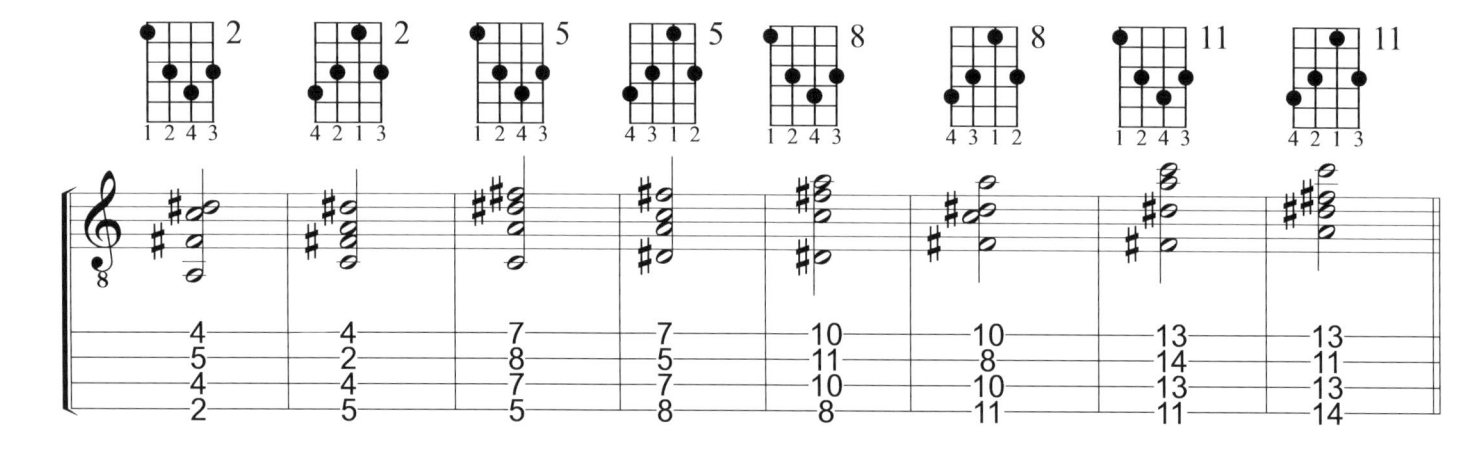

Asus4 - Asus2 - Aadd9 - A7sus - A5

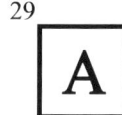

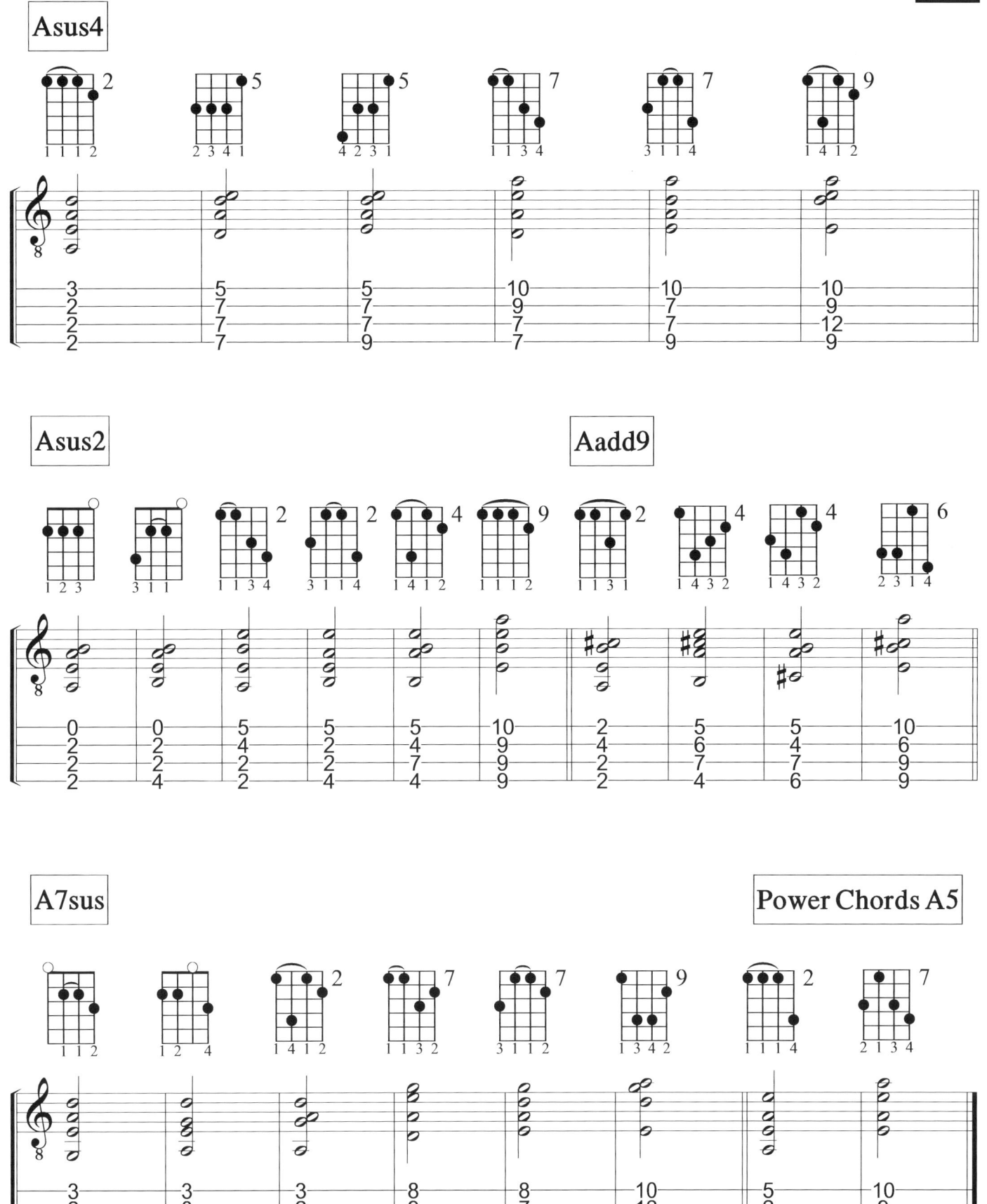

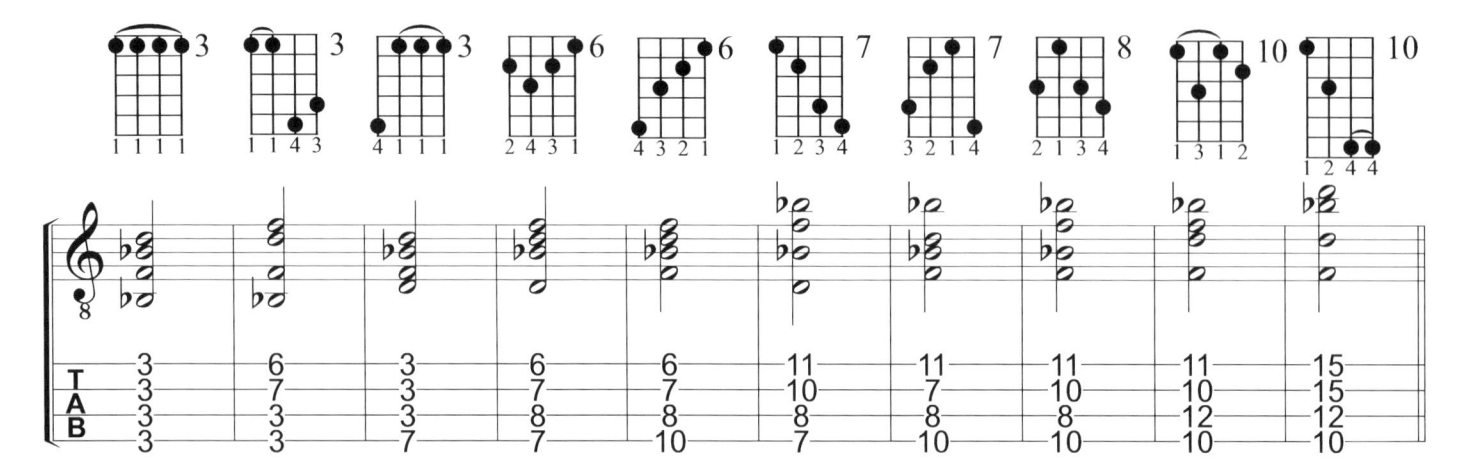

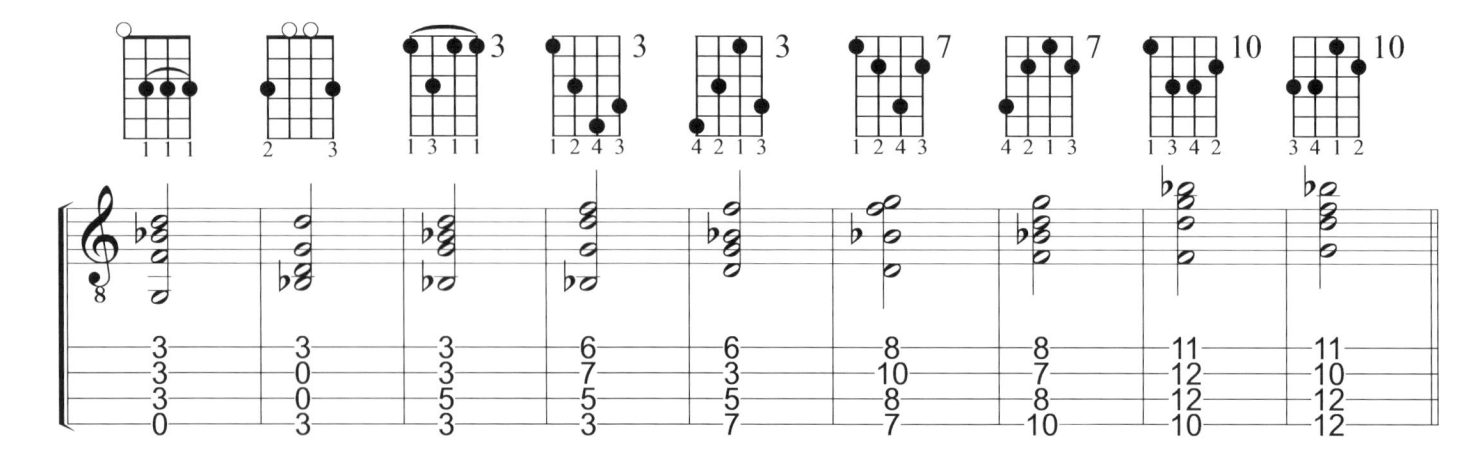

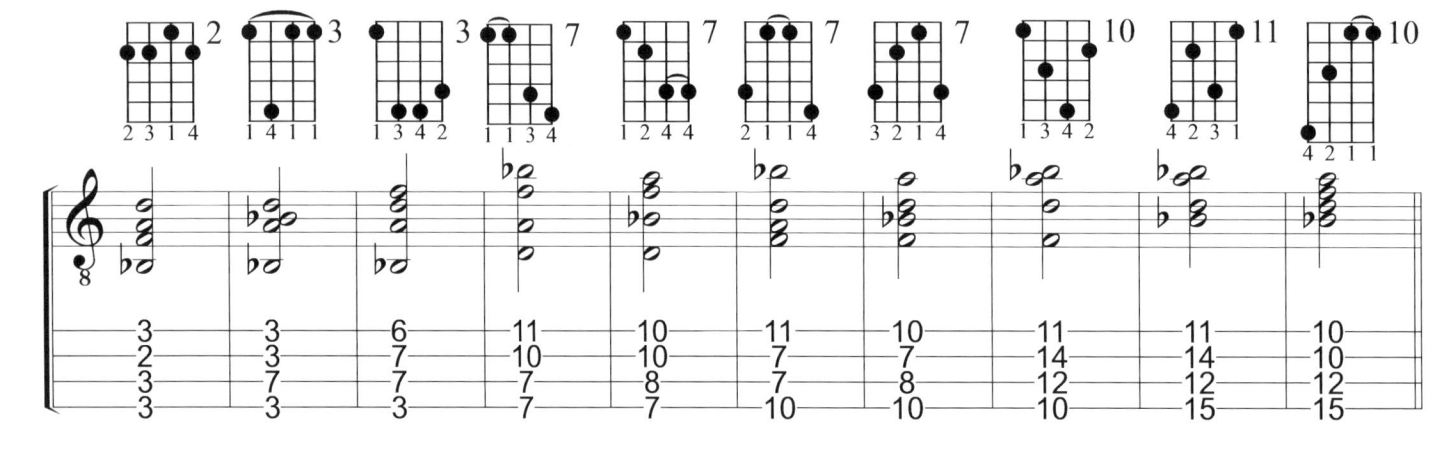

B♭ Major - B♭6 - B♭Maj7

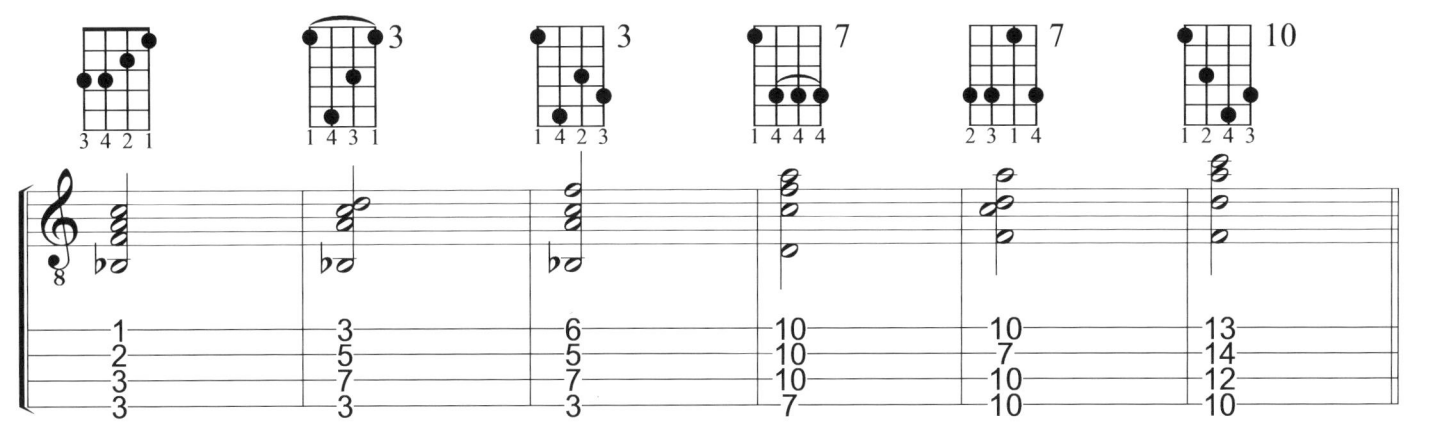

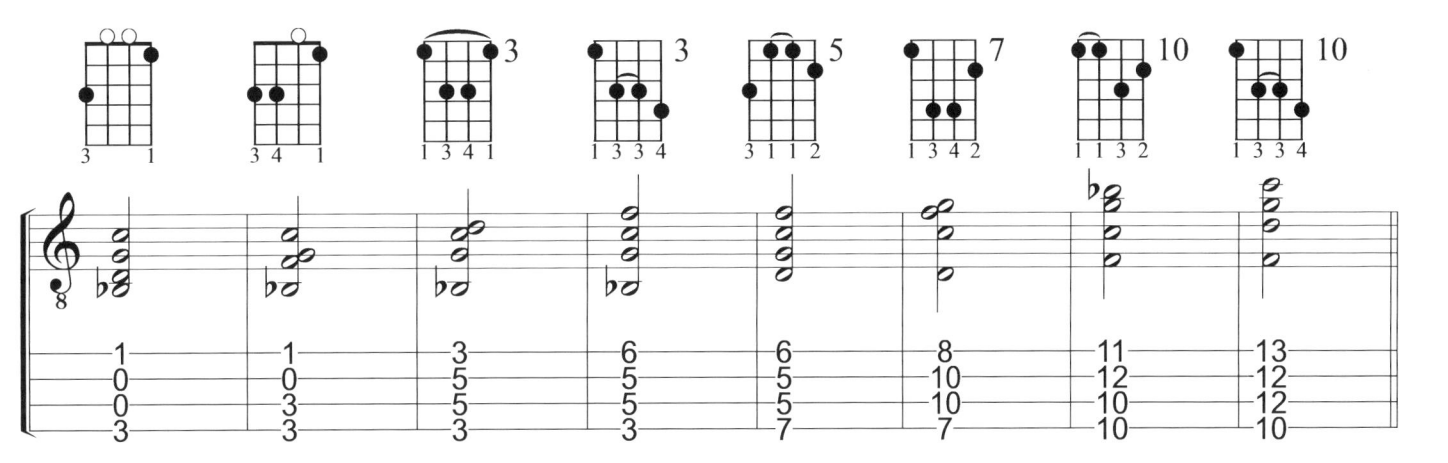

B♭maj9 - B♭6/9 - B♭ augmented+

B♭

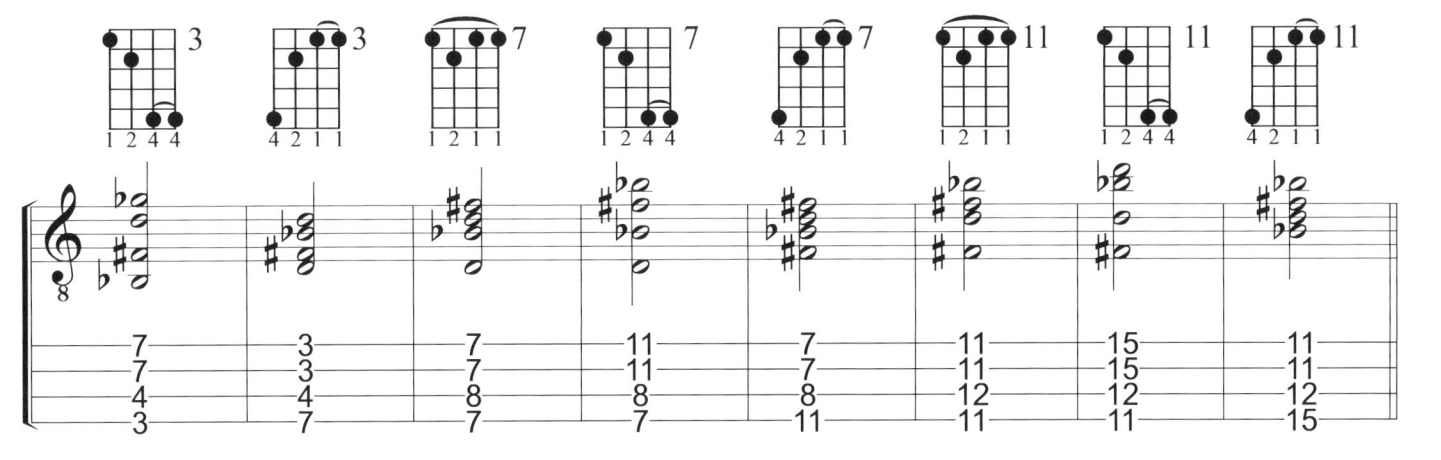

B♭maj9

B♭6/9

B♭ Augmented (B♭+)

Bbm - Bbm6 - Bbm7

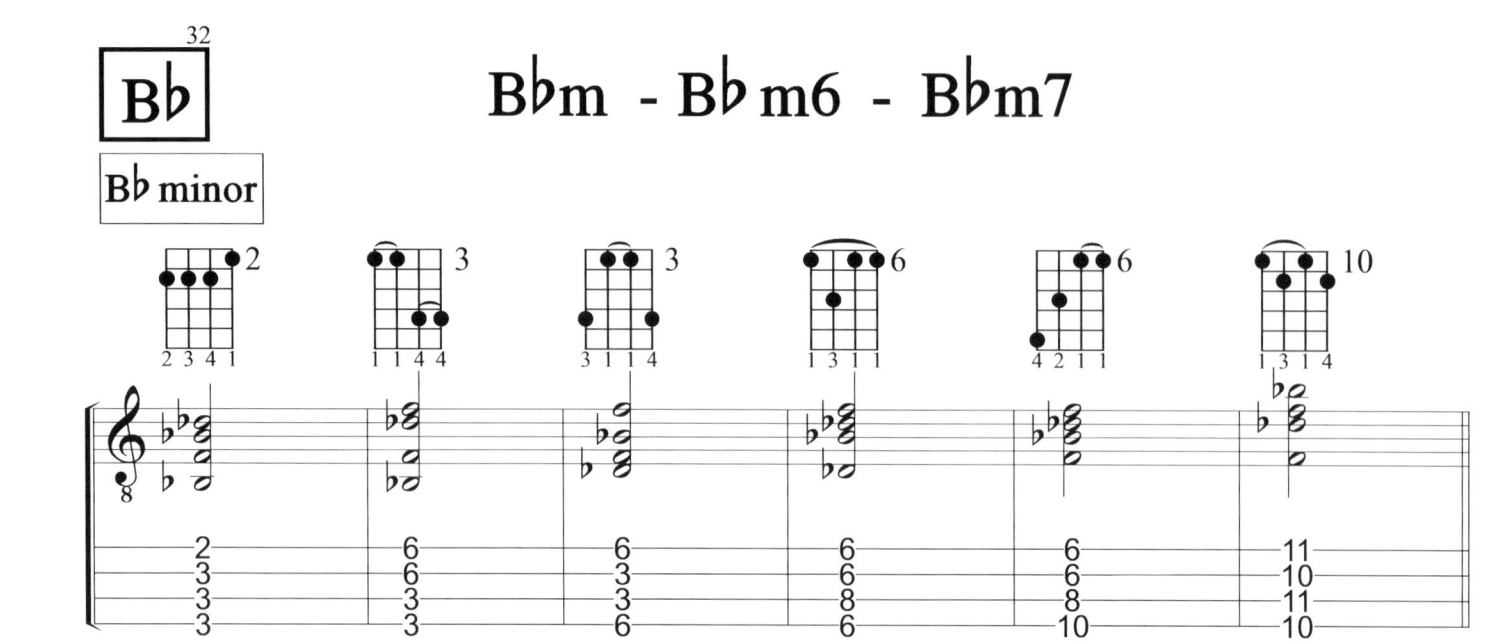

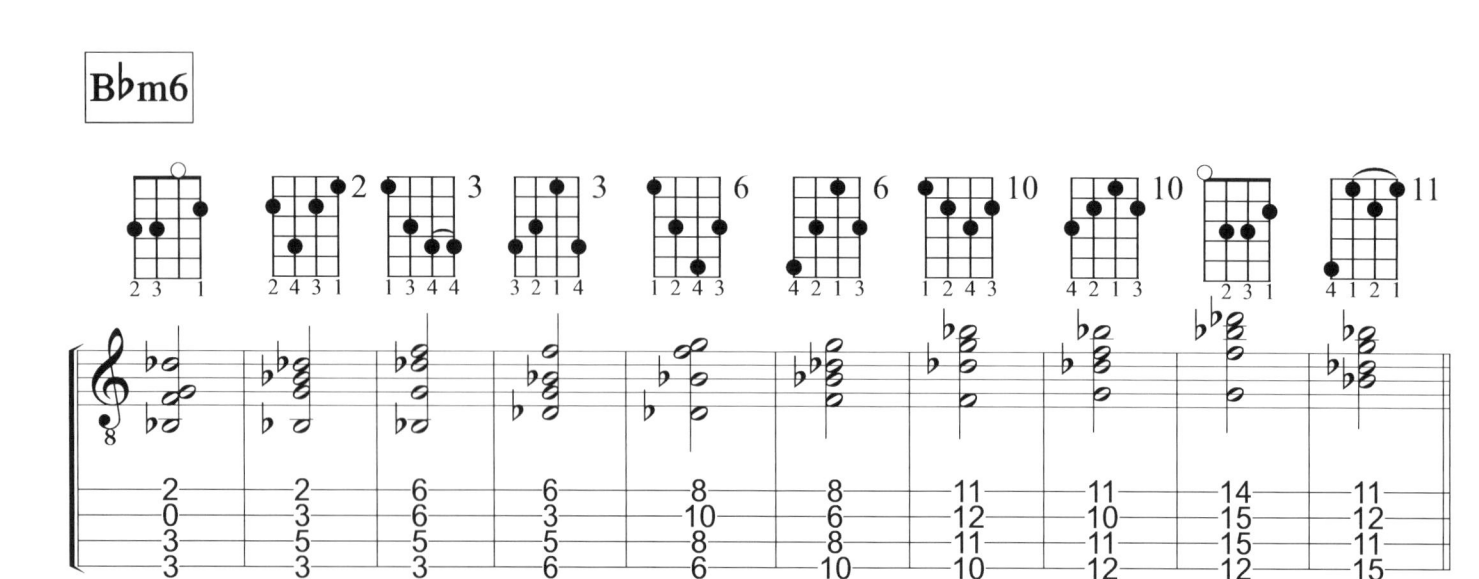

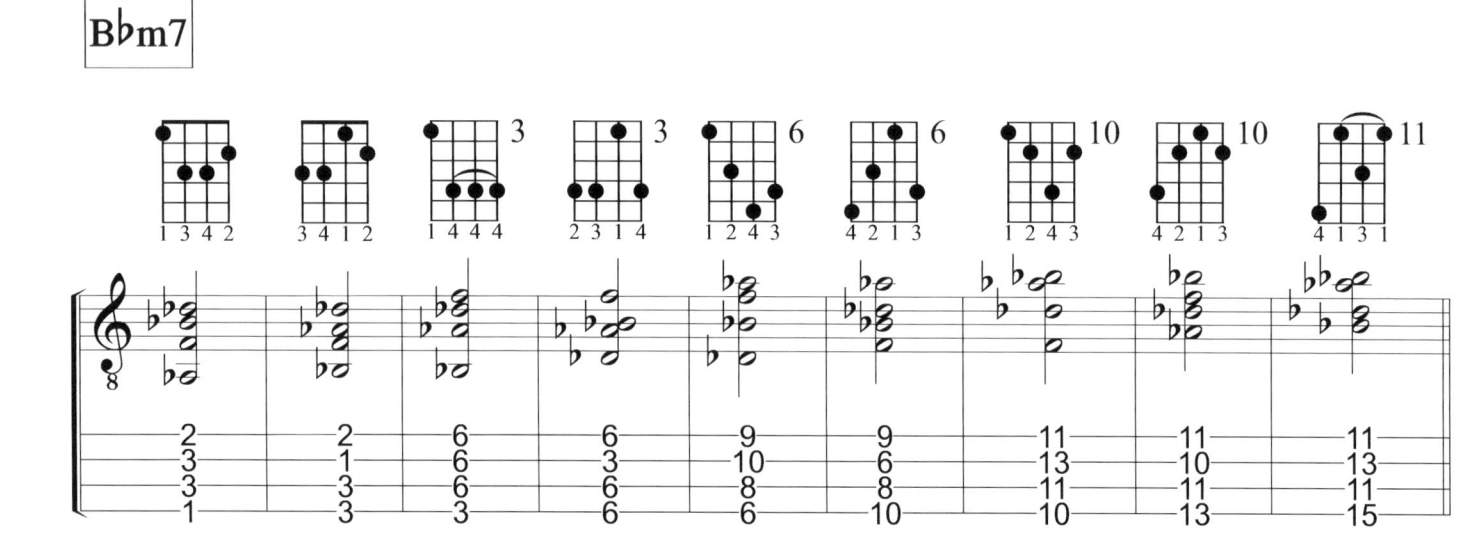

B♭m7♭5 - B♭m9 - B♭m11 - B♭m(maj7)

B♭

B♭m7♭5

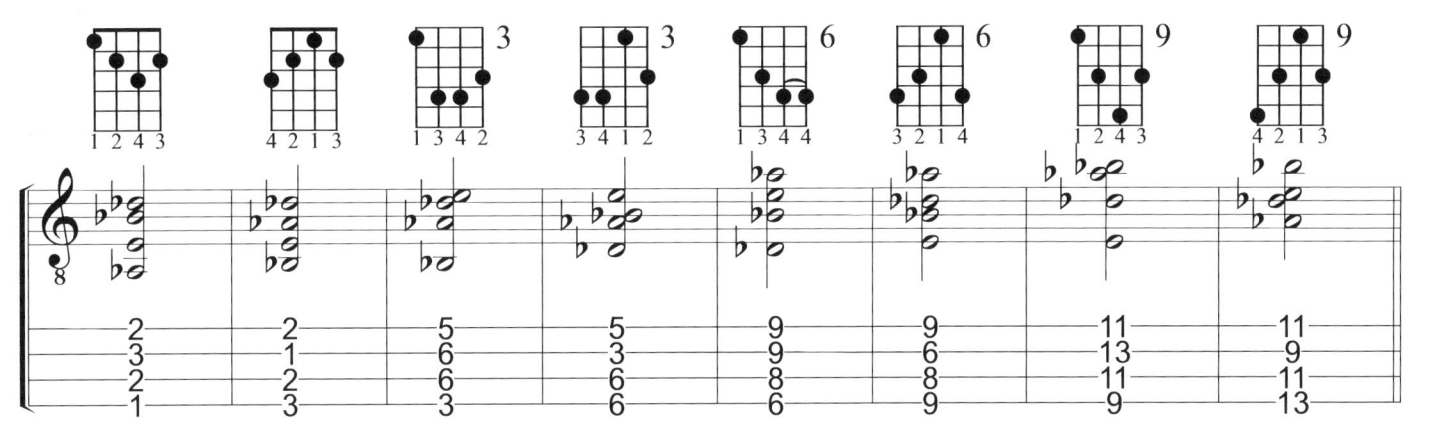

B♭m9

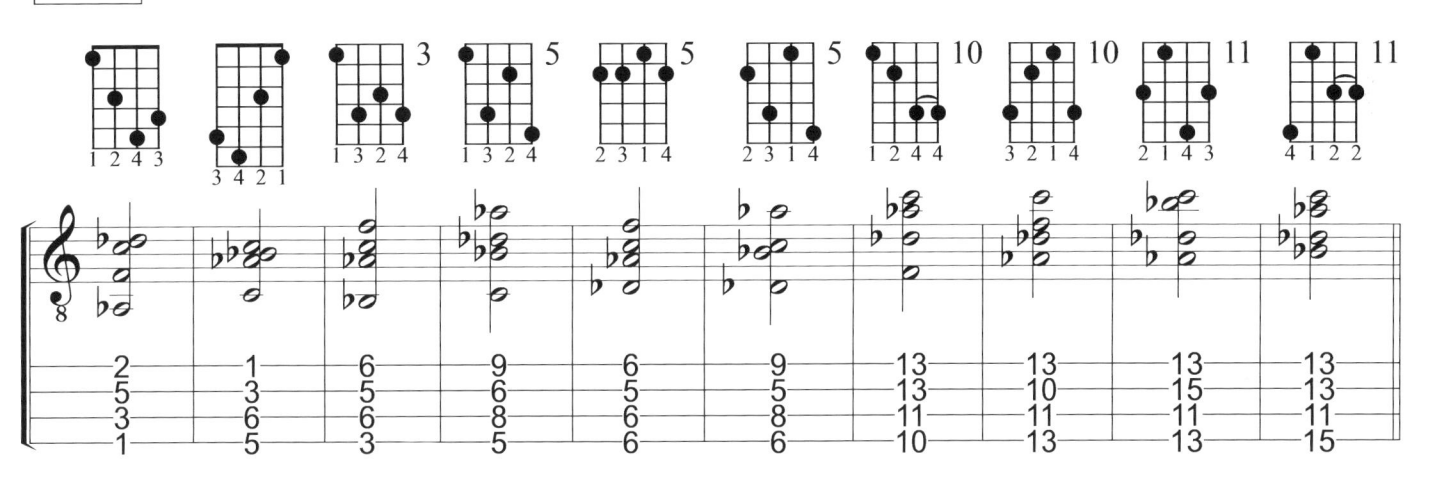

B♭m11

B♭m(maj7)

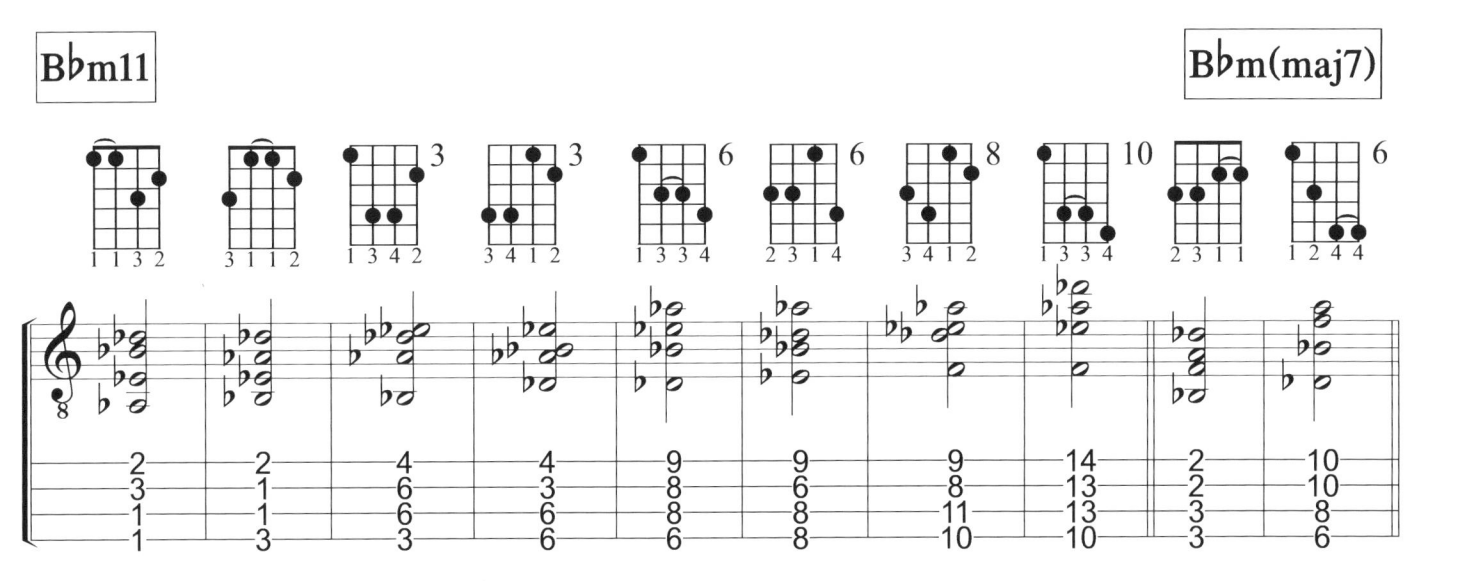

Bb7 - Bb9 - Bb13

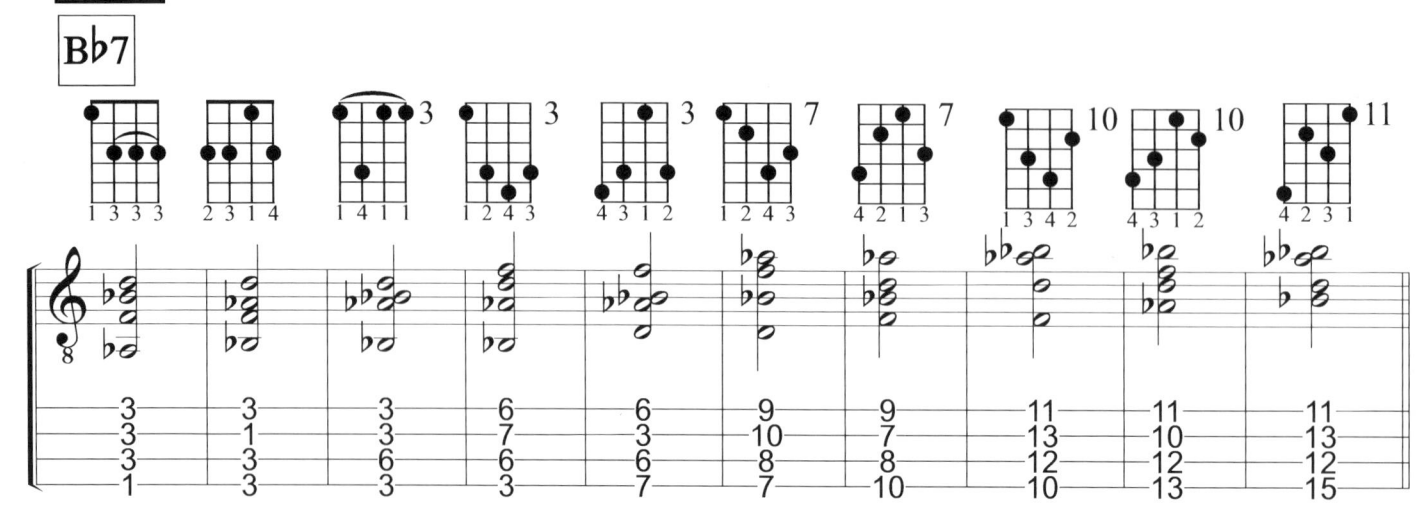

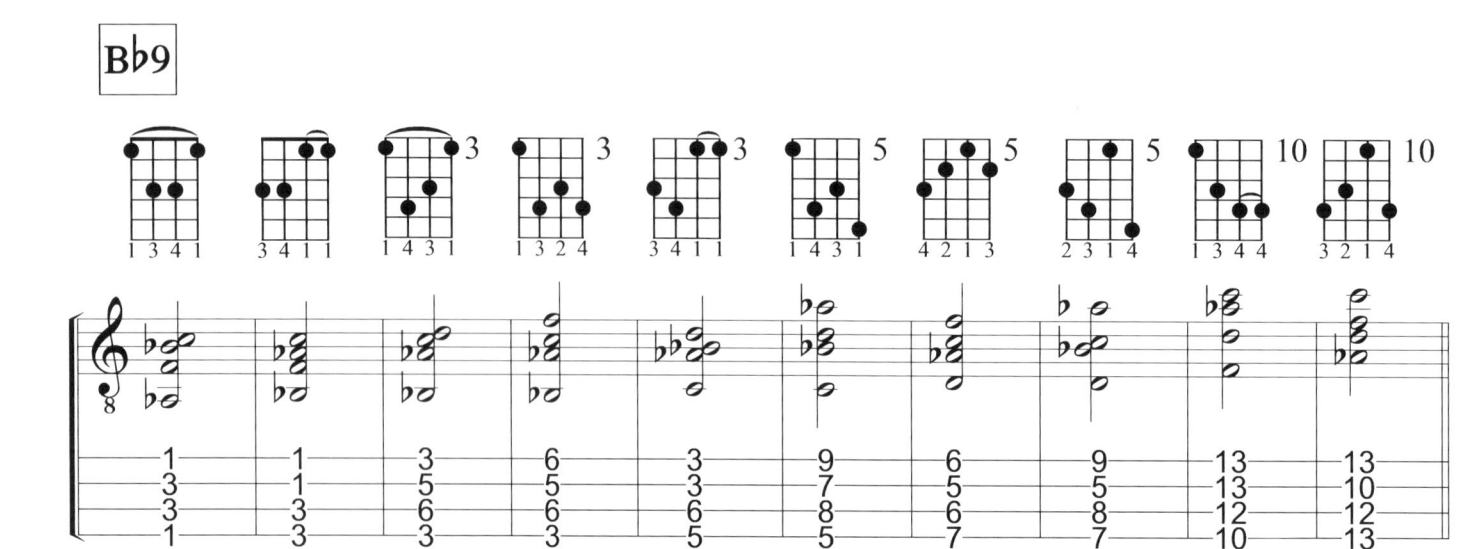

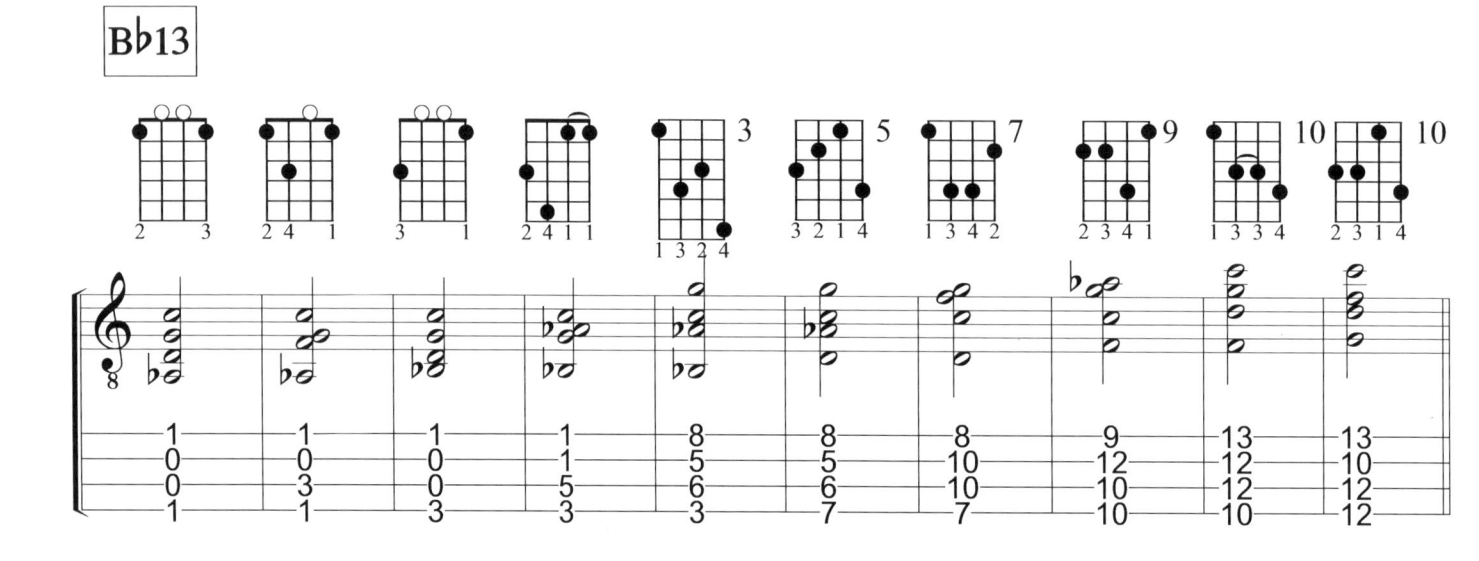

Bb7b5 - Bb7#5 - Bb7#9

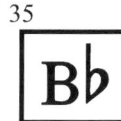

Bb
35

Bb7b5

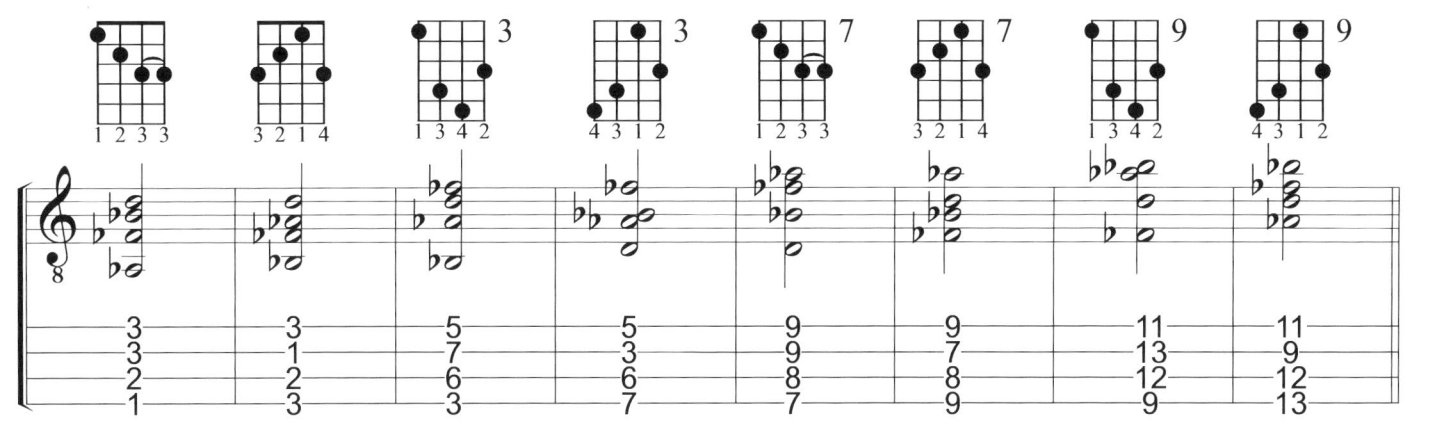

Bb7#5

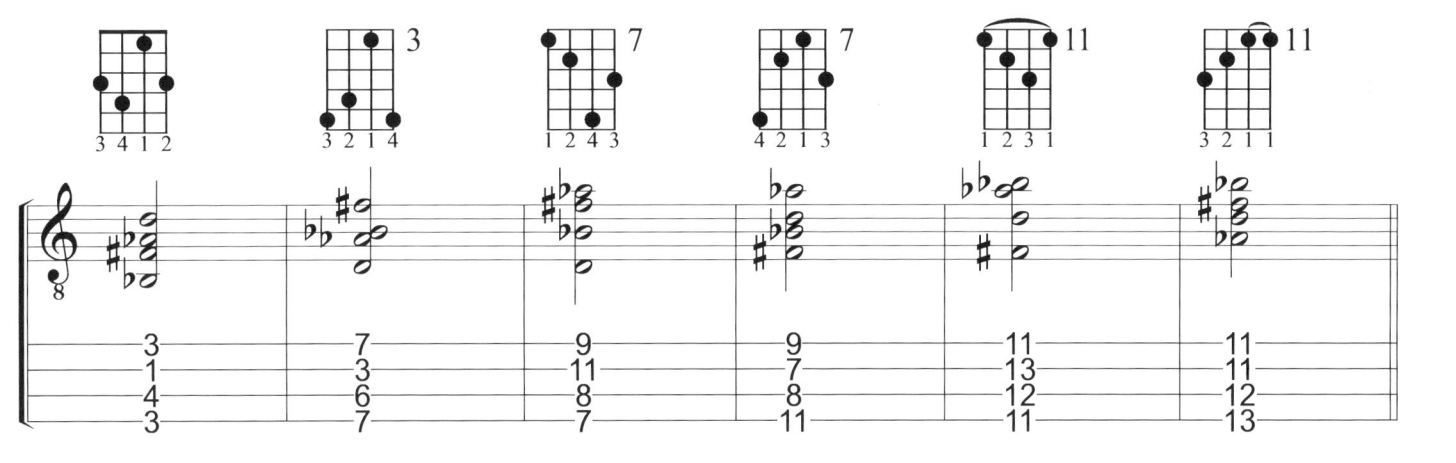

Bb7#9

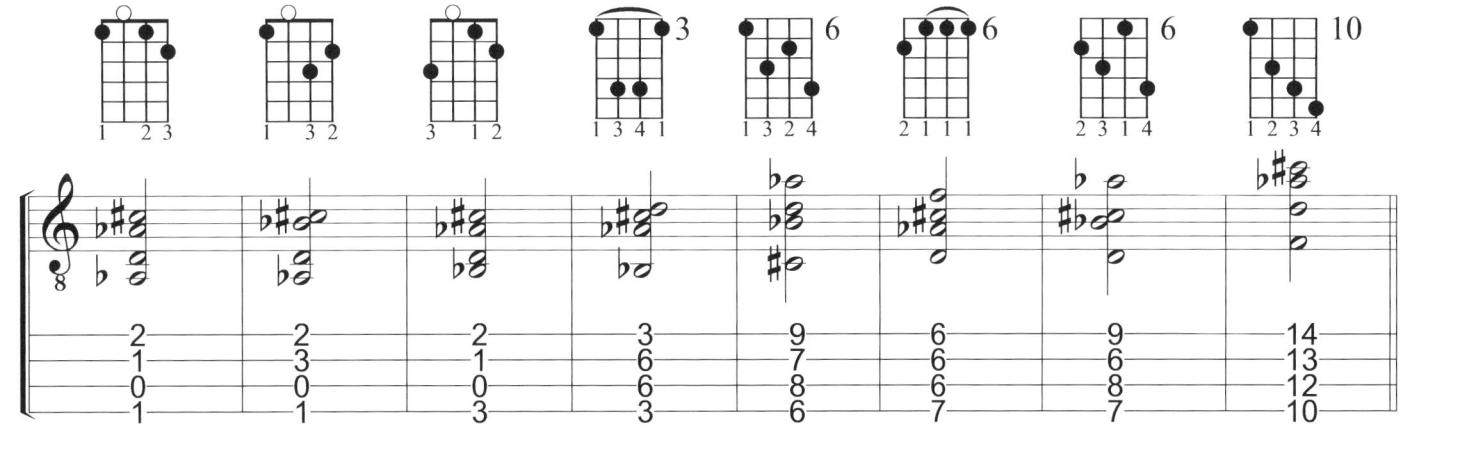

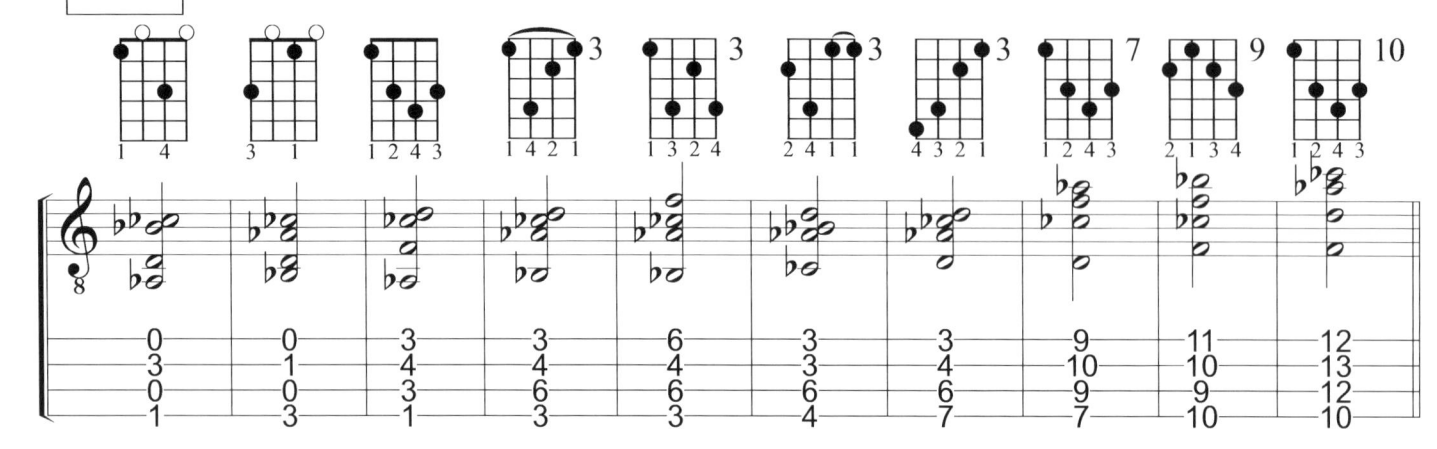

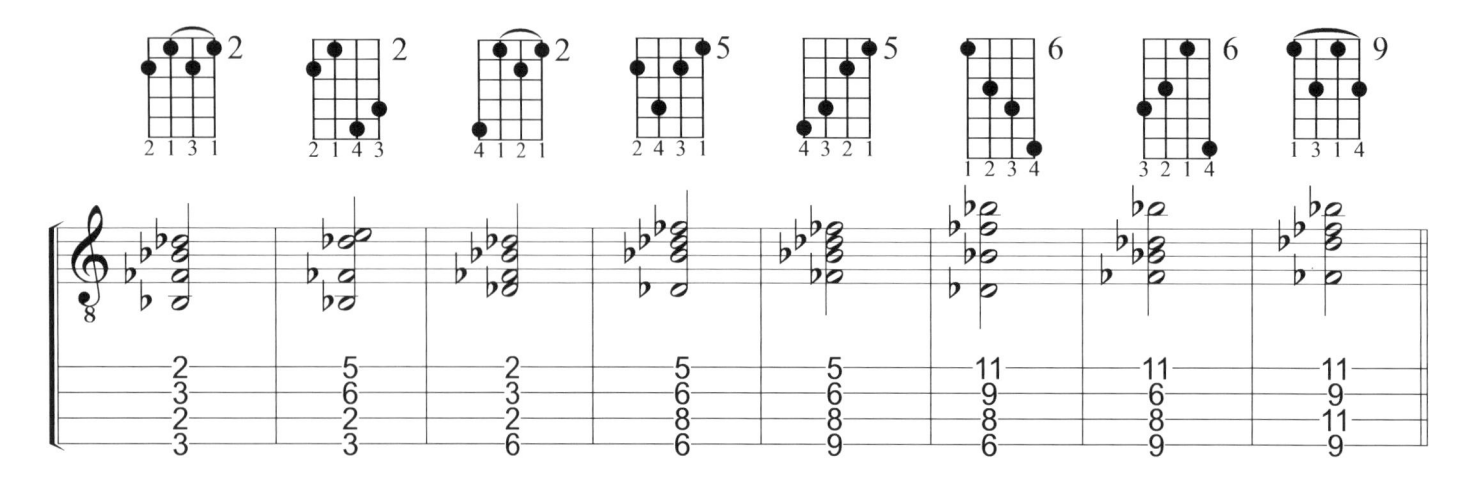

Bb7b9 - Bbdiminished - Bb°7

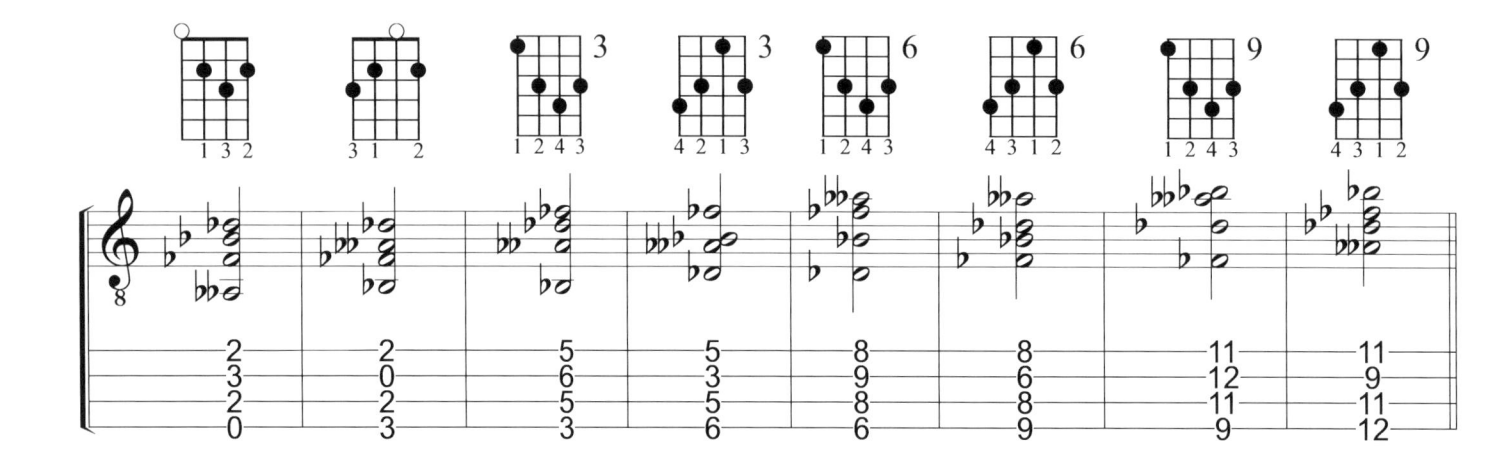

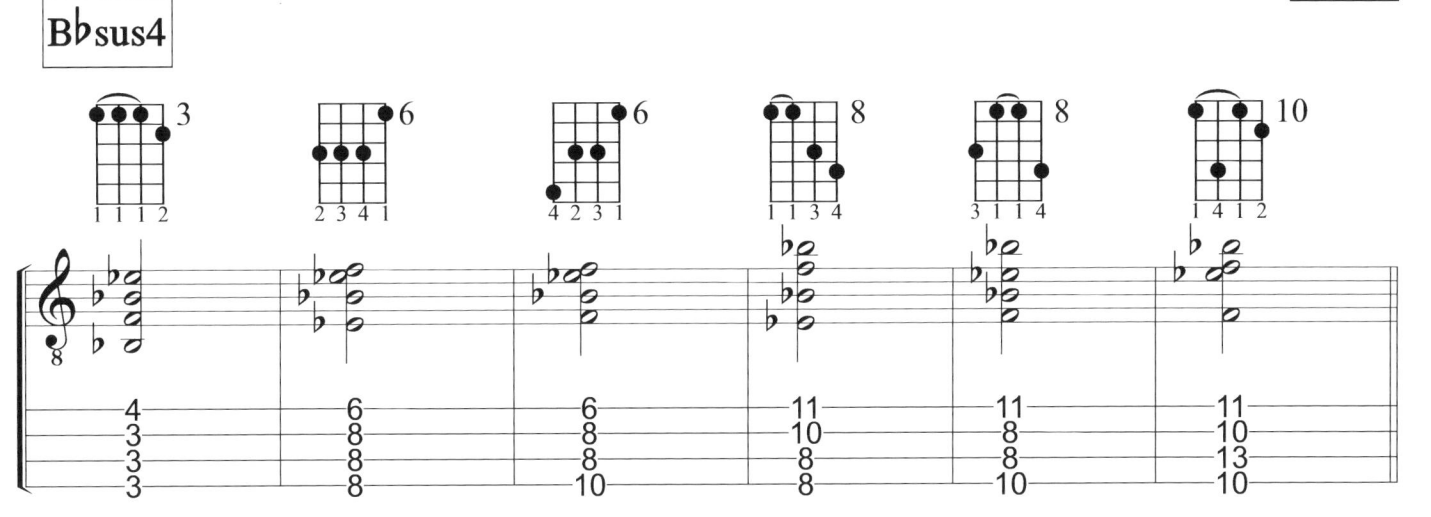

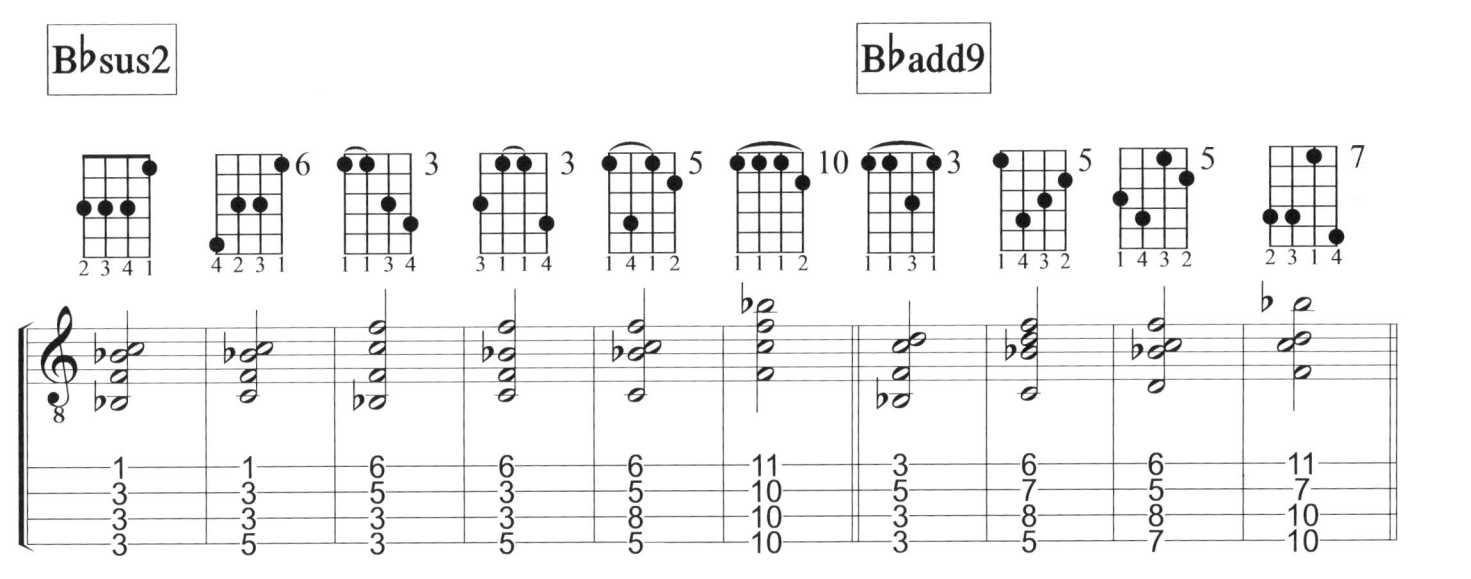

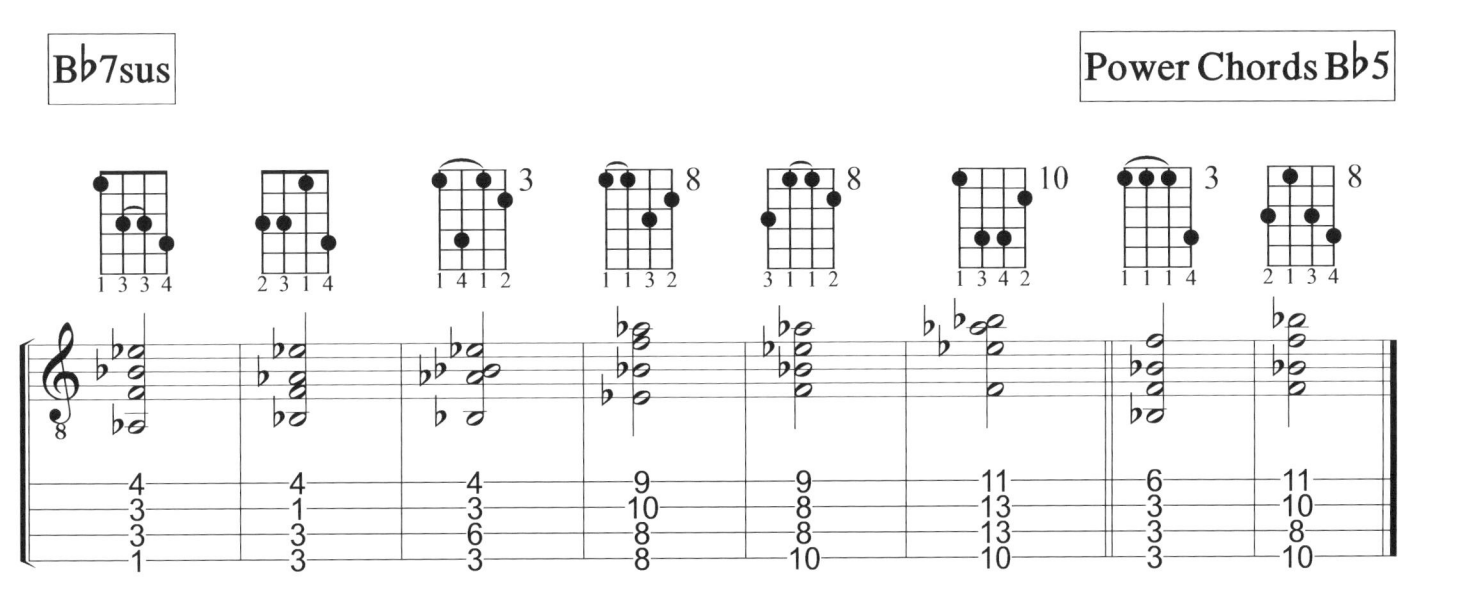

B♭sus4 - B♭sus2 - B♭add9 - B♭7sus - B5

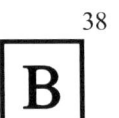

B Major - B6 - BMaj7

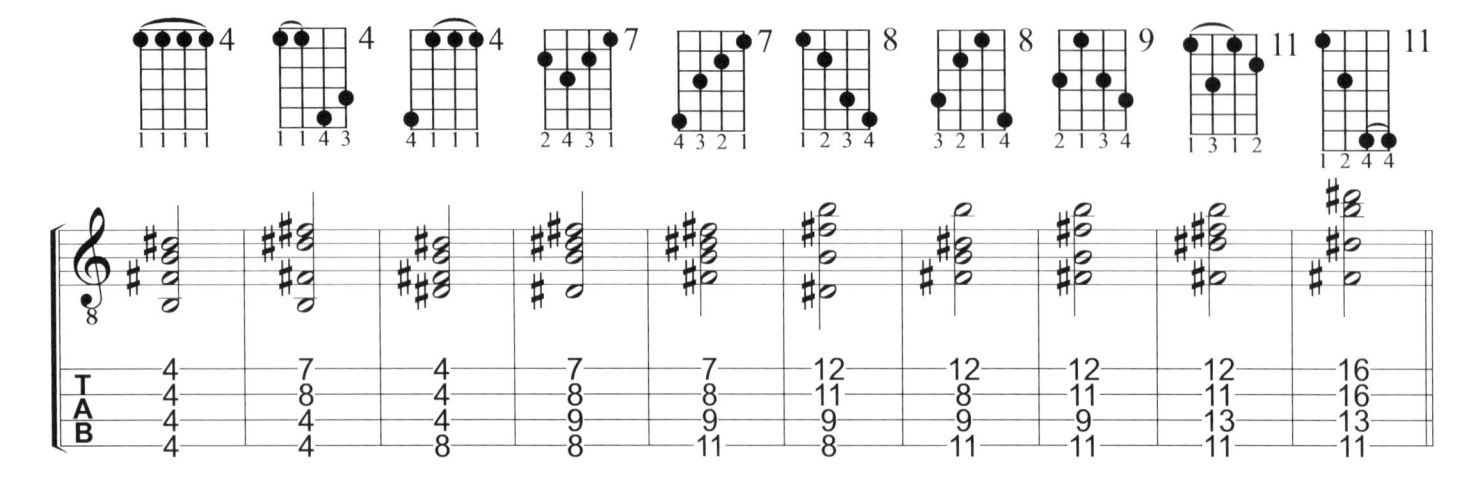

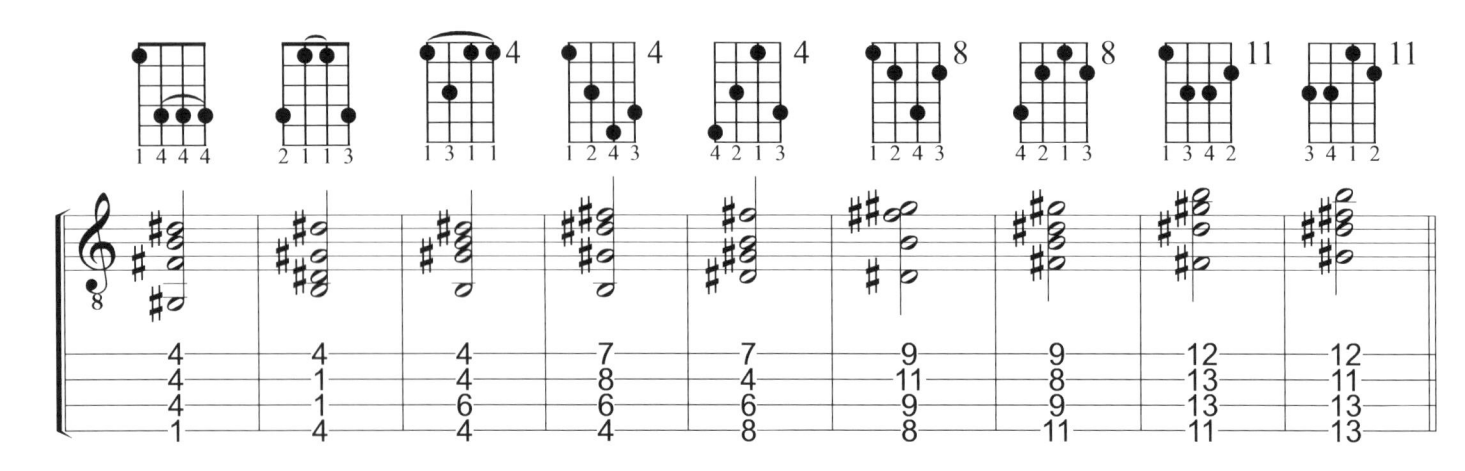

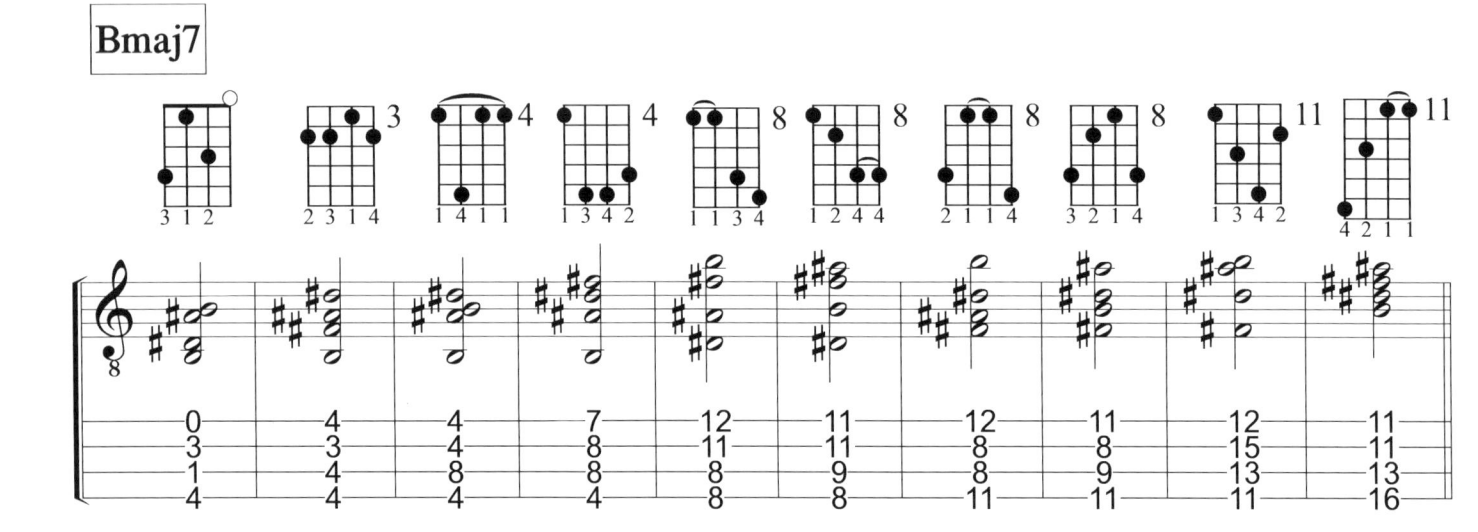

Bmaj9 - B6/9 - B Augmented +

Bmaj9

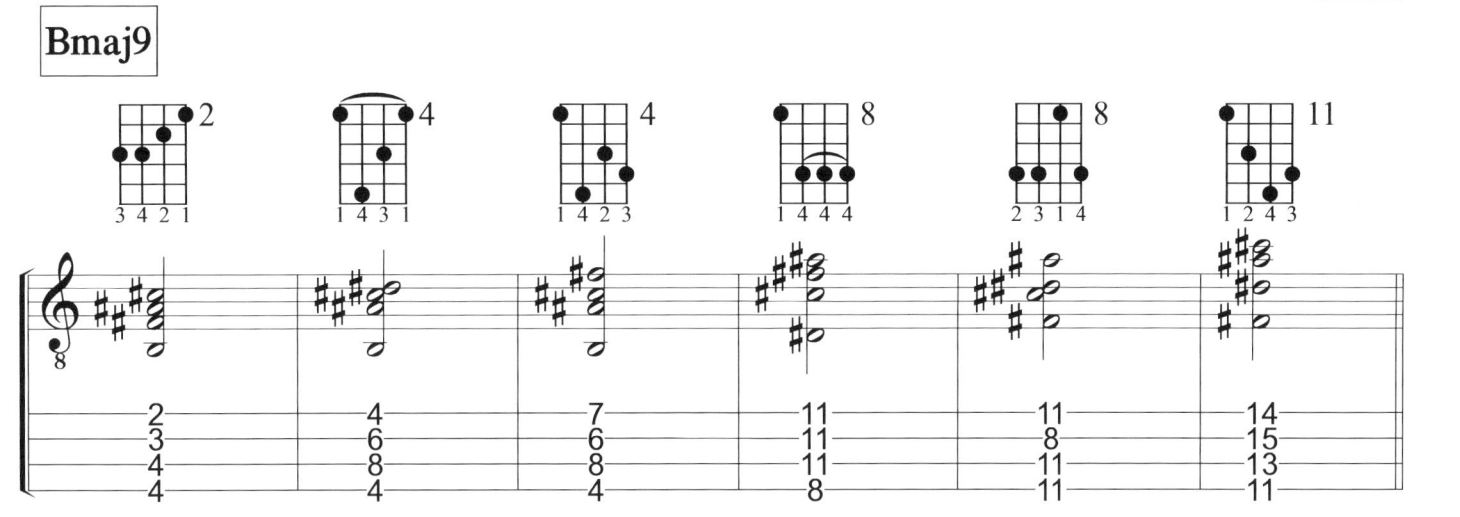

B6/9

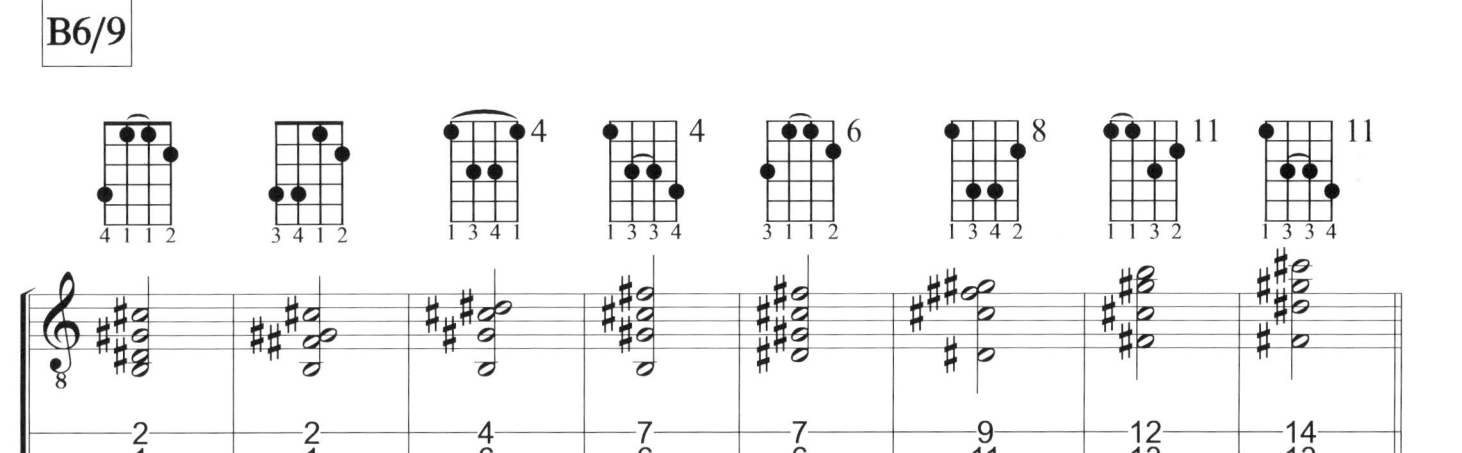

B Augmented (B+)

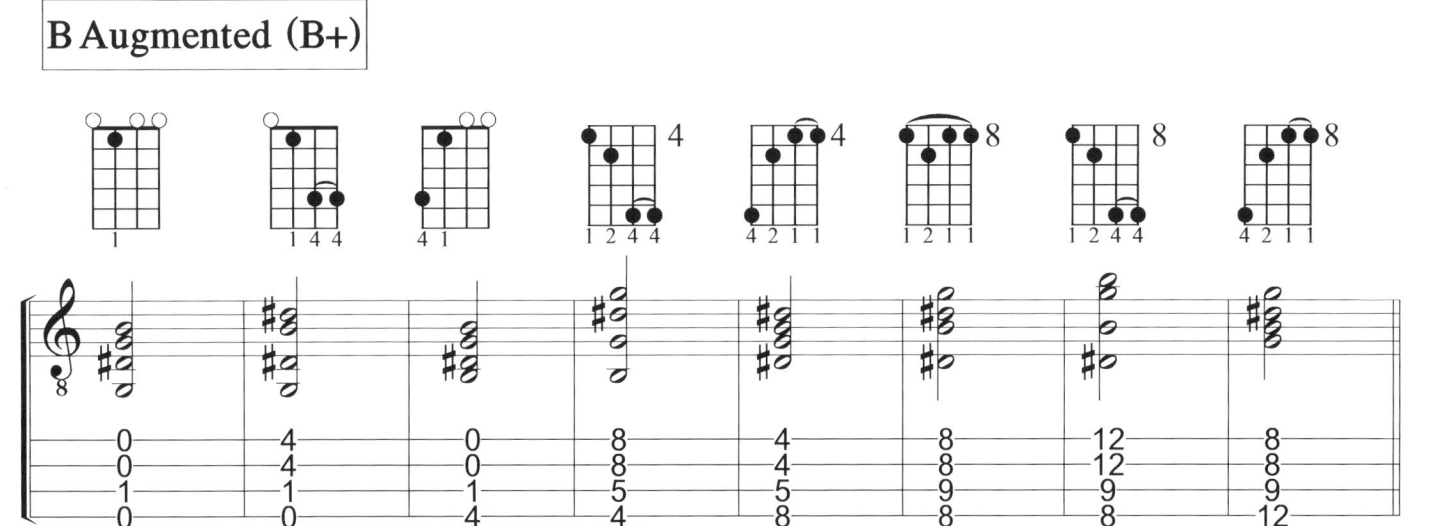

Bm - Bm6 - Bm7

B minor

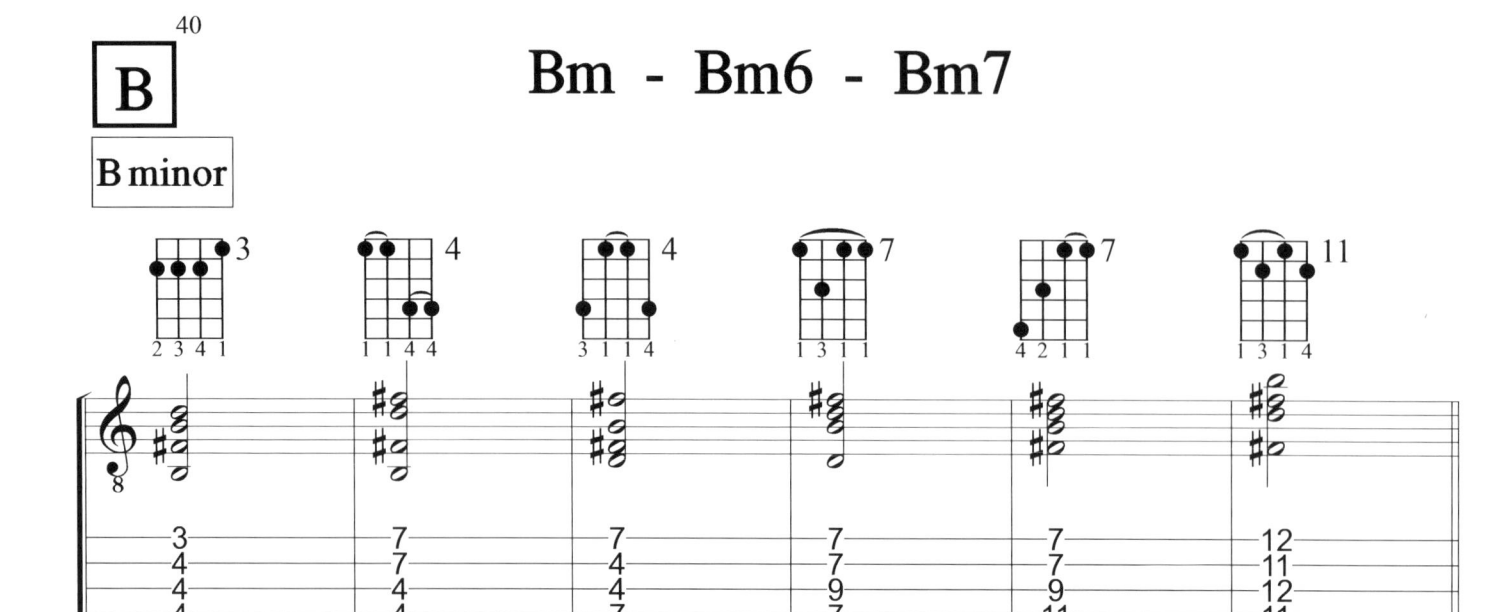

Bm6

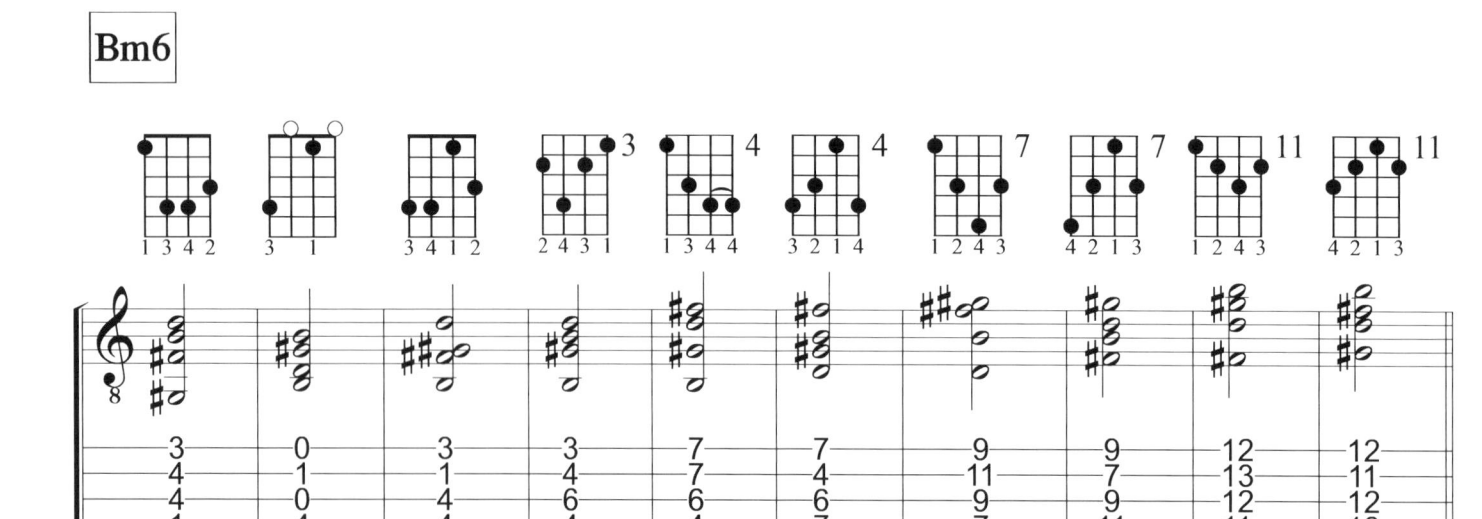

Bm7

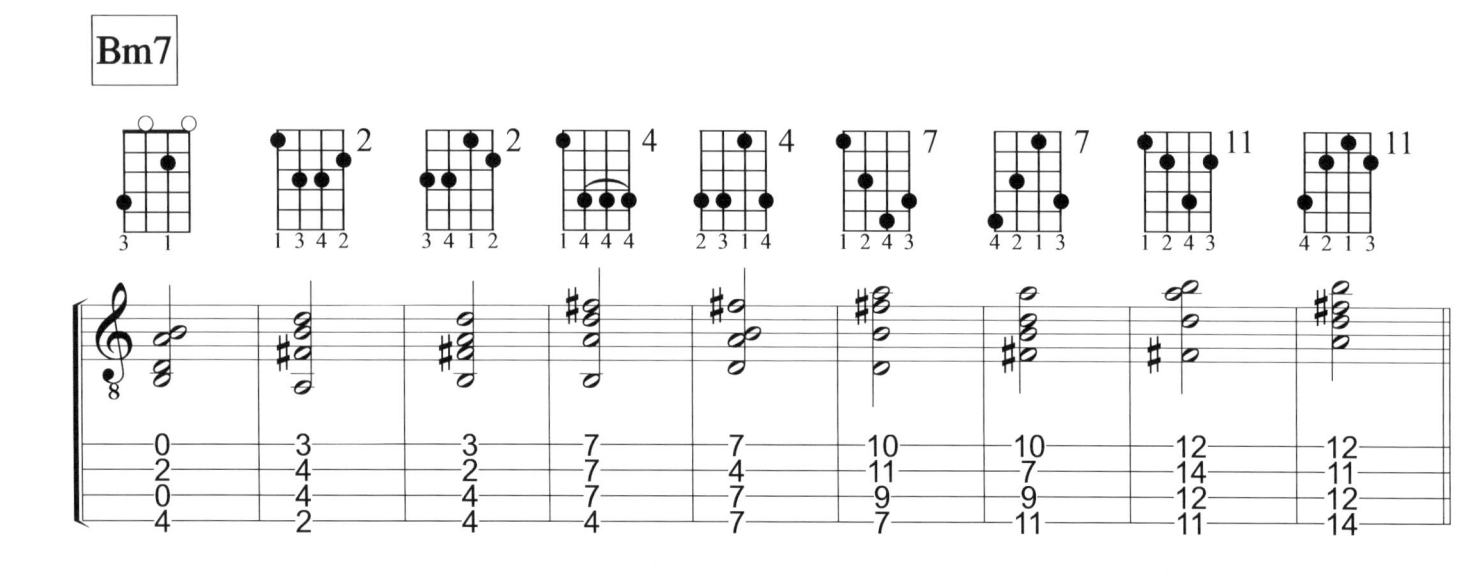

Bm7♭5 - Bm9 - Bm11 - Bm(maj7)

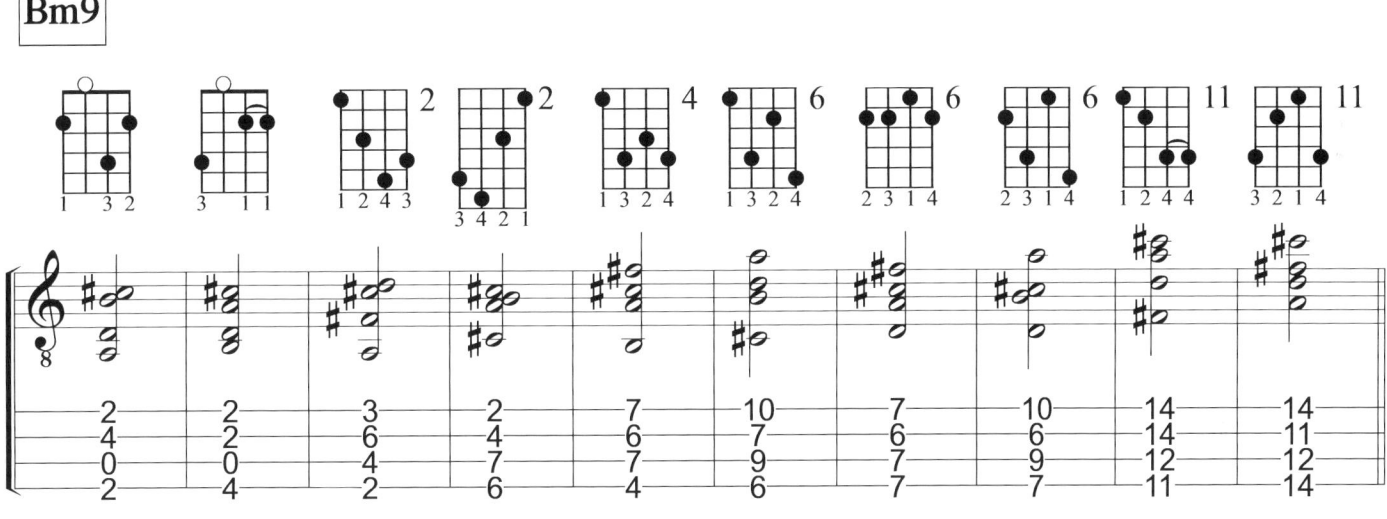

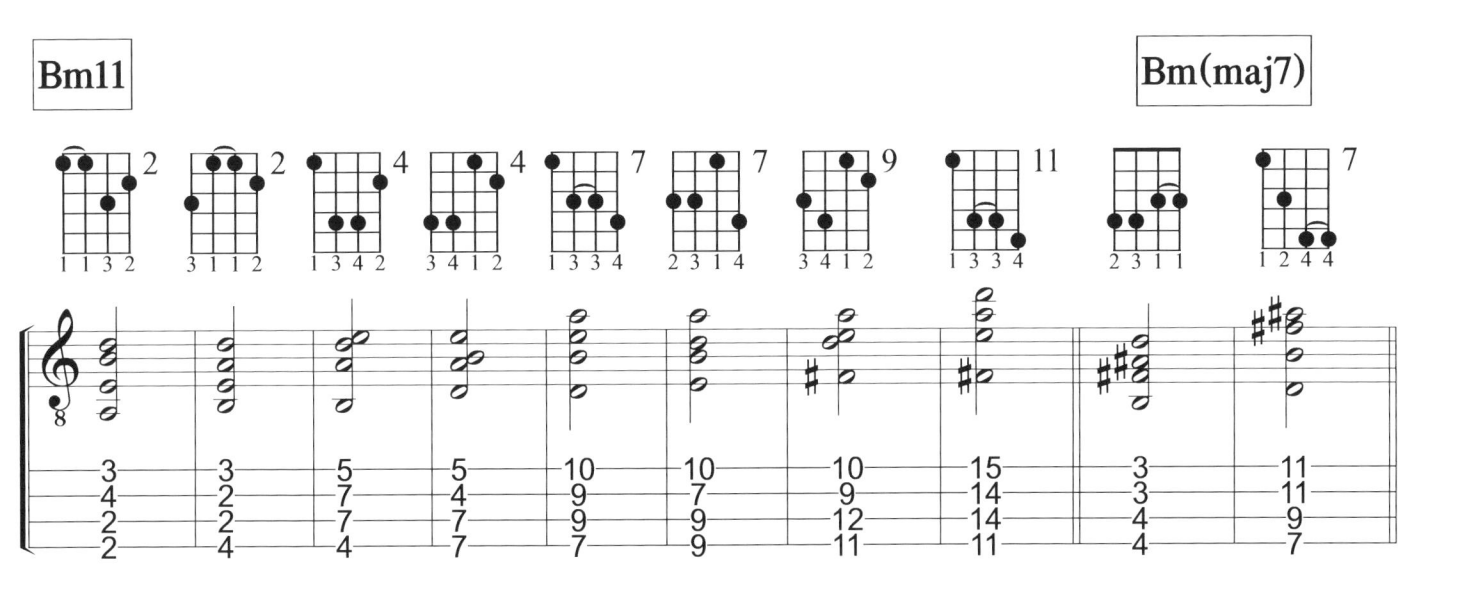

B7 - B9 - B13

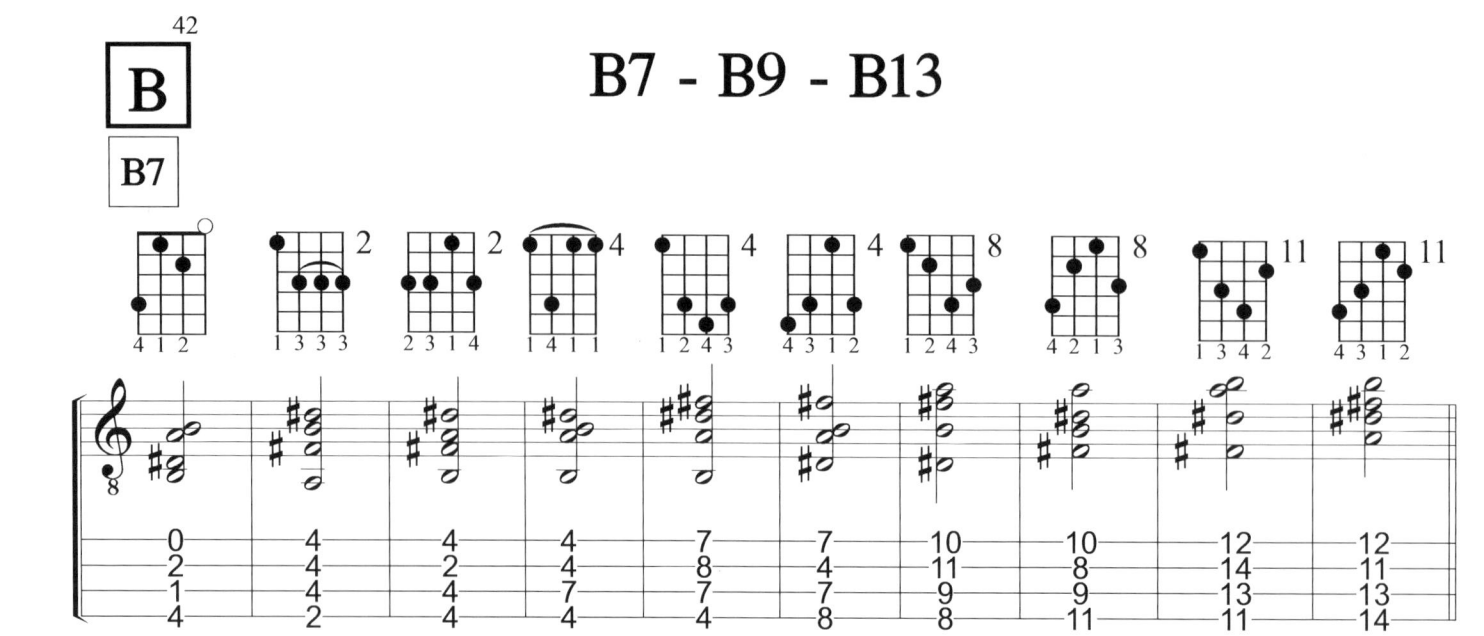

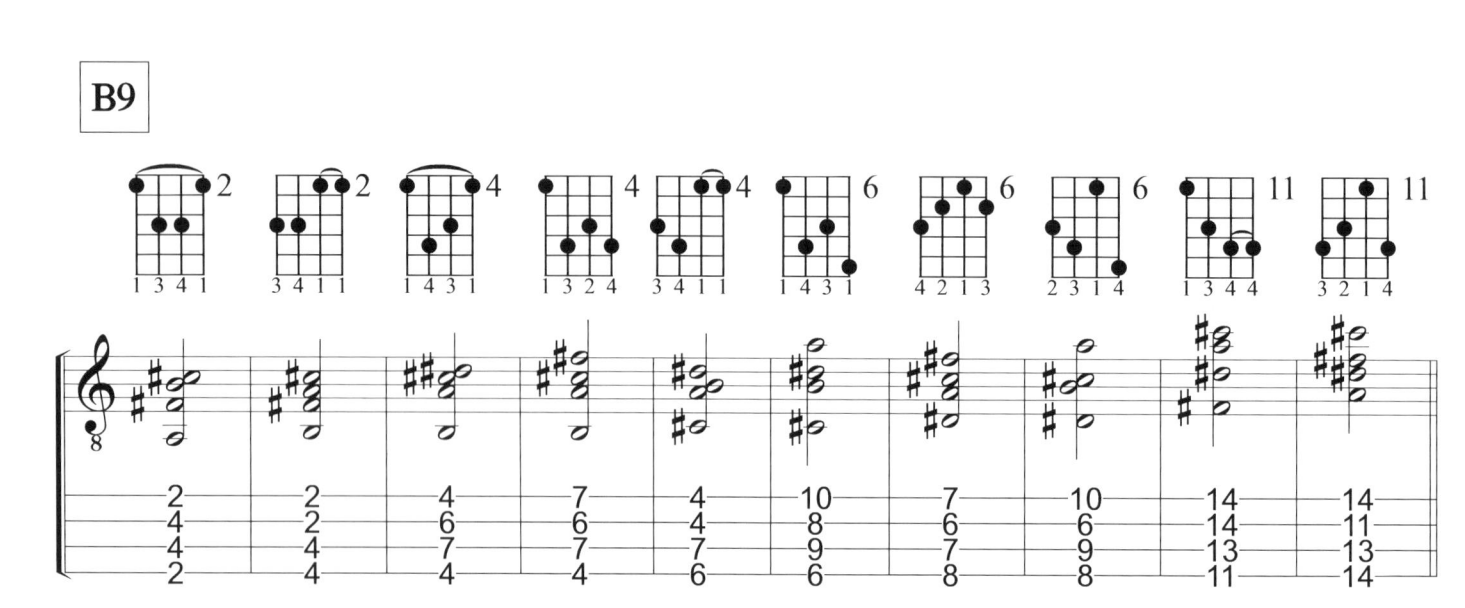

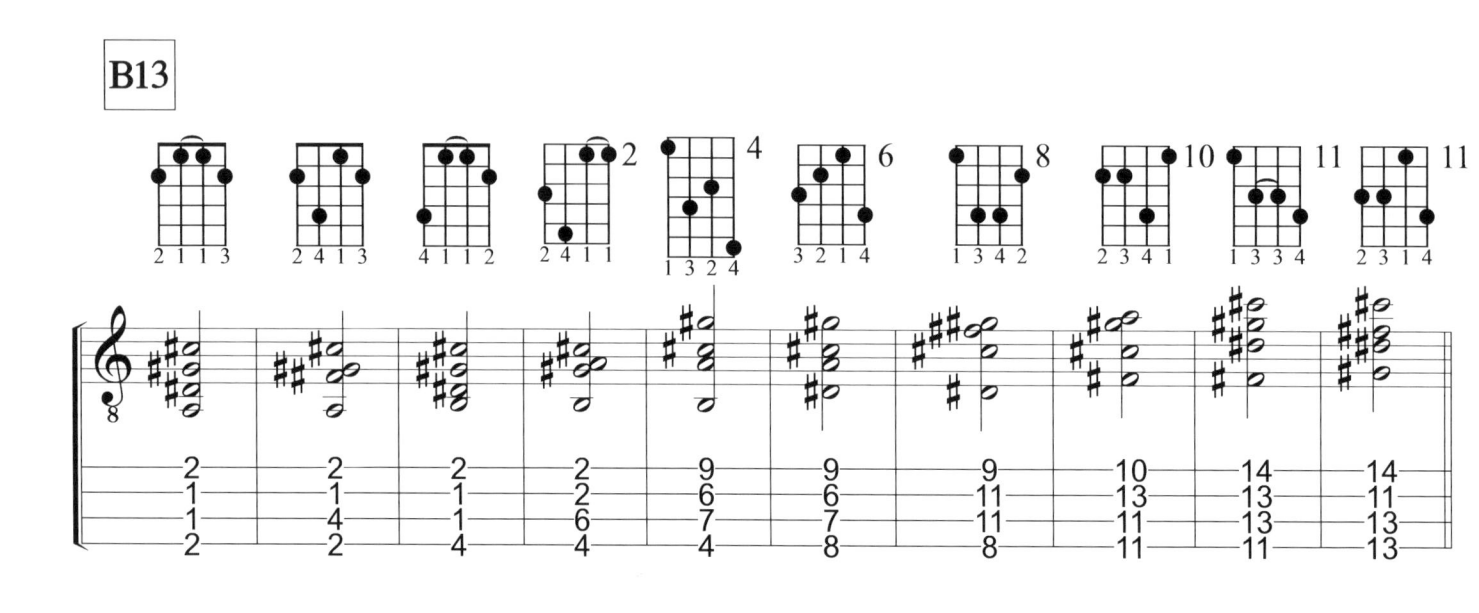

B7♭5 - B7♯5 - 7♯9

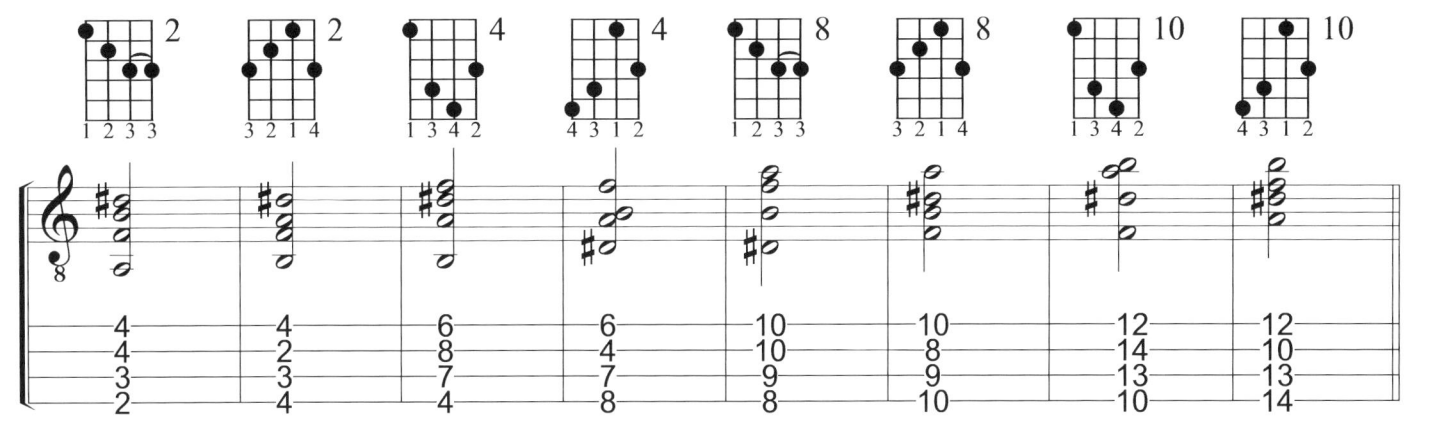

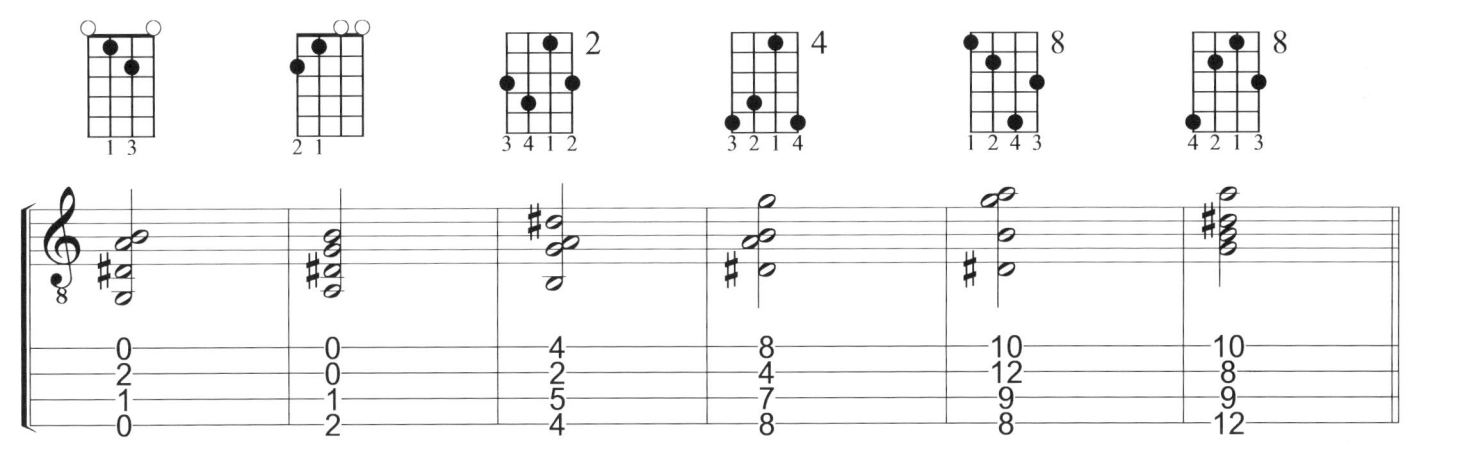

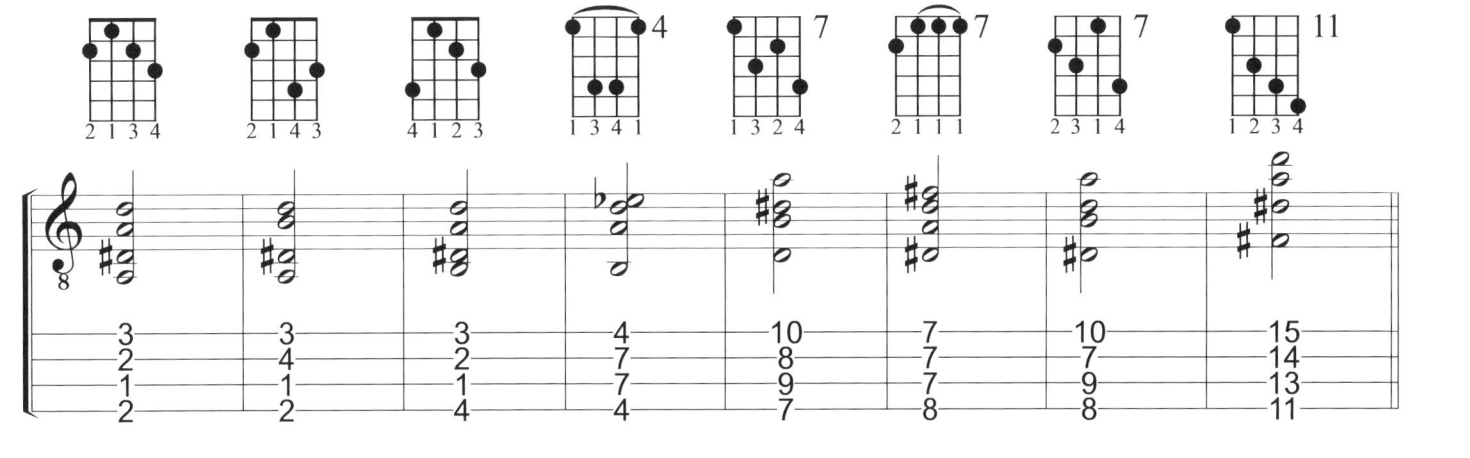

B7♭9 - B diminished - B°7

B7♭9

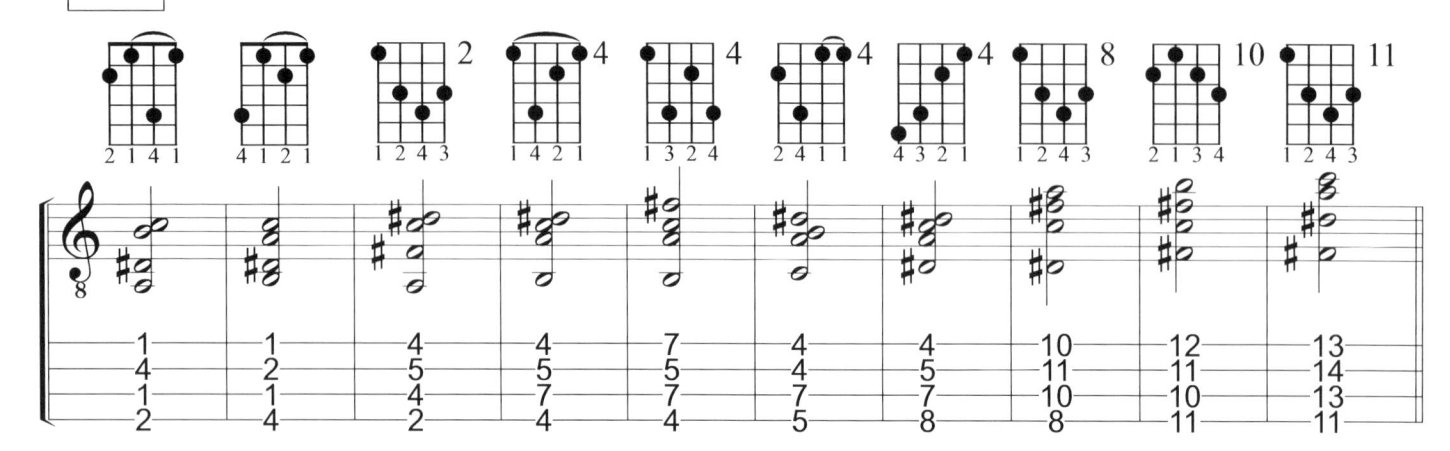

B diminished (B°)

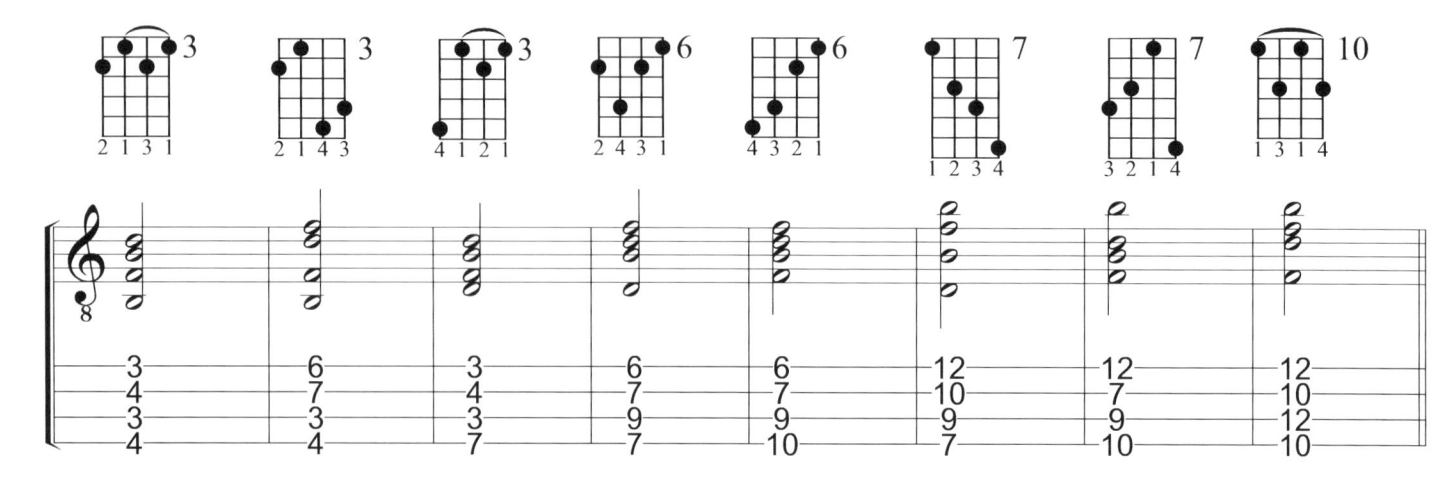

B diminished 7th (B°7)

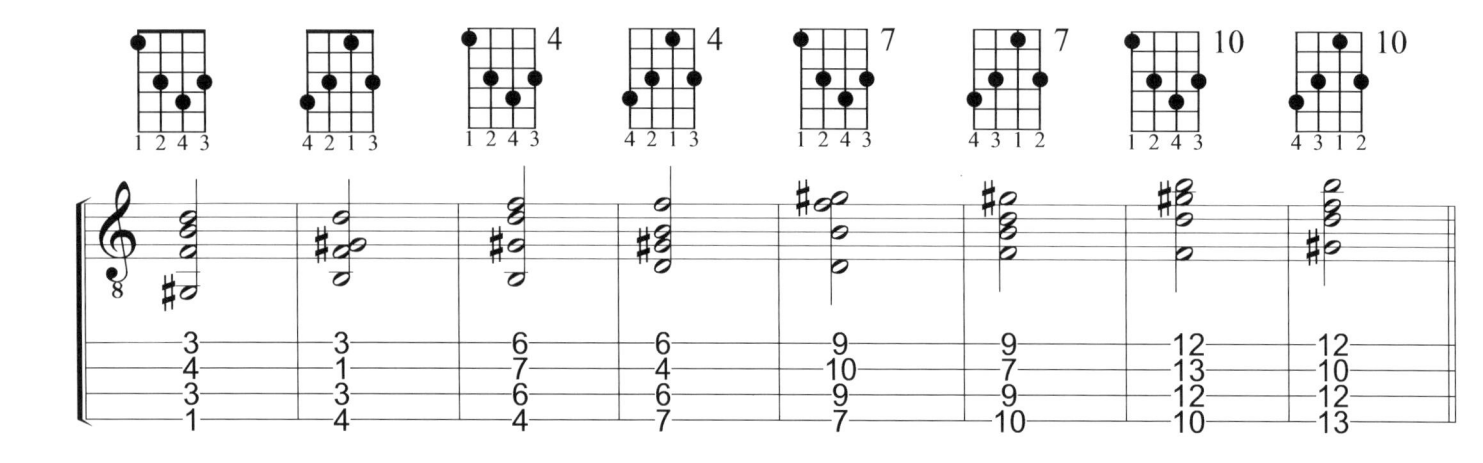

Bsus4 - Bsus2 - Badd9 - B7sus - B5

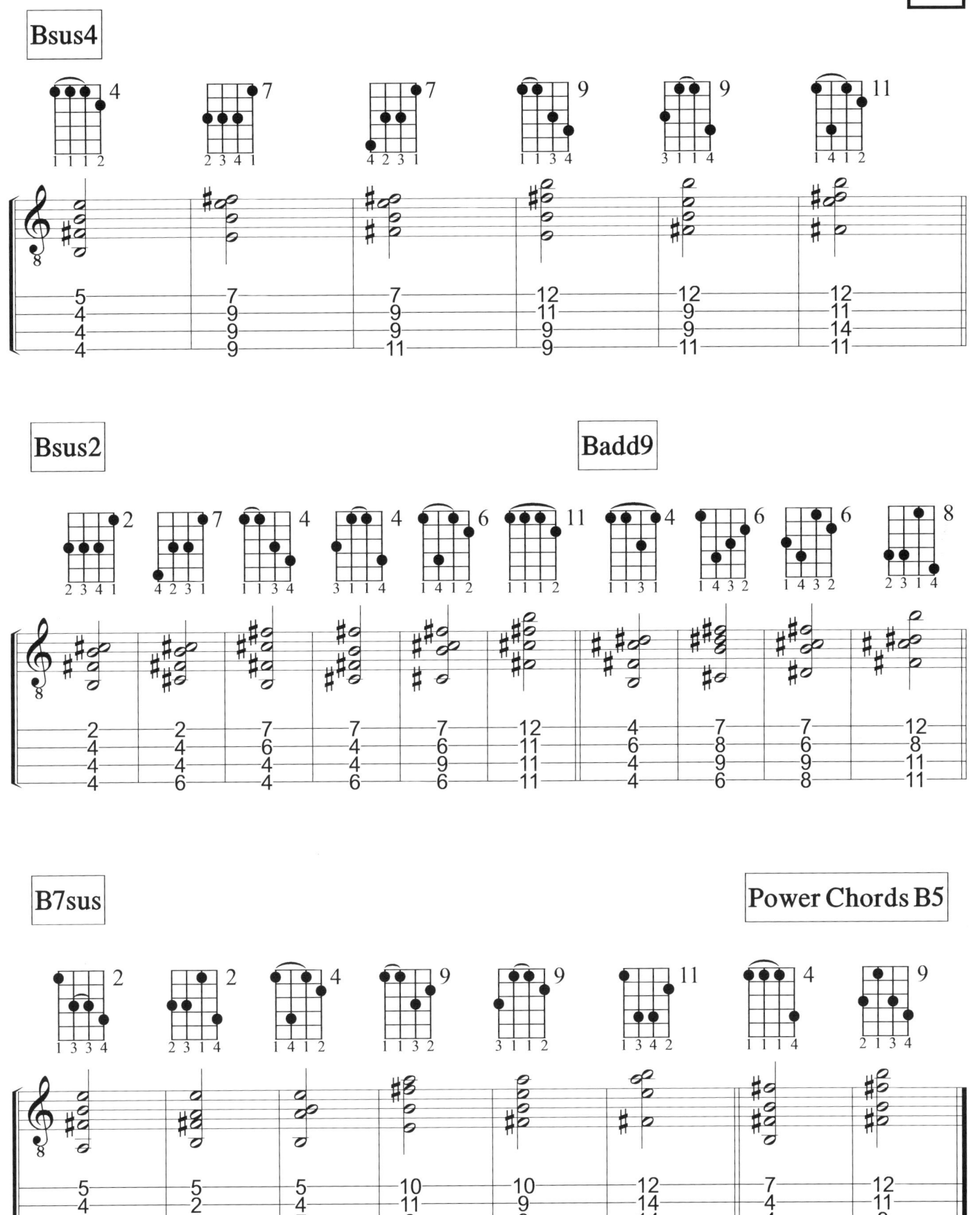

C Major - C6 - Cmaj7

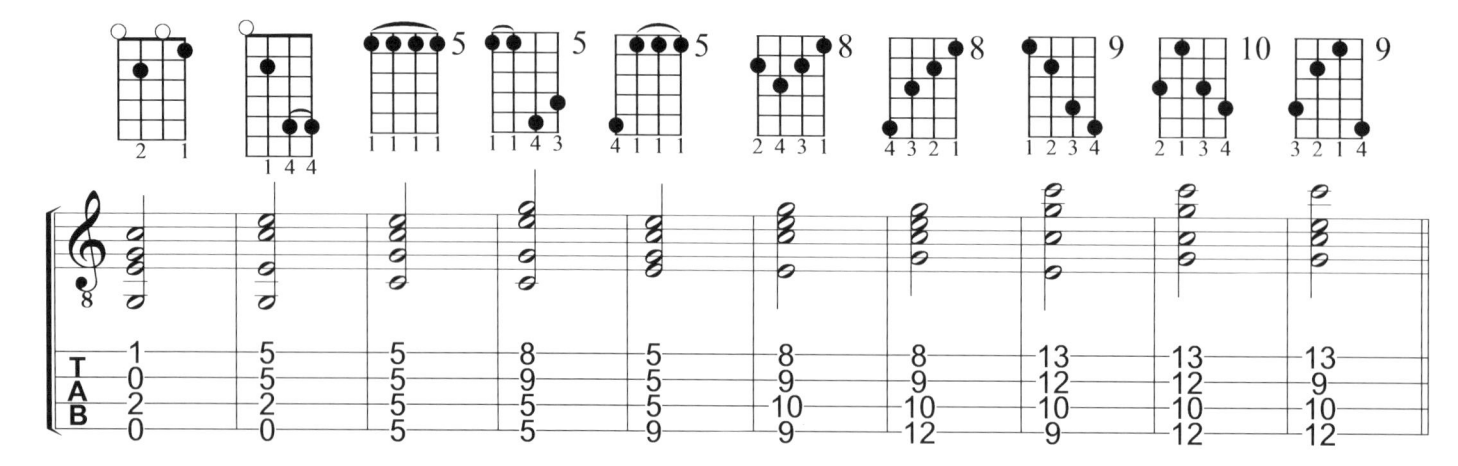

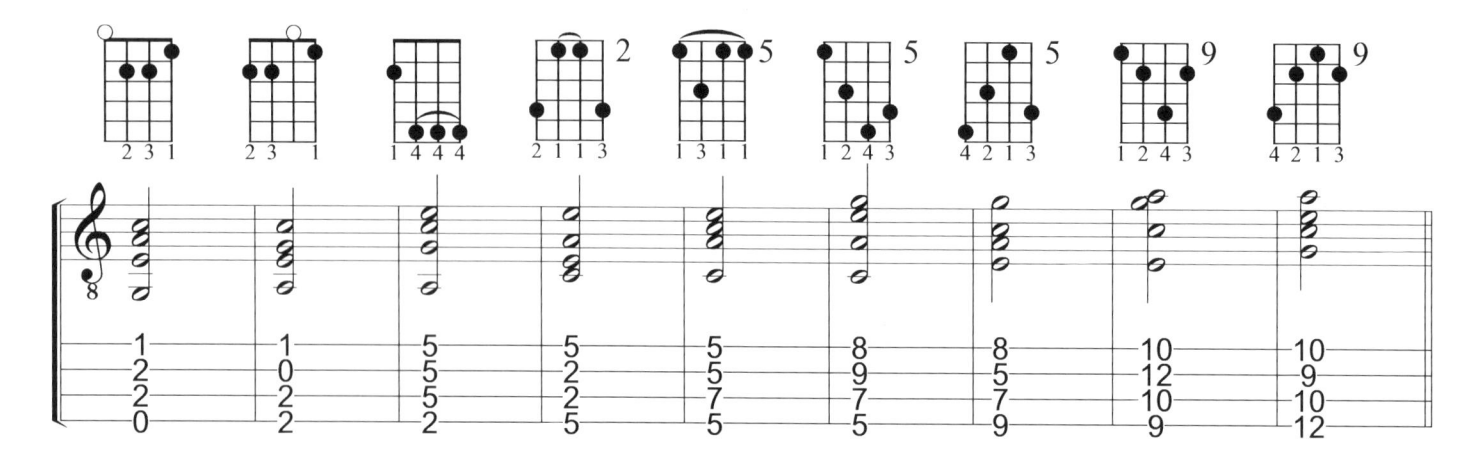

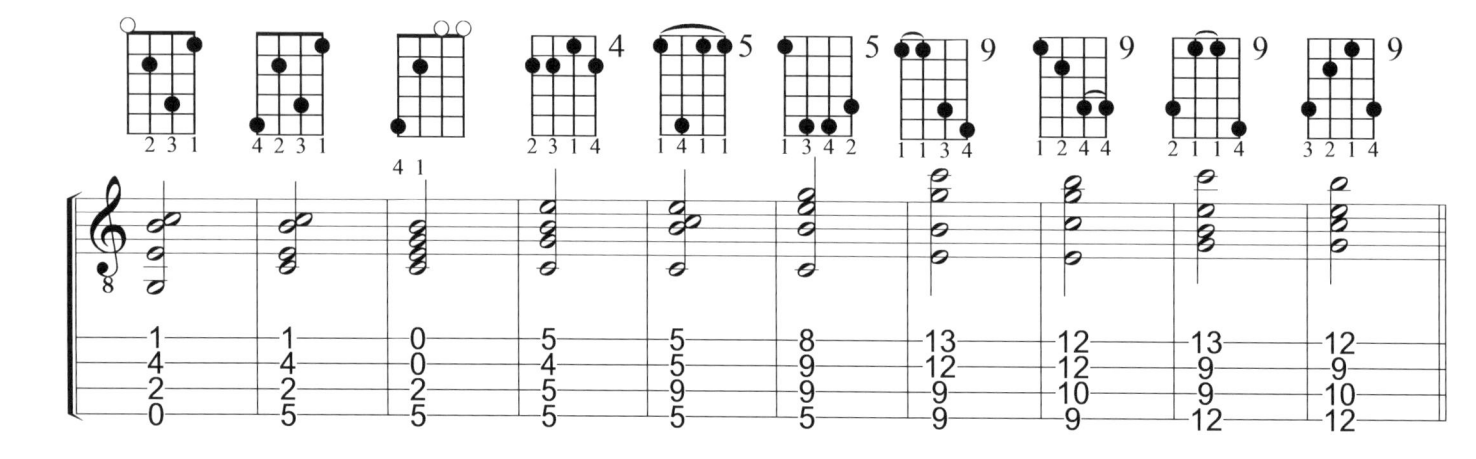

Cmaj9 - C6/9 - C+

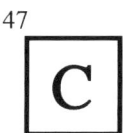

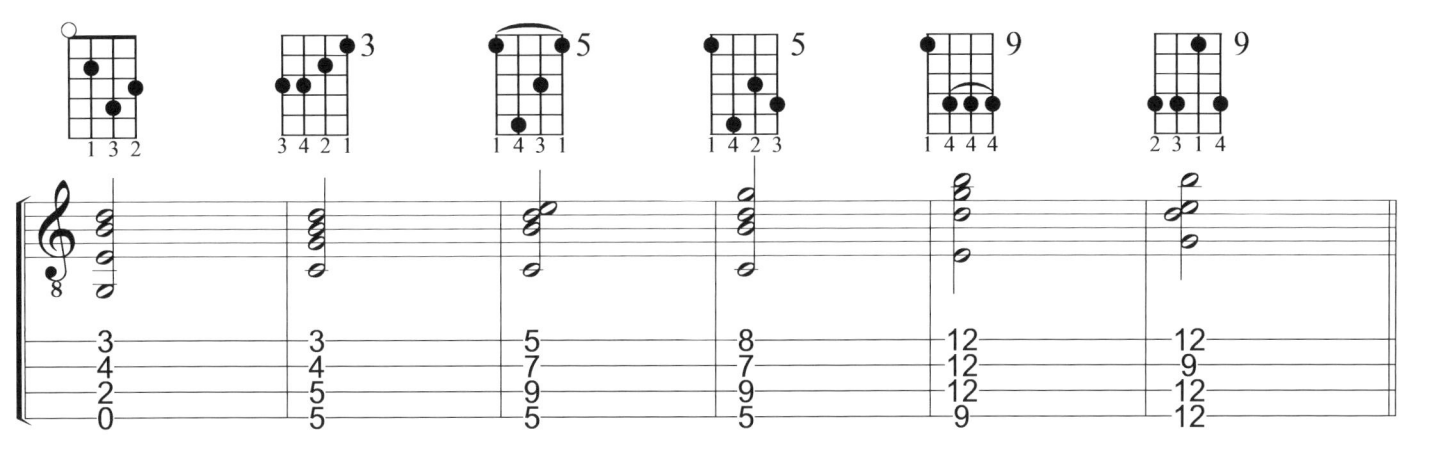

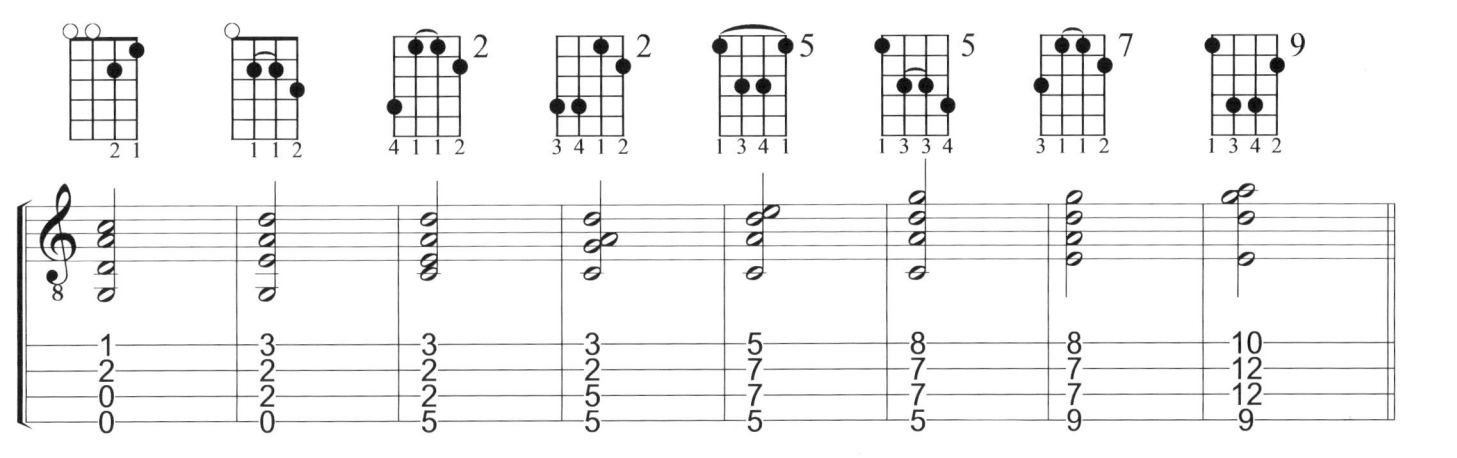

C

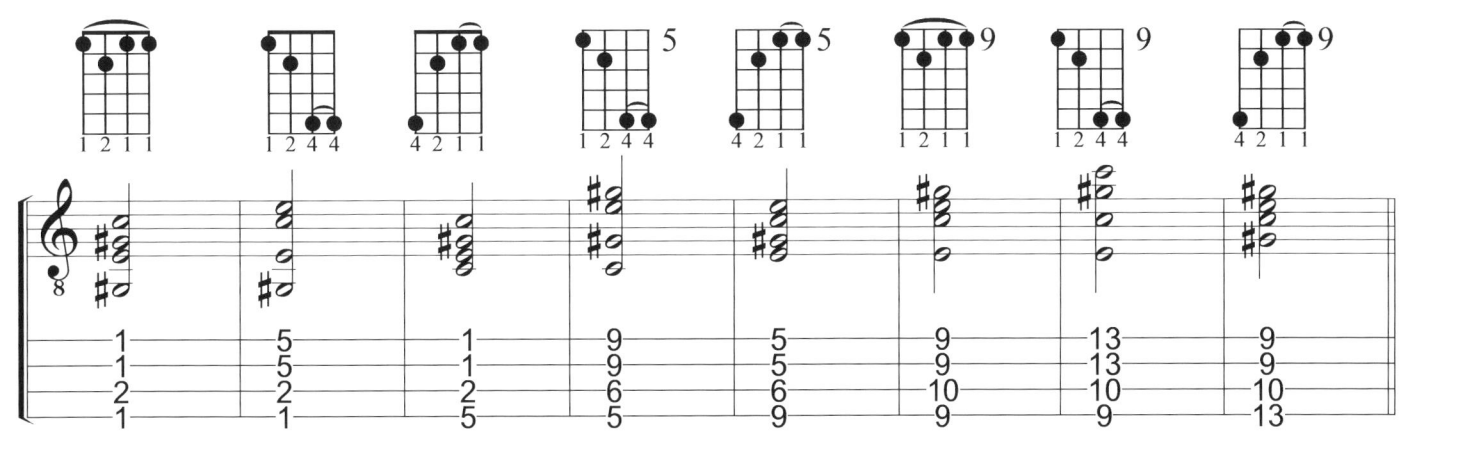

Cm - Cm6 - Cm7

C Minor

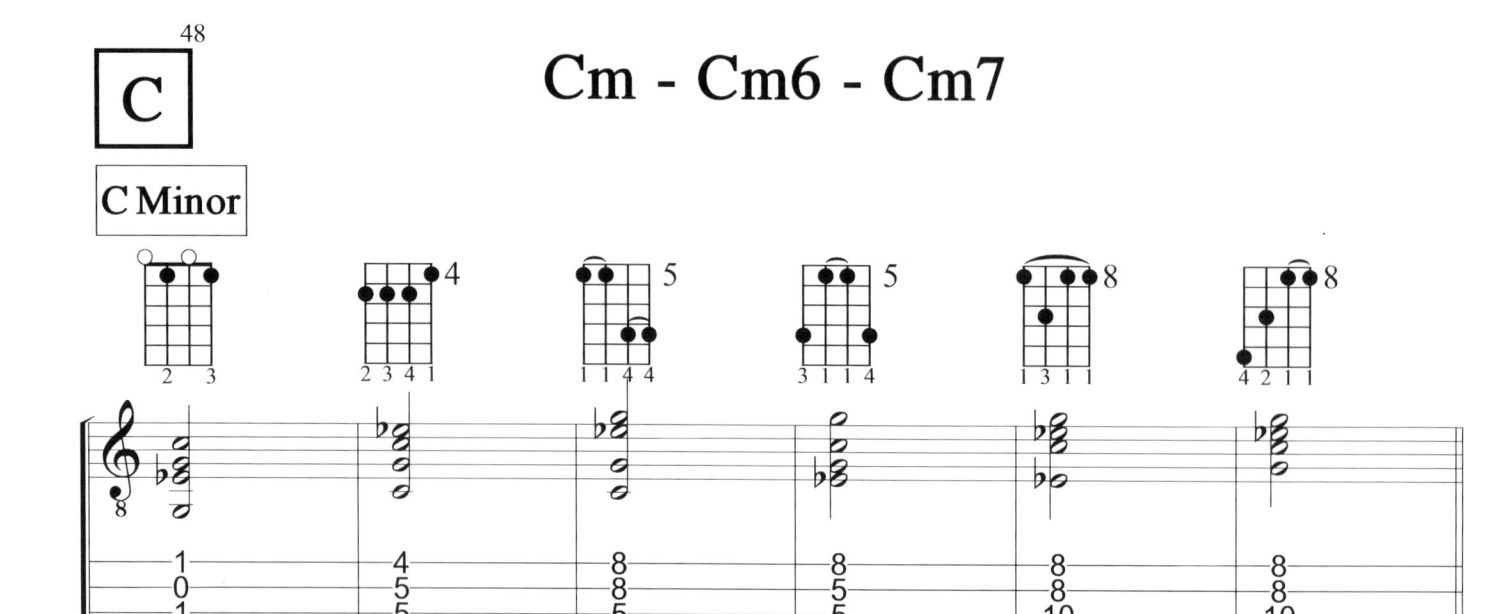

Cm6

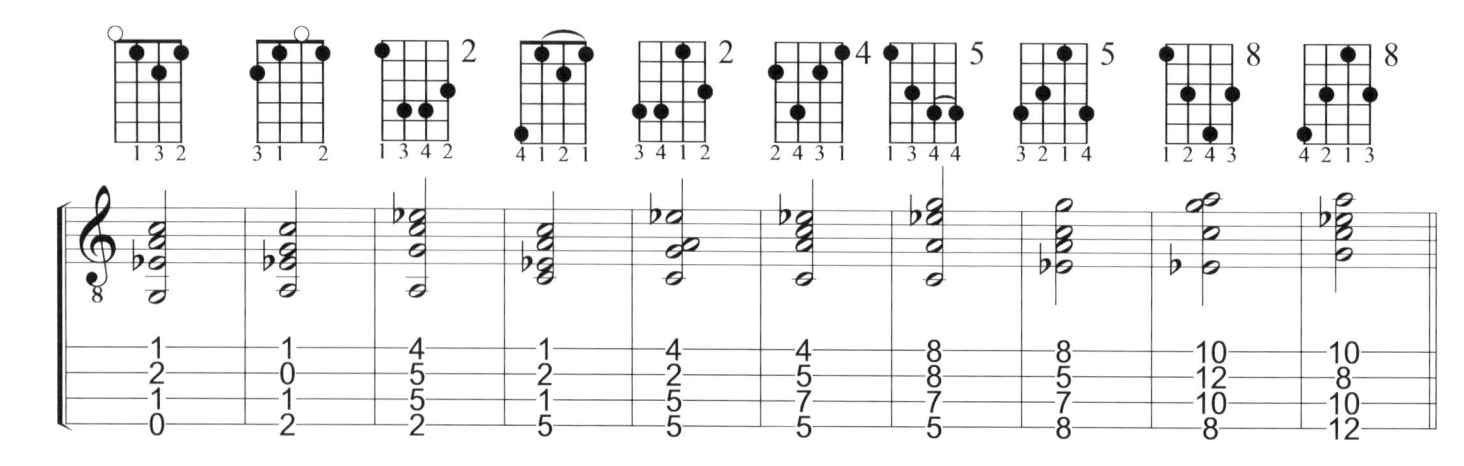

Cm7

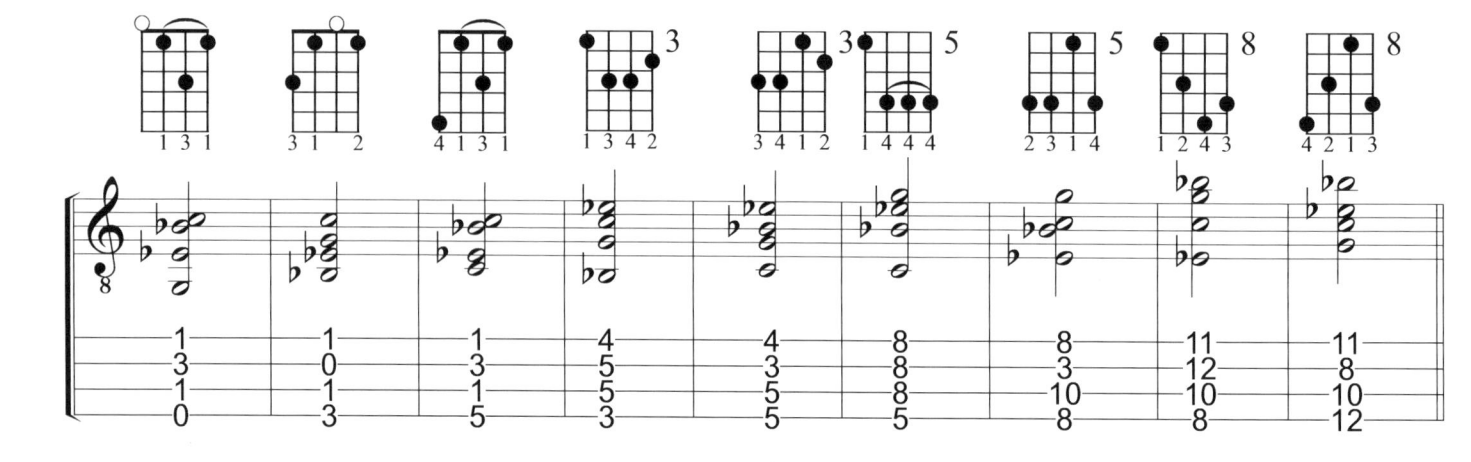

Cm7♭5 - Cm9 - Cm11 - Cm(maj7)

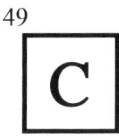

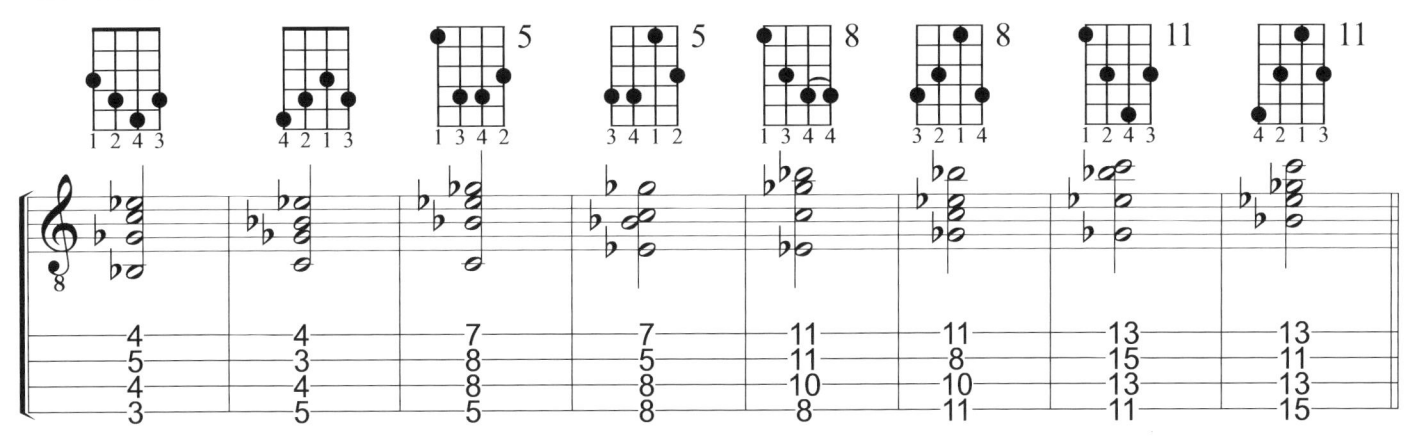

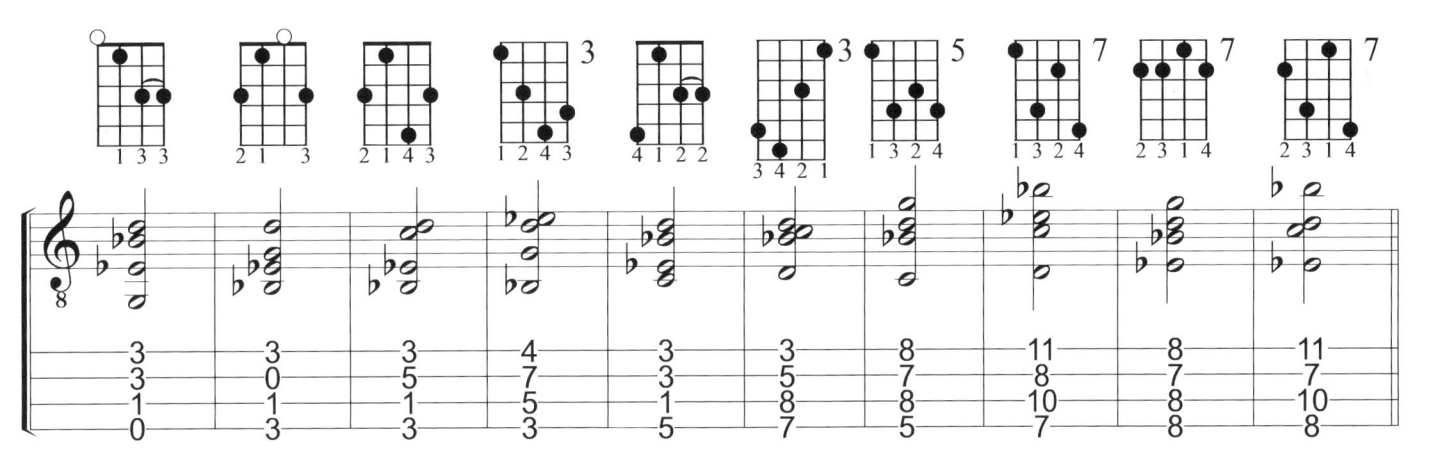

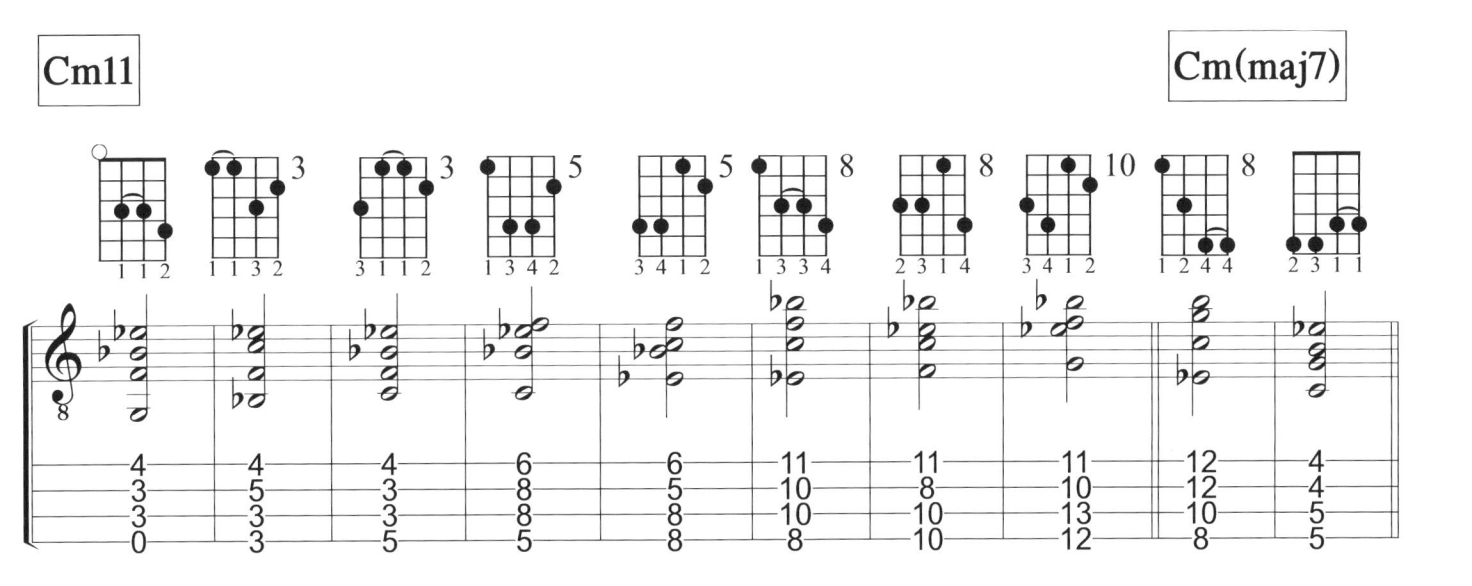

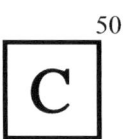

C7 - C9 - C13

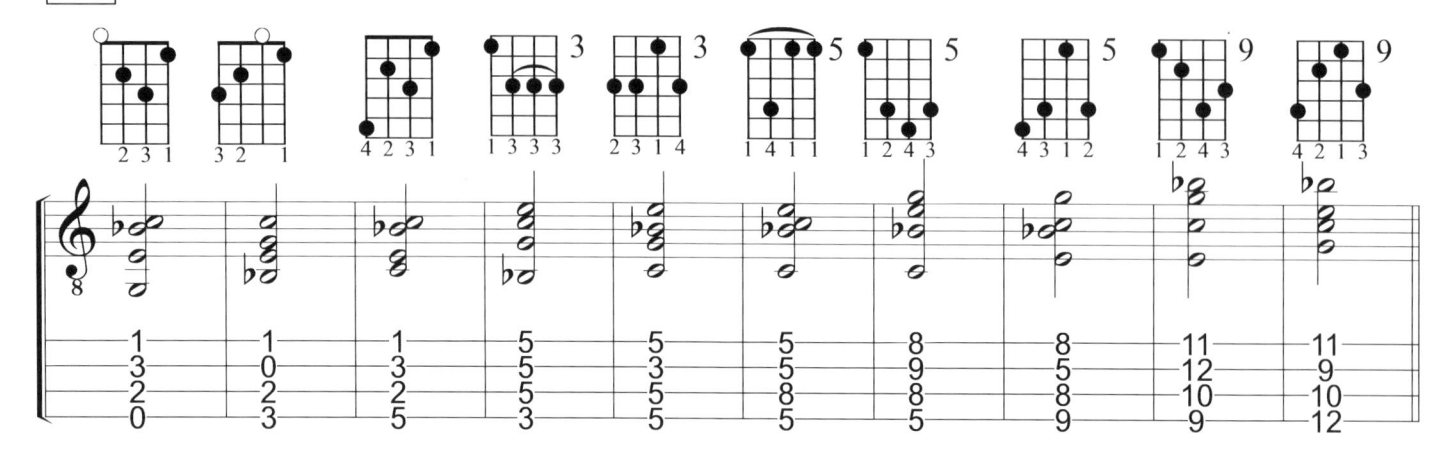

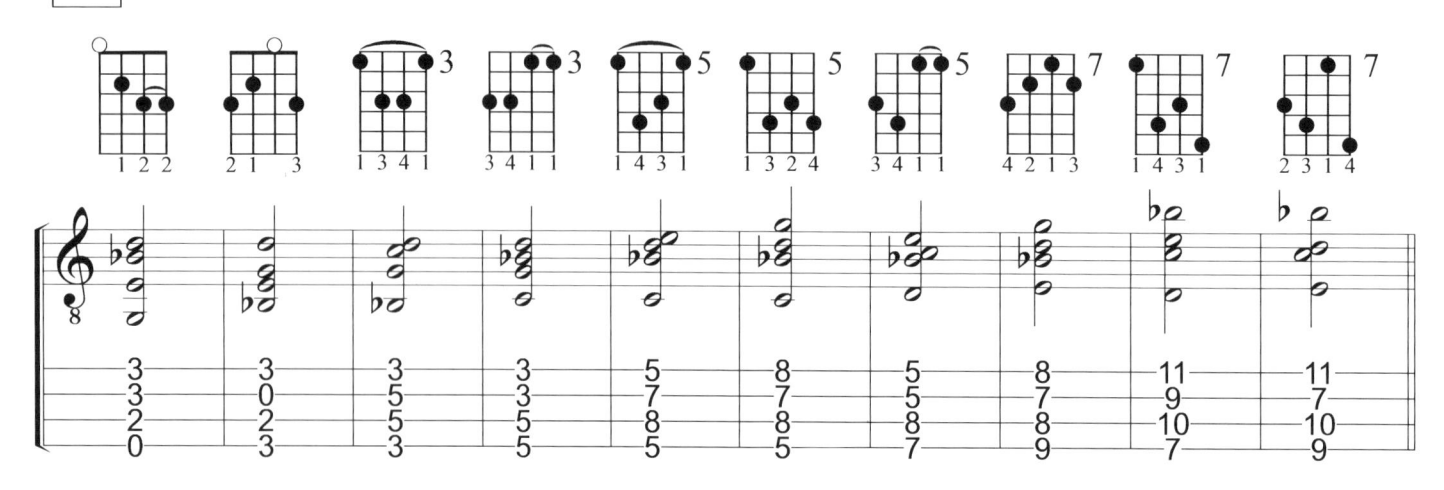

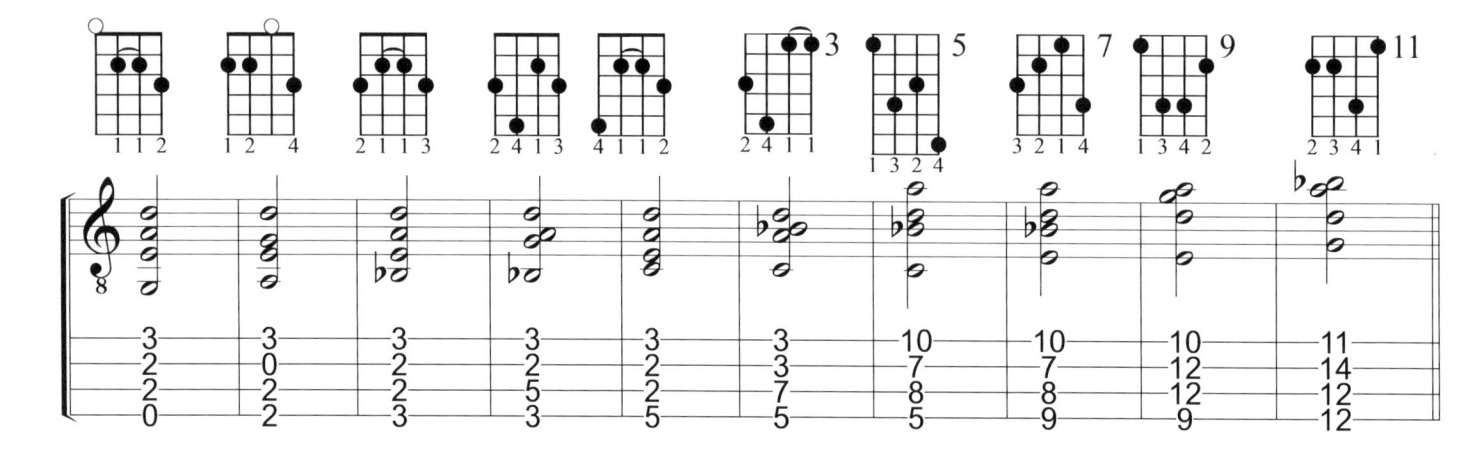

C7b5 - C7#5 - C7#9

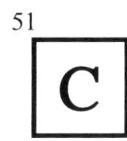

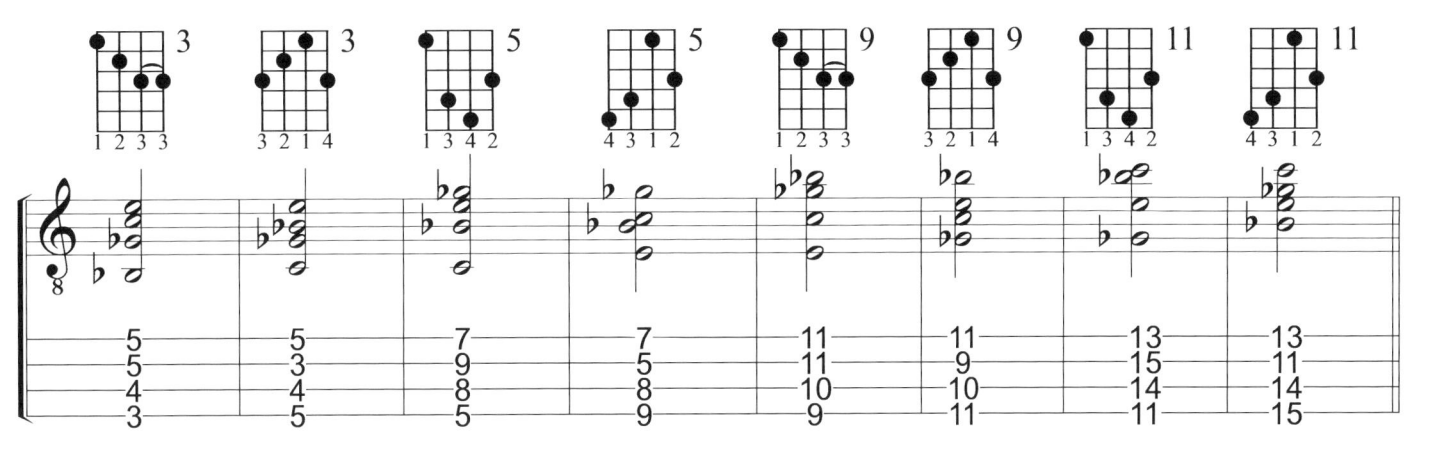

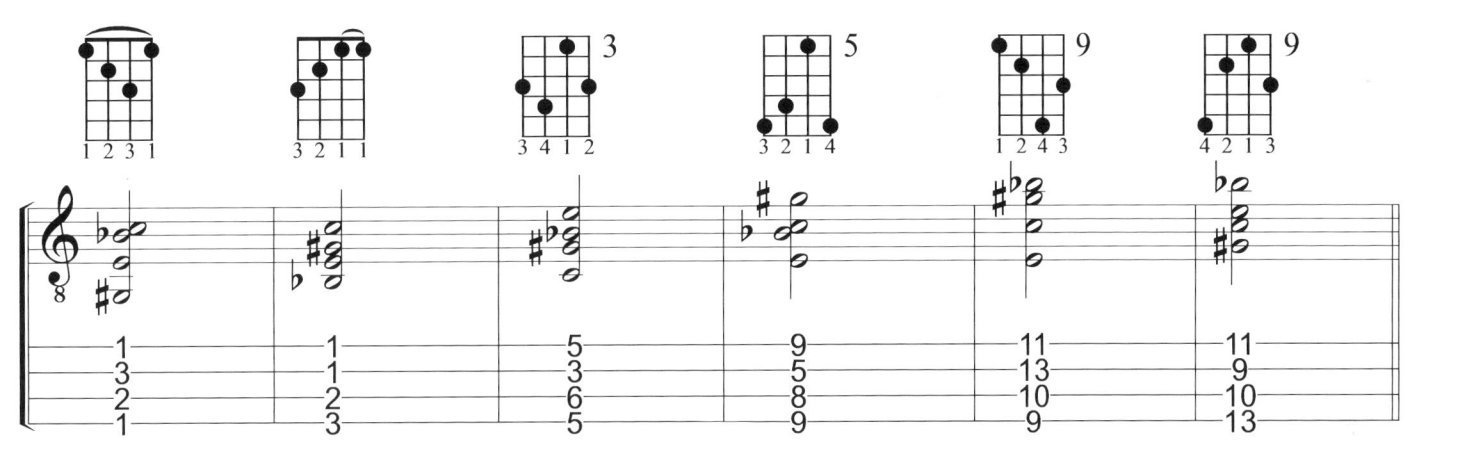

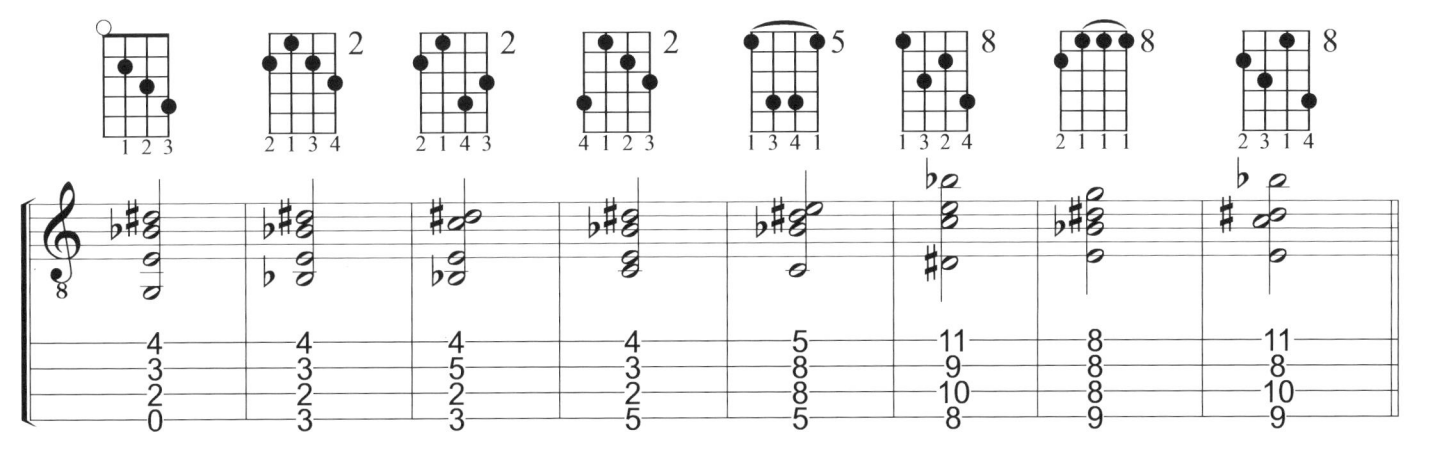

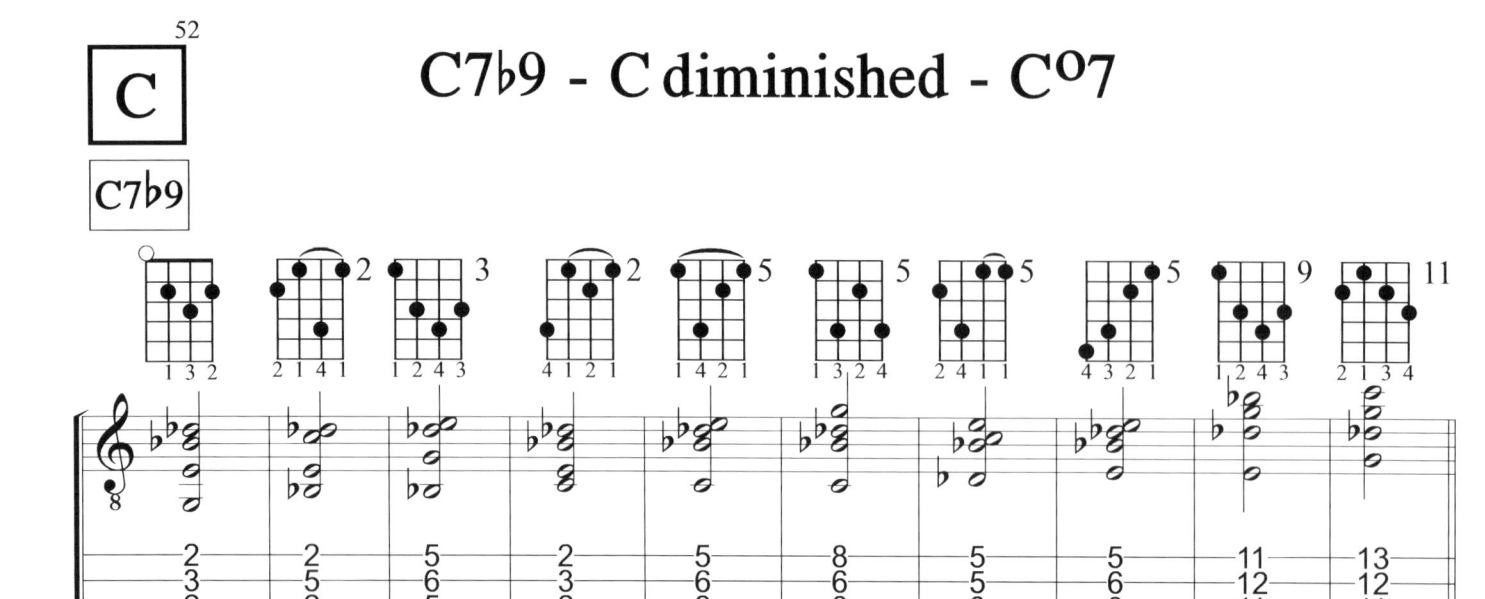

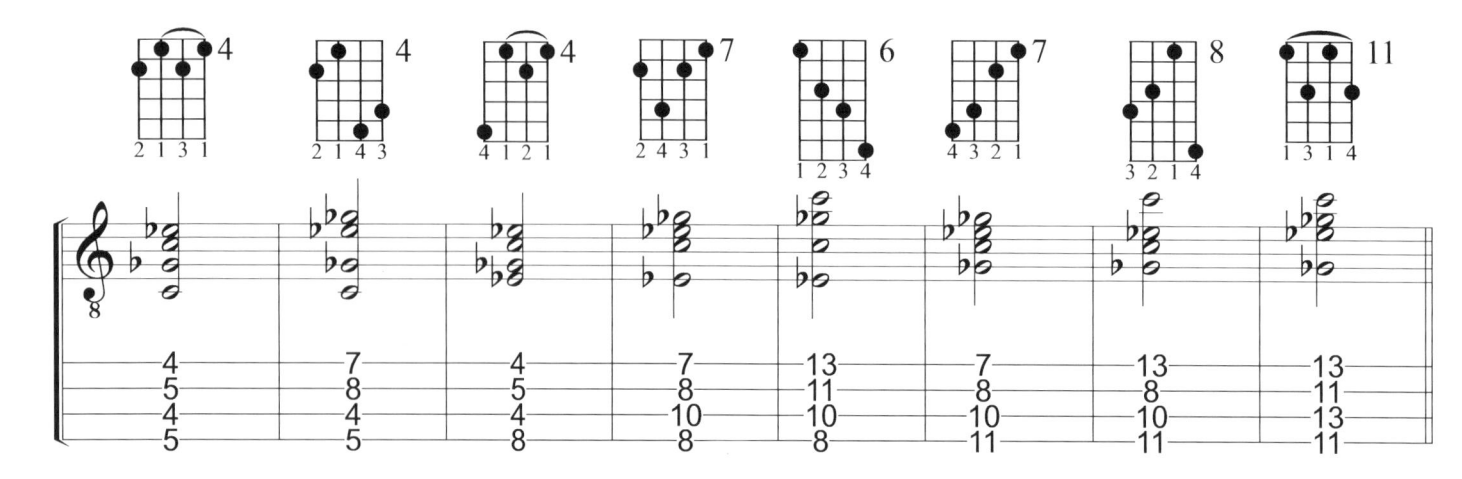

C7♭9 - C diminished - C°7

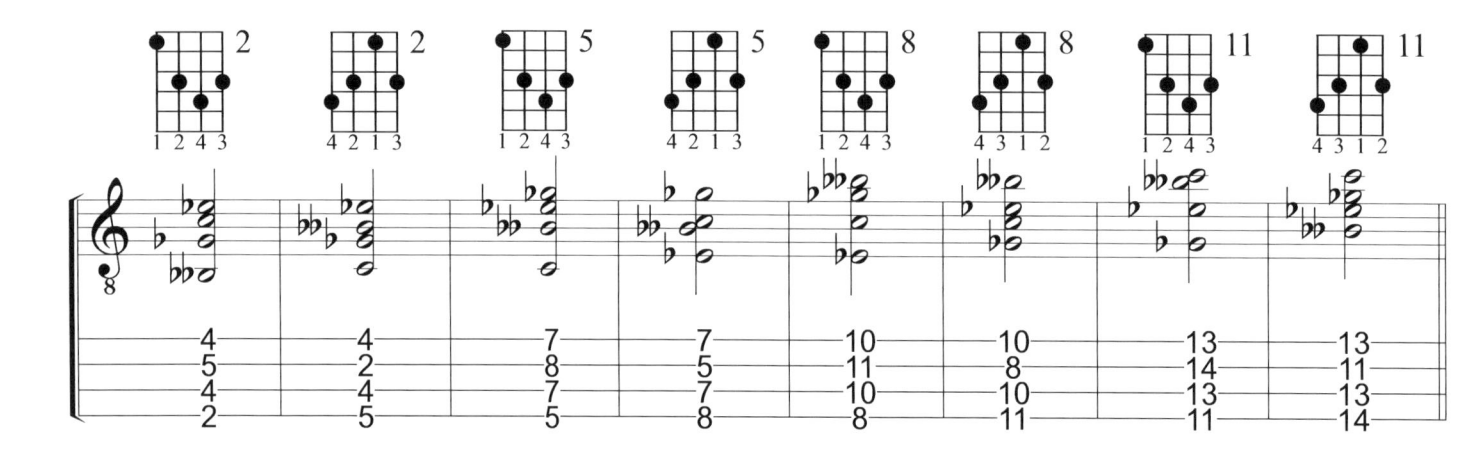

Csus4 - Csus2 - Cadd9 - C7sus - C5

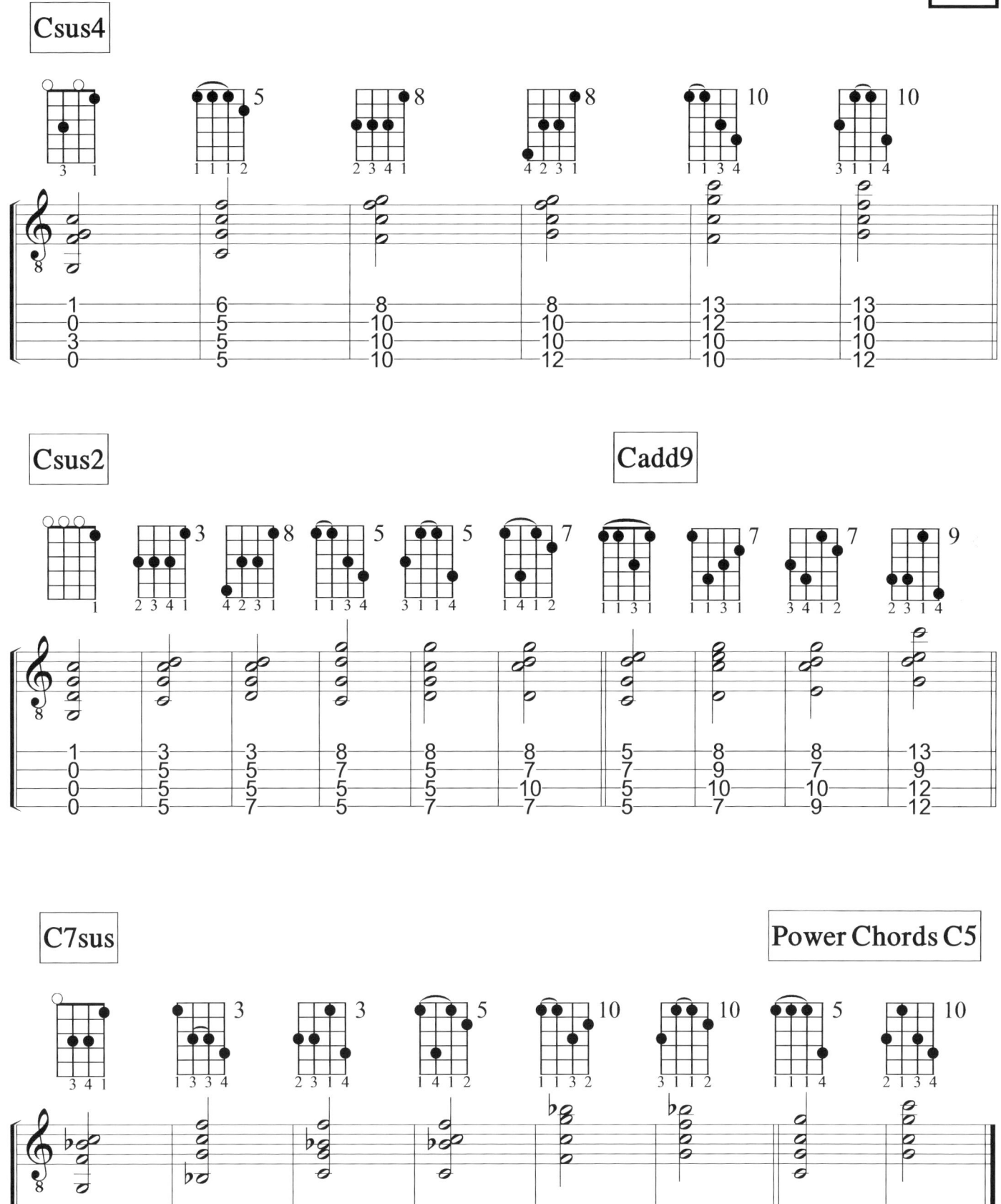

C♯ D♭ Major - 6 - Maj7

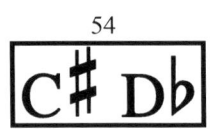

Chords are shown as either sharps or flats in the notation line.
For example, C#m is shown instead of Dbm.

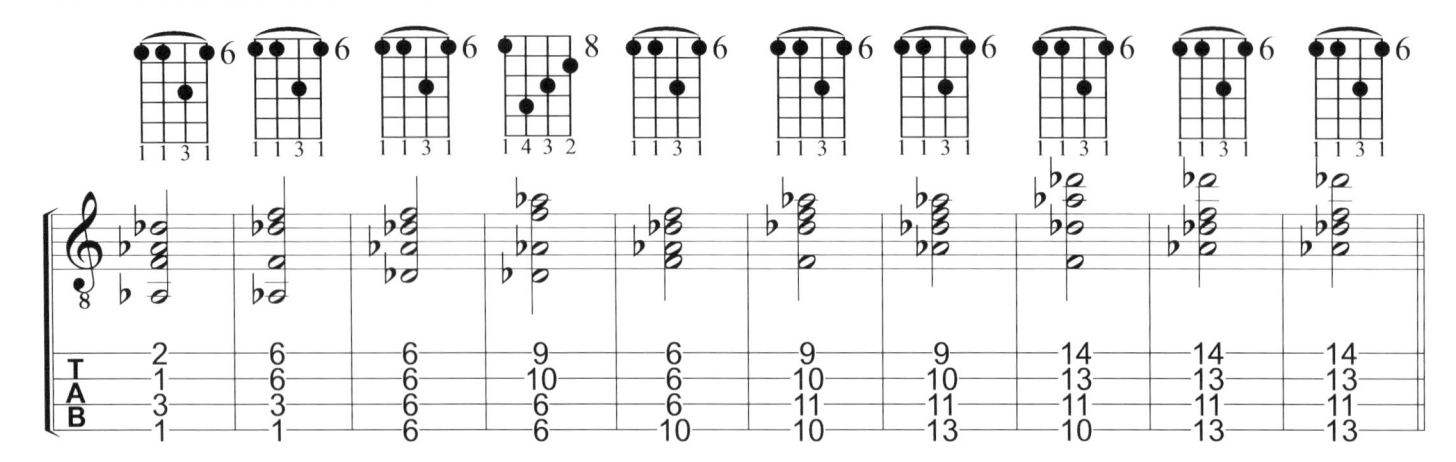

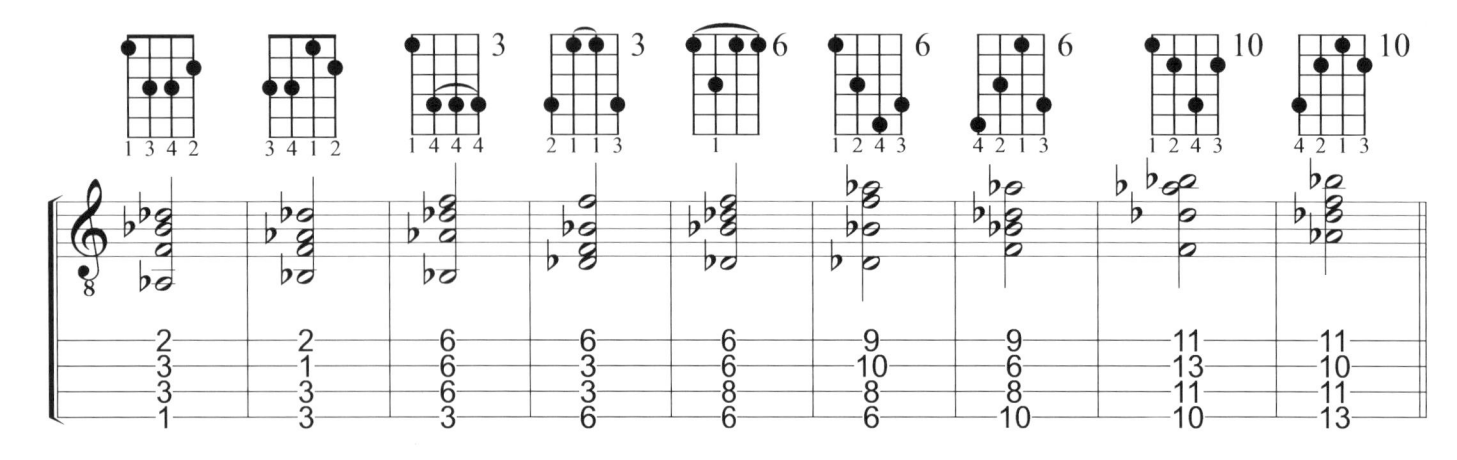

C♯ Major - D♭ Major

C♯6 - D♭6

C♯maj7 - D♭maj7

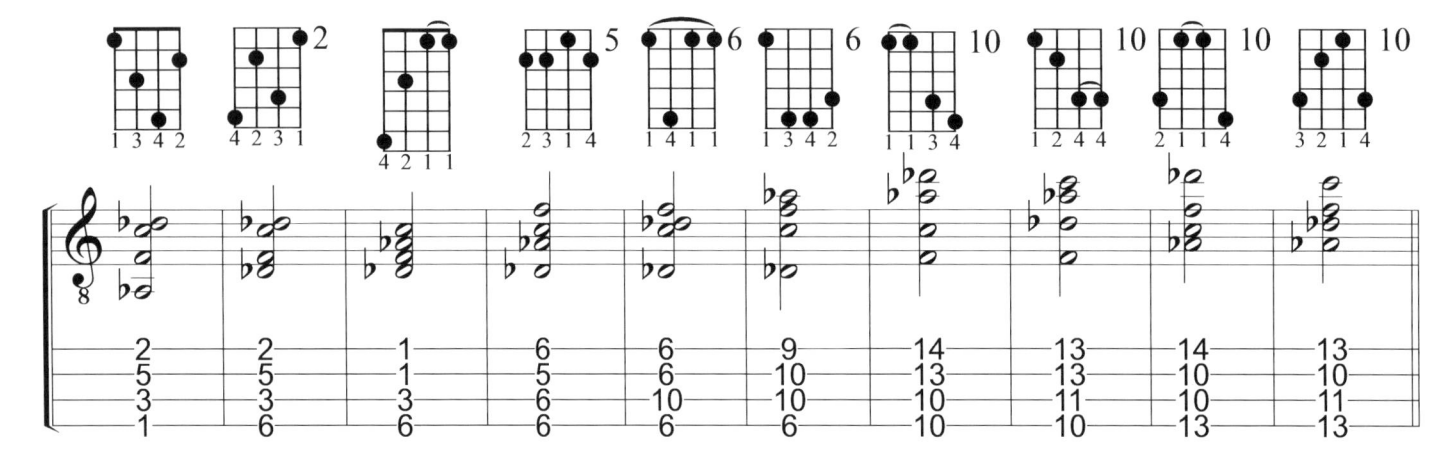

Maj9 - 6/9 - Augmented +

C# Db (55)

C#maj9 - Dbmaj9

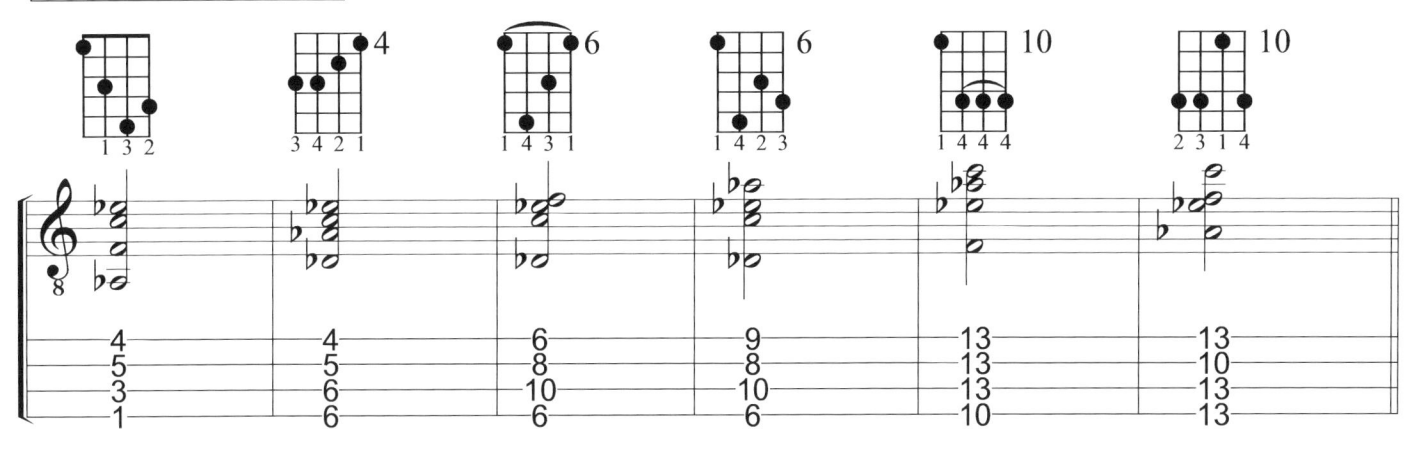

C#6/9 - Db6/9

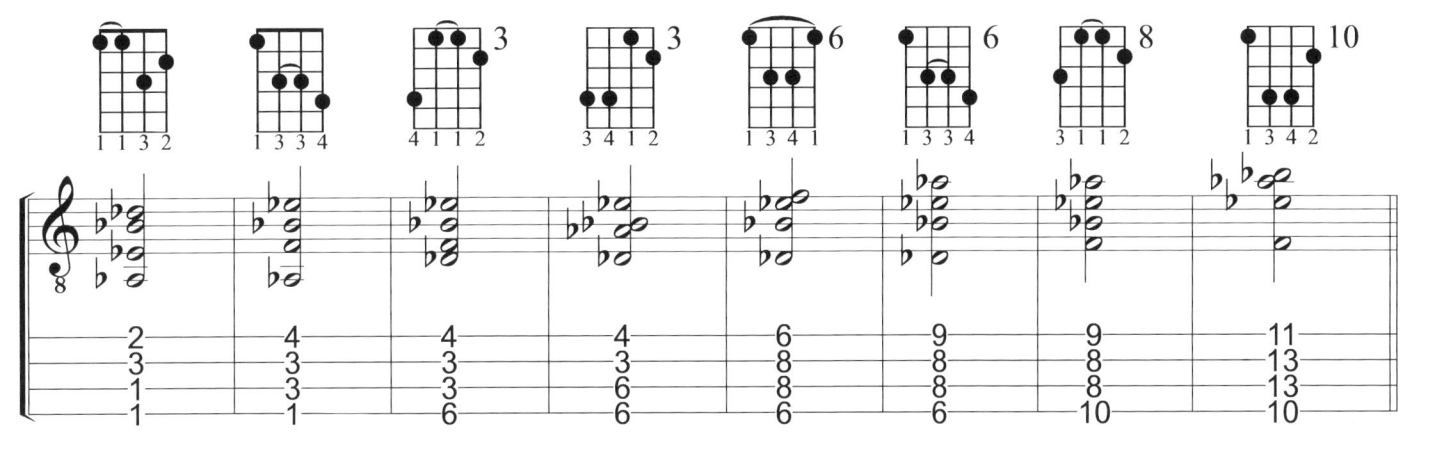

C# Augmented C#+ / Db Augmented Db+

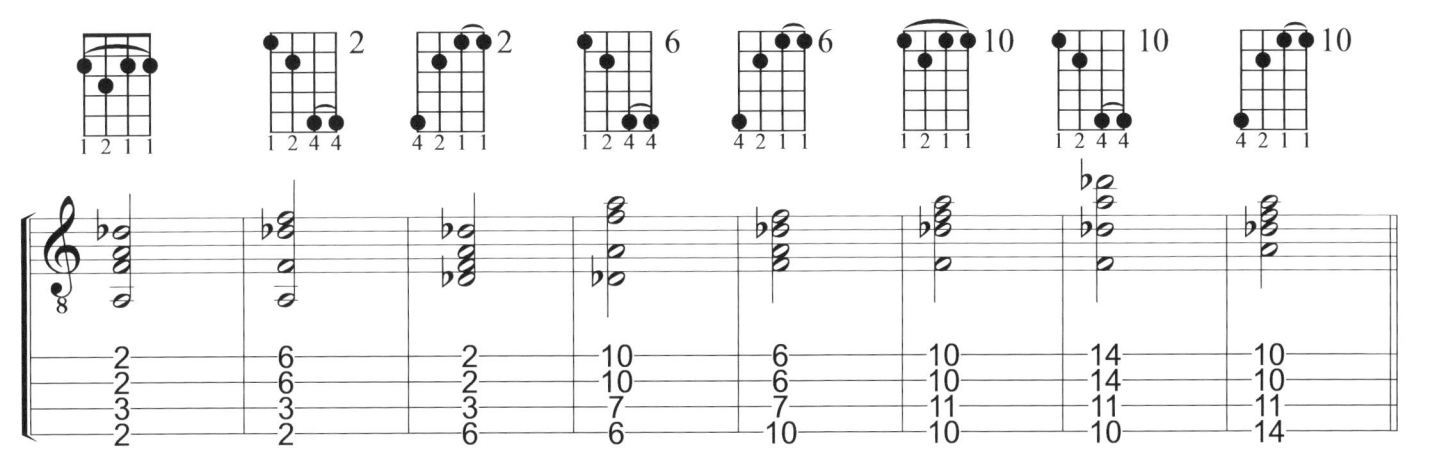

C# Db

minor - m6 - m7

C# Minor - Db Minor

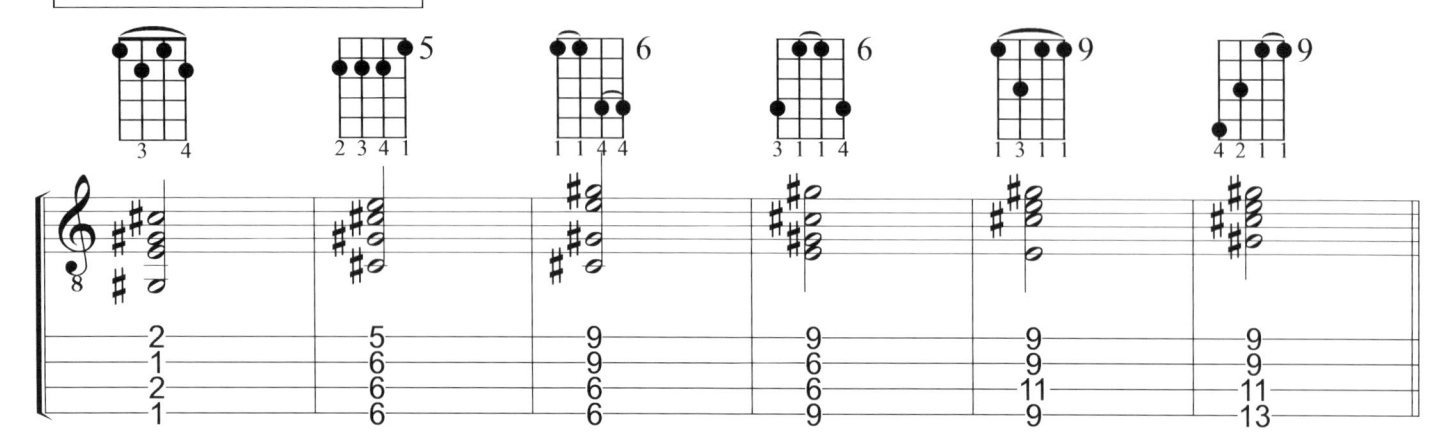

C#m6 - Dbm6

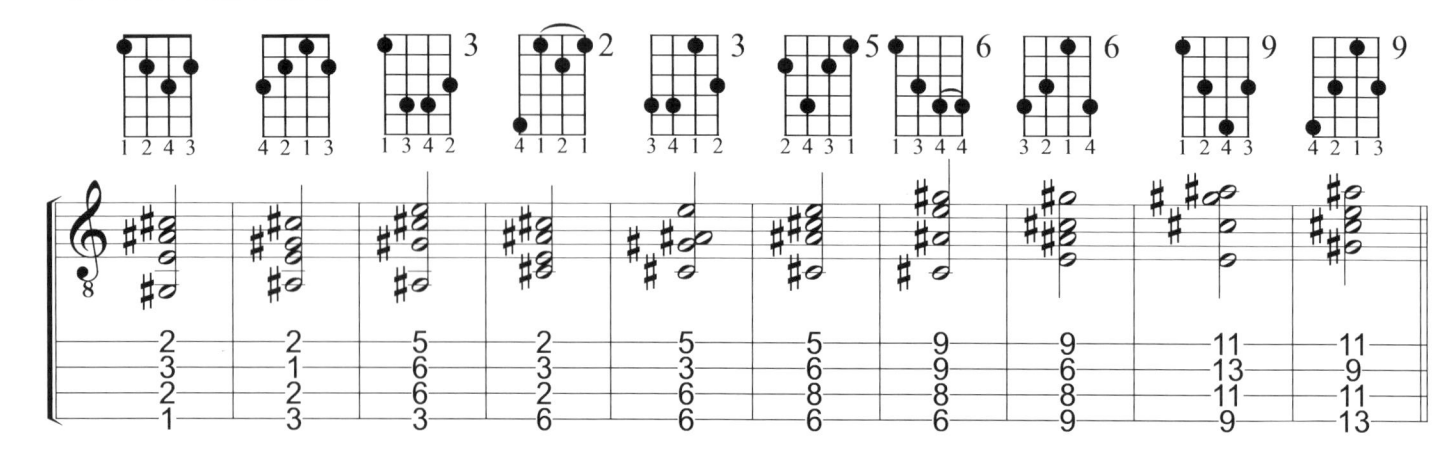

C#m7 - Dbm7

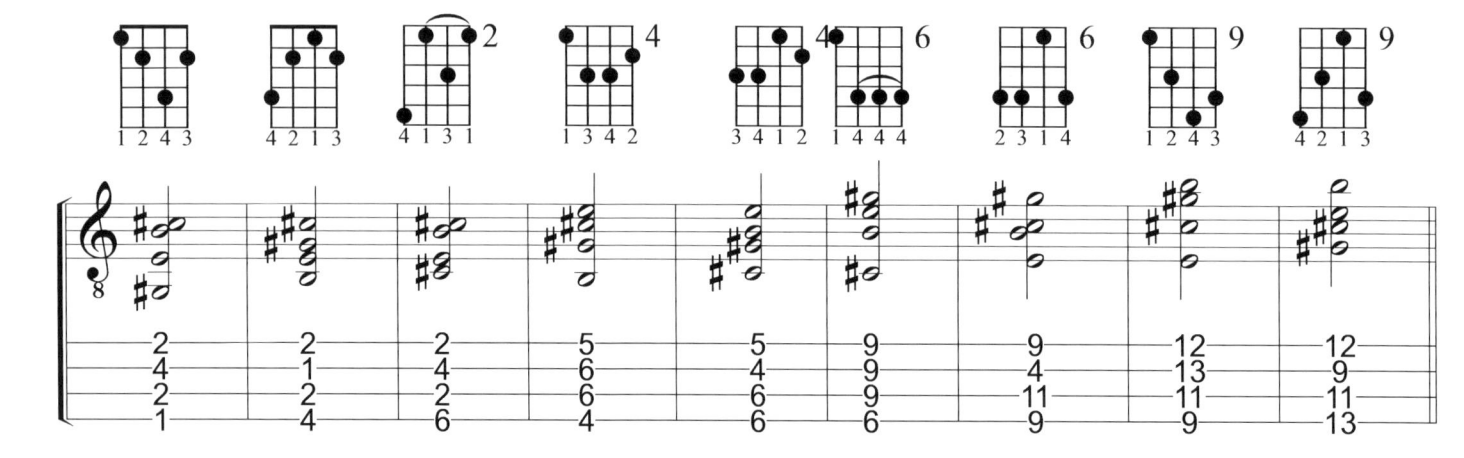

m7♭5 - m9 - m11 - m(maj7)

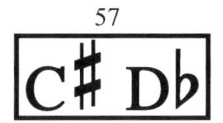

C# D♭ 57

C#m7♭5 - D♭m7♭5

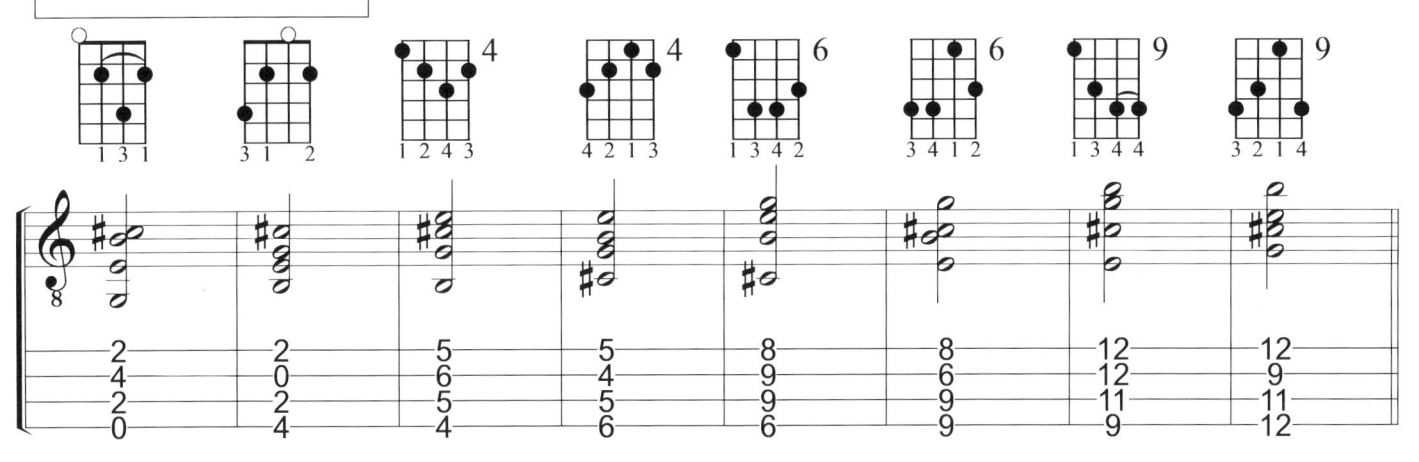

C#m9 - D♭m9

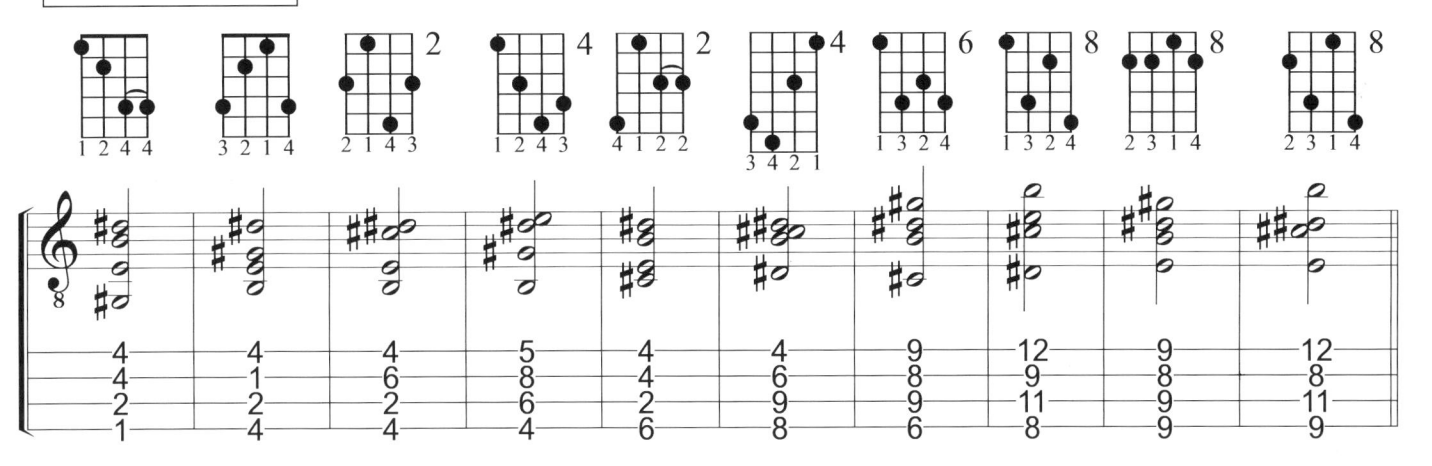

C#m11 - D♭m11

C#m(maj7) - D♭m(maj7)

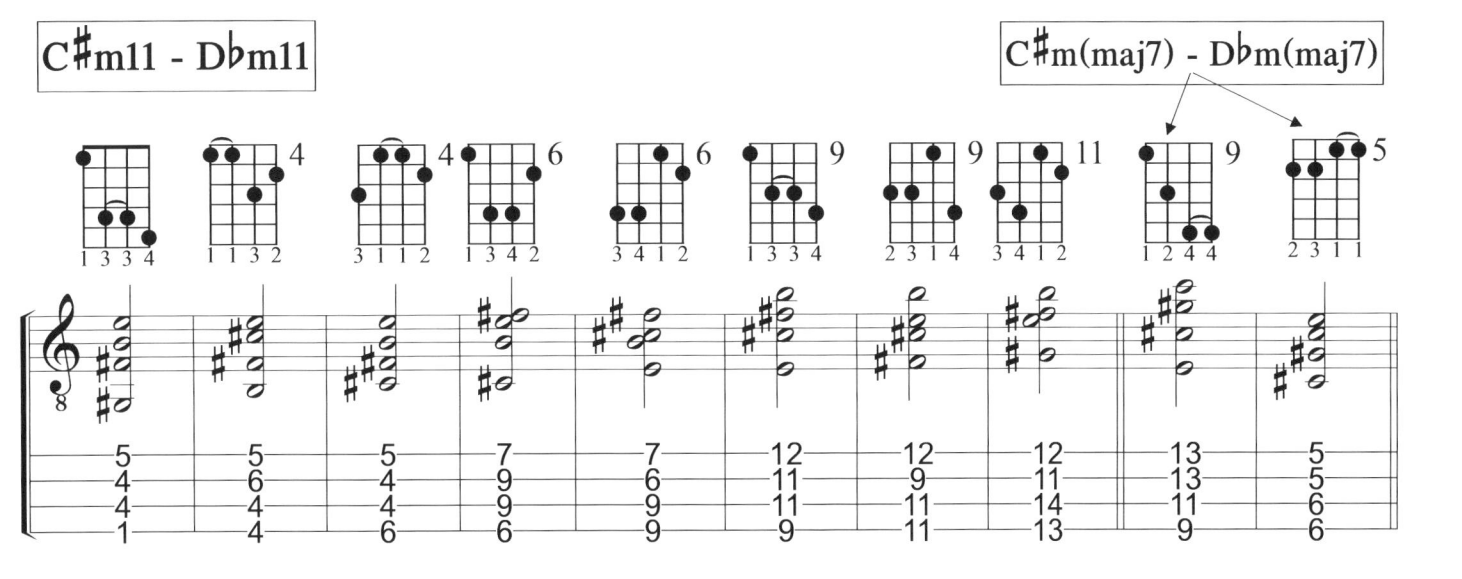

7th - 9th - 13th

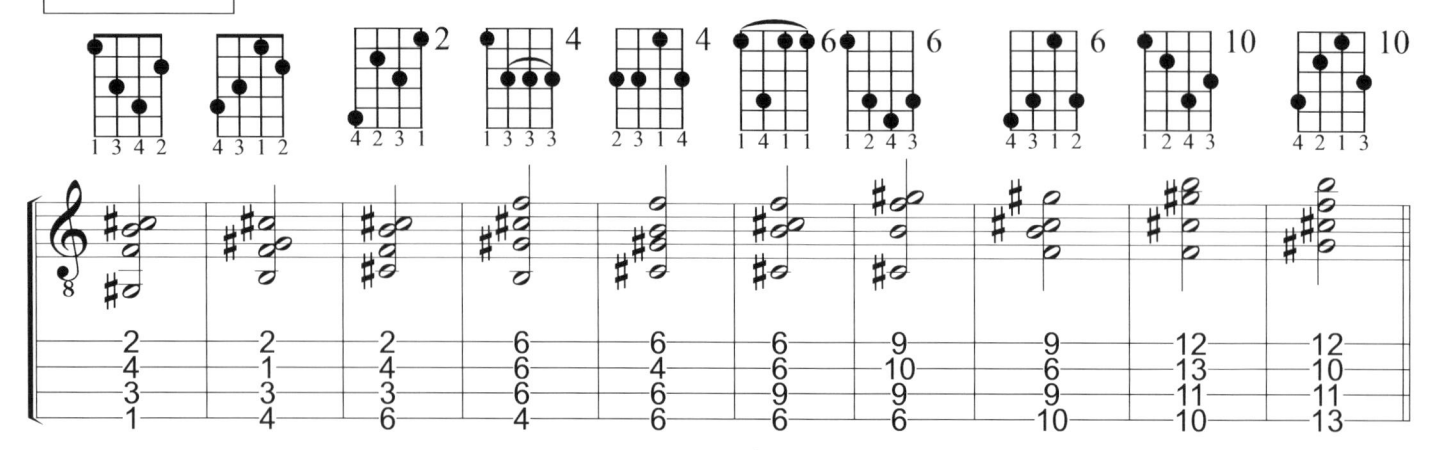

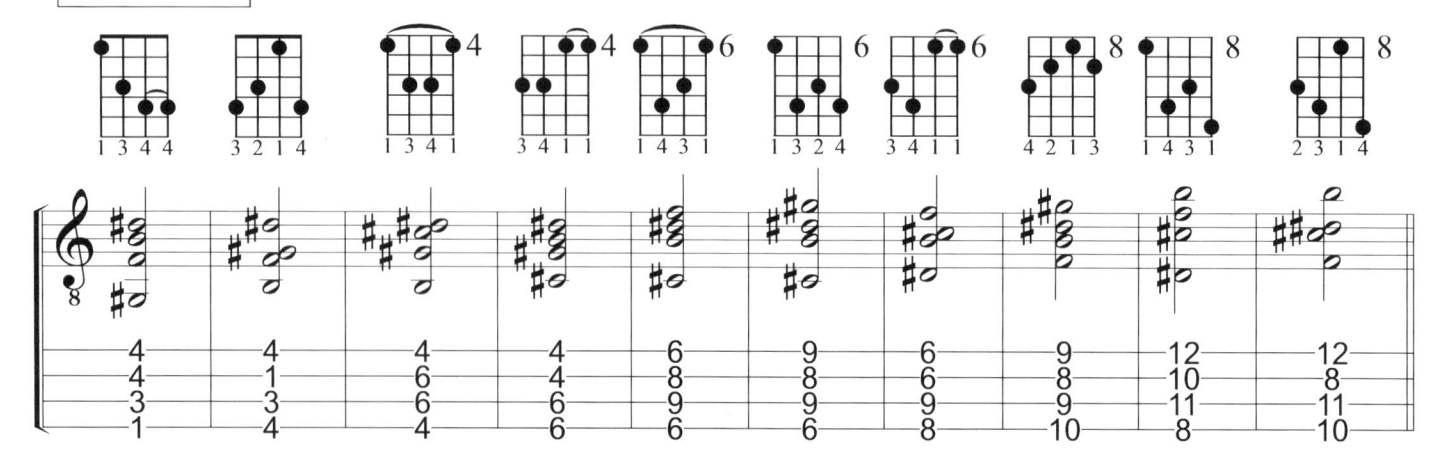

C# Db

C#7 - Db7

C#9 - Db9

C#13 - Db13

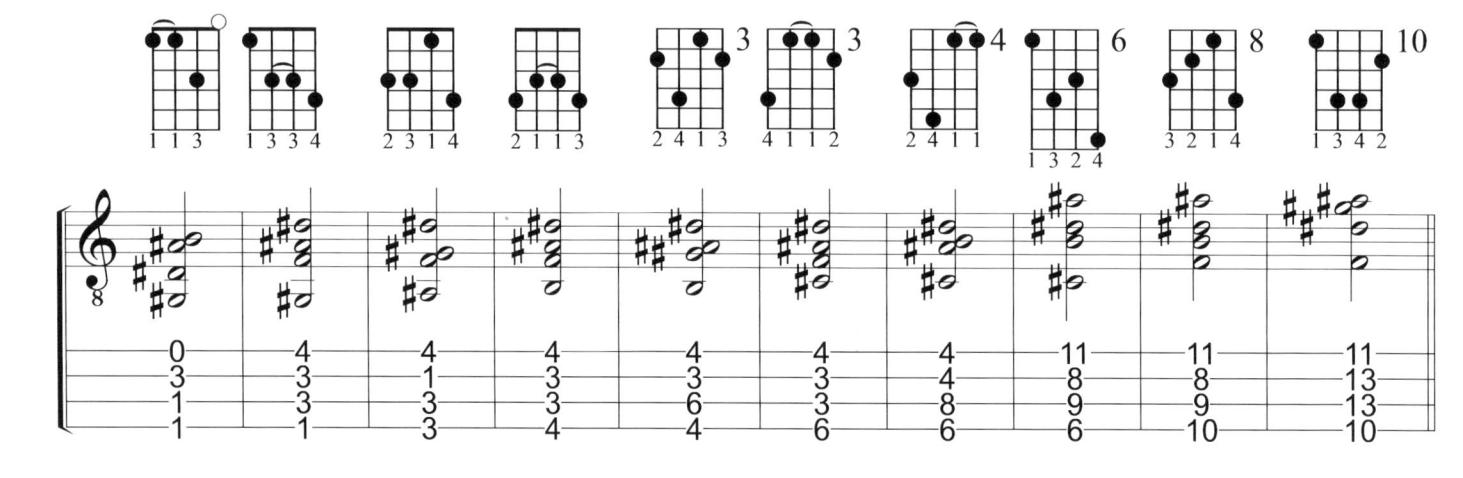

7b5 - 7#5 - 7#9

C#7b5 - Db7b5

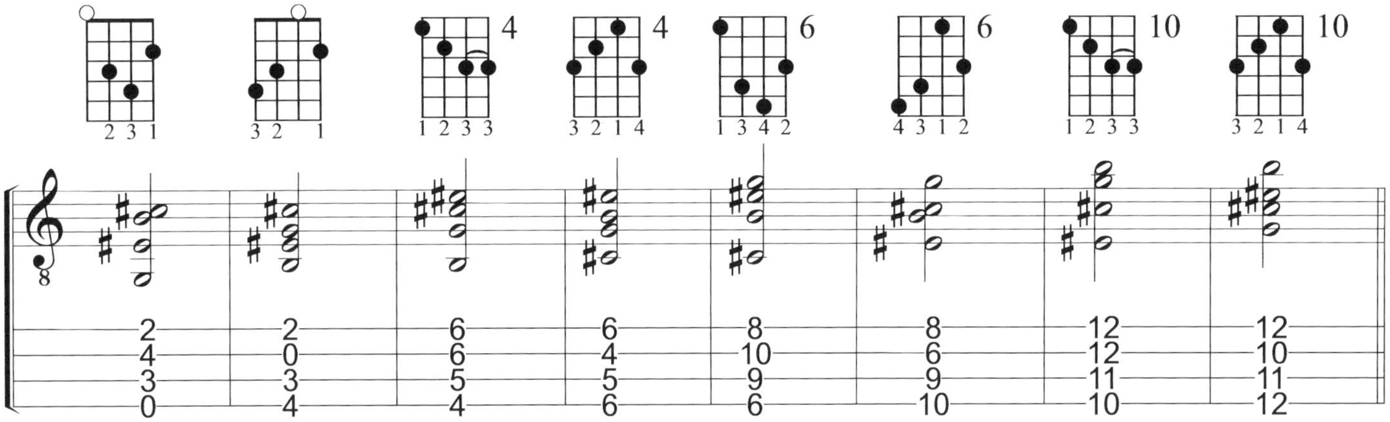

C#7#5 - Db7#5

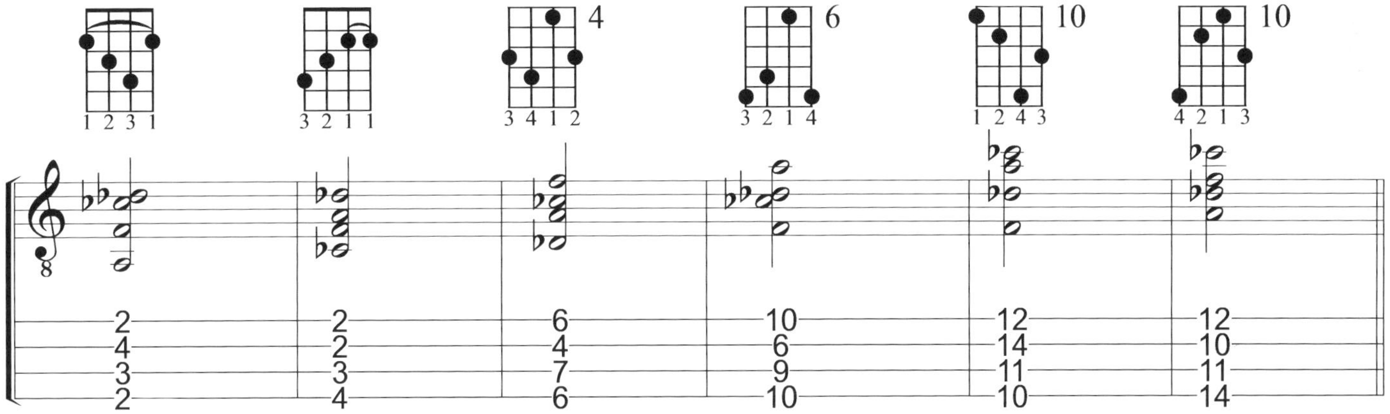

C#7#9 - Db7#9

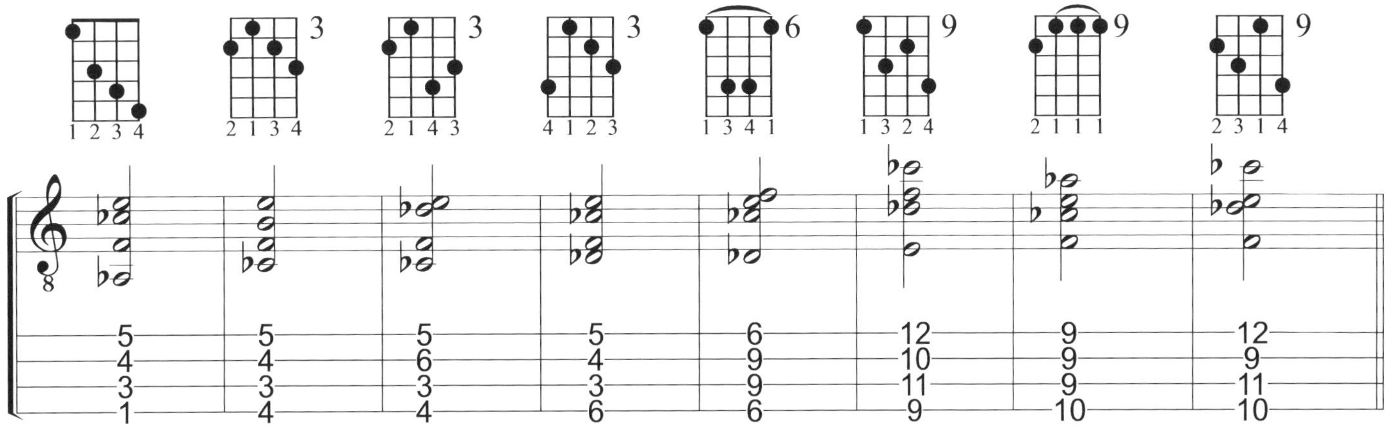

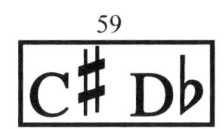

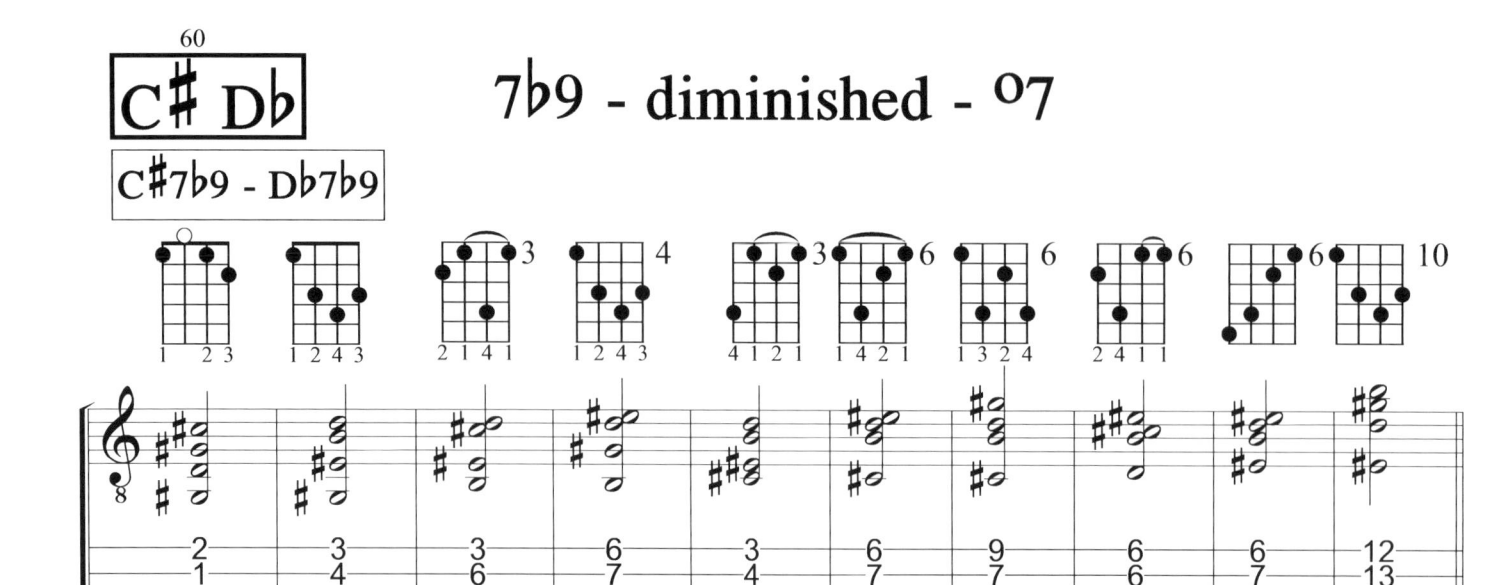

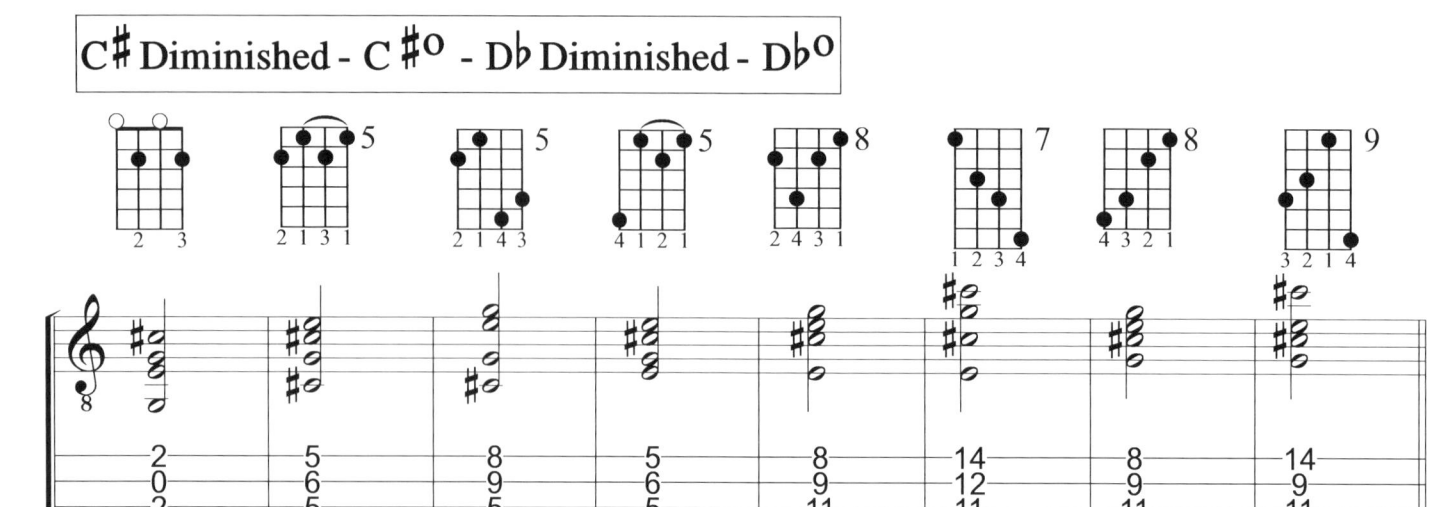

C# Db

7b9 - diminished - °7

C#7b9 - Db7b9

C# Diminished - C#° - Db Diminished - Db°

C# Diminished 7th - C#°7n - Db Diminsihed 7th - Db°7

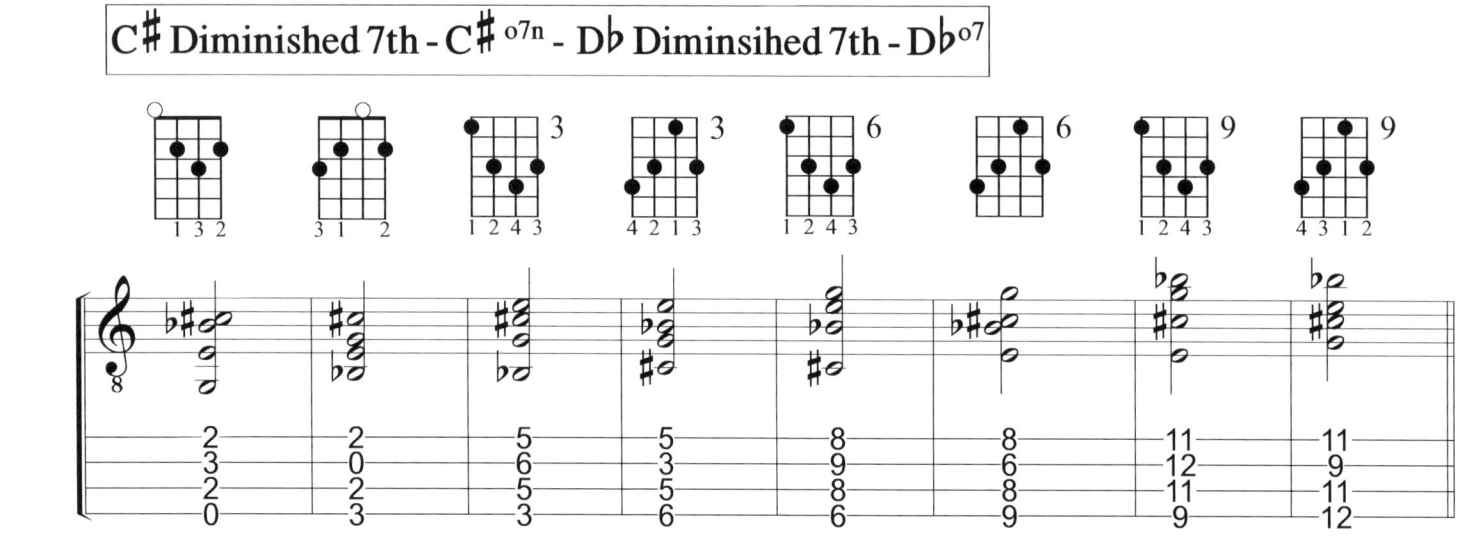

sus4 - sus2 - add9 - 7sus - 5th

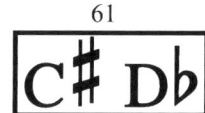

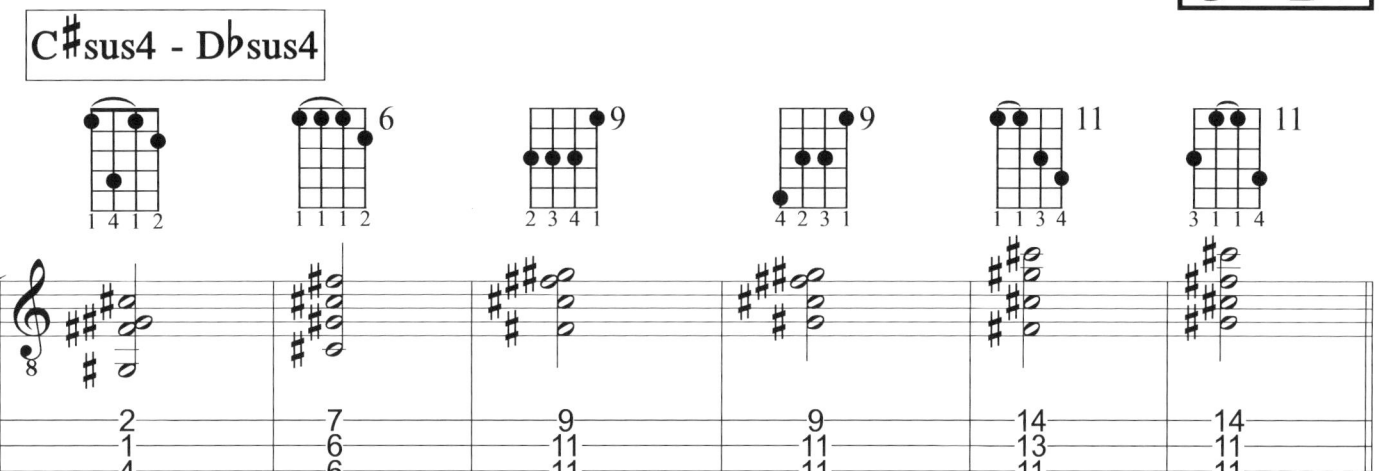

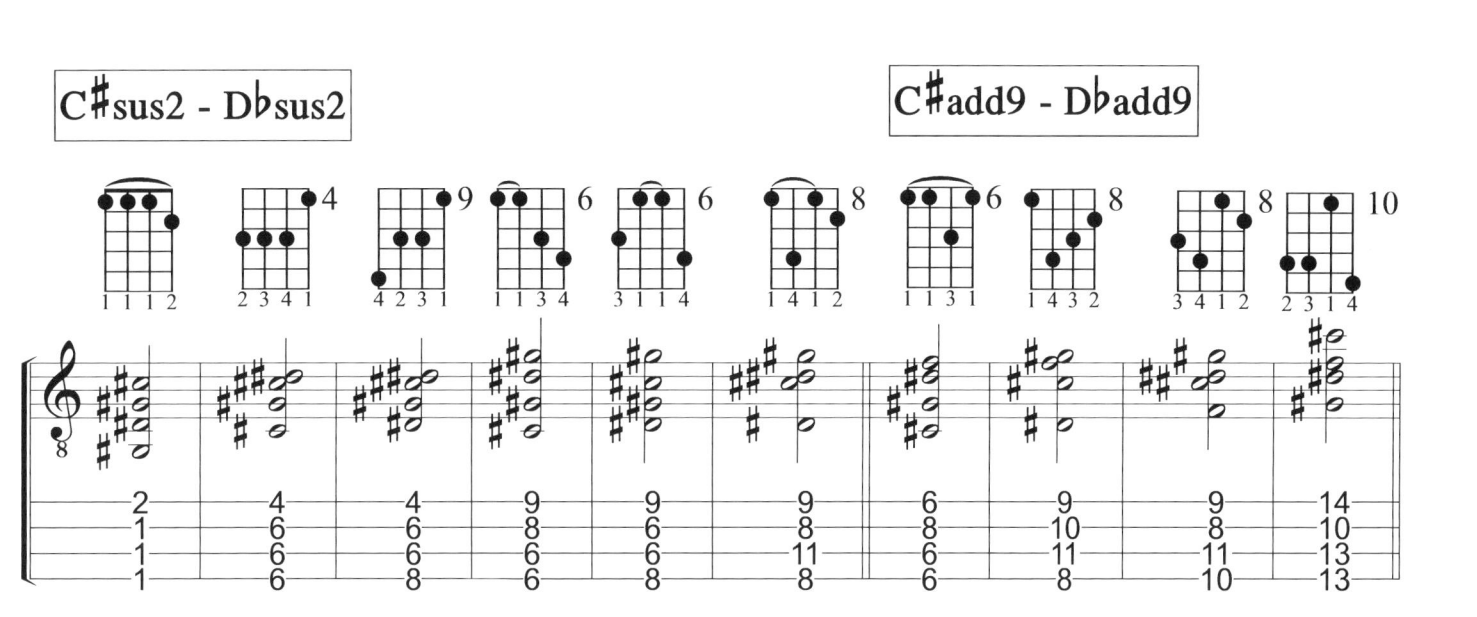

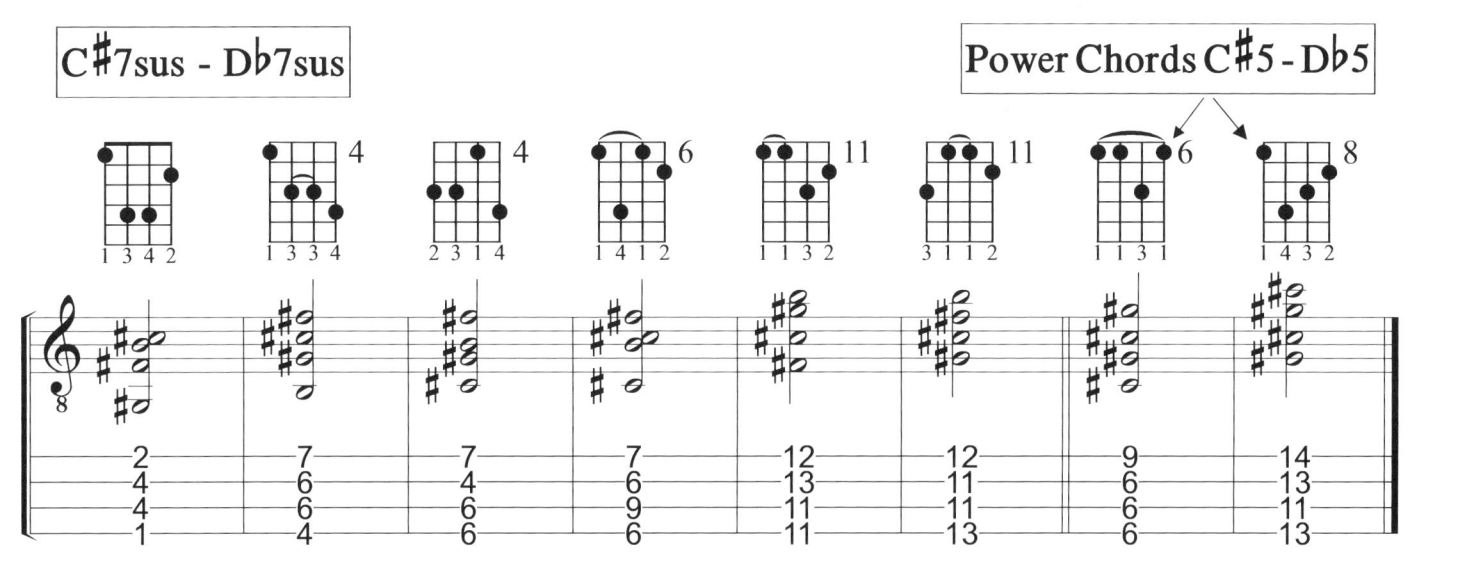

C# Db (61)

C#sus4 - Dbsus4

C#sus2 - Dbsus2

C#add9 - Dbadd9

C#7sus - Db7sus

Power Chords C#5 - Db5

D - D6 - Dmaj7

D Major

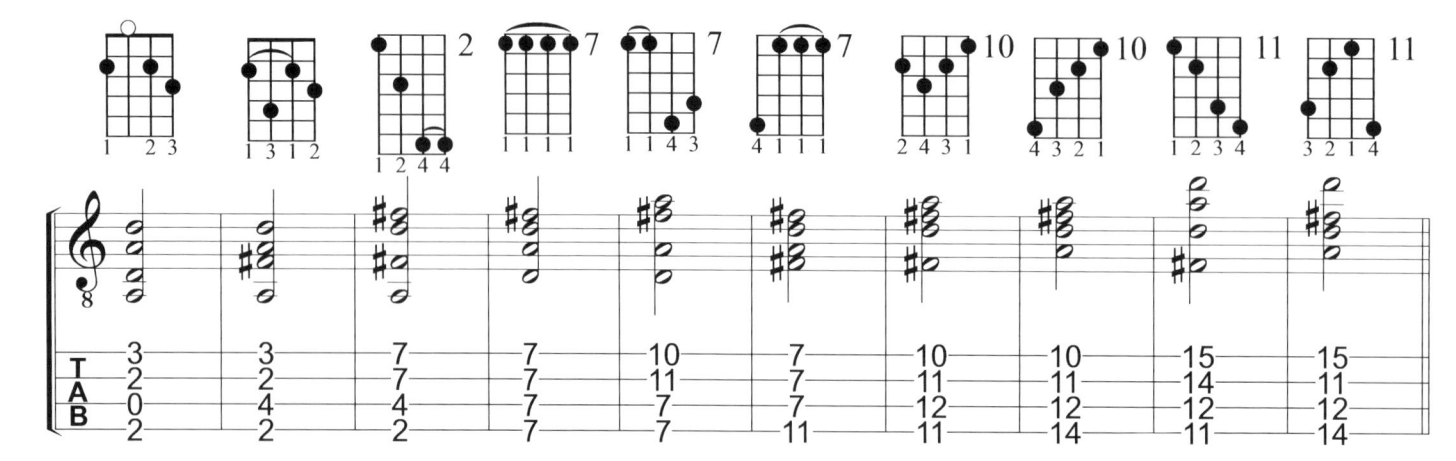

D6

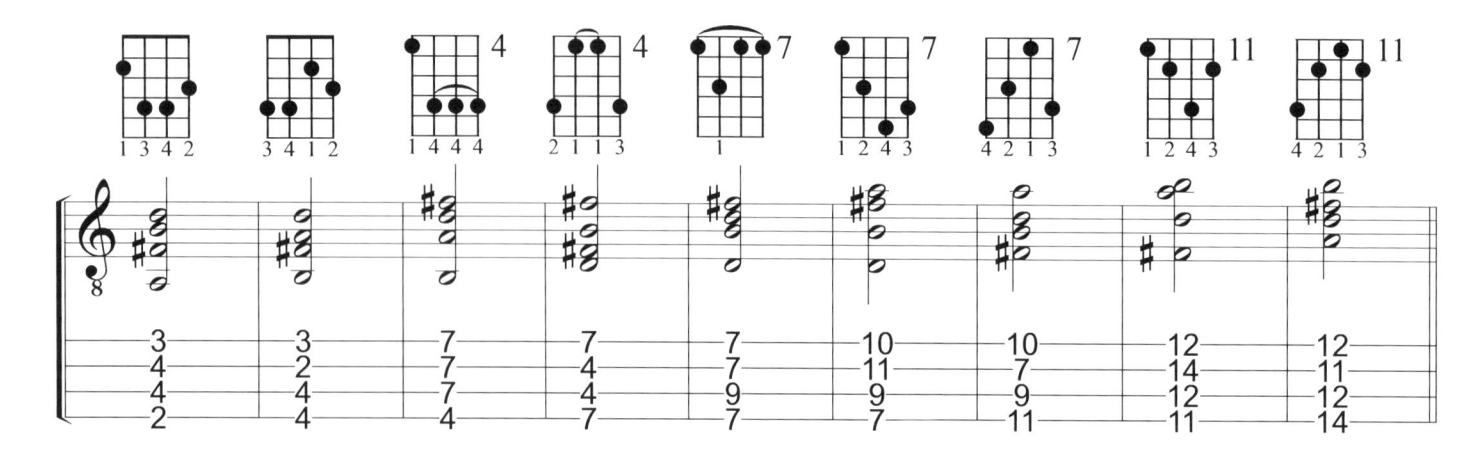

Dmaj7

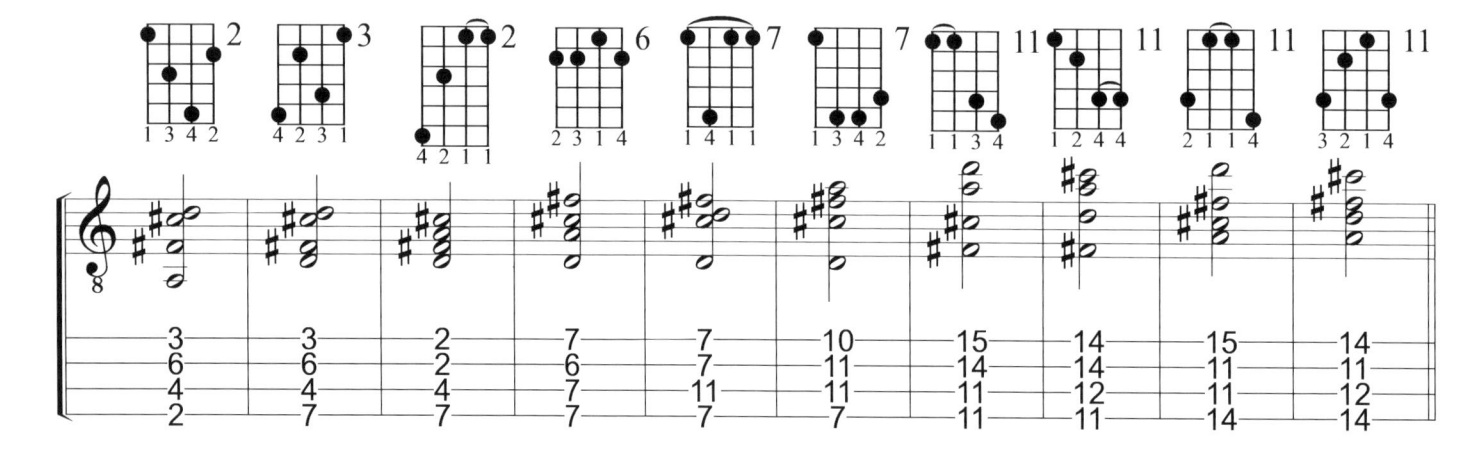

Dmaj9 - D6/9 - D+ augmented

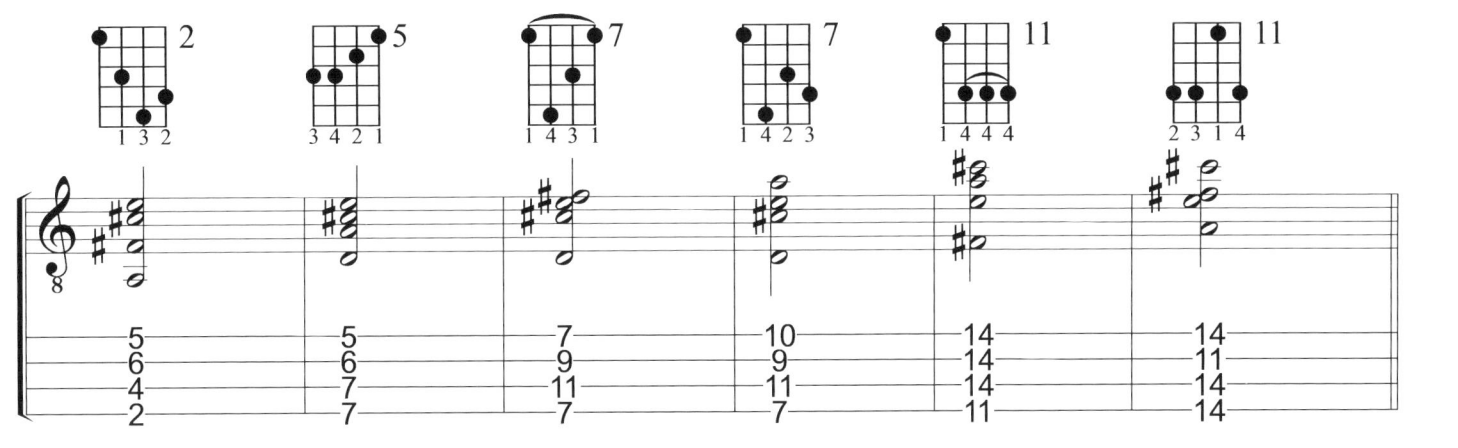

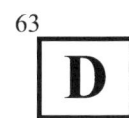

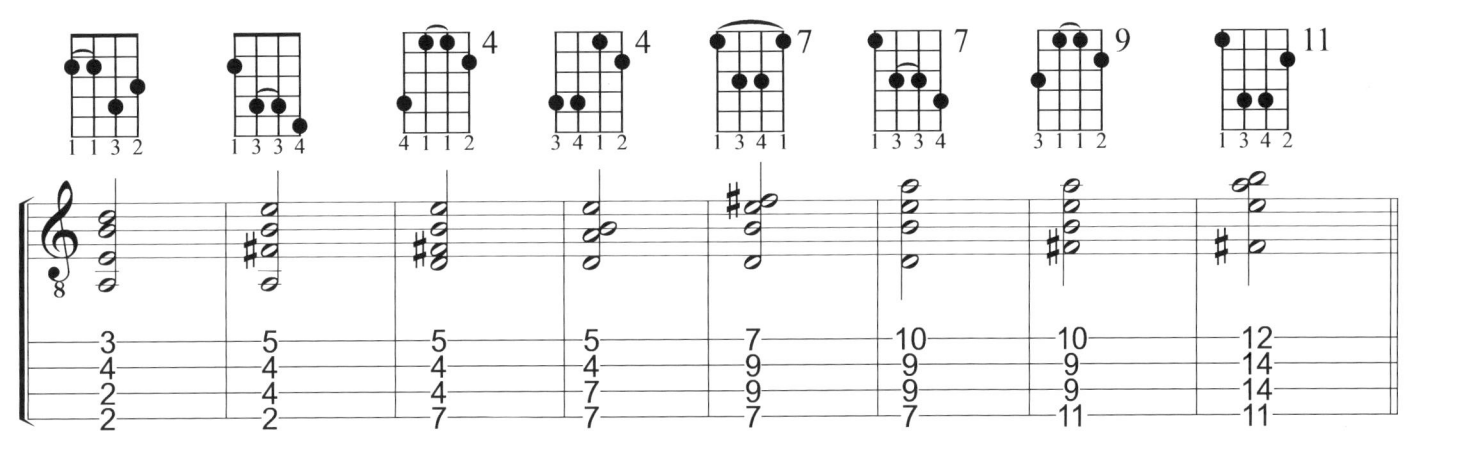

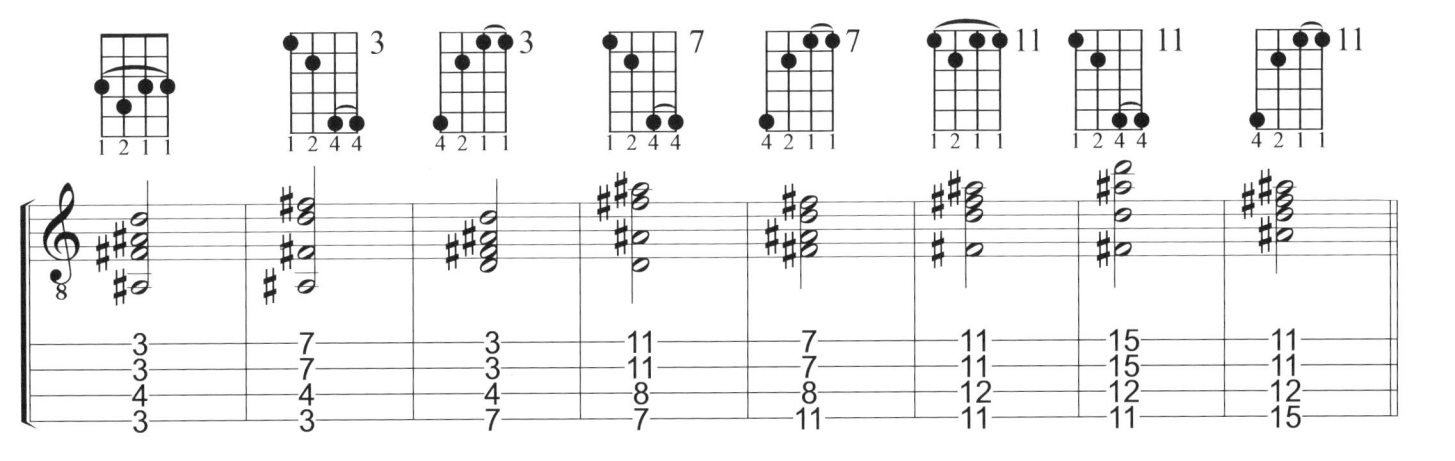

Dm - Dm6 - Dm7

D Minor

Dm6

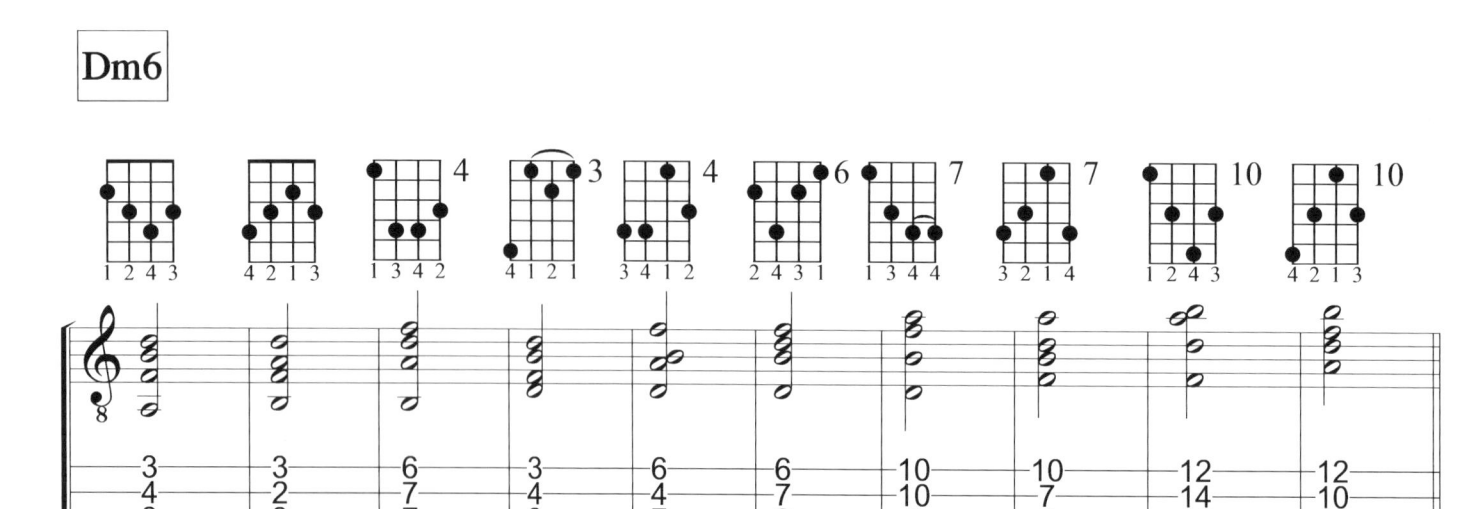

Dm7

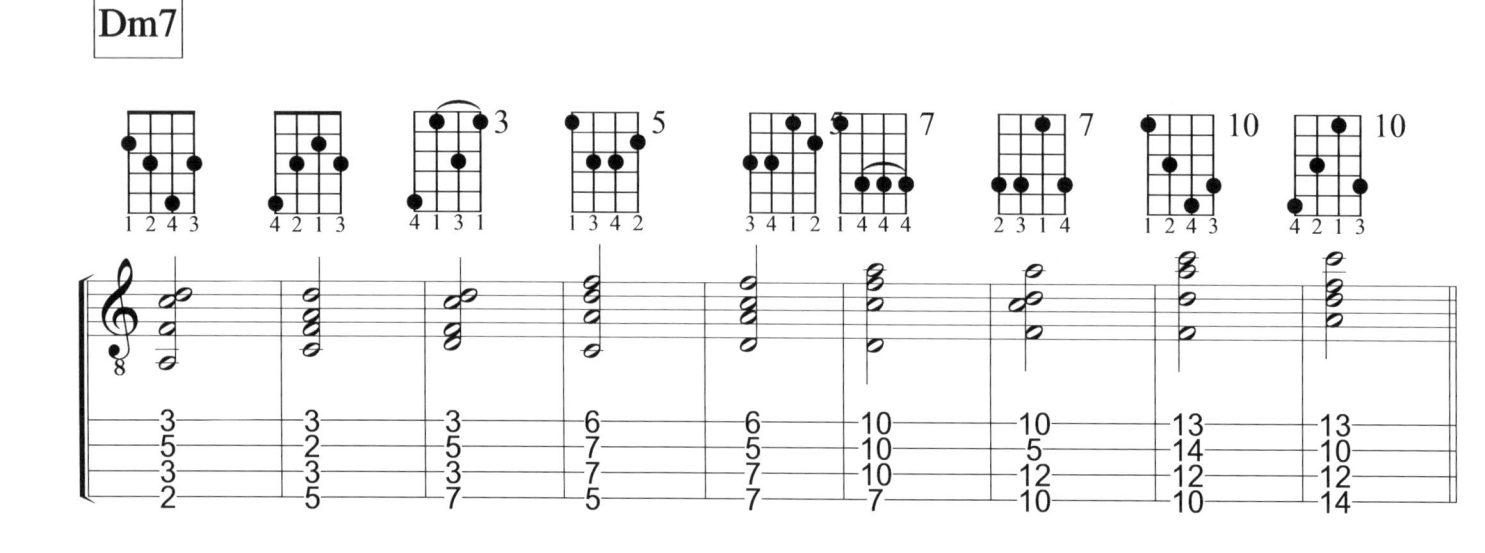

Dm7♭5 - Dm9 - Dm11 - Dm(maj7)

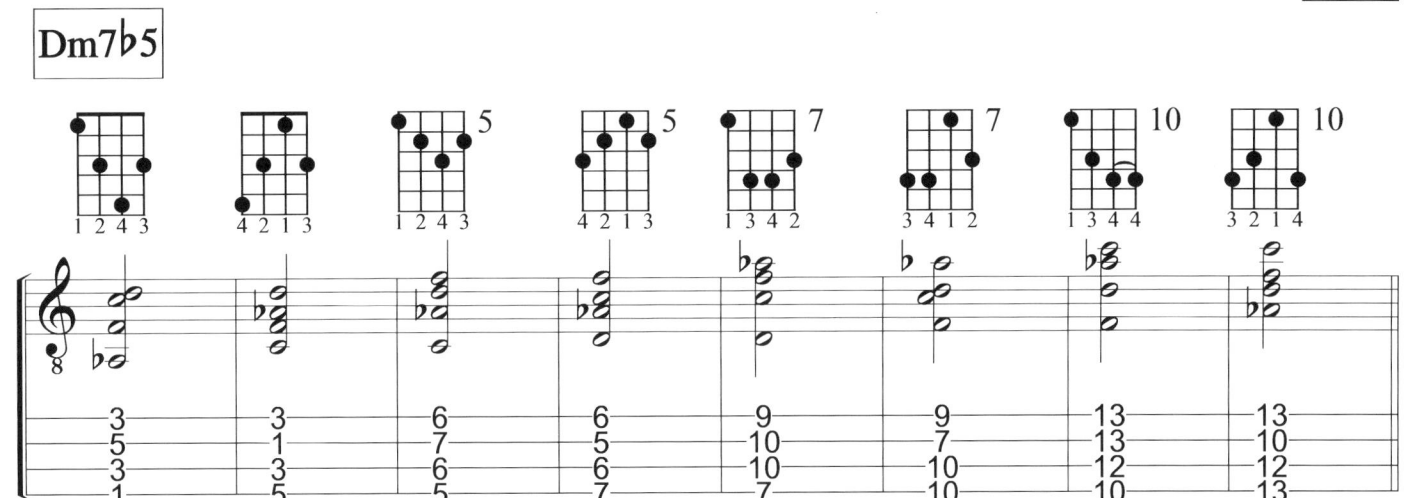

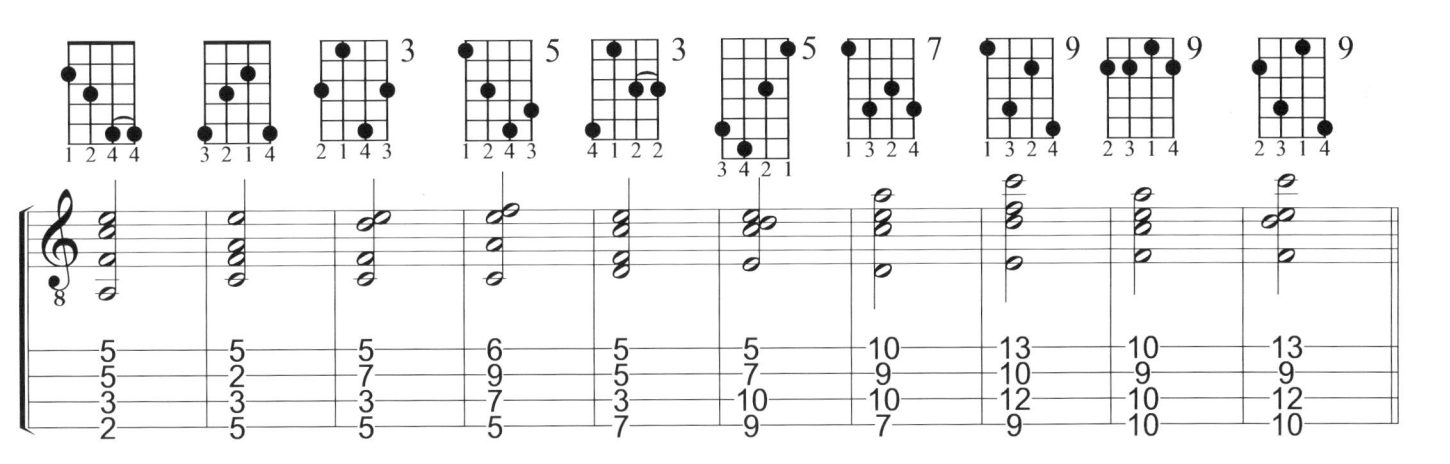

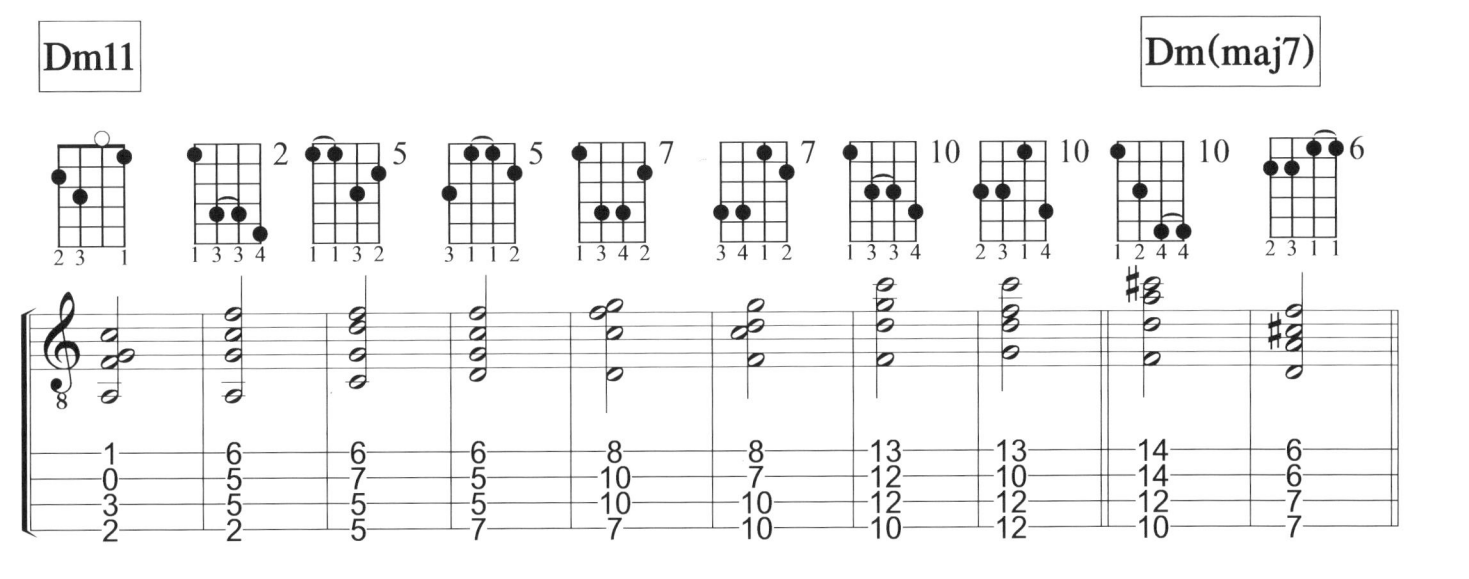

D7 - D9 - D13

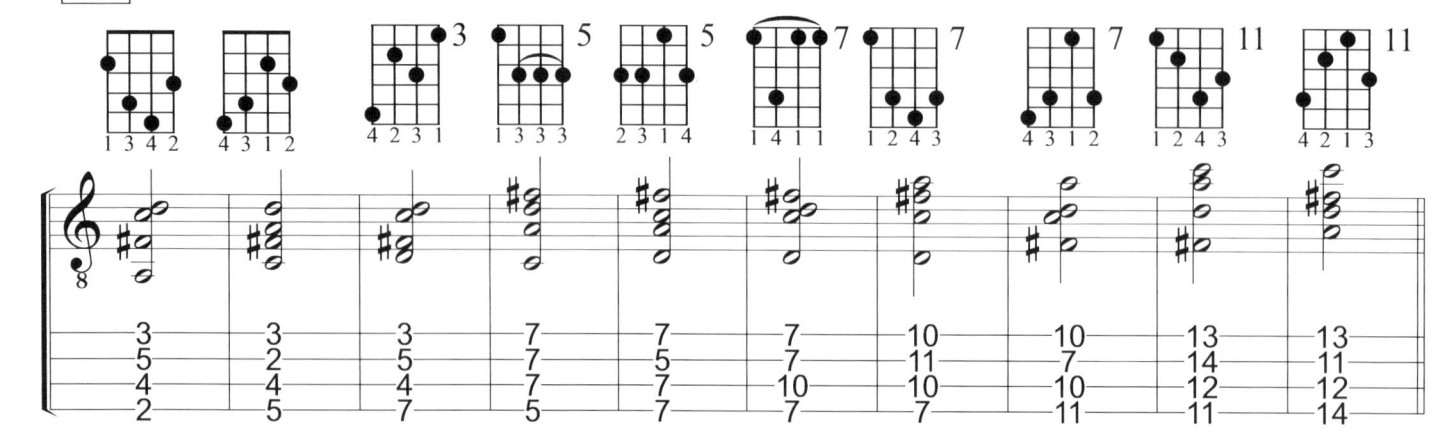

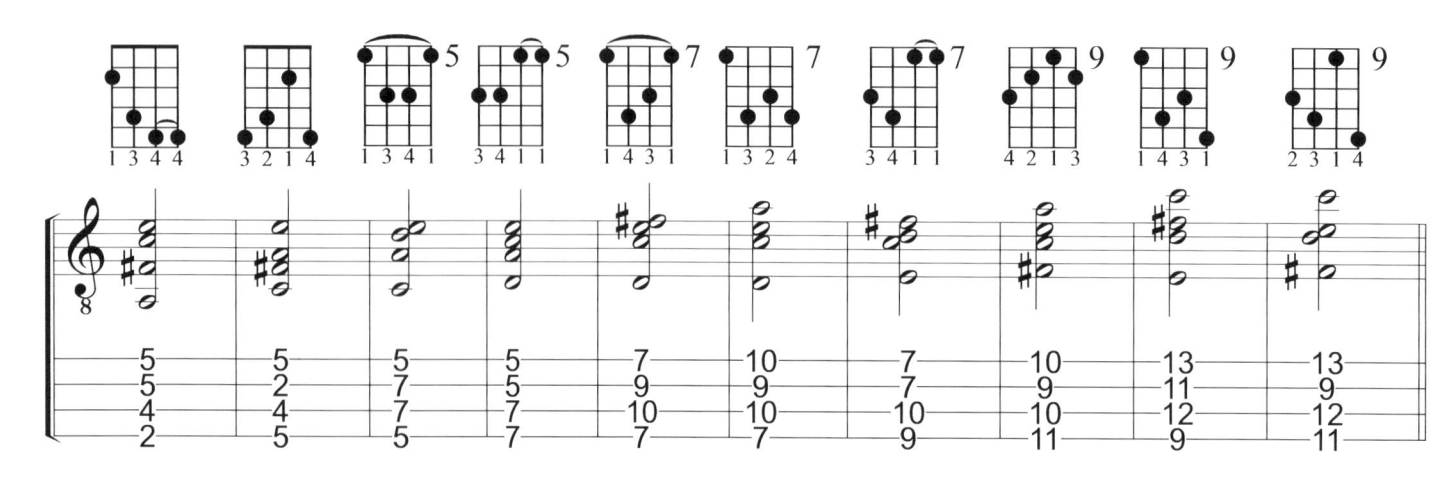

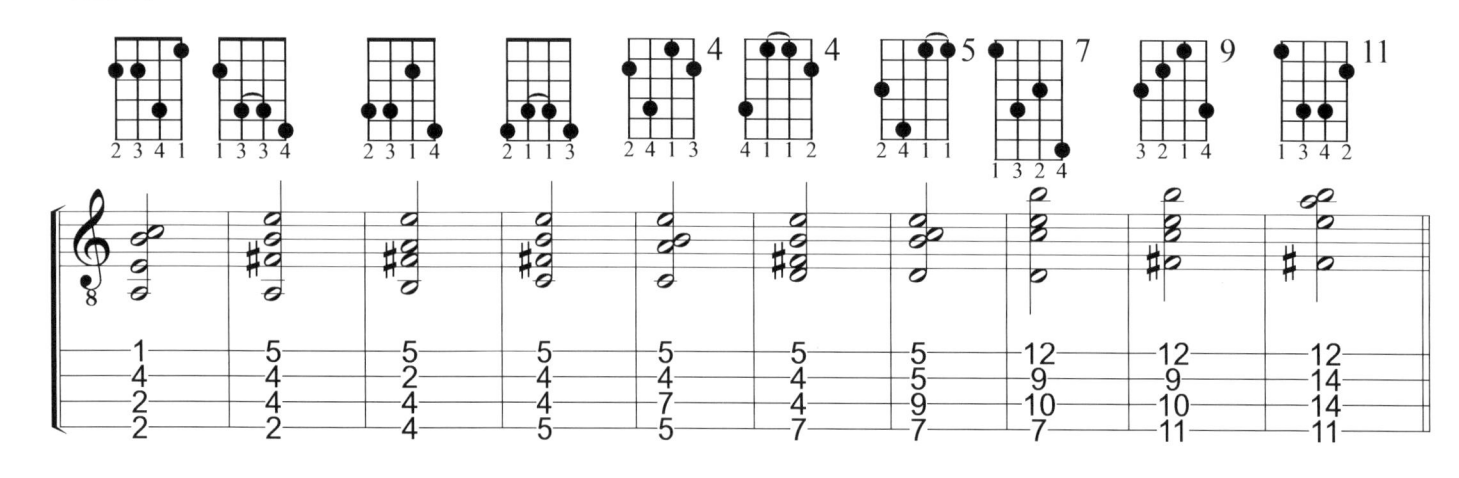

D7♭5 - D7♯5 - D7♯9

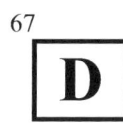

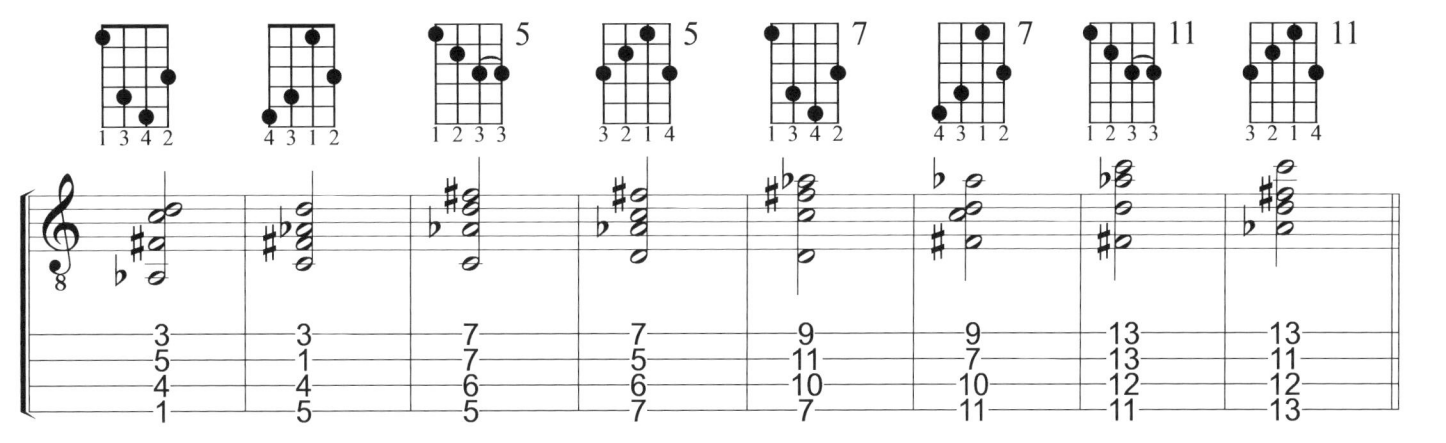

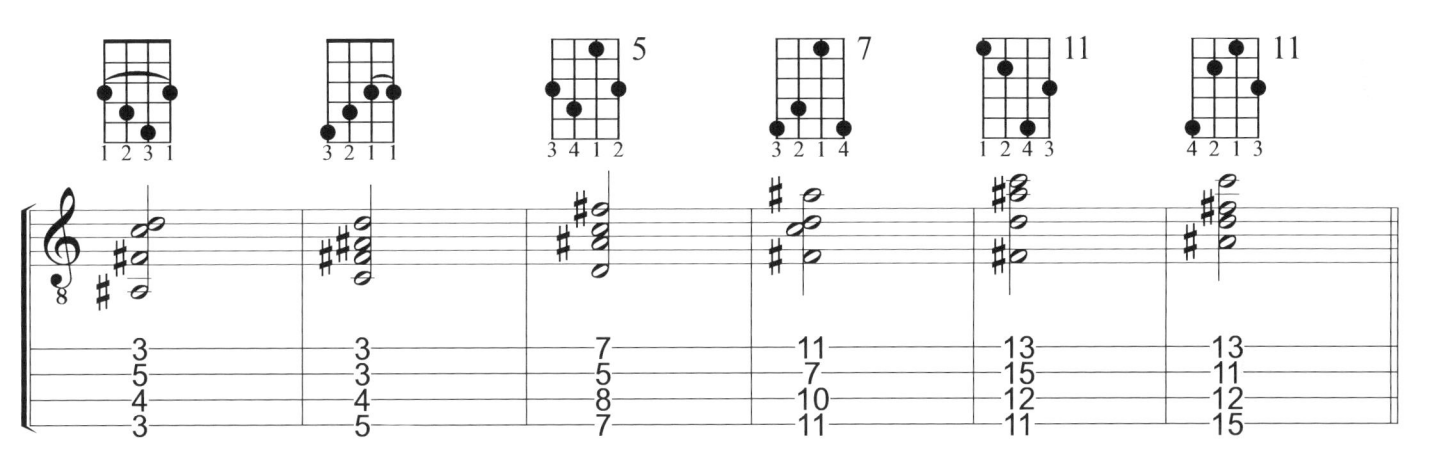

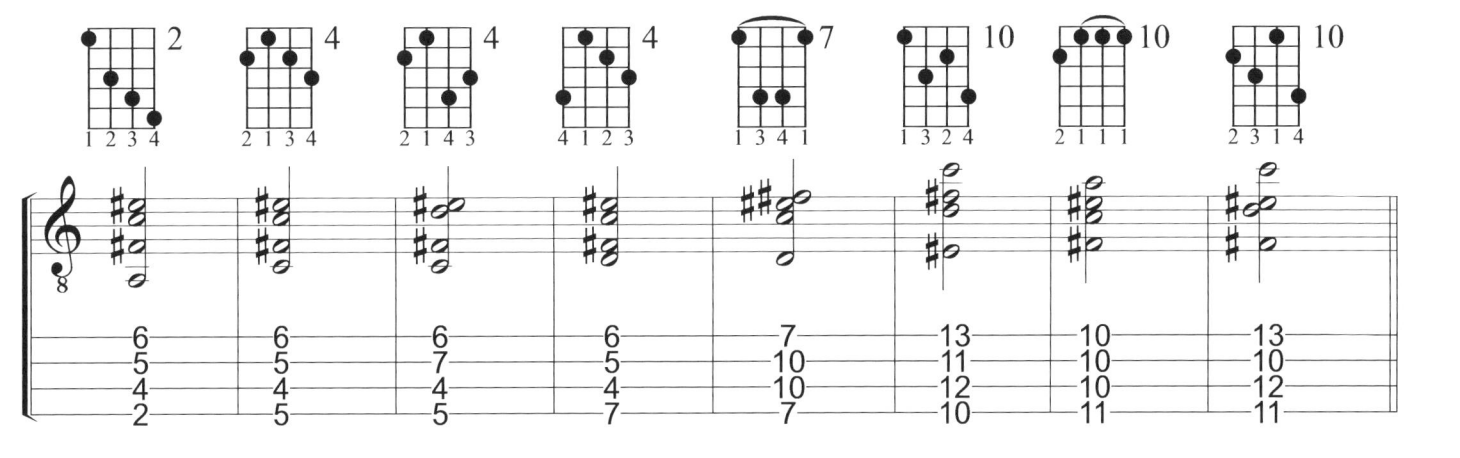

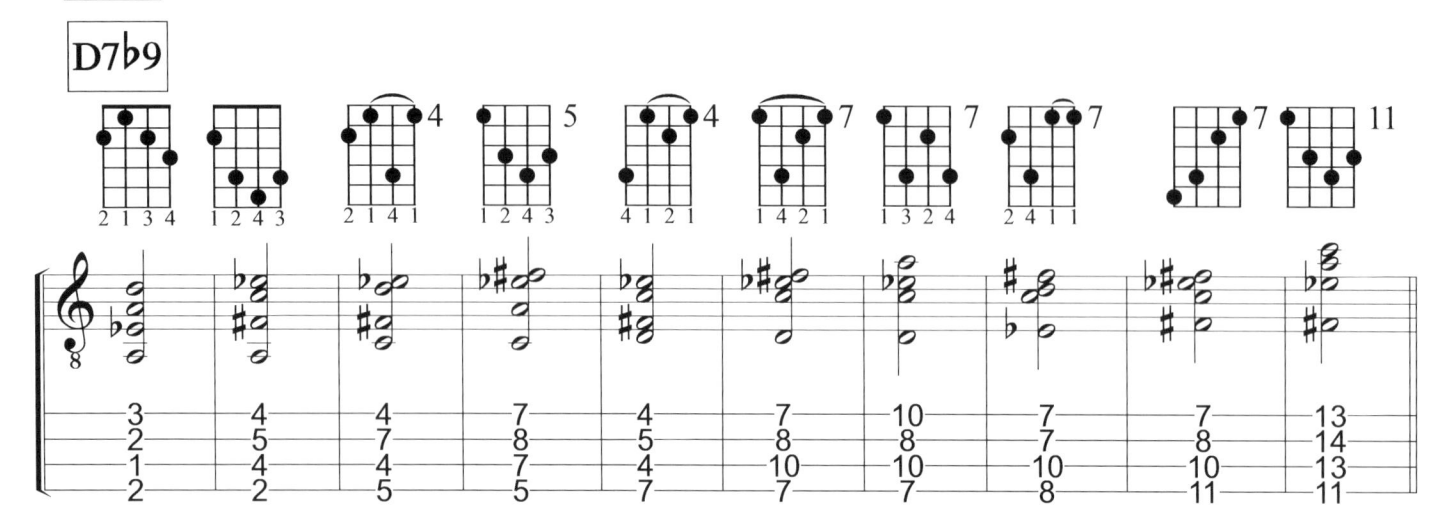

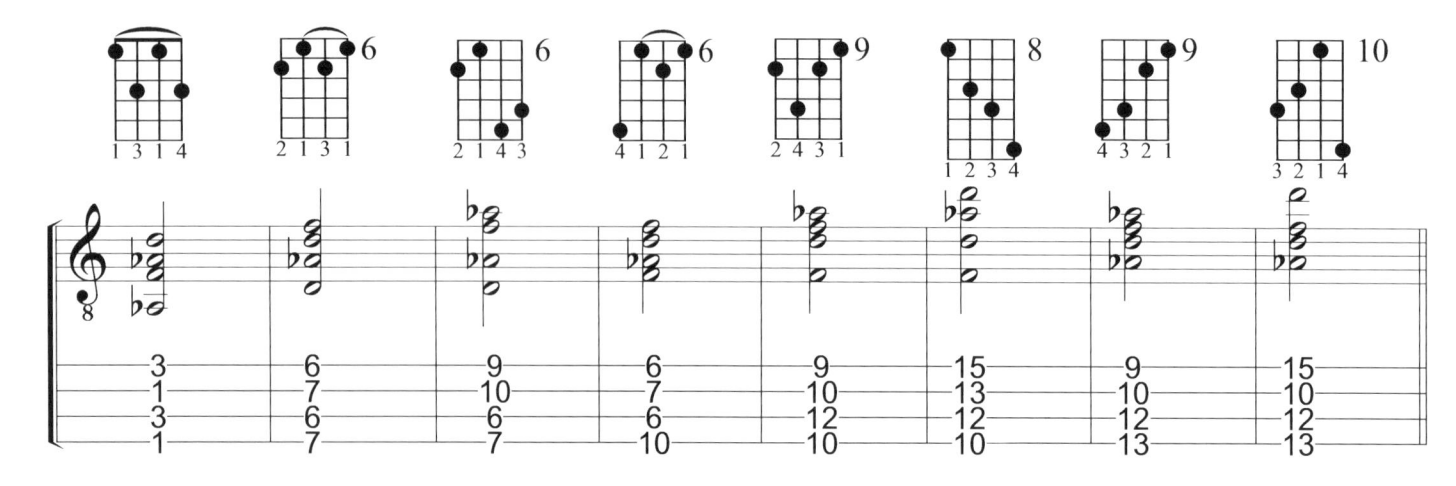

D7♭9 - D diminished - D°7

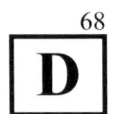

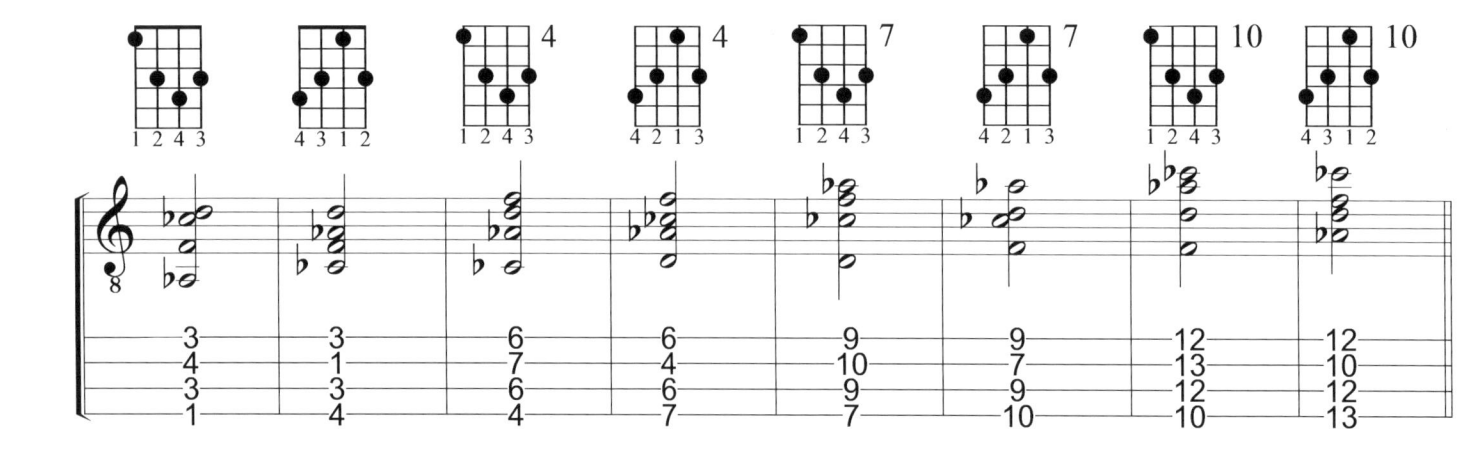

Dsus4 - Dsus2 - Dadd9 - D7sus - D5

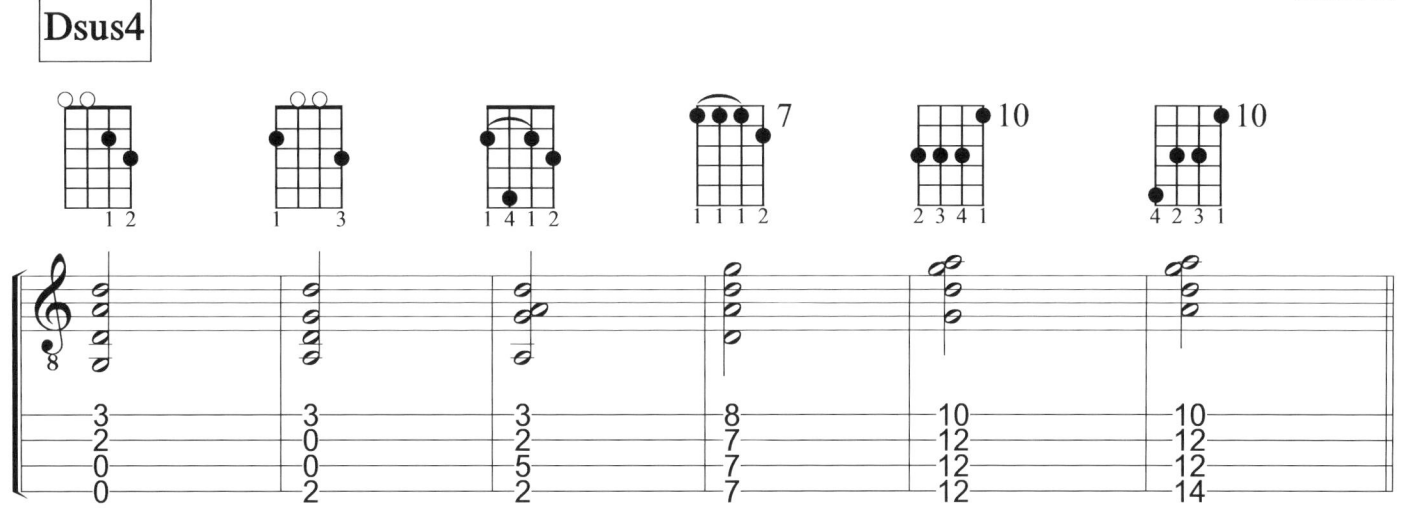

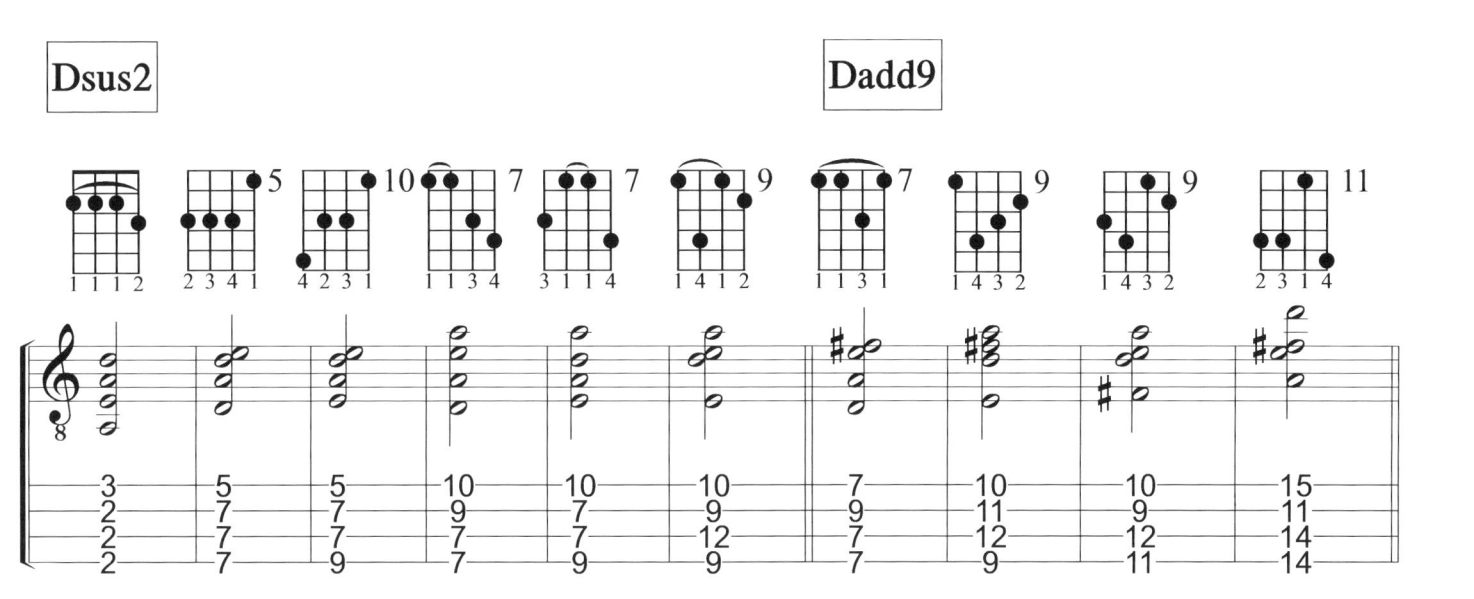

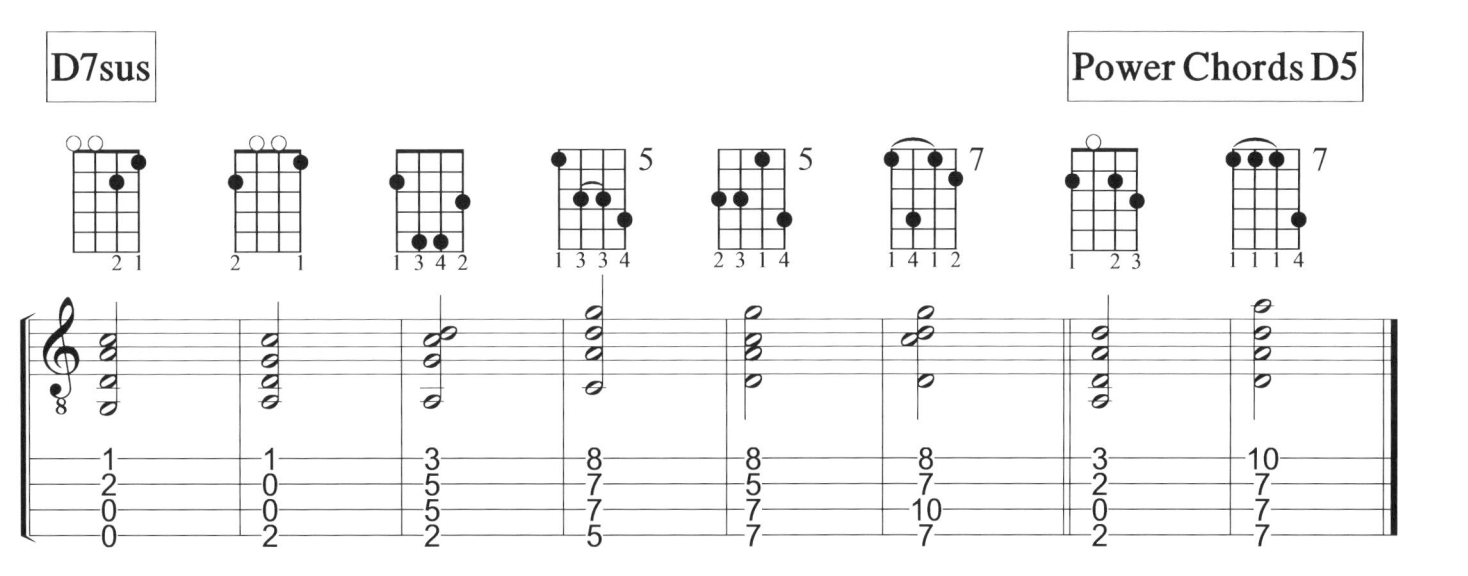

Dsus4

Dsus2 **Dadd9**

D7sus **Power Chords D5**

Eb - Eb6 - Ebmaj7

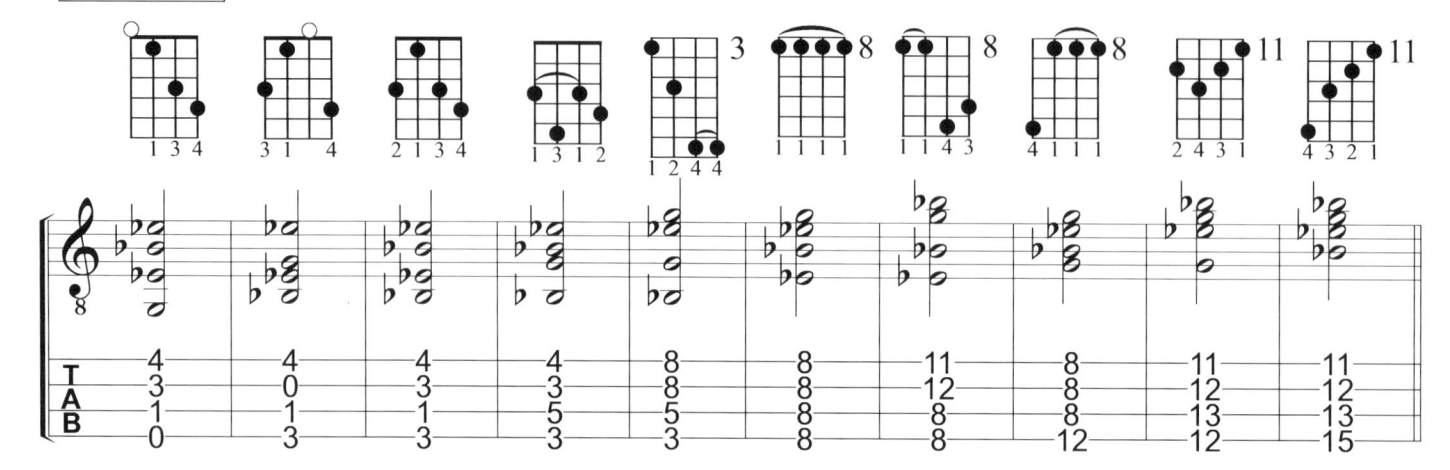

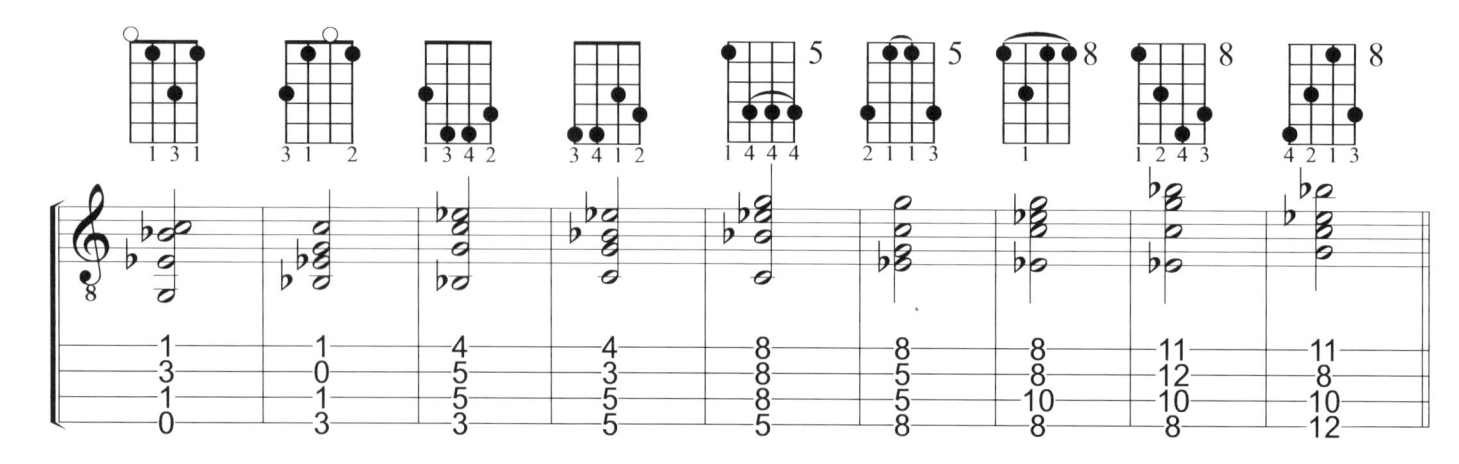

Eb Major

Eb6

Ebmaj7

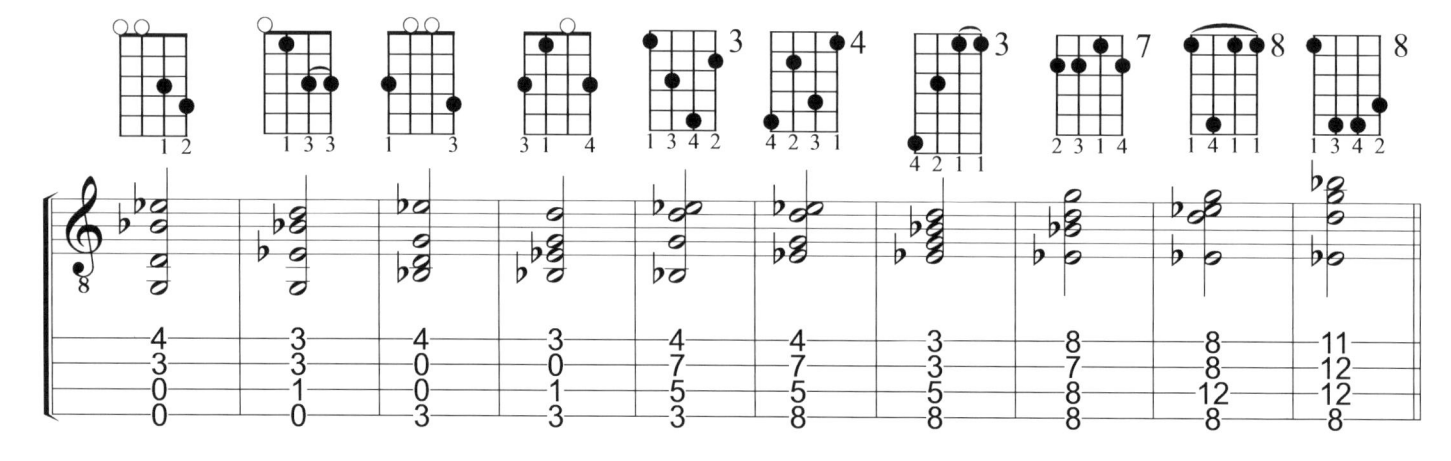

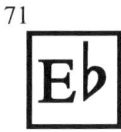

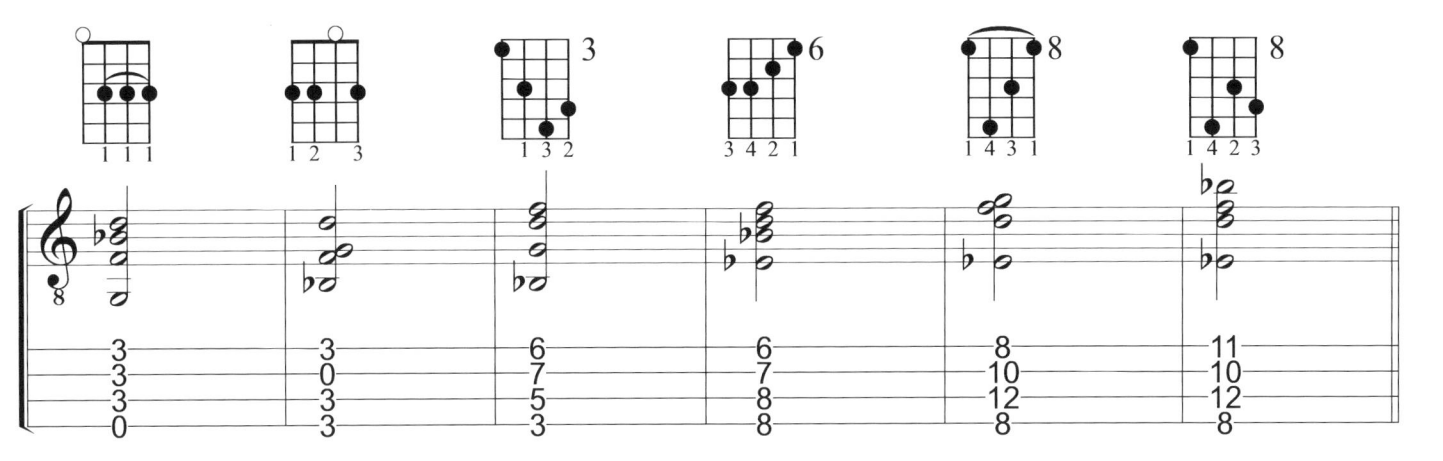

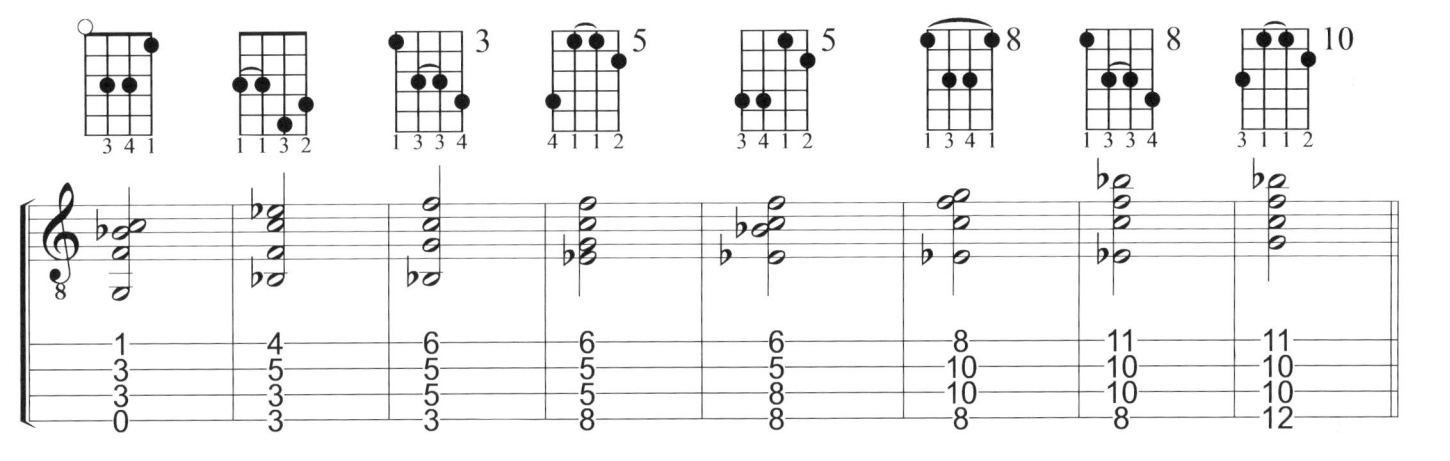

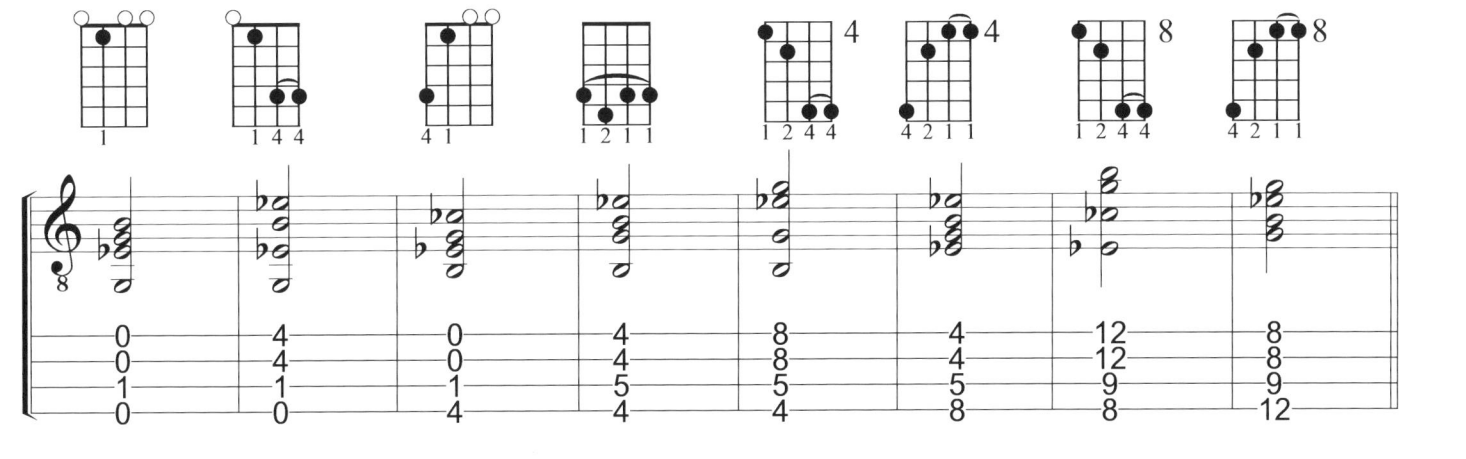

E♭maj9 - E♭6/9 - E♭+ augmented

E♭m - E♭m6 - E♭m7

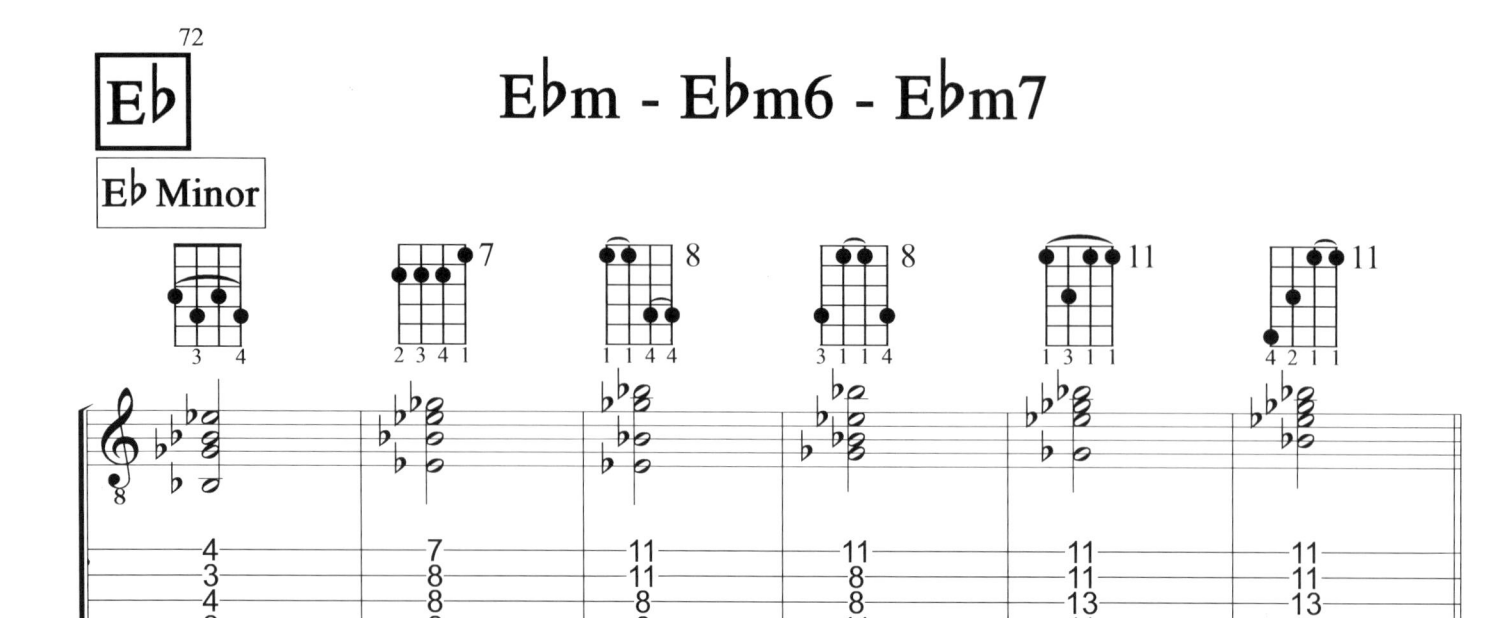

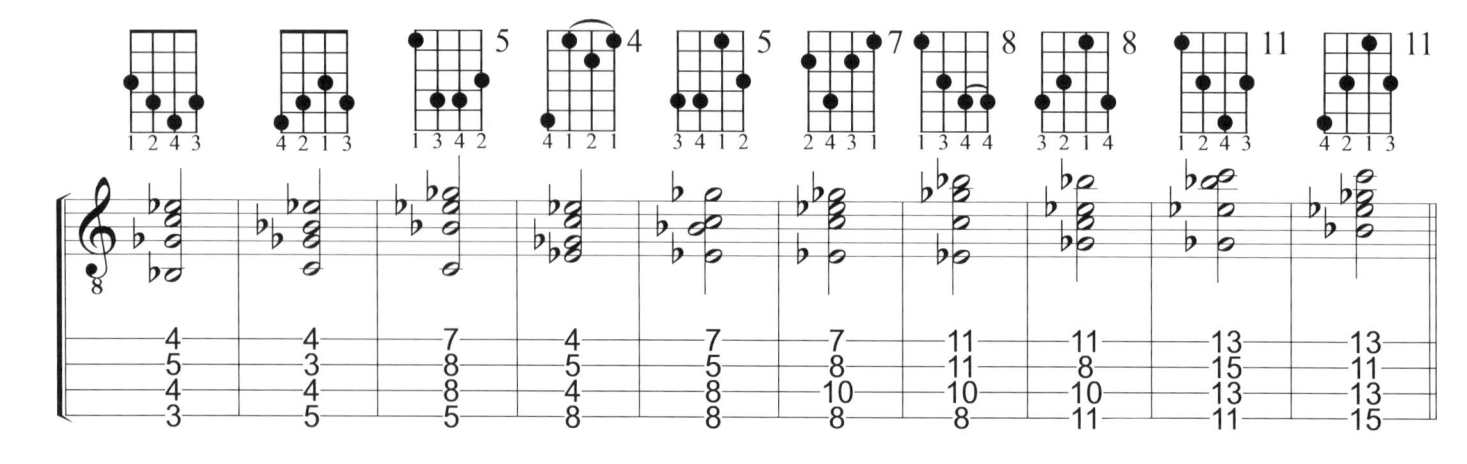

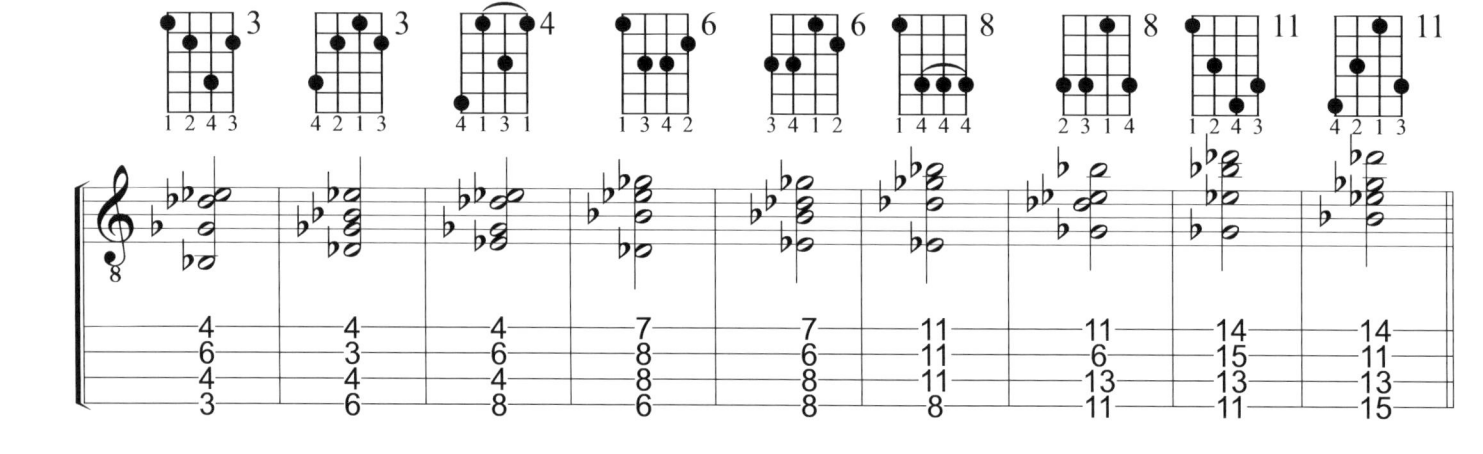

Ebm7b5 - Ebm9 - Ebm11 - Ebm(maj7)

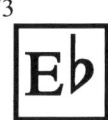

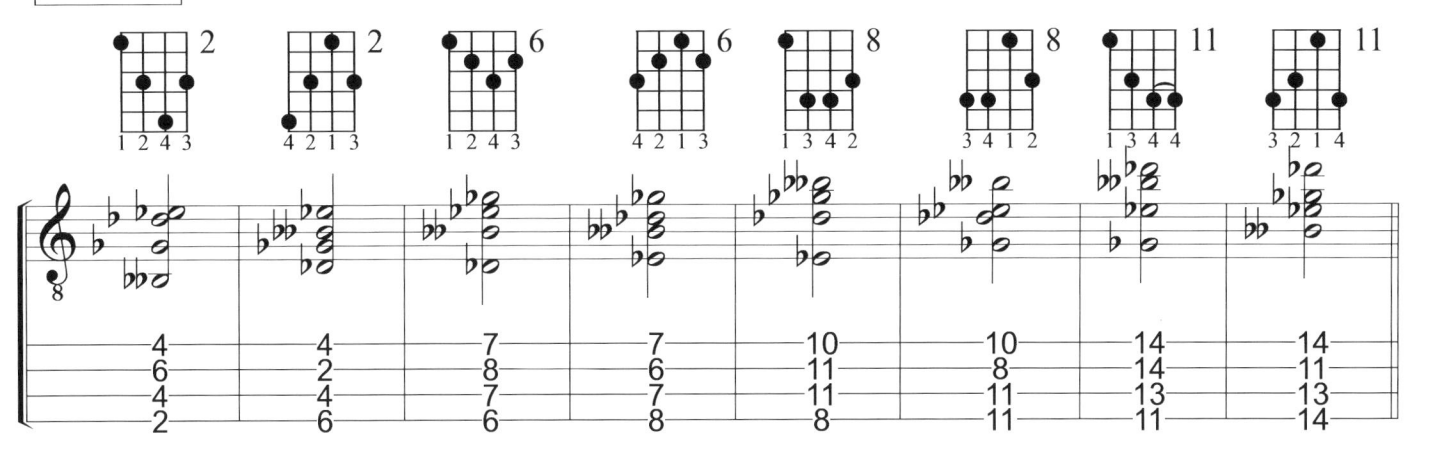

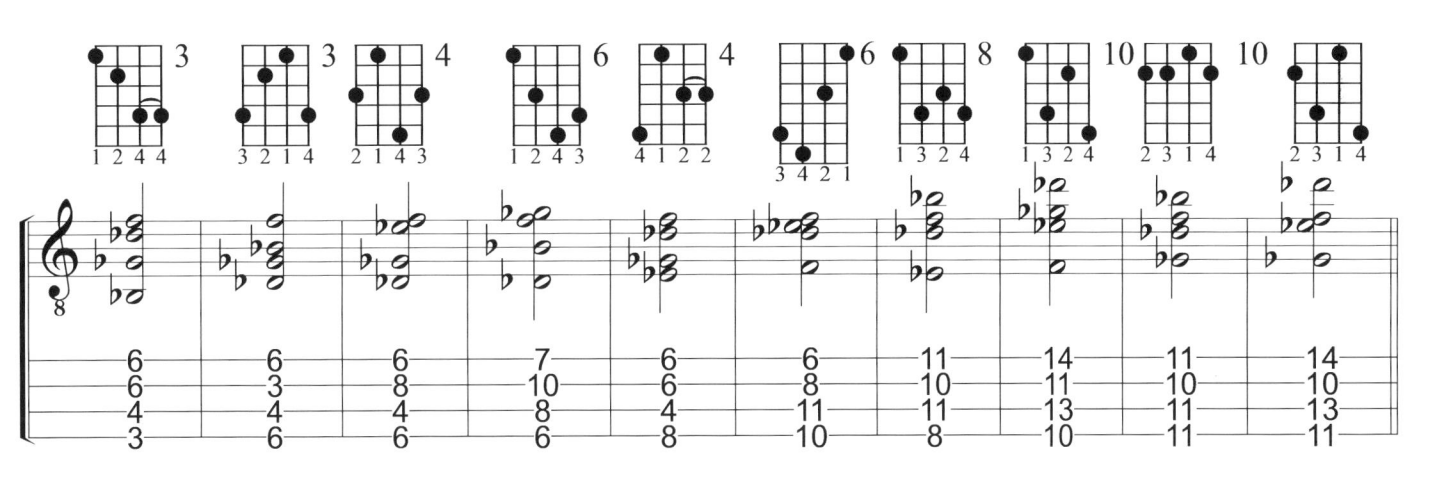

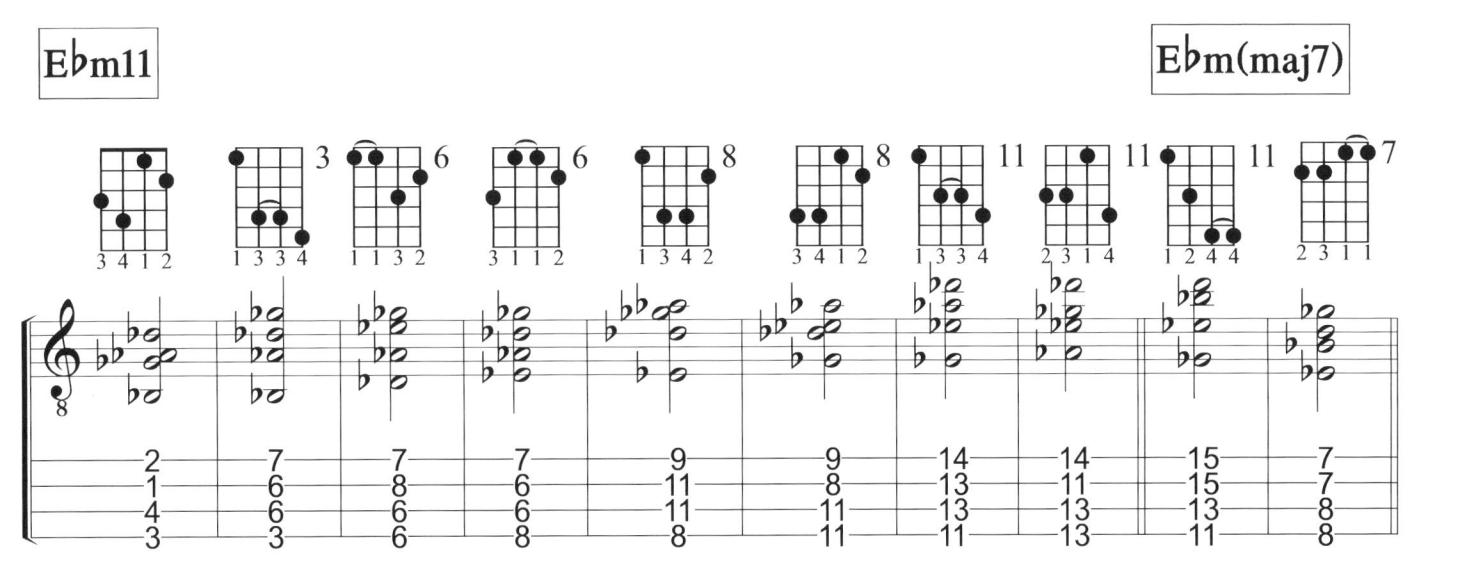

Eb7 - Eb9 - Eb13

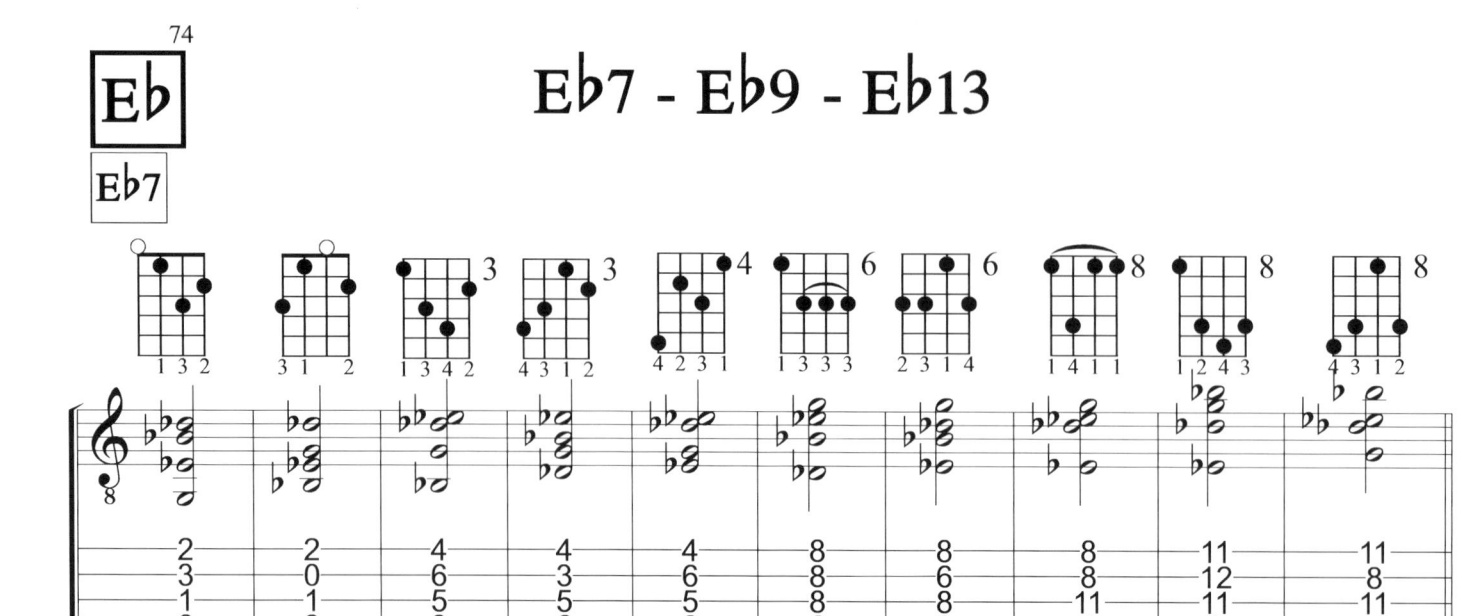

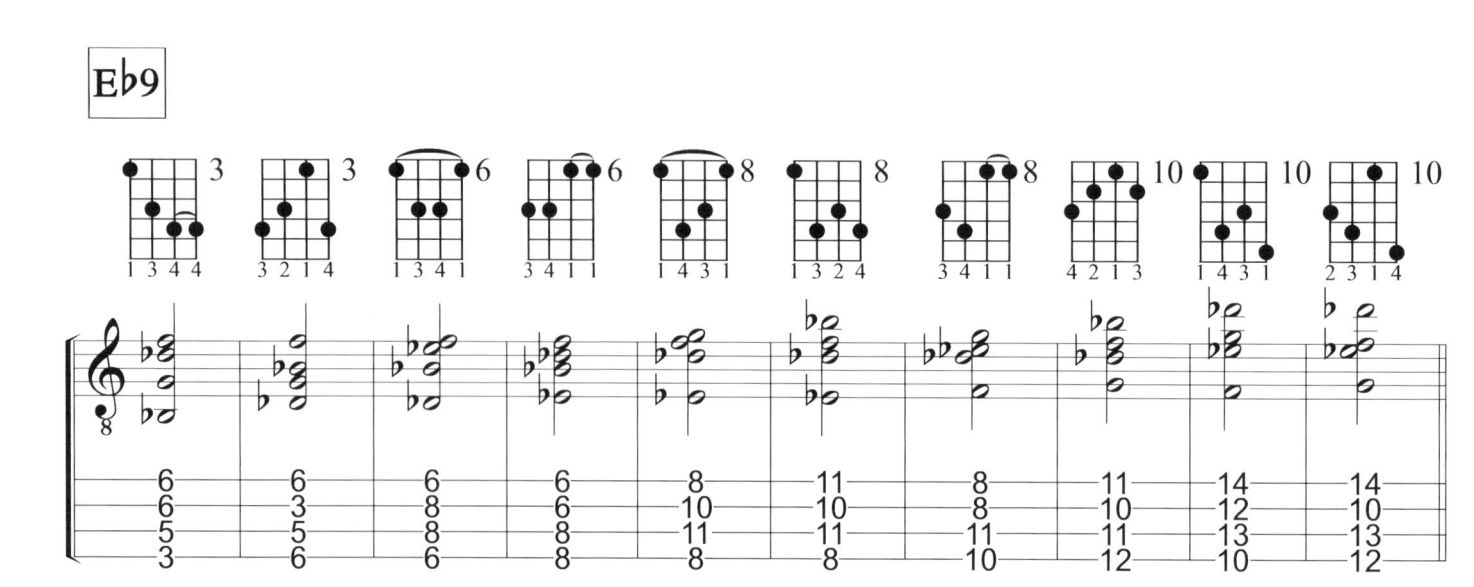

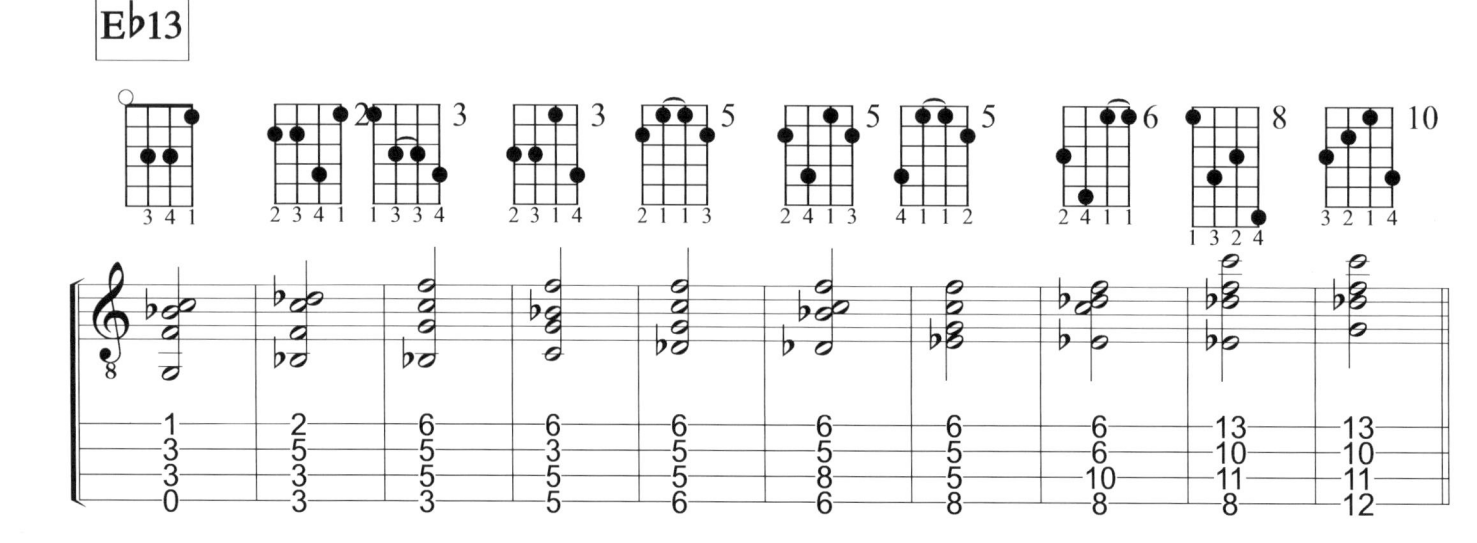

Eb7b5 - Eb7#5 - Eb7#9

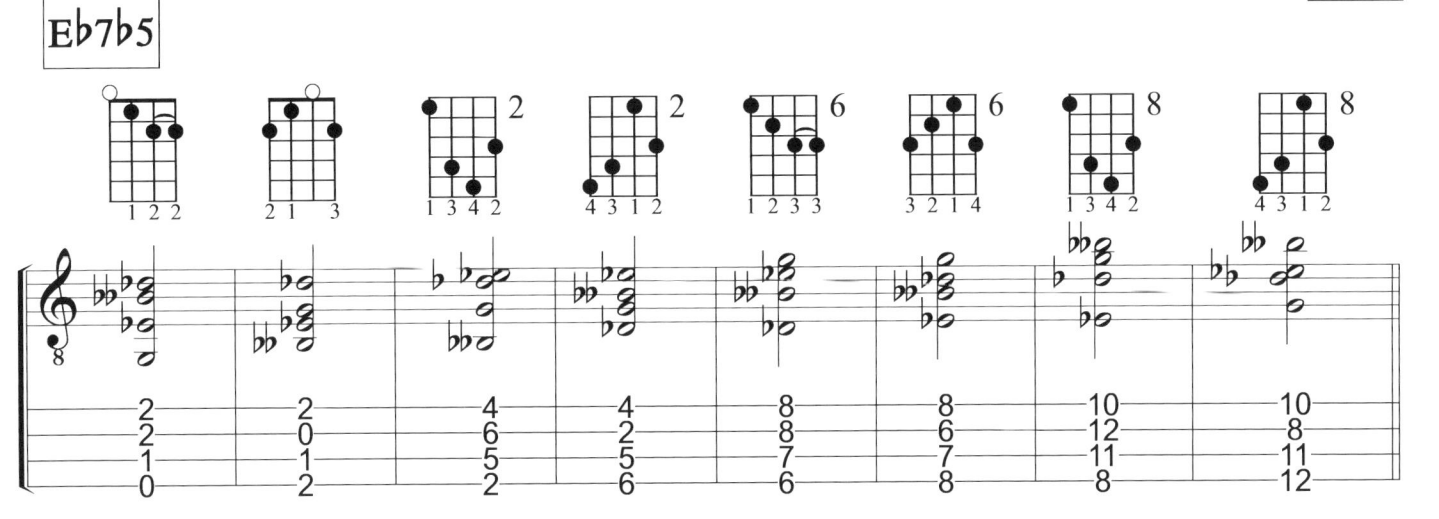

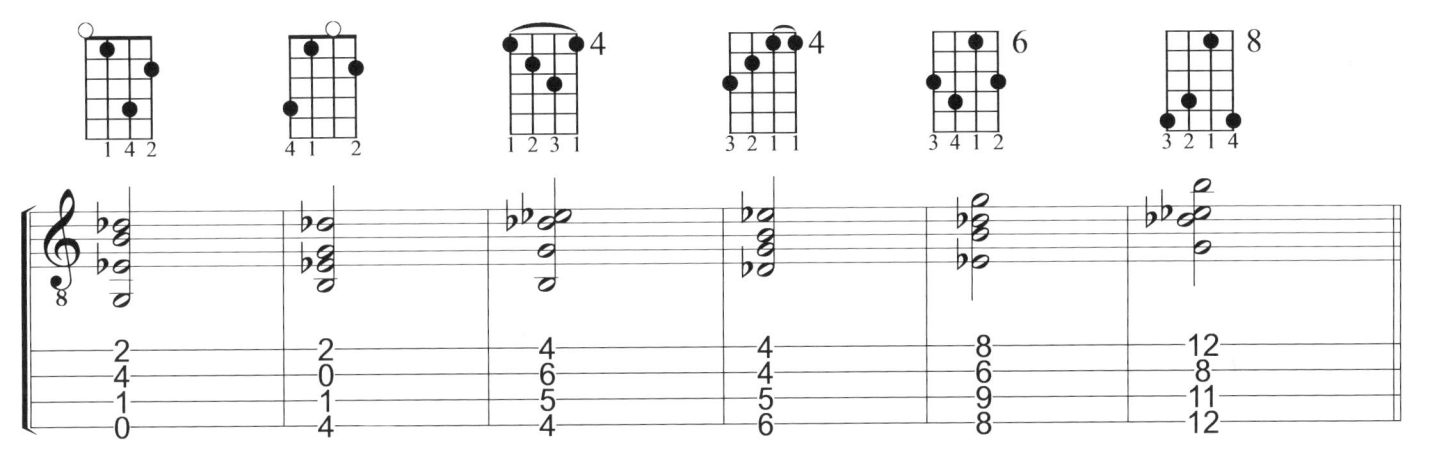

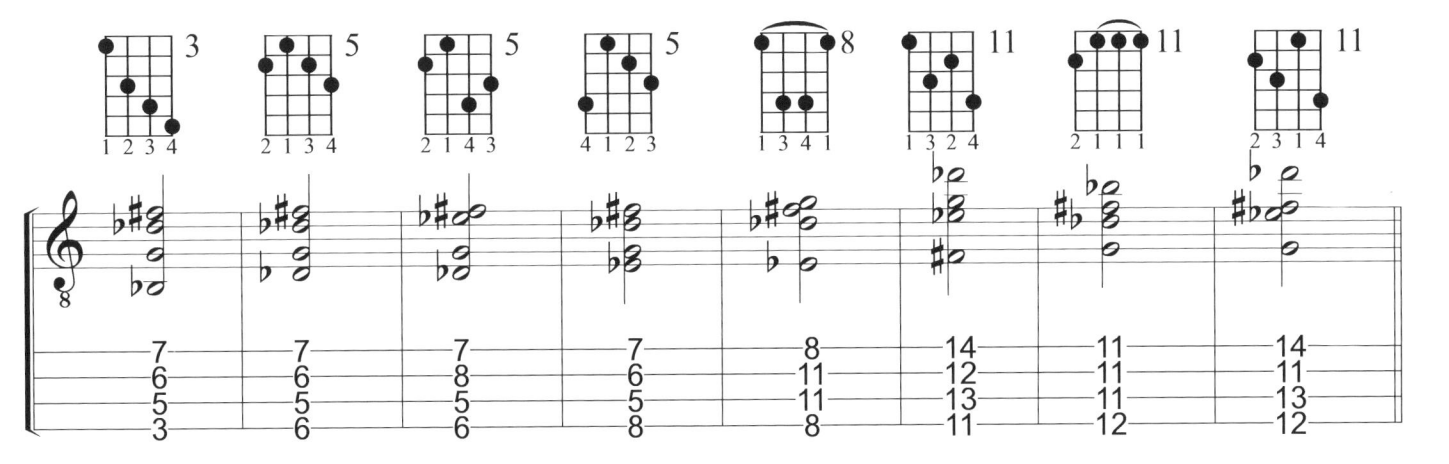

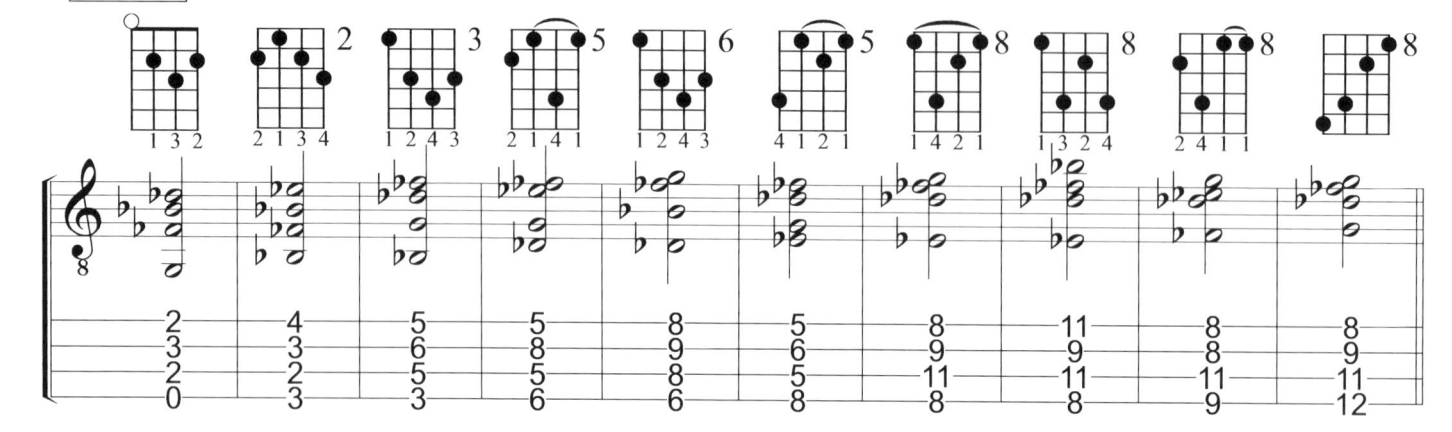

Eb7b9 - Eb diminished - Eb°7

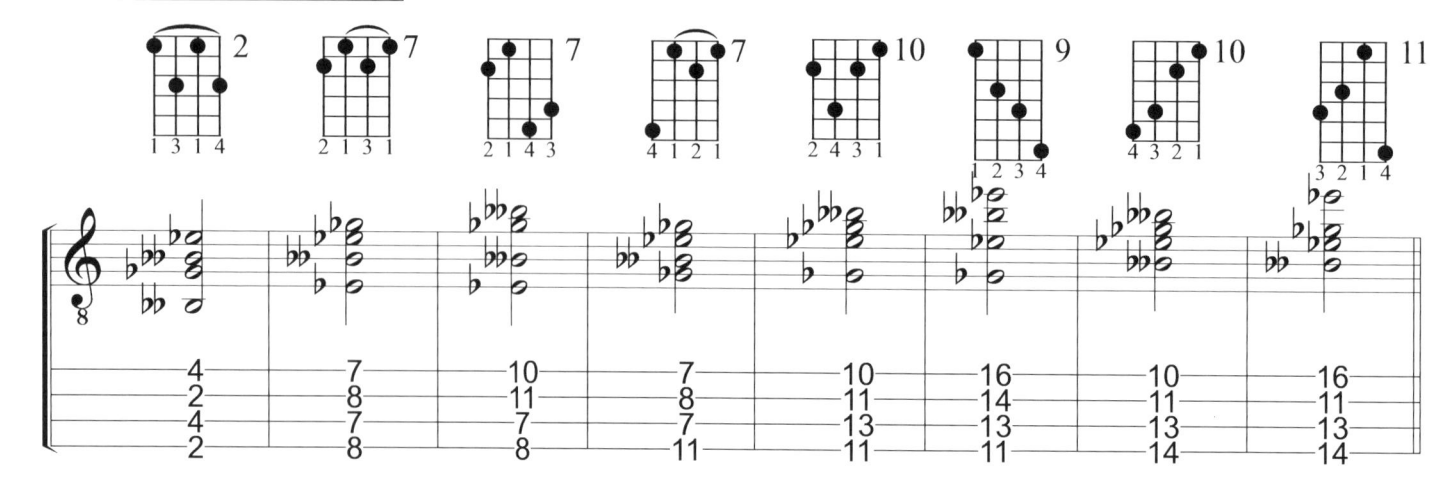

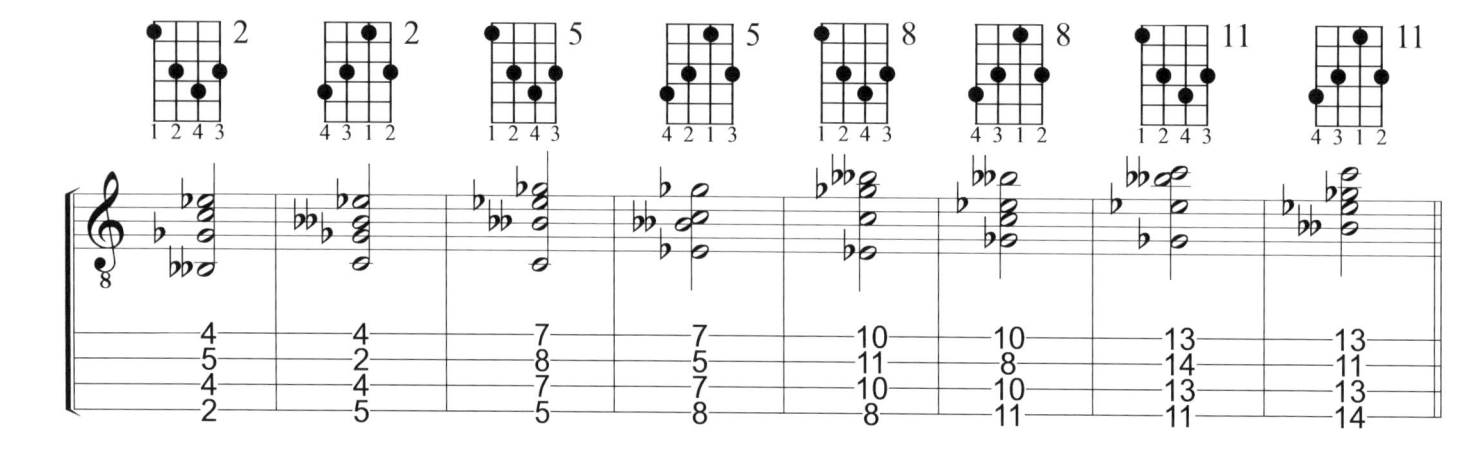

Ebsus4 - Ebsus2 - Ebadd9 - Eb7sus - Eb5   Eb

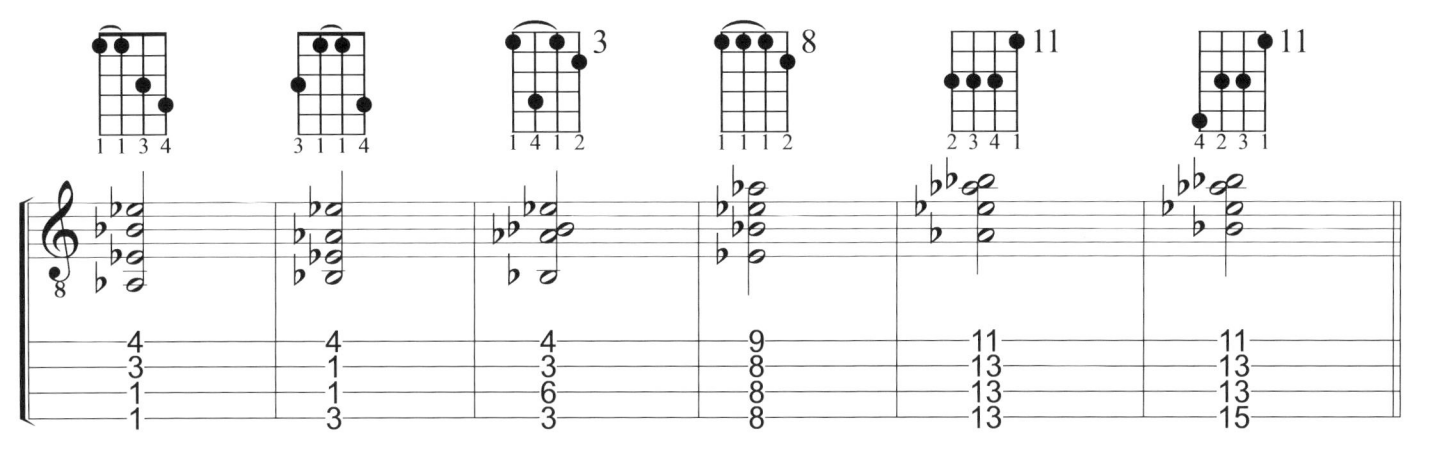

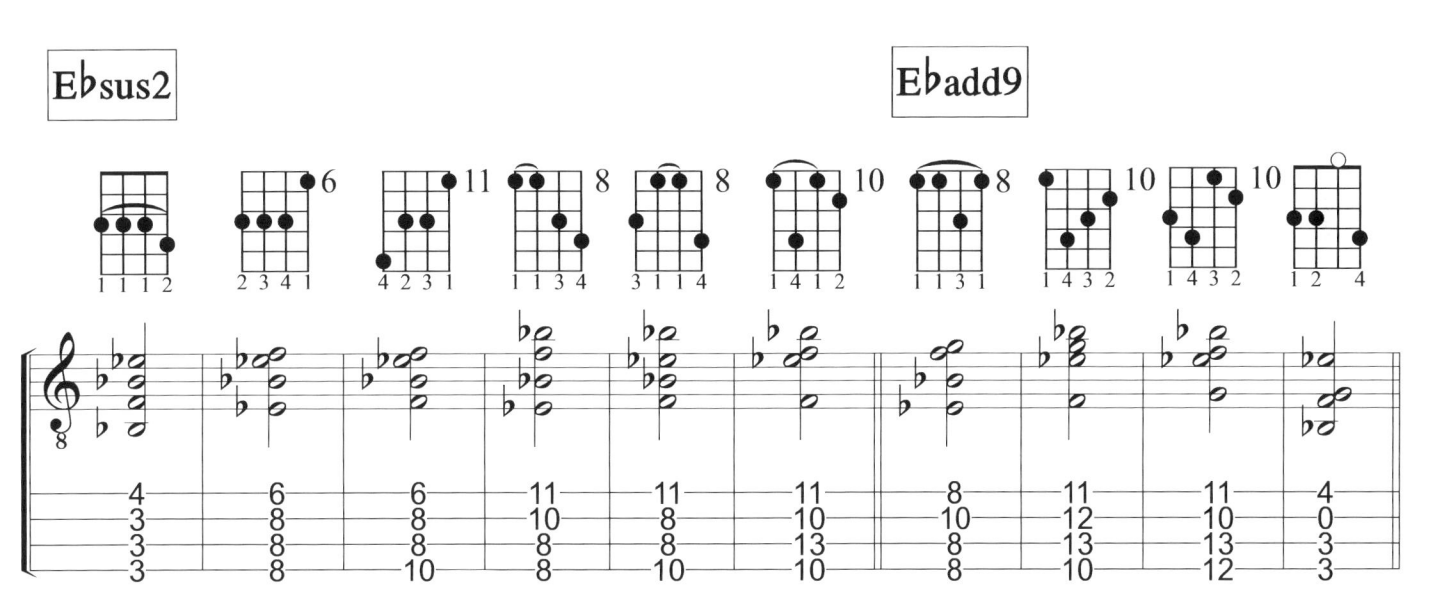

Ebsus4

Ebsus2   Ebadd9

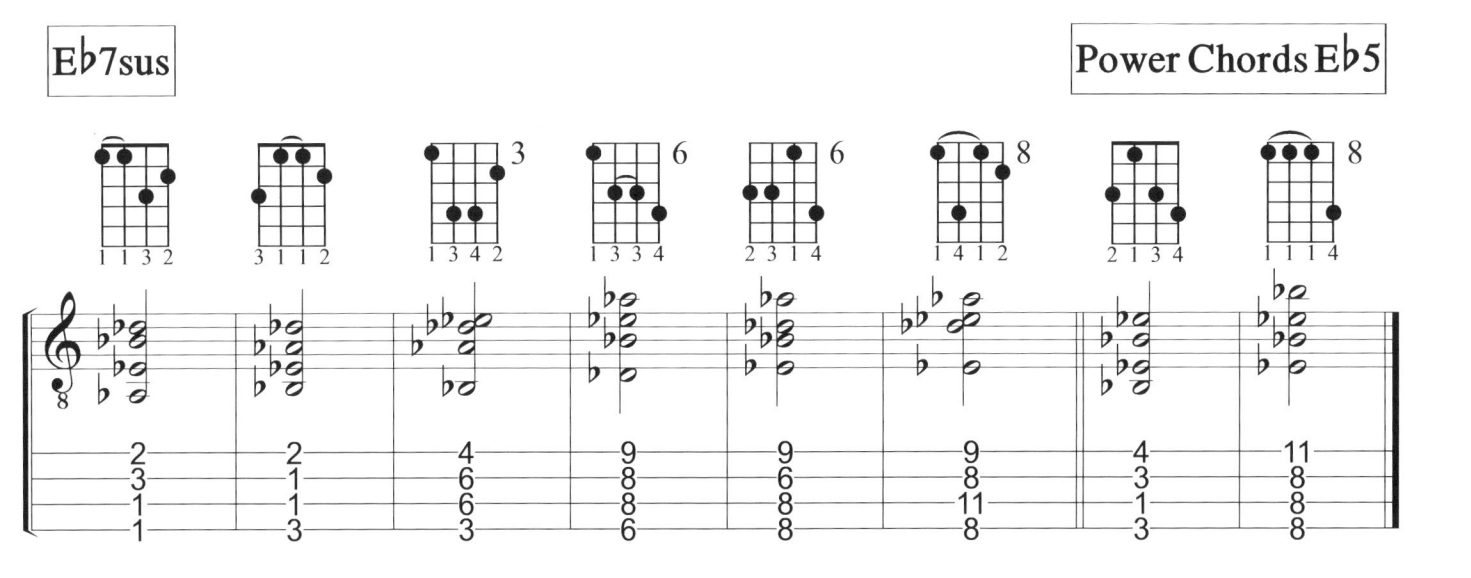

Eb7sus   Power Chords Eb5

E Major - E6 - Emaj7

E Major

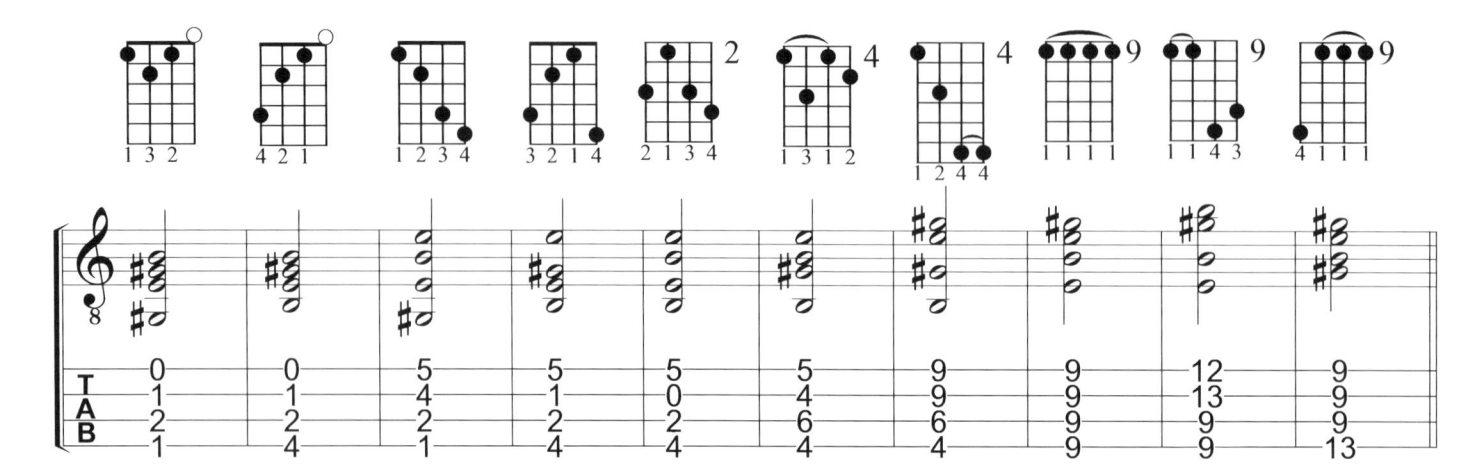

E6

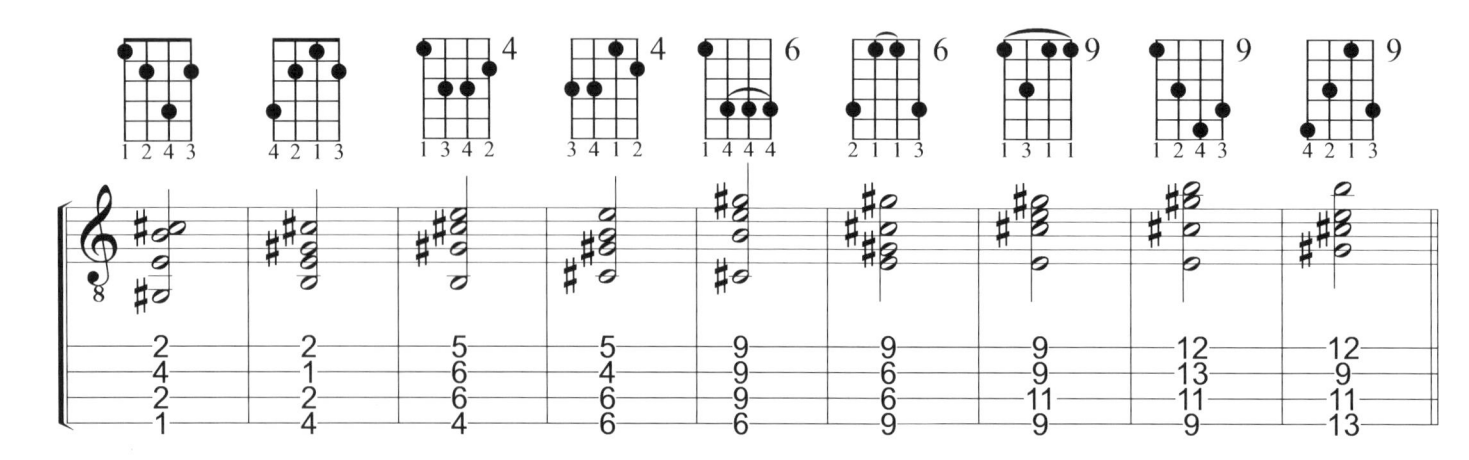

Emaj7

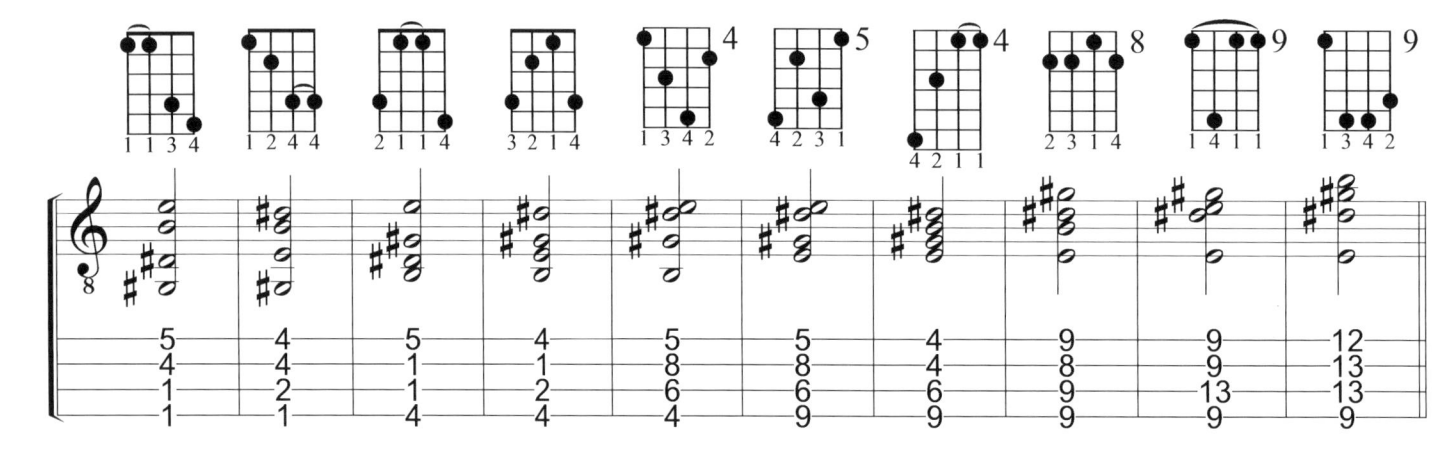

Emaj9 - E6/9 - E+ augmented

Emaj9

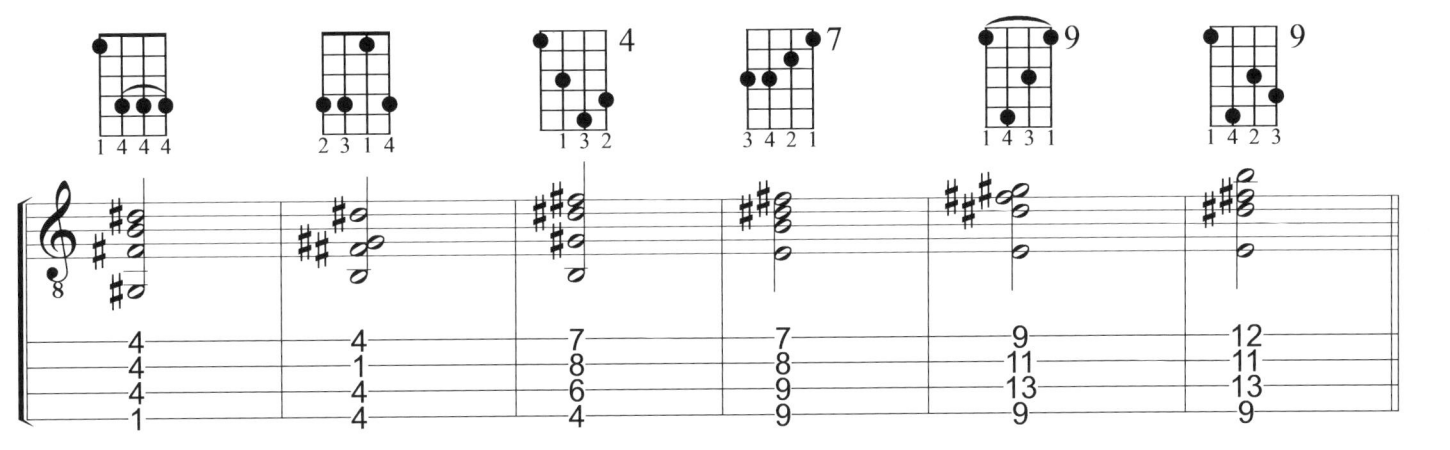

E6/9

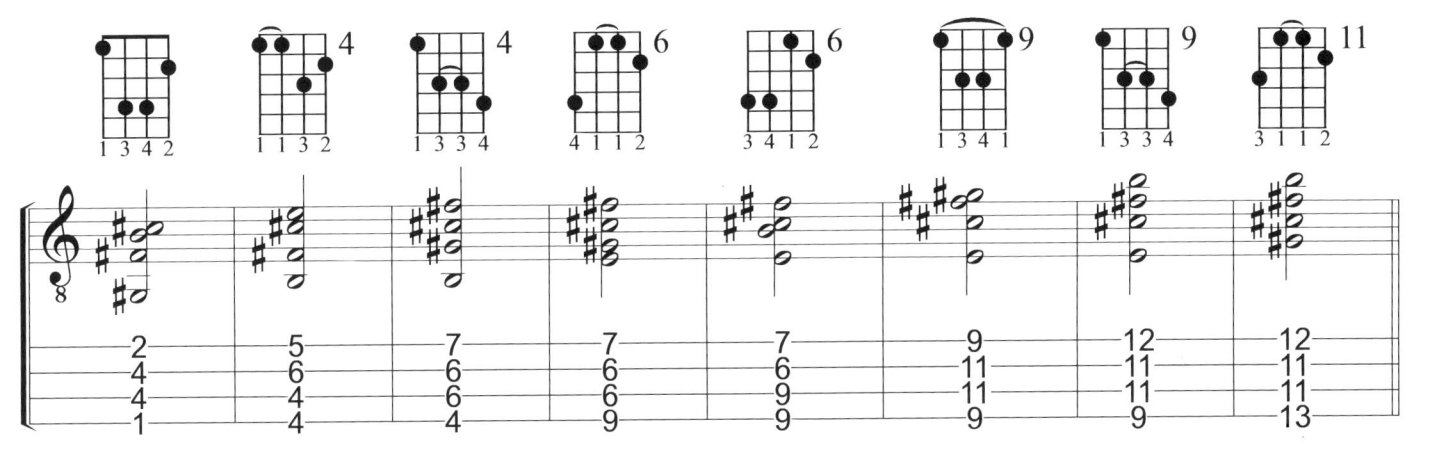

E Augmented - E+

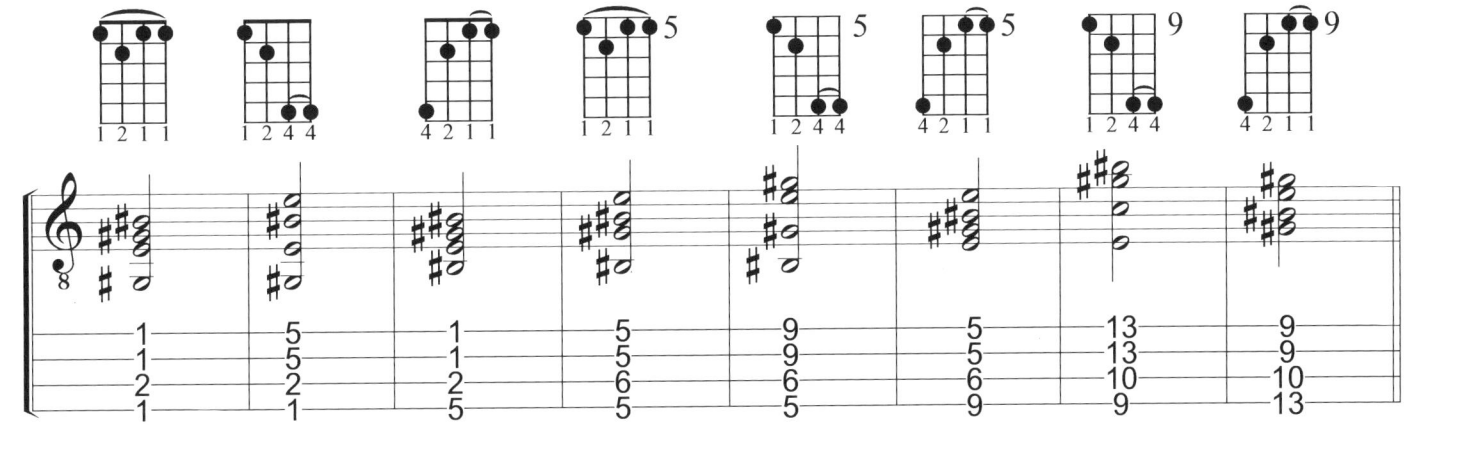

Em - Em6 - Em7

E Minor

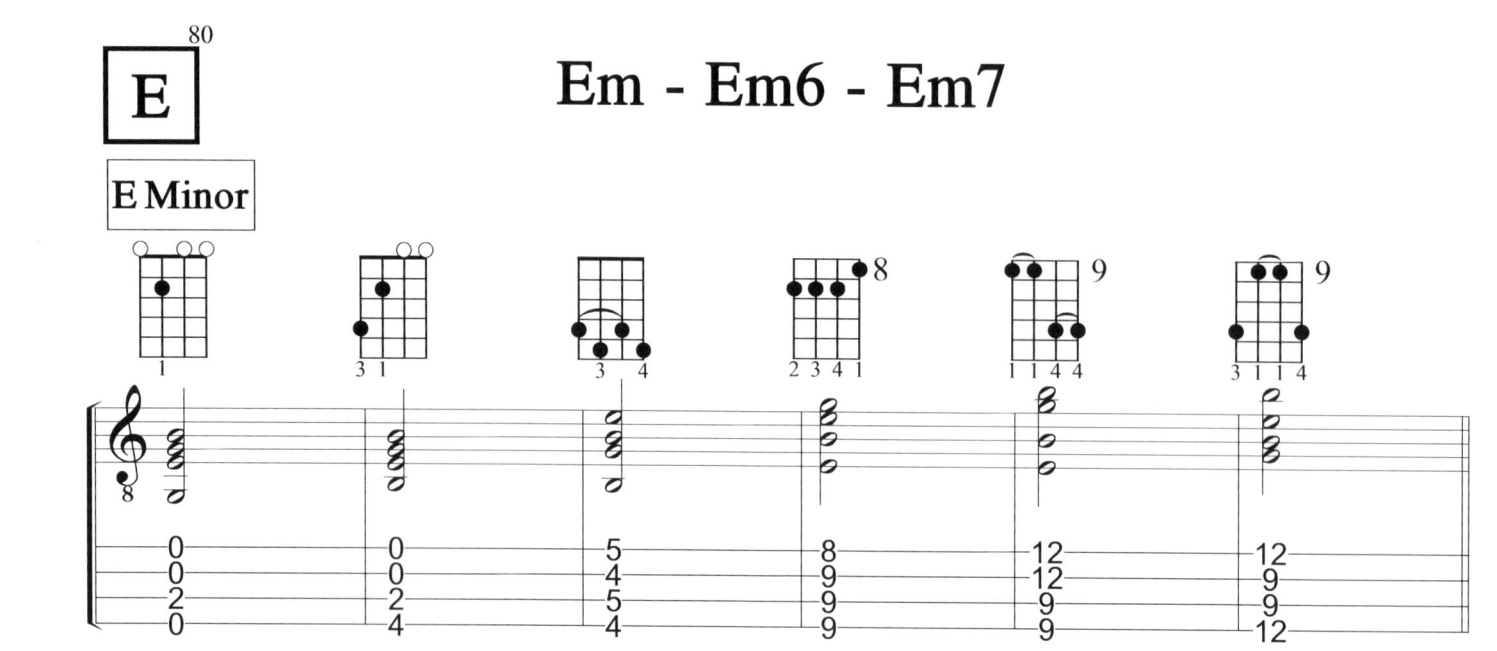

Em6

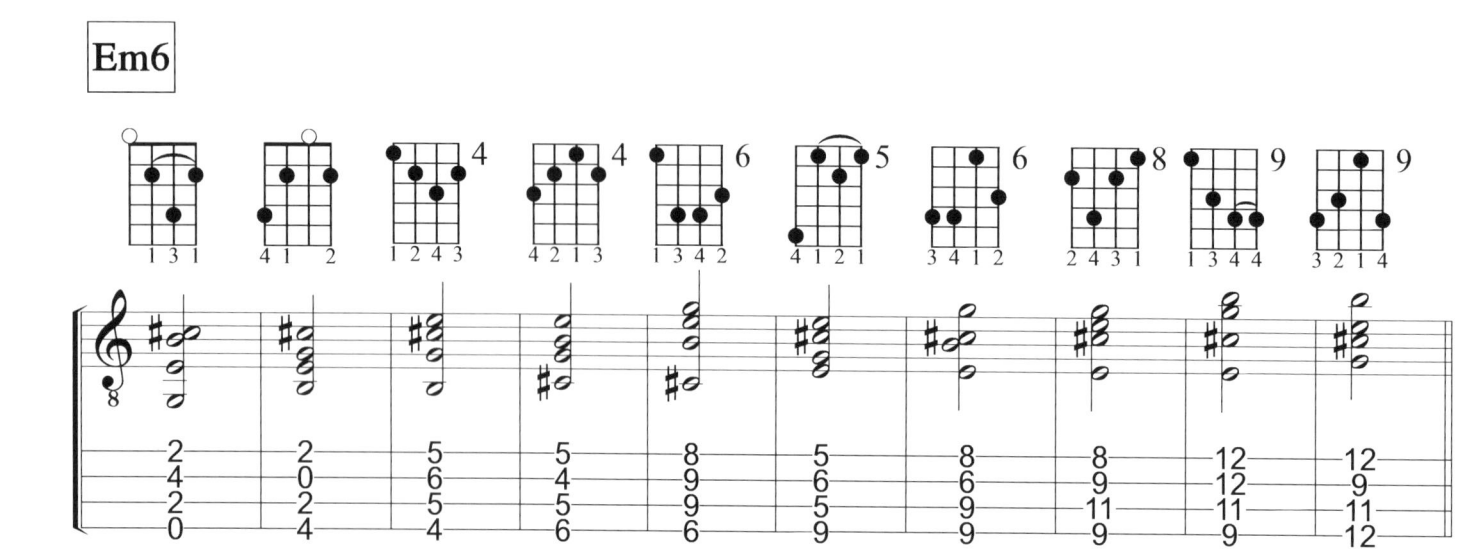

Em7

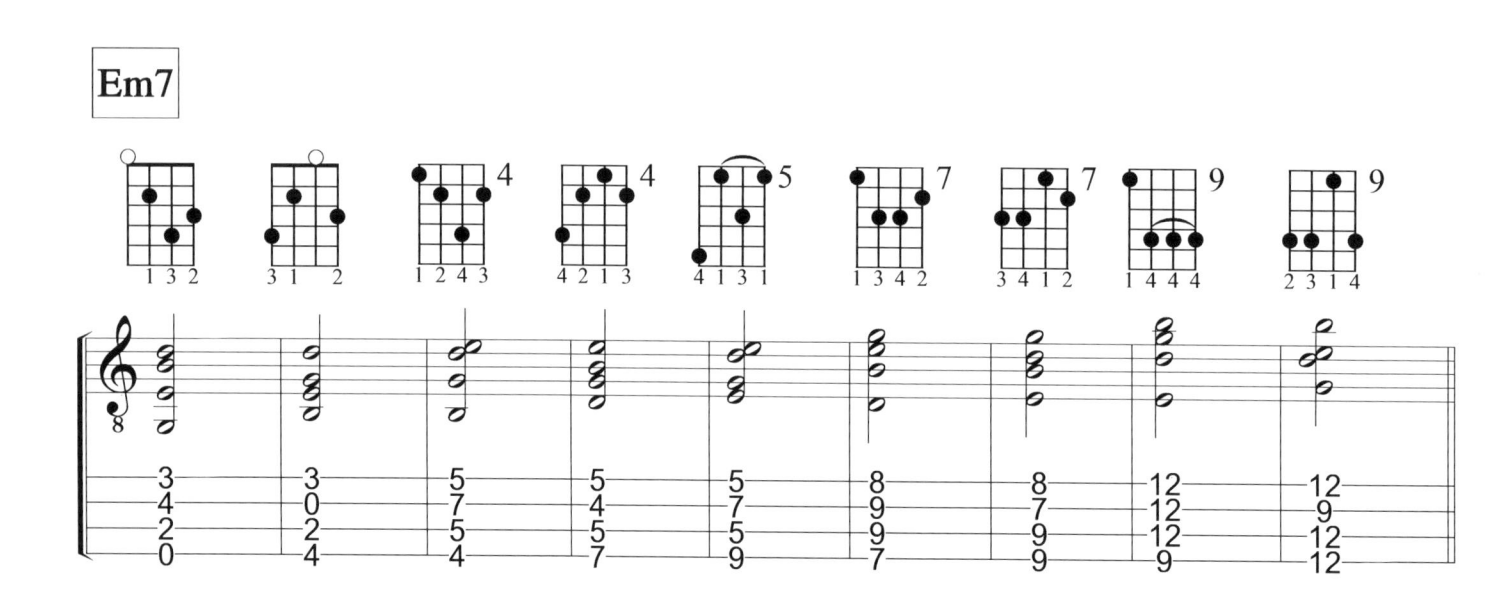

Em7♭5 - Em9 - Em11 - Em(maj7)

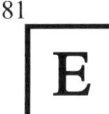

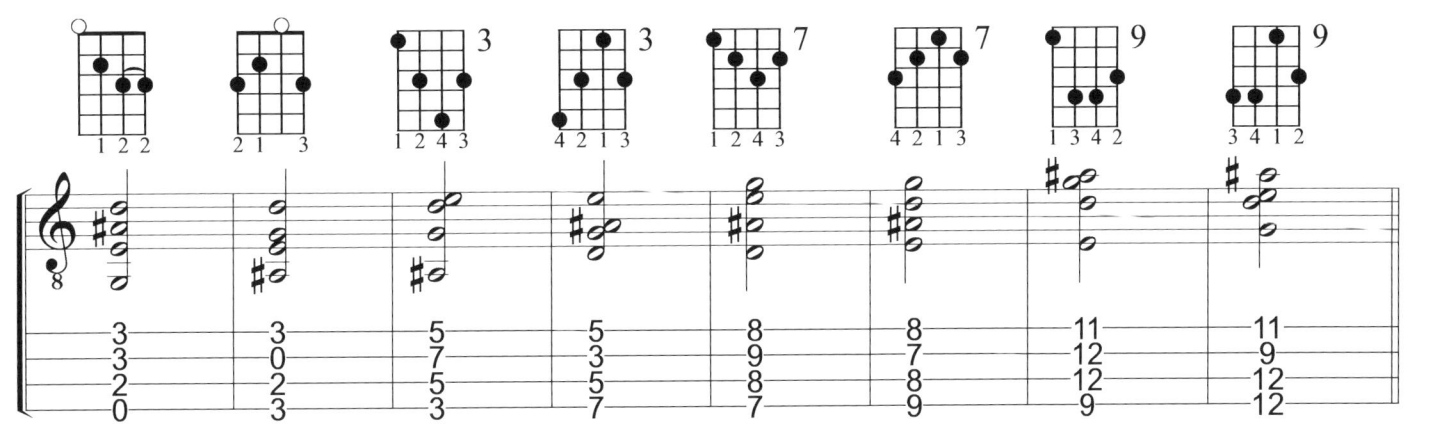

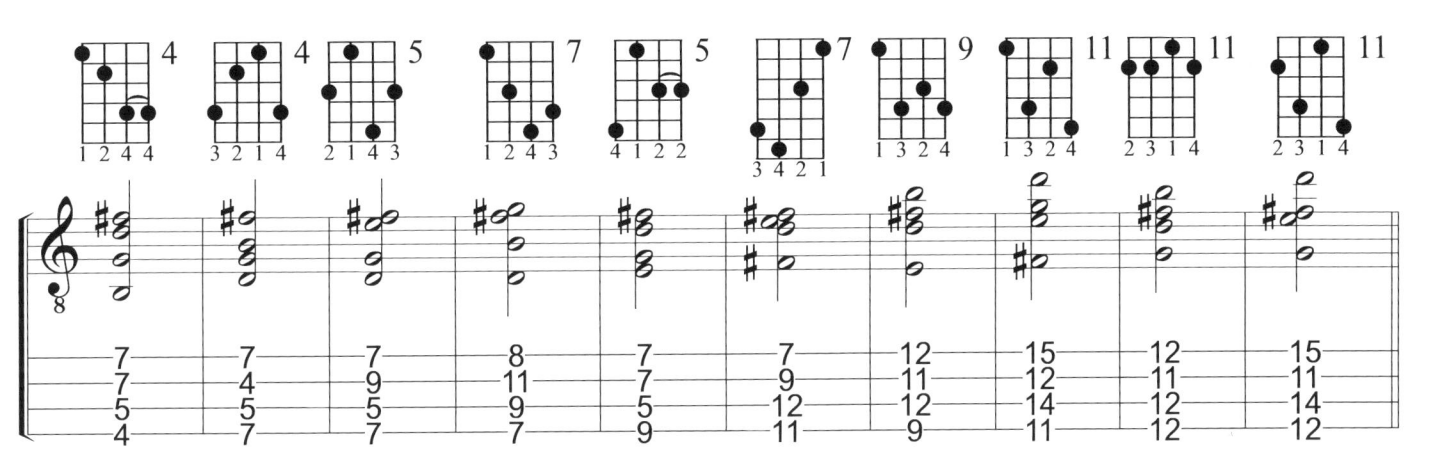

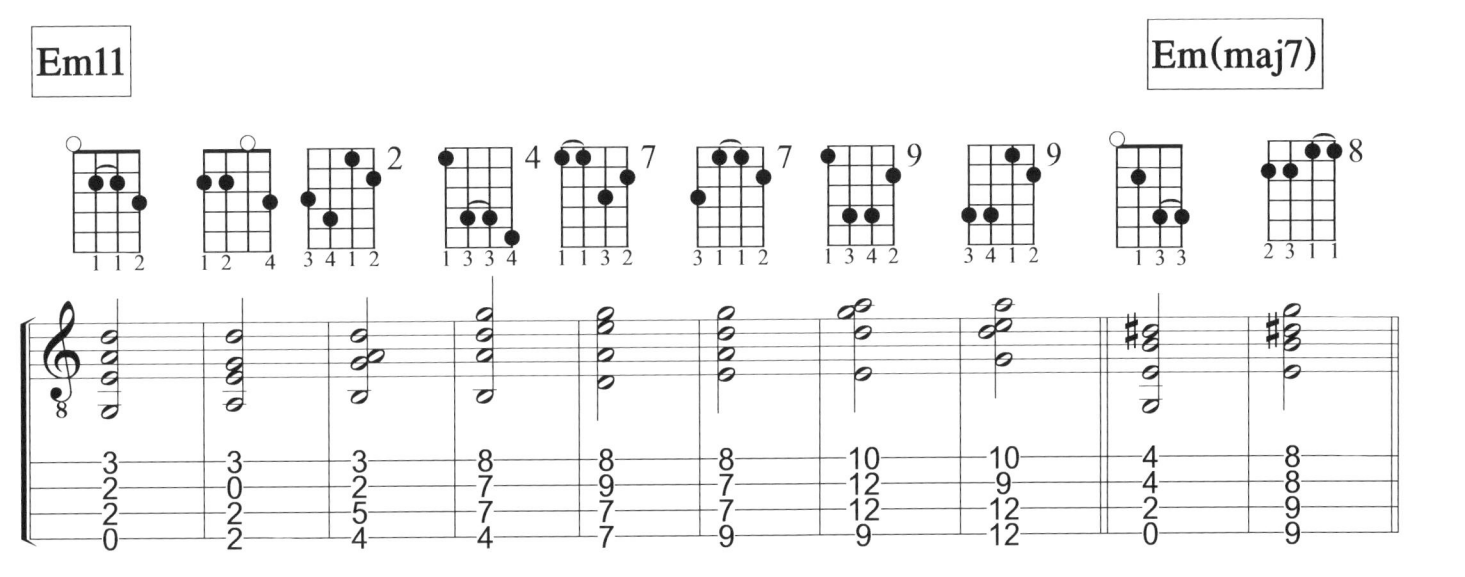

E7 - E9 - E13

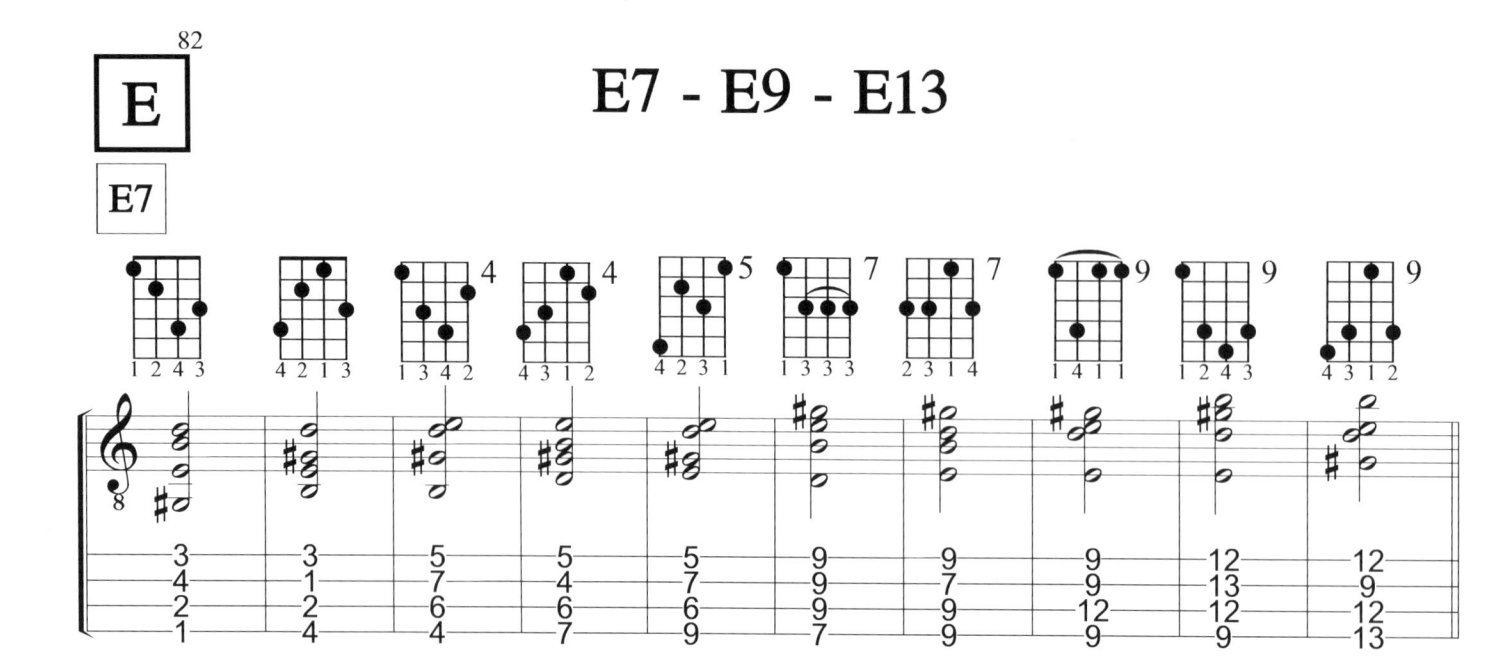

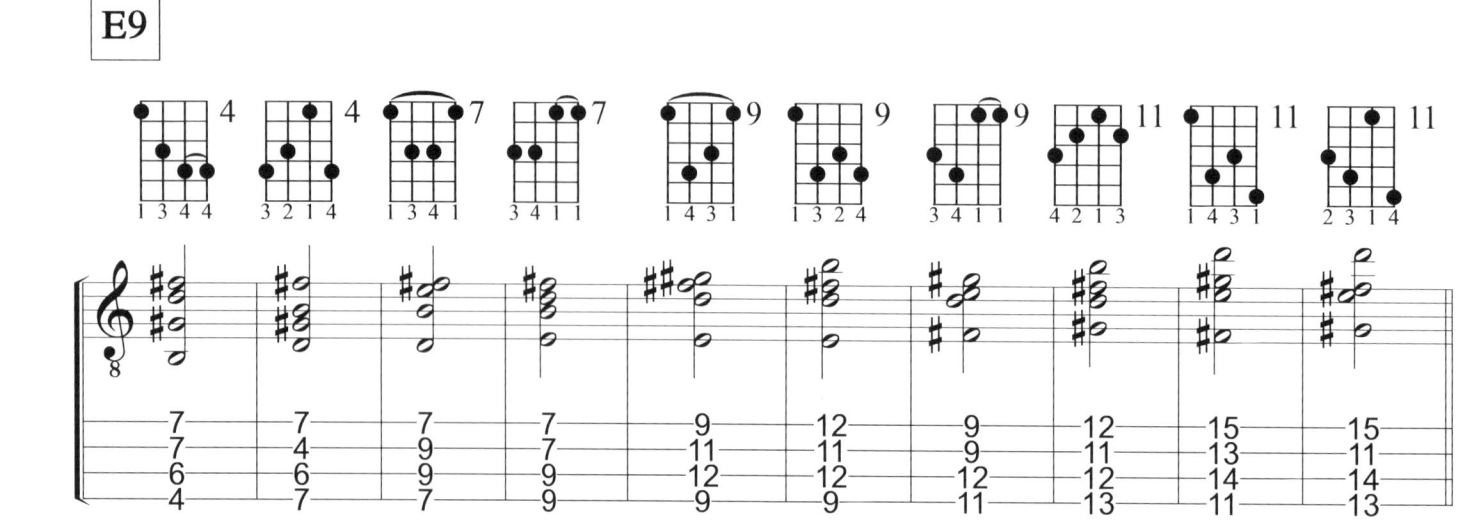

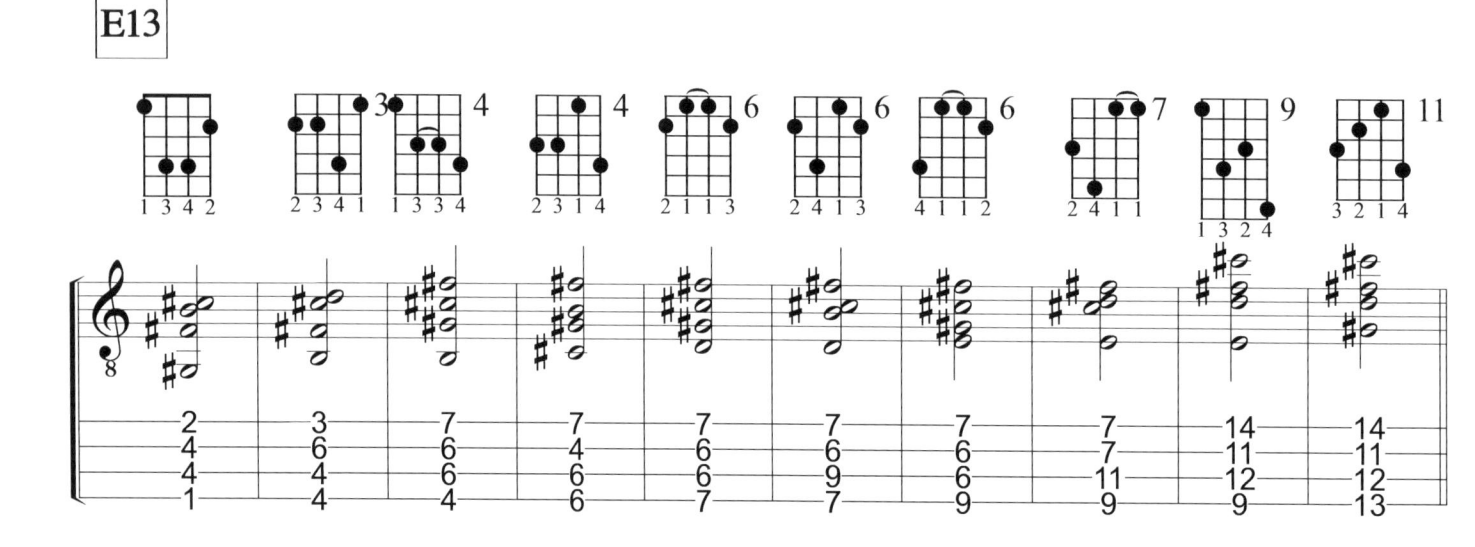

E7♭5 - E7♯5 - E7♯9

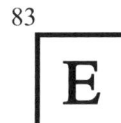

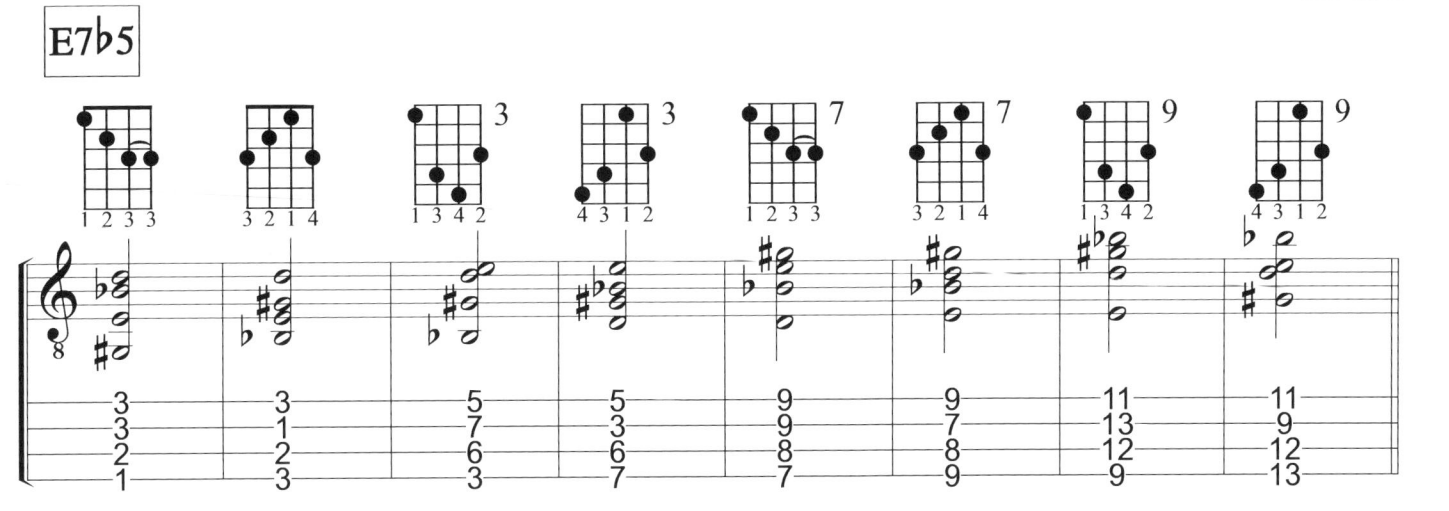

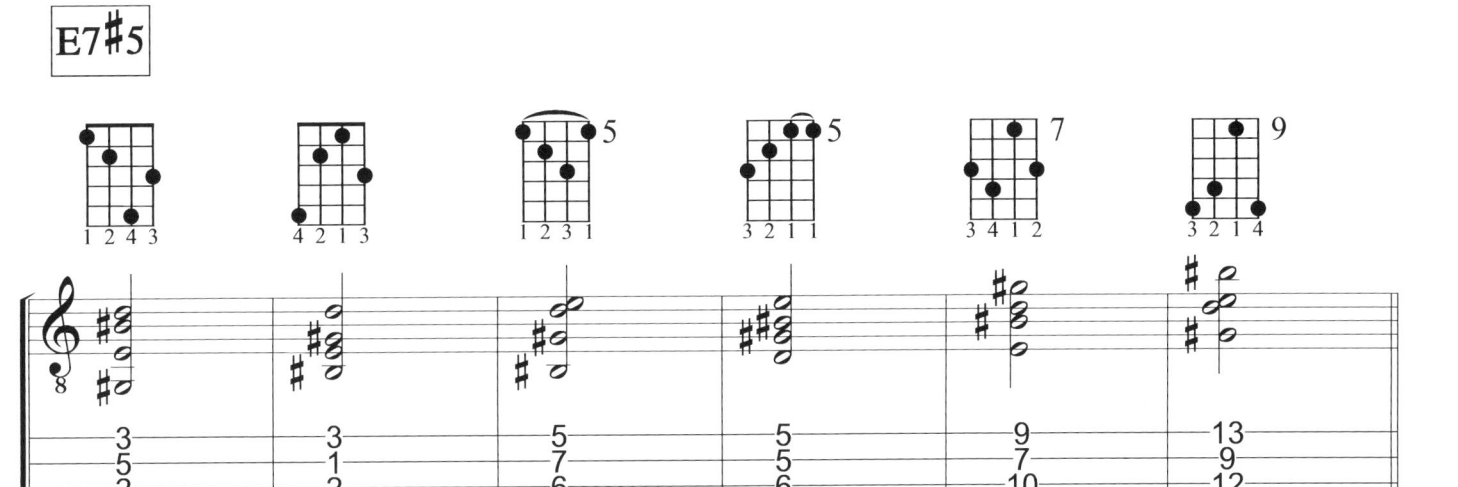

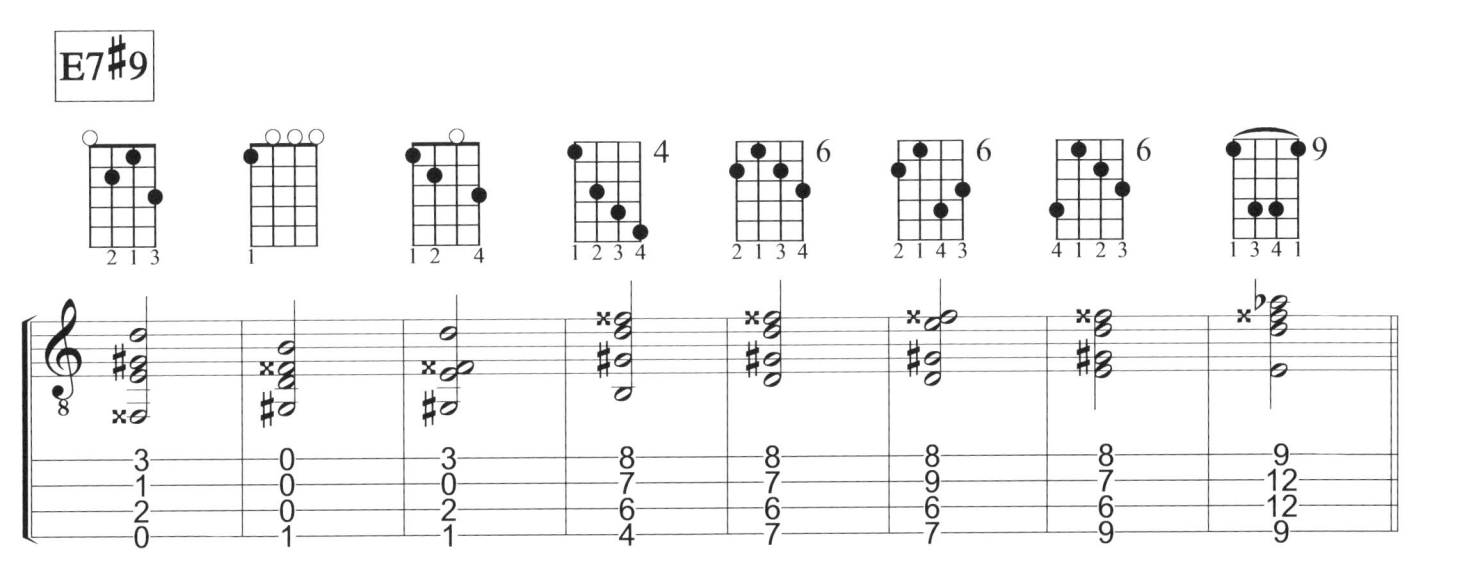

E7♭9 - E diminished - E°7

E7♭9

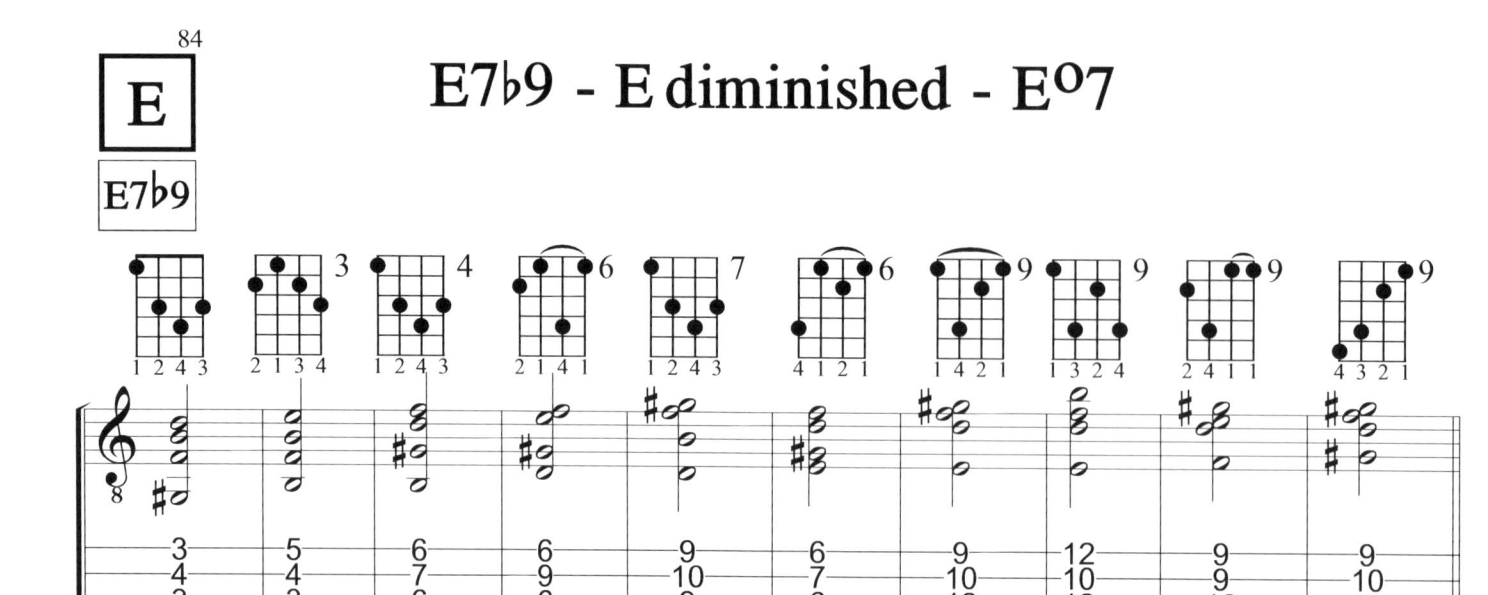

E Diminished - E°

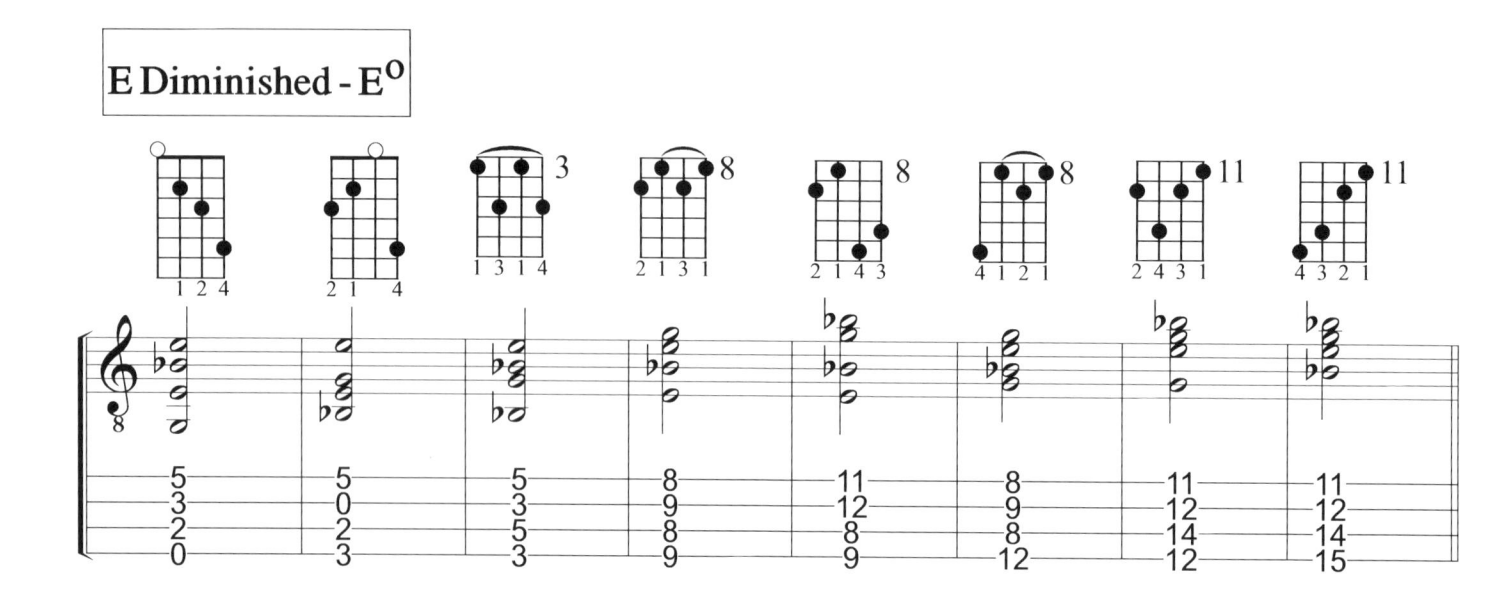

E Diminished 7th - E°7

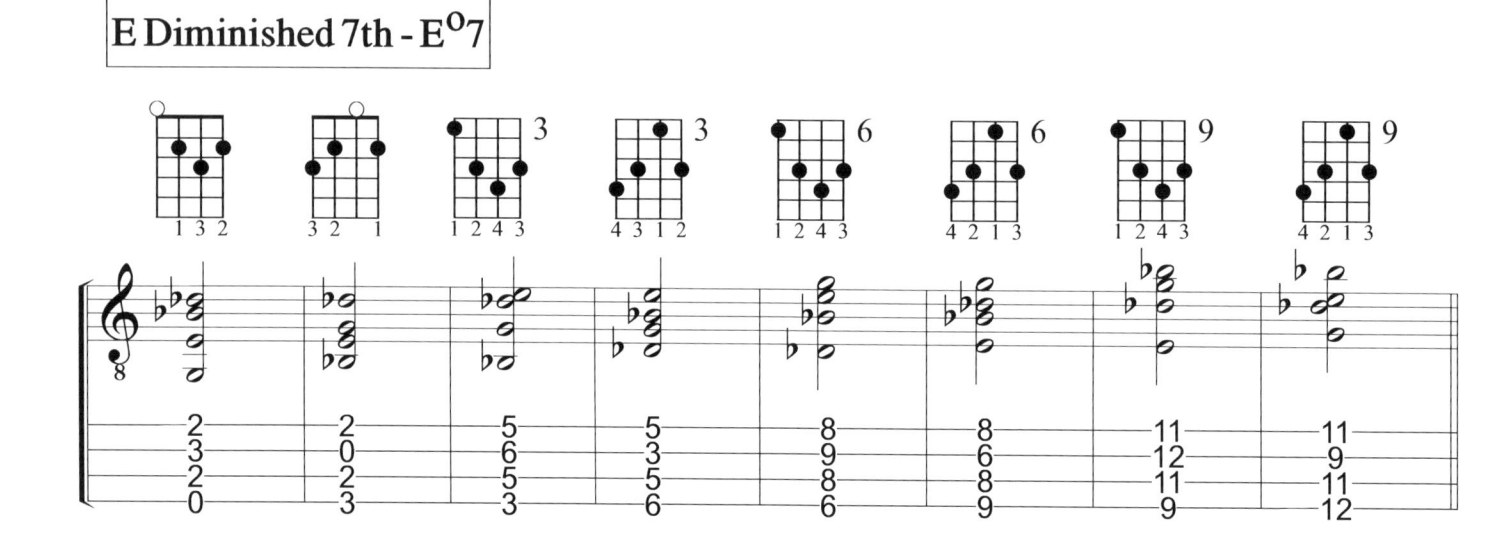

Esus4 - Esus2 - Eadd9 - E7sus - E5

Esus4

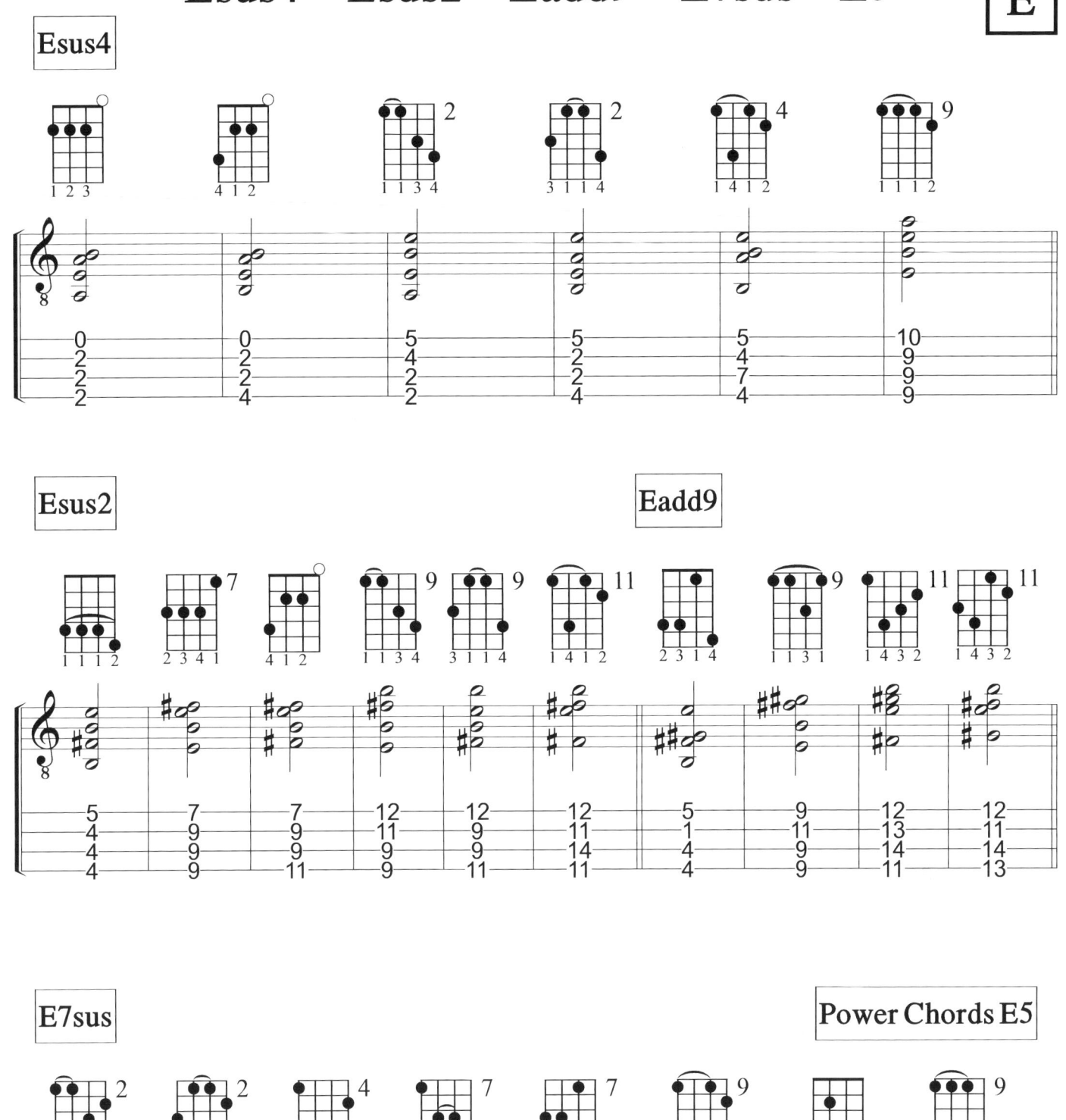

Esus2

Eadd9

E7sus

Power Chords E5

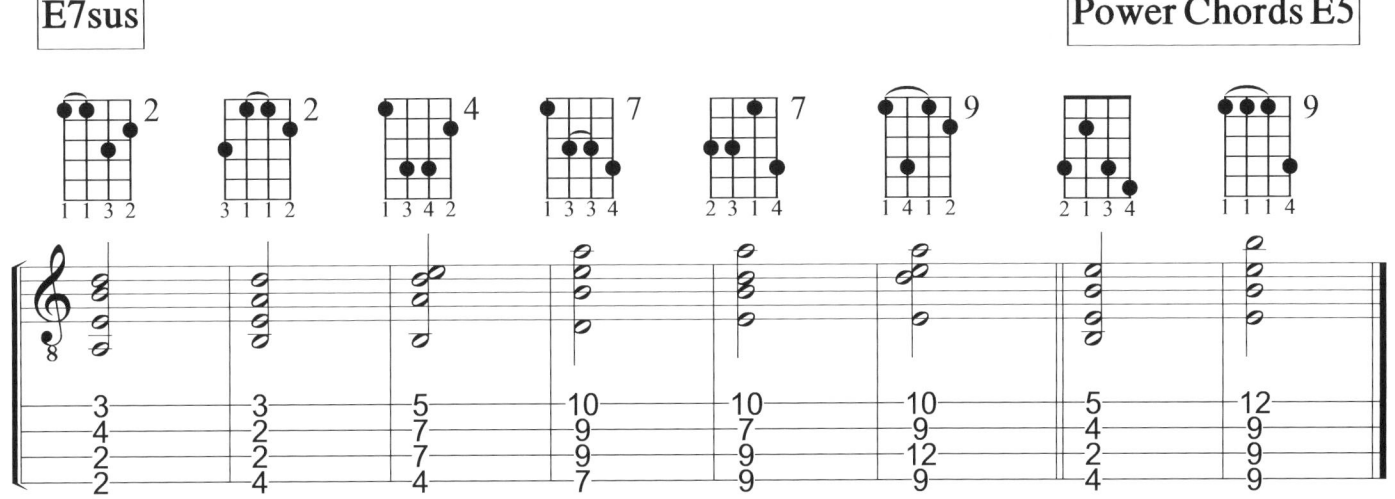

F - F6 - Fmaj7

F Major

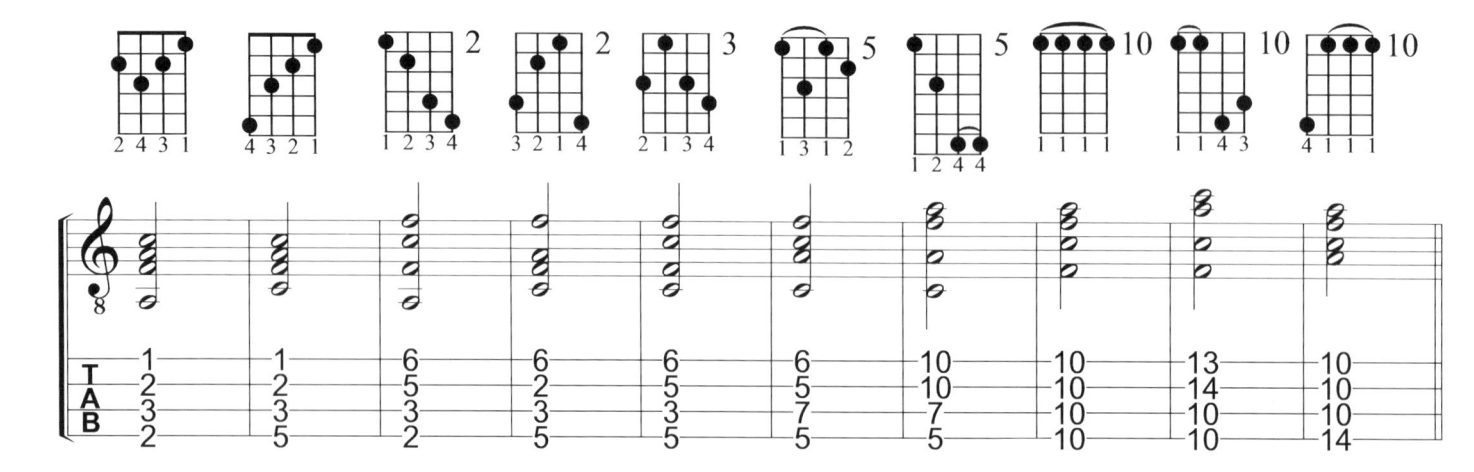

F6

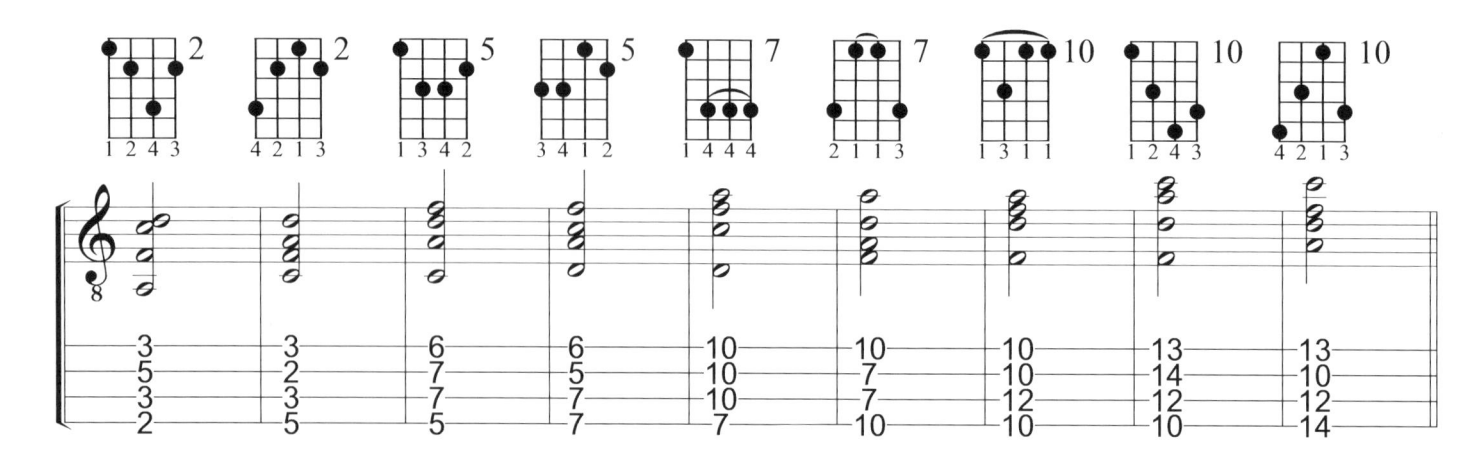

Fmaj7

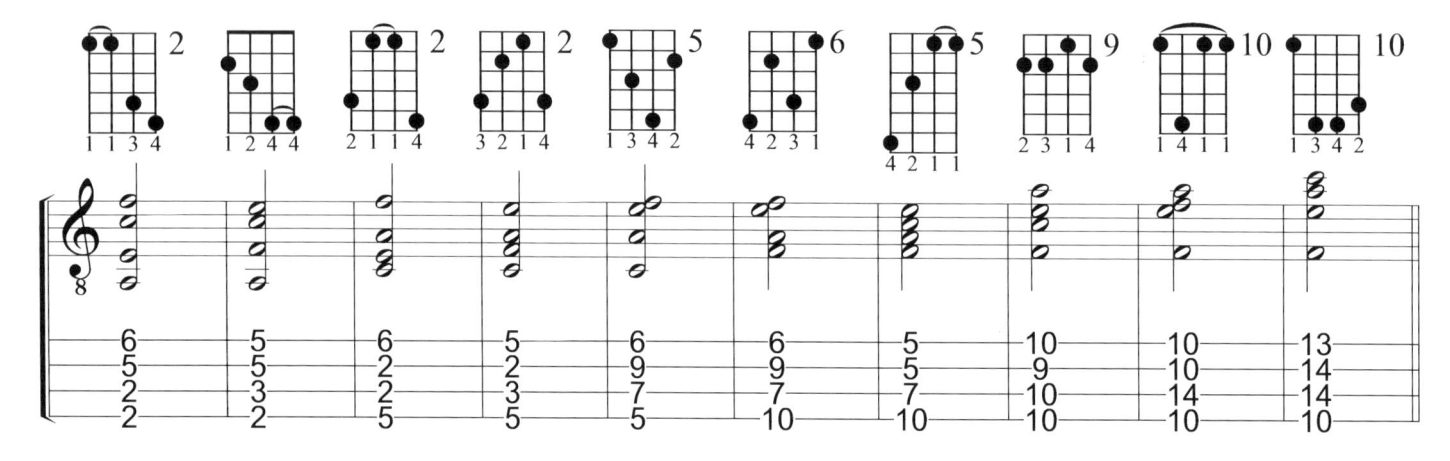

Fmaj9 - F6/9 - F+ augmented

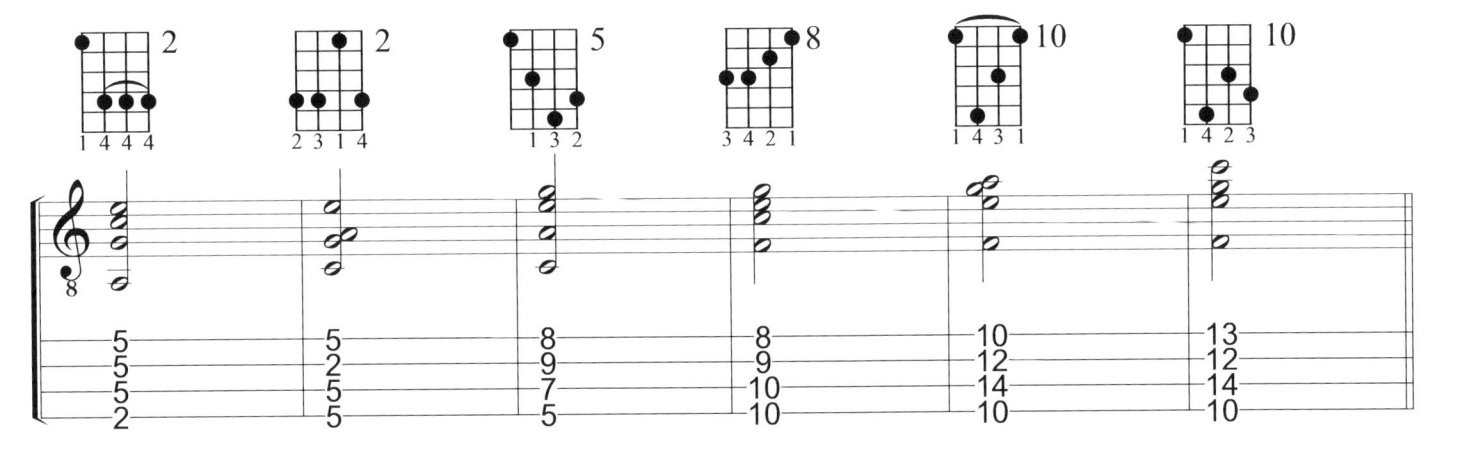

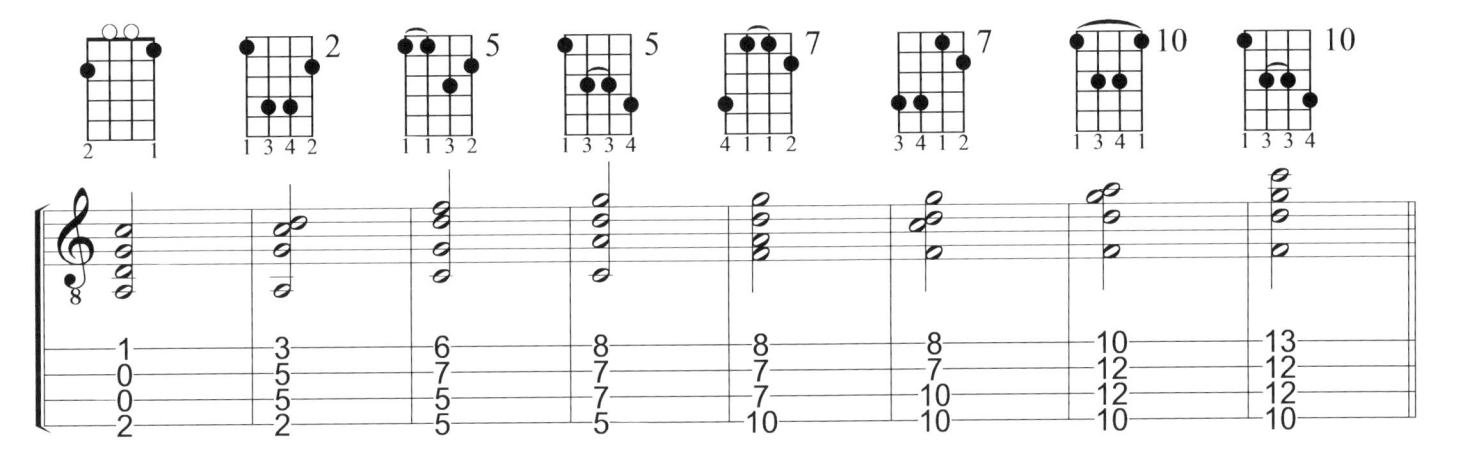

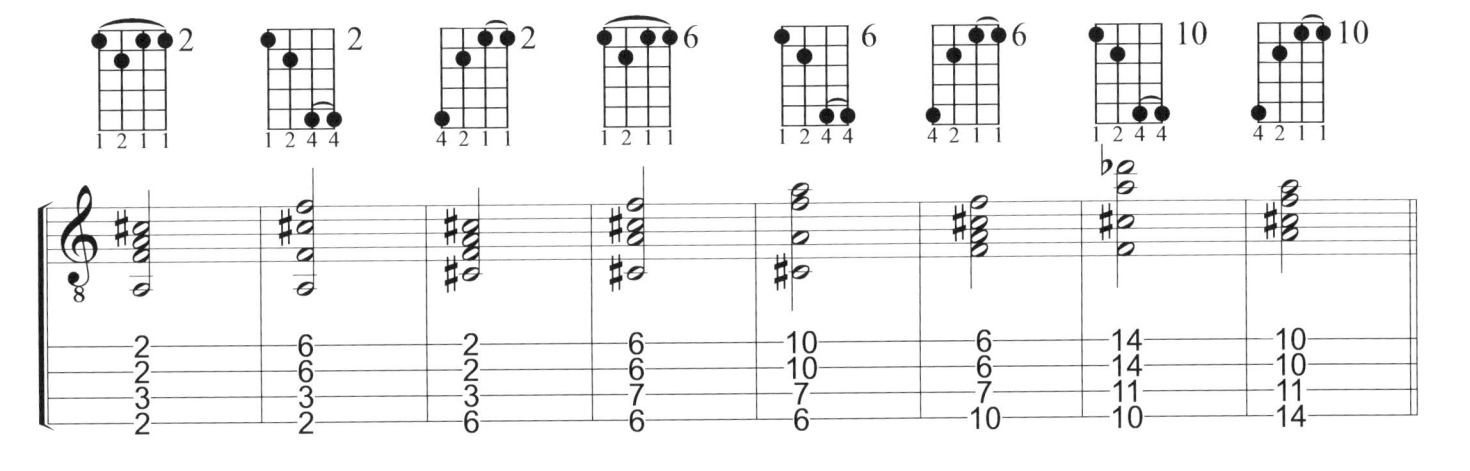

Fm - Fm6 - Fm7

F Minor

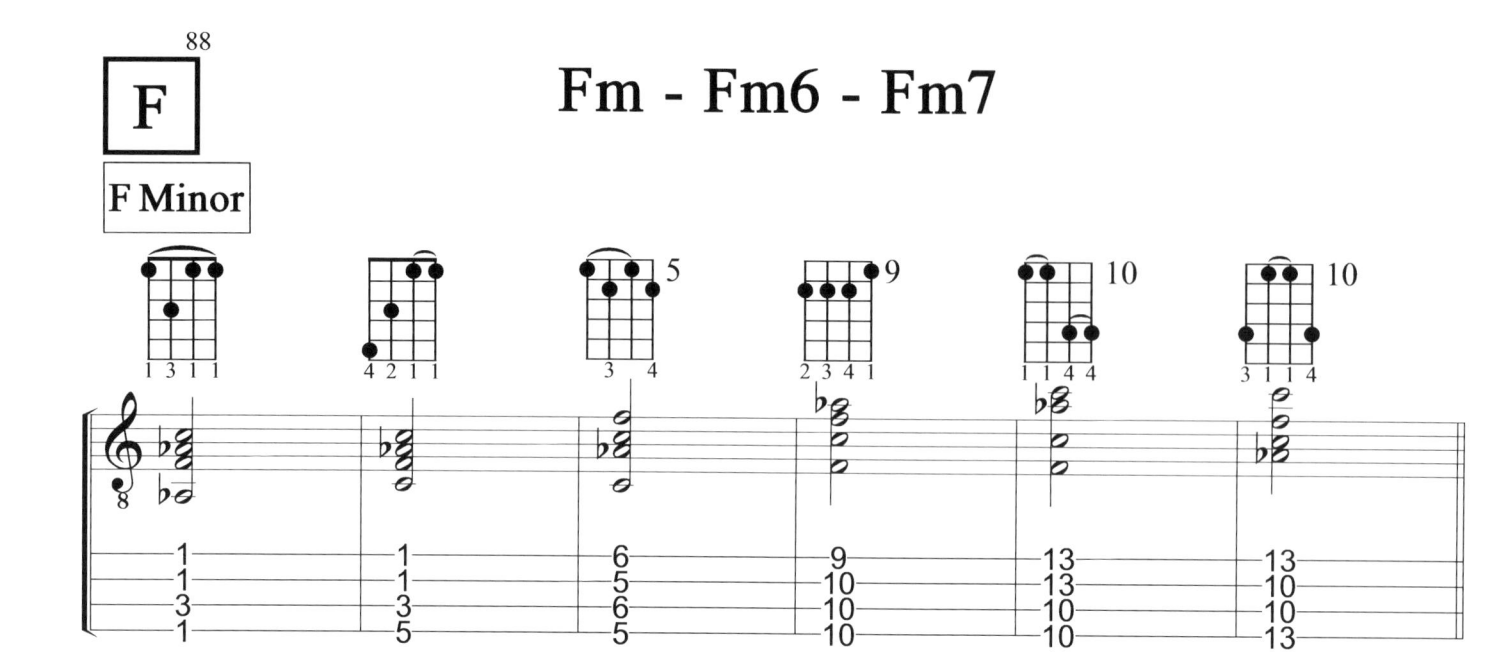

Fm6

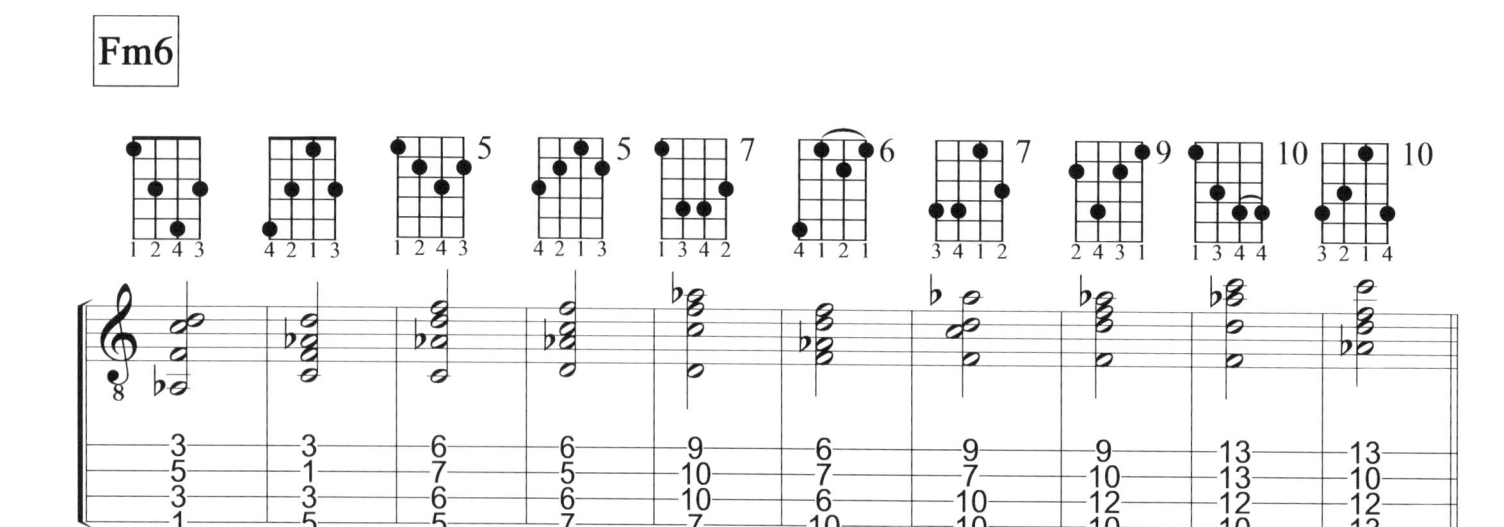

Fm7

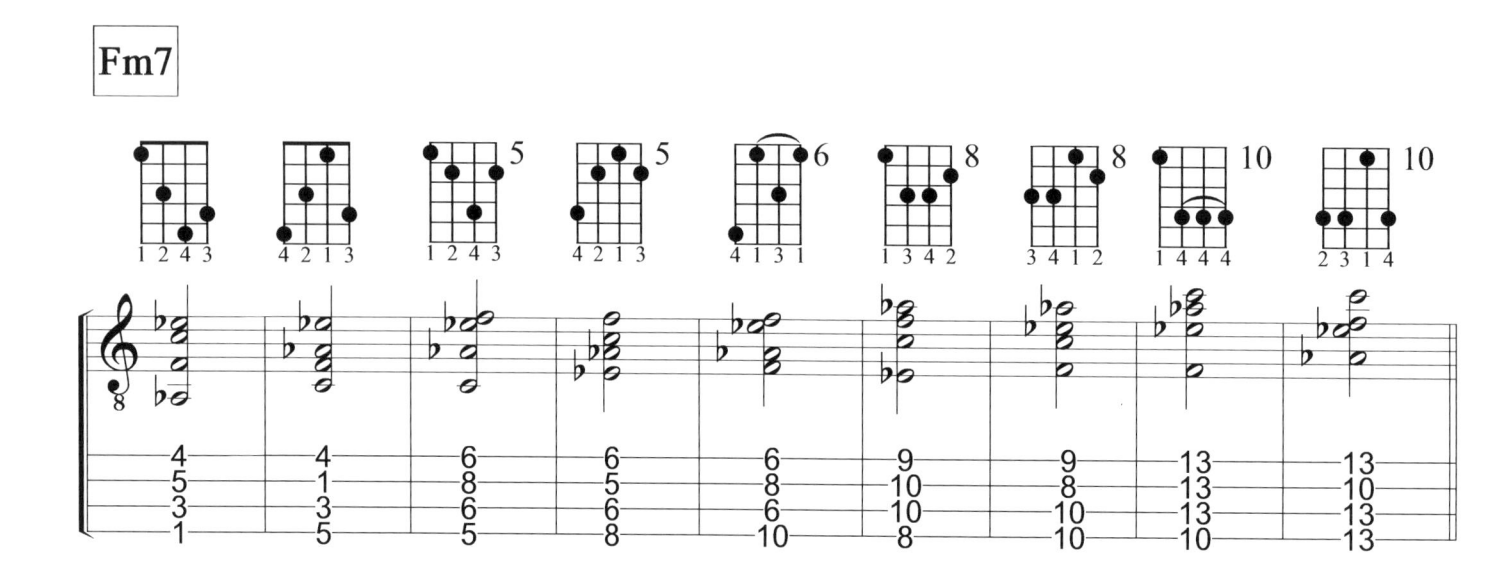

Fm7♭5 - Fm9 - Fm11 - Fm(maj7)

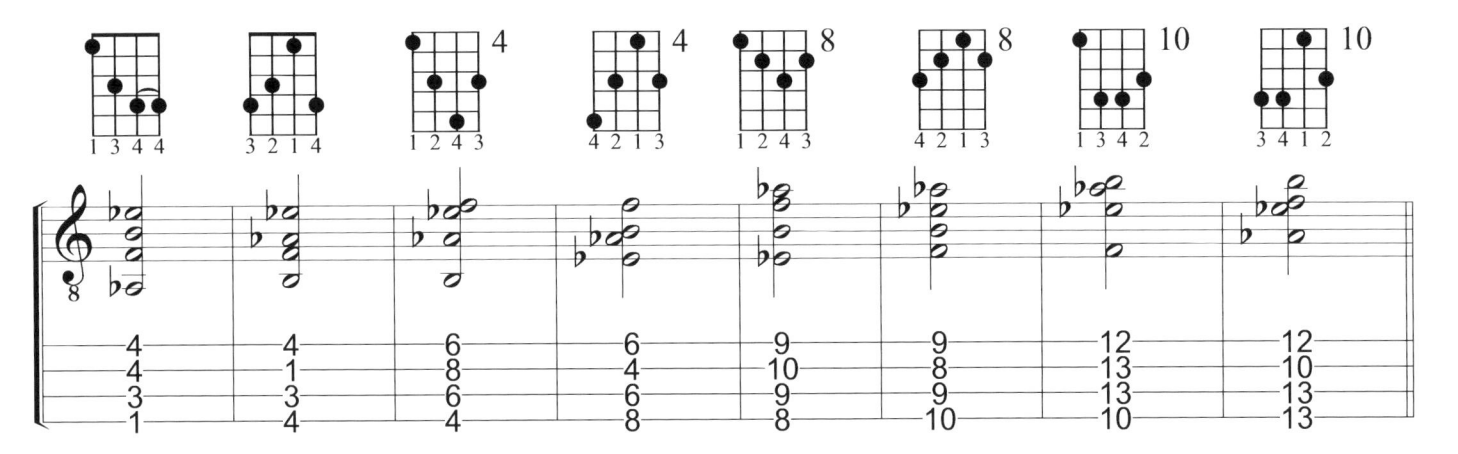

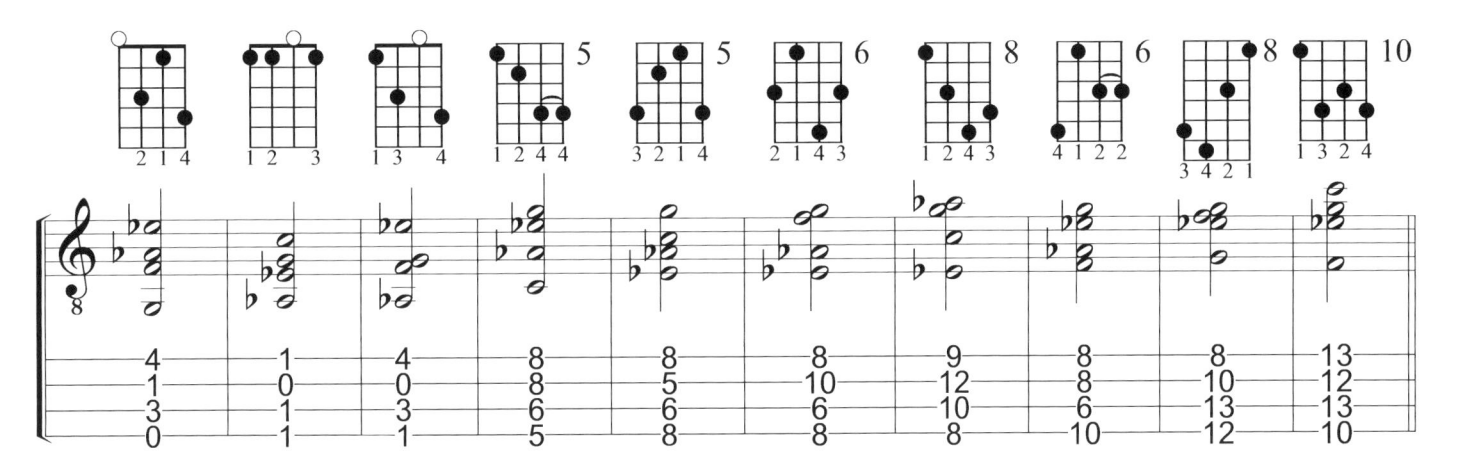

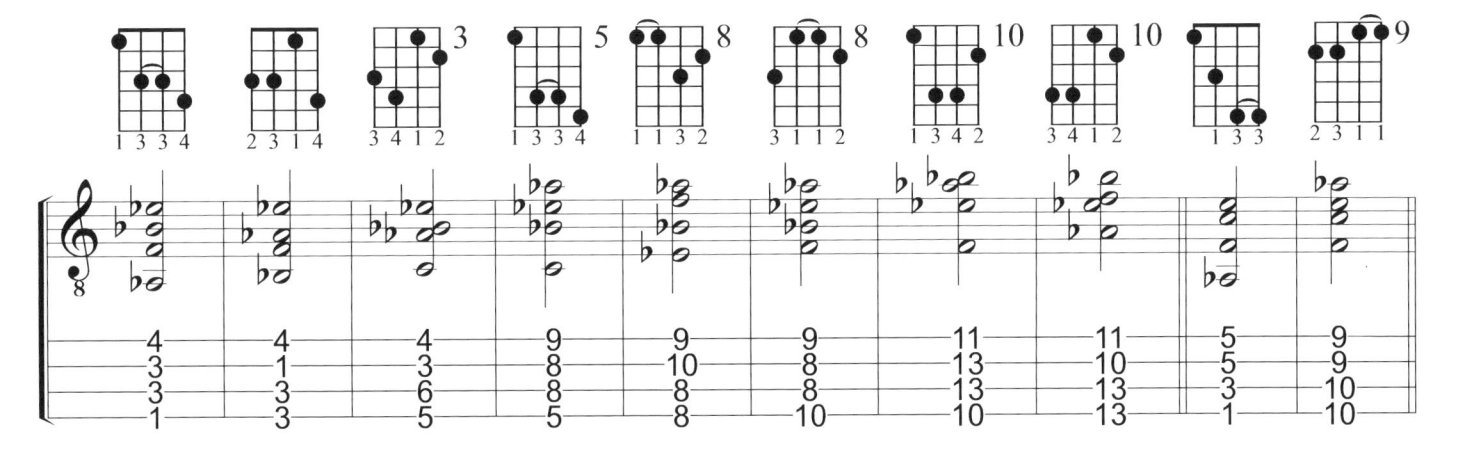

F7 - F9 - F13

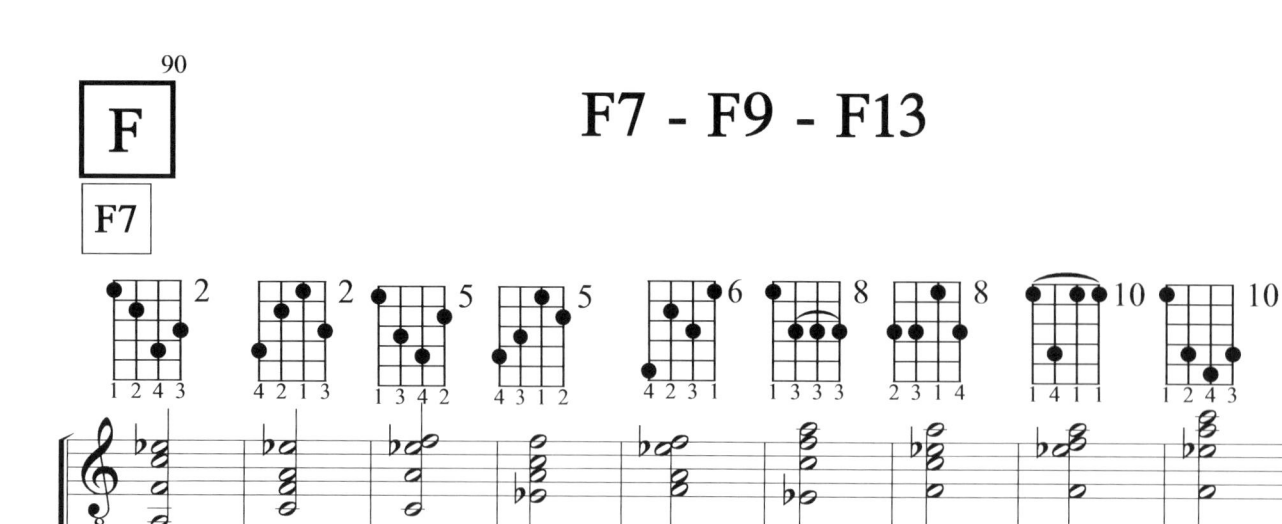

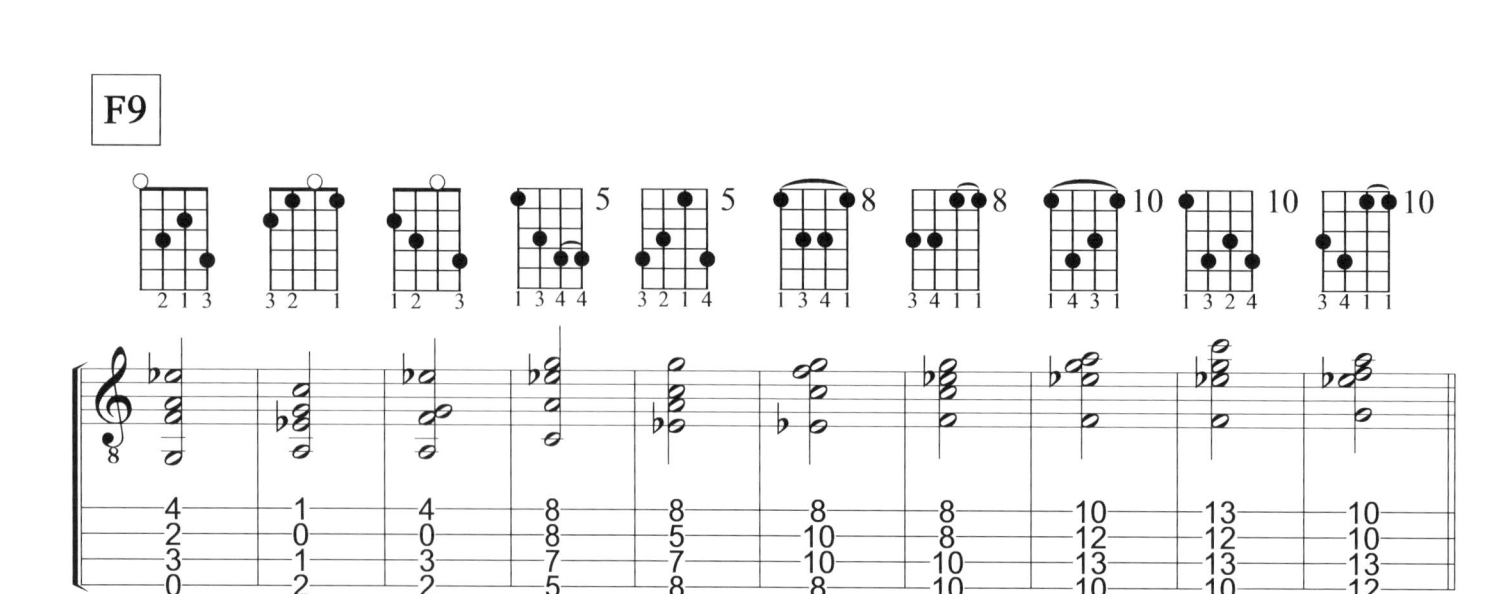

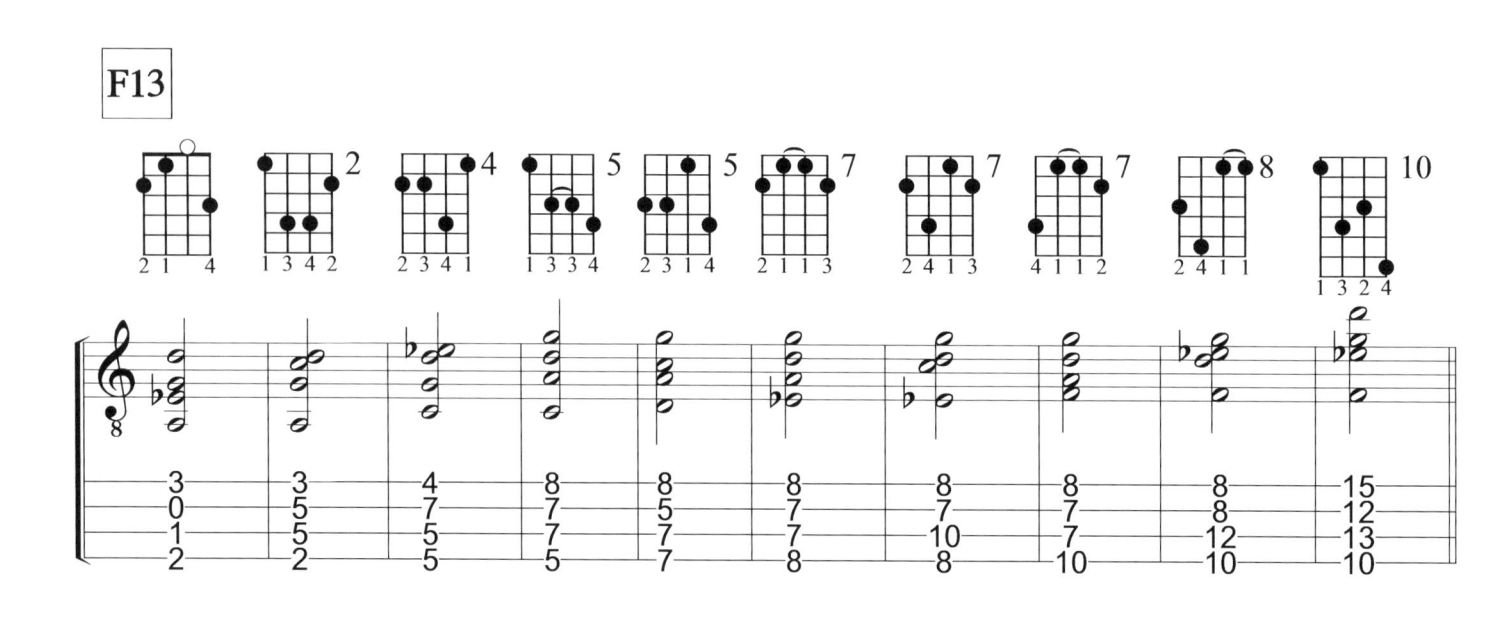

F7b5 - F7#5 - F7#9

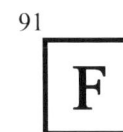

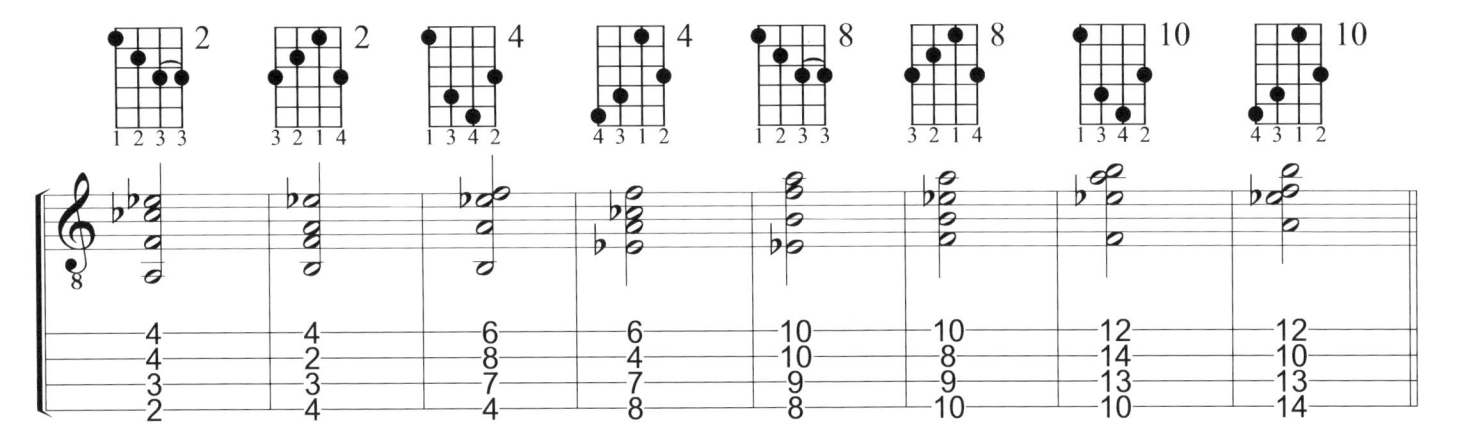

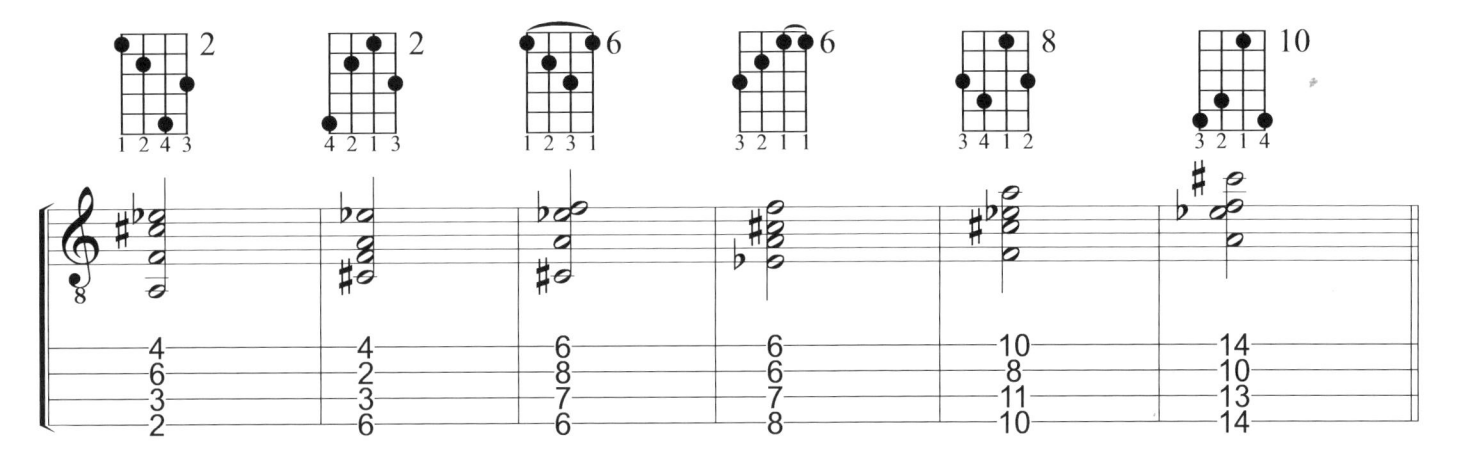

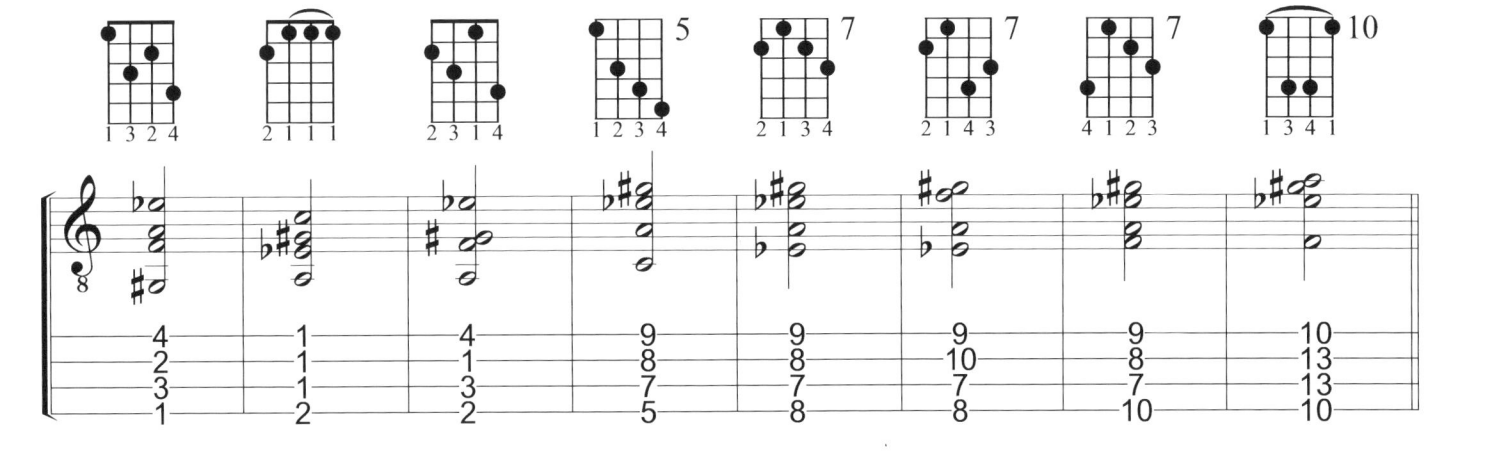

F7♭9 - F diminished - F°7

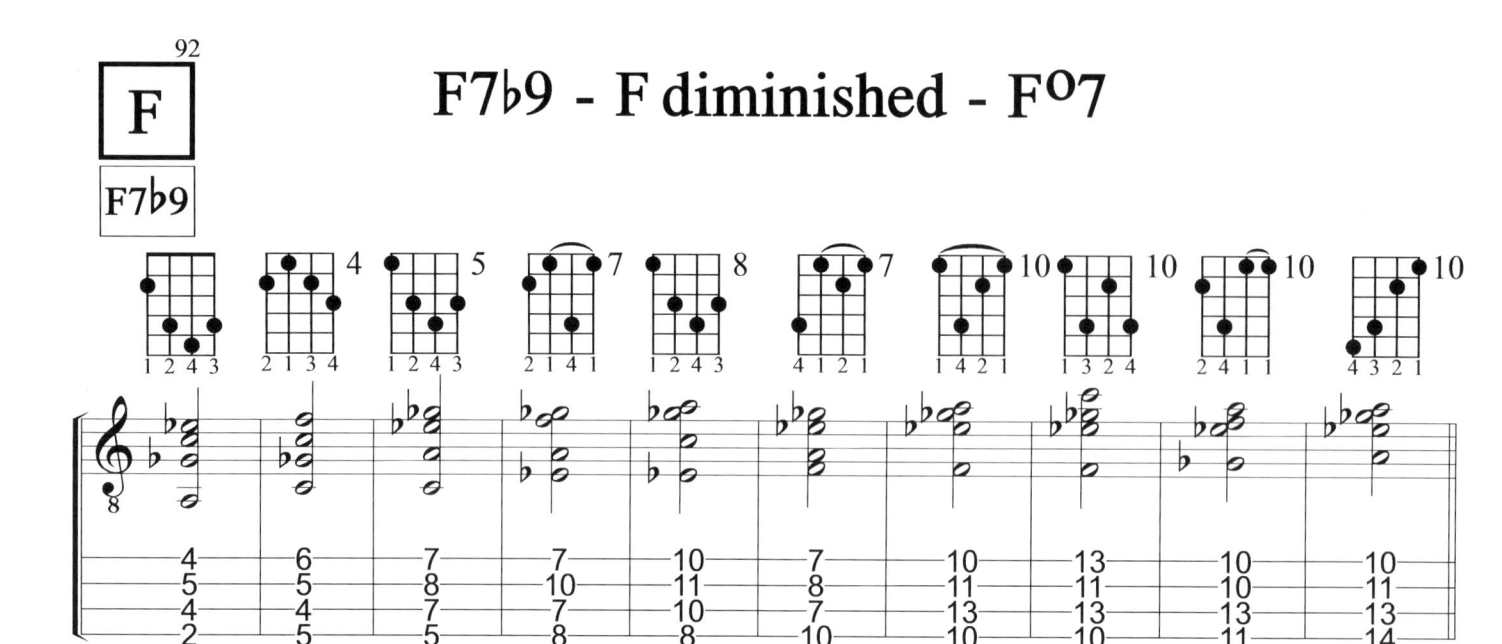

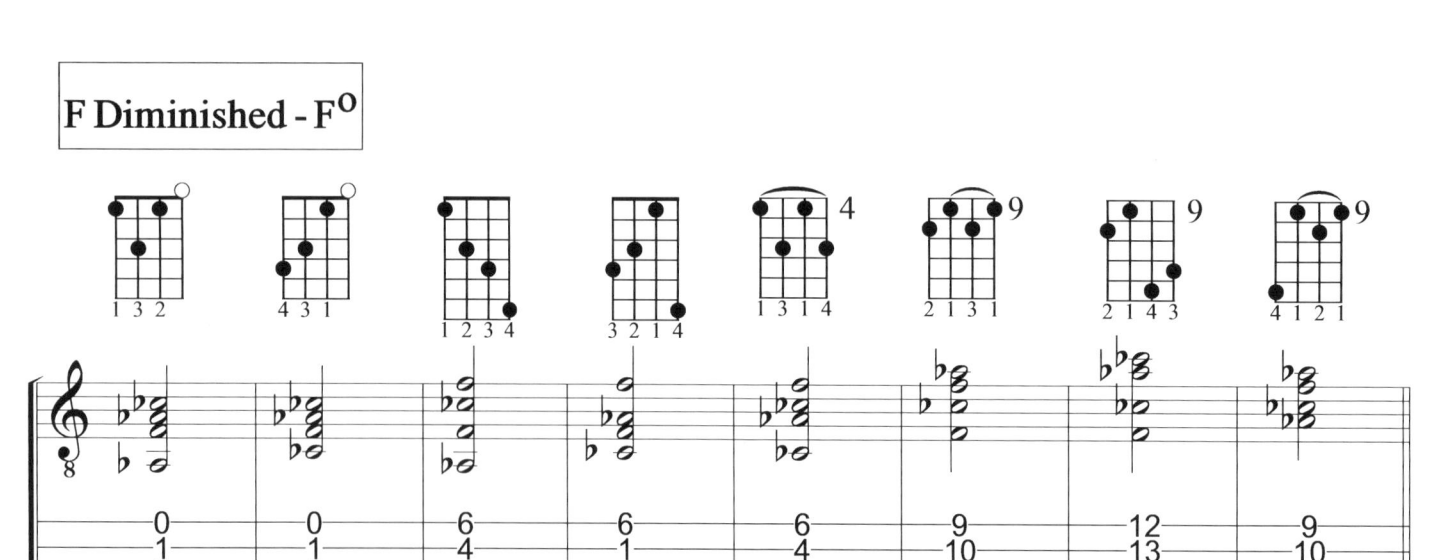

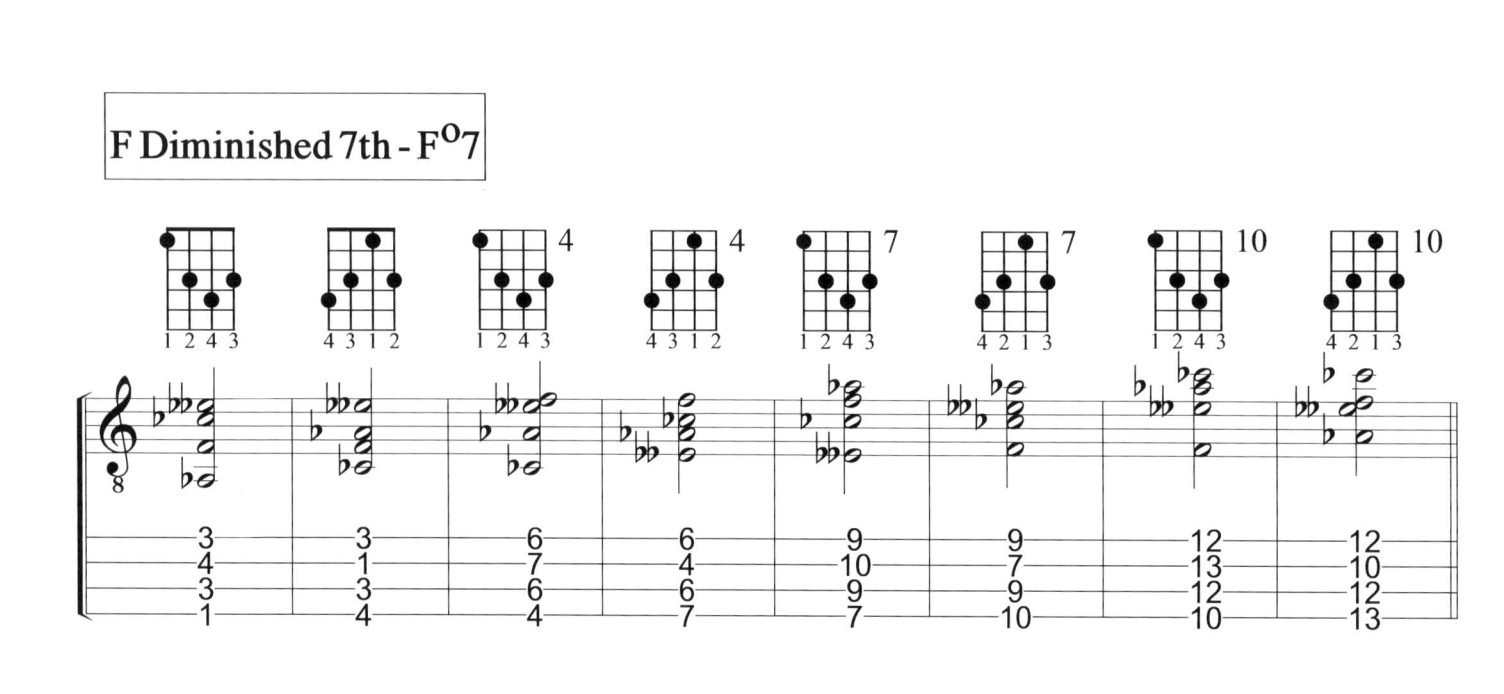

Fsus4 - Fsus2 - Fadd9 - F7sus - F5

Fsus4

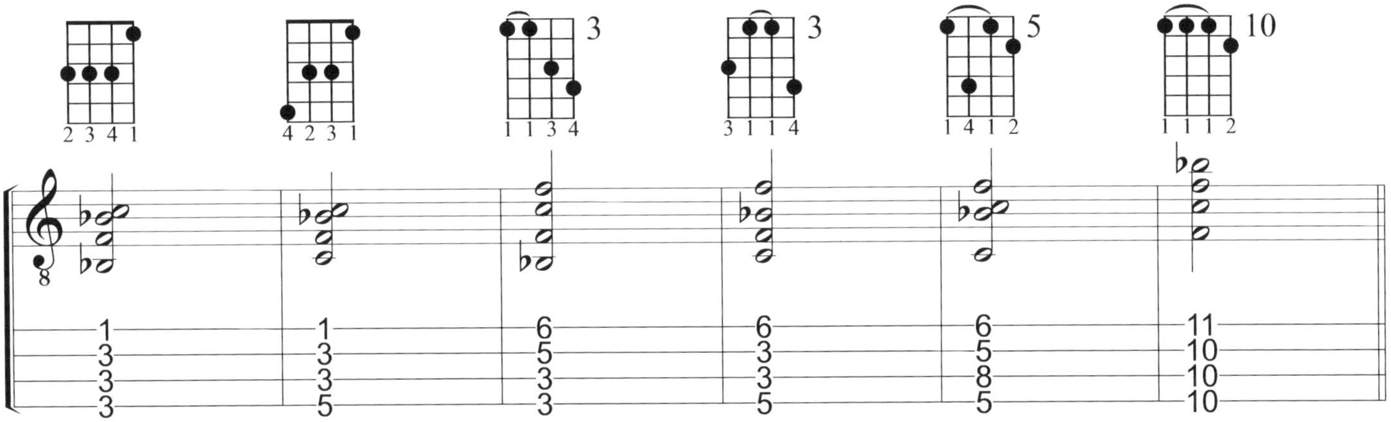

Fsus2

Fadd9

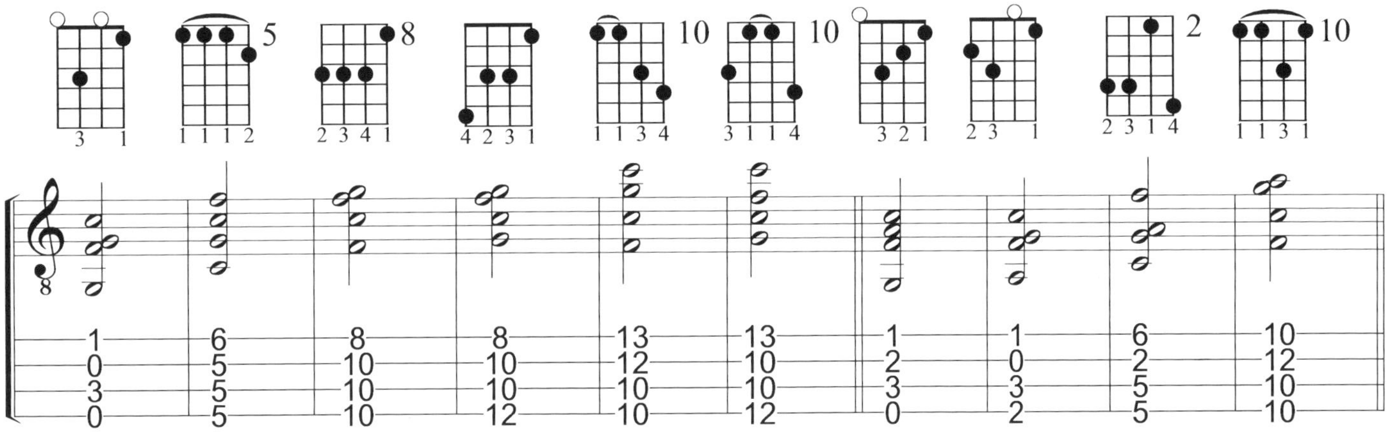

F7sus

Power Chords F5

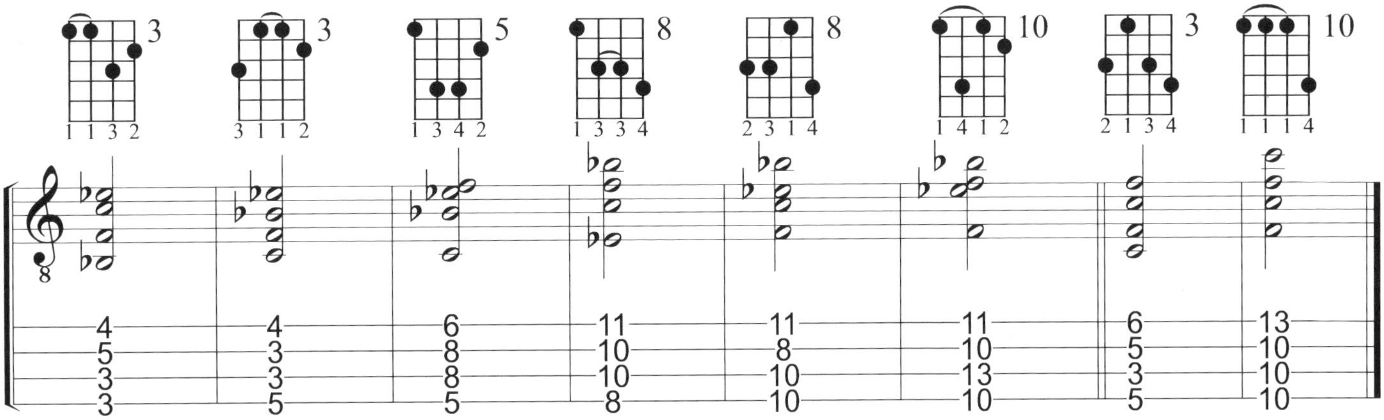

Major - 6th - maj7

F♯ G♭

Chords are shown either as sharps or flats in the notation line.
For example, F#m is shown instead of Gbm.

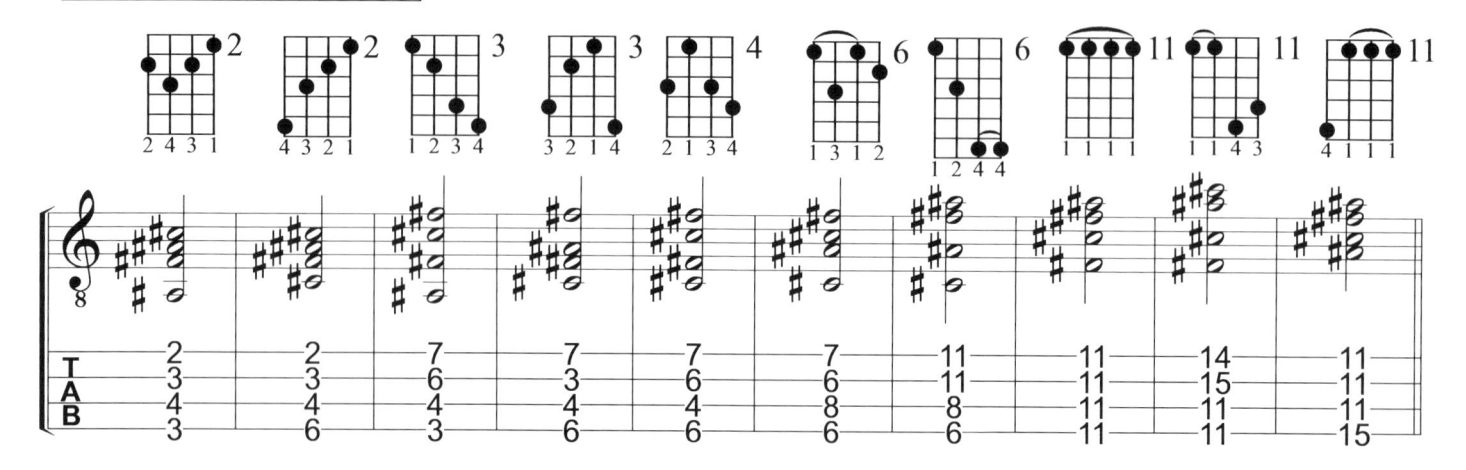

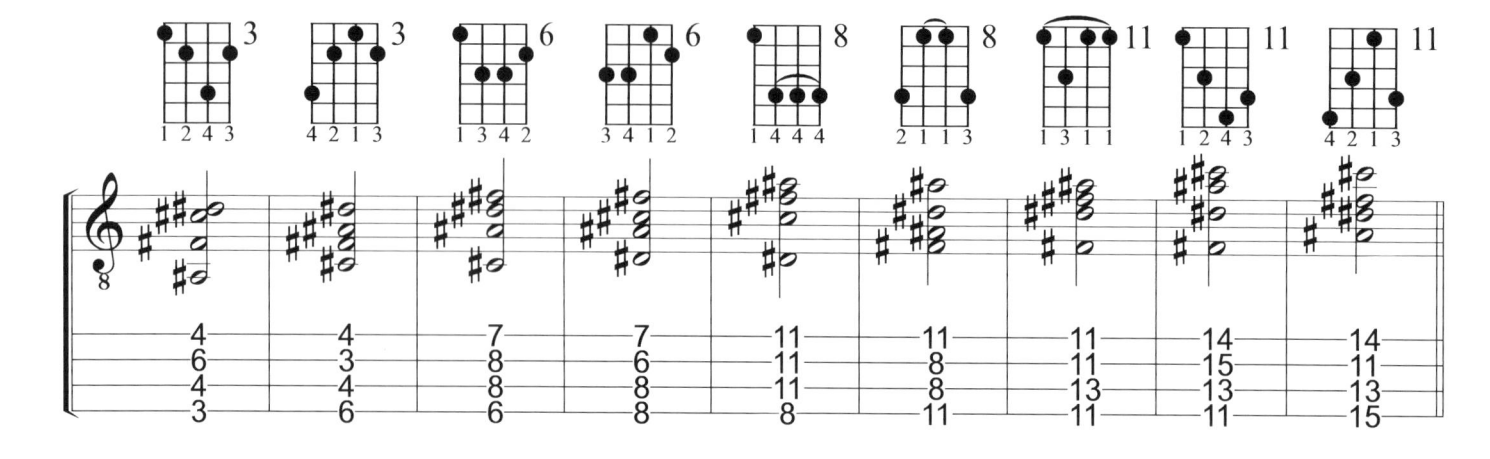

F♯ Major - G♭Major

F♯6 - G♭6

F♯maj7 - G♭maj7

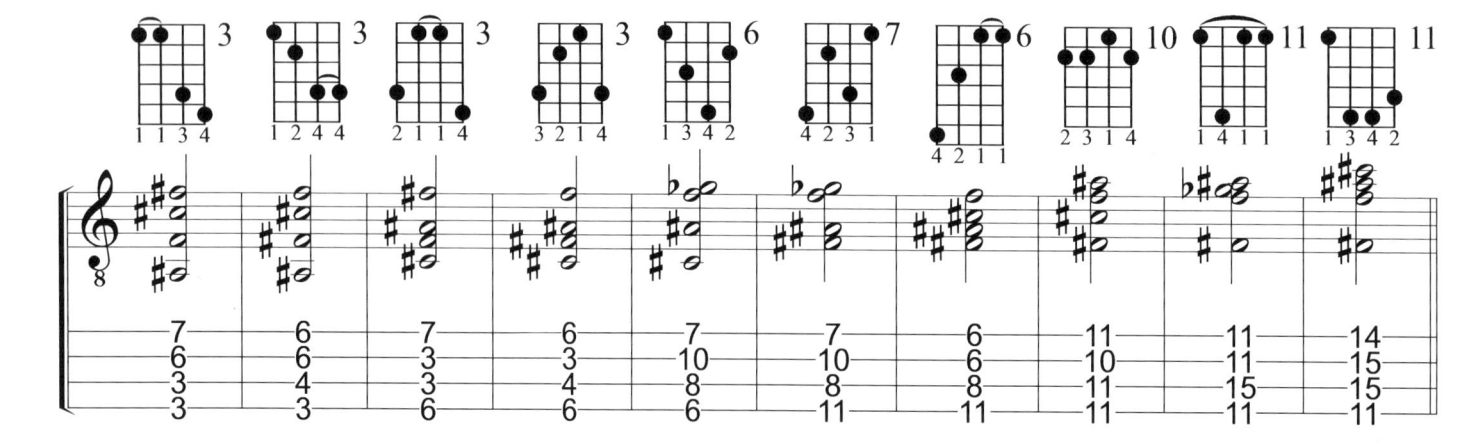

Maj9 - 6/9 - Augmented

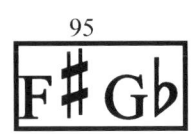

F# Gb

F#maj9 - Gbmaj9

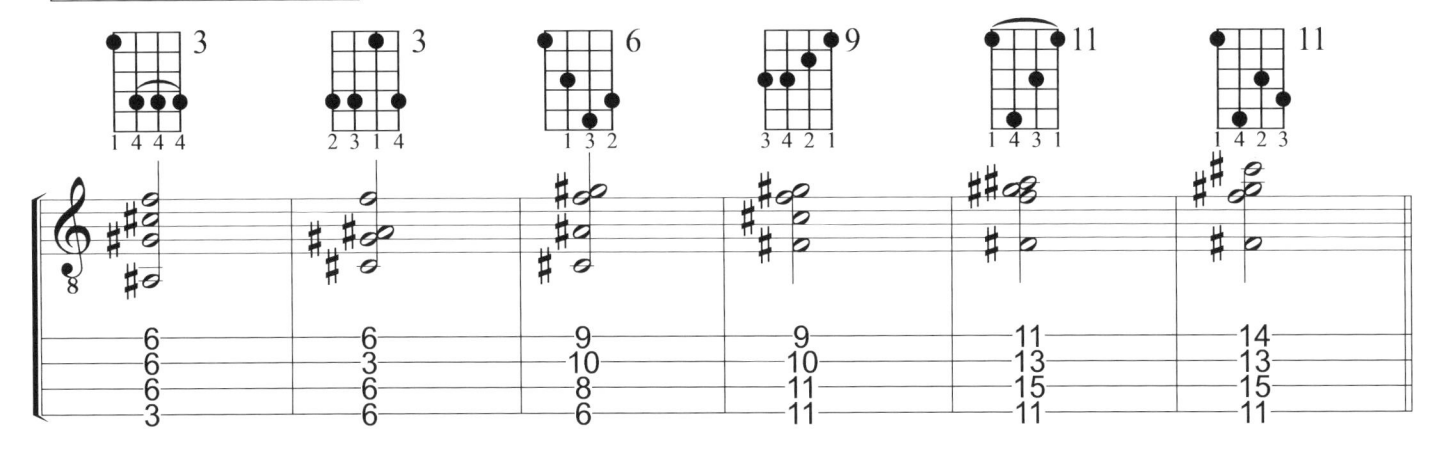

F#6/9 - Gb6/9

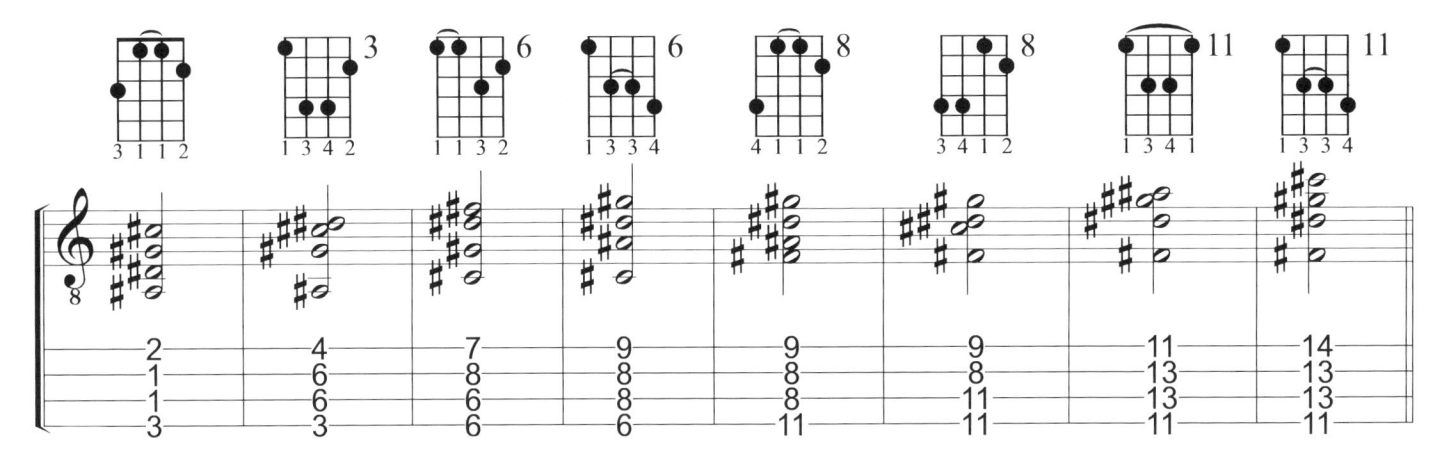

F# Augmented - F#+ Gb Augmented - Gb+

minor - m6 - m7

F# / Gb

F# Minor

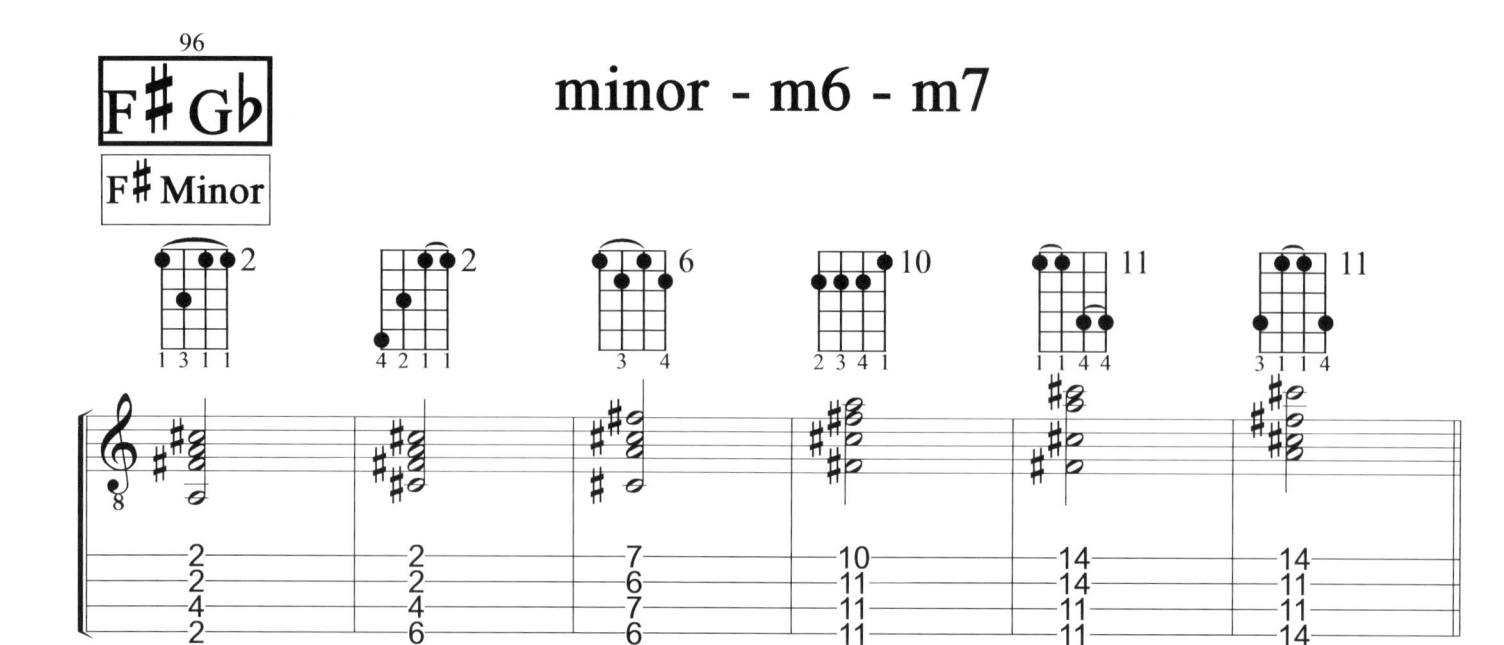

F#m6

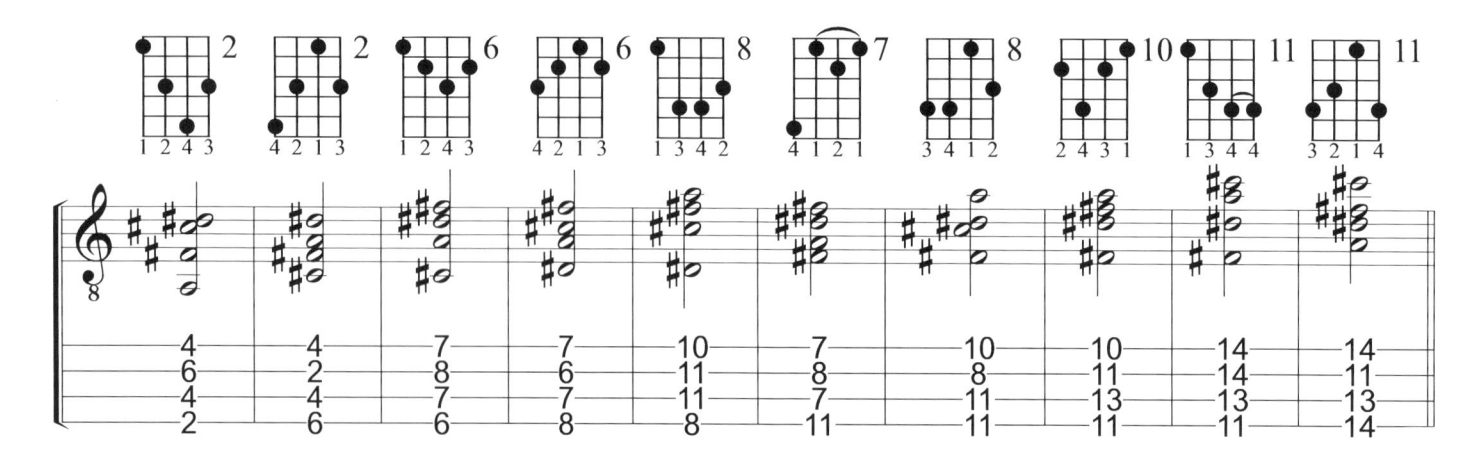

F#m7

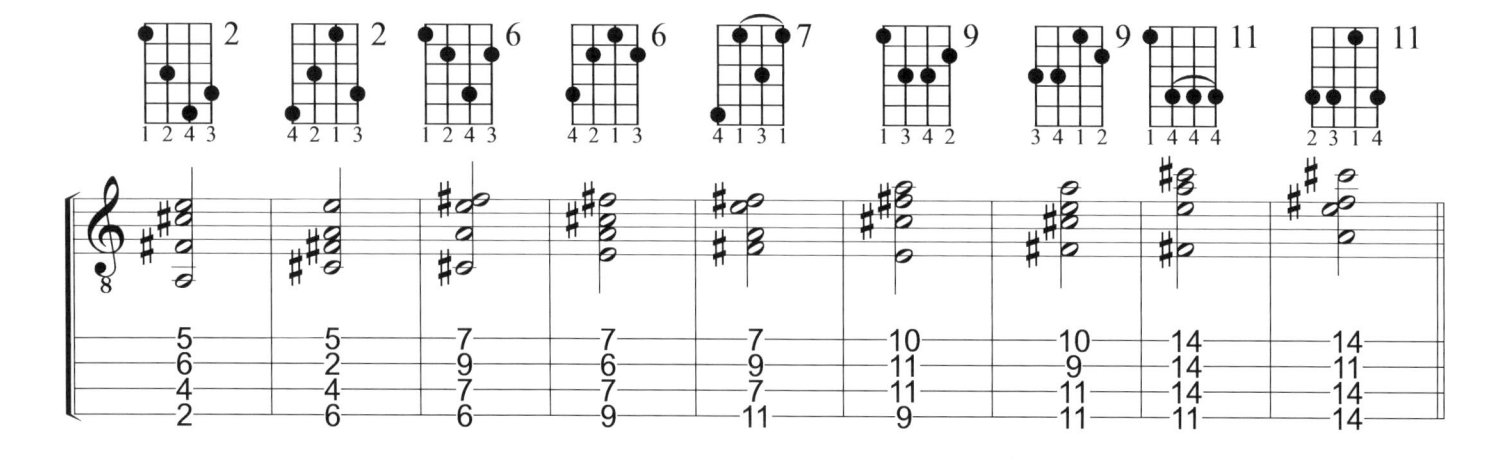

m7b5 - m9 - m11

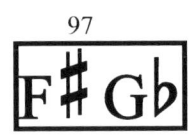

F# Gb

F#m7b5

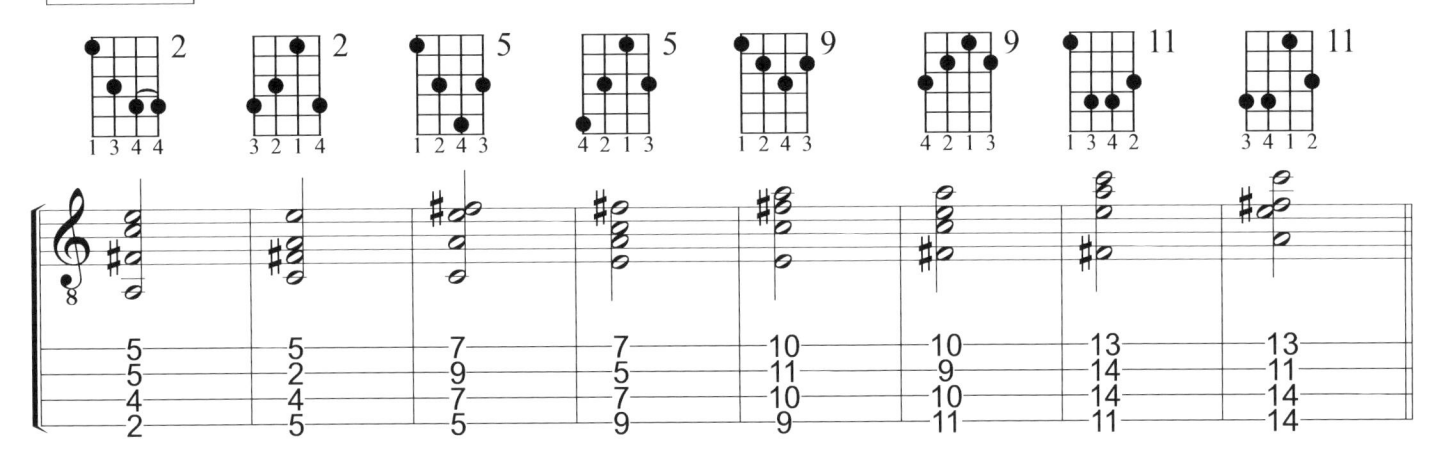

F#m9

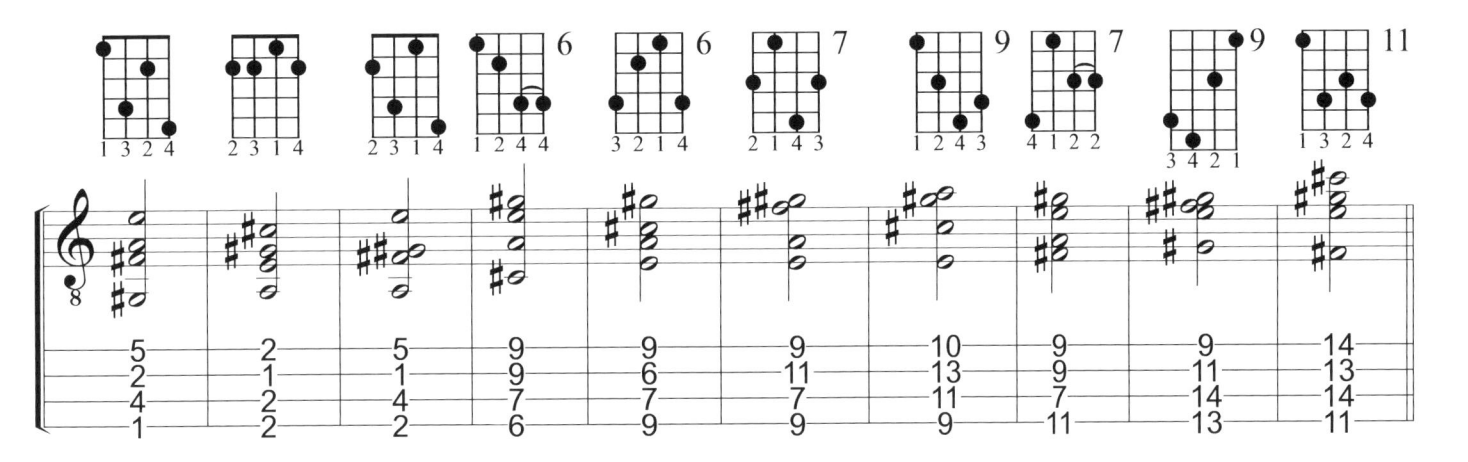

F#m11 **F#m(maj7)**

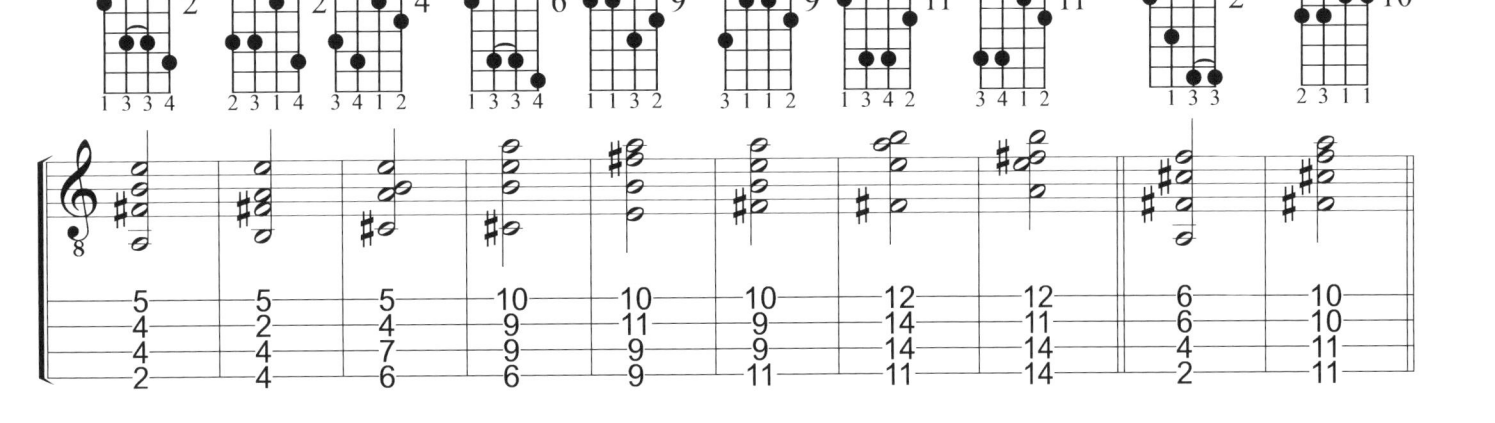

7th - 9th - 13th

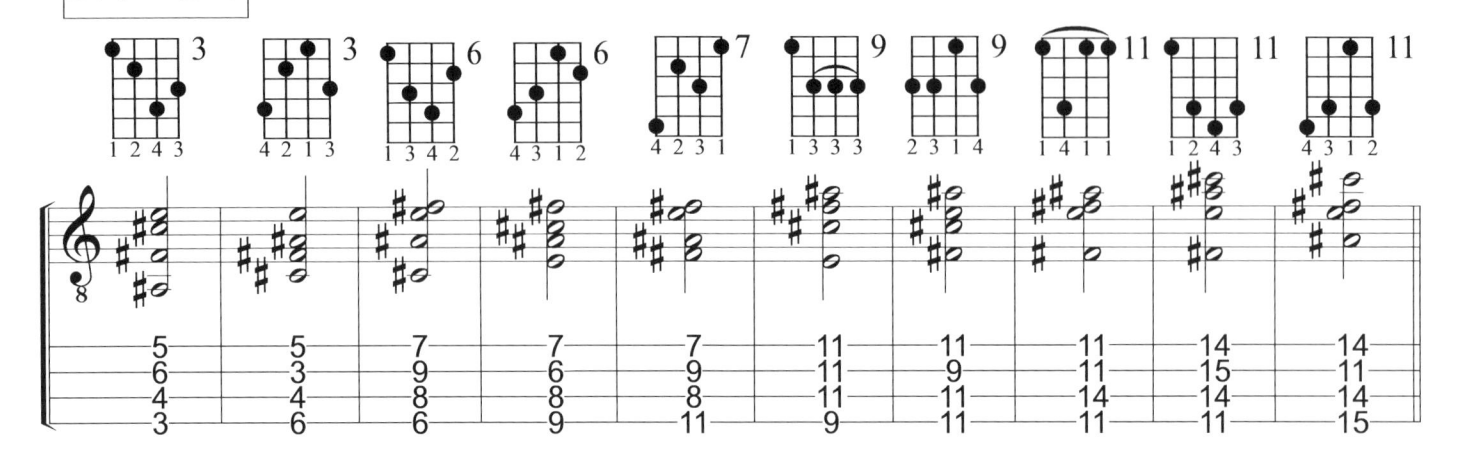

F# Gb

F#7 - Gb7

F#9 - Gb9

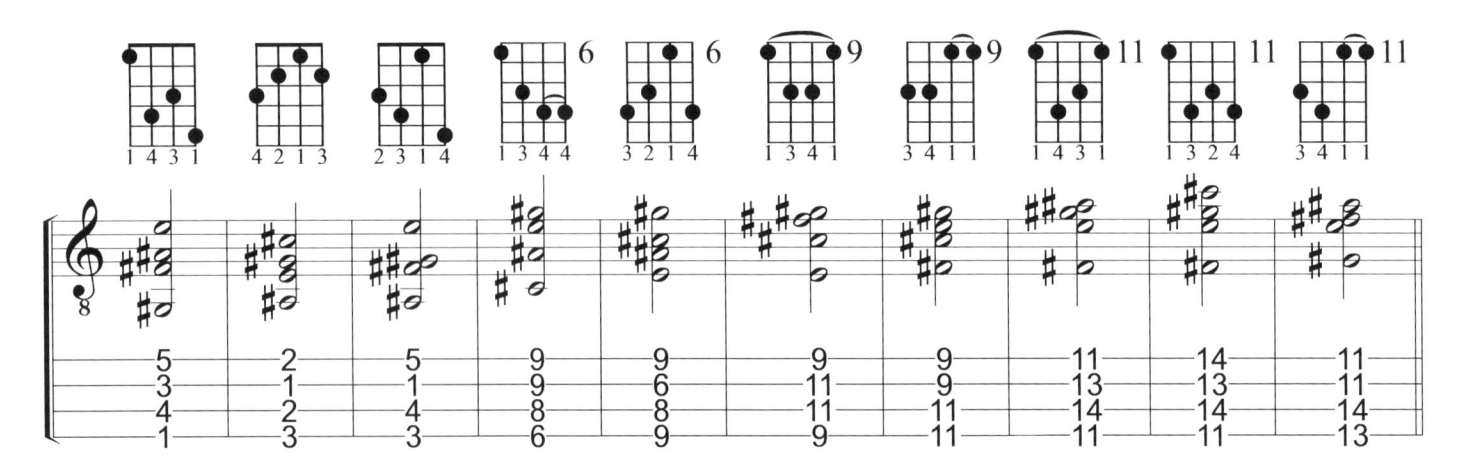

F#13 - Gb13

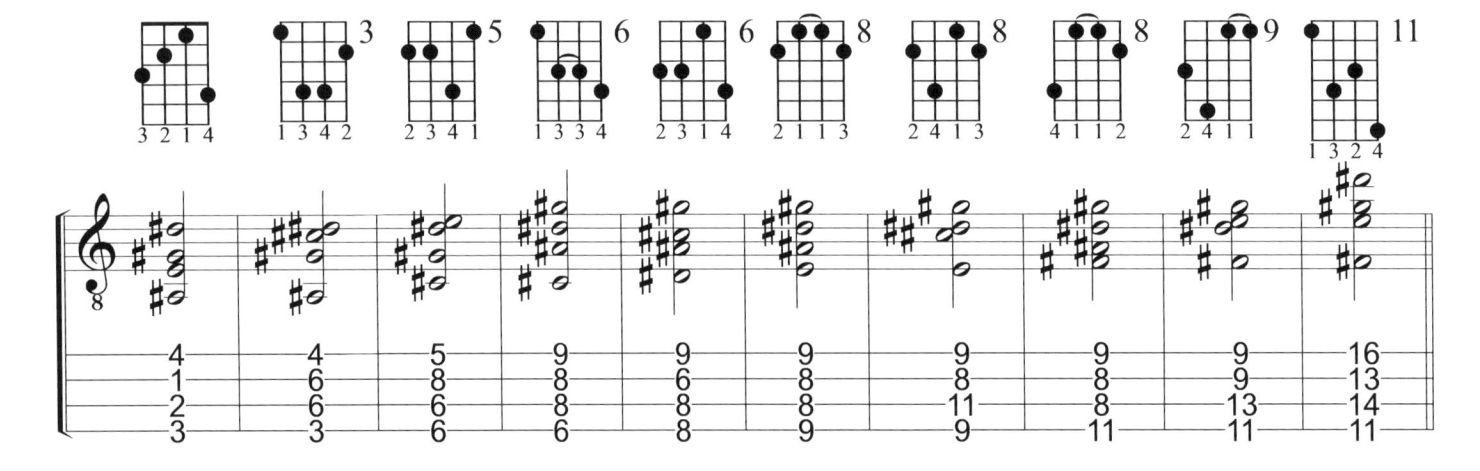

7b5 - 7#5 - 7#9

F# Gb

F#7b5 - Gb7b5

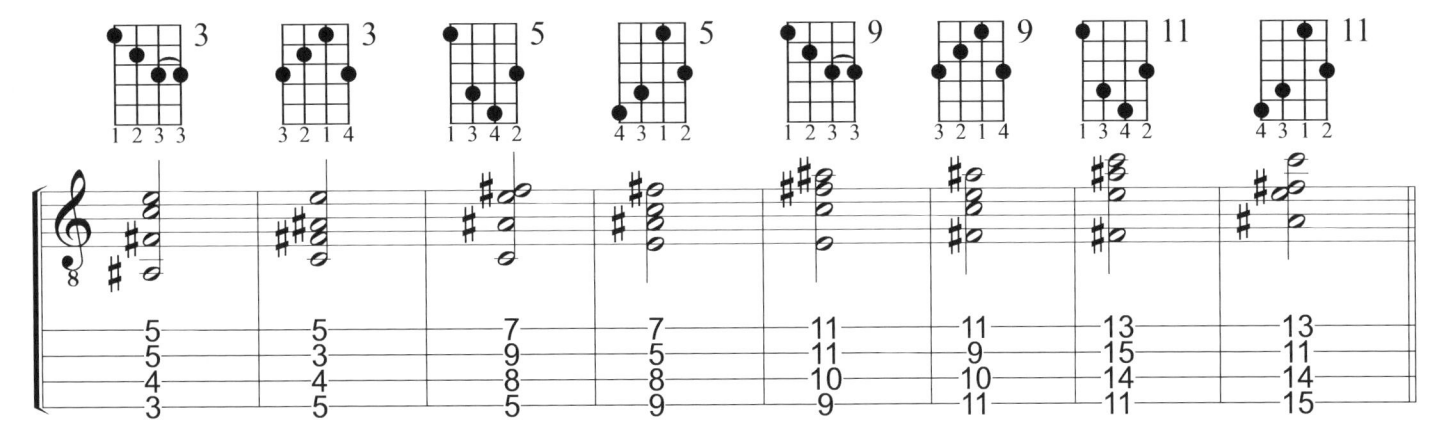

F#7#5 - Gb7#5

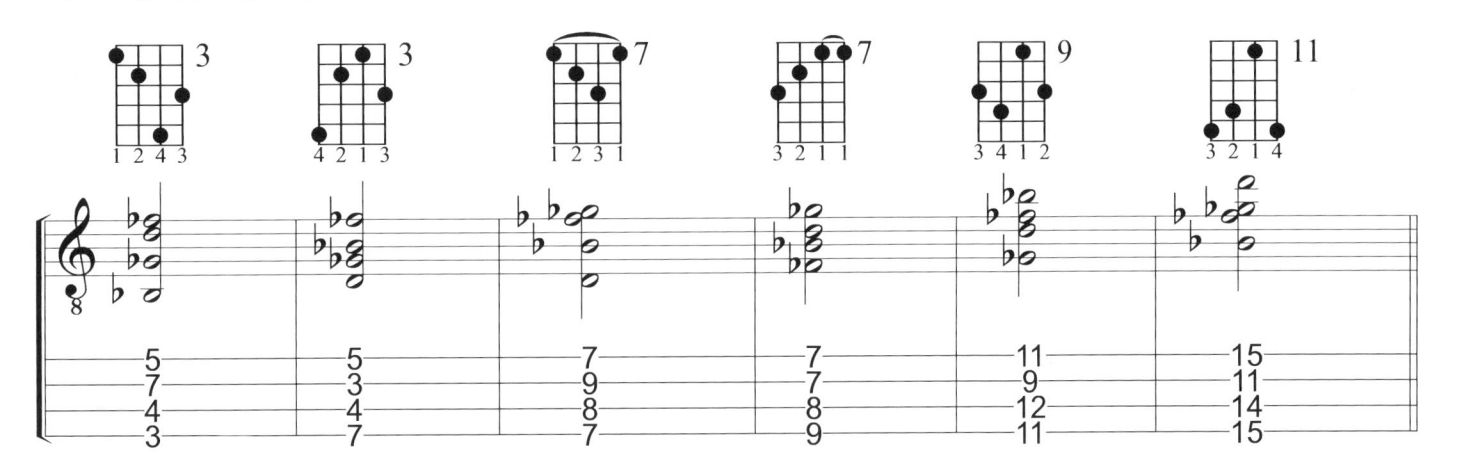

F#7#9 - Gb7#9

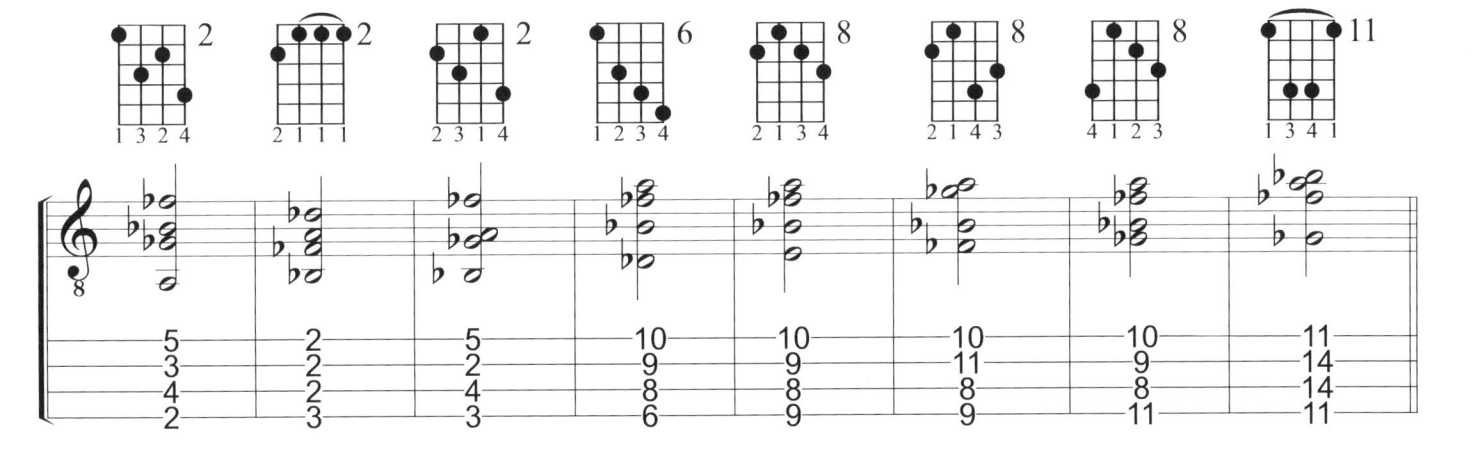

F# Gb

7b9 - diminished - °7

F#7b9

F# Diminished F#° - Gb Diminished - Gb°

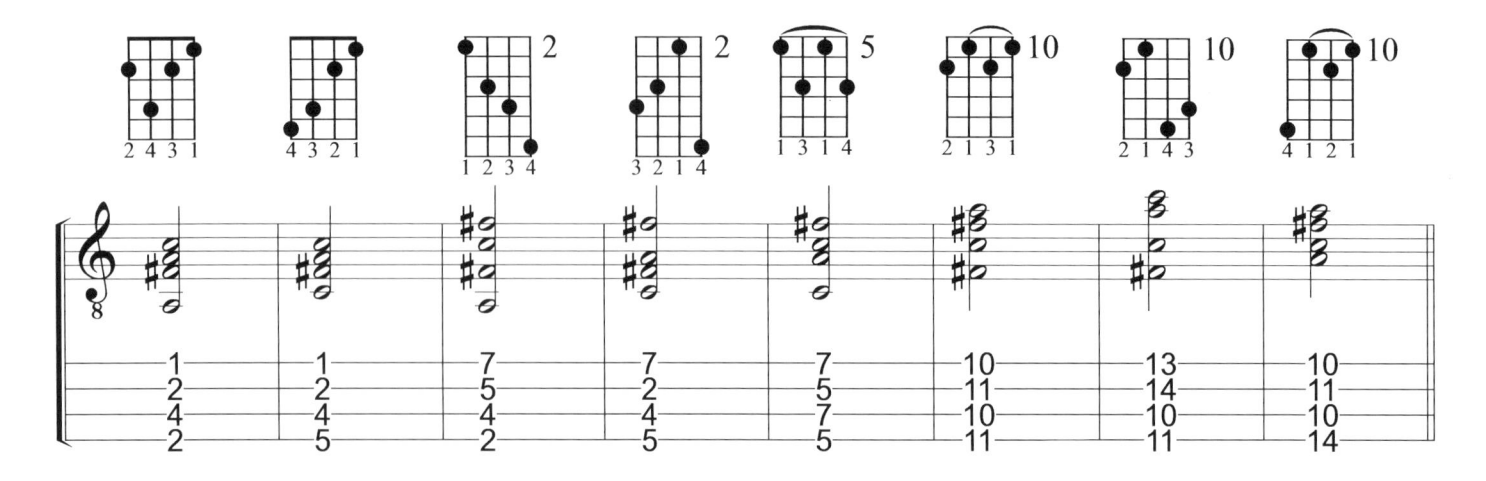

F#/Gb Diminished 7th - F#°7 Gb°7

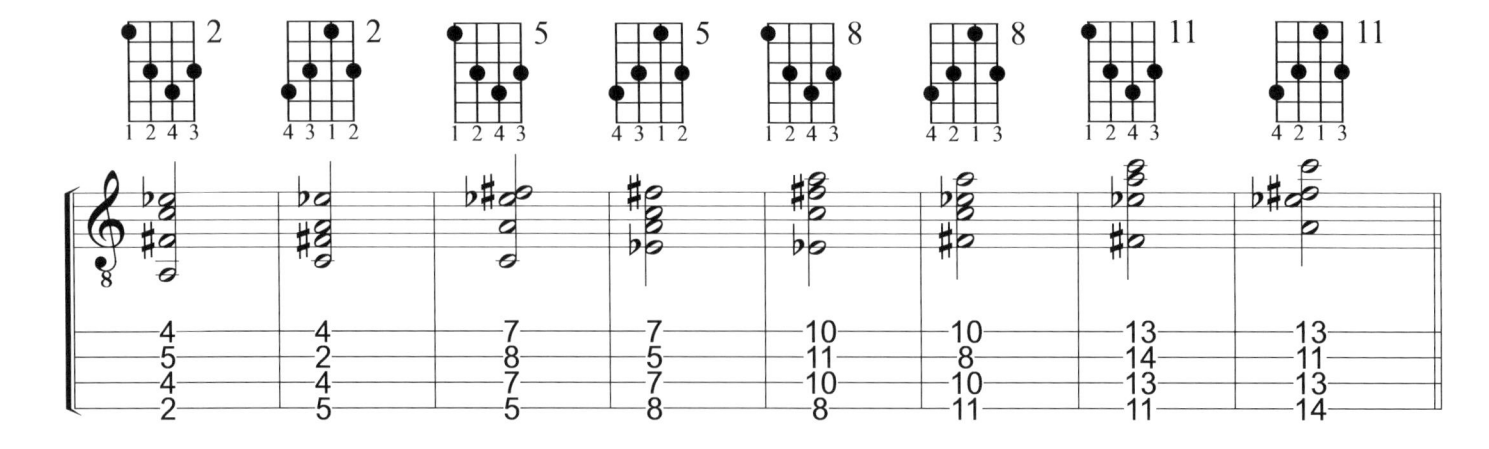

sus4 - sus2 - add9 - 7sus - 5th

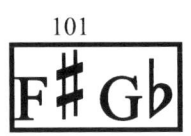

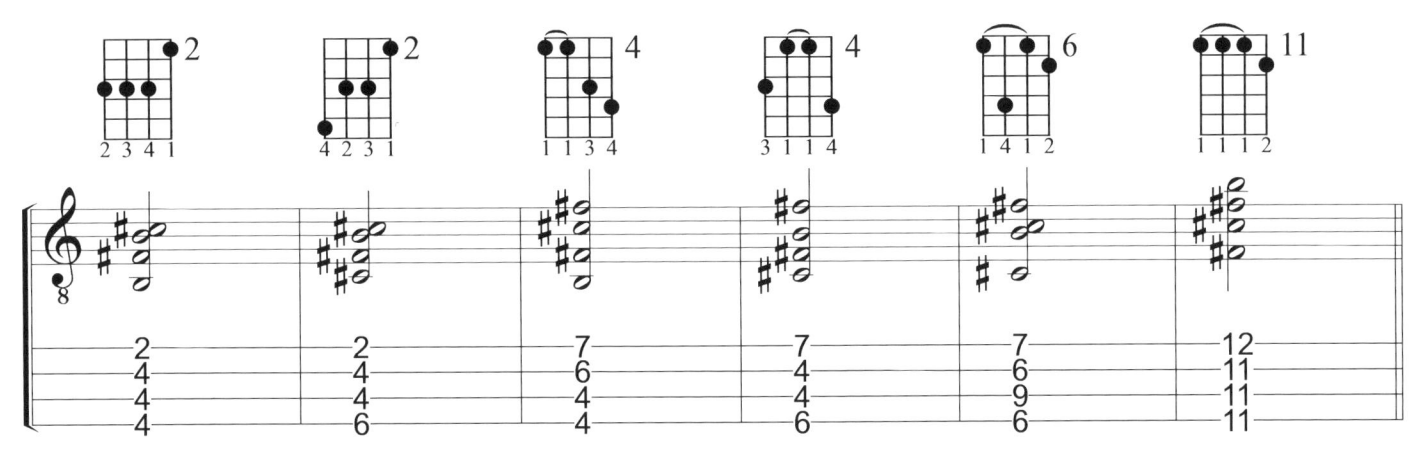

F# Gb

F#sus4 - Gbsus4

F#sus2 - Gbsus2

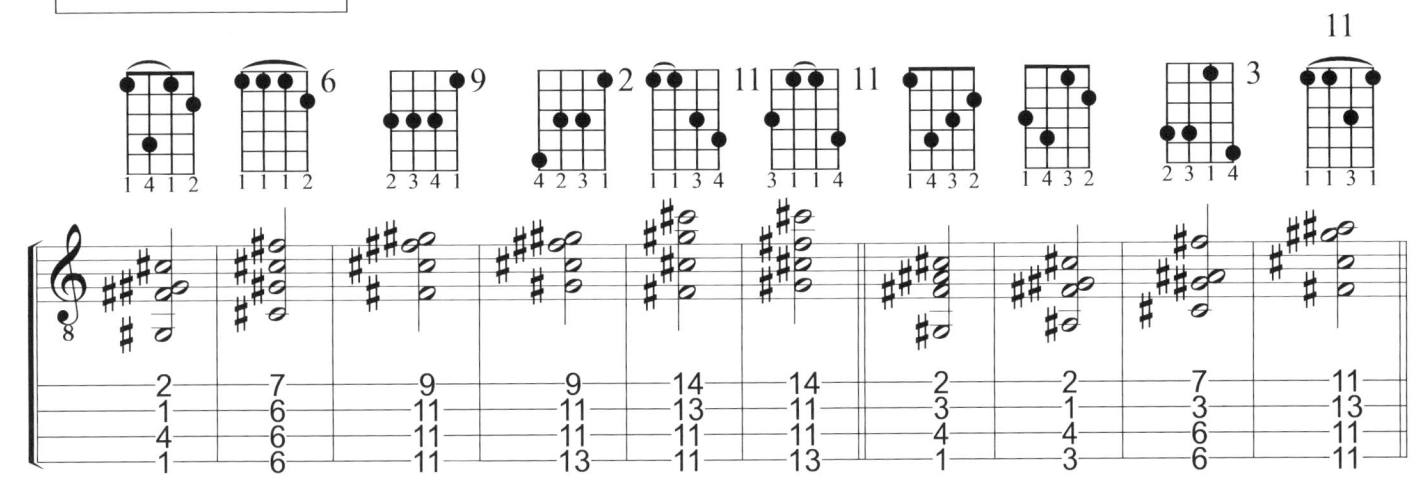

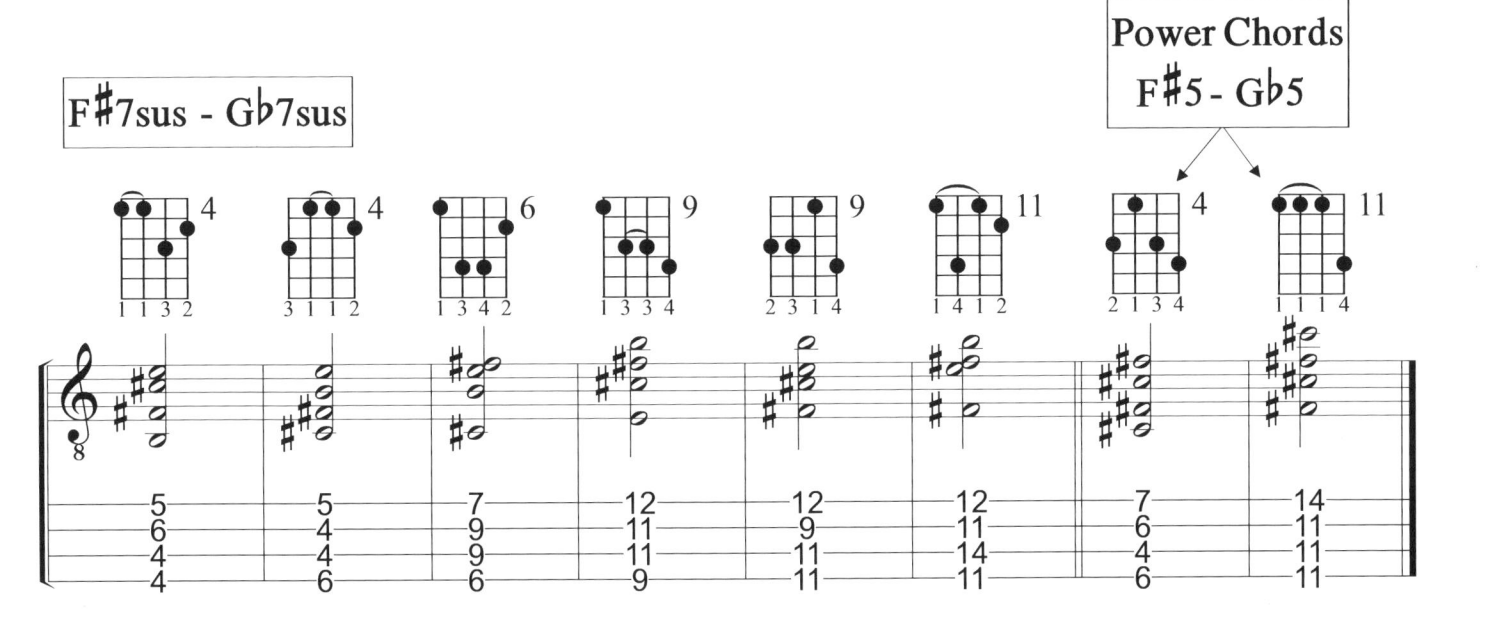

F#add9 - Gbadd9

F#7sus - Gb7sus

Power Chords F#5 - Gb5

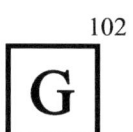

G Major - G6 - Gmaj7

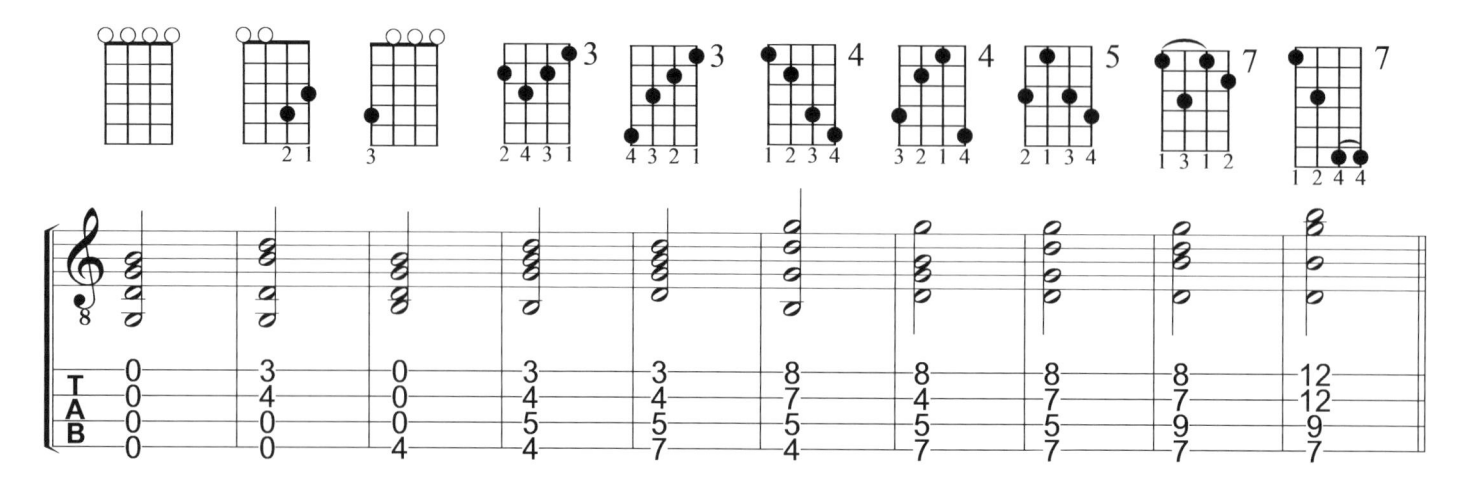

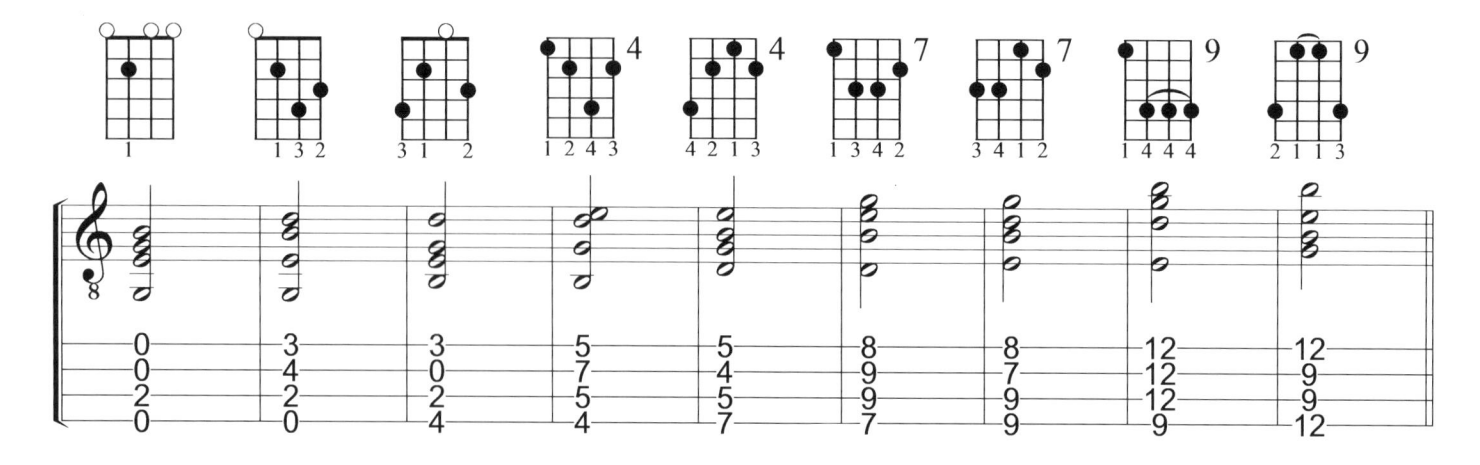

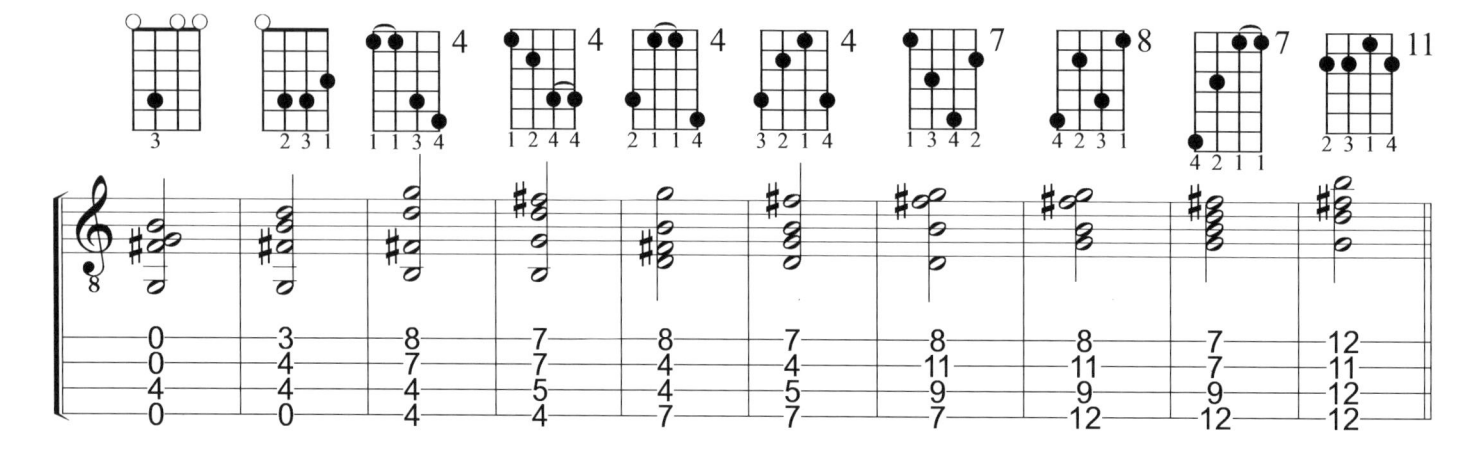

Gmaj9 - G6/9 - G+ augmented

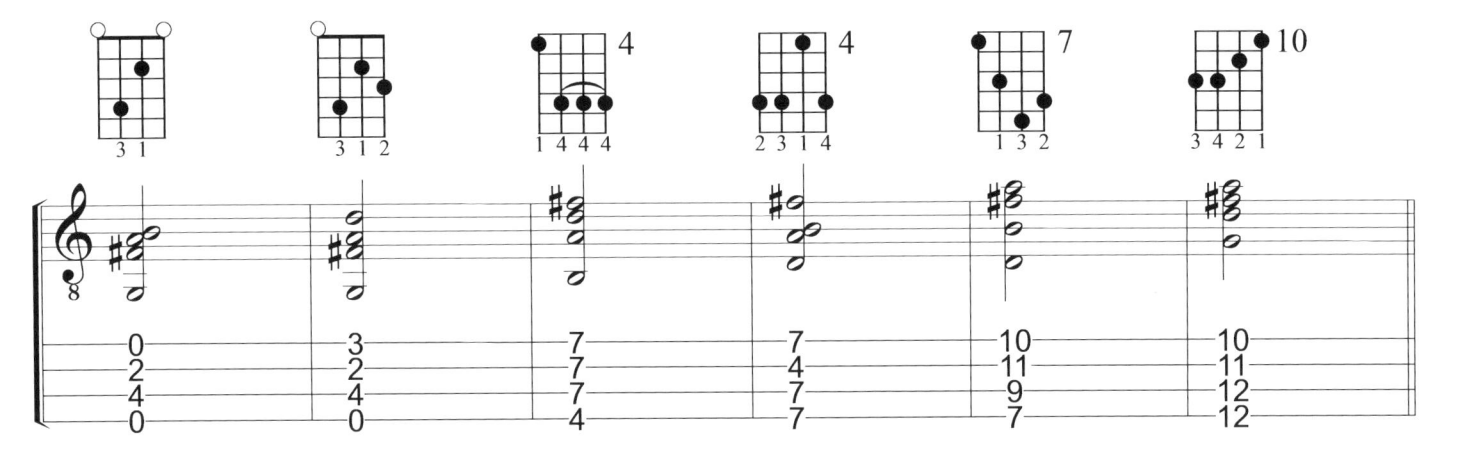

Gmaj9

G6/9

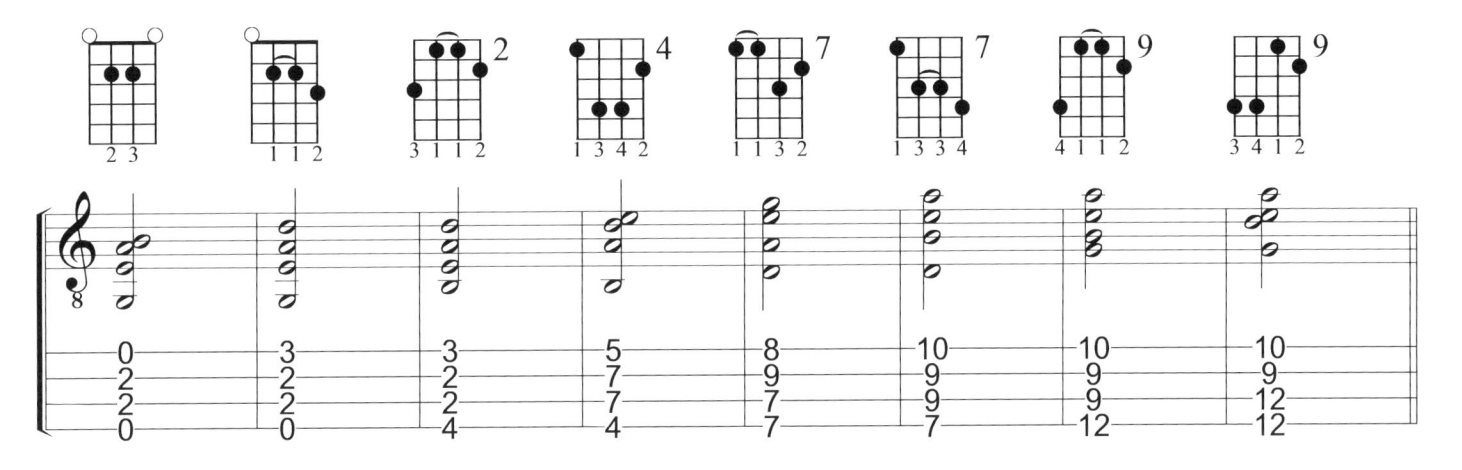

G Augmented - G+

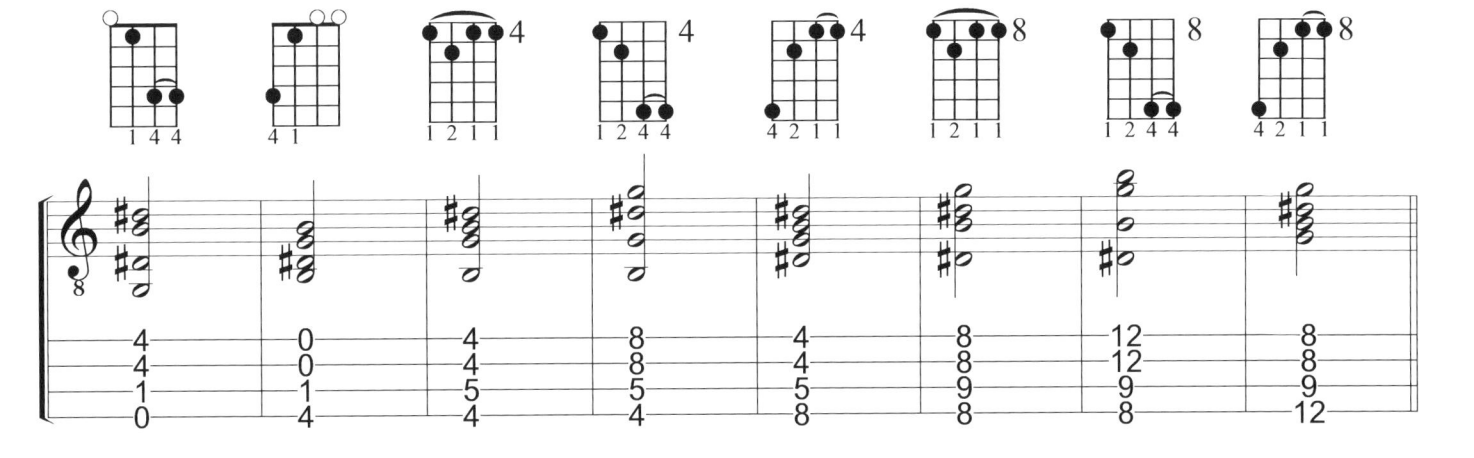

Gm - Gm6 - Gm7

G Minor

Gm6

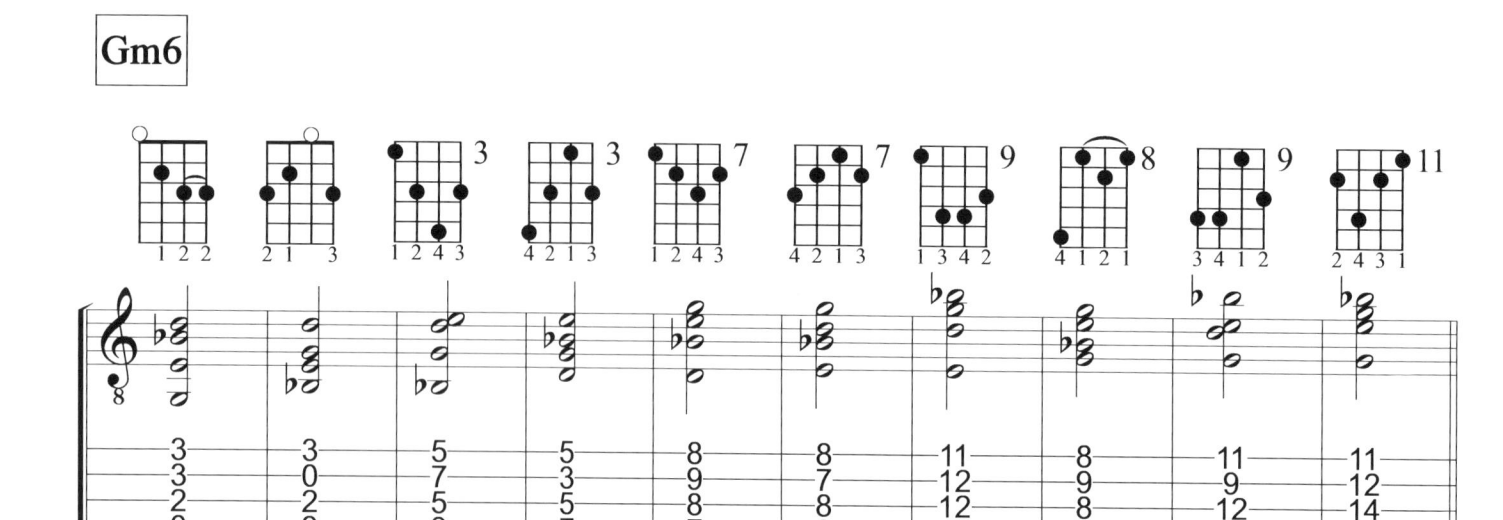

Gm7

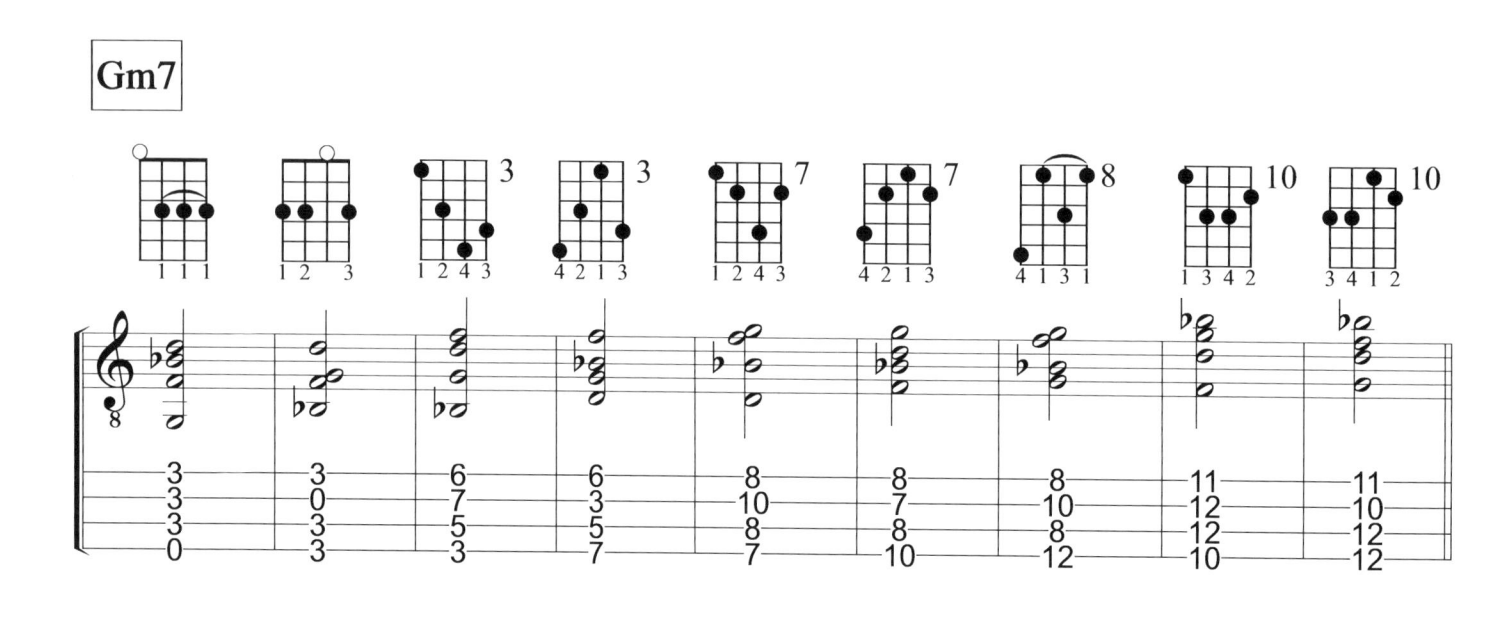

Gm7♭5 - Gm9 - Gm11 - Gm(maj7)

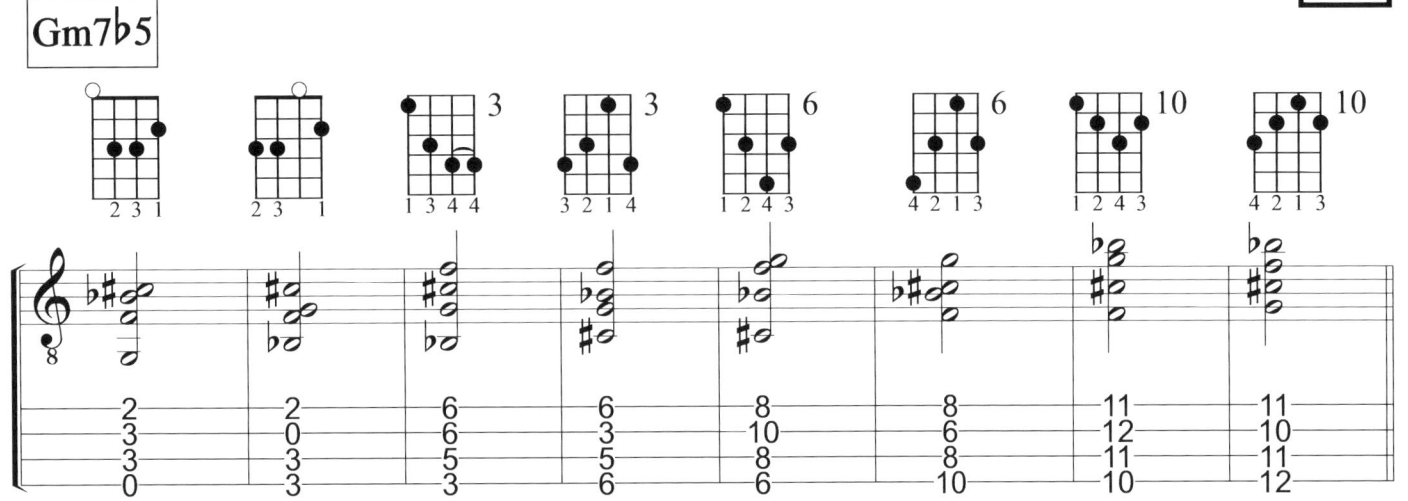

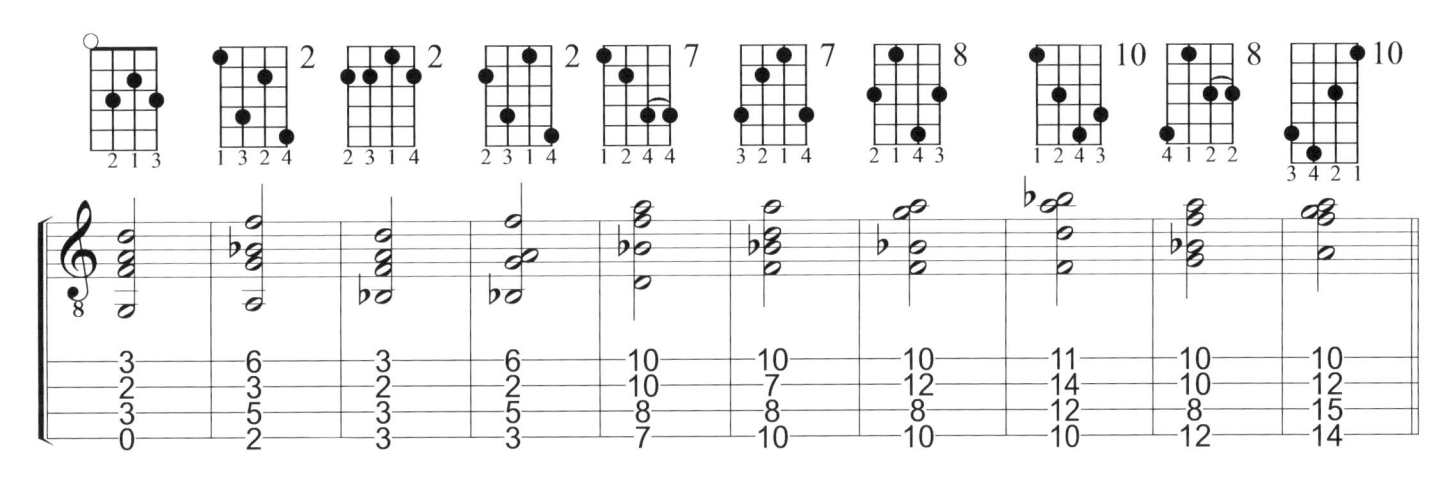

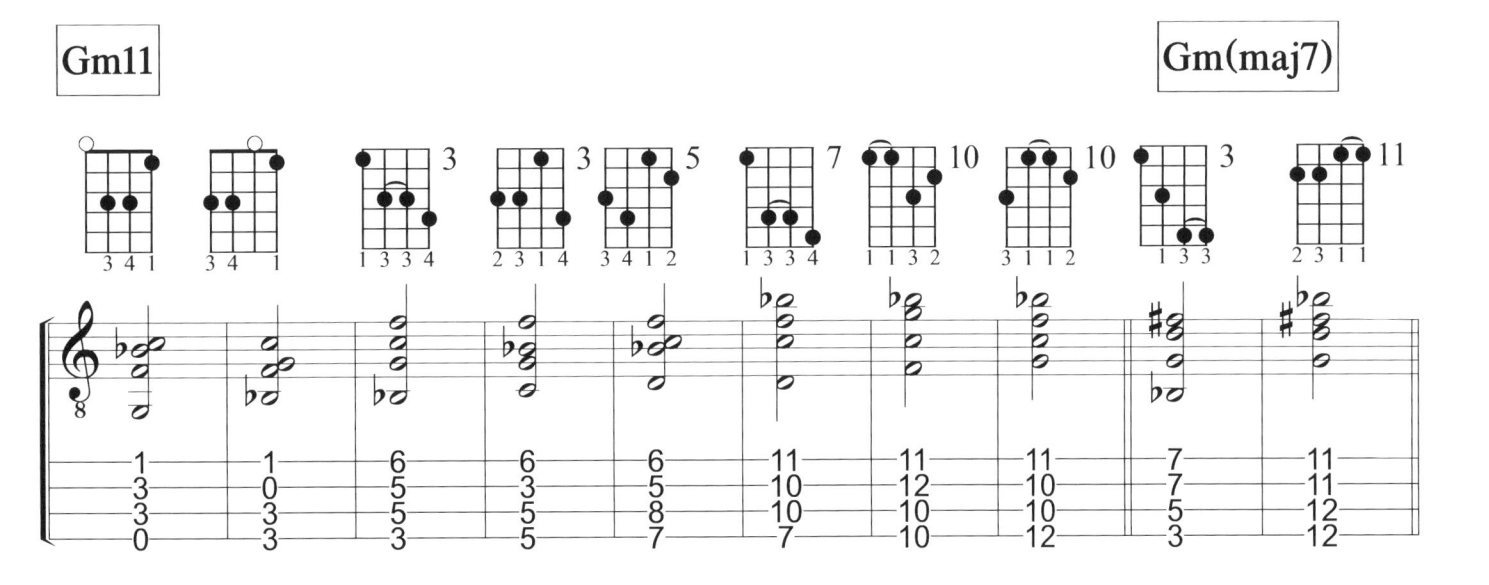

G7 - G9 - G13

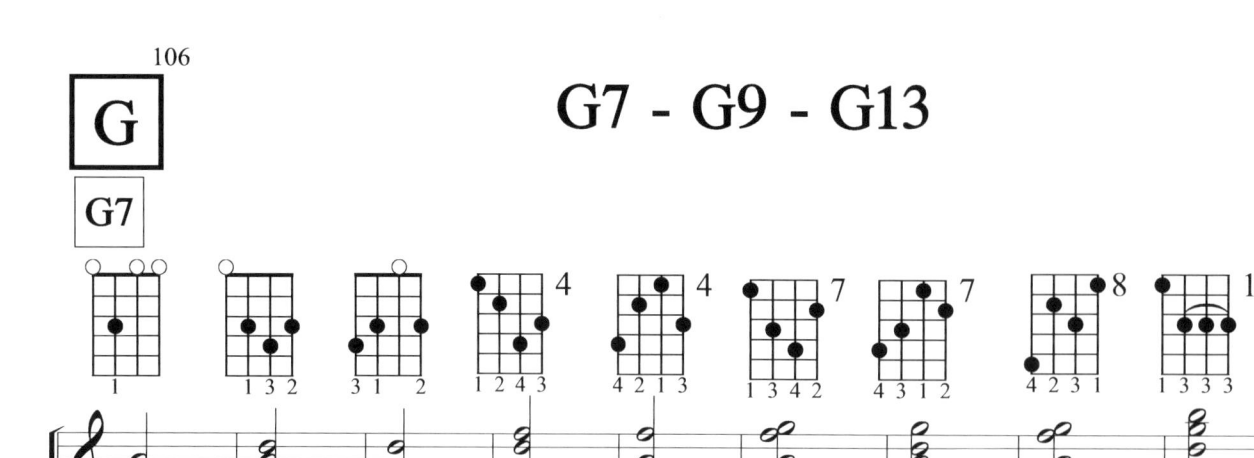

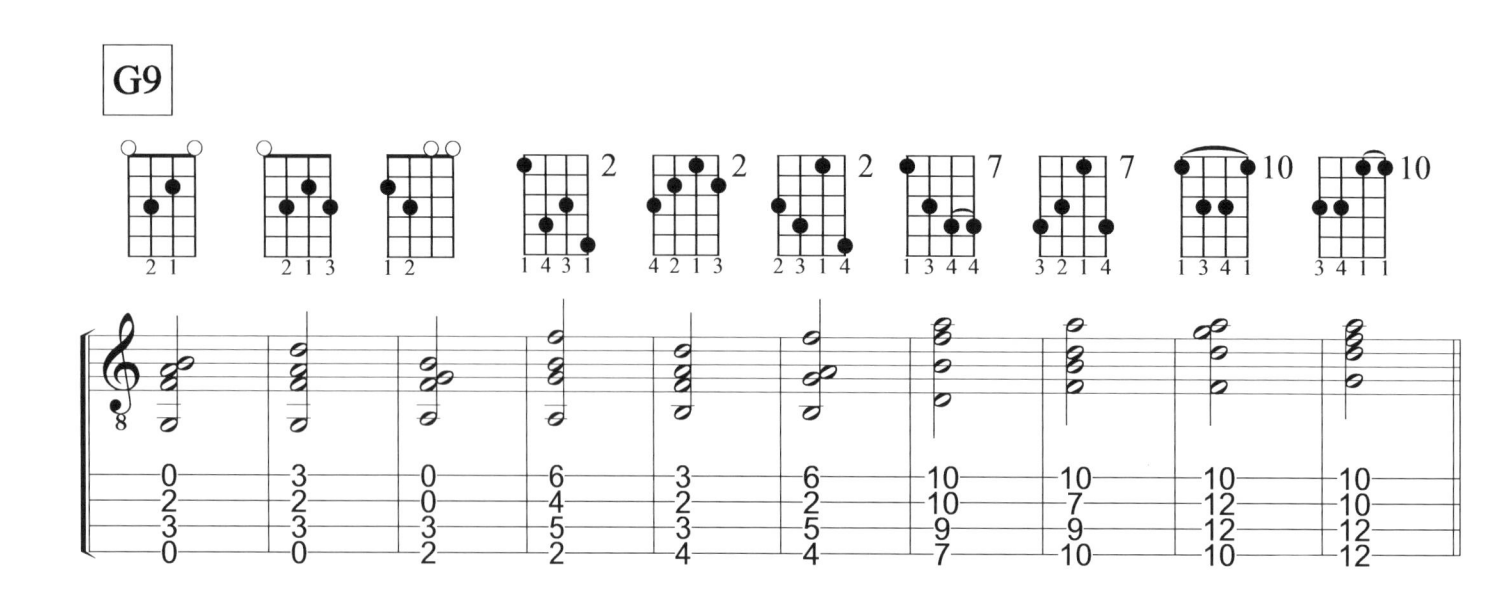

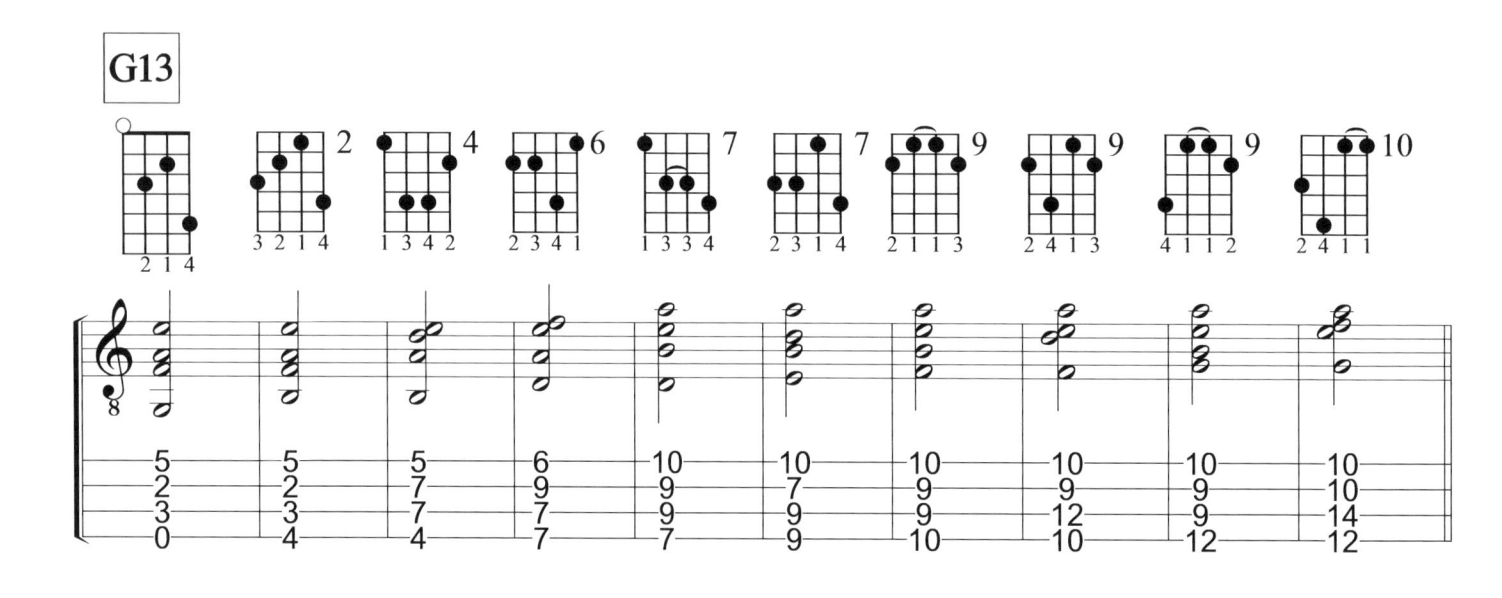

G7♭5 - G7♯5 - G7♯9

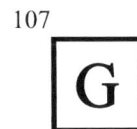

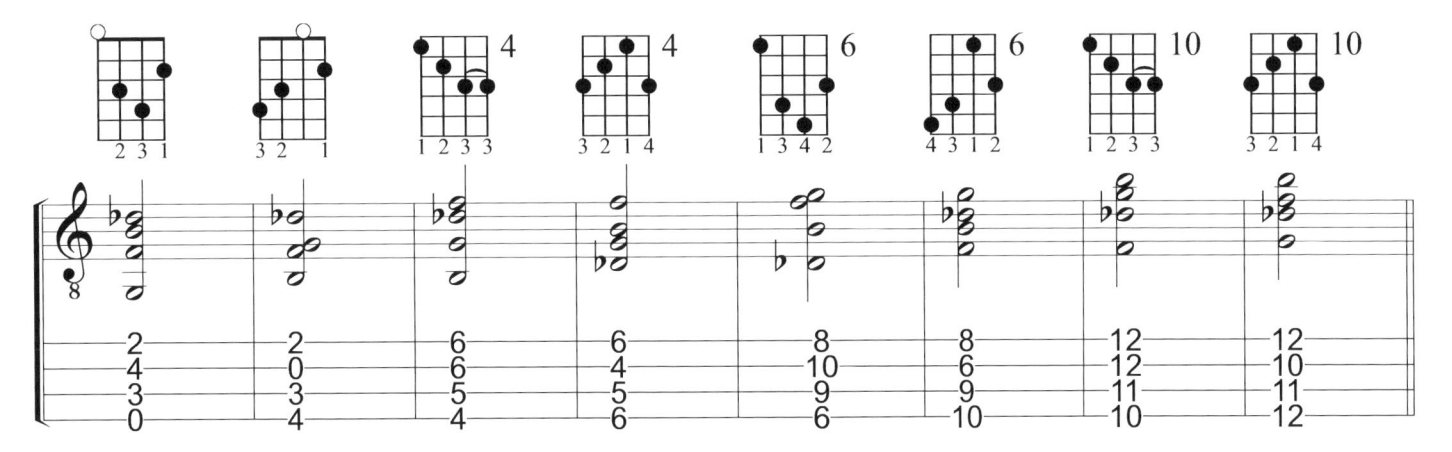

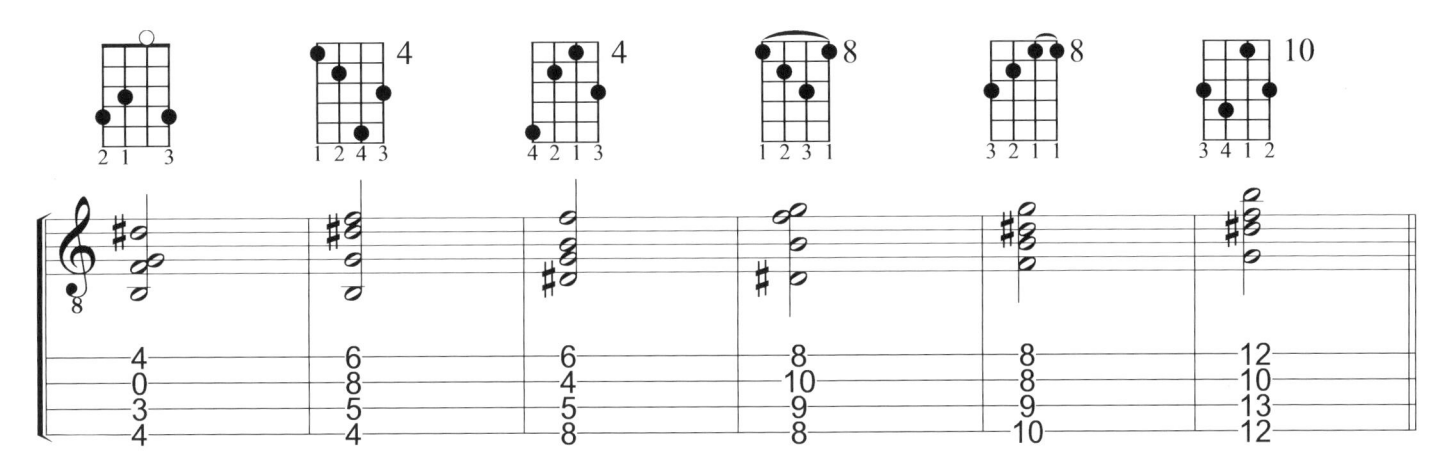

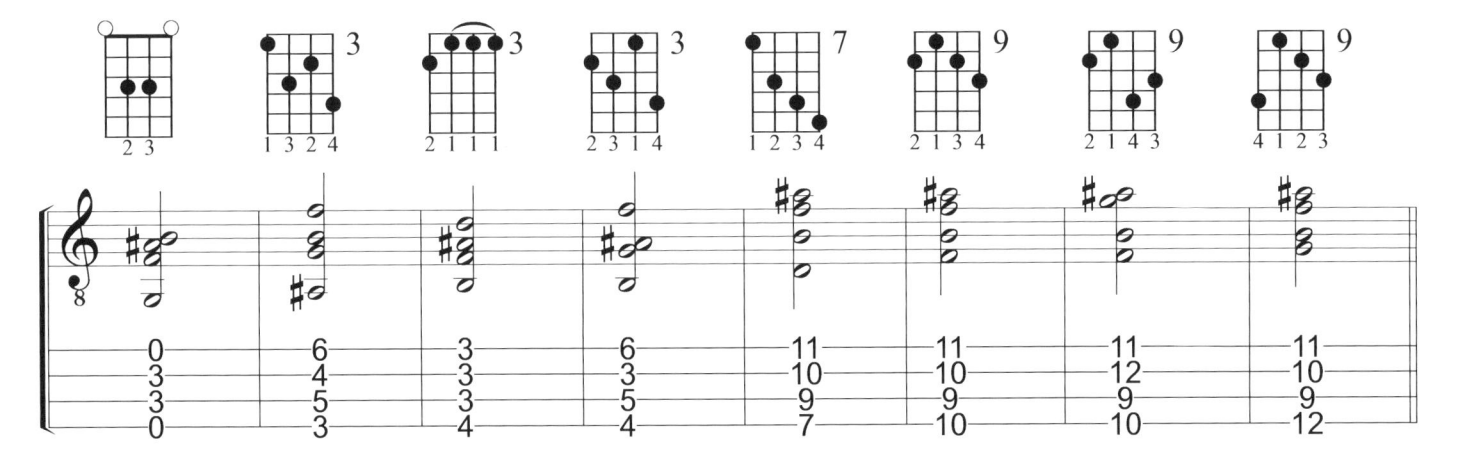

G7♭9 - G diminished - G°7

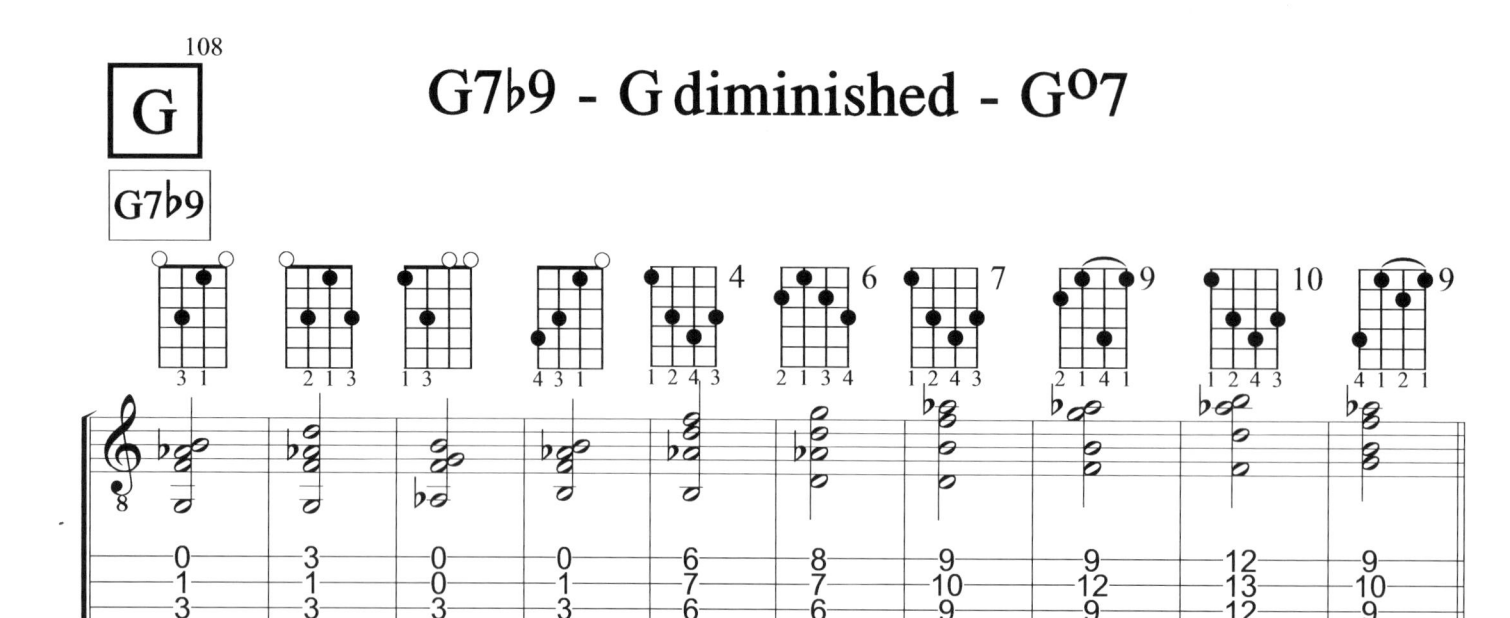

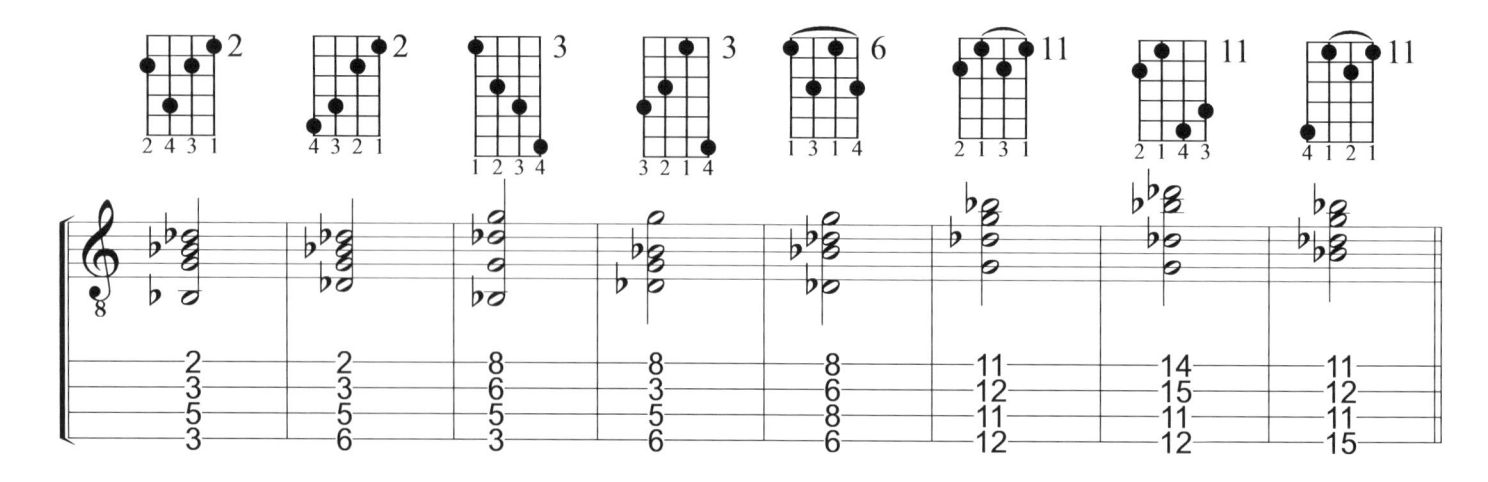

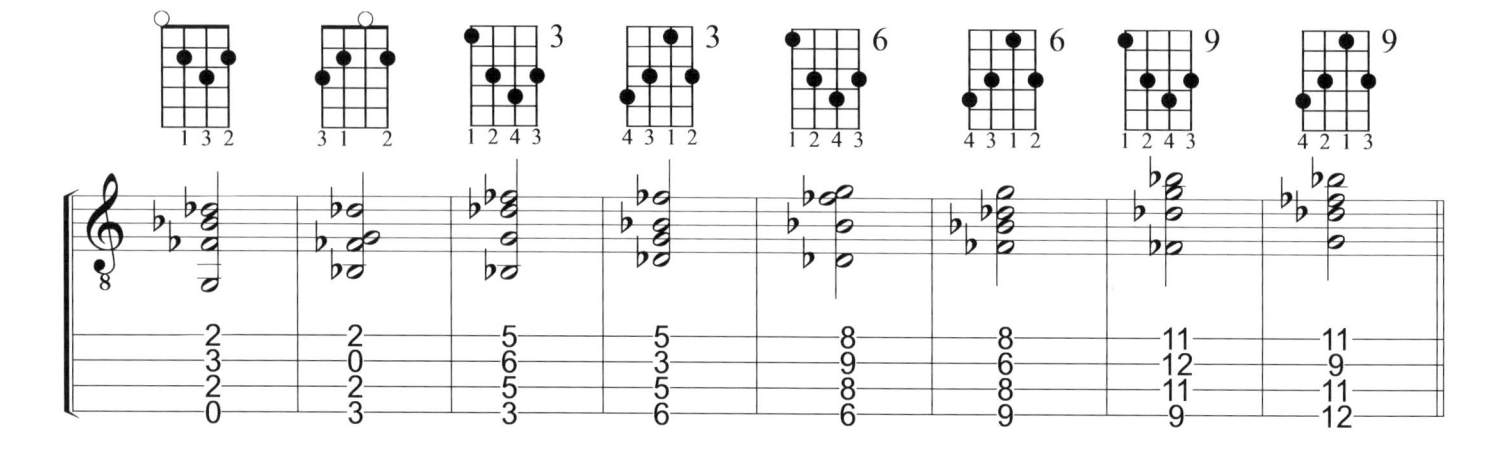

Gsus4 - Gsus2 - Gadd9 - G7sus - G5

Gsus4

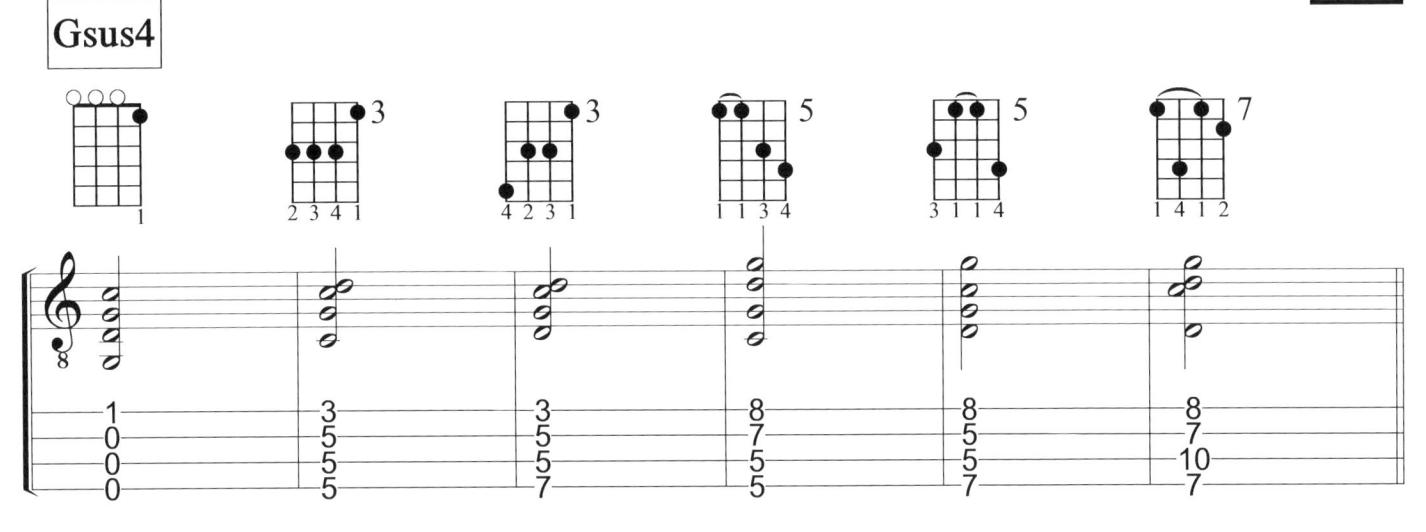

Gsus2

Gadd9

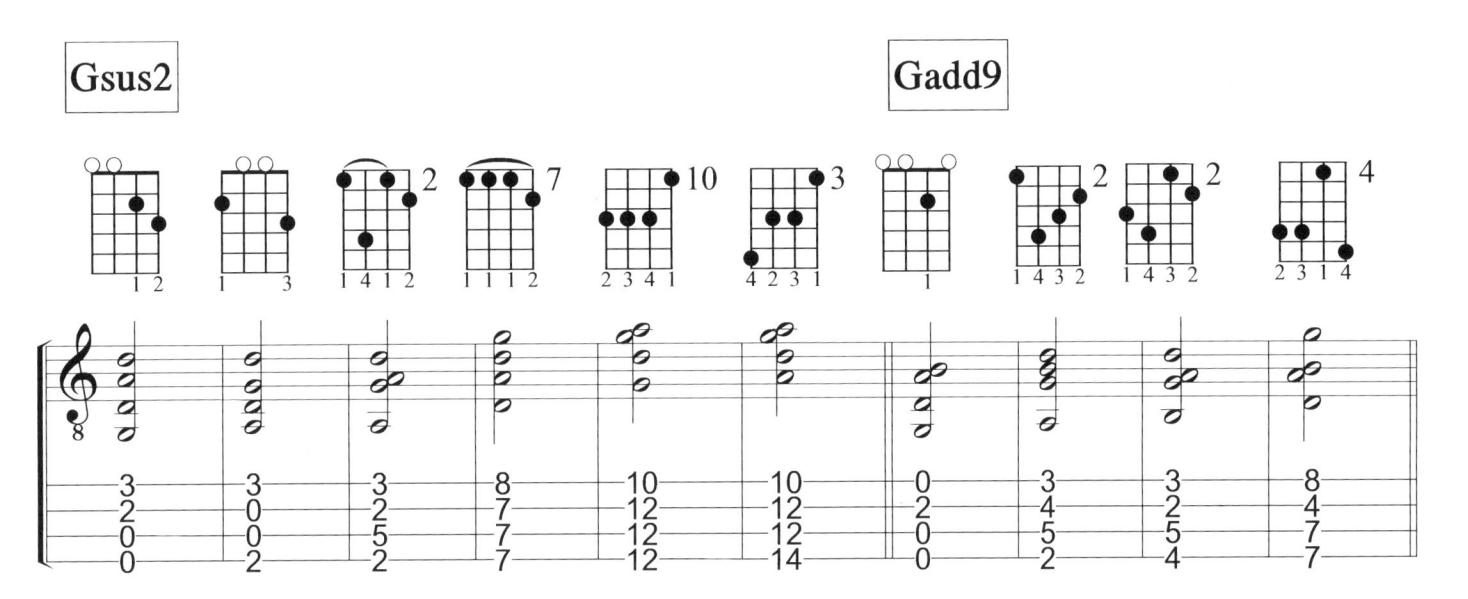

G7sus

Power Chords G5

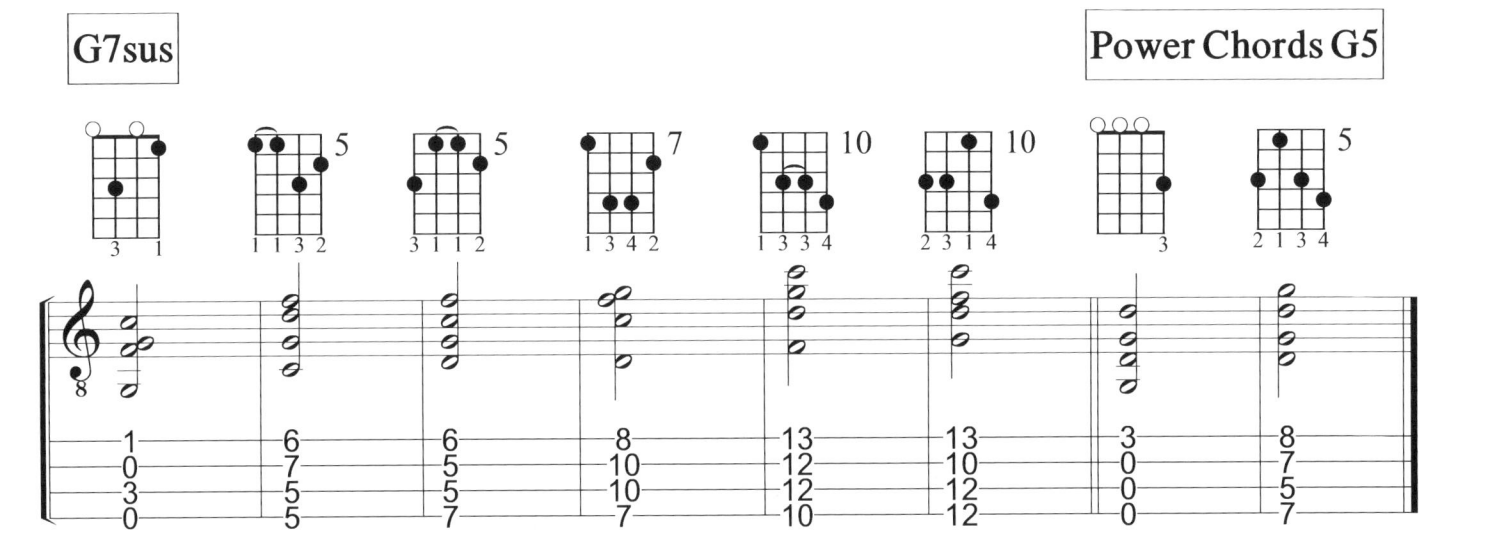

Major - 6 - Maj7

110

A♭ G♯

Chords are shown as either sharps or flats in the notation line.
For example, G#m is shown instead of Abm.

A♭ Major - G♯ Major

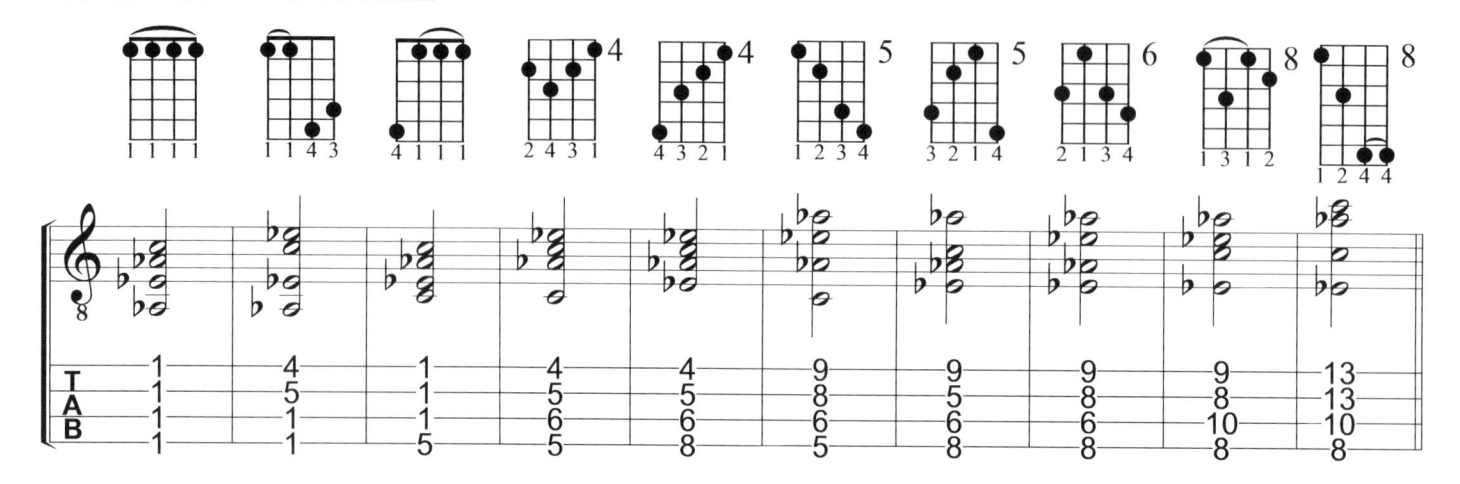

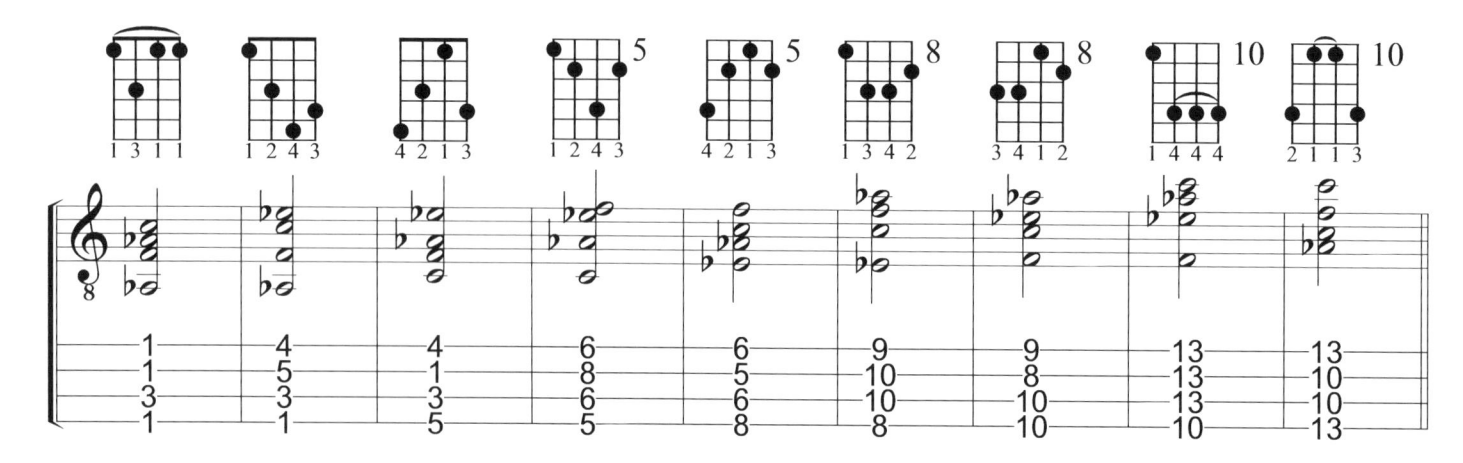

A♭6 - G♯6

A♭maj7 - G♯maj7

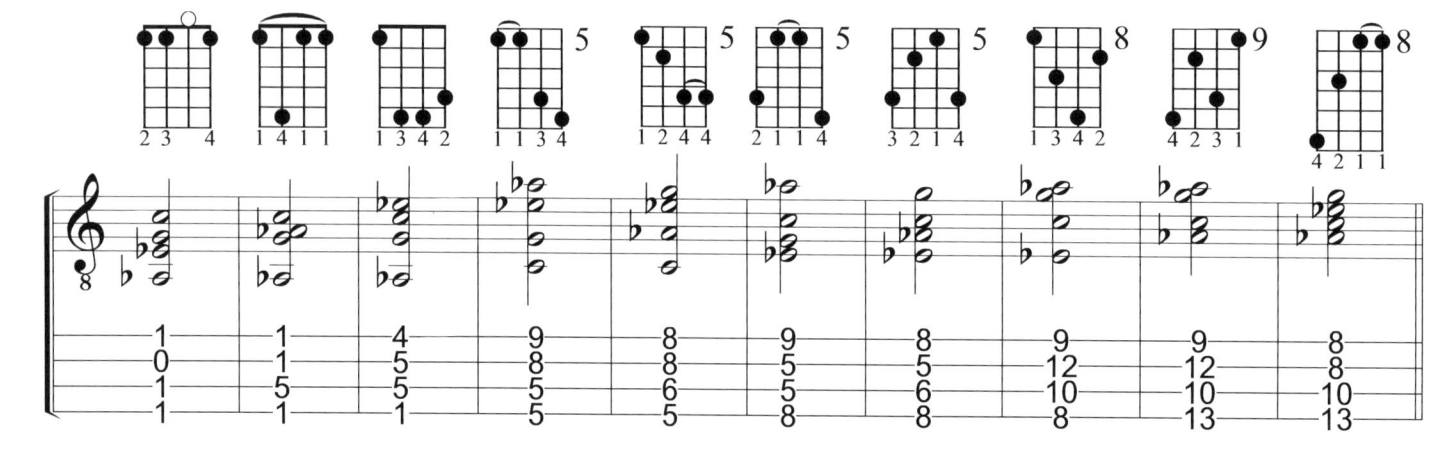

Maj9 - 6/9 - Augmented+

Ab G#

Abmaj9 - G#maj9

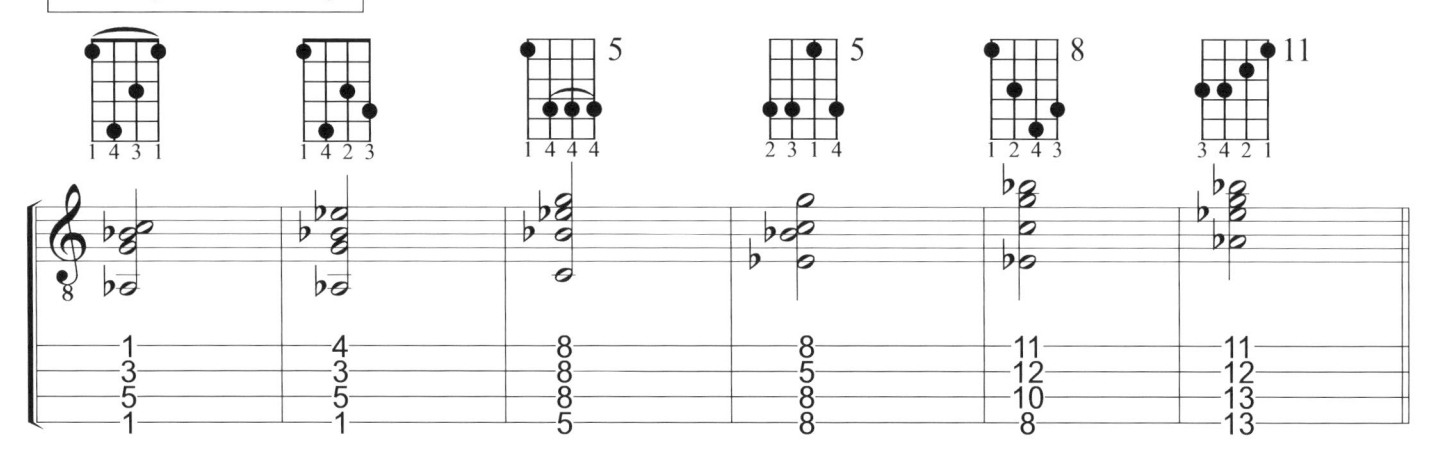

Ab6/9 - G#6/9

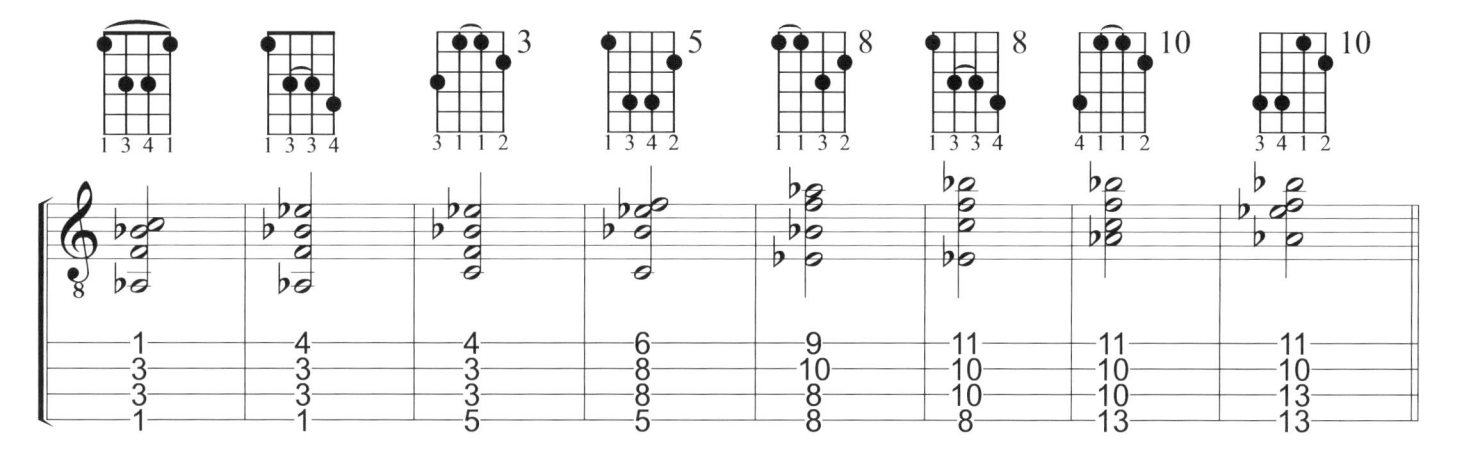

Ab Augmented (Ab+) G# Augmented (G#+)

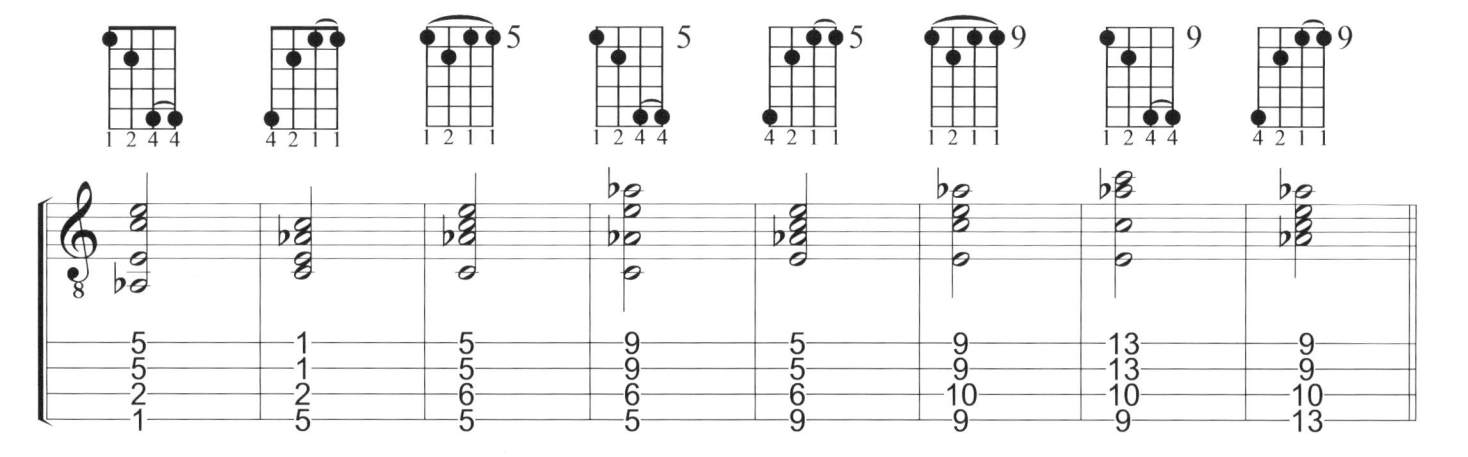

A♭ G♯ minor - m6 - m7

G♯minor - A♭minor

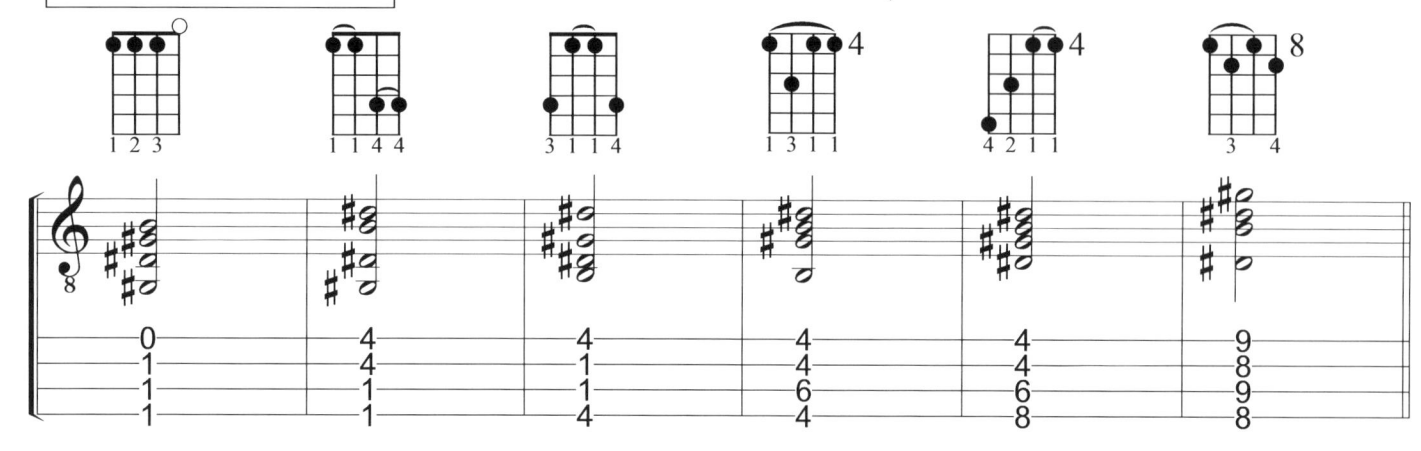

G♯m6 - A♭m6

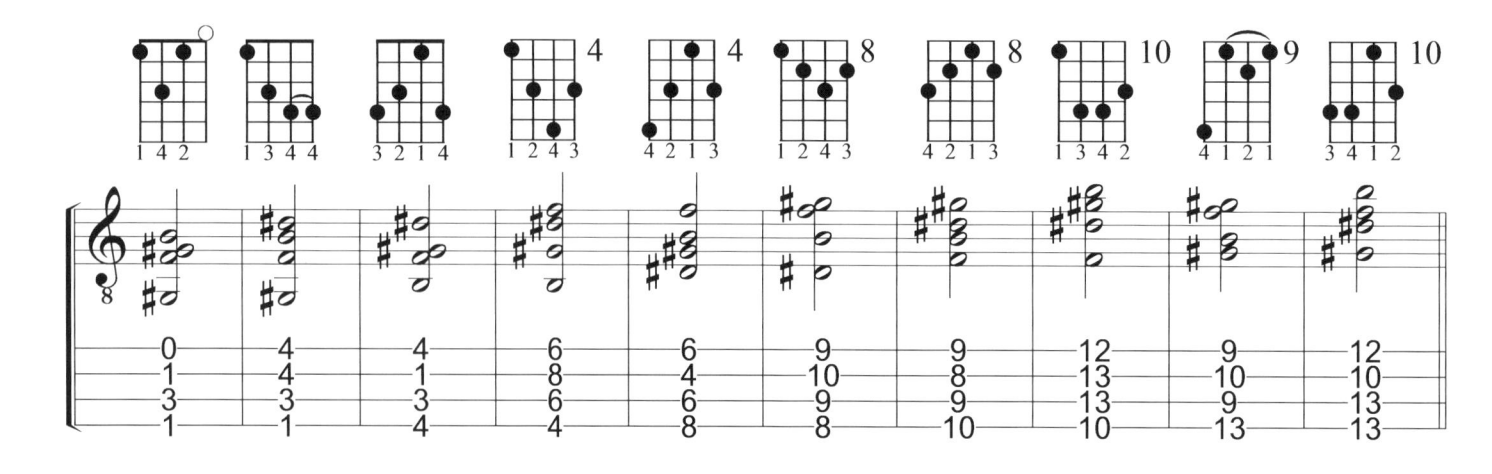

G♯m7 - A♭m7

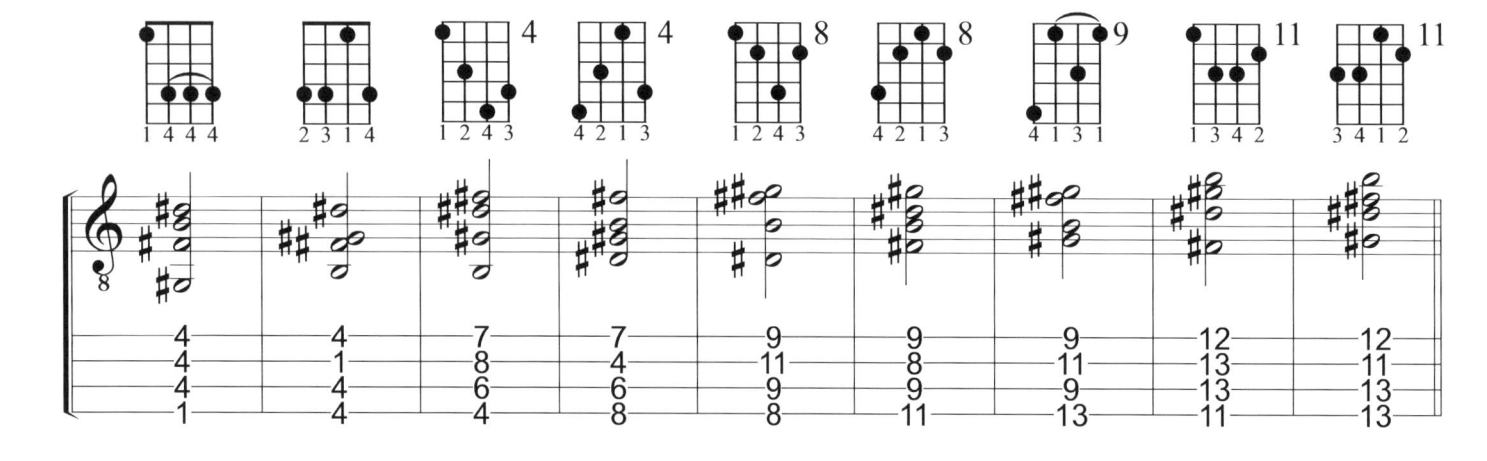

m7b5 - m9 - m11 - m(maj7)

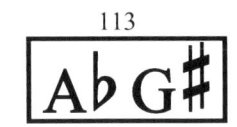

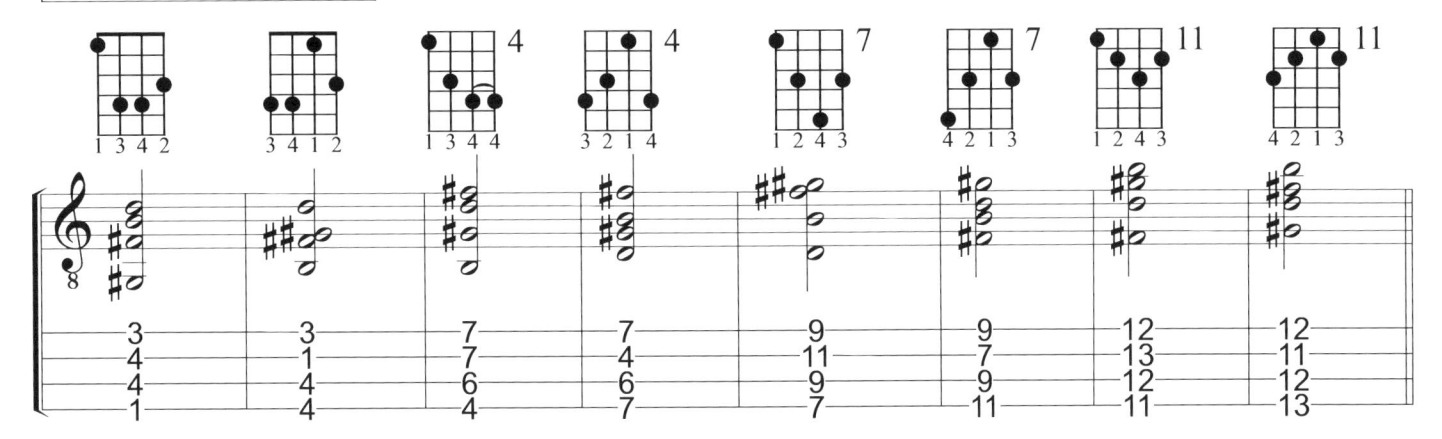

Ab G# 113

G#m7b5 - Abm7b5

G#m9 - Abm9

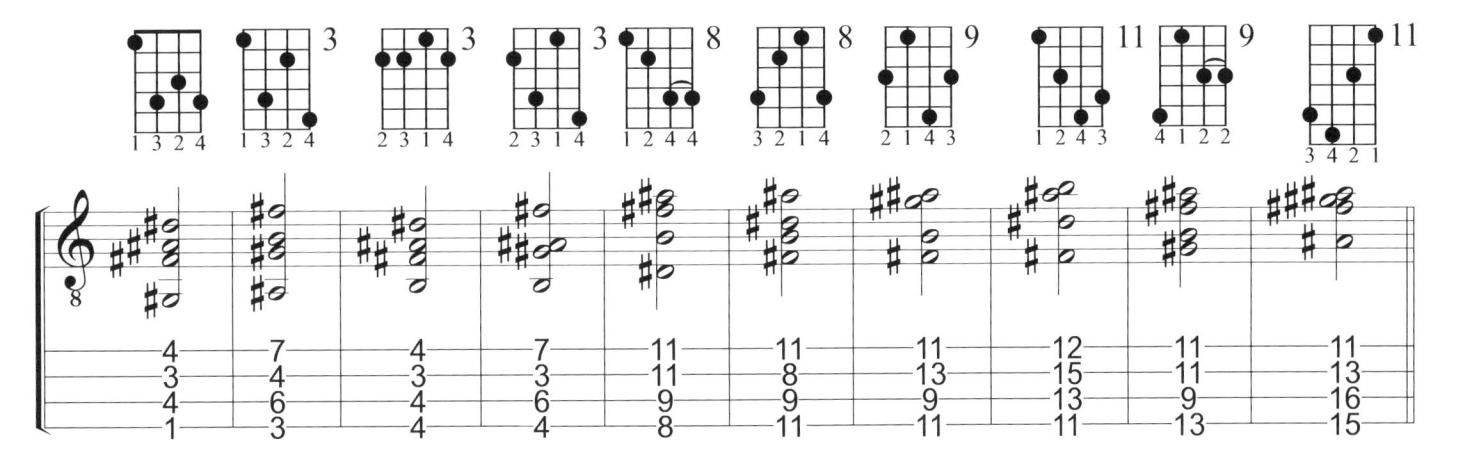

G#m11 - Abm11

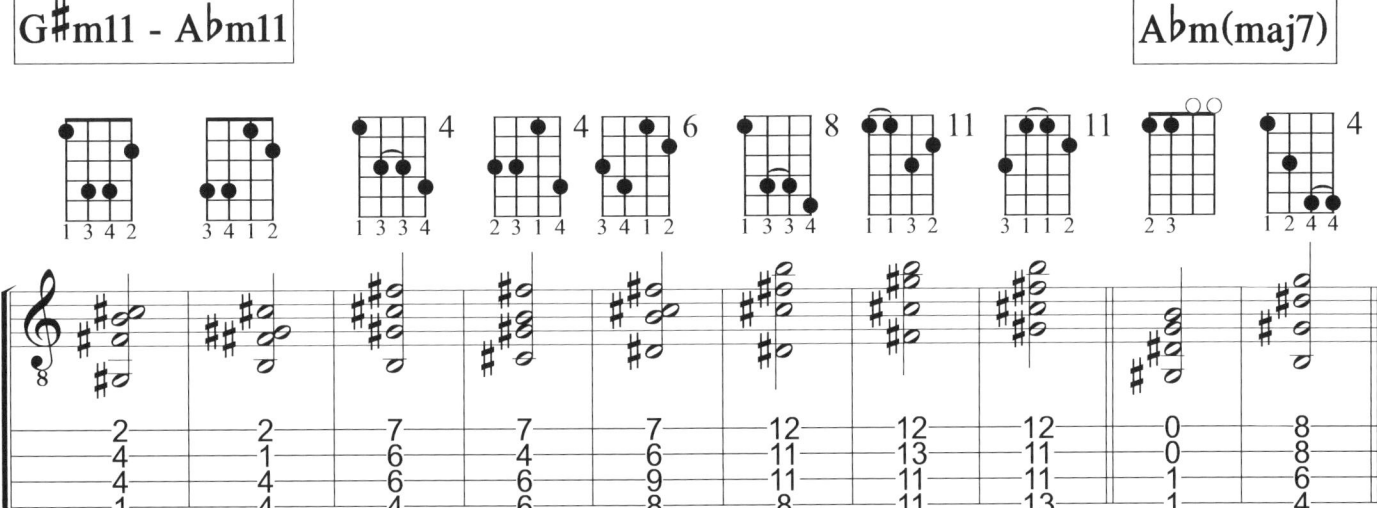

G#m(maj7) / Abm(maj7)

7th - 9th - 13th

A♭ G♯ 114

A♭7 - G♯7

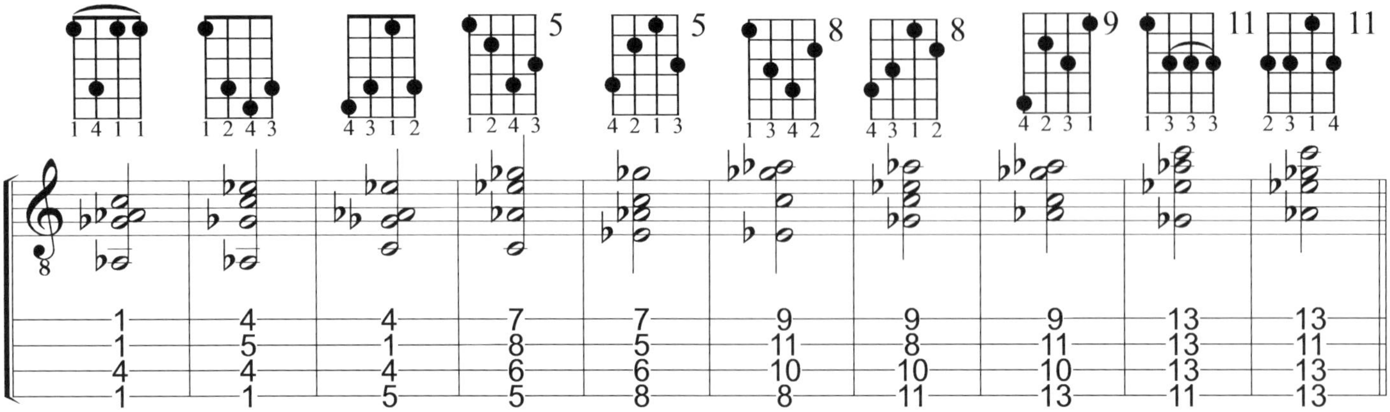

A♭9 - G♯9

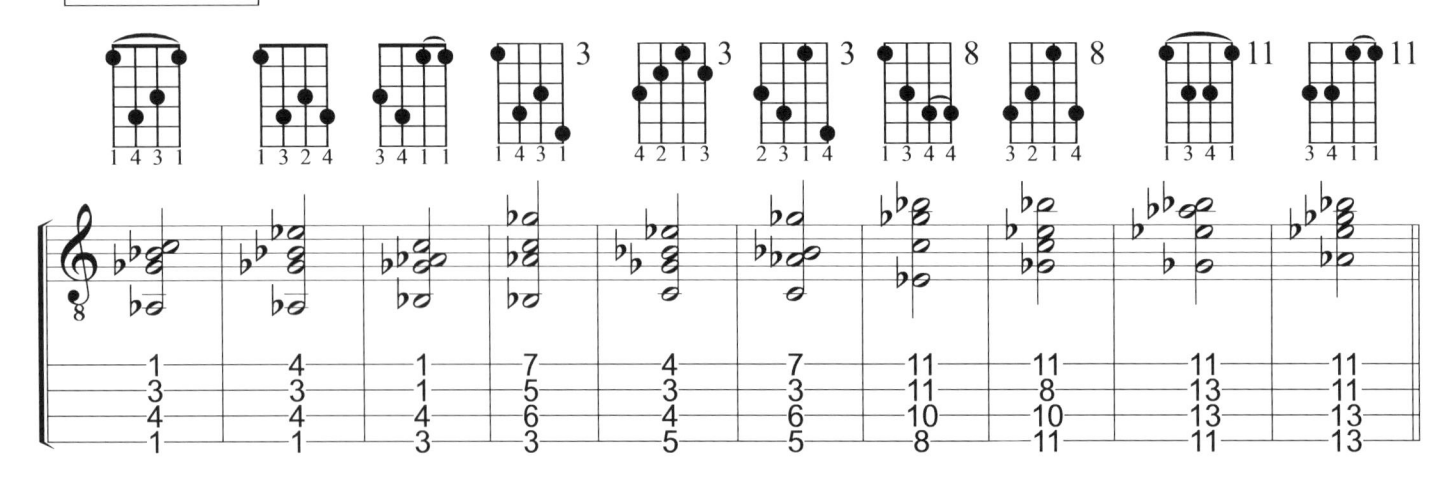

A♭13 - G♯13

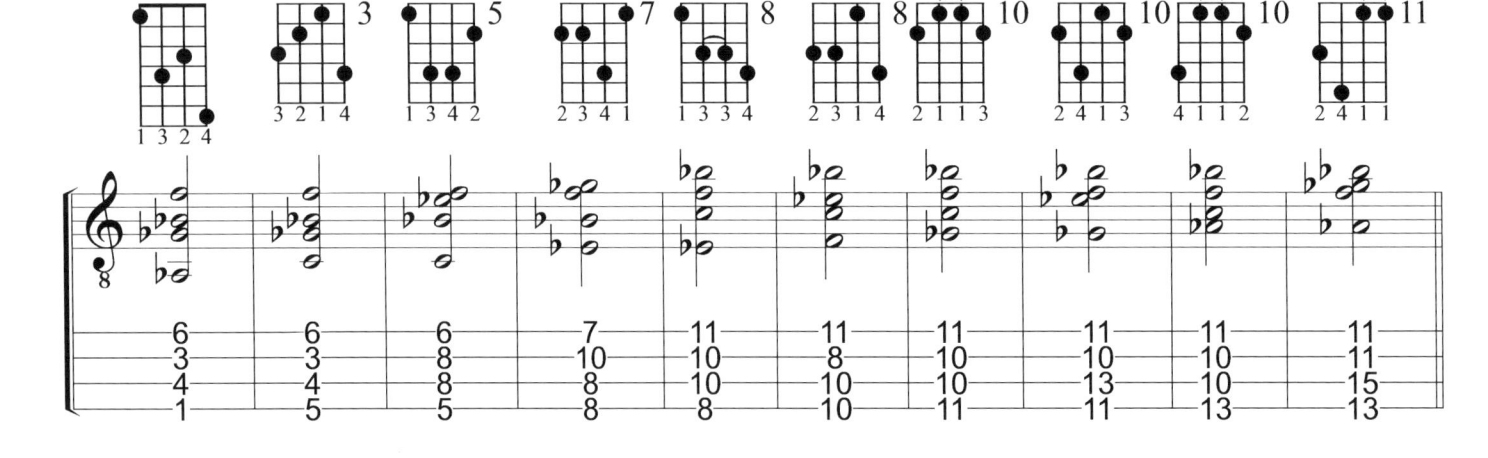

7b5 - 7#5 - 7#9

Ab G# 115

Ab7b5 - G#7b5

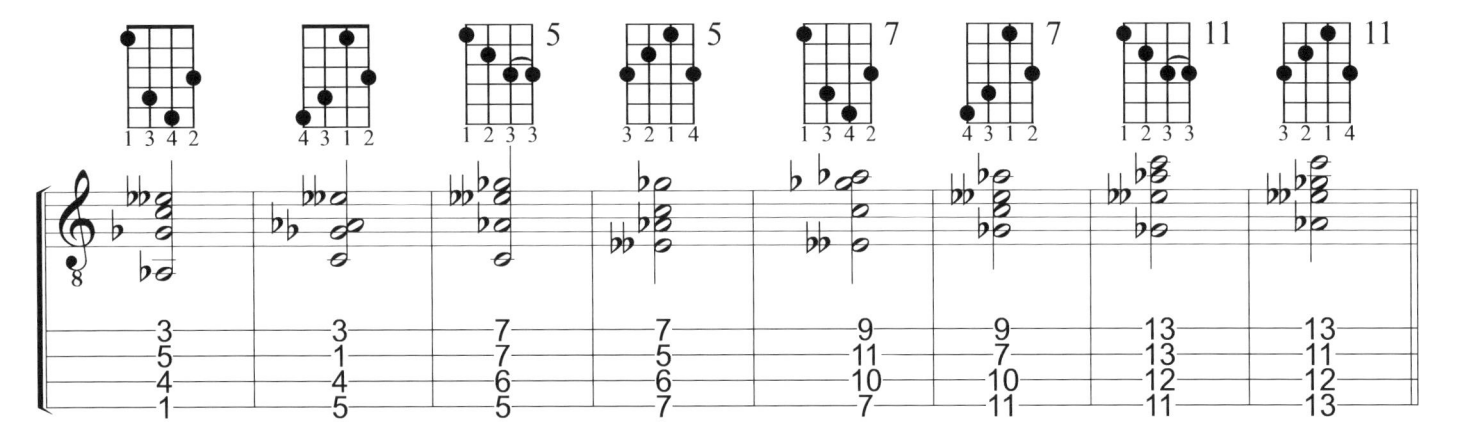

Ab7#5 - G#7#5

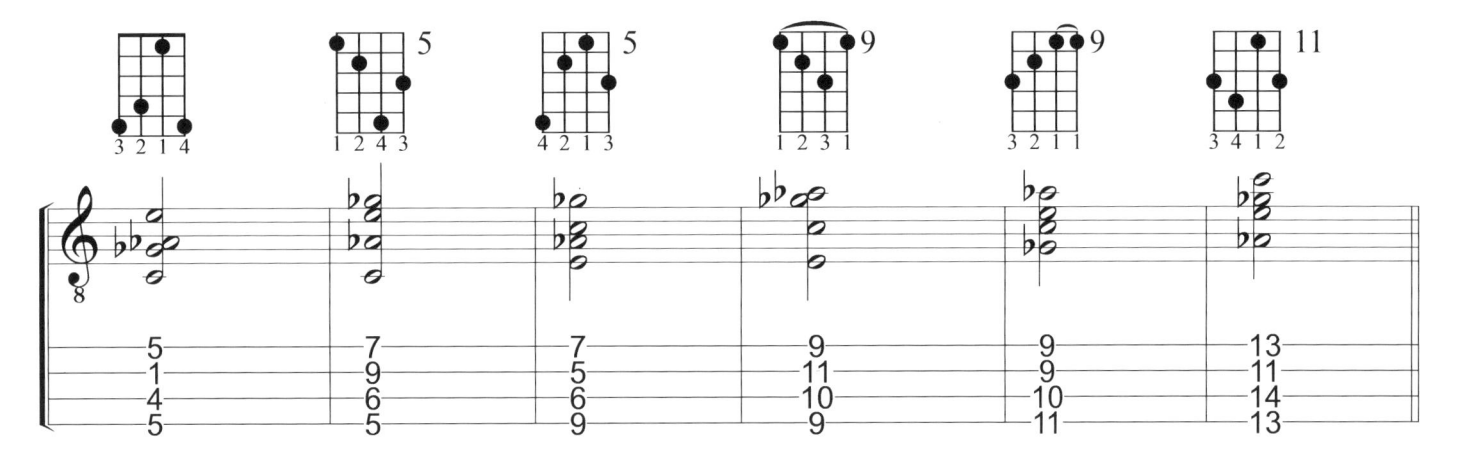

Ab7#9 - G#7#9

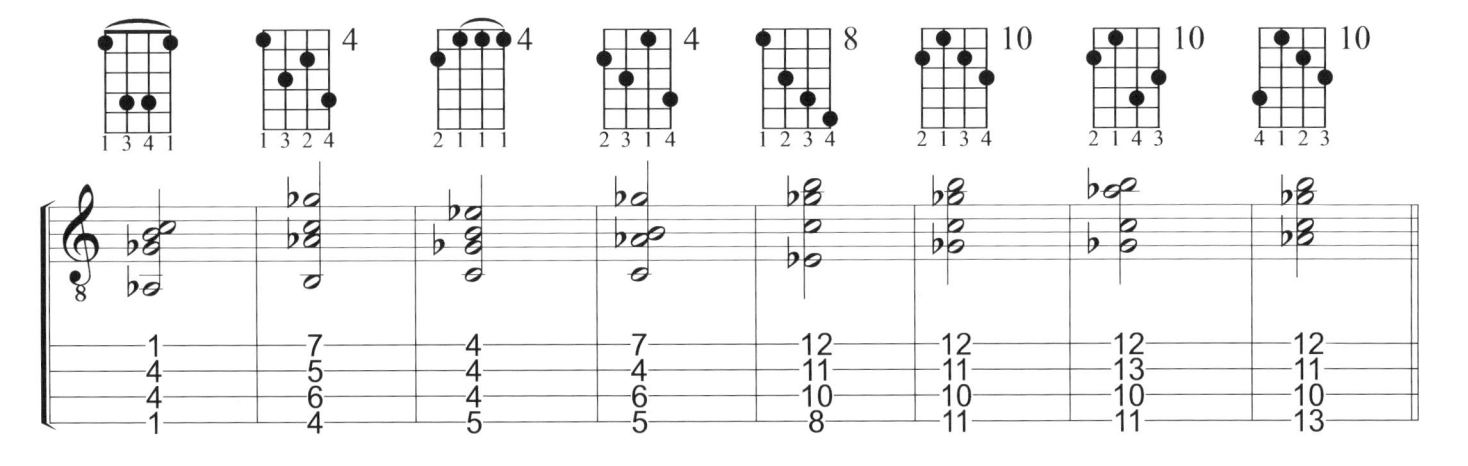

7♭9 - diminished - ○7

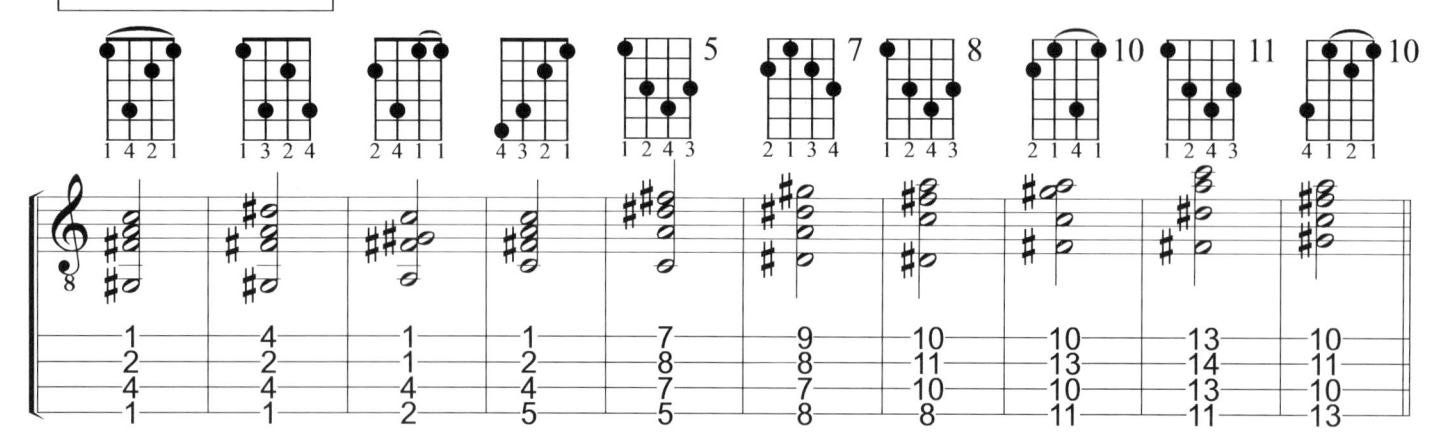

A♭ G♯ 116

G♯7♭9 - A♭7♭9

G♯diminished (G♯○) A♭diminished (A♭○)

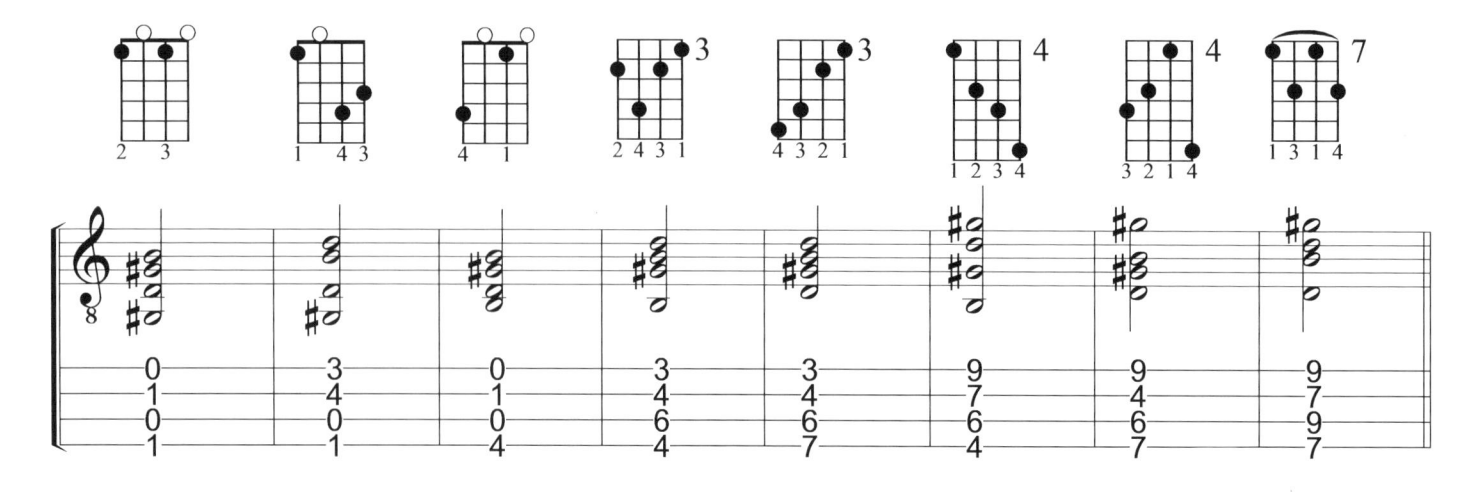

G♯diminished 7th (G♯○7) A♭diminished 7th (A♭○7)

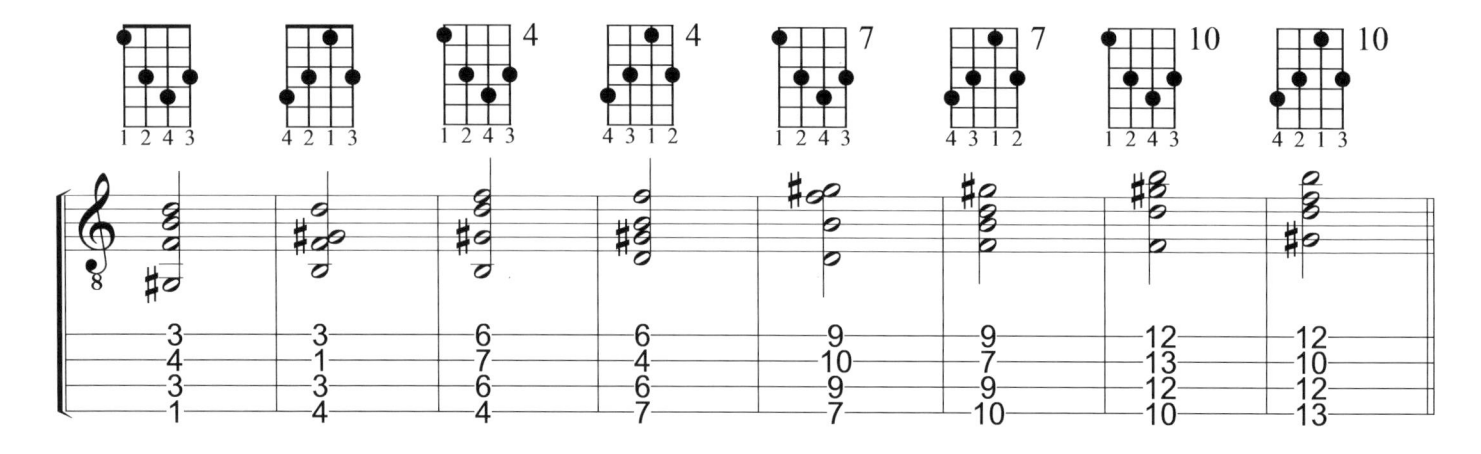

sus4 - sus2 - add9 - 7sus - 5th

A♭ G♯

A♭sus4 - G♯sus4

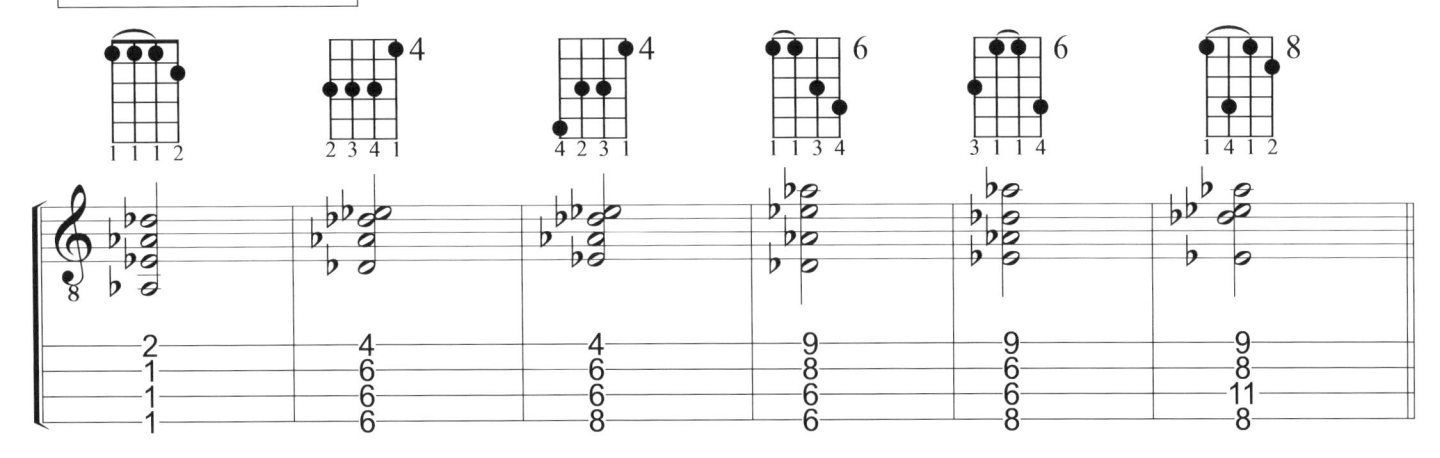

A♭sus2 - G♯sus2

A♭add9 - G♯add9

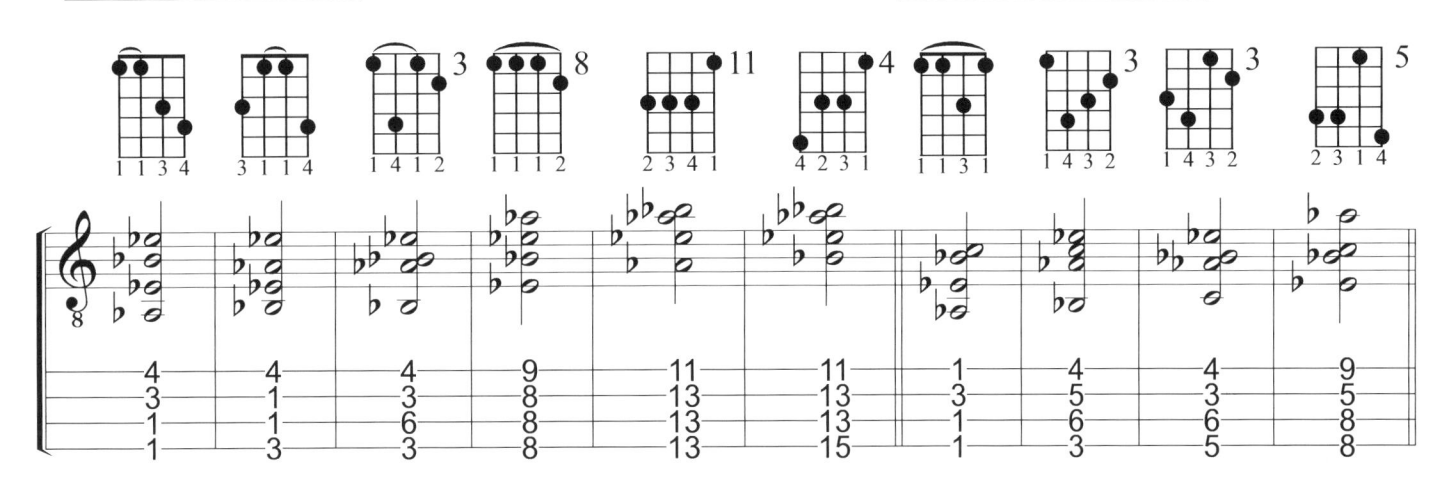

A♭7sus - G♯7sus

Power Chords A♭5 - G♯5

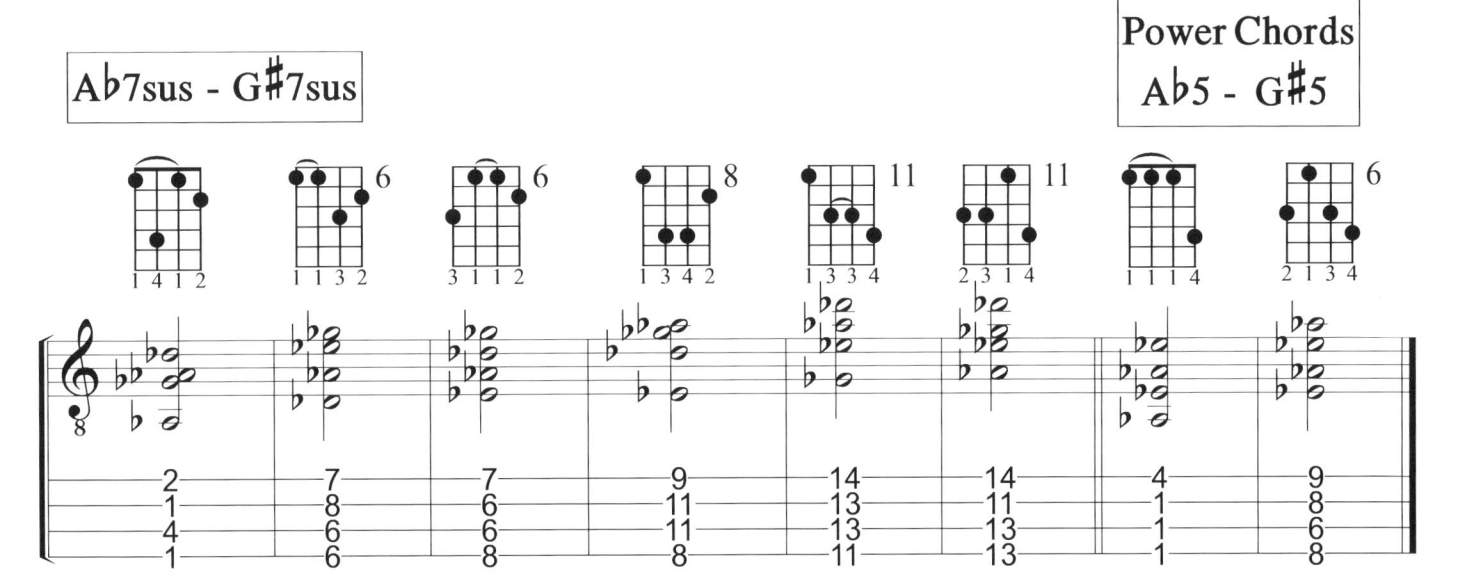

Chord Progressions and Theory

A chord progression is a set of chords played in a sequence. Each chord in a chord progression has a harmonic function that relates to a key in music. To fully understand chord progressions though, you first need to know how chords are formed. Let's start with writing out a major scale and numbering each note; in this example, we will use the C major scale:

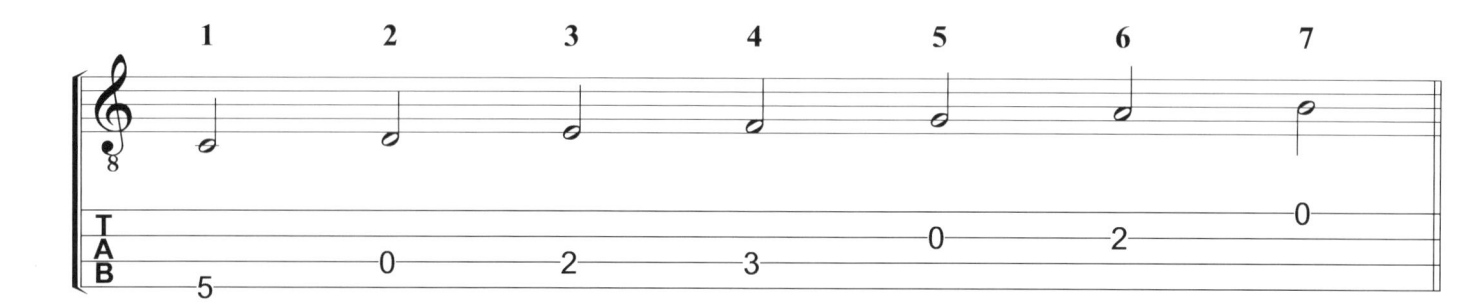

Next, let's stack two more notes on top of the original note in the scale to form a chord. When you stack the other two notes on top, make sure they are three letter names apart, or in intervals of "3rds." For example, if the note from the scale is an A, then stack a C and an E on top. These three note chords are called "triads," and when all the triads are taken from one scale, they are called "diatonic triads." Each triad in a key form a specific type of chord called either a major, minor or diminished triad depending on the distances or intervals between the notes:

TRIADS:

Major	minor	minor	Major	Major	minor	diminished
C	Dm	Em	F	G	Am	Bdim

If you stack yet another note on top of the triad, you will create a four-note chord called "7th chords." So, the 7th chord has the root note on the bottom or the 1st, the 3rd, the 5th, and 7th note above the root note:

SEVENTH CHORDS:

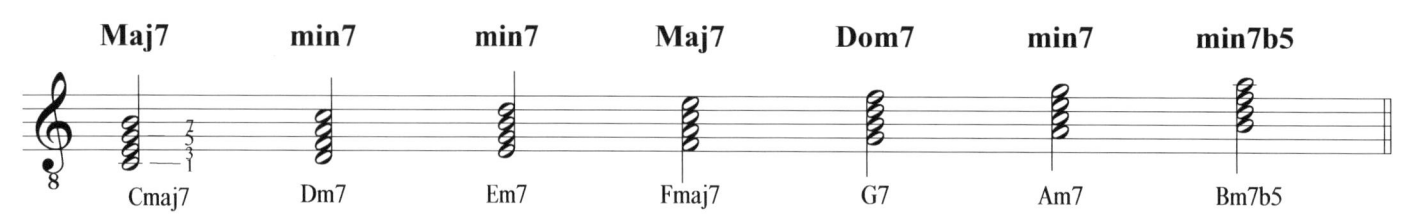

Maj7	min7	min7	Maj7	Dom7	min7	min7b5
Cmaj7	Dm7	Em7	Fmaj7	G7	Am7	Bm7b5

The initial scale used in this lesson was the C major scale, but chords can also be formed on other scales like the harmonic minor scale. The triads from the minor scale are different because they have different intervals between the notes. Here are the chords from the A harmonic minor scale, notice there is an augmented triad (+) when you build chords on this scale:

A Minor Scale:

CHORD FUNCTIONS

When you play a chord and move to another chord, a certain harmonic function is created. So, some chords will want to move towards other chords, some will want to pull away, and some will remain relatively static. There is no right or wrong way to make a chord progression, though are "inner ears" have been conditioned to hear certain chords function in predictable ways. There are acoustical reasons to explain chord progressions, but that is beyond the scope of this book. Let's classify the chords into three main functions using a major key:

Tonic function - the 1st, 3rd and 6th chord of the major scale.
Sub-Dominant function - the 2nd and 4th chord of the major scale.
Dominant function - the 5th and 7th chord of the major scale.

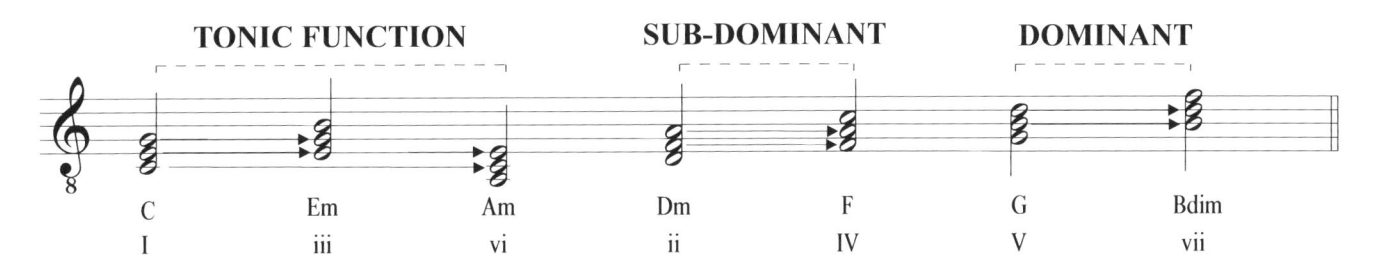

The tonic functioning chords are commonly referred to as being "stable" or like being at "home" because they share notes from the tonic "home" chord. For example, the notes in the tonic C chord are C E G, and the notes in the Em mediant chord are E G B, notice that both chords share the notes E and G. Likewise, The notes in the Am chord are A C E which share the notes C and E. So, the C, Em and Am generally share a tonic function in traditional chord progressions. Similarly, the sub-dominant and the dominant functions share notes with other chords in their group.

Chord Numbering Systems

Musicians often use a simplified system to write out chord progressions based on a number system. Each chord in a scale can be represented by a number 1 through 7. There are two systems to write the numbers down: the first and older system use "Roman Numerals" and more common in classical music, the other system is called "Nashville Numbers" and more common in blues, jazz, and popular music. Here are the chords in C major with both numbering systems:

	Major	minor	minor	Major	Major	minor	diminished
	C	Dm	Em	F	G	Am	Bdim
R.N.	I	iim	iiim	IV	V	vim	viio
Nashville	1	2m	3m	4	5	6m	7o

The Nashville numbering system can be used for all chord types including 7th chords:

Major7	minor7	minor7	Major7	Major7	minor7	minor7b5
Cmaj7	Dm7	Em7	Fmaj7	G7	Am7	Bm7b5
17	2m7	3m7	47	57	6m7	7m7b5

The number system helps to memorize chord progressions and to quickly change keys. Here is a standard 12 bar blues with both chord symbols and the Nashville numbering system:

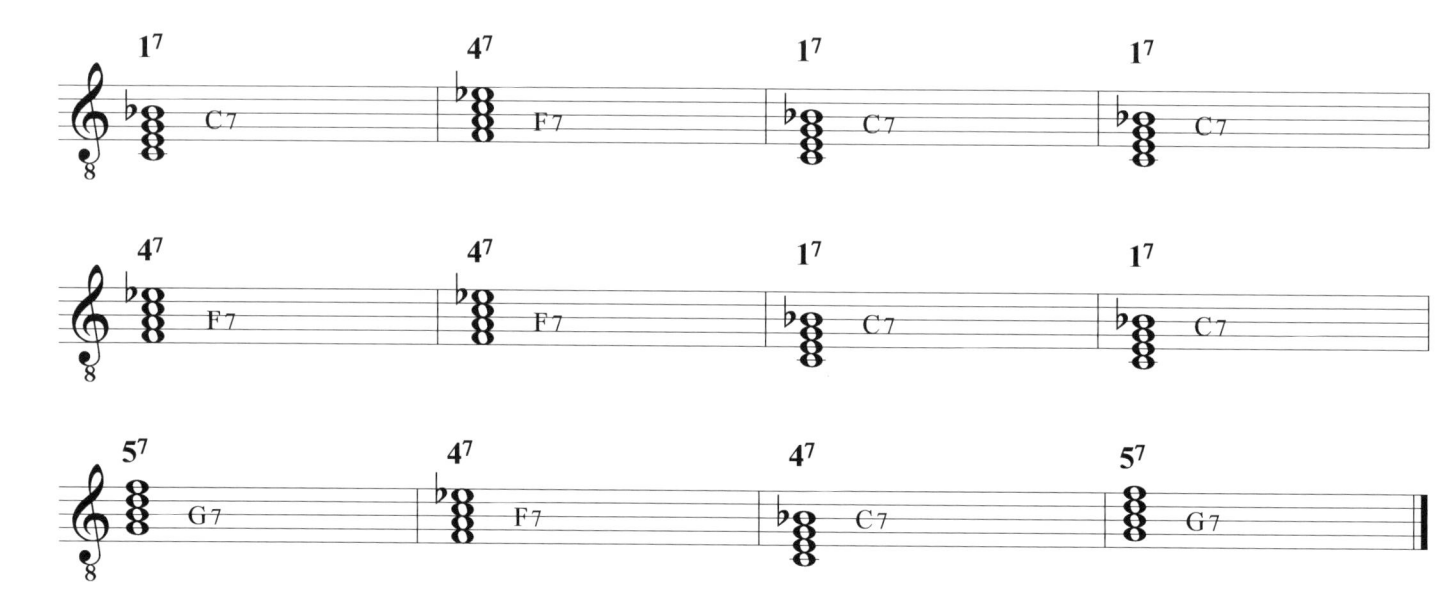

17	47	17	17
C7	F7	C7	C7

47	47	17	17
F7	F7	C7	C7

57	47	47	57
G7	F7	C7	G7

The most common jazz progression is the "2-5-1" (key of C):

Dm — **G** — **C**
2m — **5** — **1**

Here's the same progression using 7th chords:

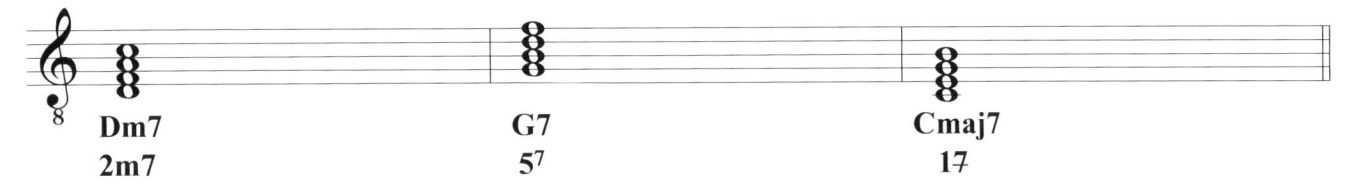

Dm7 — **G7** — **Cmaj7**
2m7 — **57** — **17**

"Rhythm Changes" is a familar chord progression used in many jazz standards. Try to memorize the Nashville numbers and transpose to a different key (chords are shown in C major).

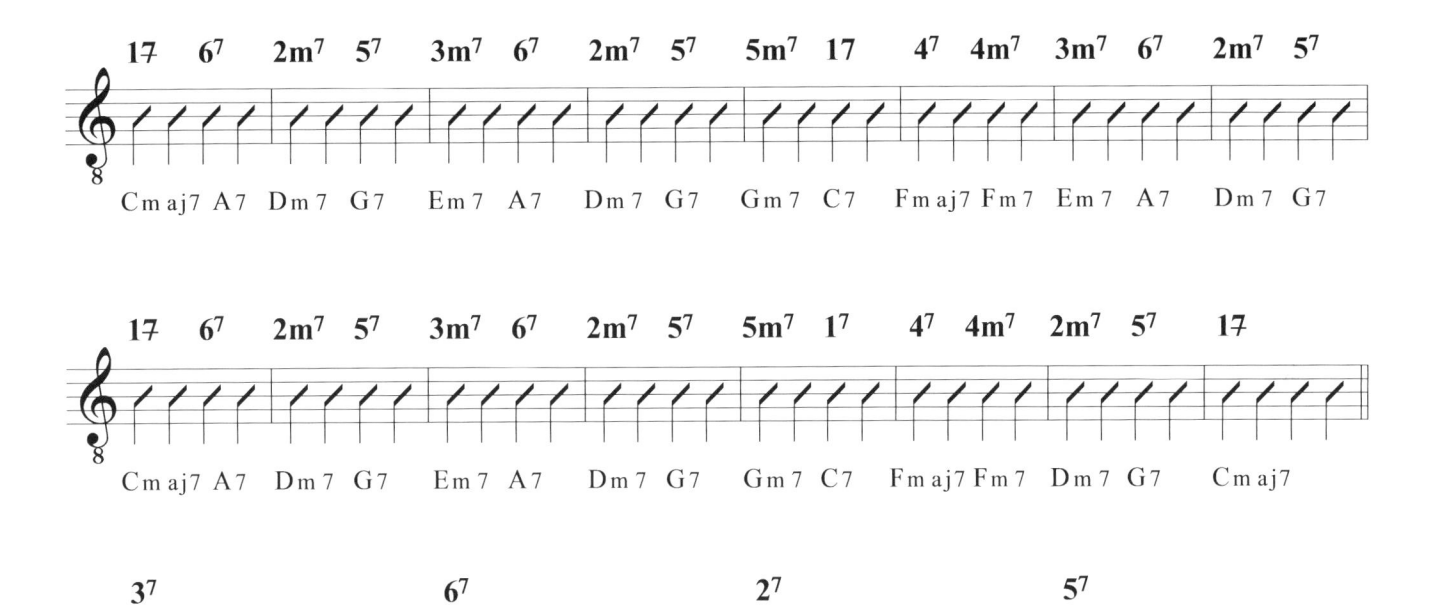

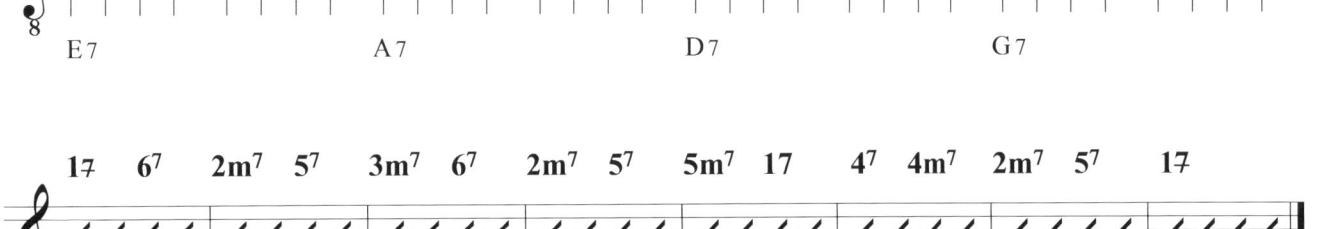

17	67	2m7	57	3m7	67	2m7	57	5m7	17	47	4m7	3m7	67	2m7	57
Cmaj7	A7	Dm7	G7	Em7	A7	Dm7	G7	Gm7	C7	Fmaj7	Fm7	Em7	A7	Dm7	G7

17	67	2m7	57	3m7	67	2m7	57	5m7	17	47	4m7	2m7	57	17
Cmaj7	A7	Dm7	G7	Em7	A7	Dm7	G7	Gm7	C7	Fmaj7	Fm7	Dm7	G7	Cmaj7

37	67	27	57
E7	A7	D7	G7

17	67	2m7	57	3m7	67	2m7	57	5m7	17	47	4m7	2m7	57	17
Cmaj7	A7	Dm7	G7	Em7	A7	Dm7	G7	Gm7	C7	Fmaj7	Fm7	Dm7	G7	Cmaj7

Understanding Chord Formulas

1) Each note in a scale can be represented by a number. In the chart below, the C major scale is written out with a number assigned for each note up to 13.

C	D	E	F	G	A	B	C	D	E	F	G	A
1	2	3	4	5	6	7	8	9	10	11	12	13

2) Each chord has a unique group of notes or "formula." For example, the major chord formula uses the 1st, 3rd and 5th notes of the major scale, so the notes in the **A** major chord are A, C# and E (see below). To make a minor chord, use the formula 1st, b3rd and 5th. Notice, the minor chord has a flat 3rd, so you must flatten the 3rd note of the major scale. That is, the A major chord has a C# whereas the A minor chord has been lowered to a C natural: A, C, and E. Here are the most frequently used chord formulas:

MAJOR (1-3-5)

A	A	C#	E
Bb	Bb	D	F
B	B	D#	F#
C	C	E	G
C#	C#	E#	G#
Db	Db	F	Ab
D	D	F#	A
Eb	Eb	G	Bb
E	E	G#	B
F	F	A	C
F#	F#	A#	C#
Gb	Gb	Bb	Db
G	G	B	D
Ab	Ab	C	Eb

MINOR (1-b3-5)

Am	A	C	E
Bbm	Bb	Db	F
Bm	B	D	F#
Cm	C	Eb	G
C#m	C#	E	G#
Dbm	Db	Fb	Ab
Dm	D	F	A
Ebm	Eb	Gb	Bb
Em	E	G	B
Fm	F	Ab	C
F#m	F#	A	C#
Gbm	Gb	Bbb	Db
Gm	G	Bb	D
Abm	Ab	Cb	Eb

DOMINANT 7th (1-3-5-b7)

A7	A	C#	E	G
Bb7	Bb	D	F	Ab
B7	B	D#	F#	A
C7	C	E	G	Bb
C#7	C#	E#	G#	B
Db7	Db	F	Ab	Cb
D7	D	F#	A	C
Eb7	Eb	G	Bb	Db
E7	E	G#	B	D
F7	F	A	C	Eb
F#7	F#	A#	C#	E
Gb7	Gb	Bb	Db	Fb
G7	G	B	D	F
Ab7	Ab	C	Eb	Gb

MAJOR CHORDS

NAME	ABBREVIATION	CHORD TONES
major	USUALLY NONE or "M"	1 3 5
major sixth	6	1 3 5 6
major seventh	maj7	1 3 5 7

major ninth	maj9	1 3 5 7 9
major sixth ninth	6/9	1 3 5 6 9
major seventh # eleven	Maj7#11	1 3 5 7 9 #11

MINOR CHORDS

NAME	ABBREVIATION	CHORD TONES
minor	m	1 b3 5
minor sixth	m6	1 b3 5 6
minor seventh	m7	1 b3 5 b7
minor major seventh	m/maj7	1 b3 5 7
minor seventh flat 5	m7b5 – (half diminished)	1 b3 b5 b7
minor Ninth	m9	1 b3 5 b7 9
minor eleventh	m11	1 b3 5 b7 9 11
minor thirteenth	m13	1 b3 5 b7 9 13

DOMINANT CHORDS

NAME	ABBREVIATION	CHORD TONES
dominant seventh	7, dom7	1 3 5 b7
dominant ninth	9	1 3 5 b7 9
dominant thirteenth	13	1 3 5 b7 9 13
dominant seventh flat 5	7b5	1 3 b5 b7
dominant seventh sharp 5	7#5	1 3 #5 b7
dominant seventh flat 9	7b9	1 3 5 b7 b9
dominant seventh sharp 9	7#9	1 3 5 b7 #9
dominant thirteenth flat 9	13b9	1 3 5 b7 b9 13

SUSPENDED CHORDS

NAME	ABBREVIATION	CHORD TONES
suspended 2nd	Sus2	1 2 5
suspended 4th	sus4	1 4 5
dominant 7suspended 4th	7sus4	1 4 5 b7
dominant 9 suspended 4th	9sus4	1 4 5 b7 9

DIMINISHED & AUGMENTED CHORDS & POWER CHORDS

NAME	ABBREVIATION	CHORD TONES
diminished	dim, 0	1 b3 b5
diminished seventh	dim7, 07	1 b3 b5 bb7
augmented	aug, +	1 3 #5
augmented seventh	aug7, +7	1 3 #5 7
power chord	5	1 5

Cigar Box Guitar Fingerboard - 4 String - GDGB

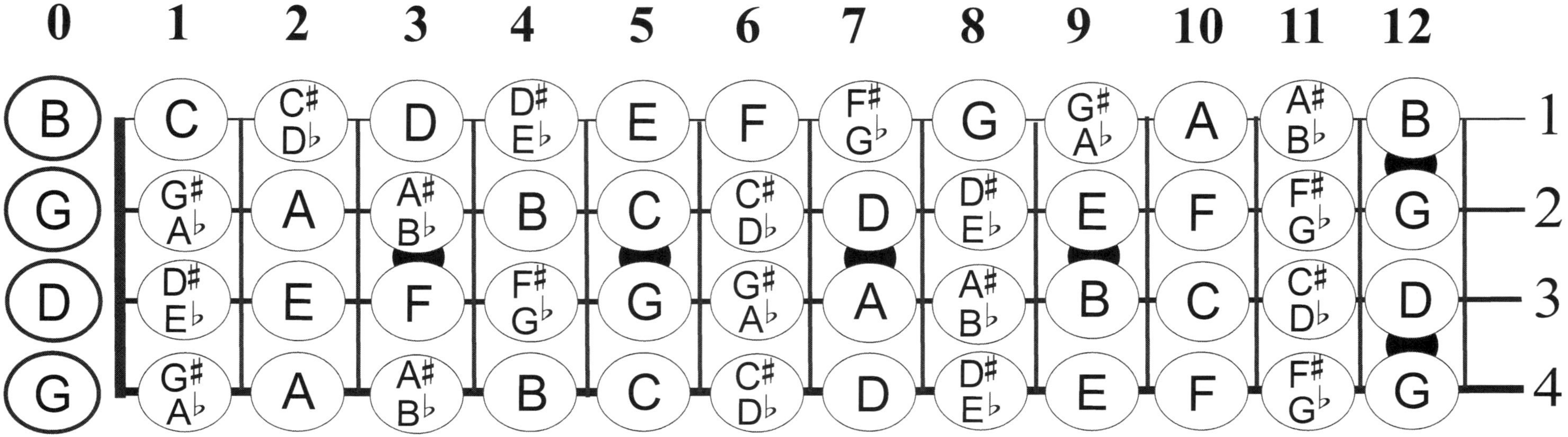

Cigar Box Guitar Interval Chart - 4 String - GDGB - Key of C

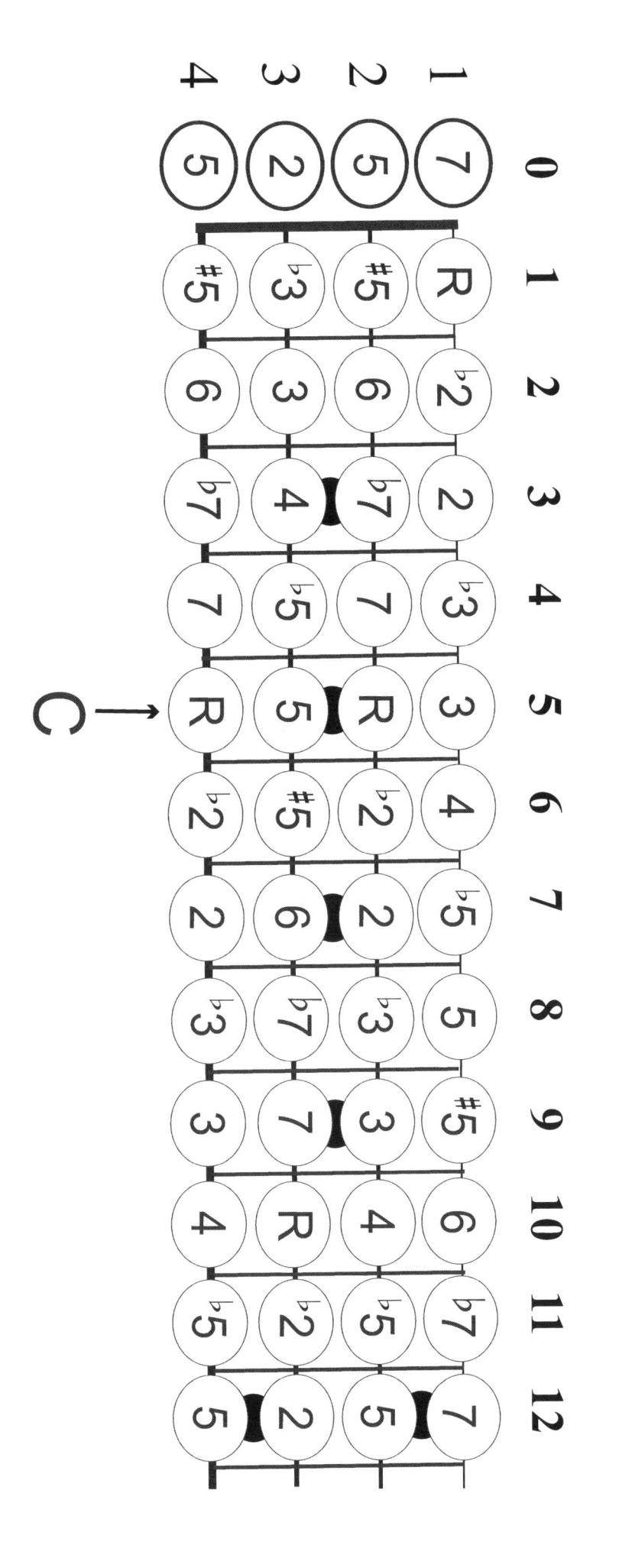

Strumming and Picking Techniques

Palm Muting - Place the left side of your (strumming hand) palm on the strings close to the bridge or on the bridge to produce a muted deadened sound. Experiment with different pressures on the string to produce different muted tones.

Let Ring - Hold a chord down while you strum and/or pick notes from the chord letting the notes ring freely. This is sometimes written as *l.r.*

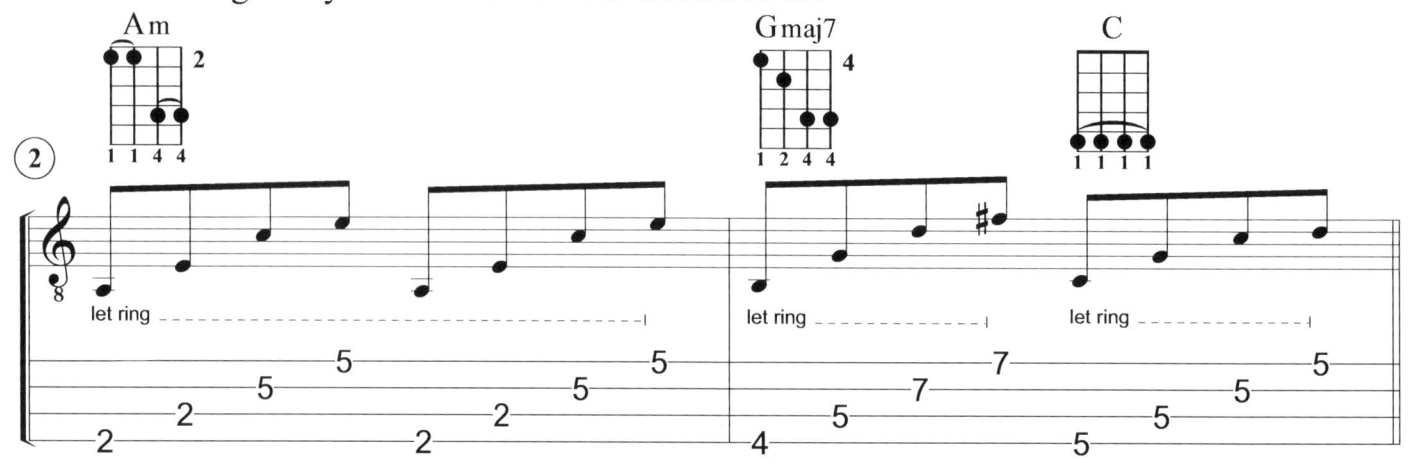

Bass Note Strum - Play a single low note then strum the chord.

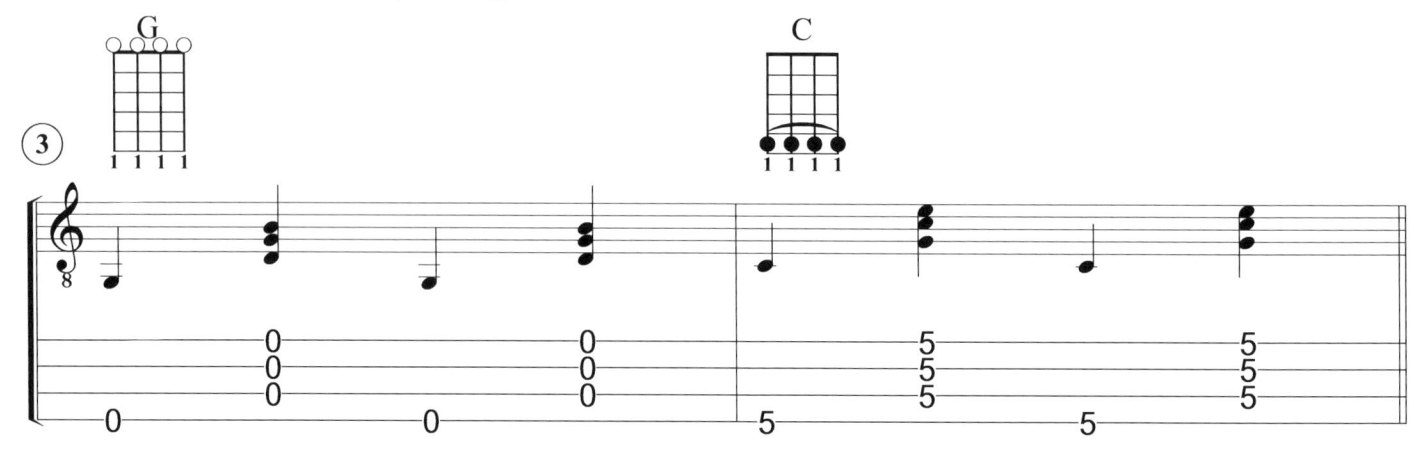

Alternating Bass Note Strum - Play a single low note, strum the chord, then play another single higher or lower note and strum the chord again.

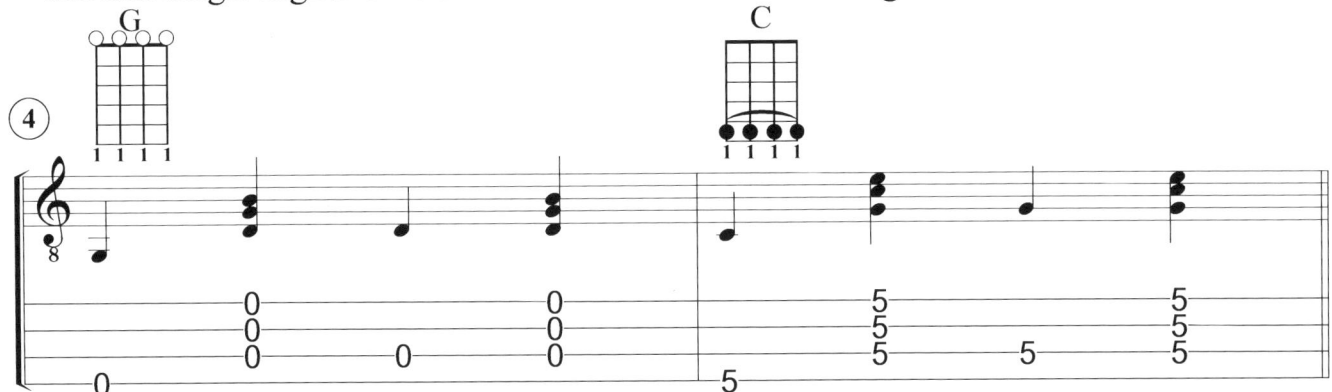

Hybrid Picking - Play with pick and fingers. In this example, play all the notes on the 4th string with your pick and notes on the 3rd and 2nd string with your fingers.

Left Hand Muting - Release the left hand string pressure stopping the notes ringing.

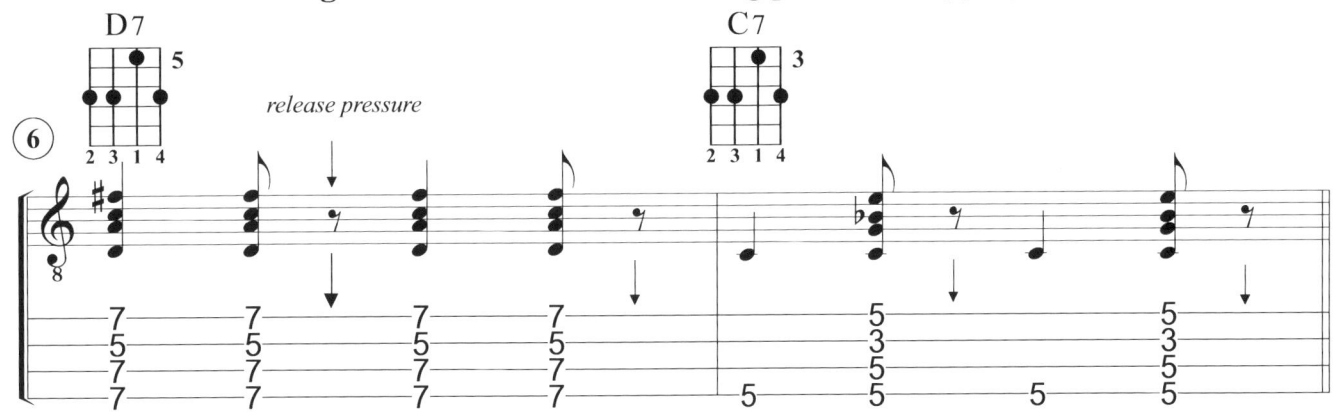

Pick Slap - Mute the strings with the left hand and strum the chord producing a rhythmic clicking sound. Pick slaps are notated with an x.

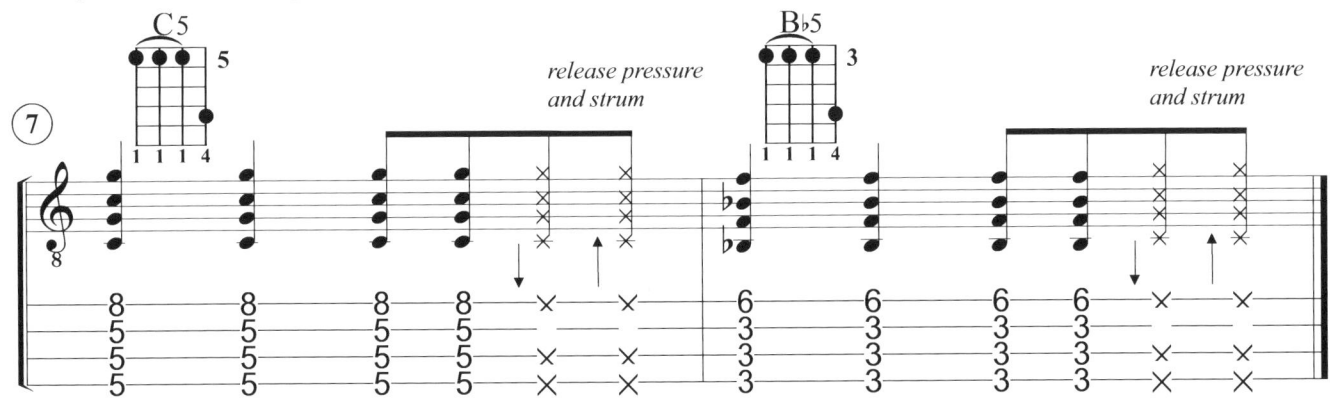

Strumming Pattern Practice

Here is an excellent exercise to practice up and down strumming. The following 15 patterns are all the variations possible using eighth notes in a measure of 2/4. The examples are using eighth notes, but sixteenth notes could easily be substituted instead. Count out loud or in your head: 1 & 2 &. If you prefer thinking with sixteenth notes, count out: 1 e & a.

Practice the strumming patterns with a single chord or with a chord progression. Repeat each pattern, make sure to keep the strumming arm moving evenly up and down, and play with a metronome if possible. If you don't have a metronome then tap your foot on the 1st beat of every bar. Practice playing a straight and shuffle rhythm.

Patterns with 4 strums

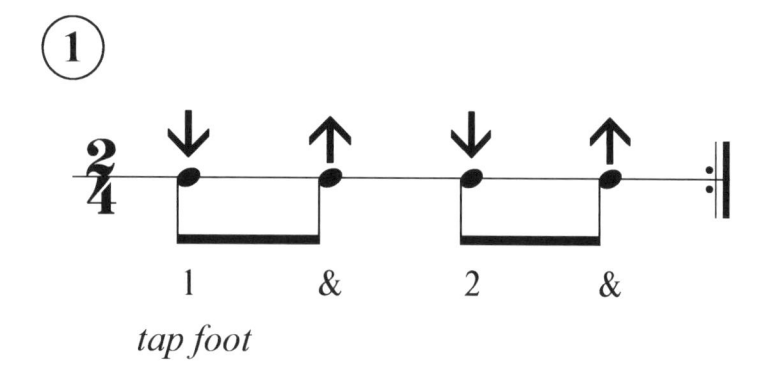

(1)

tap foot

Patterns with 3 strums

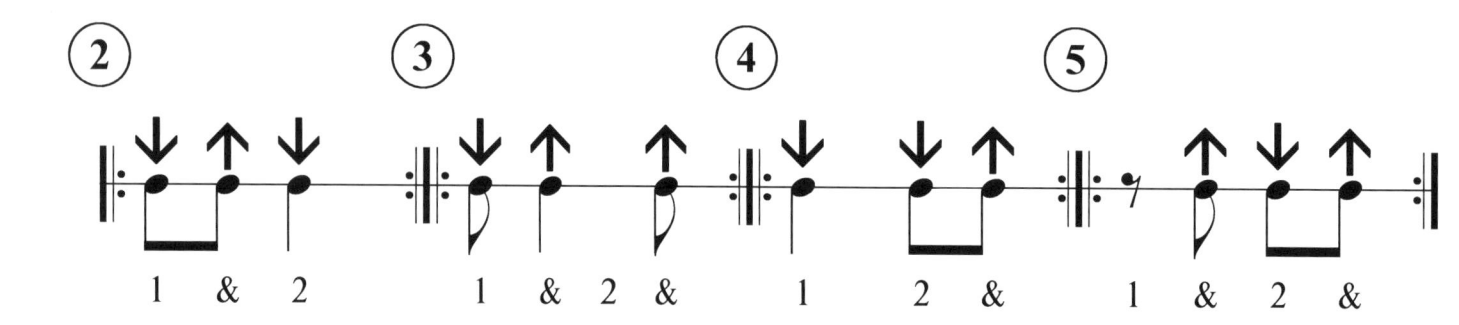

(2) **(3)** **(4)** **(5)**

Patterns with 2 strums

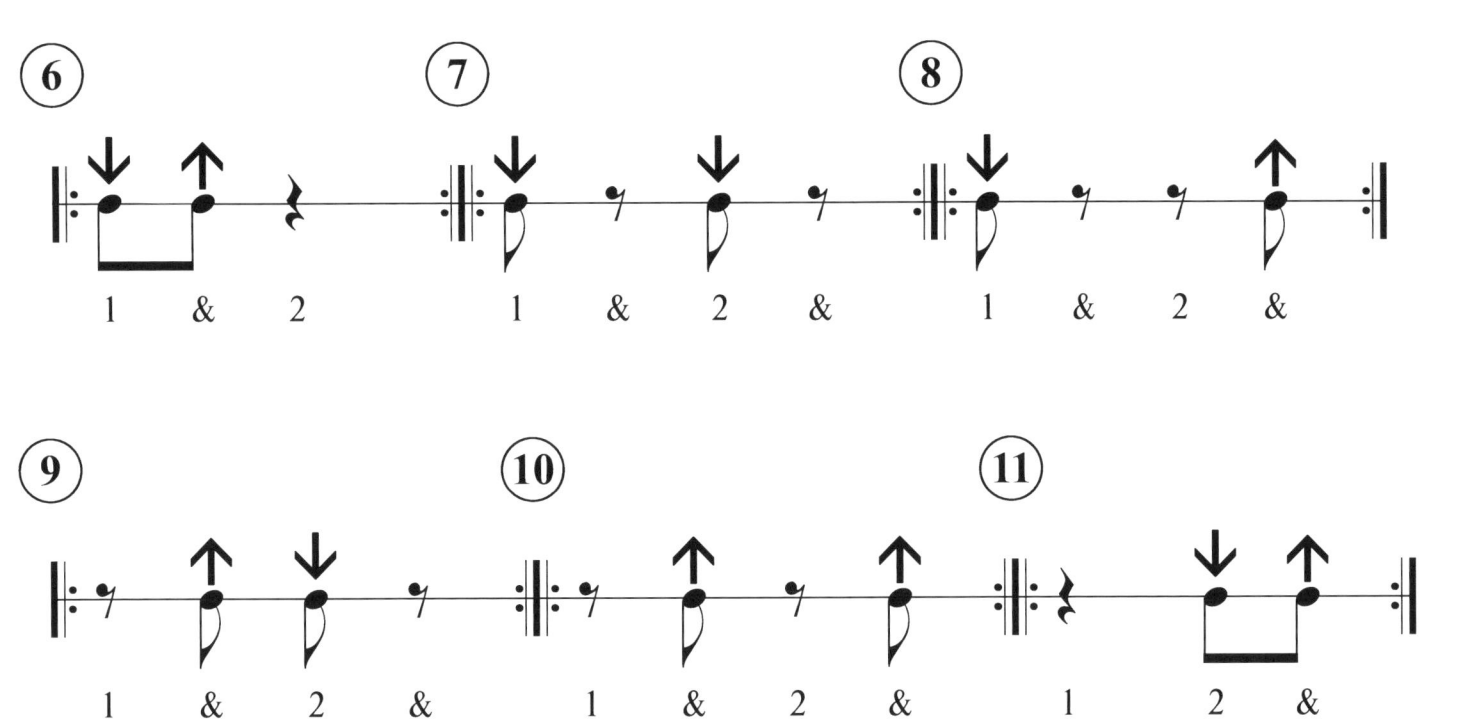

Patterns with 1 strum

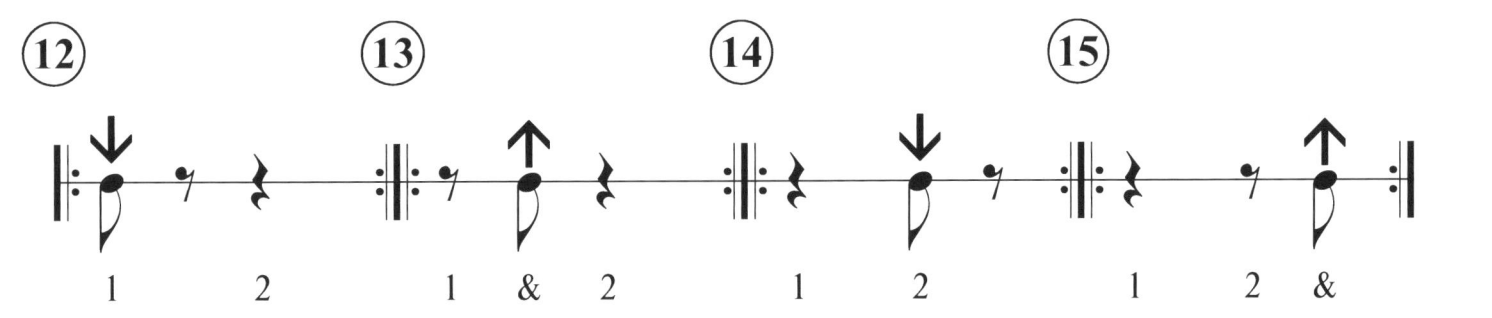

Strumming Patterns - Basic

Practice the following strumming patterns using any single chord or a chord progression. Use a metronome to help keep an even steady tempo or tap your foot.

DOWN STROKE ↓   UP STROKE ↑   ACCENT >   MUTE X

1. Down / Up Pattern. Play with even straight eighth notes or swing shuffle eighth notes.

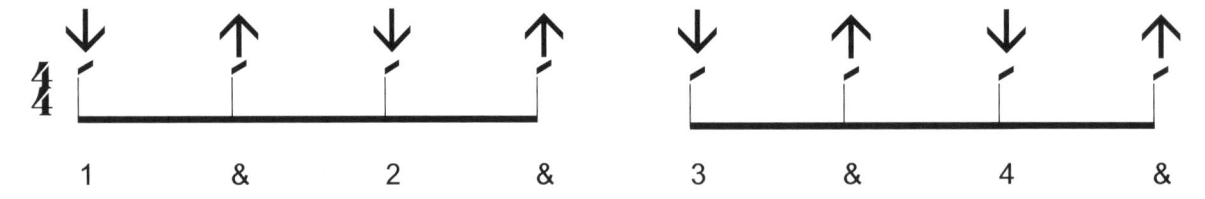

2. Down / Up Pattern with emphasis or accent on 2nd and 4th beat.

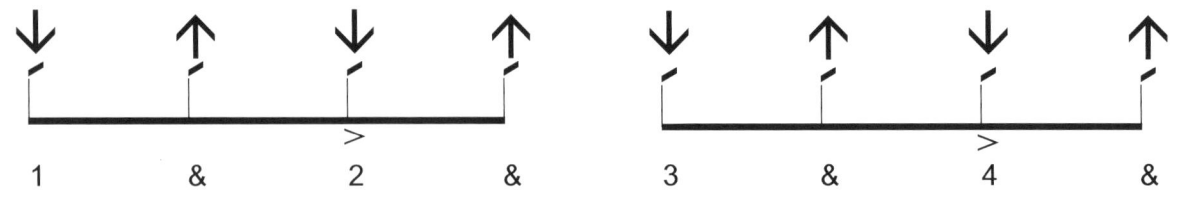

3. Left Hand Mute. Mute the strings (x) with the left hand while continuing strumming.

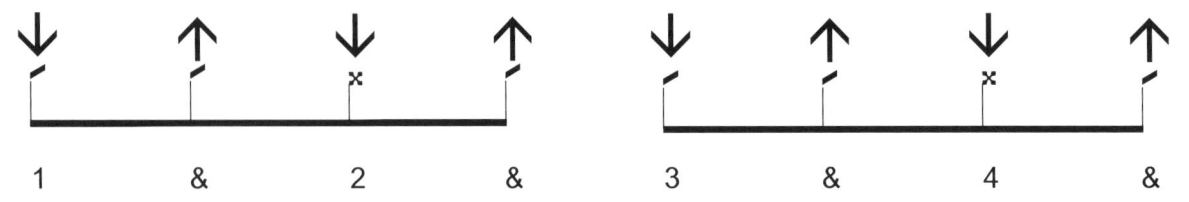

4. Accent the Up stroke.

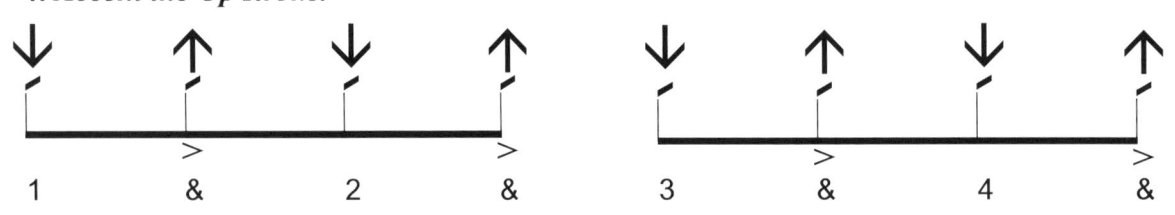

5. Tied Note. Let notes ring without playing the tied note. In this example, don't strum on beat 3.

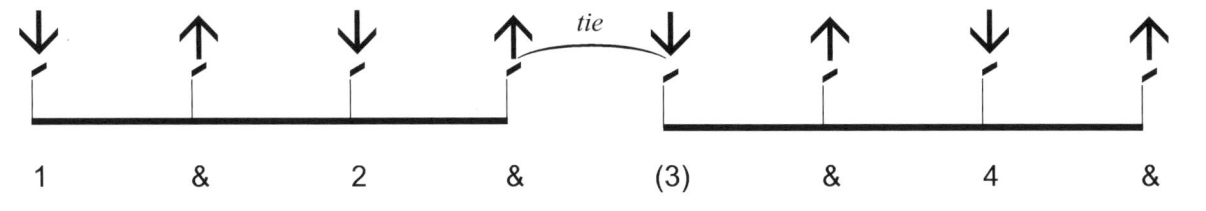

Strumming Patterns Styles

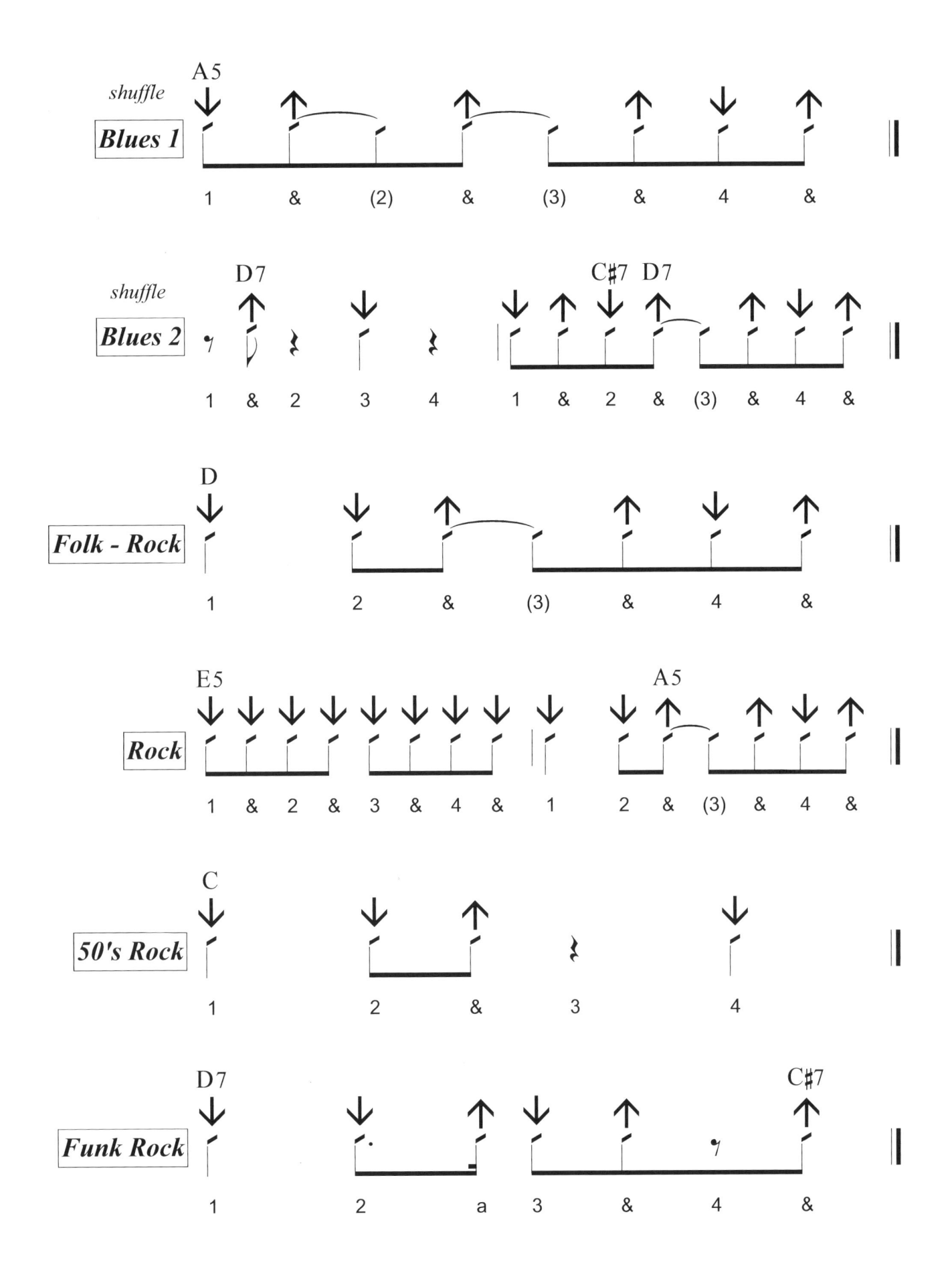

Strumming Patterns Styles

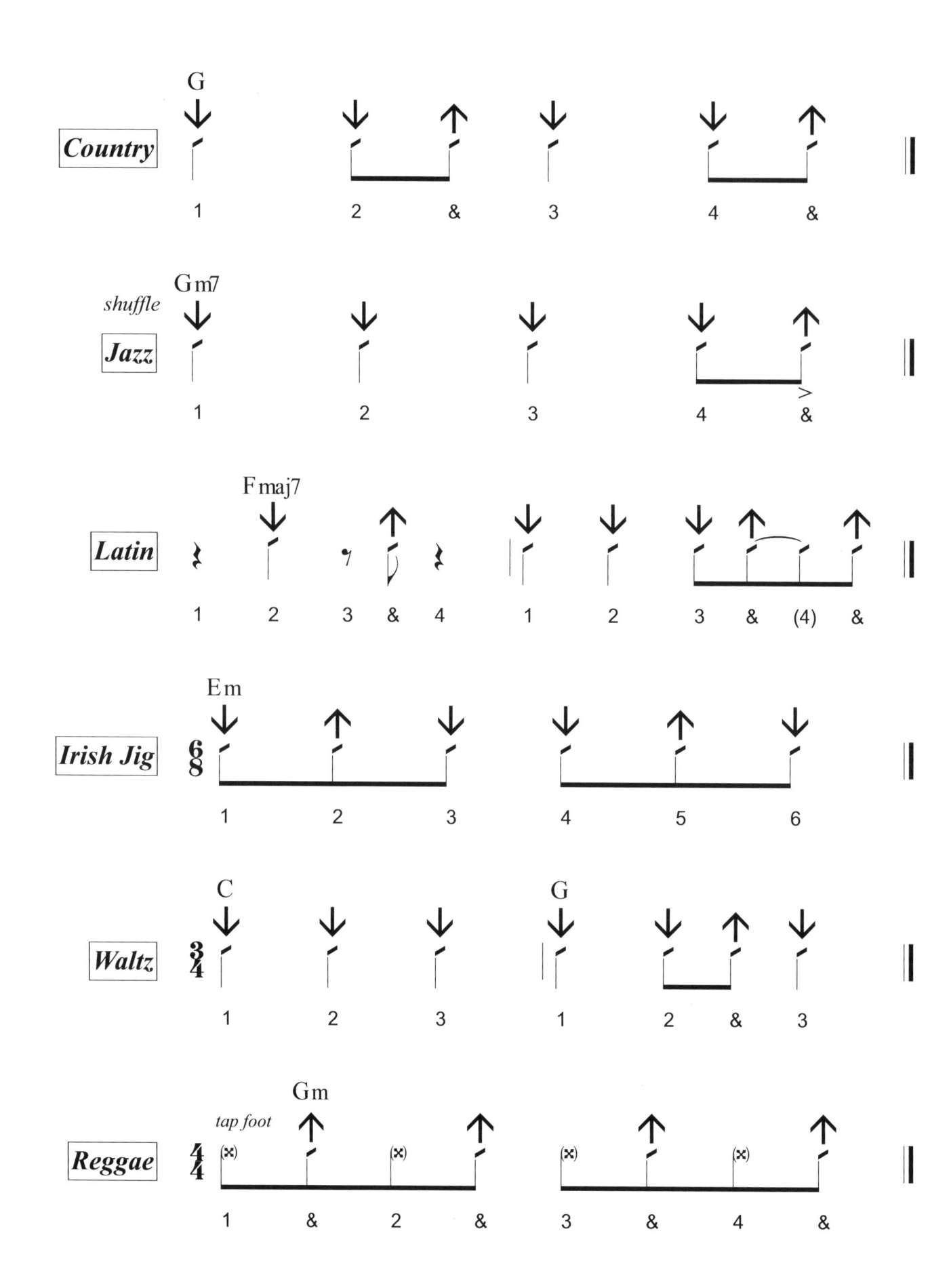

Tips for Accompanying on the Cigar Box Guitar

1. Before you begin a song, you need to know how the song's rhythm is structured. In written music, "Time Signatures" are used to group the beats. The most common time signature is four beats per measure written as 4/4. Other standard time signatures are 3/4, beats grouped in three, and 6/8 where beats are grouped in two groups of three. 6/8 is counted: 1-2-3 4-5-6.

2. Once you have figured out the time signature you are playing in, try to keep a steady rhythm going in sync with the grouping of the beats, so if you are in 4/4 time, tap your foot or count to four. Pick one of the strumming or fingerstyle patterns and practice the chords with a focus on maintaining an even strumming or fingerpicking rhythm. Keep your right hand moving as you change chords.

3. To keep a nice even flow, memorize all the chords in the song you are playing. If you already have the chords memorized, then think ahead and prepare your fingers for the proceeding chord. Most chords change at the start or middle of the measure, so prepare your fingers to land on the correct beat beforehand. As always, place your fingers close to the frets to avoid fret buzz. Practice changing chords with the chord progressions provided in this book.

4. Because the cigar box guitar only has 3 or 4 strings, you may have to simplify some chords to play songs. Substituting one chord for another helps get around this issue. A common substitution is to use the basic barre chord like a C5 in place of another chord. For example, if you have a C major or C minor chord, a simple C5 power chord substitutes for either chord. The C5 doesn't have a 3rd (the 3rd defines the major or minor quality of a chord), therefore the C5 functions as either a C major or C minor.

5. Learn several ways to play each chord in different positions. Knowing multiple chord positions gives the song variety and helps you connect chords that are nearby. Learn the most common chords in all the regular keys you play in.

12 Fingerstyle Patterns for 4-String CBG

Thumb = P   Index = I   Middle = M   Ring = A

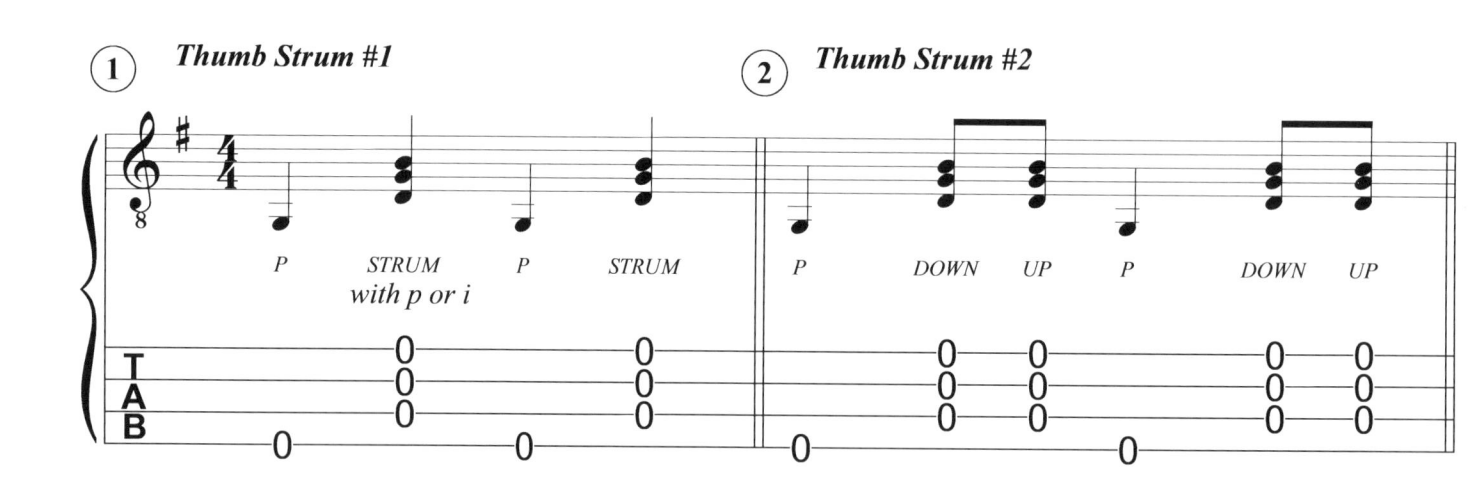

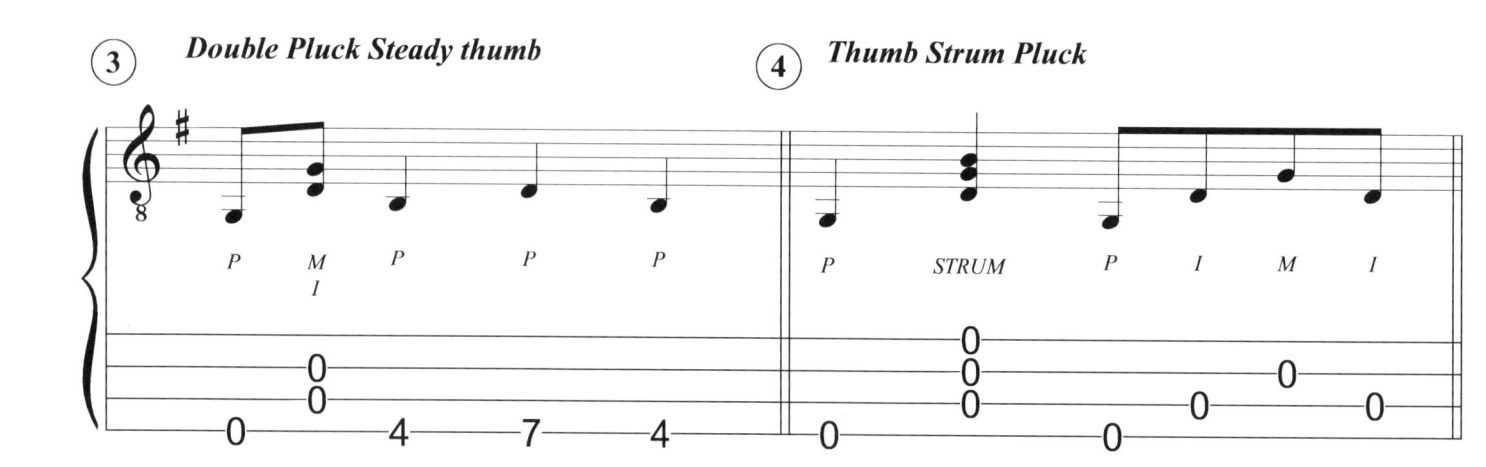

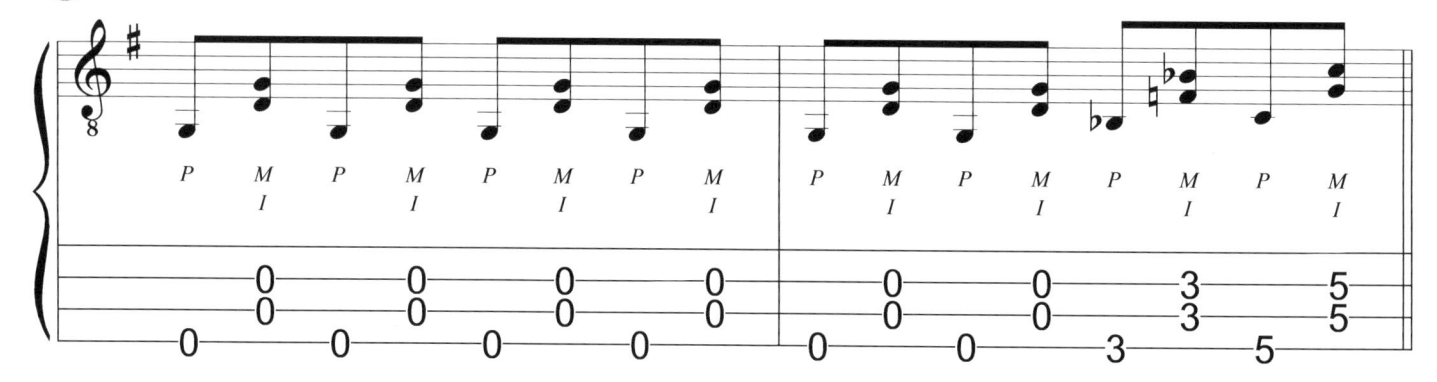

(6) *Travis Picking #1* / (7) *Travis Picking #2*

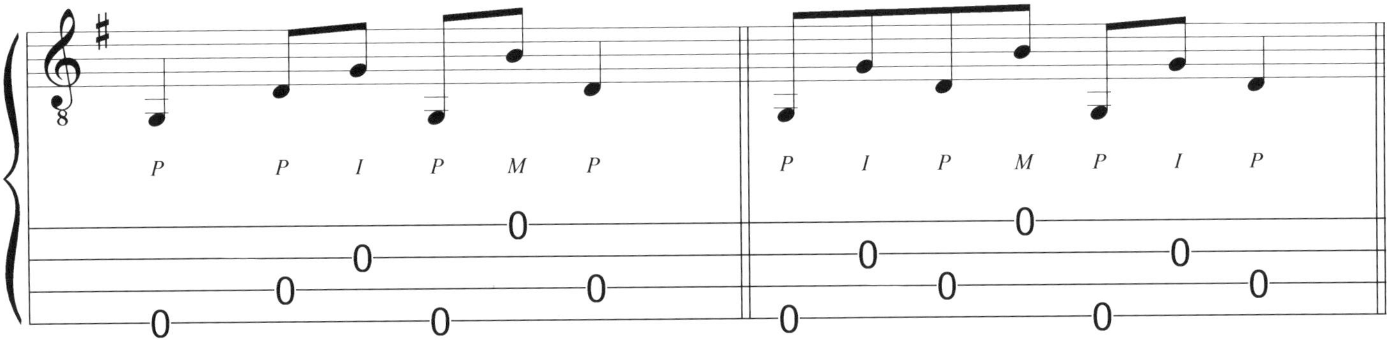

(8) *Travis Picking #3 - Pinch* / (9) *Travis Picking #4 - Double Pinch*

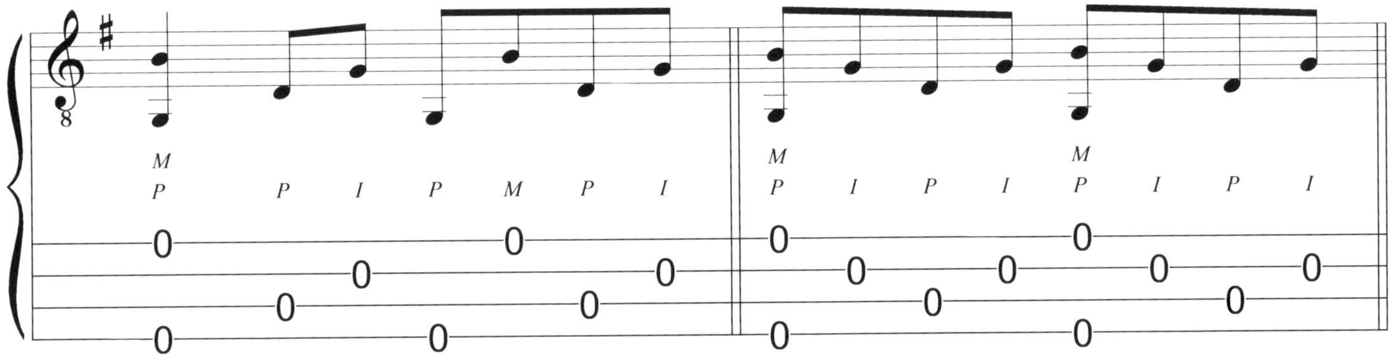

(10) *Back Beat Pinch (on 2nd and 4th beat)* / (11) *Four on the Floor - Double Pinch*

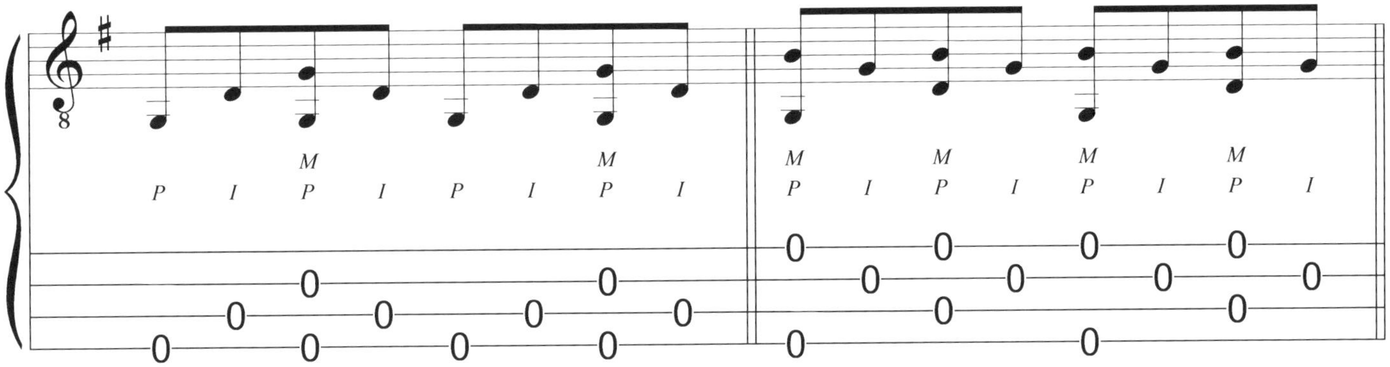

(12) *3/4 Waltz Pattern*

Blues Chord Progressions - Key of A and Am

12 Bar Blues Progression

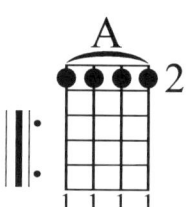

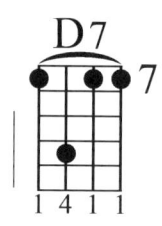

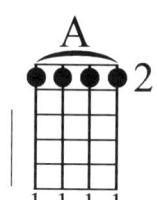

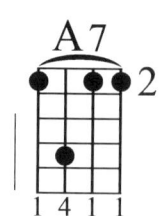

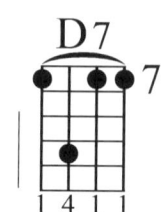

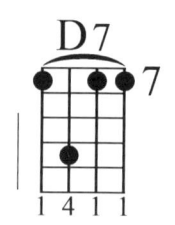

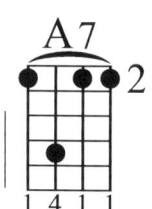

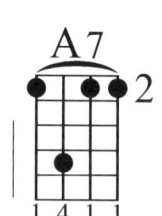

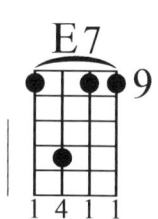

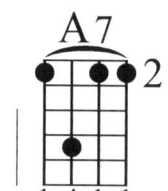

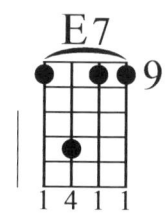

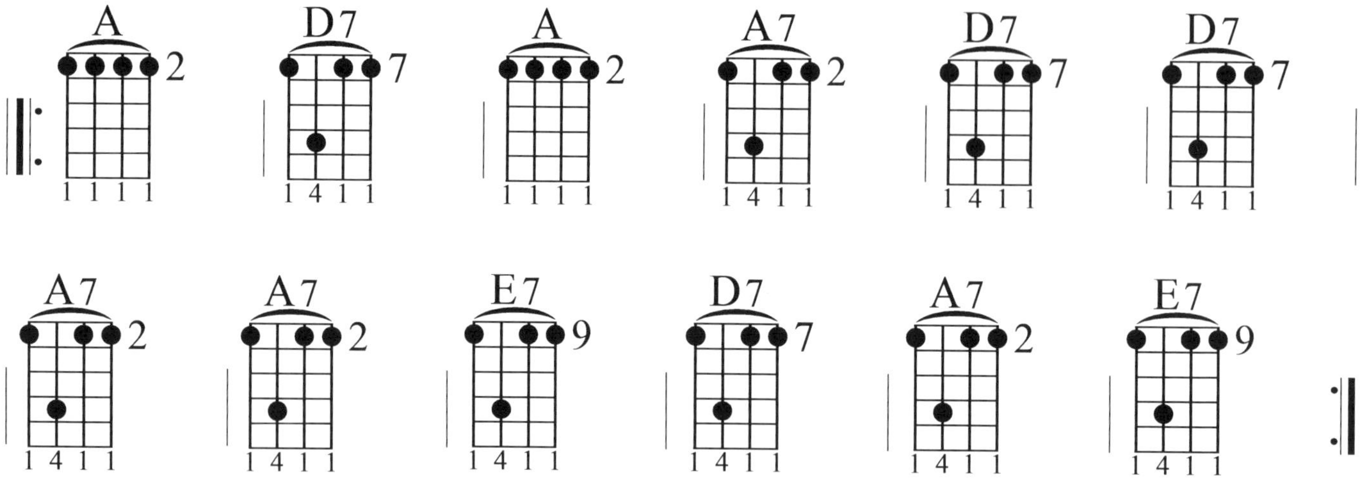

12 Bar Minor Blues Progression

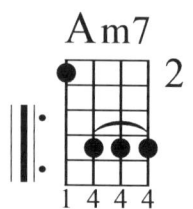

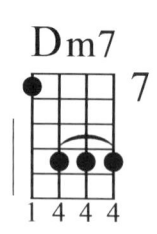

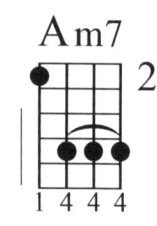

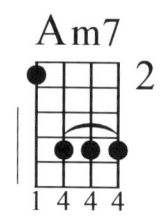

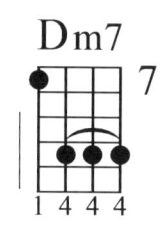

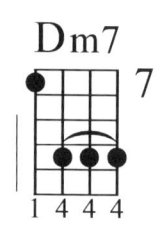

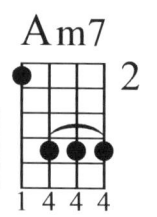

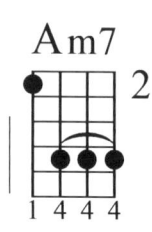

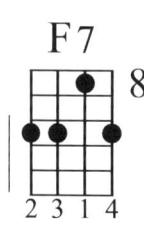

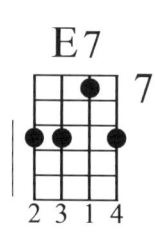

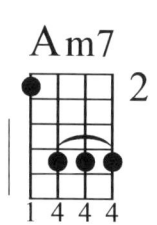

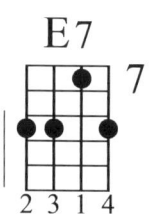

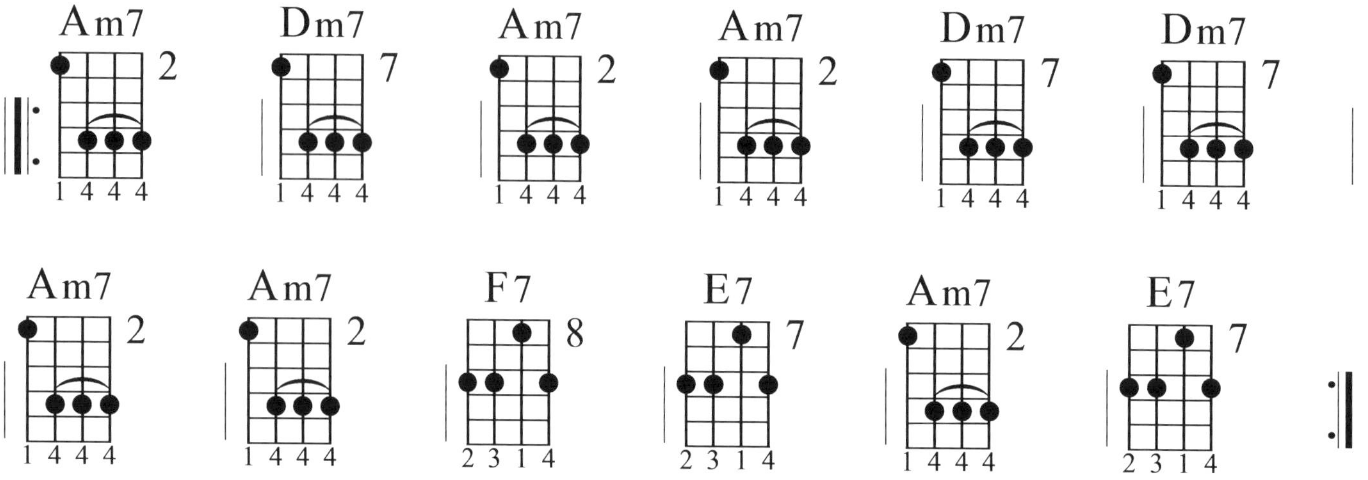

8 Bar Blues Progression

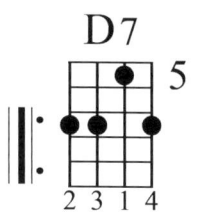

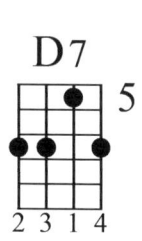

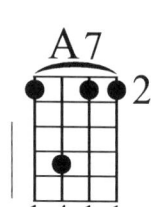

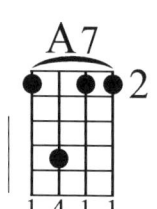

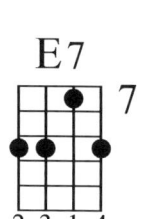

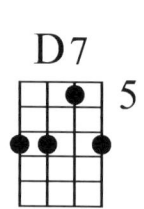

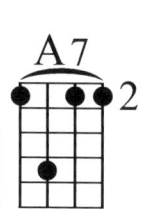

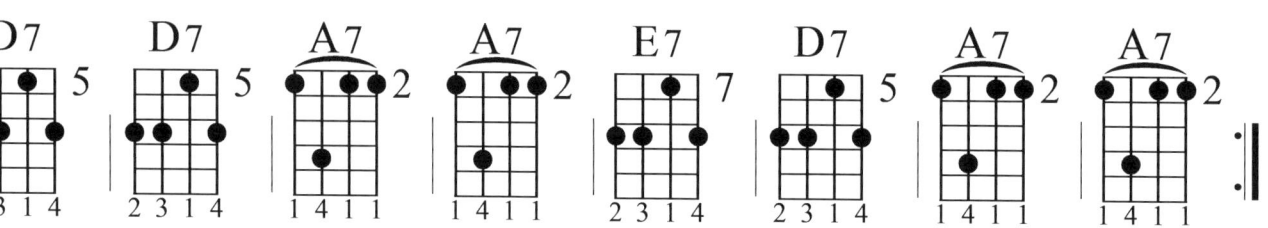

Blues Chord Progressions - Key of B♭ and B♭m

12 Bar Blues Progression

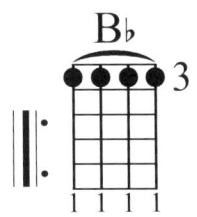

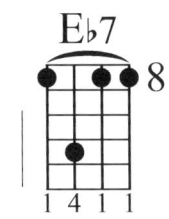

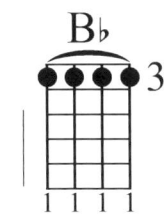

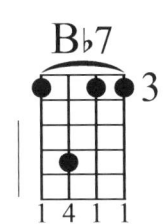

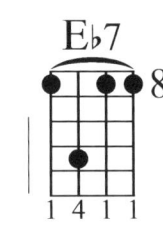

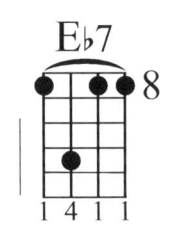

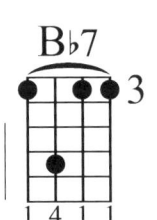

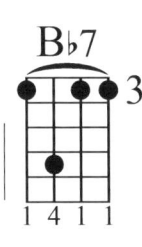

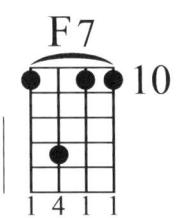

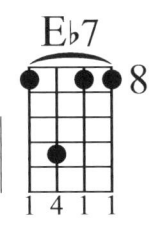

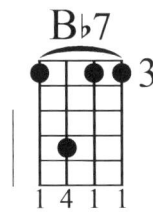

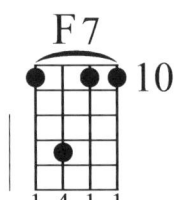

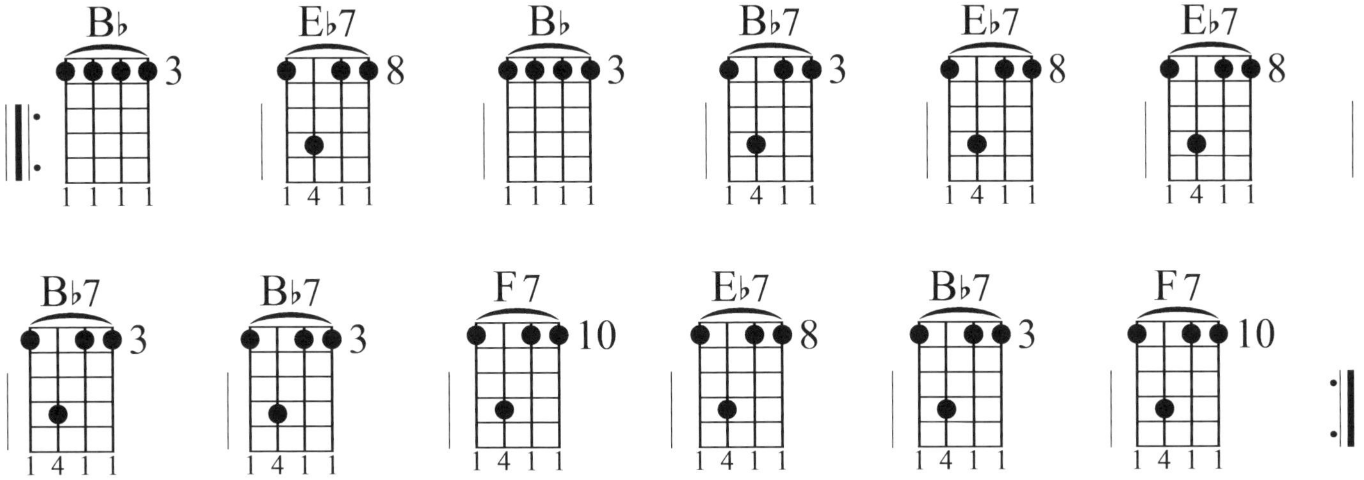

| B♭ | E♭7 | B♭ | B♭7 | E♭7 | E♭7 |
| B♭7 | B♭7 | F7 | E♭7 | B♭7 | F7 |

12 Bar Minor Blues Progression

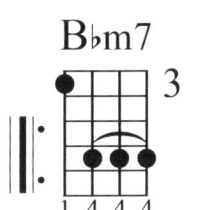

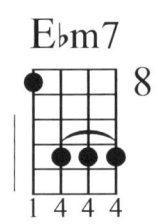

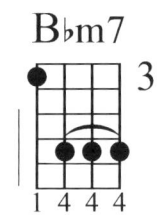

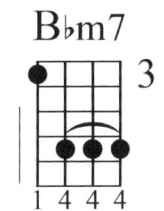

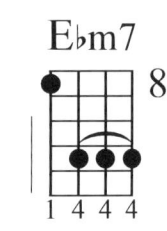

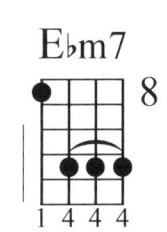

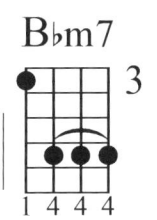

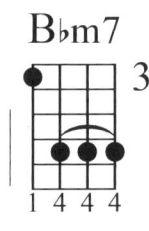

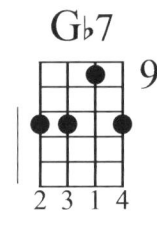

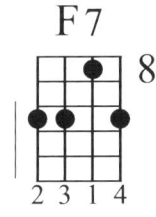

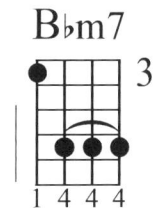

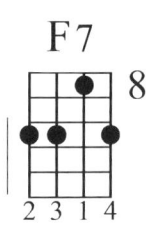

| B♭m7 | E♭m7 | B♭m7 | B♭m7 | E♭m7 | E♭m7 |
| B♭m7 | B♭m7 | G♭7 | F7 | B♭m7 | F7 |

8 Bar Blues Progression

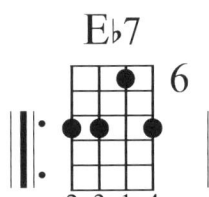

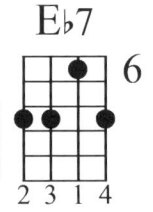

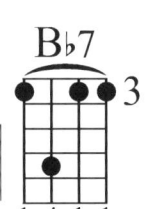

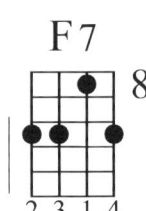

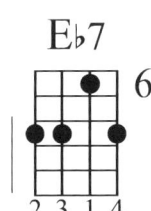

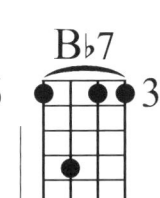

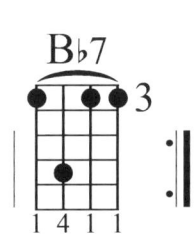

| E♭7 | E♭7 | B♭7 | B♭7 | F7 | E♭7 | B♭7 | B♭7 |

Blues Chord Progressions - Key of B and Bm

12 Bar Blues Progression

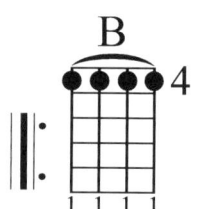

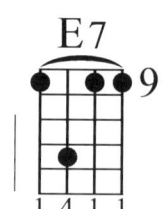

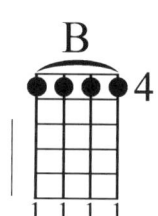

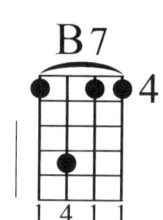

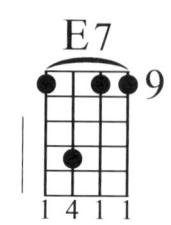

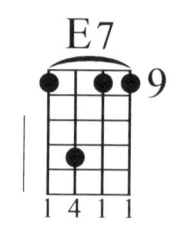

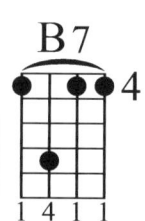

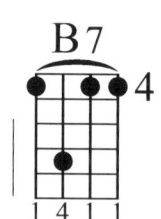

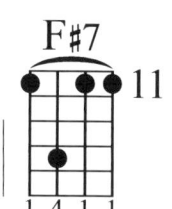

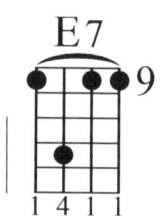

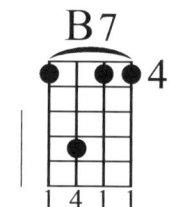

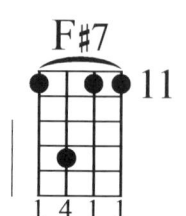

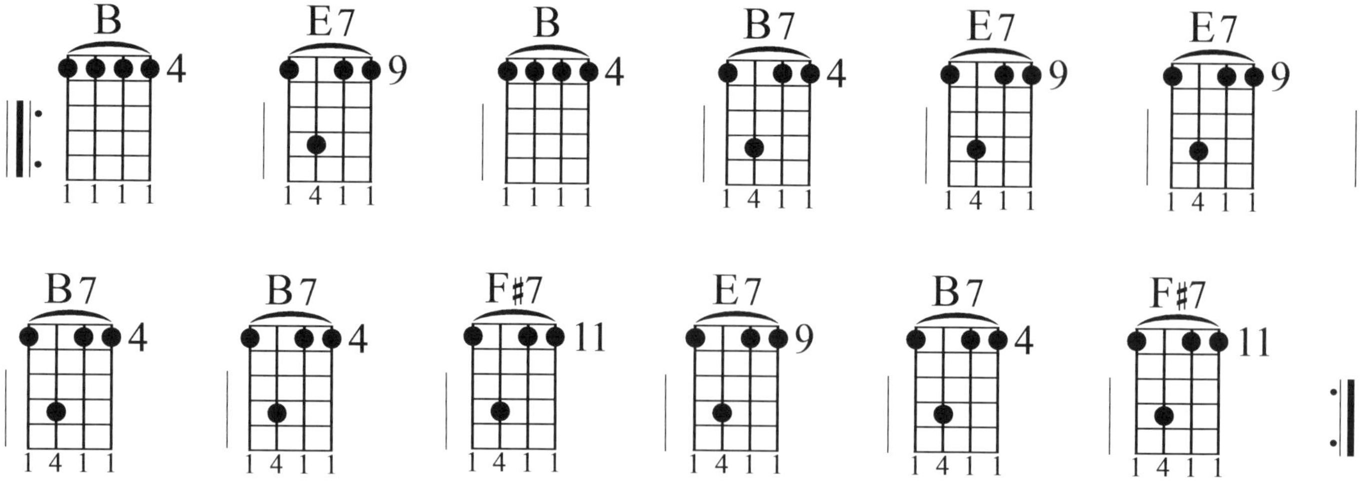

12 Bar Minor Blues Progression

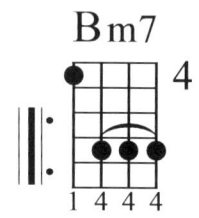

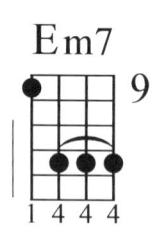

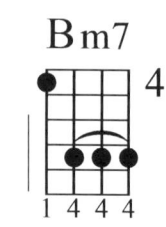

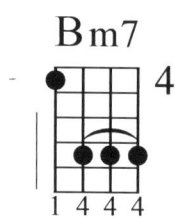

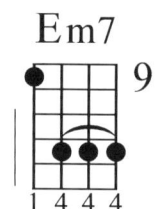

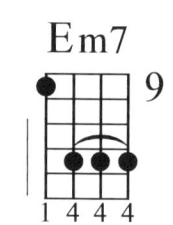

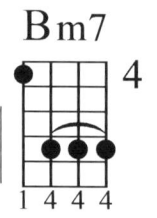

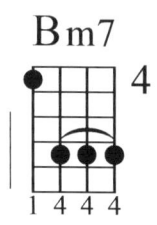

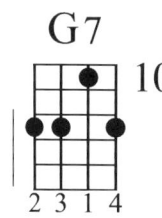

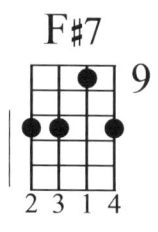

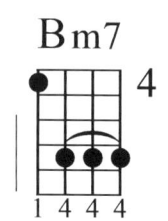

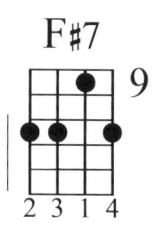

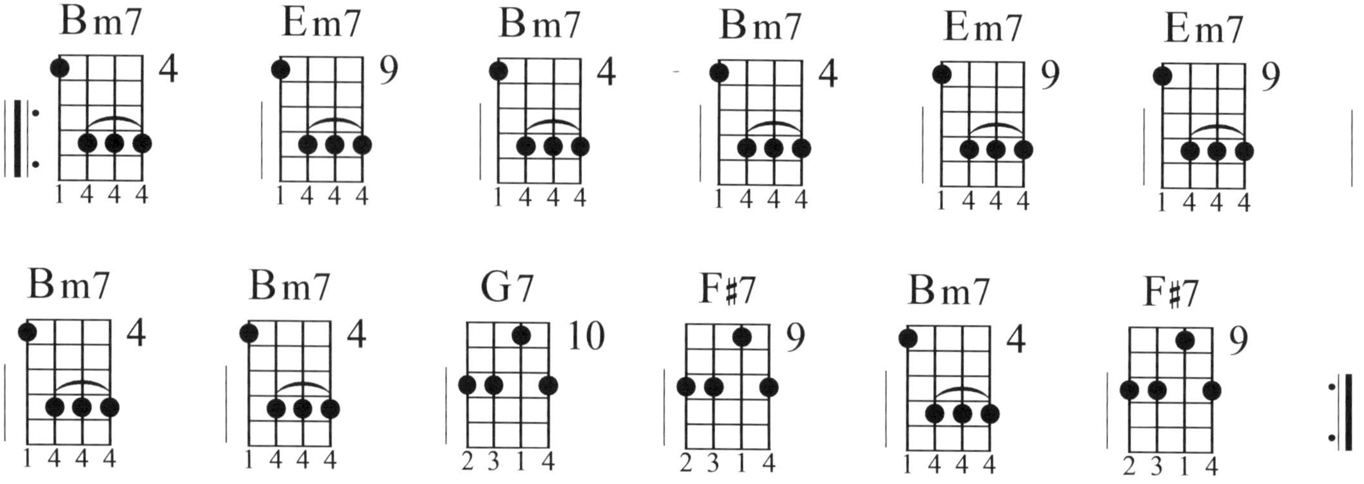

8 Bar Blues Progression

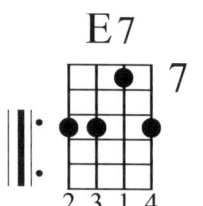

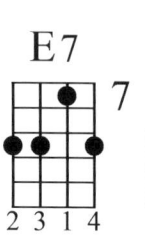

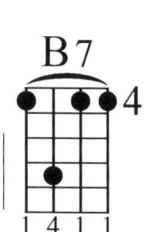

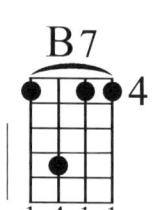

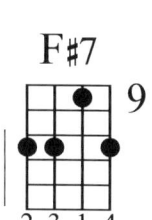

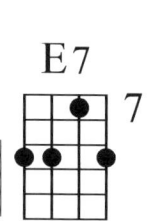

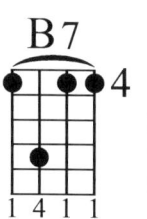

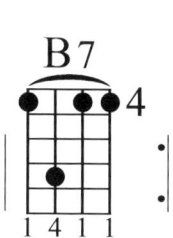

Blues Chord Progressions - Key of C and Cm

12 Bar Blues Progression

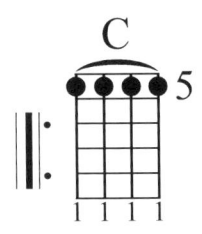

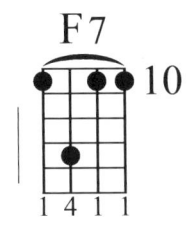

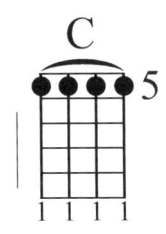

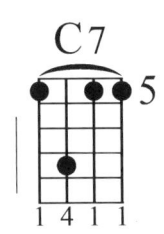

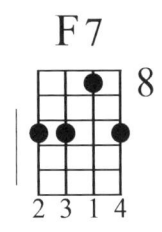

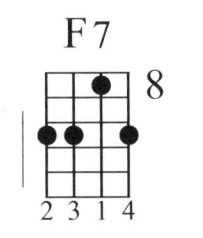

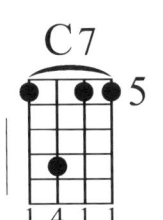

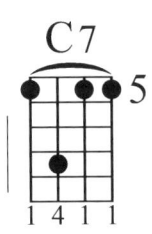

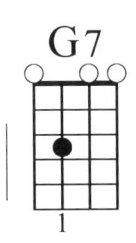

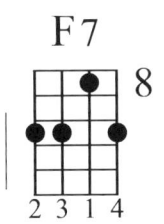

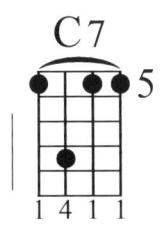

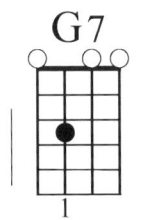

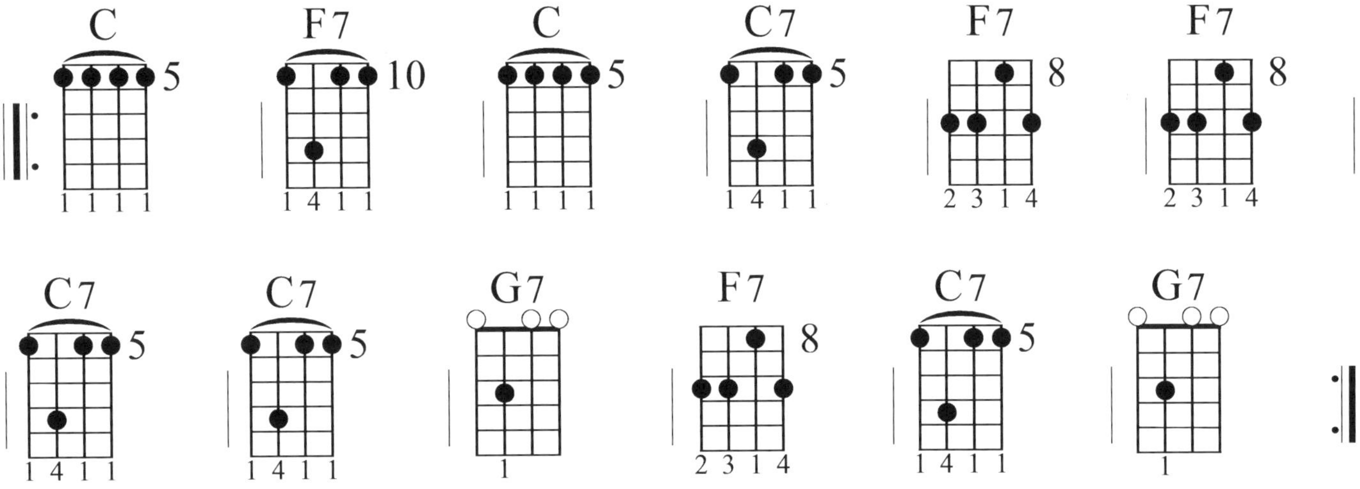

12 Bar Minor Blues Progression

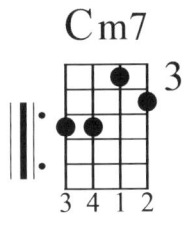

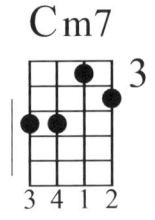

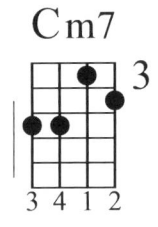

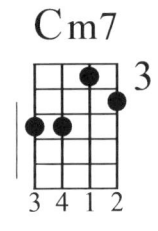

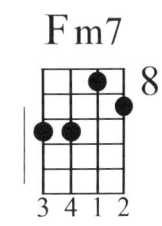

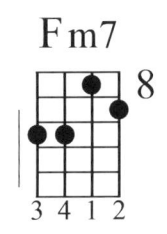

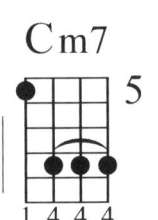

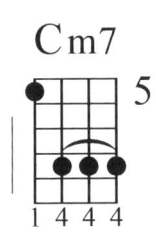

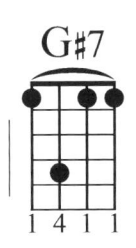

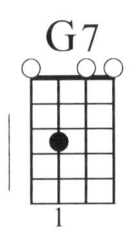

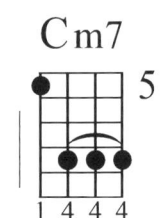

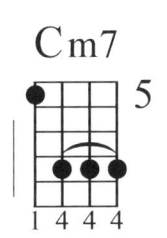

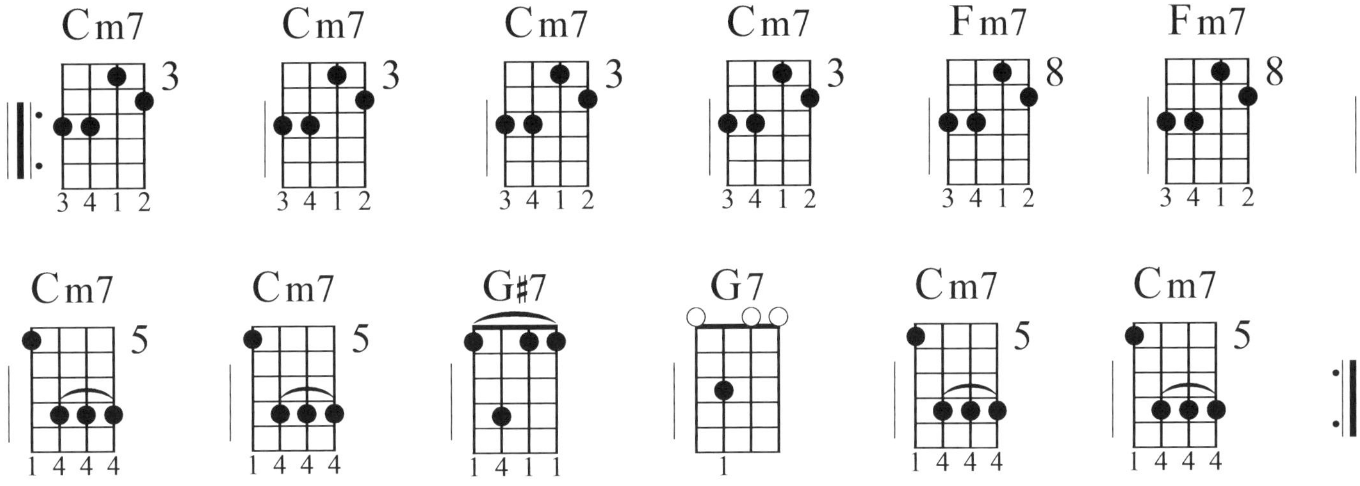

8 Bar Blues Progression

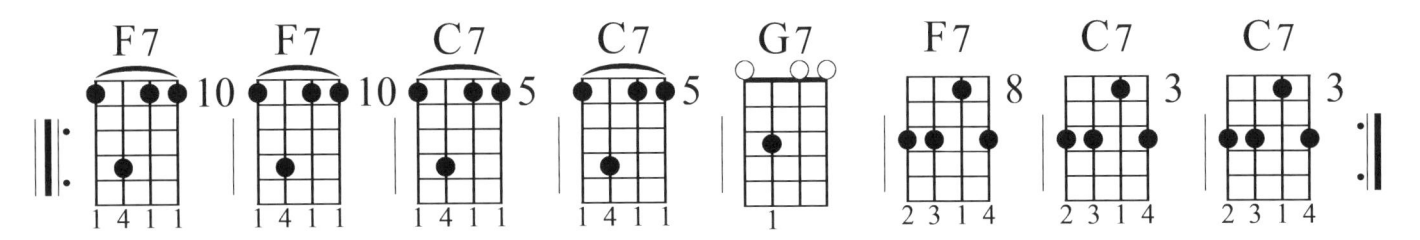

Blues Chord Progressions - Key of D and Dm

12 Bar Blues Progression

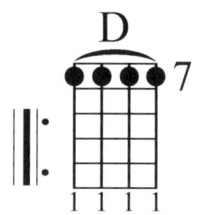

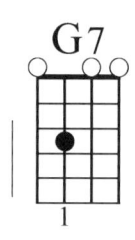

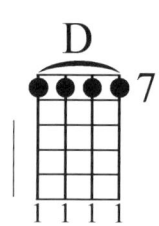

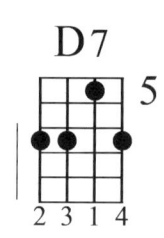

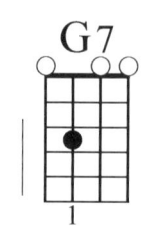

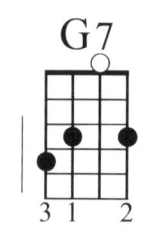

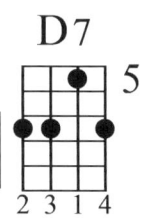

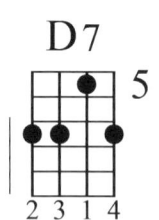

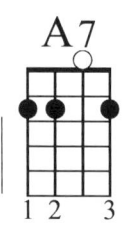

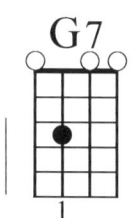

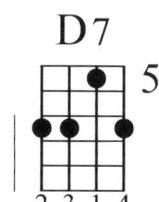

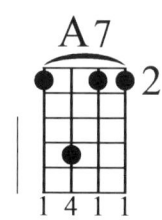

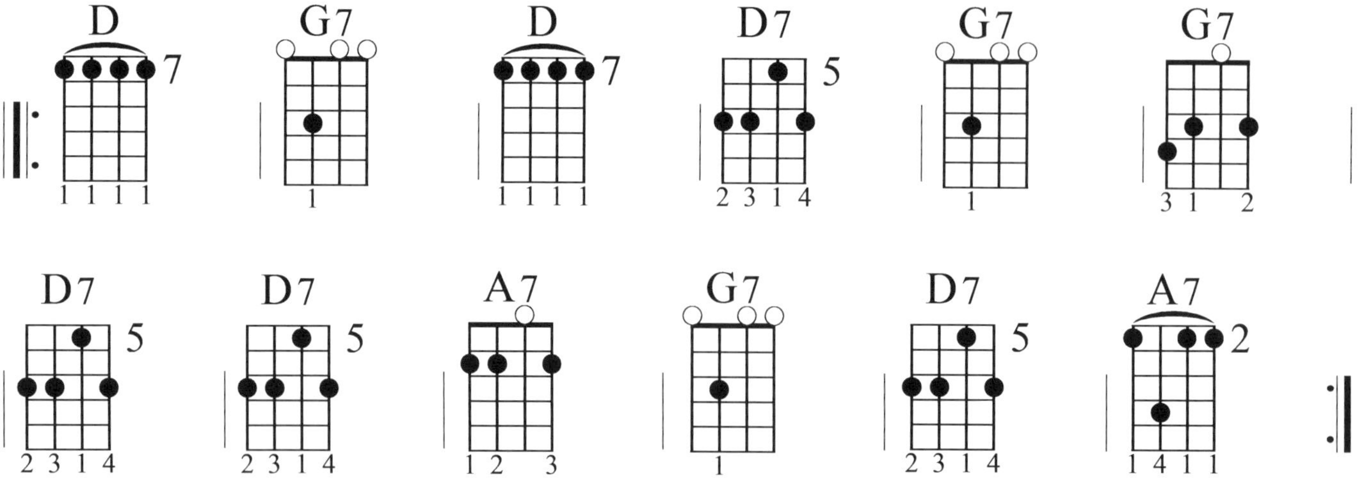

| D | G7 | D | D7 | G7 | G7 |
| D7 | D7 | A7 | G7 | D7 | A7 |

12 Bar Minor Blues Progression

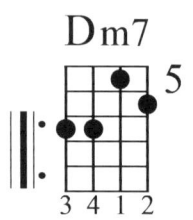

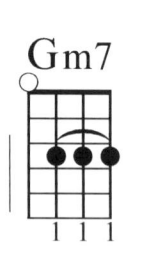

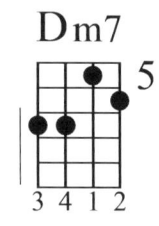

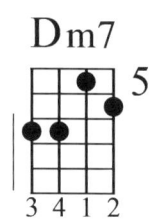

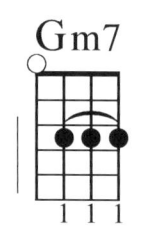

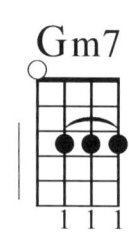

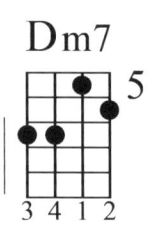

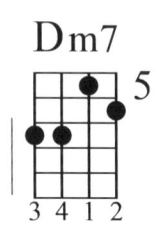

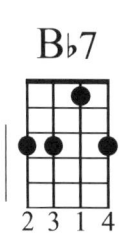

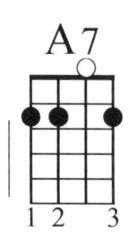

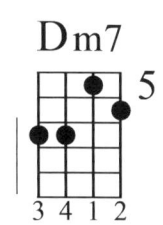

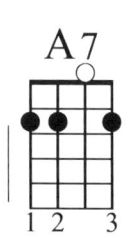

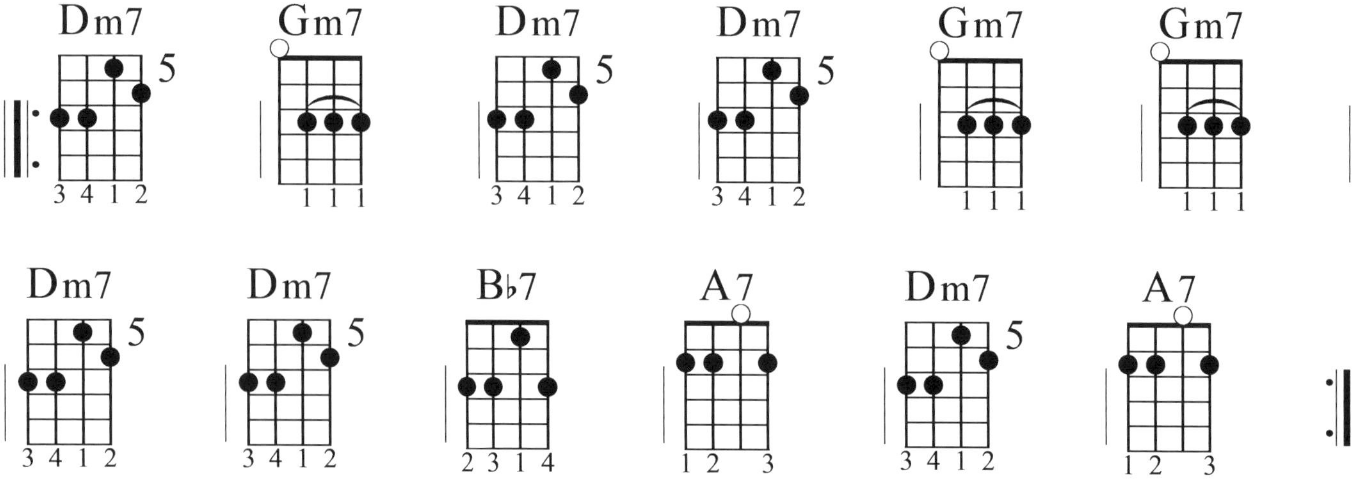

| Dm7 | Gm7 | Dm7 | Dm7 | Gm7 | Gm7 |
| Dm7 | Dm7 | B♭7 | A7 | Dm7 | A7 |

8 Bar Blues Progression

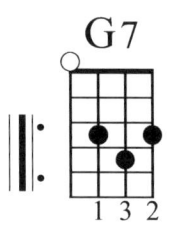

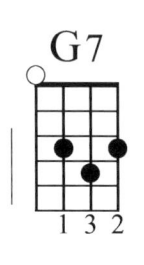

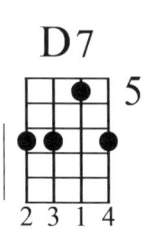

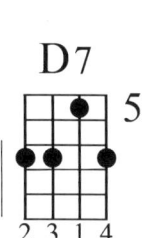

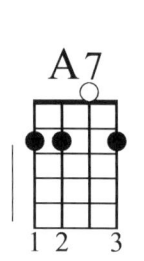

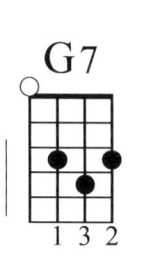

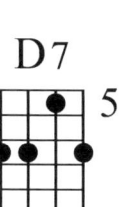

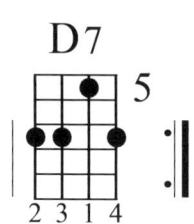

| G7 | G7 | D7 | D7 | A7 | G7 | D7 | D7 |

Blues Chord Progressions - Key of E♭ and E♭m

12 Bar Blues Progression

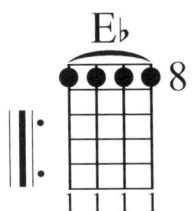

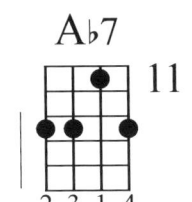

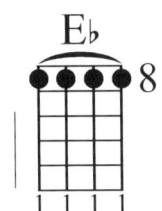

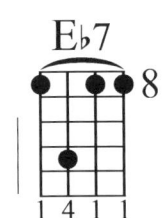

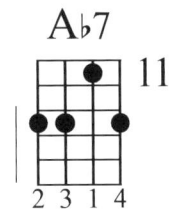

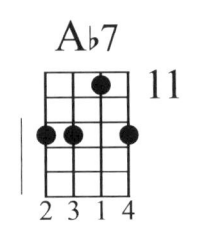

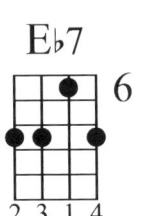

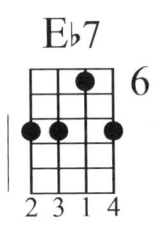

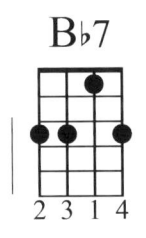

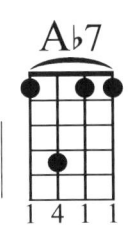

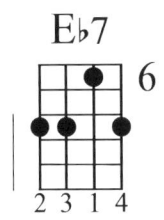

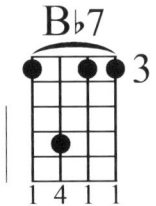

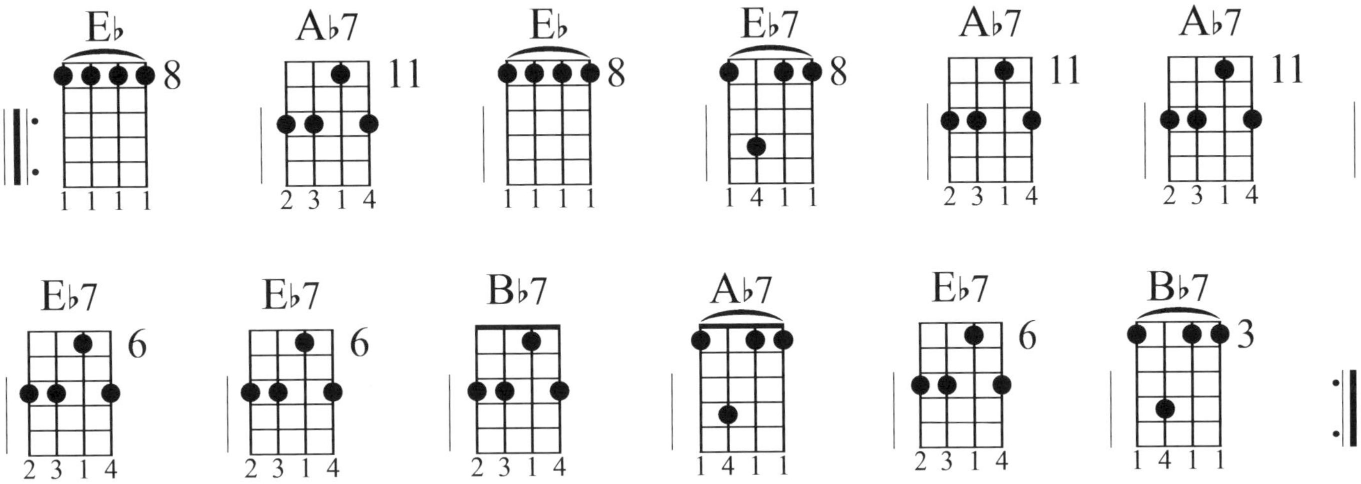

12 Bar Minor Blues Progression

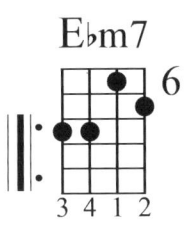

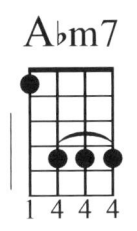

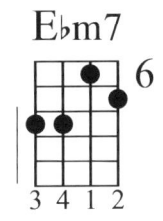

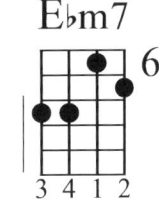

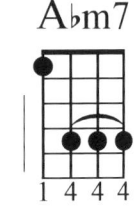

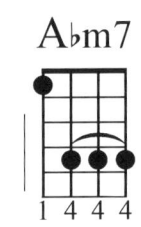

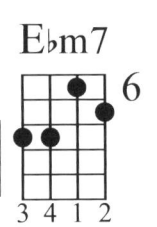

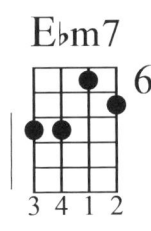

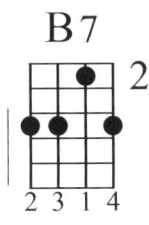

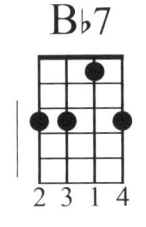

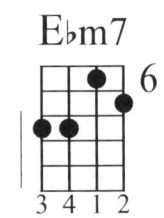

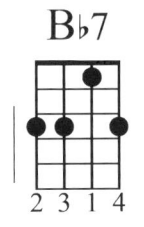

8 Bar Blues Progression

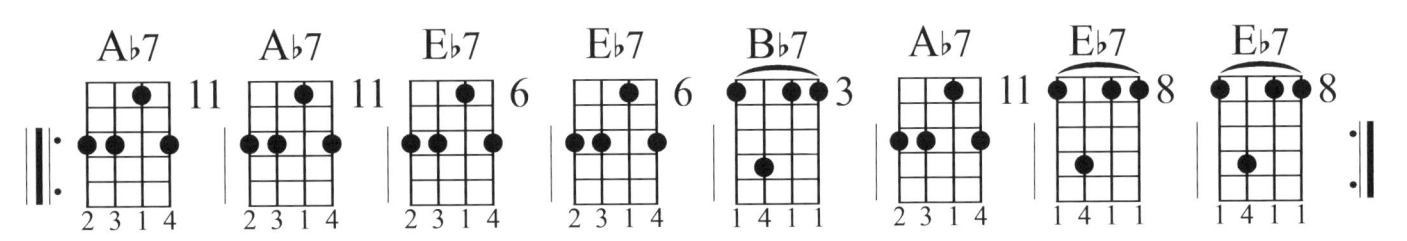

Blues Chord Progressions - Key of E and Em

12 Bar Blues Progression

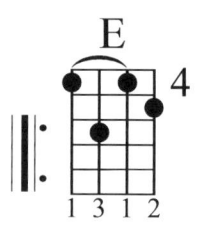

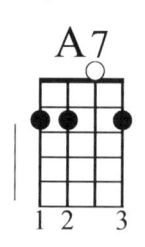

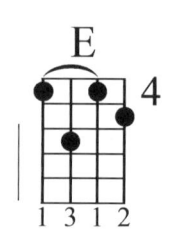

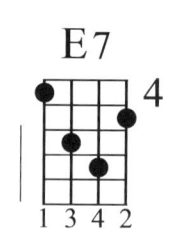

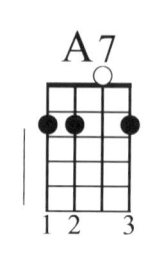

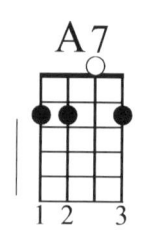

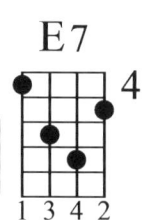

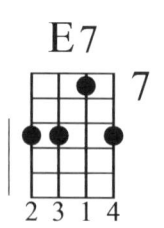

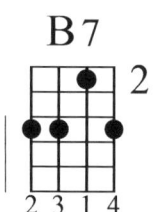

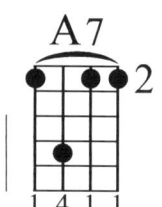

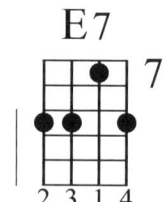

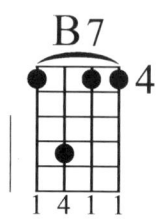

12 Bar Minor Blues Progression

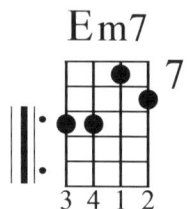

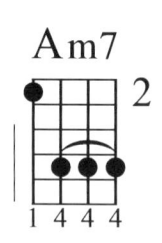

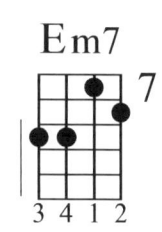

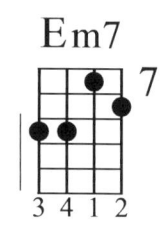

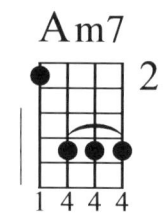

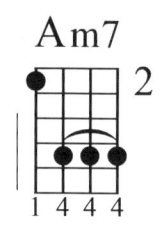

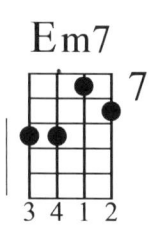

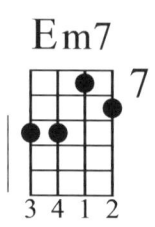

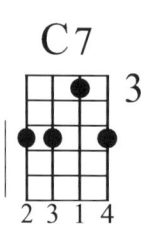

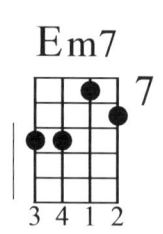

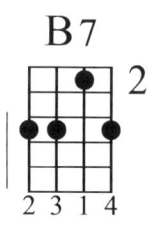

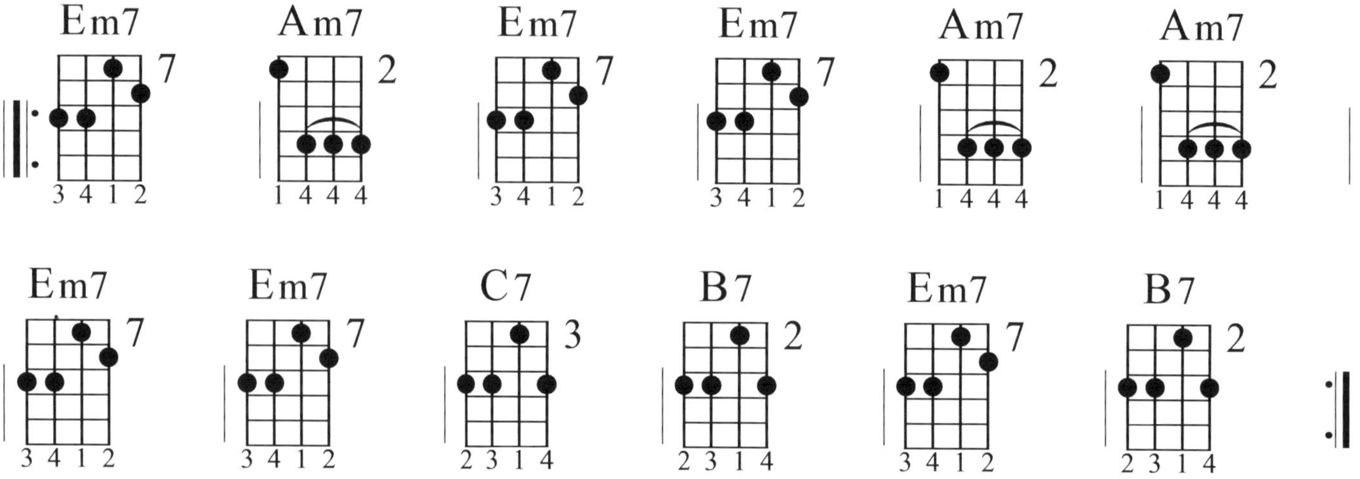

8 Bar Blues Progression

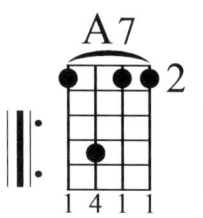

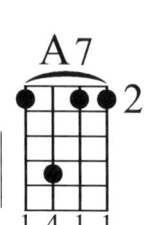

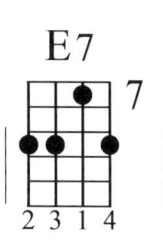

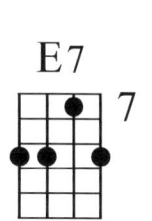

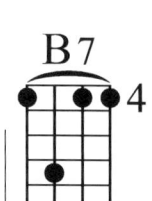

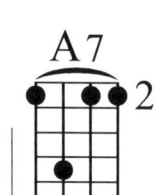

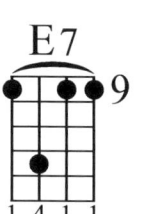

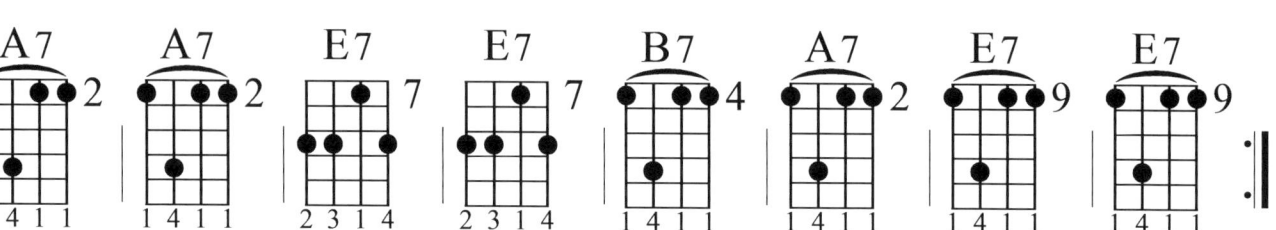

Blues Chord Progressions - Key of F and Fm

12 Bar Blues Progression

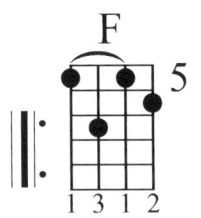

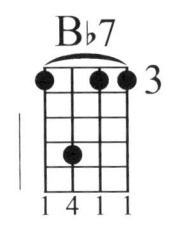

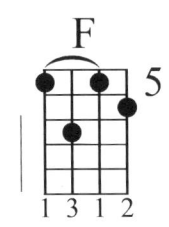

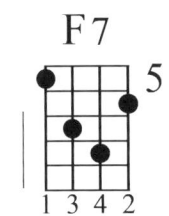

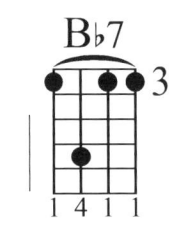

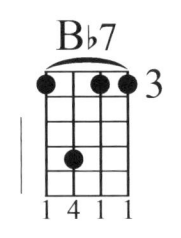

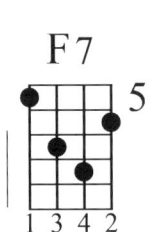

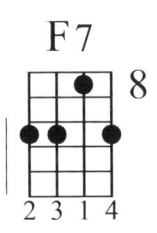

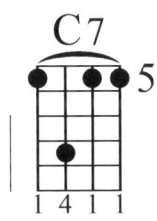

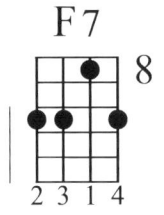

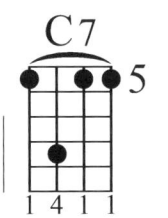

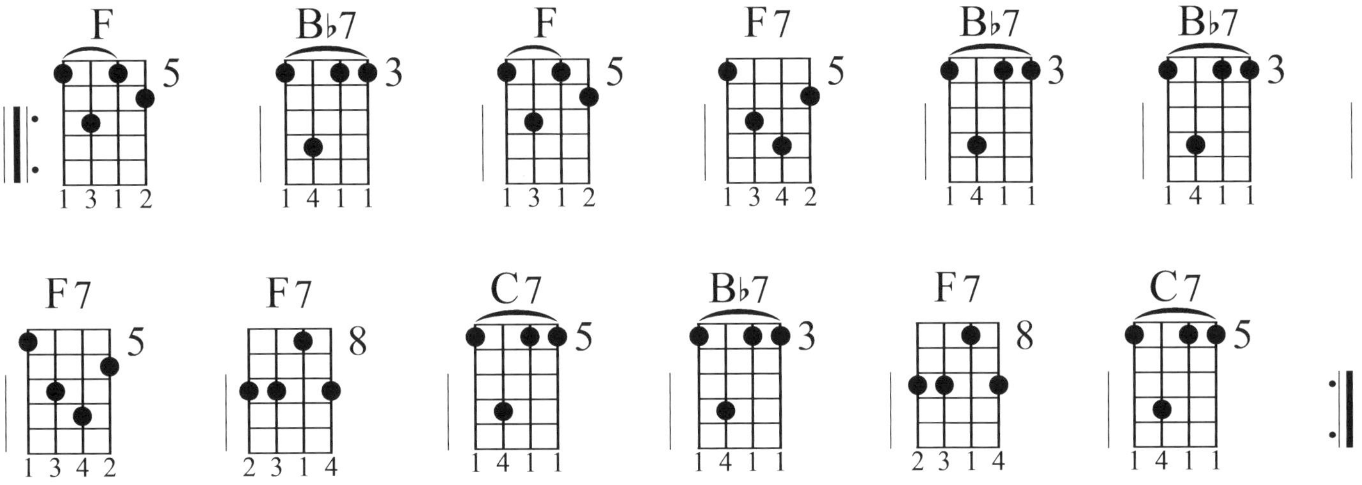

| F | B♭7 | F | F7 | B♭7 | B♭7 |
| F7 | F7 | C7 | B♭7 | F7 | C7 |

12 Bar Minor Blues Progression

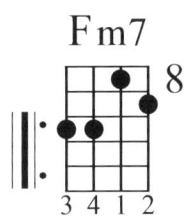

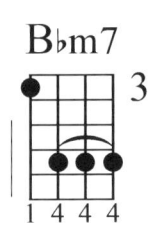

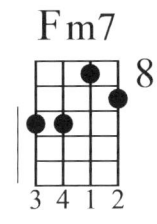

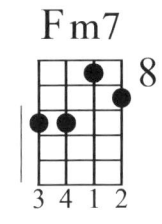

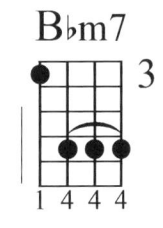

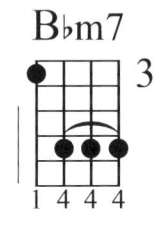

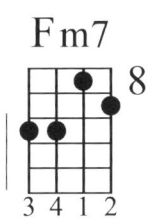

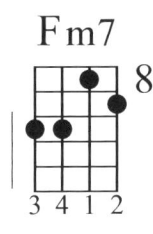

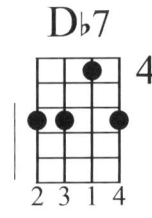

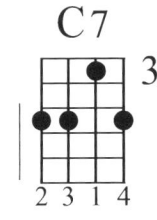

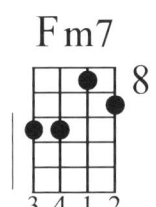

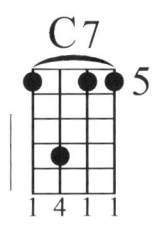

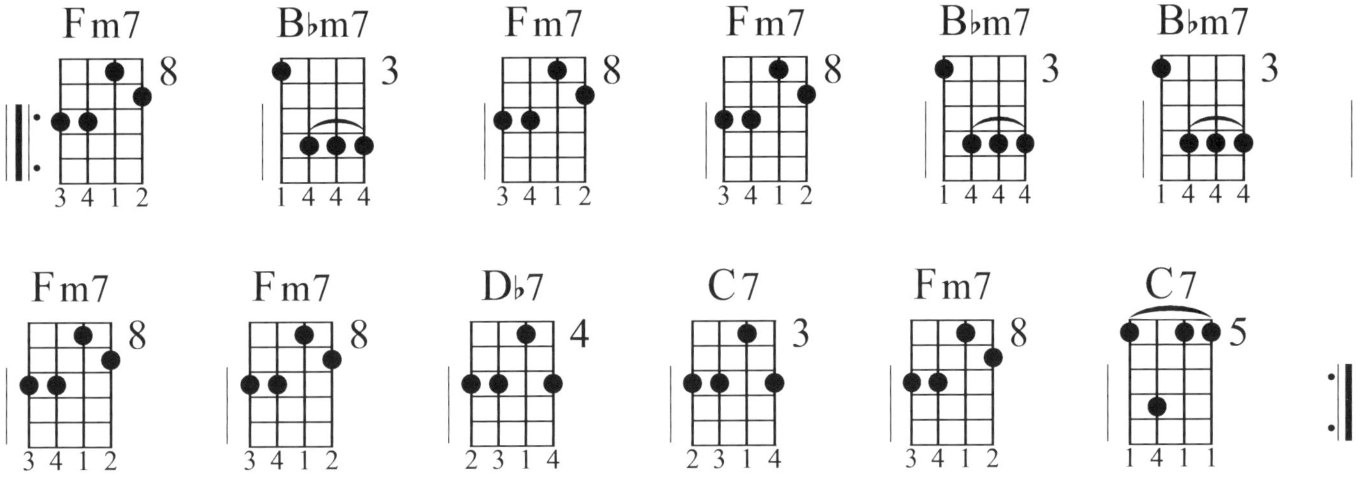

| Fm7 | B♭m7 | Fm7 | Fm7 | B♭m7 | B♭m7 |
| Fm7 | Fm7 | D♭7 | C7 | Fm7 | C7 |

8 Bar Blues Progression

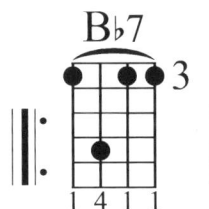

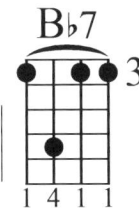

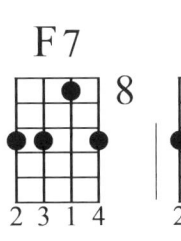

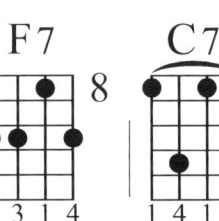

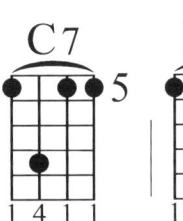

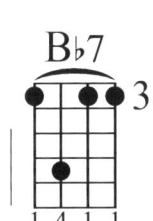

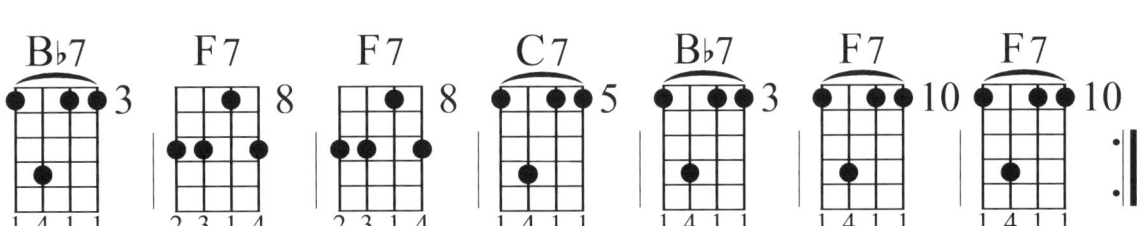

| B♭7 | B♭7 | F7 | F7 | C7 | B♭7 | F7 | F7 |

Blues Chord Progressions - Key of G and Gm

12 Bar Blues Progression

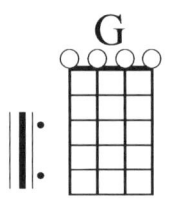

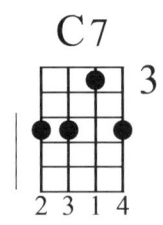

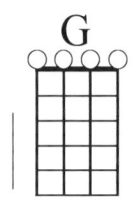

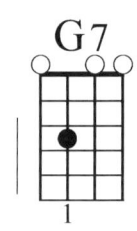

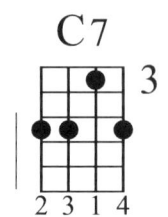

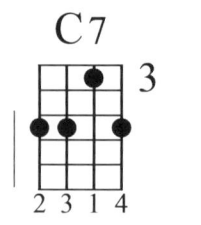

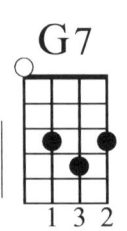

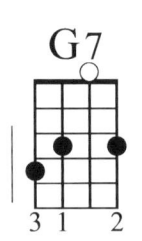

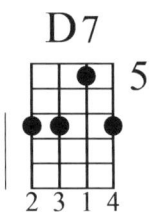

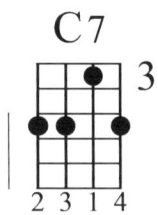

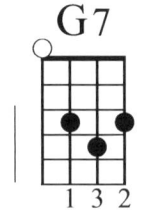

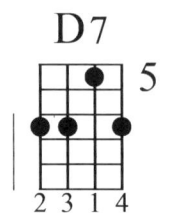

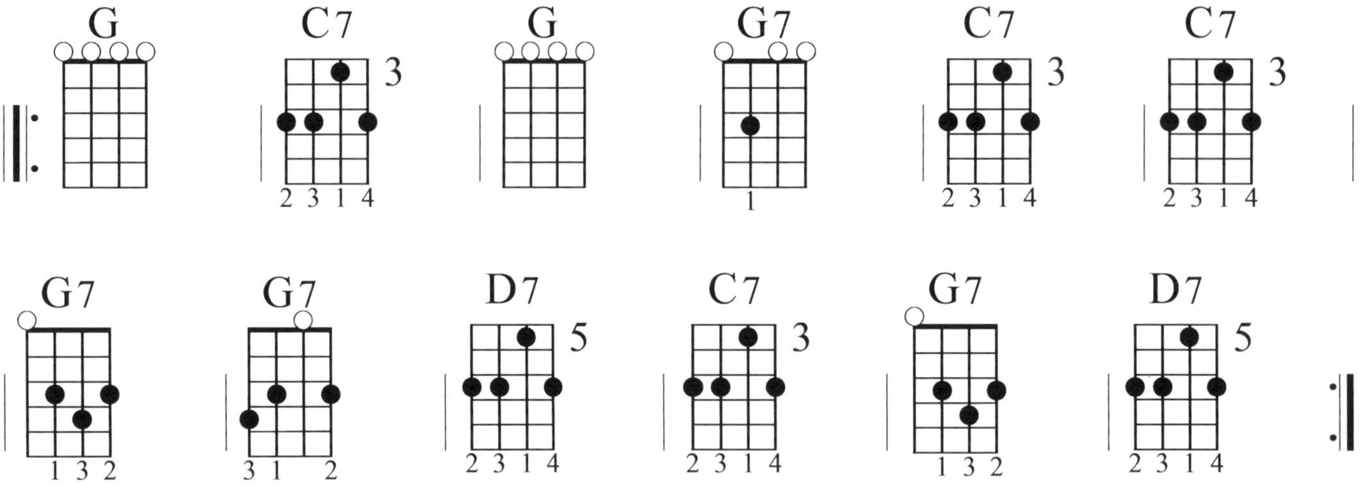

12 Bar Minor Blues Progression

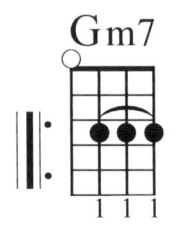

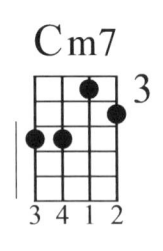

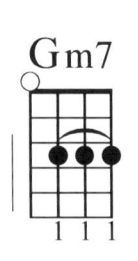

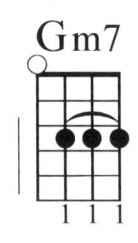

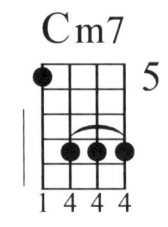

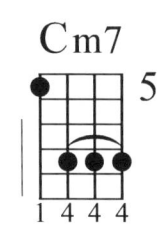

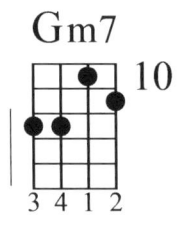

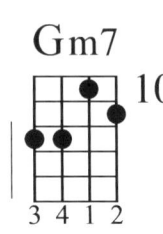

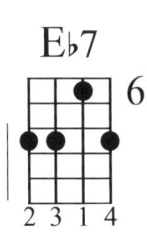

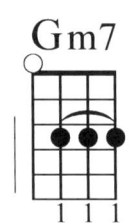

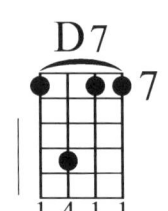

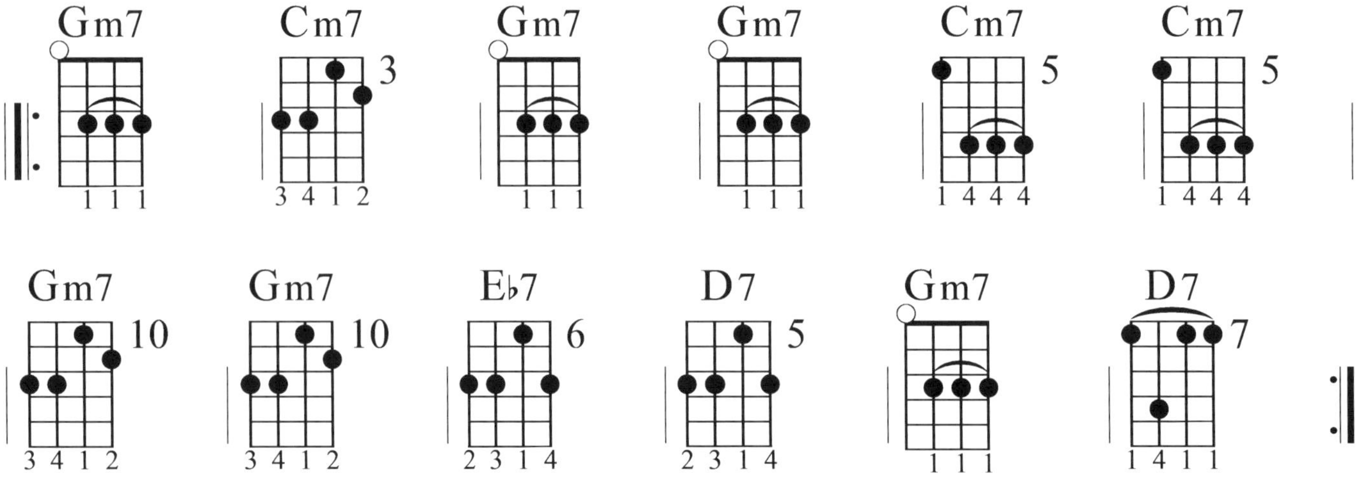

8 Bar Blues Progression

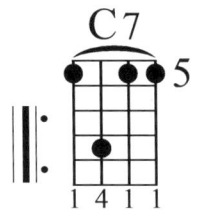

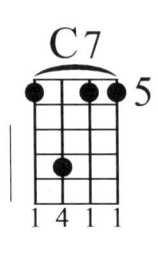

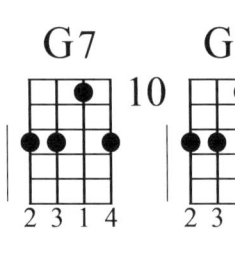

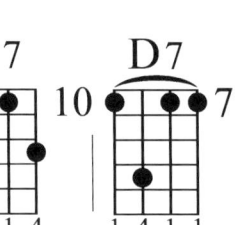

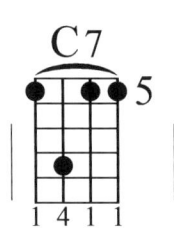

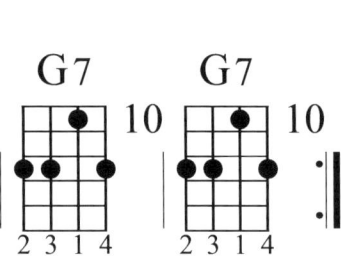

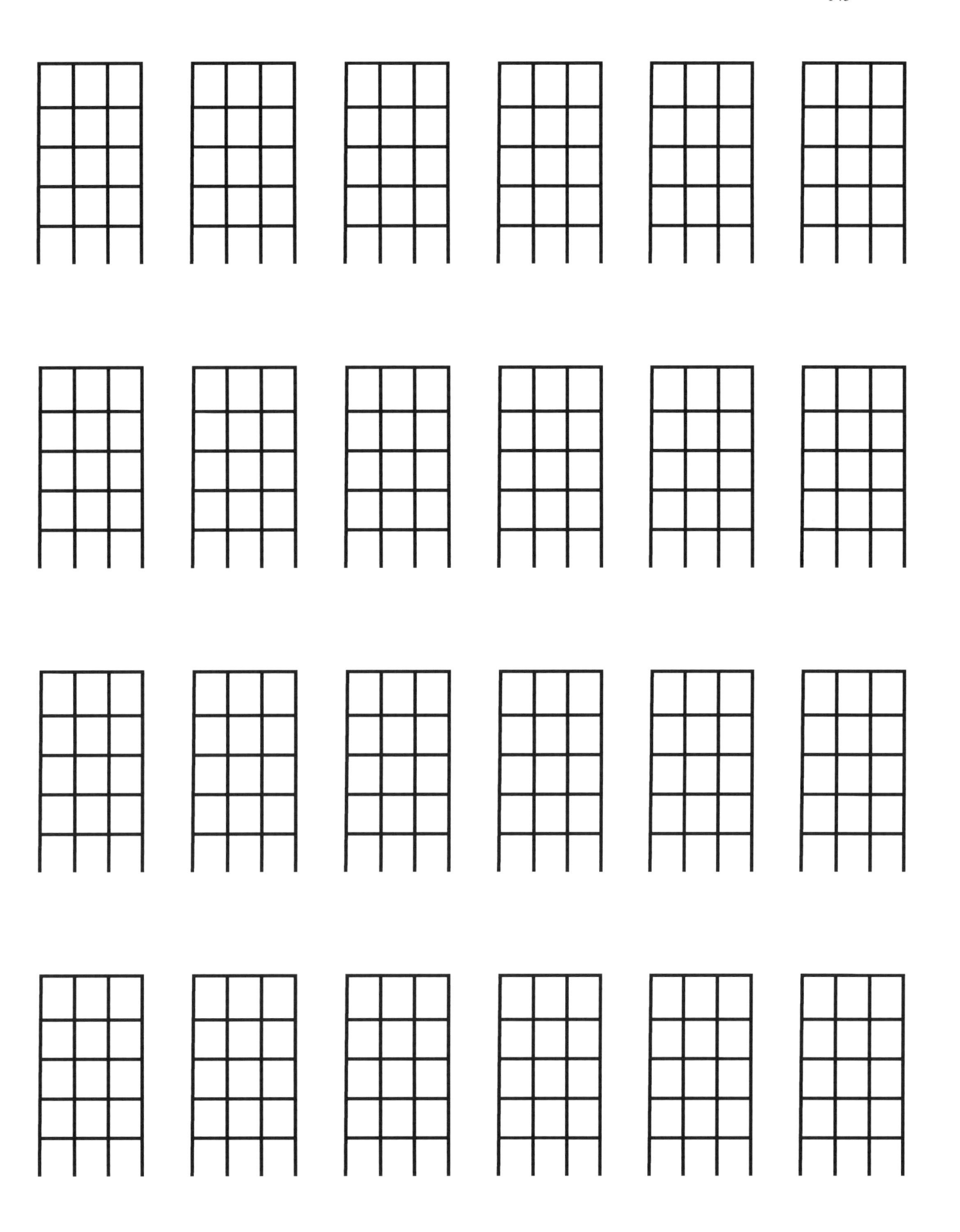

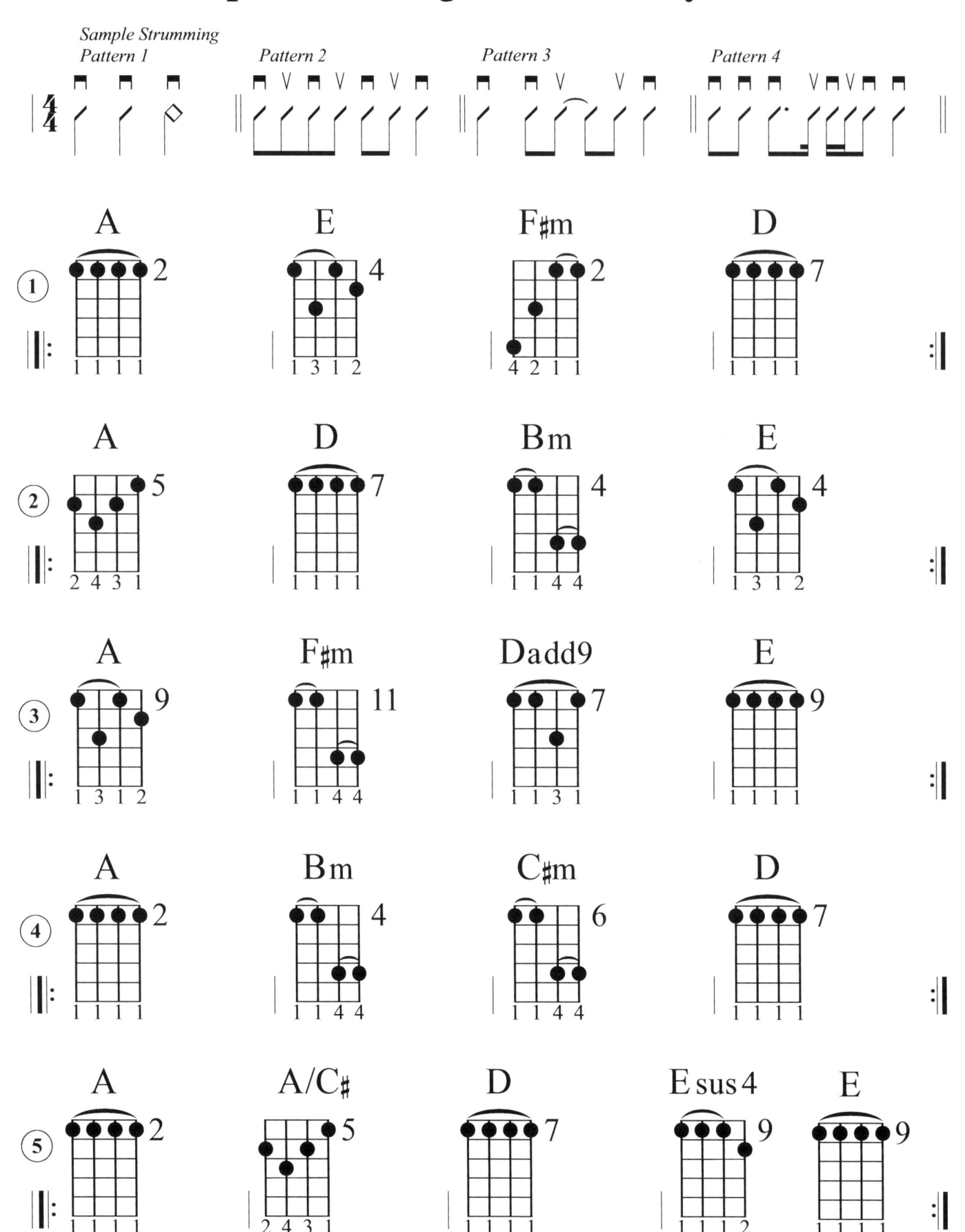

Pop Chord Progressions - Key of A

147

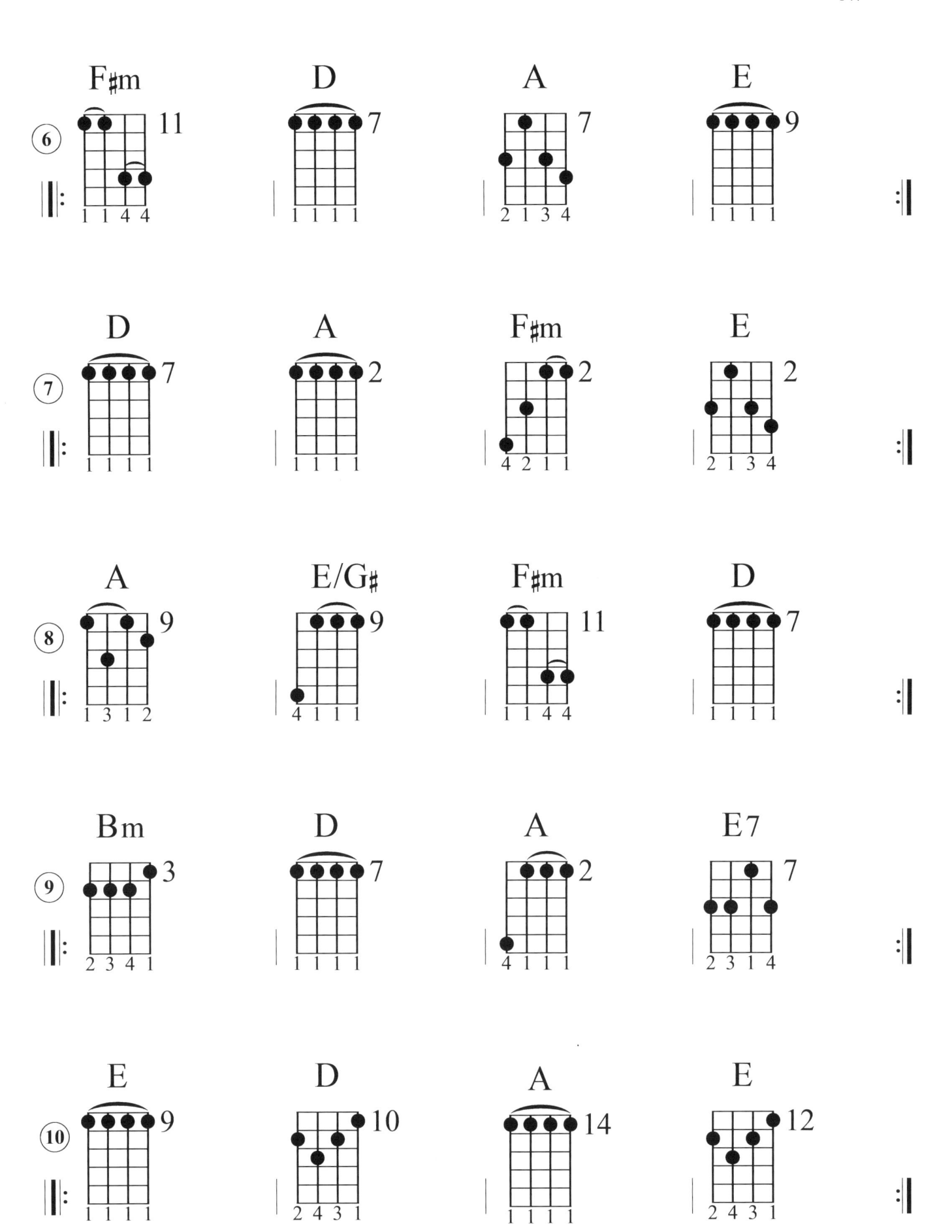

Pop Chord Progressions - Key of B♭

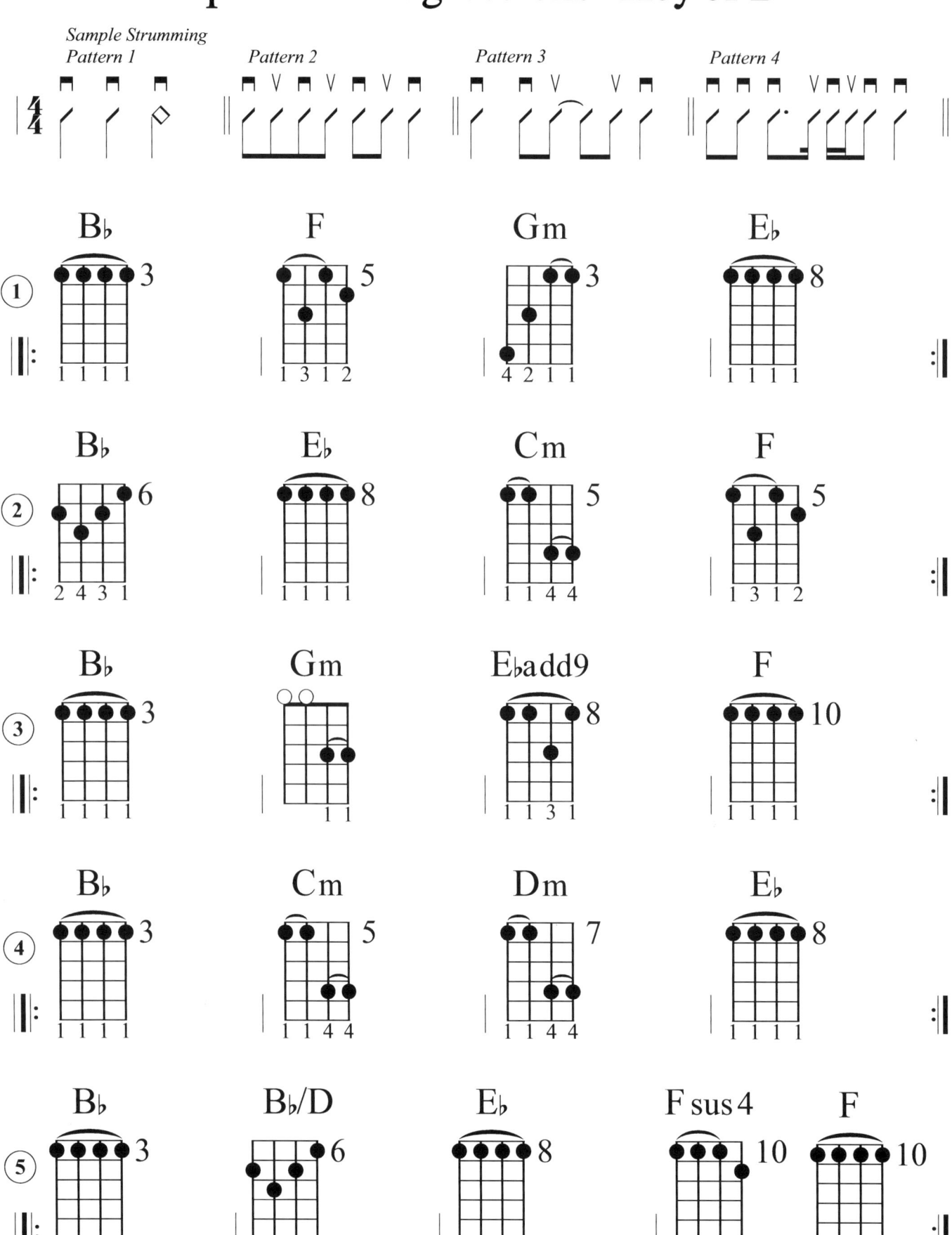

149

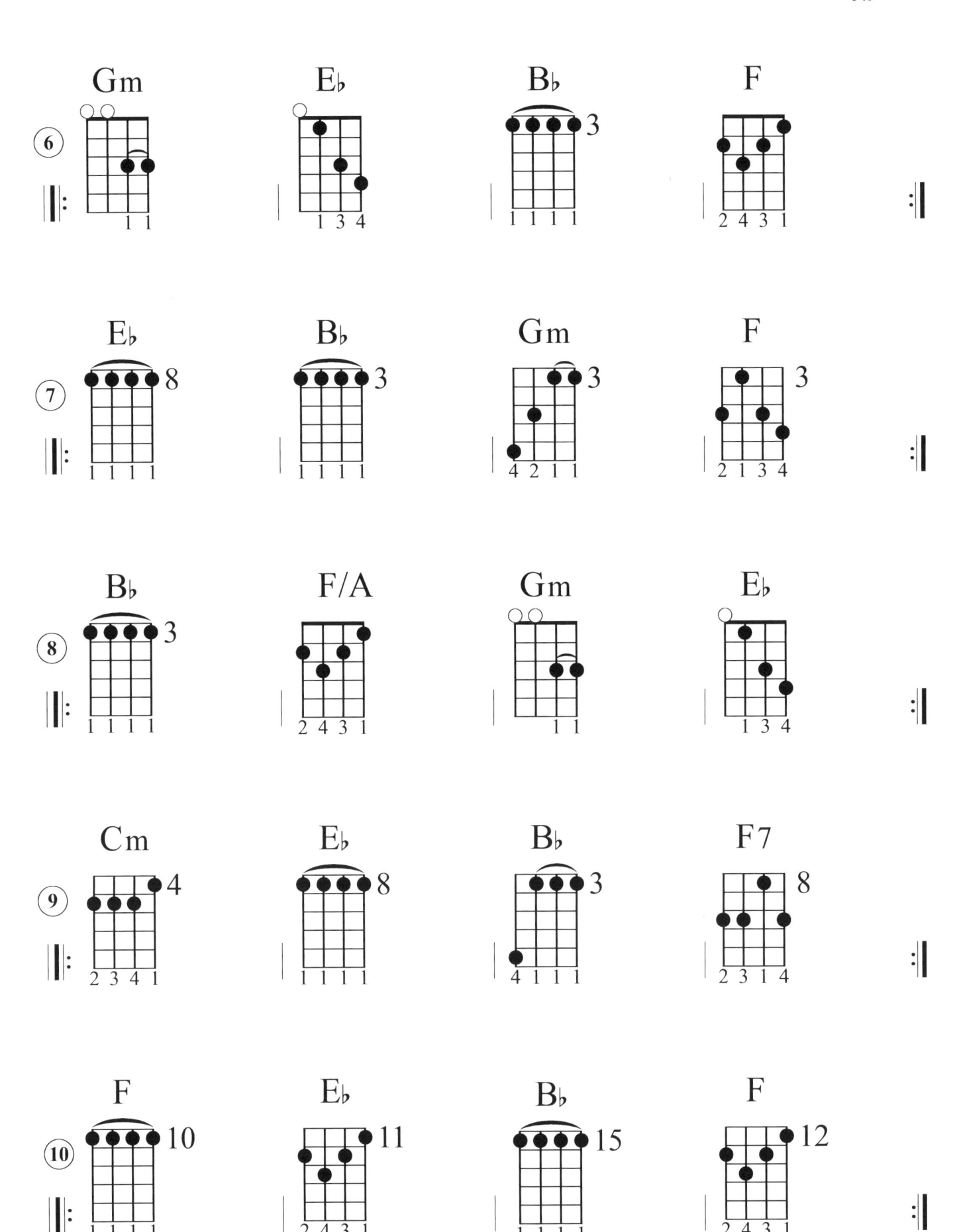

Pop Chord Progressions - Key of B

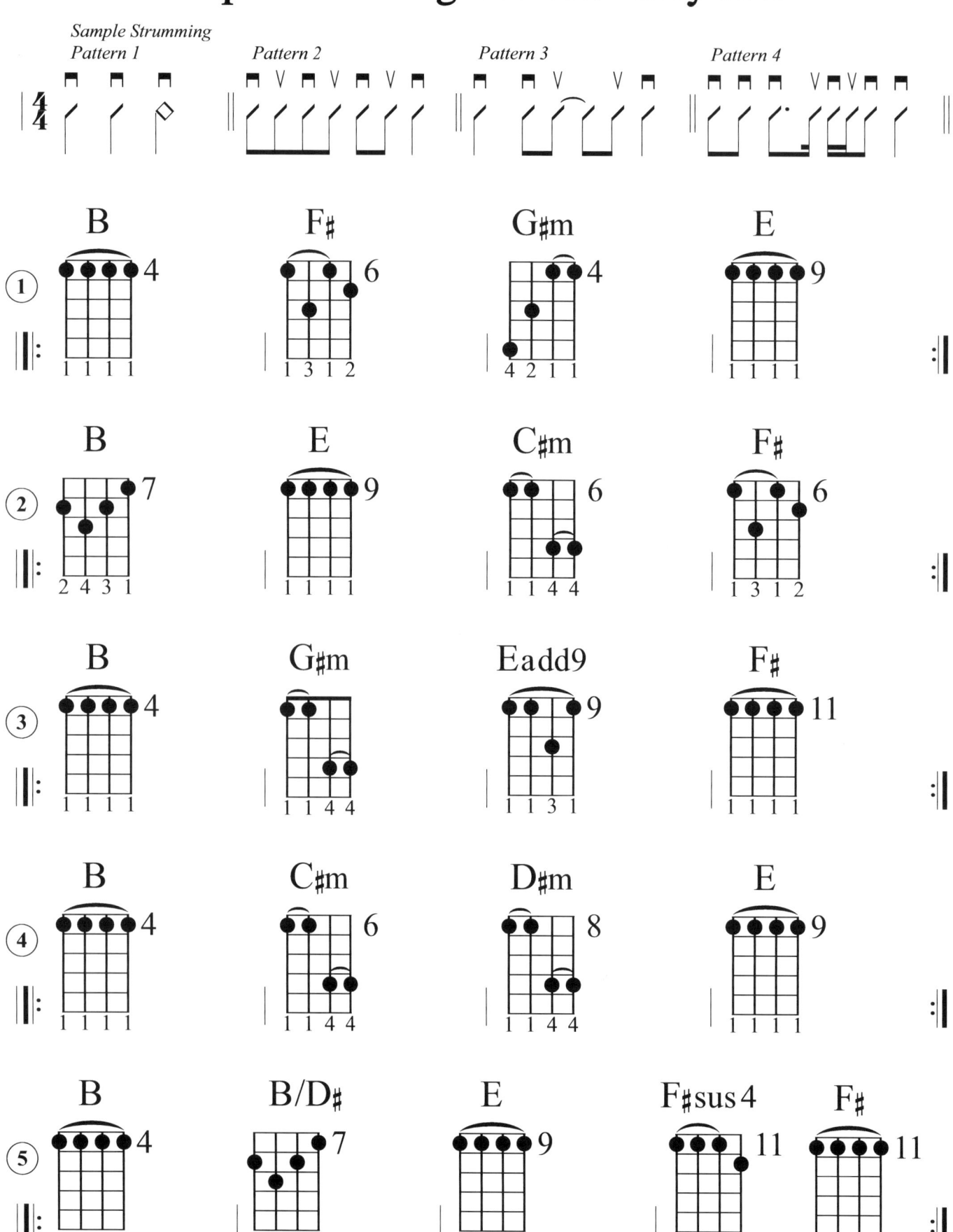

151

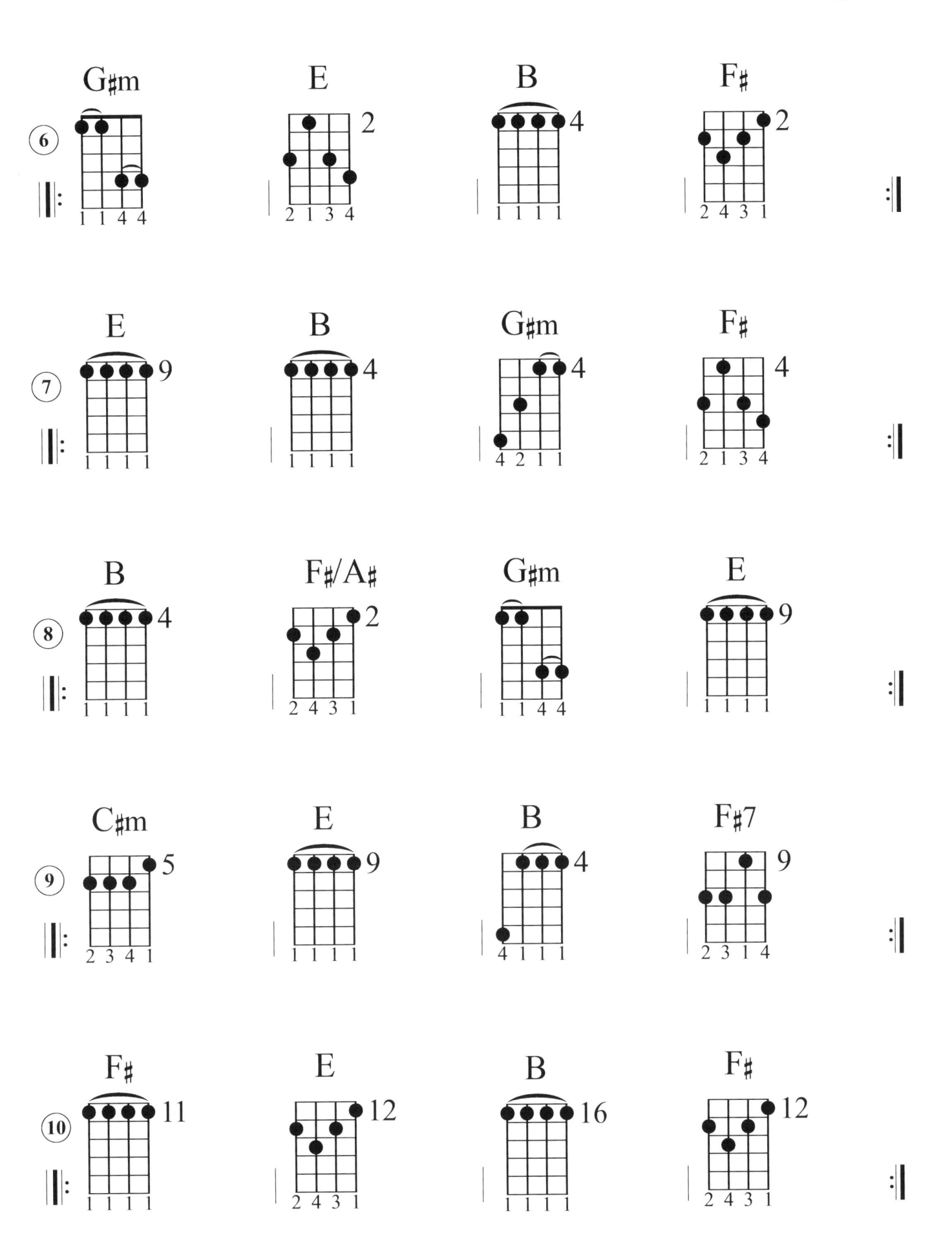

Pop Chord Progressions - Key of C

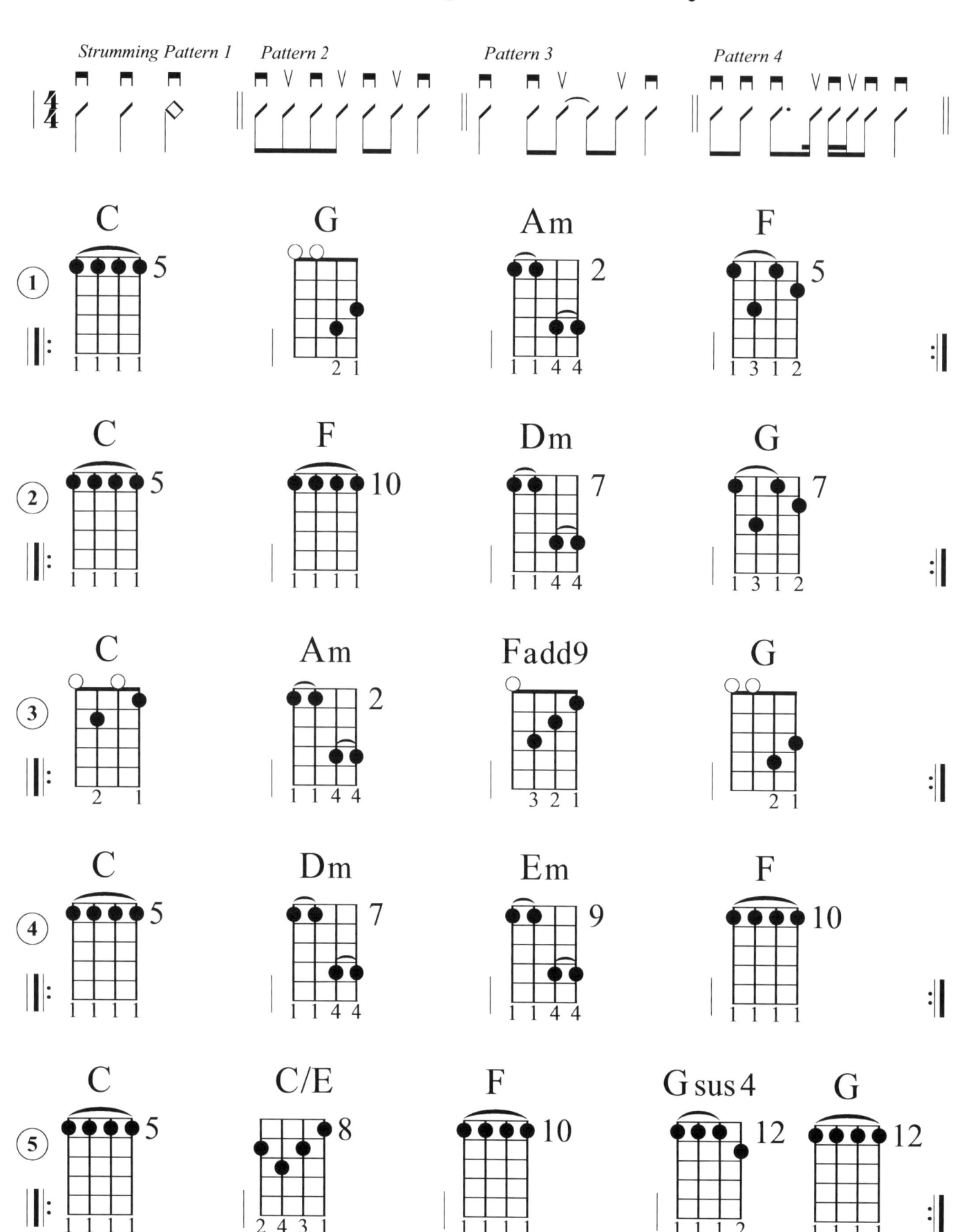

153

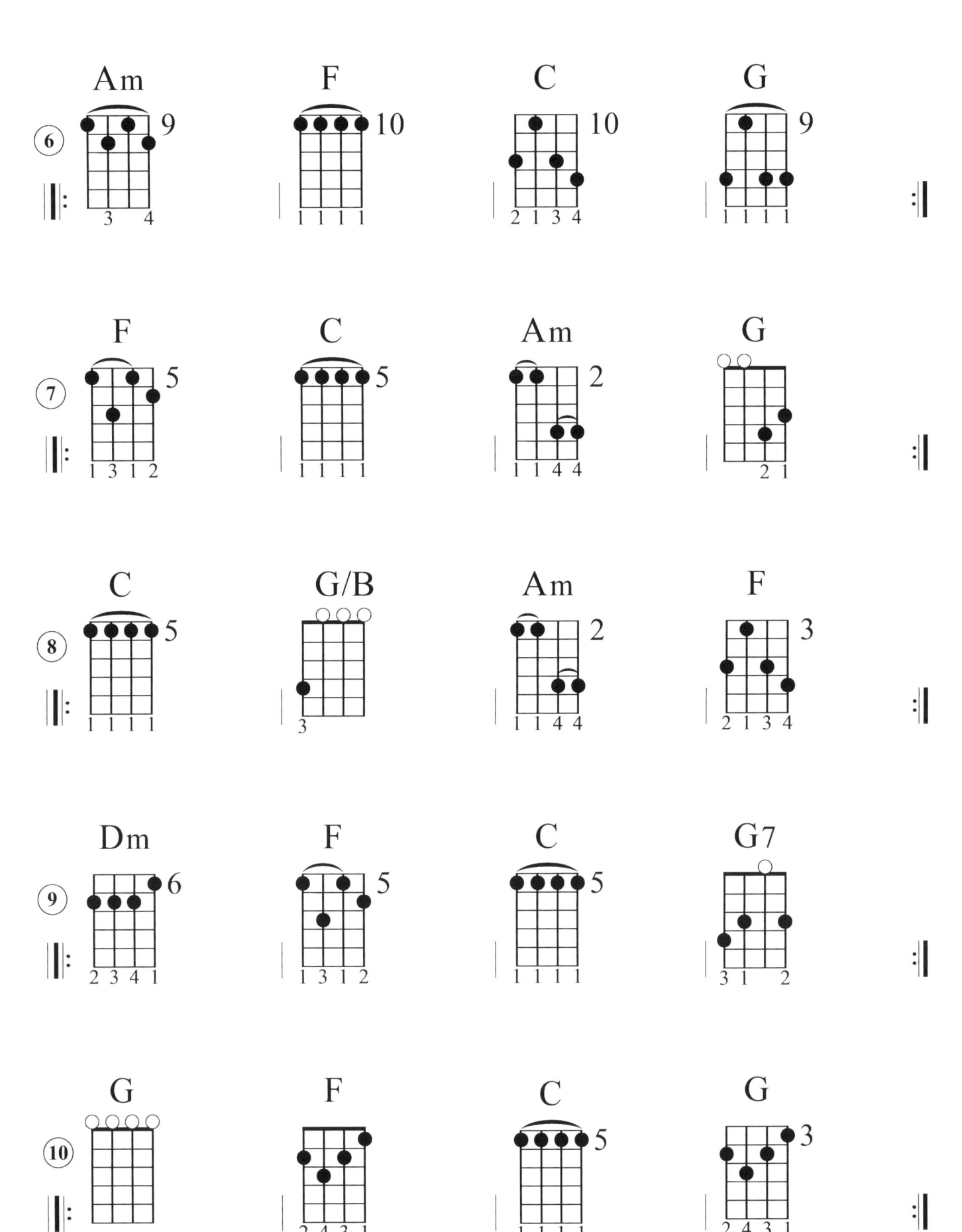

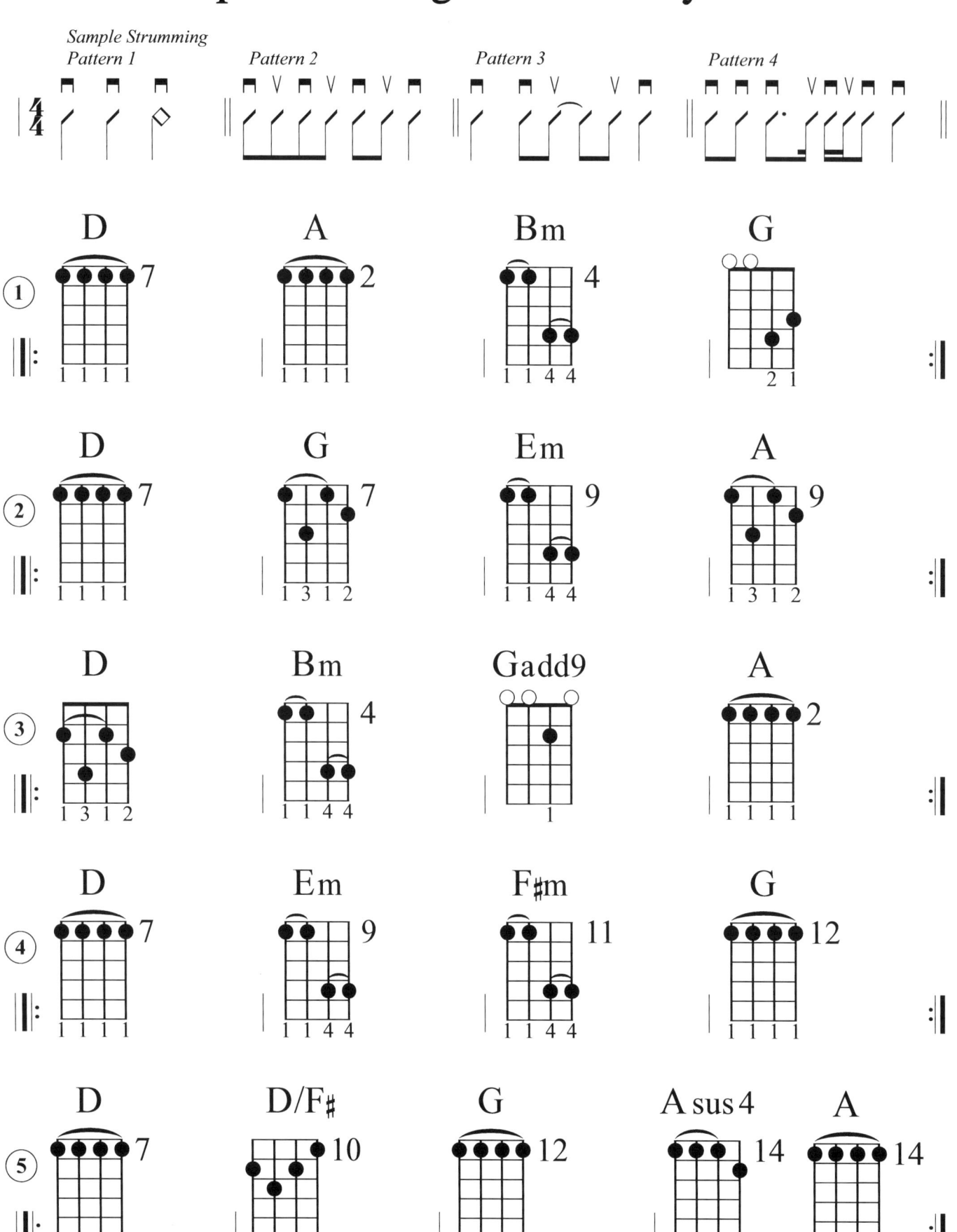

Pop Chord Progressions - Key of D

155

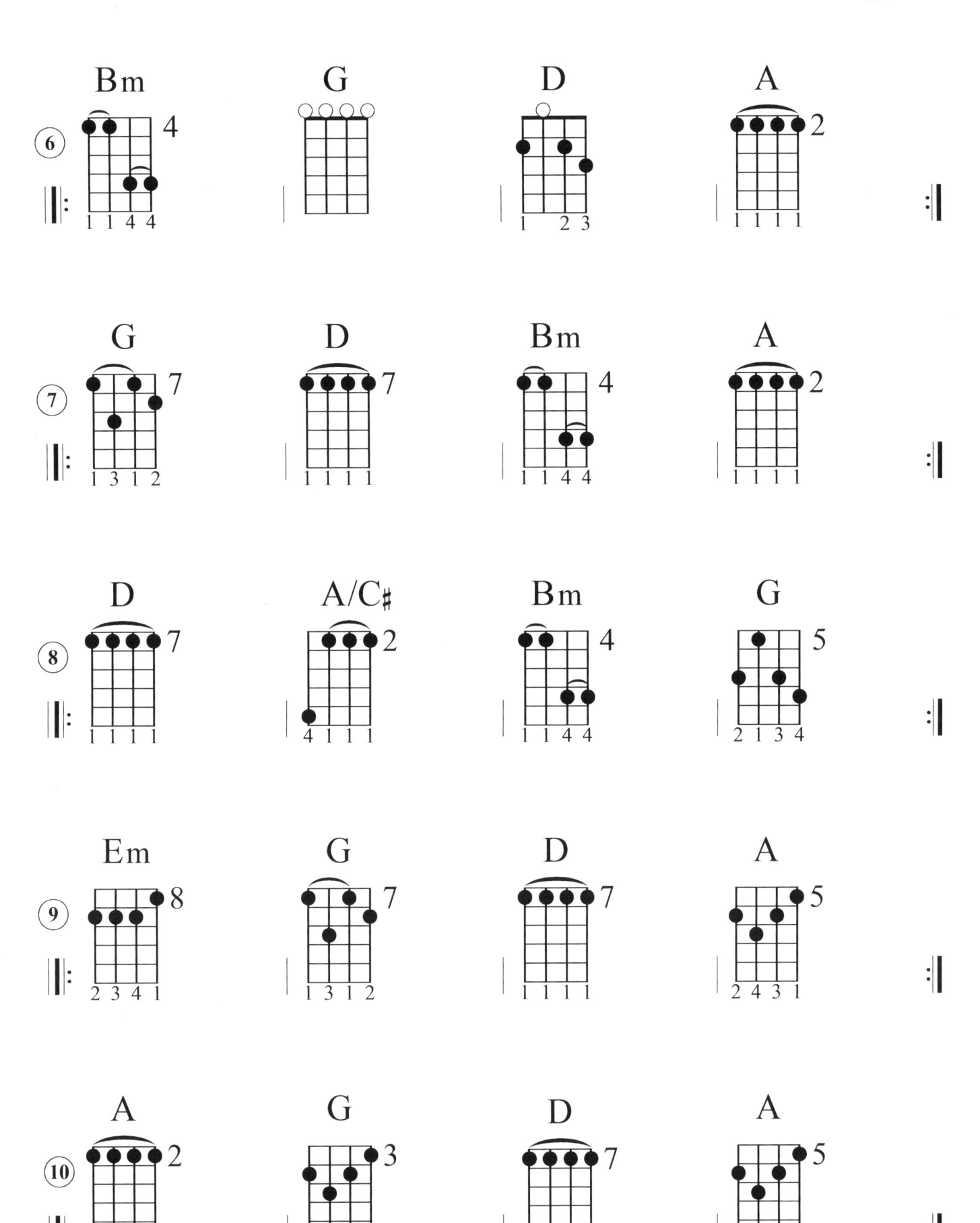

Pop Chord Progressions - Key of E

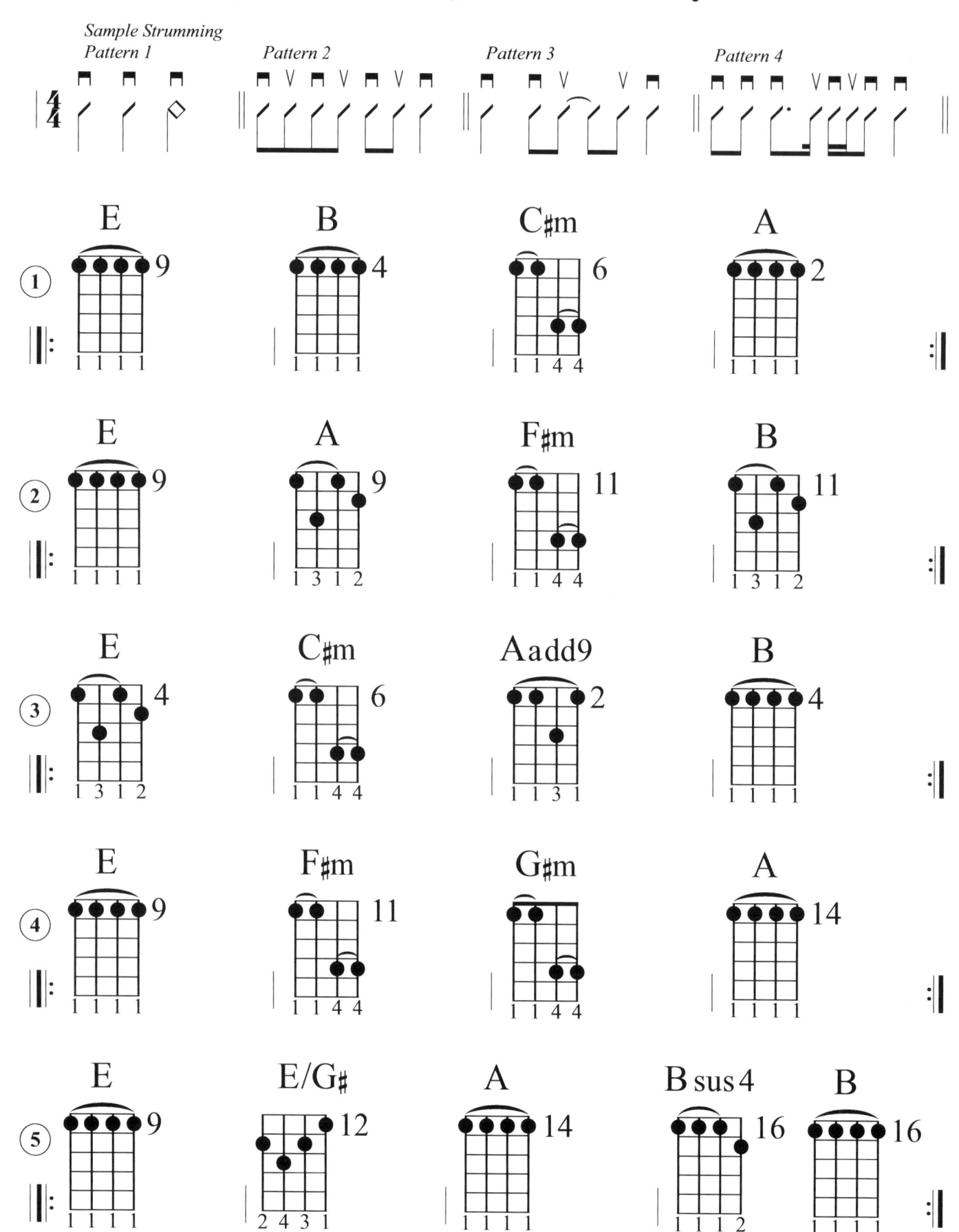

1.
E (9) | B (4) | C#m (6) | A (2)

2.
E (9) | A (9) | F#m (11) | B (11)

3.
E (4) | C#m (6) | Aadd9 (2) | B (4)

4.
E (9) | F#m (11) | G#m | A (14)

5.
E (9) | E/G# (12) | A (14) | Bsus4 (16) | B (16)

157

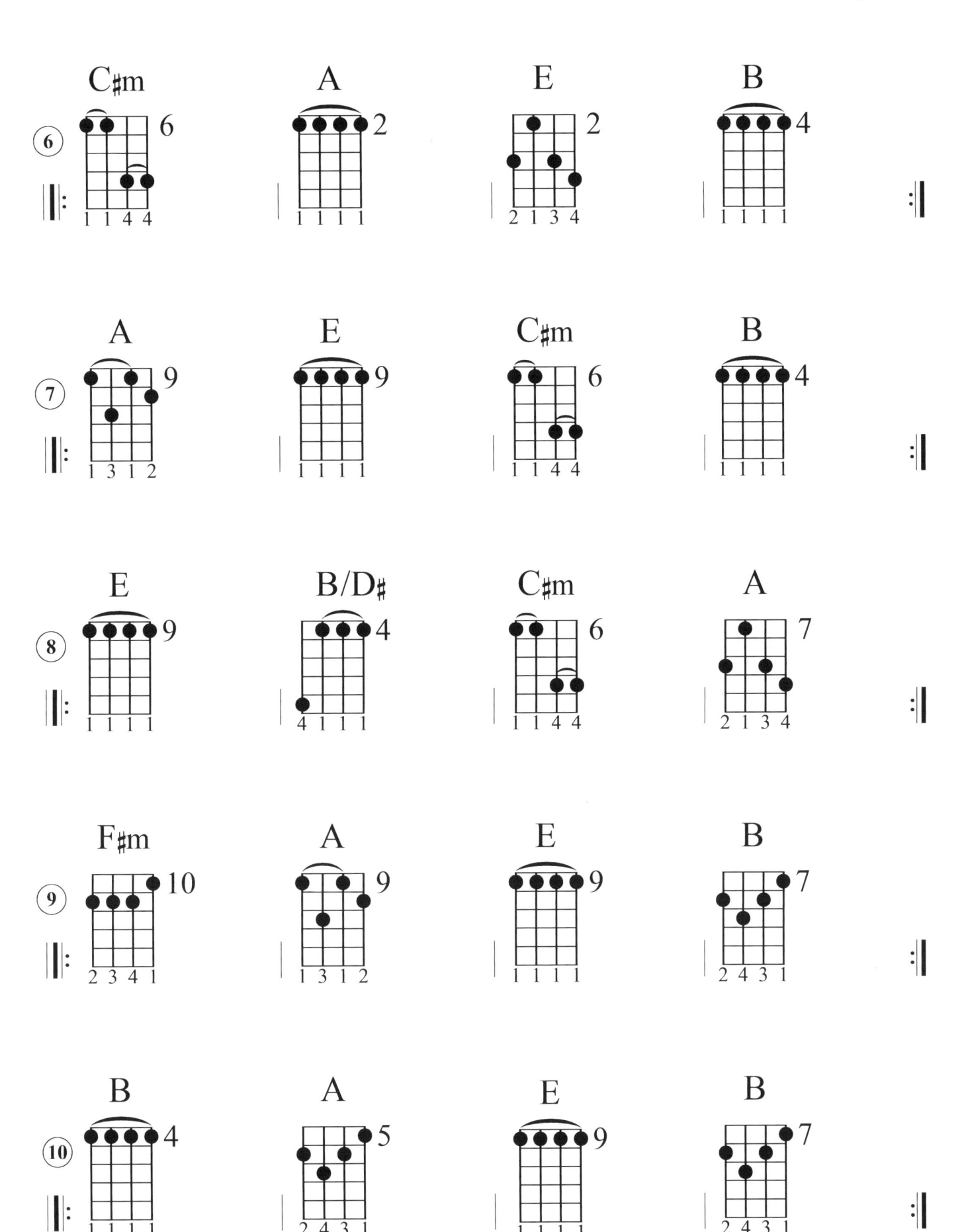

Pop Chord Progressions - Key of F

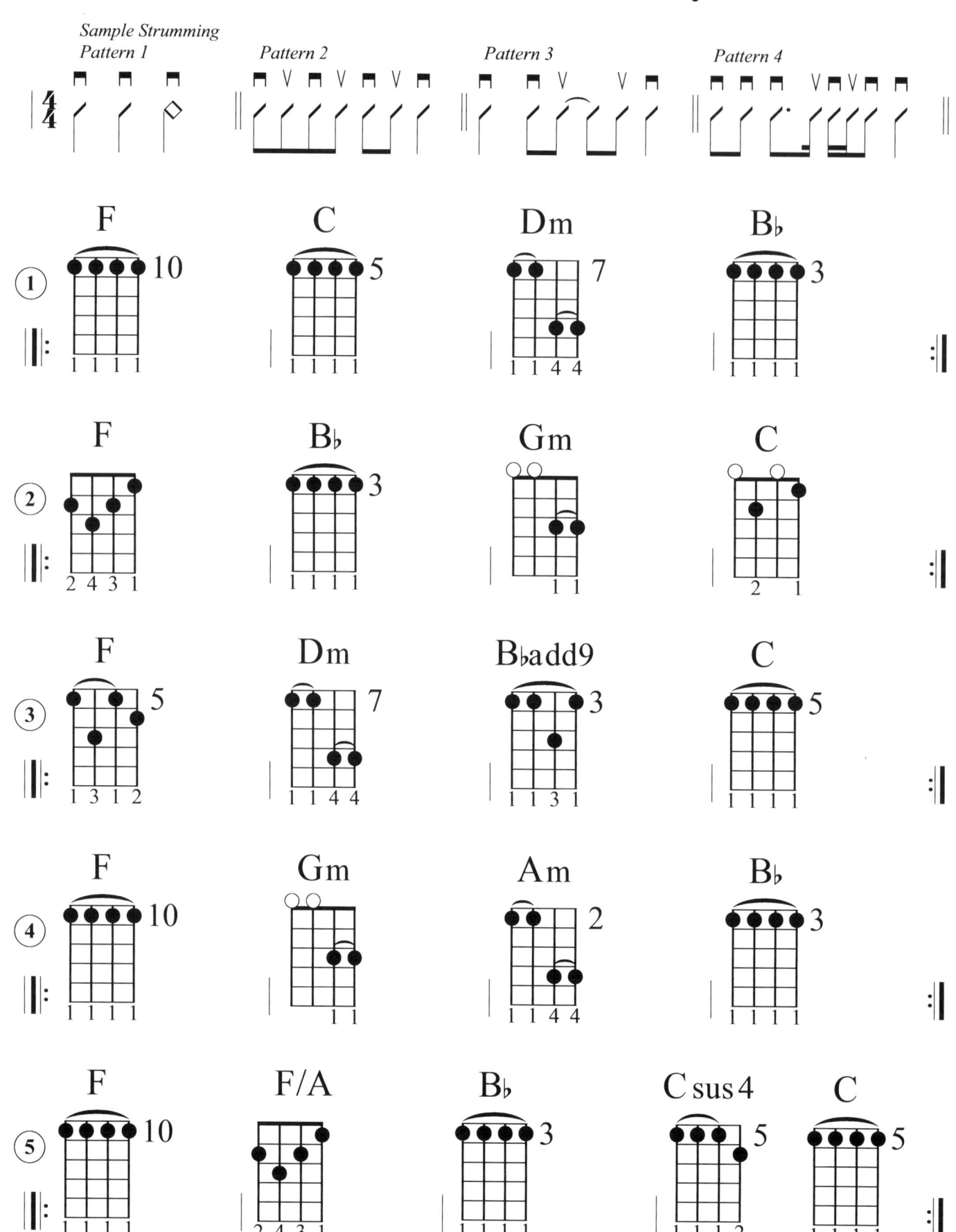

159

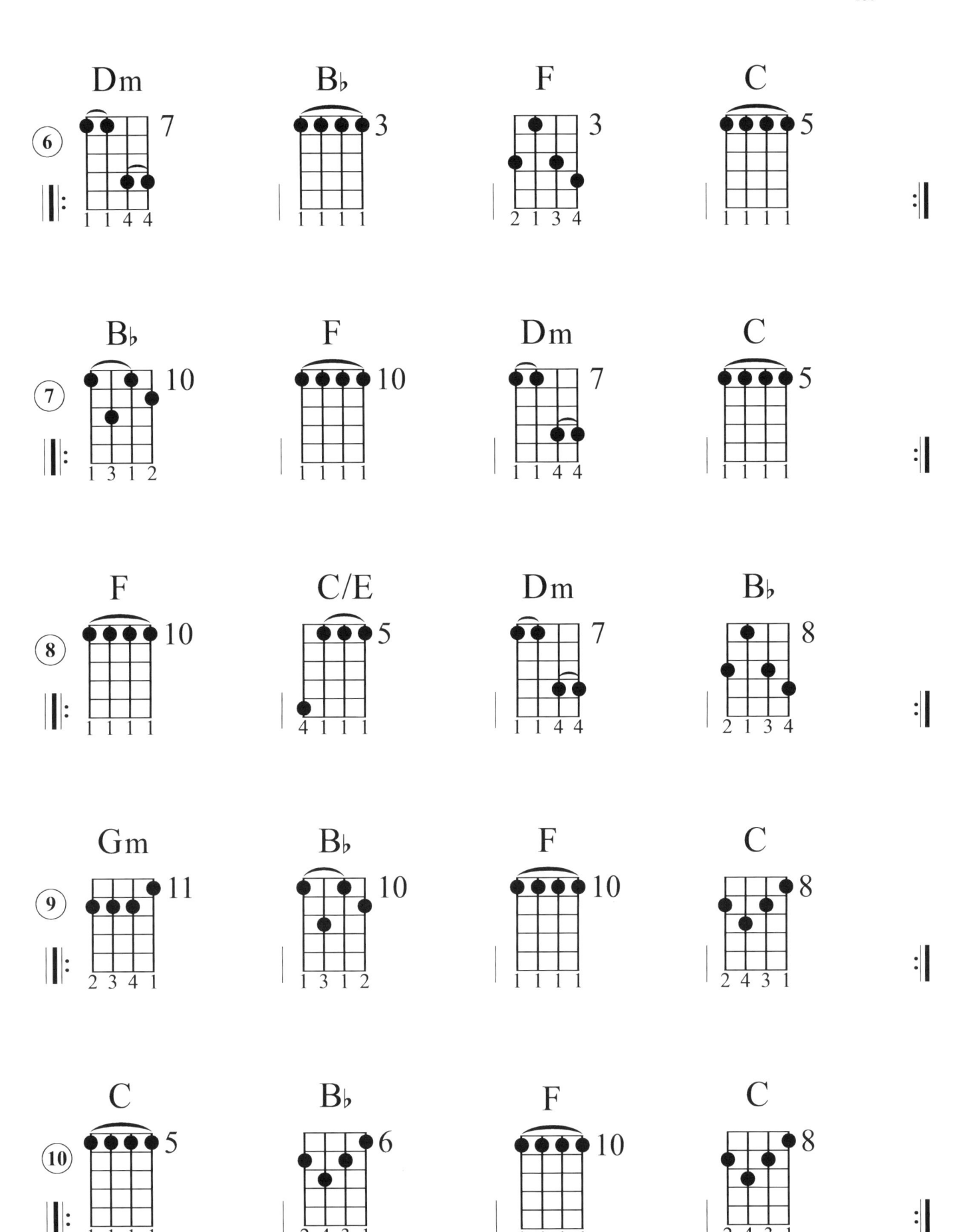

Pop Chord Progressions - Key of G

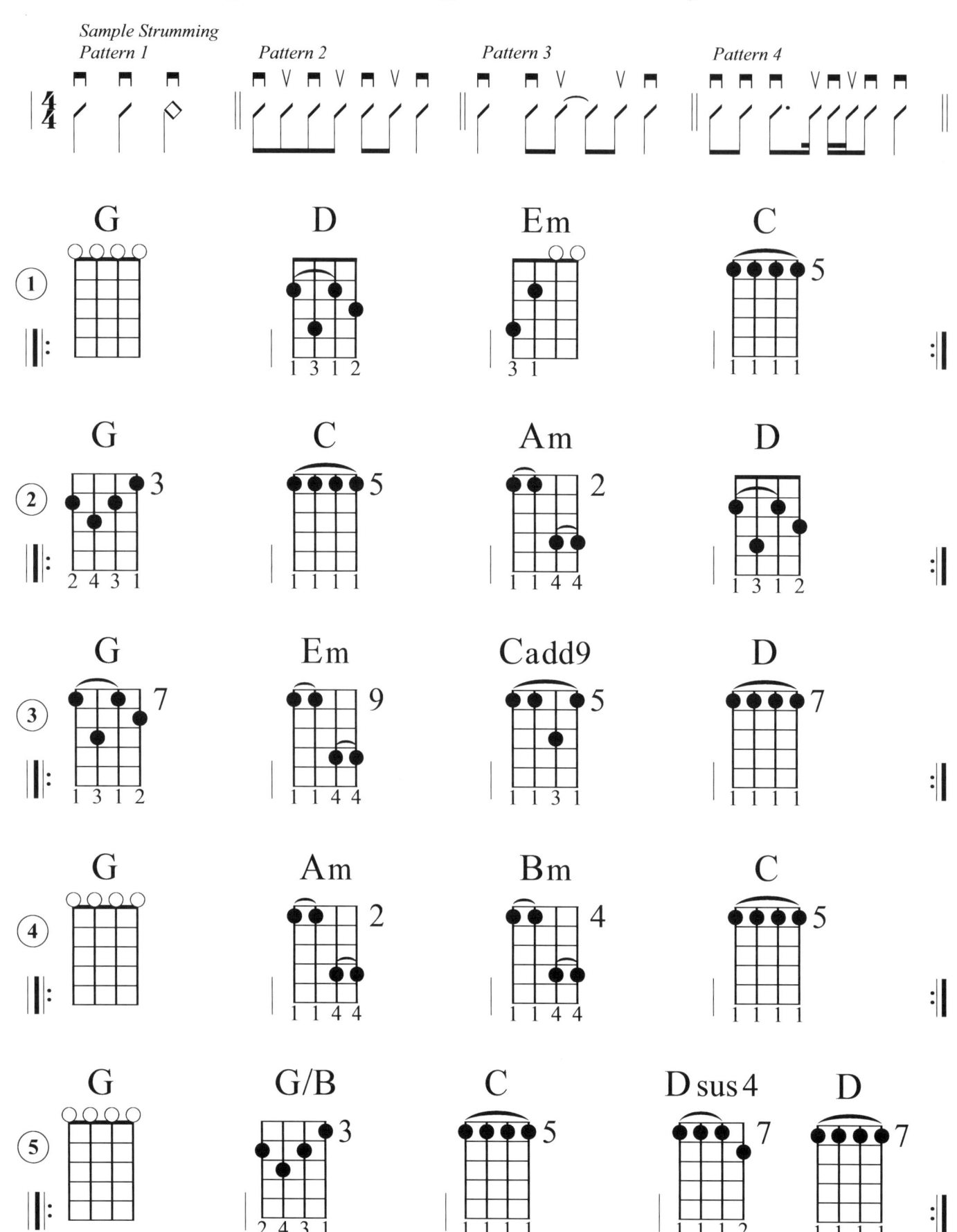

Sample Strumming Pattern 1, *Pattern 2*, *Pattern 3*, *Pattern 4*

1. G — D — Em — C
2. G — C — Am — D
3. G — Em — Cadd9 — D
4. G — Am — Bm — C
5. G — G/B — C — Dsus4 — D

161

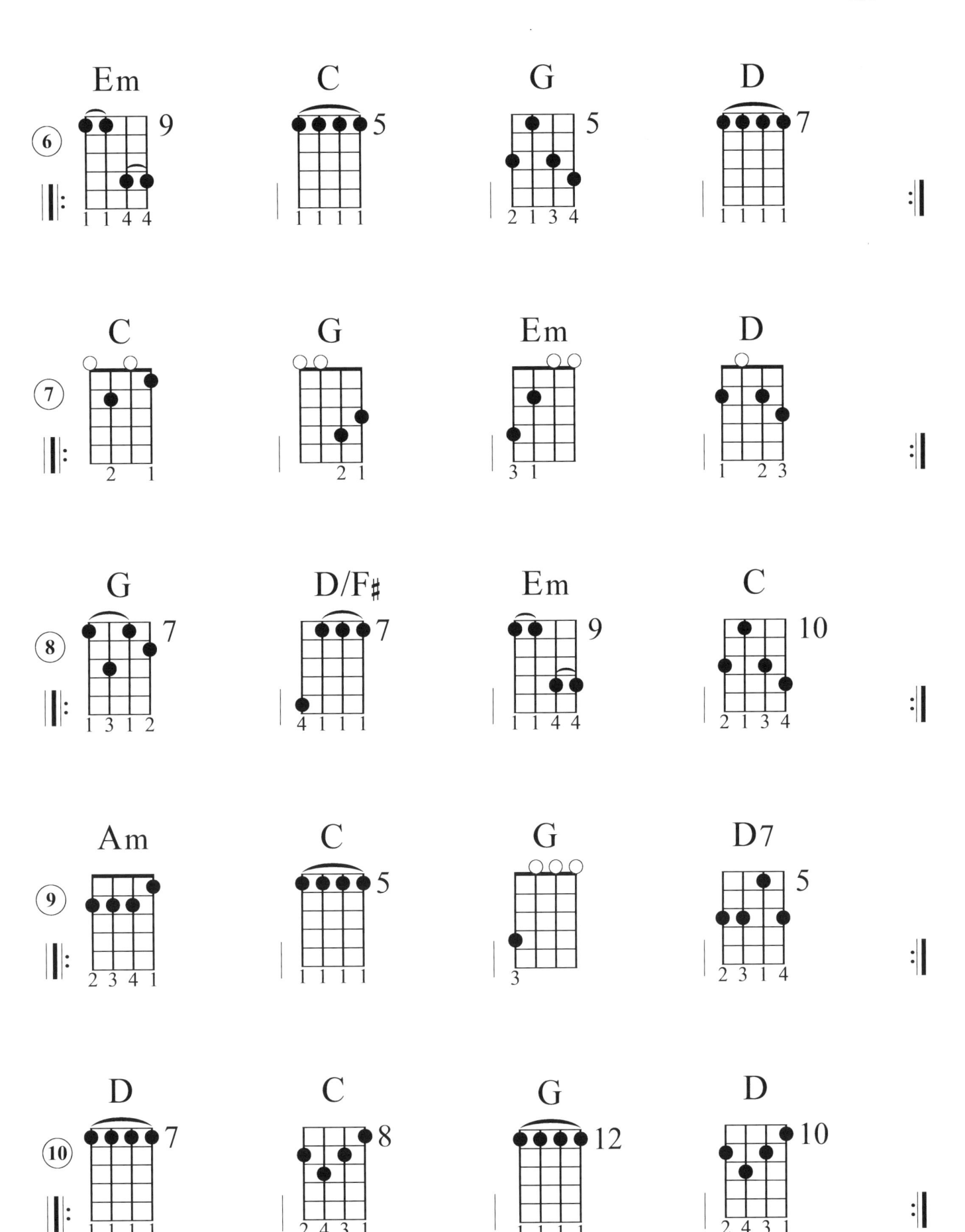

Rock Chord Progressions - A

Here are some popular rock chord progressions to practice. There are no chord diagrams, so you will need to memorize a few positions of the major, minor, and power chords (5ths) to play through the examples. I have included a fretboard diagram to help manoeuvre around the neck. Use your favourite strumming patterns or try some patterns in the strumming

1) ‖: A   E |D |A   E |D   :‖

2) ‖: A5 |D5 |C5 |F5   :‖

3) ‖: A |G |D |D   C5   :‖

4) ‖: A5   C5 |D5 |A5   C5 |E♭5 D5   :‖

5) ‖: Dm |B♭ |Am |C   :‖

6) ‖: Am |G |F |E   :‖

7) ‖: A5 |G5 |A5 |E   :‖

8) ‖: A5 |C5 |D5 |F5   G   :‖

9) ‖: A5 F5 |D5 |A5   F5 |D5   E   :‖

10) ‖: A5 C5 |A5   D5 |A5   C5 |A5 E♭5 D5   :‖

Rock Chord Progressions - B♭

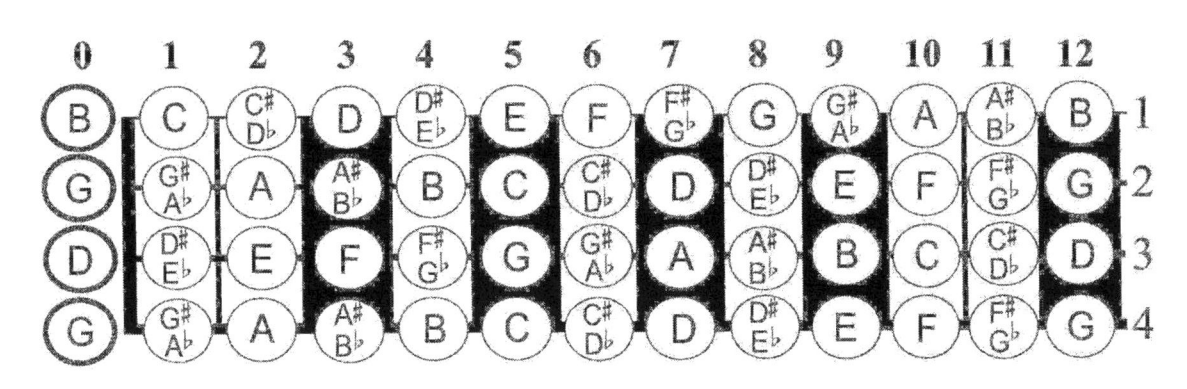

① ‖: B♭   F |E♭ |B♭   F |E♭   :‖

② ‖: B♭5 |E♭5 |D♭5 |G♭5   :‖

③ ‖: B♭ |A♭ |E♭ |E♭   D♭5   :‖

④ ‖: B♭5   D♭5 |E♭5 |B♭5   D♭5 |E5   E♭5   :‖

⑤ ‖: E♭m | B |B♭m |D♭   :‖

⑥ ‖: B♭m |A♭ |G♭ | F   :‖

⑦ ‖: B♭5 |A♭5 |B♭5 | F   :‖

⑧ ‖: B♭5 |D♭5 |E♭5 |G♭5   A♭   :‖

⑨ ‖: B♭5   G♭5 |E♭5 |B♭5   G♭5 |E♭5   F   :‖

⑩ ‖: B♭5   D♭5 |B♭5   E♭5 |B♭5   D♭5 |B♭5 E5 E♭5   :‖

Rock Chord Progressions - B

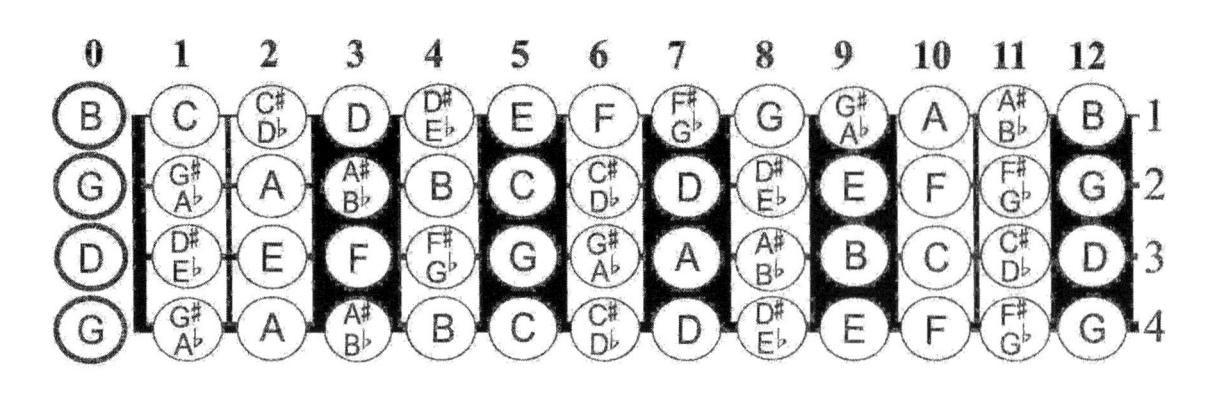

① ‖: B   F♯ | E | B   F♯ | E   :‖

② ‖: B5 | E5 | D5 | G5   :‖

③ ‖: B | A | E | E   D5   :‖

④ ‖: B5   D5 | E5 | B5   D5 | F5   E5   :‖

⑤ ‖: Em | C | Bm | D   :‖

⑥ ‖: Bm | A | G | F♯   :‖

⑦ ‖: B5 | A5 | B5 | F♯   :‖

⑧ ‖: B5 | D5 | E5 | G5   A   :‖

⑨ ‖: B5   G5 | E5 | B5   G5 | E5   F♯   :‖

⑩ ‖: B5   D5 | B5   E5 | B5   D5 | B5 F5 E5 :‖

Rock Chord Progressions - C

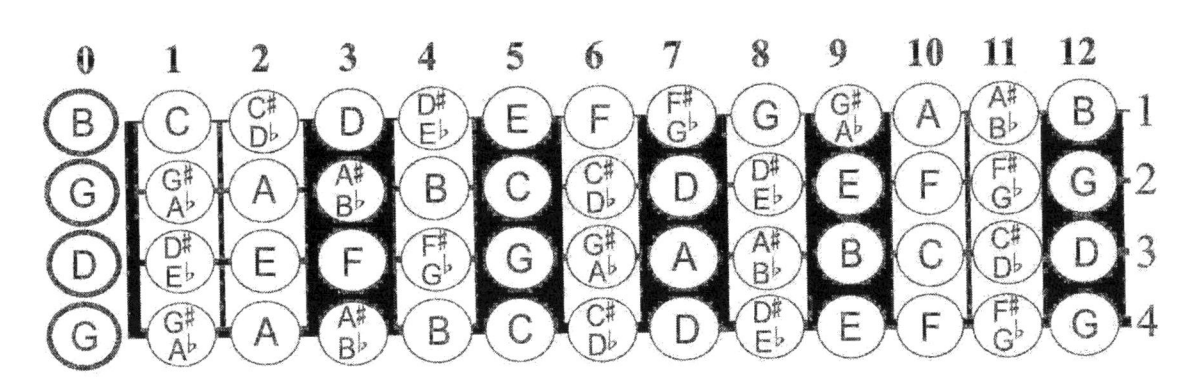

① ‖: C   G | F | C   G | F   :‖

② ‖: C5 | F5 | E♭5 | A♭5   :‖

③ ‖: C | B♭ | F | F   E♭5 :‖

④ ‖: C5   E♭5 | F5 | C5   E♭5 | G♭5   F5 :‖

⑤ ‖: Fm | D♭ | Cm | E♭   :‖

⑥ ‖: Cm | B♭ | A♭ | G   :‖

⑦ ‖: C5 | B♭5 | C5 | G   :‖

⑧ ‖: C5 | E♭5 | F5 | A♭5   B♭ :‖

⑨ ‖: C5   A♭5 | F5 | C5   A♭5 | F5   G :‖

⑩ ‖: C5   E♭5 | C5   F5 | C5   E♭5 | C5 G♭5 F5 :‖

Rock Chord Progressions - D

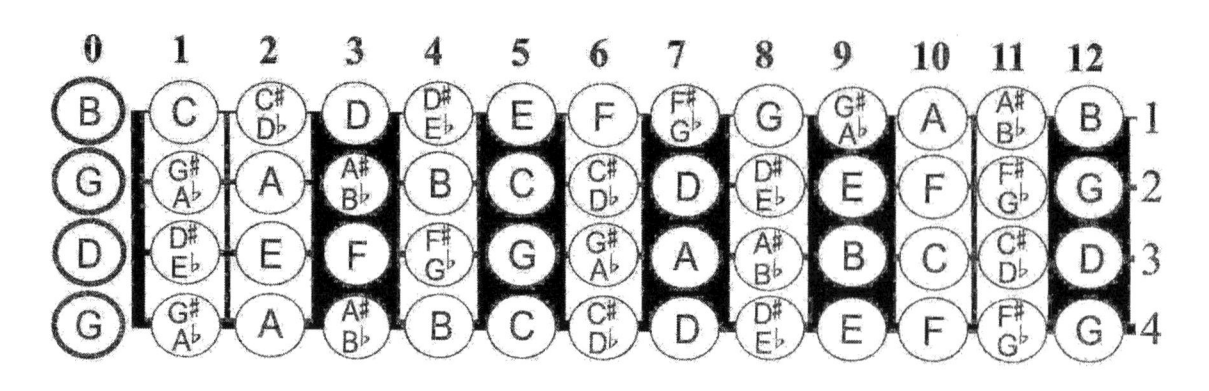

① ‖: D   A |G |D   A |G   :‖

② ‖: D5 |G5 |F5 |B♭5   :‖

③ ‖: D |C |G |G   F5   :‖

④ ‖: D5   F5 |G5 |D5   F5 |A♭5   G5   :‖

⑤ ‖: Gm |E♭ |Dm |F   :‖

⑥ ‖: Dm |C |B♭ |A   :‖

⑦ ‖: D5 |C5 |D5 |A   :‖

⑧ ‖: D5 |F5 |G5 |B♭5   C   :‖

⑨ ‖: D5   B♭5 |G5 |D5   B♭5 |G5   A   :‖

⑩ ‖: D5   F5 |D5   G5 |D5   F5 |D5 A♭5 G5   :‖

Rock Chord Progressions - E

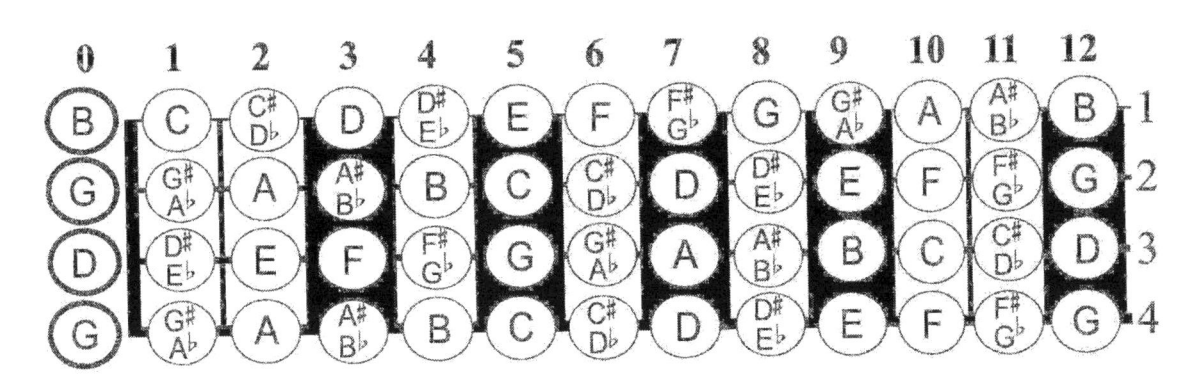

① ‖: E   B | A | E   B | A   :‖

② ‖: E5 | A5 | G5 | C5   :‖

③ ‖: E | D | A | A   G5   :‖

④ ‖: E5   G5 | A5 | E5   G5 | B♭5 A5   :‖

⑤ ‖: Am | F | Em | G   :‖

⑥ ‖: Em | D | C | B   :‖

⑦ ‖: E5 | D5 | E5 | B   :‖

⑧ ‖: E5 | G5 | A5 | C5   D   :‖

⑨ ‖: E5   C5 | A5 | E5   C5 | A5   B   :‖

⑩ ‖: E5   G5 | E5   A5 | E5   G5 | E5 B♭5 A5   :‖

Rock Chord Progressions - F

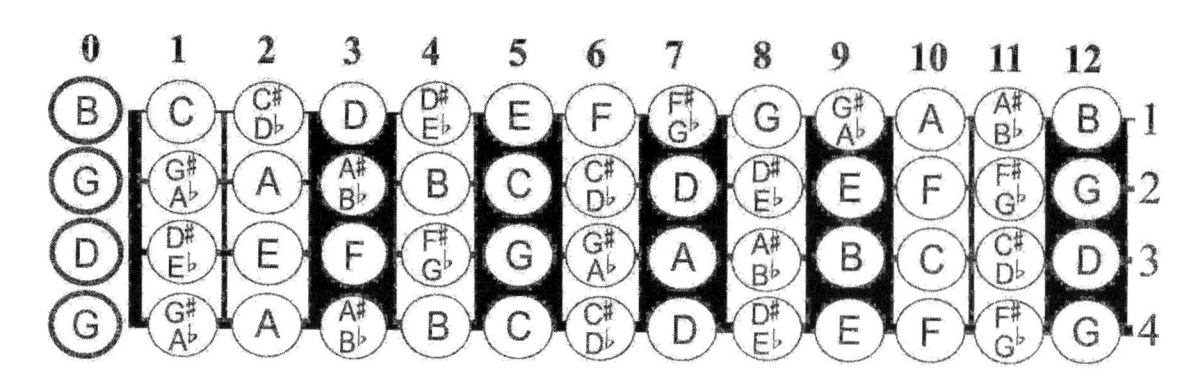

① ||: F   C | B♭ | F   C | B♭   :||

② ||: F5 | B♭5 | A♭5 | D♭5   :||

③ ||: F | E♭ | B♭ | B♭   A♭5 :||

④ ||: F5   A♭5 | B♭5 | F5   A♭5 | B5   B♭5 :||

⑤ ||: B♭m | G♭ | Fm | A♭   :||

⑥ ||: Fm | E♭ | D♭ | C   :||

⑦ ||: F5 | E♭5 | F5 | C   :||

⑧ ||: F5 | A♭5 | B♭5 | D♭5   E♭ :||

⑨ ||: F5   D♭5 | B♭5 | F5   D♭5 | B♭5   C :||

⑩ ||: F5   A♭5 | F5   B♭5 | F5   A♭5 | F5   B5   B♭5 :||

Rock Chord Progressions - G

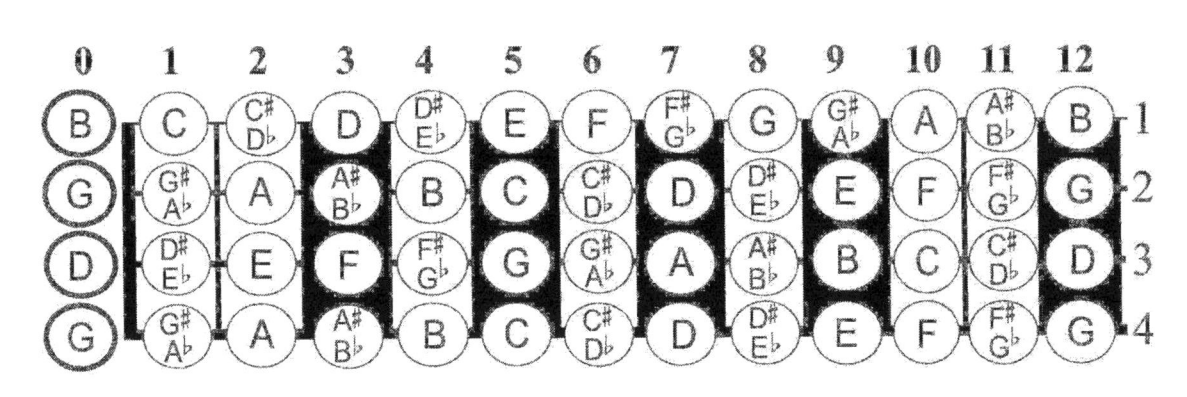

① ‖: G   D |C |G   D |C   :‖

② ‖: G5 |C5 |B♭5 |E♭5   :‖

③ ‖: G | F |C |C   B♭5 :‖

④ ‖: G5   B♭5 |C5 |G5   B♭5 |D♭5 C5   :‖

⑤ ‖: Cm |A♭ |Gm |B♭   :‖

⑥ ‖: Gm | F |E♭ |D   :‖

⑦ ‖: G5 | F5 |G5 |D   :‖

⑧ ‖: G5 |B♭5 |C5 |E♭5   F   :‖

⑨ ‖: G5 E♭5 |C5 |G5 E♭5 |C5   D   :‖

⑩ ‖: G5 B♭5 |G5   C5 |G5 B♭5 |G5 D♭5 C5 :‖

CIGAR BOX GUITAR BOOK COLLECTION

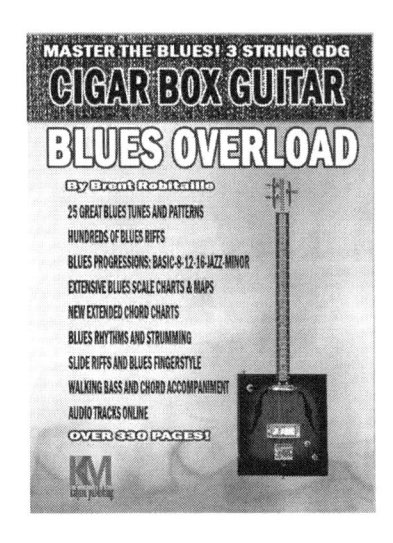

WWW.BRENTROBITAILLE.COM

More Great Music From Kalymi Publishing

THE BLUES GUITAR LOOPER PEDAL BOOK

- 2, 4, 8, 12, & 16 Bar Blues Loops
- Riffs, Bass, Chords, and Rhythm for Each Loop
- 10 Tips for Making Great Loops
- 10 Tips for Better Guitar Solos
- Blues Scales & Fingerboard Charts - Slide Guitar Exercises
- Blues Progressions & Strumming Patterns
- Free Audio Tracks Online

Improve Your Guitar Chord Playing

- 12 Tips, tricks, and exercises to improve your chord switching
- Step by step chord switching exercises excellent for beginners
- 45 common chord progressions in pop, rock, folk, and blues.
- Barre chord tips with strengthening exercises
- Master the fingerboard with triangle patterns and diagrams
- Key and capo charts to transpose from key to key

Guitar - Mandolin - Fiddle - Ukulele

WWW.BRENTROBITAILLE.COM

Made in the USA
Middletown, DE
28 April 2025